Defender

Defender
The Life of Daniel H. Wells

Quentin Thomas Wells

Utah State University Press
Logan

© 2016 by Quentin T. Wells

Published by Utah State University Press
An imprint of University Press of Colorado
1624 Market Street, Suite 226
PMB 39883
Denver, Colorado 80202-1559

All rights reserved
First paperback edition 2023
Manufactured in the United States of America

 The University Press of Colorado is a proud member of The Association of University Presses.

The University Press of Colorado is a cooperative publishing enterprise supported, in part, by Adams State University, Colorado State University, Fort Lewis College, Metropolitan State University of Denver, University of Alaska Fairbanks, University of Colorado, University of Denver, University of Northern Colorado, University of Wyoming, Utah State University, and Western Colorado University.

ISBN: 978-1-60732-546-8 (cloth)
ISBN: 978-1-64642-375-0 (paperback)
ISBN: 978-1-60732-547-5 (ebook)

Library of Congress Cataloging-in-Publication Data

Names: Wells, Quentin, author.
Title: Defender: the life of Daniel H. Wells / Quentin Thomas Wells.
Description: Logan: Utah State University Press, [2016] | Includes bibliographical references and index.
Identifiers: LCCN 2016019925 | ISBN 9781607325468 (cloth) | ISBN 9781646423750 (pbk) | ISBN 9781607325475 (ebook)
Subjects: LCSH: Wells, Daniel H. (Daniel Hanmer), 1814–1891. | Mormons—Utah—Biography. | Wells family. | Mormons—Utah—History.
Classification: LCC BX8695.W4 W45 2016 | DDC 289.3092 [B] —dc23
LC record available at https://lccn.loc.gov/2016019925

Front-cover illustration: portrait of Daniel H. Wells by C. R. Savage, Great Salt Lake City, ca. 1866

Contents

	Introduction	*vii*
1.	A Puritan Family's Progress: The Wells's Migration from England to America (1634–1814)	3
2.	Daniel H. Wells: From a Brief Childhood in New York to Frontier Life in Illinois (1814–1838)	12
3.	A Bachelor Farmer in Commerce Becomes a Married Entrepreneur and Civic Leader in Nauvoo (1839–1841)	31
4.	The Mormon Hegemony: Civic Controversy, Court Cases, and Family Conflict (1841–1844)	46
5.	The Mormon Hegemony: Disaffection and Libel Lead to Mayhem and Murder (1843–1846)	61
6.	The Decline of Nauvoo: Daniel Becomes a Mormon and Leads in the Battle of Nauvoo (1844–1846)	75
7.	The Cost of Conversion: Travels to Winter Quarters and the Trail to Great Salt Lake City (1846–1848)	95
8.	Deseret Home and New Callings: The Superintendent, the General, and the Attorney General (1848–1851)	111
9.	Six Additional Wives, a Dozen Children, and Many Enterprises to Support the Family (1851–1855)	132
10.	Fighting Indians or Feeding Them, Family Matters, and Brigham's New Counselor (1855–1857)	153
11.	The Utah Expedition, Causes and Consequences: A War of Lies and Egos, but No Casualties (1857–1858)	175
12.	The Peace Commission and War by Other Means: Church, Territorial, and Federal Politics in Utah (1858–1859)	204

13.	Family, Business, Church, and Politics in Utah while the Civil War Ravages the Nation (1860–1864)	226
14.	The Wells Family Grows and Prospers during the Civil War (1860–1864)	246
15.	Daniel's First (Incomplete) Term as European Mission President (1864–1865)	262
16.	Years of Defending Against Patient, Tenacious Raiders: Utah's Black Hawk War (1865–1868)	275
17.	Mayor of Salt Lake City: Defending the Faith, Fighting Crime, and Obtaining the Deed to the City (1868–1870)	289
18.	Mormon versus Gentile in Railroads, Business, Government, and Religion (1870–1878)	313
19.	Daniel Opposes the GLU, Defends Brigham, Escapes Drowning, and Dedicates a Temple (1875–1878)	337
20.	From Counselor to Assistant, Trapped in Court, Imprisoned, and Paraded Home (1877–1879)	355
21.	Wells Family Marriages, the Anti-polygamy Crusade, and a Second Mission in Europe (1880–1885)	373
22.	Defending against Opposition in England while Tragedy Unfolds at Home (1886–1888)	398
23.	Preparing for His Passing, President of the Temple, Death while still in Harness (1887–1891)	412
	Appendix A: The Wells Family in England and America (1484–1814)	*421*
	Appendix B: The Chapin Family in England and America (1484–1814)	*426*
	Notes	*429*
	Bibliography	*482*
	About the Author	*497*
	Index	*498*

Introduction

Daniel H. Wells awoke early on a September morning in 1846 to the sound of gunfire outside his home. He dressed quickly and saddled a white horse in the corral beside his house. Arming himself with a pair of pistols and a rifle, he mounted and rode east across open fields in the direction from which the shots were coming. Others, mostly on foot, hurried after him. They arrived at a defensive line of entrenchments and wooden barricades that spread east and west from Barlow's barn and quickly took up firing positions alongside those already engaged.

In front of the defenders a large opposing force of about twelve hundred well-armed men was advancing in a bunched column from the southeast in a determined effort to reach Mulholland Street, the main avenue leading west into the city of Nauvoo. The attackers were supported by half a dozen artillery pieces that repeatedly hurled round shot into the defenders' breastworks and beyond into their homes and farm buildings. As the oncoming troops neared one side of the line behind which Daniel stood, still astride his horse, it became apparent to him that they would overrun the severely outnumbered defenders within minutes. With that realization, he became an instant general and acted decisively to direct the course of battle.

At age thirty-three, Daniel had no military combat experience and had never fired a shot in anger at an opposing army. He did, however, have a strong knowledge of history and the strategy that some of his forbears had used in earlier American conflicts. He also knew that conflicts were usually decided by the courage of those who fought and the competence of those who led them. He had no doubt about the bravery of those around him and he determined to provide the direction they needed at the moment.

Urging his horse to a gallop, he rode swiftly to the northern end of the line where another group of men were firing at the advancing forces from too long a range to be effective. Swinging his hat overhead and shouting, he rallied the group to follow him south into the thick of the battle. Seeing the number of their opponents, only a few rose immediately to obey his call, but as the rest saw him stand in his stirrups and urge them onward while enemy bullets whined past his exposed body, they also responded. With Daniel in the lead, the company raced back over the field he had just crossed, some falling as they went, and reinforced the southern end of the line. Within an hour, as the self-appointed officer directed their fire, the defenders turned back the attacking army. His leadership would be needed even more in the following days when this temporary victory was swallowed up in defeat.

Daniel Hanmer Wells was a quintessential American. He was born in upstate New York into a family that had been in the New World for six generations prior to his arrival. Both of his grandfathers were soldiers in the Revolutionary War and his ancestors were among the early seventeenth century founders of the Massachusetts and Connecticut colonies. His parents pioneered the agricultural community of Trenton in Oneida County, New York, and he was reared to follow in his father's footsteps as a yeoman farmer.

Although he held many official titles, Daniel H. Wells never aspired to or actively sought any of the positions in which he served. During his lifetime he was chosen Hancock County constable and justice of the peace, Nauvoo City alderman, lieutenant general of the Nauvoo Legion, superintendent of Public Works, mayor of Salt Lake City, Utah Territorial legislator and attorney general, chancellor of the Deseret University, apostle of Jesus Christ, and second counselor to the president of the Church of Jesus Christ of Latter-day Saints. In most of these endeavors, which successively consumed much of his time, he worked without compensation and in all of them he was obliged to train himself on the job while supporting himself and his family with income earned from other agricultural and business enterprises.

Starting from a modest farm plot in New York, which he inherited with his mother and sisters, Daniel acquired extensive real estate holdings in Illinois. Most of his property there he turned over to members of his family and the rest he abandoned in order to move west again to the new Utah Territory. There he claimed new lands that he developed into farms and orchards in several communities. He also built and operated lumber mills, coal mines, a hardware manufactory, and stores to market the products his enterprises produced. He was one of the founders of Utah's pioneer cooperative retail enterprise, its early regional railroads, the Deseret Telegraph Company and the gas works of Salt Lake City, all of which he worked on while simultaneously serving in myriad civic and religious capacities.

Daniel ventured much further than had his father, moving almost a thousand miles from New York where he was born to Hancock County,

Illinois, before his twenty-first birthday. There he bought land, built a home, and farmed his acreage to support himself, his younger sister and his widowed mother. He quickly prospered and within a few years had married, fathered a son, and established himself as one of the leading citizens of the new town of Commerce. His career as a farmer, local magistrate, and entrepreneur was already expanding, and he appeared comfortably established in his position by the close of the year 1838.

Life changed for Daniel, as it did for all the residents of Commerce, when Mormons, members of the Church of Jesus Christ of Latter-day Saints, who were driven from their homes and hounded out of the state of Missouri by violence, crossed the Mississippi River from west to east. Communities in western Illinois welcomed the refugees and helped them establish new homes in Hancock and surrounding counties. Commerce, soon renamed Nauvoo by the leader of its new majority of residents, became the central gathering place for thousands of Latter-day Saints coming from the west and from other Mormon settlements in Ohio and New York. Within five years Nauvoo was one of the largest cities in Illinois and Daniel H. Wells was one of its business and civic leaders. He subdivided his farm, sold lots to new arrivals on easy credit, and quickly became the area's most prominent non-Mormon citizen.

But the fall of Nauvoo was even swifter than its rise, and the real estate boom that made Daniel a land-wealthy developer went bust in a new wave of violence that erupted when the political power of the Mormons became evident and conflicts with their religious practices intensified. Joseph Smith, the Latter-day Saints' prophet and mayor of Nauvoo, was murdered with his brother Hyrum and mobs attacked Mormon settlements, raping and murdering some of the inhabitants and destroying the homes and crops of many. Seeking protection in numbers, most Mormons abandoned outlying settlements and fled to the safety of Nauvoo, but their security proved short-lived. The city was also attacked and the Saints were eventually forced to leave it. By the summer of 1846, Nauvoo had become a ghost town similar to those that the Mormons had been earlier compelled to flee in New York, Ohio, and Missouri. Thousands of Latter-day Saints, now led by Brigham Young, crossed the Mississippi River and headed west toward another new home in the Rocky Mountains that none had ever seen.

Daniel H. Wells watched this exodus with conflicted feelings. He had advised the Mormons to get out of Illinois and away from the escalating violence, but he was loath to see them go because he could not go with them. He had long since been converted to the restored gospel as taught by Joseph Smith and his testimony of Mormonism had been strengthened by Smith's brutal murder.

Despite his convictions, Daniel had refrained from joining the Latter-day Saints because he felt that he could be more useful as a neutral negotiator between the Mormons and those opposing them in Hancock County. Another reason for his delay was personal: his wife was vehemently opposed to Mormon doctrines and practices and refused to accept the new religion. In August 1846, he was still trying unsuccessfully to persuade her to embrace it.

By then, Daniel's efforts as a negotiator, along with those of other would-be peacemakers had come to naught. The anti-Mormons around Nauvoo multiplied in number and massed small arms and artillery for an assault on the city center. The few hundred citizens still left in the city could not long repel such an invasion and their opponents, aware of the strength of their position, refused any settlement.

Daniel's efforts to convert his wife were also fruitless. She refused to join the church or to leave her Nauvoo home for an unknown destination. Faced with the stark choice of repudiating his own faith or losing his family, his home, and all his worldly wealth, Daniel made his decision publicly and without any reservations.

On August 9, 1846, as his coreligionists fled westward and an armed force prepared to attack Nauvoo, Daniel H. Wells was baptized and confirmed a member of the Church of Jesus Christ of Latter-day Saints. In doing so, he renounced the protestant religion of his youth, accepted the restored gospel as revealed to Joseph Smith and became an outcast from his family, none of whom would ever follow his example. He also became a hunted man, a principal target of the anti-Mormons who would shortly seize the city that he had helped to build.

Within days he was driven at gunpoint across the Mississippi River to seek refuge with the Mormon exodus. He left behind his wife, his son, his home, and all his land and business interests. He would never see any of them again.

Defender

1
A Puritan Family's Progress
THE WELLS'S MIGRATION FROM ENGLAND TO AMERICA
1634–1814

Daniel H. Wells was born in upstate New York on October 27, 1814. By the time of his birth, his ancestors had been living in America for almost two hundred years. Both his father's family and his mother's immigrated from England to Massachusetts colony in 1635. Thomas Wells stayed only a year or so in the Boston area before moving with his children to the new Connecticut colony. Deacon Samuel Chapin remained in Massachusetts for his lifetime, but his grandson Ebenezer also relocated to Connecticut. By the last third of the 1700s both families were deeply rooted there, the Wells clan in Wethersfield, Hartford County, and the Chapins in nearby New Hartford, Enfield County.[1]

Joshua Wells, Daniel H. Wells's paternal grandfather, born September 3, 1726, farmed land that he inherited from his father in Wethersfield.[2] In 1757, he married Experience Dickenson and together they had nine children, all born in Wethersfield during the years 1759 to 1773. Their youngest child, Daniel Wells, born in 1773, was the father of Daniel Hanmer Wells. Less than two weeks after Daniel Wells's birth, his mother died, whether as a consequence of childbirth complications or from other causes is not known.[3]

Although the oldest of their nine children was only fourteen at the time of Experience's death, Joshua did not remarry. He relied instead on the homemaking and parenting skills of his two eldest daughters, Experience Wells and Hannah Wells, to care for and help educate their younger siblings. They seem to have accepted this heavy burden willingly and to have performed it admirably.[4]

Figure 1.1. Mayor Daniel H. Wells, portrait by C. R. Savage, Great Salt Lake City, ca. 1866.

Joshua Wells was confident enough in the capacity of his family to manage without him (probably with the assistance of other family members and friends) that he volunteered to go to war. He was almost fifty when the Declaration of Independence was signed, older than most of those who enlisted to fight in the Revolution, but he served throughout the conflict and survived another fifteen years beyond it.[5]

As early as 1776, three years after his wife's death, Joshua Wells, along with many of his Wells, Deming, Dickenson, Goodrich, and Robbins relatives, is listed as a member of Captain H. Welles's Company of the Third Battalion of Connecticut militia headed by Col. Roger Enos.

By April 1777 he had moved to the Wethersfield Company of Captain Chester Wells in the regiment led by Col. Thomas Belden.[6]

On February 26, 1778, Joshua enlisted for the duration of the war and was assigned to Captain Joseph Walker's company in Col. Samuel B. Webb's infantry regiment.[7] This regiment and its service in the war from 1778 through the end of 1780 is described in abbreviated text in the Connecticut Military Record, 1775–1848, Record of Service of Connecticut Men in the War of the Revolution:

> One of the sixteen "additional" regiments of infantry raised at large for the "Continental Line" of [17]77, to continue through the war. Recruited mainly in Hartford County and eastern part of the State. Went into camp at Peekskill in the spring of [17]77 and served in Parson's Brigade under Putnam during movements of following summer and fall. On advance of the enemy and the loss of Forts Clinton and Montgomery, Oct., [17]77, it crossed to west side of Hudson and served under Gov. Clinton of N. Y., for a time. On Dec. 10, the regiment engaged with other troops in an expedition against L. I. [Long Island], which met with accidents, leaving Col. Webb and other officers prisoners in enemy's hands. Regt. wintered with Parson's Brigade at West Point and assisted in construction of permanent works there. Redoubt "Webb" doubtless named after the Col. In summer of [17]78 it was attached to Varnum's Brigade and marched to R. I. [Rhode Island], engaging in the battle there of Aug. 29, [17]78; commended for its conduct. Wintered in R. I. [17]78–79 and remaining there till fall of [17]79 marched to winter quarters, Morristown, N. J., [17]79–80; assigned to Stark's Brigade, Lt.-Col. Huntington commanding. Present at battle of Springfield, N. J., June 23, [17]80, and during following summer served with main army on the Hudson. Upon a memorial of Col. Huntington, the Assembly of Conn, on 2d Thursday of May, [17]80, adopted the regt. as one of the "Conn. Line" and a Committee of Congress in Camp Preakness, N. J., June 23, [17]80, approved the measure. It was designated the 9th Regt. and went into winter quarters. [17]80–81, with the Division at Camp "Connecticut Village" above the Robinson House. There it was re-organized for formation of [17]81–83.[8]

At the beginning of January 1781, Webb's regiment, now designated the Connecticut Ninth, was consolidated with the Connecticut Second

Regiment to form the new Connecticut Third Regiment. Joshua Wells remained in the army, serving in the company of Captain Samuel W. Williams, and is listed on the paymaster's rolls as being present with his unit for the entire year. He marched with his regiment to Yorktown and there participated in the final major battle of the Revolution in October 1781.[9]

Joshua remained with the victorious army throughout 1782 and was finally mustered out of service, after a period of paid leave, in January 1783.[10] He returned home to find his family had come through the war relatively unscathed. None of his children had married, but all had cooperated as a unit to run the family farm and provide for their own needs, while at the same time sending what logistical support they could to the revolutionary cause.[11]

Joshua Wells resumed his active leadership as patriarch of the family and continued to operate his farm as, one by one, his children married and began their own families.[12] Daniel Wells, the father of Daniel Hanmer Wells, was the last sibling to marry in 1799, a few months after his father Joshua's death at age seventy-one.[13]

Prior to the date on which Joshua Wells signed his will, Daniel Wells and his older brother Gideon borrowed money from him against their coming inheritance to finance a trip to the "Western Territory," which had been ceded to the United States by the Treaty of Paris that ended the Revolutionary War in 1783. They probably departed Wethersfield in the spring of 1795. Gideon left his wife Emily and two young sons at home; Daniel was still unmarried, although he was already making plans.[14]

They arrived after a journey of some 630 miles, in Marietta, Northwest Territory (located in the southern tip of present-day Ohio). Marietta was one of the first settlements founded after the northwest area was formally organized as a US territory under the Northwest Ordinance in 1787. There was a well-established trail to this destination, but as yet no road sufficiently wide for a wagon. Consequently, the Wells brothers traveled mostly on foot leading pack animals loaded with tools and equipment they would need.[15]

They immediately established claim to some land and began clearing it for farming. They probably intended to pay for this property using warrants given to their father, Joshua Wells, in partial payment for his Revolutionary War service. These land warrants were authorized for veterans by Congress and, under provisions of the Northwest Ordinance, could be used for purchases in the Ohio basin. Gideon apparently stayed in Marietta only one summer before returning to his wife and family in Wethersfield, but Daniel remained over two years, developing his claim in spring, summer, and fall months and teaching school in the winters.[16]

Daniel's relatively extensive education is confirmed not only by his being hired to teach the children of other settlers, but also by a letter he sent to Miss Honor Francis, the young lady with whom he had "kept company" before his western adventure and whom he married after his return. This letter was written when he had been over eighteen months in Ohio and was obviously longing to return to his family and his true love.

> Mrs. Honor Francis,
> Wethersfield, Connecticut.
>
> Marietta. December 12th, 1797
>
> Dear Honor:
>
> It is with pleasure I write to inform you that I enjoy my health very well, hoping you are enjoying the same blessing.
>
> I have had hopes of receiving a letter from you once more but waiting till I was out of patience I write again to let you know I have not forgot you but not able to say but you have me. I should be sorry to hear such news for it is my design to enjoy a happy life together if possible and I hope you will join me with pleasure. I should be glad to pay you a visit this winter but the journey is long and so tedious to attempt I hope their will be no friendship lost by neither of us for my not coming. I should be fond of living where I could enjoy your company as in former times, if I thought it would be for our advantage hereafter. I have not determined to settle in this country that induces me to tarry here so long, but I want to see more of it before I return.[17]

Daniel may have returned from Ohio by the time Joshua Wells died in Wethersfield in August 1798, but if not, news of his father's death surely brought him home.

Six months after Joshua's death, Daniel Wells and Honor Francis, who was born in September 1774, married in Wethersfield on March 26, 1799[18] and almost immediately embarked together on a new westward journey. They did not, however, return to Marietta or to any other settlement in the Northwest Territory. Daniel's decision to abandon his claim in Ohio, as he wrote Honor in late 1797, was probably based on his observation that the area was too remote and too dangerous because of continual Indian threats. It was reinforced by the fact that his father's eligibility for land warrants redeemable in the Northwest Territory expired at his death. Since Daniel would now have to purchase his land for cash, he determined to choose a more civilized site nearer to his and Honor's long-established family base in Wethersfield.[19]

The place they chose was the Holland Patent in Oneida County, New York. It was located a few miles north of Utica. Land in the Holland

Patent, so named for the Holland Land Company which owned it, was first offered for sale to new settlers in 1793 after title to the property was cleared and transferred to the Dutch owners of the Company.[20] By the time Daniel and Honor Wells arrived in mid-1799, a number of farms were already established, but plenty of good land remained available for purchase. They settled on a tract in the town of Trenton, which had been organized in 1797, among a number of neighbors who had also come from Connecticut. These included the Wolcott, Storrs, Hubbard, Willard, Rockwell, and other families from Hartford and Wethersfield. Both of these towns were only about 215 miles away from Trenton over developed roads that made the transport of both goods and people much easier than in the far west.[21]

Daniel Wells purchased 102 acres next to the farm of William and Ephraim Storrs from William Johnson for the sum of $665. The deed is dated December 28, 1800, but Daniel and Honor had probably been living on the property and building a home for a year or more under a rental agreement until Daniel's inherited property in Wethersfield was sold and the money forwarded to him.[22]

A few years later Daniel added another fifty acres of land to his holdings. This parcel was purchased directly from the owners of the Holland Land Co. for $365 and was transferred to Daniel by a deed dated January 19, 1807 and signed by Adam G. Mappa, the attorney for all of the absentee owners. The new acreage was located on the opposite side of Wethersfield Road from Daniel's original purchase and on lower ground. He continued to farm the original plot, on which his home was also built, and constructed a barn and other outbuildings on the lower piece. The surrounding meadowland was mainly used as pasture, although he probably intended to plow and sow some of it when he had sons old enough to assist him. Subsequent events did not make that plan feasible.[23]

Eliza Wells, Daniel and Honor's first child, was born in 1800. Four additional daughters were born in Trenton during the following years as Daniel developed his property and prospered as a farmer. Pamela Wells arrived in 1803, Abigail Wells in 1805, Lucy Ann Wells in 1809, and Honor Francis Wells in 1812.[24]

In September 1812, less than three weeks after the birth of her fifth child, Honor Wells died, likely as a result of complications from childbirth. She was eleven days short of being 38 years old. Her body was laid to rest in the Holland Patent Cemetery less than three months after the United States declared war on Great Britain.[25]

The War of 1812, which commenced with the signing of the congressional act in favor of it by President James Madison on June 19, 1812, was not popular in New York or in the rest of the northeastern US. Business and commercial interests opposed the closing of trade with Britain and were fearful of a blockade of American ports. Farmers, such as Daniel Wells, and other rural New Yorkers were less concerned about the economic aspects of the war, but anxious lest it be fought in their back yards by English forces invading southward from Canada.

In the event, it was the Americans who invaded Canada, despite the small size, lack of training and inexperience of the US Army and its associated state militias. Gen. William Hull led a force of about one thousand untrained and poorly-equipped militia across the Detroit River in July 1812 and occupied the Canadian town of Sandwich. A month later Hull's troops retreated to Detroit where they surrendered to a force of British regulars, Canadian militia and Native Americans. The Americans soon launched a second invasion of Canada in the Niagara isthmus of western New York where they attempted to establish a foothold on the western side of the Niagara River. United States forces, consisting of regular army and New York militia troops, were again defeated at the Battle of Queenston Heights on October 13, 1812 by a combined force of British regulars, Canadian militia, and Mohawk warriors.[26]

Although an early biographer of Daniel H. Wells states that his father Daniel Wells left his Trenton farm "for a short period at the call of his country to serve as a soldier in the War of 1812," there is no historical evidence to support this claim. No person from Oneida County named Daniel Wells is recorded as serving in either the regular army or the New York militia during the war. While it is possible that Daniel was a member of the 1812 Niagara expedition into Canada, it seems unlikely that he would leave his five young daughters so soon after the death of their mother.[27]

It is more reasonable to conclude that Daniel did not feel comfortable leaving his children, all of whom were under twelve years of age at the time of their mother's death, even for a ninety day summer enlistment, the shortest period for which he could have served. He probably volunteered, along with his neighbors, to defend their homes and property should the British follow up their defeat of the American invasions of Canada with a thrust into Oneida County or the surrounding area, but this possibility never materialized.[28]

Daniel was only thirty-nine at the time of Honor's death and, unlike his father, who was forty-six when his wife died, was not resigned to rearing his children alone after her passing. The population of Oneida County was not large and the number of eligible women only a small fraction of the total, but Daniel had to search only as far as Sangerfield, some thirty miles southwest of Trenton, to find a suitable prospect. She was Catherine Chapin, born 1788, who had just turned twenty-four when she began "keeping company" with the widower who was fifteen years her senior.

Catherine's family, like Daniel's, came from Connecticut. She was born in New Hartford, about twenty-five miles northwest of Wethersfield where the Wells clan had lived for generations. She was the eldest surviving child of David Chapin, born 1762 in New Hartford, and his wife Ruth Seymour, born 1767. David Chapin was a direct descendant of Deacon Samuel Chapin, born 1598 in Paignton, Devonshire, England, who immigrated to Massachusetts in 1635, the same year that Thomas Wells arrived in the colony. Like Wells's descendant Joshua Wells, David Chapin was also a Revolutionary War veteran.[29]

On March 1, 1778, David Chapin enlisted as a private for a period of three years in a Connecticut regiment of the "Connecticut Line," serving in Captain Joseph Walker's company. His enlistment at age fifteen was three days after that of fifty-one-year-old Joshua Wells in the same company.[30] Both men were fifth generation descendants from the original immigrants to North America in their respective families. There is no record that Joshua Wells and David Chapin were acquainted prior to beginning their military service together, but they doubtless became comrades during the following years. David was near the age of Joshua's three oldest sons, Joshua Jr., Levi, and Gideon. He had never known his father and his stepfather was past sixty when he married David's mother. He would have seen Joshua as a father figure, someone to turn to for guidance and counsel as they fought together through the long conflict.[31]

David Chapin marched with Joshua Wells and the rest of the Fourth Connecticut Militia Regiment through the campaigns described earlier in this chapter: to Long Island in December 1777; to Rhode Island in the summer of 1778 and into battle there on August 29; to Winter Quarters in Morristown, New Jersey, in the fall of 1778; and into the Battle of Springfield on June 23, 1780. After the Springfield battle, the regiment served in New York along the Hudson River through the summer of 1780 and went into Winter Quarters at the Connecticut Village camp in the fall of that year. David's period of service drew to a close during the winter of 1781 and, perhaps at the urging of his older companions, he decided not to re-enlist. Having served his country through three years of war, his fellows may have encouraged him to go home and marry so that he could bring new citizens into the country he had helped create.[32]

David was honorably discharged from service at Newburg, New York, on February 19, 1781. While Joshua Wells and the rest of his old regiment joined with other elements of the Continental Army and French forces under the Compte de Rochambeau for the march south into Virginia and the climactic Battle of Yorktown, David returned to his New Hartford home and his family. For him, though not yet for the country, the war was over.[33]

David Chapin married Ruth Seymour in New Hartford, in 1784. Their first five children were born there between 1786 and 1793. David worked on the parcel of land left to him by his father to support himself and his family, but it was not a large holding and provided only a modest income.[34]

In early 1795 the Chapin family moved to the newly surveyed town of Sangerfield in Chenango County, New York. David Chapin was one of the original residents who organized the community at its first town meeting held on April 7, 1795. He was among the town officers chosen, being elected as Constable and Collector along with Jonathan Porter.[35]

David and Ruth Chapin had three additional children after their move to Sangerfield, bringing their total family to eight. Their oldest child, Archer Chapin, died early in 1799, but the remainder of the family fared well in their new community.[36]

Catherine Chapin, the eldest daughter, had just turned seven years of age when the Chapin family arrived in Sangerfield. She appears to have received a good basic education as she taught school later in her life. Since she was only two years old when Daniel Wells left New Hartford, she could not have known him there, but it seems likely that he was at least aware of her existence and was known to her family in Sangerfield before he traveled there to seek her hand in marriage early in 1813. Daniel's father Joshua may have maintained his wartime friendship with Catherine's father and other members of the Chapin family. The journey from Trenton required a long day's ride, both going and returning, and would only have been worth making if Daniel was assured of a welcome at its end.

His courtship of Catherine was brief, a few hours spent together on the occasions when he could visit before returning to work his farm during the spring planting and summer growing seasons. But despite the age difference between them, they were well matched. After the fall harvest, on November 30, 1813, Daniel Wells and Catherine Chapin were married in Trenton. She became mistress of his household and stepmother to his five daughters. Their first child, Daniel Hanmer Wells, was born the following year on October 27.[37]

2
Daniel H. Wells
From a Brief Childhood in New York to Frontier Life in Illinois
1814–1838

With five older half-sisters to watch over him, pamper him, and circumscribe his every move, Daniel's early years must have been both a pleasure and a challenge for the only son. From all evidence, he handled the circumstances of his birth well and established a close relationship with all of his siblings that lasted throughout their lives. He never referred to any of them as step-sisters nor did he regard himself as a step-brother to them. His middle name was taken from his sisters' grandmother, Elizabeth Hanmer, and his ties to the Hanmer family were as extensive as those with his own mother's family, the Chapins.

The birth of Catherine Chapin Wells, Daniel's younger sister, in 1818 may have drawn some attention away from him temporarily, but he seems to have been from his arrival the central figure in the family, upon whom much love and affection were showered and of whom great accomplishments were expected. Catherine soon became his adoring younger sister in much the same manner or even more so than his older siblings.

Little is known about Daniel's education because he did not write about it and no records of the early schools in Oneida County exist. He attended the first school in Trenton, which opened in 1802 and was well established by the time he was of age to go there. The original log and lumber school was replaced with a stone structure about 1824 and this building still stands on a small plot between the Wells and Rockwell farms. The school was convenient for Daniel to attend as well as for his mother to teach at, which she did during some of the years when her own children were students there.

Figure 2.1. The one-room school built in 1825 on Wethersfield Road (now Route 365) in Trenton that Daniel H. Wells attended and his mother taught in. It was restored in 2015.

Daniel may also have been a student at the first school in nearby Deerfield, a log cabin erected in 1807, in which Aaron Reed was the first teacher. "The earliest schools were 'gotten up,' sometimes by a teacher looking for occupation, at other times by parents seeking to provide means of education for the children." All of them were one room buildings in which the quality of instruction was largely determined by the credentials and classroom ability of the teacher.[1]

Hamilton Oneida Academy which began in 1793, was granted a charter as Hamilton College on May 26, 1812, but there is no evidence that Daniel attended this institution. By the time he reached his teen years, he was already operating the family farm and hiring himself out for wages to help support the family.[2]

Daniel received a basic education at school, attending during the winters and working on the farm in the summers. His formal learning was supplemented by his father, who had himself taught school in Ohio, as noted previously, and by his well-educated mother.

He was a good student, but not overly enamored of learning. Lionel Willard, a schoolmate, remembered when, "as a little, red-headed boy, [Daniel] was perched on a high bench in the old schoolroom, and, while dozing one afternoon, tumbled off the bench, greatly to his own consternation, and much to the merriment of the rest of the school."[3]

Daniel and his family, like most of those from Wethersfield who settled in Trenton, were Methodist Christians and attended church services faithfully in keeping with the tradition of their Puritan forebears. The Rev. Mr. Fish, who was the first preacher to visit the town, was also Presbyterian and found several like-minded people already living there who urged him to stay. He became the first pastor of the church formed in 1797. The congregation struggled financially in its early years, but by the turn of the century had become well established.

The Rev. J. Taylor, writing in his journal in 1802, says of Rev. Mr. Fish: "He is a sensible, judicious man, and appears to be doing great good, and has but a poor reward." In addition to describing his visit to the Trenton church, Taylor notes that the town school has fifty children attending "who have a good teacher. Many of the children have no catechism and their parents are unable, in some instances, to procure the necessary school books. Four families nearby are destitute of Bibles and are poor."[4]

Just before he turned twelve, Daniel H. Wells's life changed dramatically. His father, who was only fifty-three, died suddenly of natural causes in September 1826. He left most of the crop on his farm unharvested and his only son responsible, with the help of his sisters and neighbors, to complete the task. From that time on, Daniel's mother Catherine took charge of the family and he became foreman of the farm. Daniel's childhood ended abruptly and he shouldered the burden of an adult.[5]

At the time of their father's death, three of Daniel's sisters were twenty-one or older, two were teenagers, and the youngest, Catherine, was eight. None of the older girls had as yet married and all were still living at home. The 150 acre farm was easily capable of providing for eight people, but Daniel H. Wells faced the same challenge as his father in trying to work it alone. The younger Daniel was large for his age and very strong, but even so, the amount of land he could plow, sow, tend, and harvest by himself was considerably less than what he had available. He wisely decided to limit the acreage planted and turn the rest to pasture where he raised animals that could be used by the family or sold for cash. This plan proved successful and the Wells farm sustained its owners adequately for the next seven years.

Daniel also hired himself out at harvest time in order to earn extra cash for the family's needs. In this endeavor he was frustrated by the tradition that a boy should not be paid wages equal to those of a man. As one of his sons, Junius Wells, later expressed it, "he never understood why, simply because he was a boy, though he did a man's work, he only received a boy's wages for his labor. He worked for [William] Storrs at fifty cents a day, but the men got a dollar."[6]

Storrs acknowledged Daniel's ability and work ethic, telling Junius Wells in 1874, "his vivid recollection of the hardworking youth who lived next door and often helped them at their haying. He said that though young Daniel Wells was only a boy in years, he was large of stature and always kept up with the men at work. He had seen him many a time wipe the sweat from his brow and dash it in streams from his fingers." Although the inequity of half-pay for boys was admitted, the tradition was maintained.[7]

None of Daniel's sisters married until 1836, some three years after he left the family farm and went west, but four of them were courting or engaged to the men they would eventually marry by the summer of 1833. Long engagements were the norm in the conservative Wells family, either to give adequate time for the couple to become deeply attached to one another or, more probably, to allow the prospective husbands to acquire land and build a proper home before starting a new family.

As his sisters prepared for marriage, they all desired to have the inheritance left them by their father, Daniel Wells. Since he made no will, his property, consisting principally of his 150 acre farm, was divided equally among his widow and each of his children. In order for the heirs to receive their portions in cash, the farm was sold for the sum of $1,350 to Oliver Coombs, a Wethersfield native who had moved to Trenton about the same time as Daniel Wells. He was the father of Joseph Coombs whom Lucy Ann Wells was courting and would marry a few years later.[8]

At the time of the sale, Daniel, as well as his sisters Honor and Catherine, had not reached the age of twenty-one and his mother Catherine was appointed guardian for the three infants under the law. Honor Wells turned twenty-one the next year and received her share, but Daniel did not come of age until 1835 and Catherine not until 1839. Until then, their money was held in trust by the New York court that approved the disposition of Daniel's estate.[9]

Unwilling to wait for his majority, Daniel prepared to leave New York soon after the sale of the farm was completed in June 1832. His mother and his younger sister agreed to accompany him and, in the spring of 1833, they departed for Ohio.[10]

Rather than going to the southern part of Ohio, as his father had done in 1795, Daniel proceeded almost directly west from Trenton to Buffalo and thence southeast along the southern shore of Lake Erie to the Cleveland area. His choice was strongly influenced by the fact that the easiest travel and best accommodations were to be had along the Erie Canal, which was completed in 1825 and had by 1833 become the established transportation route to the western part of the country.

It is possible that the family traveled by water, shipping as freight the equipment and supplies they would need to start farming life in a new community. The toll on the Canal and Lake Erie for passengers was

1½ cents per mile, including board, and for freight, eight mills per 100 pounds per mile. At those rates, three passengers with a ton of goods could travel for a fare of about 20 cents per mile including meals and sleeping quarters for the trip. The distance from Syracuse to Cleveland is 390 miles and the total fare would have been around $78.[11]

Though small by modern standards, this was a substantial sum for the Wells family and was high enough that they likely opted for a cheaper but slower journey by wagon over the rough roads that paralleled the Canal and the lakeshore. Land travel from Trenton to Cleveland required about four weeks, twice the time needed to go by water, but the cost was no more than a fifth of the boat fare.[12]

Whether by water or road, Daniel and his family arrived in northern Ohio in the late spring of 1833 and he immediately began searching for suitable farmland to purchase. The results were disappointing; they had arrived too late. Most of the best land was already claimed by others and that which was available for sale was priced too high for Daniel to afford the acreage he needed to support his family. By midsummer he had determined that Ohio was not the place where he wanted to settle and was making plans to push further west.[13]

Realizing that he would not have enough time to reach a new destination and still get in a crop before winter, Daniel opted to stay the remainder of the year in Ohio and continue west in the spring. He found living accommodations in the area and a job teaching school, the income from which provided for their needs until the following year.[14]

Many years after the event, Daniel related to one of his sons an incident that occurred during his brief stint as a teacher in Ohio. It reveals his hot temper and his recognition of his need to control it.

> When I was a very young man teaching school in Ohio, before coming to Nauvoo, one of the boys in the class, as big and strong as I was, used to make fun of my red hair, which was then considered a real calamity, and would call me red head whenever he passed me by, thus causing a titter and threatening to destroy the discipline of my school. The boy, ignoring the warning, called me red head at the first opportunity and, losing my temper, I made good my threat and dealt him a blow that sent him sprawling upon the floor, where he lay perfectly still and unconscious, and I thought surely he was dead, and I said: "I have killed him and ruined my own life just because I lost my temper," but the boy revived, for which I was truly thankful, and I vowed I would never again lose my temper.[15]

In the spring of 1834 the Wells family moved west again. This time the entire route was overland through Ohio and Indiana to the southern tip of Lake Michigan and then across Illinois to the banks of the Mississippi River and a tiny village named Venus. The reason why Daniel chose this town, which was founded by white settlers about 1827 on the site of an Indian encampment named Quashquema, is best explained in his own words:

> I started west to find a place to locate in, having but little means, and I wished to go where land was cheap so that I could get a farm and a home. First I went to Ohio and looked around there; and the next year went to Warsaw [Illinois] where a sale of lots had been advertised. Arrived there a few days after the sale, still there was yet some land for sale, but it did not suit me. I then heard of more settlements a little farther up the river at what was afterwards called Nauvoo. I went there and looked around, and rented a place on which I located. In the course of the season I bought a piece of land of 80 acres.[16]

Hancock County, in which the town was located, was created in 1825 out of land that were originally part of the so-called "Military Tract" set aside by Congress to reward veterans of the War of 1812. Settlement in the area was slow to develop until after the defeat of hostile Indian groups during the Black Hawk War in 1832. Daniel may have heard of the place from advertisements or word-of-mouth promotions put out by the absentee land owners Captain James White, A. White, and J. B. Teas, who held most of the property and were offering plots for sale at reasonable prices with easy credit terms.

About the time Daniel and his family arrived in western Illinois in early 1834, White and Teas laid out a street plan for a town, which until then consisted of randomly placed cabins and farms, on the lower bank of a large bend in the Mississippi River. Venus, the original name, was changed to Commerce in an attempt to increase its commercial appeal. The effort was only minimally successful in attracting new residents and investors, mainly because the town site was on low-lying land that was frequently flooded when the river was high and became a swampy breeding ground for malaria-bearing insects when it was low.

Most of the early settlers were farmers who preferred to locate on the flat prairie land stretching east from the bluff above the river. Daniel also chose this area for his farm and purchased an 84 acre plot from Samuel Gooch for $450. Gooch had received the land as a patent from the federal government as a result of his service in the War of 1812.[17]

Because Daniel was not yet of age to receive his inheritance, he purchased the land as a joint tenant with his mother, Catherine Wells, and her inheritance from her late husband provided the down payment on the property. The balance was made due in December of 1835, two months after Daniel's twenty-first birthday.

During the growing season of 1834, Daniel was able to plant and harvest a crop on some of his new land, and also built a cabin in which the family spent the following winter. No written account exists of the family's pioneer year in Illinois, but much can be inferred from a surviving letter written by Catherine and Daniel to their sister Pamela and other family members in New York. It is dated July 7, 1835, a little over one year after their arrival, but was written in sections over a period of several days.

> Commerce, July 7th 1835
>
> Dear Sister Pamela
>
> We received your and A[bigail]'s kind letter two weeks ago which made us very happy. We had wrote a short time before and sent papers which probably you have received long before this. D[aniel] came in this noon with a letter and 8 papers from E[liza] and L[ucy] which has done us a heap of good (as the suckers say) . . . [A slang term for Illinois residents. It was not then a negative reference.]
>
> Perhaps you would like to know how we are situated. At present bub[brother] D[aniel] is up the river two miles getting stone. I expect him home every minute to help me milk. And ma took up her work and went to our nearest neigh[bor] to drink tea and I am all alone sitting by the door where when I look up I see our pretty garden which is close by the door. We have had peas this 3 weeks and a prospect of having them four weeks longer. We have fine lot of cabbages, also onions beets carrots teomatus beans [indecipherable] peppers cucumbers radishes lettuce and I have a few flowers. So you see we have every thing that is good and some that is not. We milk eight cows, have milked ten, make a cheese every other day, and ma keeps school. They was to have me but chose ma on account of government [Catherine was then 16]. She has from 20 to 30 scholars and amongst it all we keep pretty busy. Ma has two dollars a quarter. I wish I was with you a going to school. Have no good school short of 30 or 40 miles. I am not yet married to an indian but D[aniel] talked some of selling me. He was offerd 5 horses for me by an indian. [Like Daniel, Catherine had red hair which made her a rare and valuable woman to an Indian.] I have

been to several parties this spring and have danced. Give my love to grandma grandpa and all the rest. Do write soon. C. H. W. [Catherine Wells] . . .

Dear Sister,

I improve a rainy day to finish a letter Which Catherine has commenced. Not but that I could write one myself, but that this may contain all that we have to tell. I find that setling in a new country is attended with many disadvantages deprivations and inconveniences which are not expected or thought of until tried. Things that we must have and cannot do without comfortably are numerous and come very high, but I have no reason to be discouraged yet for labor is high as well as produce of ever kind, and my health is good. The great difficulty is I cannot improve and get things to get along with as fast as I wish without money. Credit, I have more than I wish, I sometimes think, however, it is very convenient so long as it can be kept good, which requires, you know, like vegetation in a drouth, occasional refreshings to keep from drying up.

If you have ascertained whether I can get my share of money by Power of Attorney or agency I wish you to let me know. Also who to invest with said power, i.e. who will be willing to take the trouble, for I had better pay some one to do it for me, if I can, this fall than to go myself. Not but what I should like to go, but cannot afford it if it can be done without. I shall want it at all events, to make the last payment for our land the 1st of Dec . . .

The country is selling quite fast so that the neighbors are plenty. Carthage the county seat is 18 miles out in the Praire and 2 years ago was nor laid off. [It] has now 30 or 40 houses and continues to grow. Commerce also improves and will I am confident become quite a place. It was rather sickly here last season and also throughout the West so far as I could learn. It has been quite a wet season so far. I do not know what effect it may have on the health of the place this year. At present it is healthy and I believe will be one the safest of any where.

The Garrison [in Michigan, later Iowa Territory on the west side of the Mississippi River] makes everything very scarce and labor high. They are obliged to have 418 tons of hay delivered from the Praire on that side, and help will be very scarce. The Draggoons have gone out on the campaign will return in Sept. [They] will have many an Indian story to tell when they return. Indians are not so plenty here as you imagine. They have gone up the River. They are very different from those Oneidas more savage. They dance for liquor, sing their War songs, and swing their Battle axes over your head. If you jump, it is fine sport for them, if not they think you are brave. When they kill any body they make the print of a man's hand on their blanket with red paint. Its not uncommon to see them swing the scalps of their enimies when they dance. With their heads shaved faces painted decorated in the most curious manner, bells on their legs, I don't know what I should call them if I did not know and should meet them by myself. You must have patience or you never will read the half of this letter . . .

Remember me to all my relations and acquaintances. Per Your affectionate brother,
Daniel H. Wells

Send [news]Papers. We would if we could get them. Don't work too hard because you are alone. I think every time I see a boat land how glad I would be to see some of my old friends. I look among the Passengers to see if there is not at least one that I know, but all are strangers. DW[18]

While frontier life had its difficulties for civilized New Yorkers, Daniel was obviously pleased with his new farm and the community that was growing up around it. The economy of Commerce and Hancock County was expanding as new settlers purchased land in the area or received bounty acreage as a reward for their war service. The newcomers had all the basic needs for food, shelter, and other essentials that the Wells family experienced after their arrival the previous year. They were now in a position to supply some of the foodstuffs, clothing, and other products that were in demand and prospered accordingly. Catherine wrote Pamela about their varied sources of income, some of which were much different than had existed on their Trenton farm.

> I have taken in shirts to make from the garrison. Have made twenty, get from 75 [cents] to a dollar apiece . . . Excellent market for everything. Daniel sold 200 bushels of corn last week for 50 cents per bushel, and 30 bushels of oats at the same price. He had sold a good many oats before at forty-five. We have sold fifty dollars worth of fish this winter.[19]

Daniel did not return to New York during the winter of 1835 due to the expense and the amount of time the thousand mile journey would have required. His request that Pamela find someone in Trenton to whom he could give power of attorney to settle his inheritance took longer to accomplish than he expected. A second letter sent from Daniel and Catherine in March 1836 indicates that the matter was still not settled by that time.

> Commerce, March 12th, 1836
>
> Dear Sister,
>
> For weeks and months have I looked for an answer to the letter which I sent with power of attorney to do my business. I received one but you had not then received mine. I hope it has not miscarried. If I do not receive it soon shall write to [William] Storrs and give him the power att[orney]. He has not writen to me as yet but you say he will do the business.[20]

Daniel obtained an extension of the due date for the final payment on his land. Samuel Gooch, his creditor, had relocated to Madison County, Illinois, where he was pursuing additional land deals. He did not apparently mind the delay of payment for a few months, but Daniel was impatient for a resolution that would give him a debt-free title.

Pamela also wrote that their sister Abigail had announced her marriage to Stephen Rockwell of Trenton. Daniel sent back his congratulations and chided Abigail, tongue in cheek, for not sending him, Catherine or their mother formal invitations to their nuptials. The Wells family's second year in Illinois was so successful that he now felt a trip back to New York was within their economic means.[21]

Abigail Wells was the first of Daniel's sisters to marry, and four additional family weddings occurred within a year of the Rockwells's. The next one, as related by Daniel to Pamela, happened much closer to his home, and he was able to attend.

> Commerce August 28 [1836]
>
> Dear Sister . . .
>
> Catherine is married, and we are all well. Two items of no news, I suppose you think, but it is nevertheless true, and I think if you will come here we can convince you of the fact that it is not such an all killing job to get married as it is cracked up to be. I will give you a short history of the affair and leave you to judge. You see I was out in the Praire haying and it rained on Friday night, so I came home. Well the next morning I found Woods, (or James Weston Woods, is his name) was here and that he and

Catherine were going to be married on Sunday, and sure enough they was. They just exactly walked over to the school-house arm in arm. Their attendance [attendants] followed next and Ma brought up the rear. She wanted me to walk by her side but I thought I had rather walk in the path too so I went behind her. Well we got there at last and there we staid until the preacher preached and sung and prayed, and then they just got up, they did, and cleared away a seat so they could all sit together and then and there they was all standing up, they was, and he married them. That is all, except they come back again and we had some excellent cake, the best I have tasted this long while. I like to forget to tell you, the preacher came over home and some of the neighbors and took dinner and that night I had the greatest notion to go and see some of the girls I ever had in my life, but I was afraid I should not know how to act so I thought I would go to bed & be ready to go to work in the Praire haying again the next morning, as I did. And it is work work all the time.[22]

Catherine's new husband, James Weston Woods, from Middlesex, Massachusetts, was eight years older than his wife and was just starting his career as a self-trained attorney. He would subsequently practice in Illinois, Iowa, and Missouri for more than forty years and become known under the name J. W. Woods Esq. as one of the area's most prominent figures. Shortly after marrying Catherine, he established himself in Burlington, Iowa Territory, and pursued his legal practice from there.

Daniel's inheritance was finally settled before the end of 1836, and he paid off his land debt with the proceeds.

Daniel also began, out of necessity, to get acquainted with the law. He was elected constable for Hancock County a month or two after becoming eligible to serve on his twenty-first birthday. He did not seek the office, but his neighbors, as he wryly put it in a letter, "cotcht me up on a pin hook and elected me so I was obliged to serve."[23]

The following year he was elected justice of the peace for Hancock County, and served in the Commerce area so that residents there did not have to make the forty mile round trip to Carthage, the county seat, in order to have legal matters heard and documents witnessed. Daniel was well regarded among his neighbors and, although he did not seek these offices, he was repeatedly re-elected to them and chosen for other positions as well.

Ere he was twenty-one years of age, he was elected constable, and soon afterwards justice of the peace. He was also elected second sergeant in the first organization of the militia of the district; and so great was the confidence of all parties and sects, including the Catholics, in his integrity and impartiality, that he was often selected as arbitrator of differences between neighbors, and administrator of the estates of deceased persons.[24]

Daniel remained a justice of the peace for more than ten years, not relinquishing the office until he left Illinois. As a justice, he acquired the designation "Squire" by which he was known throughout the remainder of his life. Although he later held other positions of higher rank and greater responsibility, including legislator, general, and mayor, he was called "Squire Wells" by almost everyone who knew him.[25]

As was often the case in western states with small populations and newly organized counties, Daniel served as both constable and justice of the peace without any formal legal training. His education included basic legal concepts and an understanding of the Constitution, but he had to learn the duties of his offices on the job. He had some experience in court procedures from pursuing his own affairs after the death of his father and he learned from others who came into his court.

Most of the lawyers and government officials in Illinois were self-taught and Daniel followed their examples by studying on his own to improve his legal knowledge. His education in law was undoubtedly helped by input from his brother-in-law James Weston Woods. Mr. Woods, as Catherine usually referred to her husband, was four years older than Daniel and often brought his wife and family to Commerce to visit relatives and pursue his work. While there, he guided Daniel's studies from his own experience and lent him scarce legal books from which the young justice markedly improved his understanding.

Another Illinois lawyer with whom Daniel established a friendship was Abraham Lincoln. They became acquainted in April 1839 when Lincoln visited Hancock County as defense attorney for William Fraim, a man accused of murder in Schuyler County who secured a change of venue for his trial because bias against him existed in the area where the crime was committed. Daniel was called to serve on the jury and, according to the story he later told, when he met the future president, Lincoln exclaimed, "Prepare to die! I swore that if I ever met a man who was uglier than I am, I would shoot him." To this the young squire replied, "Shoot away. If I am as ugly as you are, then I don't want to live."[26]

Such an introduction naturally led to a closer association between the two men who were, aside from Daniel's blazing red hair, similar in appearance and temperament. Lincoln was five years older and several inches taller, but had commenced his law practice in Springfield in 1836, the same year that Daniel became a justice of the peace in Hancock County.

The evidence against Fraim was overwhelming, as he had been seen to stab a man named Neathammer in the chest during an altercation at a tavern in the town of Frederick. A witness testified to the facts and, the jurors' friendship with the defense attorney notwithstanding, Fraim was convicted in April 1836 and hanged a month later.[27]

Church meetings were held frequently in the Wells home beginning soon after their arrival in Commerce. One of the preachers who often presided at these services was the Rev. Charles Robison, born 1785. He was a native of Oneida in Madison County, New York, who moved to the southern part of Indiana about 1807, thence to Cincinnati, Ohio, about 1810, and farther west to Illinois in 1823. He obtained land in Sonora Township, located south of Commerce and built a home for himself and his large family of twelve children near the Mississippi River. Robison was one of the first sixty-five settlers who organized Hancock County in 1827. Like most American evangelical preachers of the time, he was a part-time, self-called minister who recognized only the authority of the Bible in his teaching. He adhered to Methodist doctrine, but the services he hosted were open to those of any Christian denomination.

Robison's wife, Jerusha Rebecca Kellogg, who was also born in 1785, died in Hancock County on August 23, 1836, leaving the Rev. Robison with six minor children, the youngest only nine years old.[28]

Catherine Wells, Daniel's mother, was the same age as the Rev. Robison and had become friends with him through his numerous visits to her home. She was still an attractive woman at age fifty-one and the widower lost no time in turning their relationship into an offer of marriage. Catherine accepted with the same alacrity her daughter had shown in marrying J. W. Woods after only a brief courtship. Rev. Charles Robison and Catherine Wells were married on February 7, 1837 and she moved to his home in Sonora Township.[29]

Their marriage lasted only three and a half years as Charles Robison died on October 4, 1840, leaving Catherine to complete the upbringing of his younger children. This she accomplished with some assistance from Daniel, who established a close friendship with Lewis Robison, one of Charles's younger sons, and an intimate relationship with one of his daughters.

Whether finding himself alone and obliged to fend for himself in a home where he had formerly enjoyed the help and company of his mother and sister accelerated Daniel's efforts to find a wife is uncertain. He may have been pursuing Eliza Rebecca Robison for as long or longer than her father had shown an interest in his mother, but his suddenly empty quarters may have contributed to the speed of his proposal. One month after Rev. Charles Robison became his stepfather, he also became his father-in-law when Daniel and Eliza were married on March 12, 1837. Eliza, born June 4, 1820, in Ohio, was sixteen; Daniel was twenty-two.[30]

Figure 2.2. Eliza Rebecca Robison, Daniel H. Wells's first wife, date unknown.

The following winter Daniel and Eliza received word that Daniel's sister Honor Francis Wells (known in the family as Frank) had married Joseph D'Ortigue Raphel in November 1837. D'Ortigue, who preferred his middle name, was the son of Fontienne Raphel and his wife Lucy Goodrich, and a grandson of Revolutionary War veteran Nichol Raphel. Frank and D'Ortigue settled in Connecticut, but Frank spent much of her time in New York visiting with her family there while her husband traveled extensively on business.[31]

Daniel's increasing prosperity enabled him to easily support his new wife, expand their home and purchase some of the comforts of civilization that had not been available or affordable during the first years of his residence in Illinois. As he had written in his earlier letters, prices were high for agricultural products and wages for labor were also high in Hancock County. The Panic of 1837, which began in New York in May, had already forced the eastern states into a recession that persisted through the mid-1840s, but the farming economy of the western states was not seriously affected until 1839.

Martin Van Buren was inaugurated as president a week after Daniel and Eliza were married, succeeding Democrat Andrew Jackson, whose actions in the last days of his administration helped precipitate the panic and prolong the following recession. Van Buren continued to enforce Jackson's Specie Circular, issued as an Executive Order on July 11, 1836, which directed all government officials to accept only gold and silver specie (coined money) in payment for public lands. This policy drastically reduced purchases by speculators, many of whom had formerly paid with paper currency issued by state banks that often did not have gold or silver sufficient to back the amounts of their money in circulation.[32]

Daniel's purchase in Hancock County was not affected by the new policy since he bought from a private owner and paid with gold-backed currency from a New York bank. The decline in government land purchases over the next few years actually benefitted owners like Daniel, who had made payment and secured their deeds before the downturn began.

The Wells farm in New York sold in 1832 for $9.00 per acre. Daniel purchased his undeveloped farm in Illinois for $5.36 per acre in 1834, but the paper-money-fueled land boom in western states caused the purchases of government land to quintuple by 1836 with a corresponding rise in price. After the gold-or-silver-only payment rule was implemented, sales of government land plunged, but private sales, which could still be made using paper currency, rose and as demand increased, so did the price per acre. By 1840, when Daniel began selling some of his property, it commanded $20.00 per acre and continued to increase in value each year thereafter.[33]

The year following their marriage Daniel and Eliza's first and, as events turned out, only child, Albert Emory Wells, was born in March 1837. He enjoyed good health from the start of his life and grew rapidly in stature and the affections of his parents.[34]

A few months later Eliza Wells, Daniel's oldest sister, married Dr. James S. Ross. Eliza was thirty-six and her husband a year or two older at the time of their wedding. Immediately afterward the couple moved west to begin their life together in a new community. They did not come as far as Illinois, but established themselves in the small town of Medina, about thirty miles south of Cleveland, where Dr. Ross set up his medical practice.[35]

The growing season of 1837 was so successful that Daniel was finally able to make a visit to his family in Trenton during the early months of 1838. Owing to the distance, the difficulty of overland travel, and Albert's age, he and his mother, Eliza, did not go east, but remained in Illinois with the Robison family while Daniel was away. Catherine Woods, who had her first child, Nehemiah, in the fall of 1837, also did not accompany her brother.

Figure 2.3. Albert Emory Wells (1838–1916), only child of Daniel H. Wells and Eliza R. Robison. Photo by W. N. Stoddard, Chicago, ca. 1860.

Daniel made most of his journey on water, going by boat from Cleveland to Buffalo on Lake Erie and thence on the Erie Canal to Syracuse. Both going to New York and coming home, he visited for two weeks with his sister Eliza in Ohio. His return coincided with the birth of her first child in May 1838, as described in his letter to his sisters and brother-in-law still resident in Trenton.

Medina, April 30, 1838

Dear Brother and Sisters:

I can hardly realize that I am newly in Ohio after so long a time, but 'tis true. I arrived here Friday afternoon with my box trunk boy and bushel-all safe and sound. Our dear E[liza] well enough to meet me at the door . . .

May 11th E[liza] is the happy mother of a little son. O how thankful are we to know that she has been sustained thus far . . . The little fellow is very pretty—is not as large as yours was and not half as handsome—but has dark hair and eyes. Dr. says it looks like Lucy—E[liza] thinks it looks like Edmond—and is afraid it will act like him—and so on.[36]

Daniel completed another successful growing season after returning home in mid-May. His duties as a justice of the peace, begun in 1836, now began to consume more of his time and, although the amount earned from his services was not large, it provided a welcome supplement to his farm income. Though still young compared to most of his neighbors, he was now well-established as one of the leading citizens of Hancock County.

In the fall of 1838 two events occurred in the adjacent state of Missouri that profoundly affected the lives of the Wells family as well as those of thousands of other Illinois residents, present and future.

On October 28 Governor Lilburn Boggs in Jefferson City, the capital of Missouri, received reports of violence that had occurred three days earlier in Caldwell County in the northwest part of the state. These reports claimed that a band of Mormons, members of the Church of Jesus Christ of Latter-day Saints, had attacked a company of state militia under the command of Samuel Bogard, killing several, confiscating much of their arms and equipment, and driving the rest across a river in headlong retreat. This action, which became known as the Battle of Crooked River, was one of several confrontations between the Mormons, several thousand of whom lived in western Missouri, and their surrounding neighbors.

Both sides accused one another of firing the first shots and both sides suffered casualties in the ensuing melee, but the reports given to Governor Boggs laid full blame for the affair on the Mormons, whose own accounts either did not reach the capital or, more probably, fell on deaf ears.[37]

Governor Boggs, who was already predisposed to believe the worst of the Mormons after having received previous one-sided accounts of the so-called Mormon War in his state, did not investigate the accuracy of the information he was given concerning the Crooked River engagement, but soon after receiving it issued a state-wide executive order.

I have received . . . information of the most appalling character, which changes the whole face of things, and places the Mormons in the attitude of open and avowed defiance of the laws, and of having made open war upon the people of this state. Your orders are, therefore, to hasten your operations . . . The Mormons must be treated as enemies and must be exterminated or driven from the state, if necessary for the public good.[38]

This directive was disseminated throughout the state and the state militia, acting under an order that authorized the killing or expulsion of a whole segment of Missouri's population, rode into action against Mormons in every town and village where they could be found.

The second event occurred three days later on October 30 in the isolated hamlet of Hawn's Mill, a small Mormon settlement in Caldwell County containing perhaps a dozen cabins and other buildings. In the middle of the afternoon as the people there were working in nearby fields and at the blacksmith shop, they observed a large band of mounted horsemen approaching and quickly fled to the center of the settlement for security. The raiders included several community leaders, a county clerk, and a state legislator. They numbered 240 men and were under the command of Nehemia Comstock.[39]

> Alarmed at their hostile appearance, one of the Mormons swung his hat and cried for peace. The answer was a blast of gunfire from the leader and a shout to his men, "Shoot everything wearing breeches, and shoot to kill!"

Then came a barrage of rifle shots.

> The Mormon men called for the women and children to run to the woods. Some of the men also ran for the woods. Others took off their hats and cried "Quarter!" until they were shot down.
>
> Several made a dash for whatever weapons they could find. A few men and boys fled for cover to the blacksmith shop, which was a poor choice, because the logs were loosely put together, with large cracks between them. The raiders charged the shop and aimed through the cracks, shooting the people inside like animals in a pen.[40]

When the firing ceased after sixteen hundred rounds had been fired by the raiders and a few dozen by the Mormons, fifteen people were dead, two were dying, and sixteen were wounded (only three of them raiders). Realizing that they were threatened by further attack, the survivors dumped the bodies of the slain down an abandoned well and fled. They could not go westward, from which news of escalating violence against Mormons had already reached them, nor beyond the western Missouri settlements into unknown Indian country; they turned eastward toward the safety of civilized Illinois.[41]

The Hawn's Mill Massacre was neither the first or last atrocity inflicted on the Mormons in Missouri. Within days thousands of raiders burned Mormon settlements, raped women, plundered property, rustled or slaughtered livestock, and shot any Mormons who resisted their incursions or refused to leave the state. Joseph Smith, the Mormon prophet, and several other leaders were arrested on charges of treason; condemned to death by one militia general, Samuel Lucas, and then imprisoned after another general, Alexander Doniphan, refused to obey any order to execute them. At the same time the Mormon populace was forced to surrender their arms, vacate their homes and immediately leave Missouri.

Having driven the Mormons out, their tormentors quickly seized their abandoned property as noted by a non-Mormon who wrote to Clay County authorities on November 29 to protest what was happening.

> These demons are now constantly strolling up and down Caldwell county, in small companies armed, insulting the women in any way and every way, and plundering the poor devils of all the means of subsistence (scanty as it was) left them, and driving off their horses, cattle, hogs, etc. and rifling their houses and farms of everything therein, taking beds, bedding, wardrobes, and such things as they see they want, leaving the poor Mormons in a starving and naked condition . . . They [the Mormons] are entirely willing to leave our state, so Soon as this inclement season is over; and a number have already left, and are leaving daily.[42]

As winter snows began and temperatures plummeted, thousands of destitute and starving Mormon refugees walked two hundred miles east across Missouri, in constant jeopardy of life and limb, to reach the Mississippi River and escape from persecution. Although they did not know it then, their destination, the center point of their gathering and their religious devotion was located on the farm of Daniel H. Wells.

3
A Bachelor Farmer in Commerce Becomes a Married Entrepreneur and Civic Leader in Nauvoo

1839–1841

On April 22, 1839, while Daniel H. Wells was sitting in a Carthage courtroom listening to Abraham Lincoln's defense of William Fraim, the man accused of murder in Schuyler County, Joseph Smith, the Mormon prophet, crossed the Mississippi River on a ferry and landed at Quincy, Illinois. He was thin, ragged, and exhausted from months of imprisonment in the Liberty jail, a contrived escape, and flight from Missouri lawmen under threat of execution if apprehended, but he was free. Smith was one of the last Mormons to reach the relative safety of Illinois and, like those who had arrived before him, he found a far friendlier and more compassionate welcome than the Mormons had experienced in Missouri. The citizens of Quincy and the surrounding communities, although outnumbered and somewhat overwhelmed by an influx of over five thousand destitute and often starving refugees, did all that they could to provide temporary shelter and sustenance for the newcomers.

The Mormons could not settle permanently in Quincy or the other nearby towns in Adams County because there was simply not enough available land to accommodate their needs. Twenty-five miles north of Quincy, however, in adjacent Hancock County, thousands of acres of land were being offered for sale at reasonable prices.

Mormon leaders had already developed an interest in Hancock County in the fall of 1838 when it became evident, even before the issuance of Missouri's extermination order, that they would have to leave that state or face continuing persecution. The Mormon Elder Israel Barlow made the acquaintance of Isaac Galland, one of the principal land speculators in Hancock County, while the Mormon exodus was beginning and told him that they were in dire need of new lands on which to settle. Galland suggested Commerce, much of which he owned, as a possible home for the Latter-day Saints. On his recommendation, Barlow and David Rogers visited the town and reported favorably on it and the surrounding land to Joseph Smith, then still imprisoned in Missouri. They noted that, in addition to his Illinois property, Galland owned some twenty thousand acres of the "Half Breed Reservation" lands in Iowa Territory, just across the river from Commerce. Galland assured the Mormons that this land could also be bought on easy terms. After reviewing their report and learning that church members were already buying plots in the Half Breed Reservation, Smith wrote an open letter to them on April 4, 1839 recommending that they contract with Galland for purchase of his holdings.[1]

Elder Sidney Rigdon, First Counselor to Joseph Smith in the Presidency of the church and thus second in authority to Smith, was the first church member to reside at Commerce. He purchased the two-story stone house that Galland had built near the river and the surrounding property in April 1839. He took immediate possession and moved his family there from Big Neck Prairie where he had been renting temporary quarters.

On May 1, 1839, Joseph Smith purchased Hugh White's farm in Commerce, which consisted of about 135 acres situated on the river bank directly west of Daniel H. Wells's property, for $5,000. The price was about $37 per acre, almost seven times what Daniel had paid for his acreage five years earlier, and reflected both the effects of the Panic of 1837 and the continuing inflationary use of paper money not backed by gold or silver.

On behalf of the church, Joseph Smith also purchased about 560 acres of Isaac Galland's Commerce property for $9,000. The price per acre of $16 was much lower than the cost of the White farm and was probably agreed to by Galland to improve his prospects of selling the Mormons more of his land in Iowa Territory, for which his title was seriously flawed, at the same or a better price. Galland joined the LDS Church in July 1839, thus further securing his business relationship with Joseph Smith and other Mormons. His baptism also gave him forgiveness among Church members for previous sins that he was widely accused of by others, including theft, counterfeiting, membership in the Massac outlaw band, and a self-admitted lack of personal integrity.[2]

Unlike Daniel H. Wells's farm, which began on the top of a bluff about half a mile from the water's edge and extended eastward, most of the White and Galland tracts, as well as a third purchase of about five hundred acres made by Joseph Smith from Horace Hotchkiss, were on the west and south slope of the bluff that descended gradually to the river. This lower ground was thickly grown with brush and timber and contained many swampy areas that flooded when the river was high and became stagnant when it receded. To become the beautiful city that the Mormons desired, Commerce and its environs would require an enormous input of labor and money, but the Saints, impoverished and in poor health as most of them were, proved equal to the challenge. As soon as the purchases were secured and Joseph Smith had moved his family into a small cabin on the Galland property, they began to gather there and the makeover commenced in earnest.[3]

It began with a new name: Nauvoo, meaning beautiful, which was designated by Joseph in mid-1839 and made official when the Commerce post office was renamed in early 1840. The Saints immediately began, under their leaders' directions, to clear the land, drain swamps, plant crops, and build homes.[4]

Joseph and his older brother Hyrum laid out an extensive plan for a new city. The Commerce grid, which consisted of about twenty-four blocks with streets set at a northwest to southeast angle from the river front, was discontinued and a new grid of 160 four-acre blocks was created with streets running north-south and east-west in straight lines. So rapid was the growth of Nauvoo that more than two hundred additional blocks, including all of Daniel's eighty-four-acre farm, were added to the city during the next year.[5]

Demand for one-acre city lots was strong and prices for them rose rapidly. By 1840 Joseph Smith, as its trustee-in-trust, set a cap of $500 on the price of city lots owned by the church. This was a high figure, but private owners sold their property for more and the prophet's edict provided enough revenue from sales that the church could deed a free lot to any family left destitute or disabled by the persecution in Missouri.

As Nauvoo began to develop around his farm, Daniel planted his crops and continued to pursue his duties as a justice of the peace. 1839 was his fifth growing season in Commerce and he was planning on many more equally bountiful. He had not intended to sell any of his property, but to use its agricultural profits as a base from which to acquire larger holdings. By the fall of the year, however, the Mormon influx of new residents compelled a change of strategy.

The Wells farm was located about a half-mile from the Commerce steamboat landing, well outside the original grid of streets laid out for the town by Hugh White. But the new Nauvoo map placed the Wells farm in the center of the city and made the lots within it the most desirable in the area. The selection in early 1840 of Block 20 on the western edge of the Wells Survey, as it was soon known, to be the site of the Mormon temple further defined the Wells property as the center point of Nauvoo.[6]

Acknowledging the fact that rural Commerce had almost overnight changed into urban Nauvoo, Daniel divided his farm into eighteen city

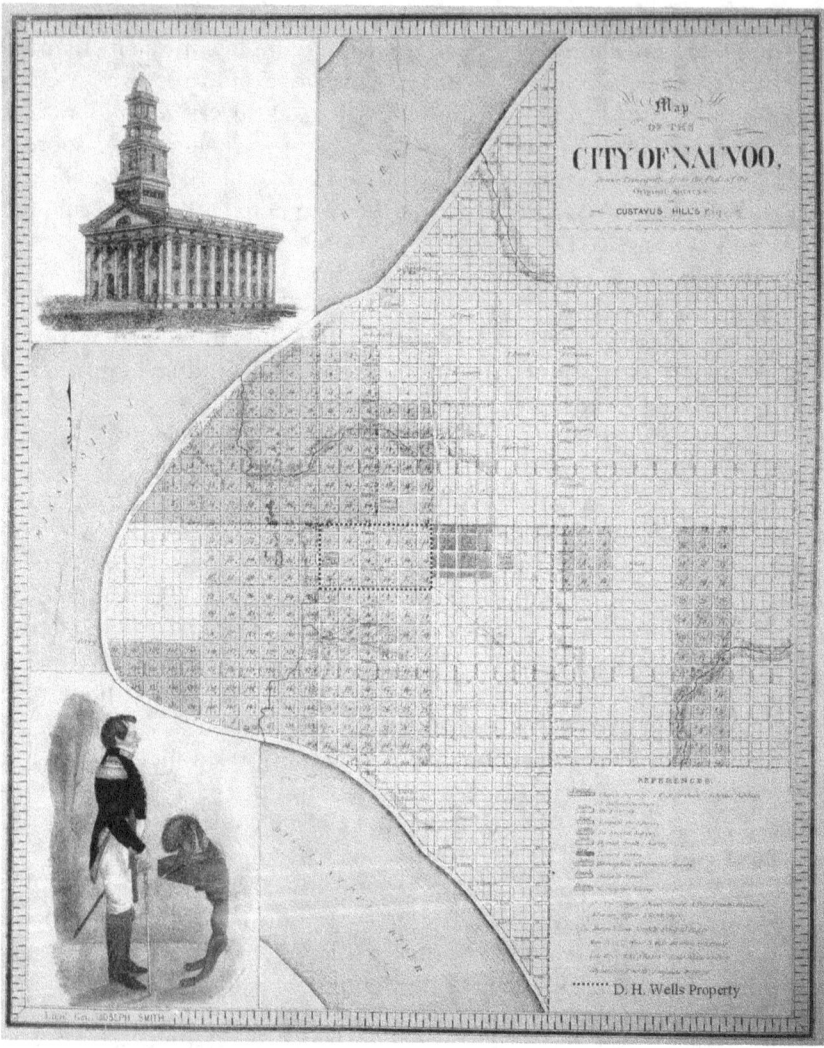

Figure 3.1. Map of the City of Nauvoo by Gustavus Hill, reproduced by Nauvoo Restoration, Inc., the Church of Jesus Christ of Latter-day Saints.

blocks, each containing four one-acre lots, plus six smaller plots, each containing two one-acre lots, and offered them for sale to new residents. He was joined by several other landowners who subdivided their property near Nauvoo, among whom were Davison Hibbard, George W. Robinson, Benjamin Warrington, and the partnerships Herringshaw and Thompson, and Spears and Worthington. The prices Daniel charged and the credit terms he offered were somewhat better than those of his competitors.

He owned, among other pieces of property, eighty acres of land on the bluff. This he platted into city lots and let the poor and persecuted refugees have them at very low figures, and on long time for payment. This endeared him to the people and determined the location of the chief part of the city, and of the Temple, which was built on land that had belonged to him.[7]

Remembering the credit that was extended to him when he arrived in Illinois, Daniel frequently agreed to minimal down payments with the balances to be paid over several years as the new owners prospered again after their losses in Missouri. He also accepted paper money rather than only specie, which few Mormons had. Daniel's good business judgment in riding the western Illinois land boom enabled him to profit handsomely from it.

Before the scale of the coming land boom in Hancock County became evident, Daniel sold part of his farm in June 1839 for $200. By February 1840 he realized that he had sold too much acreage for too little and too quickly. He bought the parcel of property back for $1,000, willingly giving the owner a 500 percent profit for having held it little more than half a year.

Daniel completed the survey of his land in April 1840 and immediately had the subdivided plat added to the official Nauvoo city survey made the previous year. As he received payment for lots sold in the Wells Survey, Daniel purchased additional plots of land further out on the eastern side of the city. These he held until their value had increased sufficiently for him to realize a profit from their sale. So rapid was the growth of Nauvoo and rural Hancock County around it that he was often able to double his investment in a parcel within a year or two.

> The four-acre Temple block he deeded to the Trustee-in-Trust for $1,100, a modest sum. However, the Temple made the neighborhood more desirable, and many of Wells's lots brought as much as $1,000.[8]

By 1843, the "Hill," as the part of Nauvoo situated on the bluff overlooking the river had come to be known, had developed into a business district that rivaled or even exceeded the southern Main Street frontage on the "Flat" section nearer the river that had been intended by Joseph Smith and other church leaders to be the commercial center of the city. In February of that year a proposal was made in the city council to establish two markets, one along Main Street in the Flat and another along

Figure 3.2. Nauvoo looking northeast from the "Flat," near the river toward the temple on the "Hill." From an 1846 daguerreotype that was taken from a second-story window.

Mulholland Street on the Hill. Joseph Smith opposed this proposal, saying to the Council:

> The upper part of the town had no right to rival those on the river. Here, on the bank of the river, was where we first pitched our tents; here was where the first sickness and deaths occurred; here has been the greatest suffering in this city. We have been the making of the upper part of the town. We have located the Temple on the hill; and they ought to be satisfied. We began here first; and let the market go out from this part of the city; let the upper part of the town be marketed by wagons, until they can build [their own] market.[9]

The two-market proposal was not passed but the Hill continued to prosper and grow more rapidly than the Flat because it was higher, drier, and therefore healthier. The price of building lots on the Hill also remained somewhat lower.[10]

It is impossible to determine how much actual cash Daniel H. Wells received from his multiple land transactions, given the fact that many of the lots he sold were still partially or entirely unpaid for when he left the city. The temple block purchase was paid in full, as Mormon doctrine held that the building could not be dedicated or used for its intended purposes if any debt remained against it. Most early purchasers probably also completed payment for their land, although some not for considerable time after buying it. Orson Pratt and his wife Sarah, in partnership with his brother Parley P. Pratt, one of the Twelve Apostles in the church, bought Lot 2 of Block 9 in the Wells Survey from Daniel H. Wells in May 1842. The final payment of $300 was made on February 14, 1843.[11]

There is no deed conveying this lot from Daniel to Parley P. Pratt recorded in the Hancock County records. Carthage, the county seat, was a long horseback ride from Nauvoo and many deeds given by Daniel H. Wells and other land developers were simply held by the purchasers for later recording when they were in Carthage. These deeds, known as "dresser-drawer deeds" after the location where they were often kept, caused confusion about ownership of land in Nauvoo and sometimes cost the true owners dearly when the Saints were driven out of the city and anti-Mormons claimed lots for which no recorded deeds existed.

Parley P. Pratt was fortunate to have made his purchase from Daniel, who honored all of his land deals and even re-issued some deeds in order to help the new owner hold or sell his property. When Pratt left Nauvoo in February 1846, he left Ezra Bickford in charge of selling all of his property. The deed for Lot 2, Block 9 from Daniel H. Wells to Ezra Bickford, issued some fourteen months later on April 12, 1847, was probably given to recognize Pratt's ownership of the property. Bickford may have shown Daniel a dresser-drawer deed that Daniel himself had given to Pratt when he sold the land to him in 1843. Two months after Bickford was deeded ownership of the land and house, he sold it to William Quarter for $850. Pratt had estimated its value a year earlier at $7,000.[12]

Like Pratt, other Mormons trying to sell out in 1846 in order to join the Saints' western exodus, were hard hit, as evidenced by the experience of Samuel Bennion and his wife Mary Bushell.

> We arrived at St. Louis on the 20th day of May [1845] near night. Stopped the first night in the Stone House at the landing. Next day the s[aints] were putting the Capstone on the Temple, and my brother John brought his team, took us to his house or shanty seven miles east of Nauvoo where I bout 85 acres of land of Daniel H. Wells, the same summer. Had it fenced and built a good two story Brick House with six apartments in it. Hauled thirty two thousand bricks from Nauvoo. Cost of house was one thousand dollars. During the summer my father, myself and wife and two children, John R. and Elizabeth were sick with the ague and fever. On the 18th day of

February 1846, our little daughter Elizabeth died of the same. Buried in the Nauvoo burying ground, near Nauvoo, and put a large headstone on her grave.

May 1846, I sold my house and farm for two hundred and fifty dollars ($250.) part trade.

On the 19th day of May 1846, we left our Nauvoo home to go West somewhere. Myself, wife, son, and father, brother John and his wife Esther Wainwright and two children, Samuel R. and Mary.[13]

From the time he first met Joseph Smith in May 1839, Daniel H. Wells became close friends with him and his brothers, as well as with other Latter-day Saint leaders. Like his forbears, Daniel was a Methodist, a Christian faith that included many members strongly opposed to Mormon beliefs and some who had been prominent in opposing the Mormons in New York, Ohio, and Missouri. But Daniel accepted the Mormons as friends, business associates, and fellow Christians without concern for doctrinal or political differences he may have had with them. He saw them as a religious people who had been wrongly treated in Missouri and who should be welcomed and encouraged to build their communities again in Illinois.

The Mormons, and Joseph Smith in particular, also had high regard for Daniel. Though he was a Gentile, as LDS people referred to all persons not of their faith, and remained such throughout the entire period of Mormon prominence in Illinois, they liked him. He was well-respected as one of the original settlers and was drawn into numerous business ventures with Mormons. Within a few months of their arrival in Illinois, Mormons constituted a majority of the residents of Hancock County and could exercise political dominance there almost at will. Despite this, Daniel became one of the few Gentiles elected to office in the city government, and continued to serve as a justice of the peace until he left Nauvoo.[14]

In the fall of 1839, Joseph Smith and three other Mormons went to Washington, DC, to seek redress from the federal government for wrongs done to the Mormons in Missouri. The trip accomplished nothing except to convince the Mormon leader that President Van Buren, who granted him an interview, was "not as fit as my dog for the chair of state."[15]

When Joseph returned to Nauvoo, the city was rapidly expanding and afflicted with many of the growing pains of a new metropolis. Malaria, temporarily restrained by cold weather that reduced the mosquito population, reappeared in the summer of 1840 and took many more lives. Crime, especially theft and property destruction, also increased. Citizens of Missouri blamed every depredation in that state on Mormon raiders whom they claimed were returning to extract revenge for wrongs previously done them. Around Nauvoo, criminal acts were often credited to marauders from Missouri who continued to harass Mormons and steal what they could from them. As some of the perpetrators were apprehended, Daniel's workload as justice of the peace increased. This responsibility and his new career as a land developer soon left him little time for farming.

Until the middle of 1839, Daniel's justice court had mainly handled cases brought by the early non-Mormon residents of Hancock County. His court book includes disputes involving Isaac Galland, Oliver Granger, Davison Hibard, Lewis Robison, Amos Davis, Theodore Turley, Hiram Kimball and Ethan Kimball, C. W. Lyon and Windsor P. Lyon, and Stephen Markham.

After the Mormons arrived in Commerce, their land agents and bishops were also frequently involved in land debt disputes, including Peter Haws, Isaac Morely, Alanson Ripley, Newel K. Whitney, Joseph L. Heywood, and Vinson Knight.[16]

In the summer Daniel received word that his sister Lucy Ann Wells and Joseph Coombs had finally married and settled on a farm in Trenton near the home of the groom's father Oliver Coombs. Despite an invitation from Daniel to move west to Nauvoo or a nearby location, the Coombs family stayed close to their New York roots. Over the next ten years they had four children, all born in Oneida County. Joseph became a "daguerrotyper" around 1847 and began to make his living producing portraits using the new photographic process. In pursuit of that occupation he eventually moved his family to the town of Ripon in Fon Du Lac County, Wisconsin, where a fifth child was born in 1851.[17]

As his business interests prospered, Daniel became more politically active. He was a lifelong Whig and his views thus coincided, for the most part, with those of the Mormons who now constituted the majority of voters in Hancock County and a significant bloc in the state. Although church members were free to vote as they pleased, most were heavily influenced by the fact that Governor Lilburn Boggs of Missouri and President Martin Van Buren were both Democrats. Keenly aware that Boggs had issued the extermination order against the Mormons and of their prophet's often-expressed opinion of Van Buren's "insolence and iniquity," the Saints voted overwhelmingly for Whig candidates in the election of August 1840. The only Democrat they supported was James H. Ralston, who was running for Congress and had previously befriended Joseph Smith. In this race, Daniel H. Wells voted for the Whig candidate, Abraham Lincoln, but his choice was overwhelmed by the Mormon majority and Ralston was elected.[18]

Nationally, the Whigs prevailed and William Henry Harrison was elected to the presidency over Martin Van Buren, the Democrat who had treated the Mormons with such callous disregard.

Having demonstrated their political muscle in the election, the Mormons moved quickly to secure local control of Nauvoo to themselves. A charter for the City of Nauvoo, patterned after the one granted by the Illinois legislature to Springfield the previous year, was drawn up by Joseph Smith and presented as a bill to the 1840 session of the state legislature by John C. Bennett, a recently baptized convert who had become a close advisor of church leaders. By the time the charter was voted on, both of the major political parties were vying for Mormon support and it was passed by both houses without even the requirement of a complete reading on the floor of either. Stephen A. Douglas and Abraham Lincoln both voted in favor of it and the latter, holding no animosity for the lack of Mormon support in his congressional bid, also congratulated them on the bill's passage after the vote.[19]

Governor Carlin signed the charter bill on December 16, 1840 and it went into effect in February 1841. John C. Bennett was elected as the new city's first mayor and Daniel H. Wells was chosen one of four aldermen on the city council. He was the only non-Mormon among the mayor, aldermen, and nine council members elected.[20] He was reelected in 1843 and served until the Nauvoo Charter was revoked in 1845. He was the only city officer to serve for the entire duration of the Nauvoo Charter and the only non-Mormon ever elected as an alderman. Two other non-Mormons, Sylvester Emmons and Benjamin Warrington, served as City Council members from 1843 to 1845.[21]

The charter defined the duties of the mayor and aldermen as including those of justice of the peace. Consequently, Daniel became a justice of the peace within the City of Nauvoo as well as a justice for Hancock County as a whole. He appears to be the only city officer who actually served as a justice of the peace, all city cases being referred to him for adjudication, in addition to many county cases. Appeals from justice courts could be made to the Illinois Circuit Court in Carthage, the Hancock County seat. This was the legal process that in 1844 caused Joseph Smith to be first tried before Daniel H. Wells and then taken to Carthage where he was murdered before his appeal could be heard.[22]

Once he was chosen alderman, city business became a major factor in Daniel's life. The City Council voted to found a university and elected a slate of twenty-three regents, among them some Gentiles. Daniel was named to a committee to choose a site and draw up plans for the university. The site was selected and plans formulated, but other priorities delayed construction. Some courses were taught during 1841 and 1842, but succeeding events eventually doomed completion of the university structure in Nauvoo. The project was revived when the Saints reached Utah Territory and became the University of Deseret in 1850 with Daniel again serving as a member of the Board of Regents.[23]

Appearing before the City Council on May 1, 1840, Joseph Smith asked that a cemetery be created outside the city limits and readied for use. Deaths were occurring frequently in Nauvoo and the immediate need for a burying ground was evident. A motion to purchase ten acres was carried and Daniel was appointed with two other councilors to locate a site and buy the land with city funds. A suitable property on the south side of Parley Street about two miles east of Drury Street was quickly decided upon and the cemetery became available before the end of the month. One of the first graves placed in it was that of Edward Partridge, the first Presiding Bishop of the Church of Jesus Christ of Latter-day Saints, who died May 27, 1840 at age forty-six. Others soon followed and what is today known as the Old Nauvoo Burial Grounds contains almost thirteen hundred known graves[24]

Another Nauvoo Charter–based organization that Daniel became part of was the Nauvoo Legion. This military group was authorized by Section 25 of the Nauvoo Charter as a unit of the Illinois State Militia under article V of the State Constitution.[25]

The Illinois Militia Code of 1833 closely followed the 1792 Act of Congress, which provided for universal military obligation. Section 1 of the Code stated:

> All free white male inhabitants resident in this State, who are or shall be of the age of eighteen and under the age of forty-five years . . . shall severally and respectively be enrolled in the militia . . . and every such person . . . shall . . . provide himself with a good musket, fuzee or rifle . . . The field officers . . . shall be armed with a sword and pair of pistols, and the company officers with a sword.

Section 2 provided for the organization of the militia in divisions, regiments, battalions, and companies, according to counties with Hancock County in the Third Brigade of the Fifth Division. Section 3 set out the officers for the militia, with a major general to head a division; a brigadier general, a brigade; and a colonel a regiment. There was no authorization for rank higher than major general.[26]

The organization of the Nauvoo Legion was begun as soon as the charter went into effect. Within six months it numbered over fifteen hundred men and a year later over two thousand, making it by far the largest militia unit in Illinois. Most of the officers were Mormons and included Joseph Smith as lieutenant general, commanding, with his brother Don Carlos Smith and John C. Bennett as major generals.

When the Legion was organized, Daniel H. Wells was appointed commissary, a staff position under General John C. Bennett in which he labored to secure and maintain adequate arms, equipment and supplies for the organization's members. A city ordinance provided penalties for those who failed to serve as required by the State Militia Code, and Daniel was also mustered as a member of the Legion ranks who attended required drills and parades. But he was never a line officer of the Legion in Illinois, even though he later led the only significant military action by the citizens of Nauvoo, their defense of the city against the attack of an armed mob.[27]

The Legion represented the Mormons' security in Illinois; its strength gave them some assurance that the depredations inflicted upon them in the past would not be repeated. Having failed to obtain any help from state and federal military forces to defend their rights or property or any redress for the destruction and slaughter that ensued when government officials ignored their pleas for protection, the Saints enthusiastically supported their own military force that was visibly powerful enough to ward off any physical threat. The Legion never lacked for recruits and its officer corps and enlisted companies were continuously expanded to accommodate its increasing numbers.

Martial displays and ceremonies were a much-loved form of entertainment among Americans, who had no fear of military forces composed of citizens like themselves. Members of the Legion also reveled in the military pageantry of the organization. Its marches, parades, drills, and training were as much for recreation and display as for the development of martial skills. Officers sported beautiful uniforms, polished high-quality weapons, and handsome mounts; Joseph Smith led parades accompanied by a personal bodyguard of twelve mounted men in white uniforms; companies of men vied with one another in the precision of their drill and the smartness of their uniforms; and all of the processions were accompanied by well-played martial music. The Legion's exhibitions and parades rapidly became one of the most popular attractions in the area, drawing not only crowds of Nauvoo residents, but hundreds more from nearby communities, many of whom arrived for a day of sight-seeing on Mississippi excursion steamboats.[28]

Some saw the Nauvoo Legion's numbers as a possible threat and a demonstration of growing Mormon political power. Other companies of state militia were jealous of the rifles and artillery pieces which Daniel, in his role as commissary, was able to obtain for the Legion while longer established units had only muskets. The numerical strength of the Legion, its evident discipline, and its members' strong allegiance to Joseph Smith soon roused the concern of non-Mormons. Joseph himself did not allay this concern when he made belligerent speeches suggesting that if people continued to molest the Saints, they would establish their religion by the sword and he himself would become a second Mahomet.[29]

Such statements, probably not made in earnest, but out of frustration for the previous unrectified wrongs done to his people, nevertheless alarmed those who observed the intense loyalty that the prophet inspired. As one Hancock County non-Mormon wrote in May 1841:

> . . . they must and will take the world. And if they cannot do it by preaching they will by the force of arms they therefore incorporate militerry tacticks with their religion it is said they train Saturday and are well disciplined . . . it is said they take the liberty to tell the people that they now come with the Bible in their hands but ere long they will come with the sword also by their side.[30]

Residents of Warsaw, a river town about twenty miles downriver from Nauvoo, watched the growth of trade and river traffic in the new city with envy. Ministers of other sects, particularly Presbyterians, Methodists, and Baptists, some of whom had labored in the area for years with small congregations and few converts to their faiths, were stunned to see the enormous growth of the Church of Jesus Christ of Latter-day Saints, and were quick to denounce its prophet as a charlatan and its members as deluded fanatics. Their anti-Mormon comments and sermons were spread and enhanced by those who feared the Saints' economic and political power as well as old enemies from Missouri who frequently traveled to Illinois in hopes of recapturing Joseph Smith or wreaking further havoc on his followers.

A few non-Mormons, in and around Nauvoo, held liberal views toward their Mormon neighbors. One of these was Lewis Robison, the younger brother of Daniel's wife Eliza. Lewis married Clarissa Duzette in December 1839 and thereafter continued to make his home in Nauvoo. By contrast, the Rev. Charles Robison, father of both Eliza and Lewis, who had married Catherine Wells after the death of his first wife, refused to live among the Mormons and removed his family across the Mississippi River to Iowa to avoid contact with them. Soon afterward, he died at age fifty-five, leaving Catherine, twice widowed, to care for his teenage children, all of them safe from the heretical doctrines of the charismatic Joseph Smith.[31]

Charles Robison's early death had a profound effect on Eliza Wells and set her determination to further his missionary work in the Methodist faith. That determination, which included pushing her son Albert to follow his grandfather into the ministry, would dramatically affect the future course of her marriage to Daniel, who did not share her antipathy toward Mormons.

Even before her father's death Eliza was, like him, opposed to Mormon theology without knowing much about it. The Rev. Robison did not listen to Mormon proselyting and insisted that his family also avoid any spiritual contamination by rejecting outright Joseph Smith's claims to divine inspiration. All the Robisons except Lewis dutifully followed his instructions and even he did not investigate Mormon doctrine until years after his father's passing.[32]

Eliza withdrew from any unnecessary contact with her Mormon neighbors. Even though Daniel was now one of the leading citizens of Nauvoo and a prominent member of its government, he and Eliza did not socialize with the Mormon members of the City Council or with the leadership of the LDS Church. By the end of 1840 Daniel knew personally almost every Mormon male who resided in Nauvoo and was acquainted with many of their wives, but Eliza had met few of her neighbors and had developed friendships with none of them. She was close to Daniel's sister Catherine, who resided with her husband J. W. Woods in Burlington, Iowa, and was a frequent visitor in their home. She also visited with Daniel's mother who lived for a time after Charles Robison's death in West Point, Iowa, but eventually moved back to Nauvoo to be nearer her son. Beyond family connections, none of whom were Mormons, Eliza rarely ventured.[33]

In October 1840, the congregation assembled for the general conference of the LDS Church responded to an epistle issued by the First Presidency of the Church in August stating, "it is necessary to erect a house of prayer, a house of worship of our God, where the ordinances can be attended to agreeably to His divine will, in this region of country." Church members resolved, "That the Saints build a house for the worship of God, and that Reynolds Cahoon, Elias Higbee, and Alpheus Cutler be appointed a committee to build the same."[34]

Soon after the conference the committee contacted Daniel H. Wells whose property on top of the bluff overlooking lower Nauvoo and the river was the obvious best choice for the temple site. Daniel agreed to sell all four one-acre lots of Block 20 in the Wells Survey, bounded by Wells St. on the west, Knight St. on the north, Woodruff St. on the east, and Mulholland St. on the south, to the Church. The transaction seems to have been made on a handshake between Daniel and Joseph Smith, the trustee-in-trust for the church, but the actual deed to Block 20 was not transferred to the Trustee-in-Trust for the $1,100 sale price until almost eighteen months later in February 1843. The informal but absolute nature of the deal indicates the mutual trust and regard Joseph and Daniel had for one another.[35]

On April 6, 1841, the four cornerstones were laid in impressive ceremonies which commenced with Joseph Smith reviewing two cohorts of the Nauvoo Legion at 9:00 am on the parade ground. Approximately ten thousand persons attended the services at which all four cornerstones were laid in succession by those holding various offices in the church hierarchy. Following the ceremony the whole assembly walked to the Legion parade ground where the all-day event concluded after Joseph Smith and John C. Bennett each addressed the crowd. Daniel H. Wells attended this event, but because he was not a Mormon, he did not participate in the ceremonies. His wife was not present.[36]

4

The Mormon Hegemony
Civic Controversy, Court Cases, and Family Conflict

1841–1844

The period 1841 to 1844 was a time of great gain and of great loss for Daniel H. Wells and for Nauvoo, the city in which he was now a central figure. A continuing inflow of Mormons from around the country gathering to Hancock County plus the arrival of thousands of new church members from England, who had been converted through the missionary efforts of the apostles, kept Nauvoo growing at a rapid pace. Daniel's land sales gave him a continuing source of income, and his wealth multiplied as the price of lots in the Wells Survey increased.

Daniel still thought of himself as a farmer and listed that as his occupation, but in fact he now did little planting and harvesting himself. He was a charter member of the Nauvoo Agricultural and Manufacturing Association created by the Illinois legislature in February 1841 and, like many founding members of that association, had become more of a "gentleman farmer" who rarely put his own hand to the plow. The plentiful supply of labor in Nauvoo enabled him to hire others to farm his land, either for cash or for a portion of the crop. This arrangement enabled him to earn a profit from his land while at the same time offering employment to men who needed the wages.[1]

Few of these rental agreements were written and of those that were, fewer still survive, but an example made by Davison Hibbard with Jeremiah Mackley and Stephen Chase gives the essentials of the type. It is a sharecropping agreement signed November 26, 1840 for eight acres of tillable ground for a period of two years under which Mackley and Chase are to:

. . . cultivate the said premisis in a complete and agricultral manner and fence the same on the North and west with a good and sufficient fence and deliver to the party of the first part in good order & in proper season one tenth part of all the produce raised on the said premises the first year and one eighth part the second year ending 1842.

Hibard retained the option to sell his property out from under the renters "by paying a resonable compensation for the labour done."[2]

In addition to his other justice of the peace responsibilities, Daniel was frequently called upon to prepare affidavits, swear those who declared them, and attest to the signatures or marks made on them. Along with other City Council members, he also attested to the accuracy of deeds recorded in the Nauvoo City Court books and later in the Hancock County Court records.

During the spring of 1840, Daniel sent his widowed mother east to visit her daughters Pamela, Lucy Ann, Frank, and Abigail who were still living in Trenton. She traveled alone, as both Daniel and his sister Catherine were too busy to accompany her. She made most of the trip by water, going from St. Louis to Pittsburgh by steamboat on the Mississippi and Ohio rivers, then overland to Cleveland and by steamboat from there to Buffalo and Utica on the Erie Canal. Her round trip transportation cost totaled $87, a sum that would have been difficult for Daniel to manage a few years earlier, but which was now easily within his expanded budget.

Hardly had Catherine Wells Robison returned to Nauvoo when letters arrived telling of the death of Eliza Wells Ross in New York where she and her husband were visiting family. Her death, only four years after her marriage to Dr. Ross, left him with their only child, three-year-old Henry W. Ross. Since he could not adequately care for his son due to the demands of his work, Pamela Wells, who at age thirty-eight was still unmarried (and remained so until her death in 1857), agreed to raise her nephew as her own and immediately took him into her home.

Eliza's death was a serious blow to Daniel, who had always been close to his sisters. His letter to Pamela, written after receiving word of Eliza's passing indicates his grief and also the depth of his belief in a physical resurrection in which he would see her and other family members again.

Dear sister Pamela,
Catherine has just gone home & kept her letter for me to finish. It is truly trying to think that we are never more on earth to see

our sister Elisa. One more link which binds us to earth is broken; how afflicting: If I were to follow the current of my feelings I should stop and say I could write no more. I sometimes think that if there is only one thing more than another that should make us appreciate a glorious [im]mortality beyond the grave, it is that there we shall meet friends to be separated no more forever, where neither sorrow pain sickness or death can ever come. And herein is consolation that these away shall meet them as they were here, for I do believe that when the body is raised it assumes the same physiognomy and features that it here possessed . . .

Little did I think that when I gave her the parting hand I should never see her more . . .

I can feel for Brother R[oss] . . . How lonely must be his situation when he must be deprived of the company of his little son . . .

Yours ever D H Wells[3]

Daniel's description of an afterlife in which family members know and recognize one another and will be reunited in an eternal association together is very close to Joseph Smith's vision of extended families living together forever and shows he had already been influenced by the prophet's teaching on this subject. Daniel often related in later life that the Mormon doctrine known as the "plan of salvation" with its promise of eternal families was the most important factor in his eventual conversion to the LDS faith.[4]

In early 1842, Dr. John C. Bennett, who had been baptized into the LDS Church in the summer of 1840 and risen rapidly to become a counselor to Joseph Smith, a major general in the Nauvoo Legion, and the mayor of Nauvoo, was determined to have deceived the Saints concerning his background, his motives for joining the Church, and his personal morals and behavior. When Bennett's duplicity in falsely representing himself as unmarried, preaching false doctrine, and attempting to seduce several female Mormon women was revealed publicly, the resulting controversy quickly drew Daniel H. Wells, who was serving with Bennett in the city government, into the midst of the fray.

Hyrum Smith discovered during his missionary travels in 1841 that Bennett had a wife and children living in Ohio. When confronted, he confessed and expressed great remorse, even going to the extreme of swallowing poison to atone for his guilt. He recovered (perhaps from nothing since the draft he swallowed was his own concoction) and the forgiving prophet allowed him to retain his positions in the church, city, and legion. By the following year, however, Bennett's offenses had gone far beyond his own family.

... while mouthing the religious and moral beliefs of the Saints, he secretly found it not at all necessary to renounce the life of a profligate. One aspect of his new religion was a particular source of temptation, and he did not mind how he distorted or perverted it for his own gratification.

Before this time, Joseph [Smith] had taken several wives in the new covenant of plural marriage. Although polygamy was still denied in public in the realization that the Gentiles and most of the Saints were not yet prepared for such a radical change in the social structure, several high leaders in the church, Joseph's most loyal friends, had been taught what was to be included in the restoration of the ancient order, and some were already participating. Every attempt was made to keep plural marriages secret, but enough rumors were in circulation to make what Bennett told the sisters not altogether incredible. Bennett used his enormous prestige in Nauvoo and the fact that he was thought to be Joseph's closest friend to try to persuade the Mormon women of his choice that the prophet had sanctioned his "spiritual wifery."

Hyrum [Smith] began an investigation of the rumors about Bennett and gathered testimony that he had tried to seduce a number of women by telling them that it was "perfectly right" if kept secret, that it was one of the mysteries of God to be revealed when the people were strong enough, and that if necessary, he would give them medicine to produce abortion.[5]

When Joseph demanded to know why Bennett was using his name to "carry on your hellish wickedness," the doctor acknowledged that the prophet had never taught him such behavior. At Joseph's request, he made an affidavit and swore to it before Alderman Daniel H. Wells.

State Of Illinois, City Of Nauvoo.
Personally appeared before me, Daniel H. Wells, an alderman of said city of Nauvoo, John C. Bennett, who being duly sworn, according to law, deposeth and saith: that he never was taught anything in the least contrary to the strictest principles of the Gospel, or of virtue, or of the laws of God, or man, under any occasion, either directly or indirectly, in word or deed by Joseph Smith: and that he never knew the said Smith to countenance any improper conduct whatever, either in public or private; and that he never did teach to me in private that an illegal, illicit in-

tercourse with females was, under any circumstances, justifiable, and that I never knew him so to teach others.

> John C. Bennett.
> Sworn to and subscribed before me, this 17th day of May, 1842
> Daniel H. Wells, Alderman.⁶

On the same day, Bennett resigned as mayor of Nauvoo and withdrew his name as a member of the Church. Soon, however, he began to protest that the affidavit had been made under duress and over the next few weeks alternately feigned contrition for his behavior or denied it. On June 16, Bennett was expelled from the Nauvoo Masonic Lodge and on June 23 his excommunication from the Church was publicly announced.⁷

By then Bennett was claiming that he was a victim of persecution by Joseph Smith and that the Church was a fraud. So great was Bennett's former prestige in Nauvoo, and so vile his denunciation of his former associates there, that the City Council, who all witnessed him repeat his affidavit statements before them on May 19, made another affidavit confirming this in July. Again, Daniel, this time as Hancock County justice of the peace, swore them to their statement.

> We, the undersigned, members of the city council, of the city of Nauvoo, testify that John C. Bennett was not under duress at the time he testified before the city council, May 19, 1842, concerning Joseph Smith's innocence, virtue and pure teaching. His statements that he has lately made concerning this matter are false; there was no excitement at the time, nor was he in anywise threatened, menaced or intimidated . . .
>
> > Wilson Law, Geo. A. Smith,
> > John Taylor, Geo. W. Harris,
> > Wilford Woodruff, Newel K. Whitney,
> > Vinson Knight, Brigham Young,
> > Heber C. Kimball, Charles C. Rich,
> > John P. Greene, Orson Spencer.
> > William Marks,
>
> Subscribed and sworn to by the persons whose names appear to the foregoing affidavit, the 20th day of July, A.D. 1842, except Newel K. Whitney, who subscribed and affirmed to the foregoing this day [July 21st] before me.
>
> > Daniel H. Wells,
> > Justice of the peace within and for Hancock County, Illinois.⁸

As Bennett still continued to publish his allegations, others also testified against him, some before Daniel and some before other justices.[9]

Daniel himself finally executed an affidavit in defense of Joseph Smith's character and teachings, thus aligning himself openly with the prophet by affirming that Bennett had said nothing against Joseph until after the latter exposed him.

State Of Illinois, County Of Hancock.

I hereby certify that on the 17th day of May last, John C. Bennett subscribed and swore to the affidavit over my signature of that date and published in the Wasp, after writing the same in my presence, in the office where I was employed in taking depositions of witnesses. The door of the room was open and free for all, or any person to pass or repass . . .

I was in the city council on the 19th day of May last. I there heard him say what has been published concerning the teachings of Joseph Smith, and of his own course. I afterwards met him in company with Colonel Francis M. Higbee. He then stated that he was going to be the candidate, (meaning the candidate for the legislature) and Joseph and Hyrum Smith were going in for him. Said "You know it will be better for me not to be bothered with the mayor's office, Legion, 'Mormon,' or anything else." During all this time, if he was under duress or fear, he must have a good faculty for concealing it, for he was at liberty to go and come when and where he pleased, so far as I am capable of judging.

I know that I saw him in different parts of the city even after he had made these statements, transacting business as usual, and said he was going to complete some business pertaining to the mayor's office; and I think did attend to work on the streets.

I was always personally friendly with him, after I became acquainted with him. I never heard him say anything derogatory to the character of Joseph Smith, until after he had been exposed by said Smith, on the public stand in Nauvoo.

Daniel H. Wells.
July 22nd, A. D. 1842.

Sworn to and subscribed before me, a justice of the peace, in and for the city of Nauvoo, in said county, this 22nd day of July, 1842.

Gustavus Hills, [L. S.]
J. P. and Alderman.[10]

Daniel's statement and those of others who were witnesses to Bennett's duplicity forced him to leave Nauvoo, but he continued to vilify Joseph Smith and the Mormons long after his departure.

On the evening of May 6, 1842, the former governor of Missouri, Lilburn W. Boggs, was gravely wounded by an assassin. Despite severe injuries, Boggs slowly recuperated while authorities hunted unsuccessfully for his attacker. As the search lengthened, rumors surfaced that a Mormon might have done the deed in revenge for their persecution in Missouri. The disgraced John C. Bennett claimed that the culprit was Orrin Porter Rockwell, a bodyguard of Joseph Smith, and that both were equally responsible for the crime.

Although Joseph and Porter vehemently denied any part in the attempt on Boggs's life, and no evidence implicating either was ever presented, the false rumors multiplied and, with Bennett's avid support, eventually acquired wide acceptance among Missouri's anti-Mormons.[11]

Boggs did not see his assailant, who shot him from behind, and did not know his identity, let alone whether he acted alone or as part of a conspiracy. But he nevertheless swore an affidavit charging Joseph with being "an accessory before the fact, to an assault with intent to kill made by one Orrin P. Rockwell on Lilburn W. Boggs." On the basis of this affidavit, a request for Joseph's extradition to Missouri was sent to Illinois Governor Thomas Carlin. An order for Joseph and Porter's arrest was signed by Carlin and they were taken into custody by the sheriff of Adams County and his assistants on August 8.[12]

Joseph and Porter were taken before Daniel H. Wells in the Nauvoo Municipal Court and were released on writs of habeas corpus. The same day the Nauvoo City Council, with Daniel participating as an alderman, passed an ordinance giving local courts authority to rule on the validity of any writ served on a Nauvoo citizen. Daniel voted against this ordinance, judging that it would increase anti-Mormon feeling in the rest of Illinois, but to no avail.[13]

Governor Carlin regarded the action of the Nauvoo Municipal Court in releasing Joseph and Porter as an illegal interference of his arrest order and sent the Adams County Sheriff back to Nauvoo to execute it. On his arrival, he found both men had disappeared; Porter to Philadelphia and Joseph into hiding in and around Nauvoo where he played cat and mouse with the authorities seeking him for the next four months. Joseph finally surrendered to the court in Springfield for trial. On January 5, 1843, the court found the Missouri requisition defective in numerous ways and ordered Joseph discharged from arrest.[14]

Porter Rockwell was not so fortunate. He found Philadelphia a poor exile and upon hearing of Joseph's release he started back to Nauvoo. Traveling by steamboat from Pittsburgh, he unwisely went ashore in St.

Louis where he was recognized, arrested, and thrown in jail. He was tried in Independence a week later. Despite demands that he be hanged and fights in the justice court during his trial, he was acquitted, but still held in prison, allegedly "for his own safety." During the next nine months, he escaped twice, was recaptured, charged with jailbreak, convicted, and finally freed. A twelve-day walk across Missouri finally brought him back to Nauvoo where he appeared at Joseph's 1843 Christmas party still dressed in prison rags with bleeding feet, shoulder-length hair, and a year-old beard.[15]

John C. Bennett's continual diatribes and those of others who feared the growing economic and political power of the Saints made the state elections of 1842 a contest that pitted candidates favored by the Mormons against those who pledged to suppress their influence.

Daniel H. Wells remained an ardent Whig, but most residents of Nauvoo favored Democratic candidates, who had supported passage of the Nauvoo Charter in the state legislature the previous year. Some Whigs, including Lincoln and Douglas, had also favored the charter, but were now furious at the Mormons because they had not supported President Van Buren for a second term.[16]

For governor, the Democrats nominated Thomas Ford, a State Supreme Court Justice who knew little about the Mormons and was neutral in his feelings toward them. Ford received near-unanimous Mormon support and retained a sufficient number of other Democrats to win the election. His victory, although won without courting Mormon favor, increased the hostility of the anti-Mormons toward the Saints and helped turn the thinking of many toward illegal methods of stopping their ascendancy.[17]

Despite the growing antipathy of some neighboring communities, Nauvoo continued to expand as Mormons from around the country and new converts from England arrived almost daily. Many of the new arrivals bought lots from Daniel for homes or businesses in the Wells Survey. Between April 1839 and April 1844, membership in the LDS Church increased by more than 9,500 and a large portion of those new members, both births and converts, were added to the population of Nauvoo.[18]

On February 4, 1843, Daniel H. Wells deeded the temple property to the church's Trustee-in-Trust, Joseph Smith, upon receipt of the final portion of the $1,100 purchase price. An early winter brought the 1843 building season to a close in November, by which time the temple walls had risen to the arches of the first tier of windows all around the building.[19]

Other substantial buildings were also being erected in the city, many of them on lots purchased from Daniel on the Hill where the temple was rising.

> The community was growing rapidly, business in Nauvoo
> was expanding with shops and commercial buildings going up

Figure 4.1. Engraving of Nauvoo, as seen from Montrose on the western side of the Mississippi River, ca. 1855, after nearly all Mormons had left the city and the temple was partially destroyed.

on all sides. Solid structures of brick or timber had replaced many log cabins and temporary shelters; farms and gardens were well laid out. On June 1, the City Council passed an ordinance to establish a ferry across the Mississippi at Nauvoo. On June 2, Joseph [Smith] became the delighted half owner of the steamship Maid of Iowa and the next day organized an excursion to Quincy for his family and friends, with a band on board to provide music.[20]

In mid-1843, the state of Missouri brought another indictment against Joseph Smith on the old charge of treason that had been made against him during the last months of the Mormons' sojourn in that state. Governor Ford of Illinois, after first privately warning Church leaders that he was obliged to do so, issued a writ for Joseph's arrest. Missouri officials took Joseph into custody at gunpoint on June 21, denied him any right to counsel or a hearing in Illinois, and attempted to immediately get him across the river to Missouri. The citizens of Dixon, where the arrest was made, and Pawpaw Grove, where Joseph was later held incommunicado, were outraged at the high-handed proceedings and delayed the flight of the officers and their prisoner long enough for

Joseph's friends to bring lawyers to his defense. There followed a week of intense legal battles, the arrest of the Missouri officers by the sheriff of Lee County, and the massing of some three hundred members of the Nauvoo Legion to accompany Joseph to trial in Quincy to ensure that his rights were observed.

Joseph's arrest ended in his triumphal release when, as the party was traveling to Quincy, he told his lawyers that the closest court authorized to hear his case was in Nauvoo and they immediately, over the protests of the arresting officers, altered their destination. On June 30, Joseph, his wife Emma, his would-be jailers, and his numerous bodyguards rode into Nauvoo with colors flying and a brass band playing as hundreds of onlookers cheered his arrival. The next day, Daniel H. Wells sat with other members of the Nauvoo Municipal Court and heard the case argued. The warrant was judged to be without substance and Joseph was discharged.[21]

Governor Ford felt strongly that the Nauvoo Charter did not give the city's municipal court the power to invalidate a state writ, but he nevertheless refused to call out the state militia, as demanded by Missouri's Sheriff Reynolds to enforce his view. He castigated Joseph's lawyer for supporting the Nauvoo court's claim to jurisdiction, but he allowed its decision to stand and the writ to remain dead. He also stated he would take no further action unless a new requisition was made by Missouri.[22]

Apparently fearing such a possibility, the Nauvoo City Council passed an ordinance on December 8 making it a crime for any officer to bring a writ against Joseph Smith based on charges from Missouri and providing a penalty of life imprisonment in the Nauvoo jail for anyone found guilty of this offense. A week later another ordinance was passed requiring every warrant issued in Nauvoo to carry the mayor's signature. Even more than the Nauvoo Municipal Court's proceedings in Joseph's case, these ordinances were widely viewed as being beyond the authority of the council. Alderman Daniel H. Wells voted against them, but was in the minority and both were enacted over his opposition. Within a few months, however, cooler heads prevailed and the ordinances were repealed; this time Daniel's vote was with the majority.[23]

Another city ordinance which Daniel opposed was proposed in March 1843. It required that payment of taxes and debts in Nauvoo be made only in gold or silver specie and immediately banned all use of paper money or scrip within the city. The purpose of the ordinance, as Joseph Smith explained it, was to protect converts coming from eastern states and overseas who usually arrived in Nauvoo with their assets in coin or gold-backed currency issued by eastern banks. Having little knowledge of the weakness or failure of many western banks or of widespread counterfeiting of their notes, they were often persuaded to exchange their hard money for worthless paper or to accept payment for their labor or produce in the same form.

Daniel feared that immediately declaring scrip and paper currency, then in wide use, invalid would impoverish all those, possibly including himself, who had previously accepted it in good faith as payment for property and goods. After hearing his objections, the proposed ordinance was revised to ban new scrip from being issued or accepted, but allowing what was previously in circulation to be redeemed for value. Paper currency was also banned and made liable to confiscation through a schedule of fines, but only the passing of counterfeit money was constituted a crime punishable by a prison sentence. With his concerns thus addressed Daniel withdrew his opposition and voted with the rest of the Council when the ordinance was passed unanimously.[24]

During his long service as justice of the peace, Daniel became acquainted with literally hundreds of citizens who appeared before him as plaintiffs, defendants, witnesses, lawmen, and government officials. By 1843, Squire Wells was probably the best-known non-Mormon in Nauvoo.

Most of the cases brought before Daniel after the beginning of 1840 were disputes between Mormons. Serious criminal matters were usually heard before the Hancock County Court in Carthage; a few before the Nauvoo City Court. But smaller crimes and civil cases were better settled in the more informal atmosphere of the justice court. Daniel's reputation for honesty and fairness was such that all citizens were willing to accept his judgment and he was frequently able to work out compromises that satisfied both parties in a dispute. When such a resolution was agreed to, he would often record it in his court book in his own hand and have the parties sign the record as evidence that they had accepted his decision.

The cases were varied and sometimes startling for what the Mormons claimed was a religiously-oriented community. Conversion to their new faith did not remove the temptation to commit crimes and Daniel's judicial practice included stolen property searches; assault and battery cases (one with a female defendant); larceny and horse theft cases; swindling, perjury, and debt suits; and even a case of buildings being "broken, destroyed and carried away."[25]

The justice court had no permanent location. It was originally held in Daniel's home, but soon began meeting in various other venues in order to be closer to the participants in its proceedings. Daniel's court book records cases heard at Joseph Smith's Store, William Law's Store, Foster's Store, Amos Davis's Grocery, Galland's Store, and Colton's Brickyard. One case involved a Mississippi River steamboat and was apparently heard on board.

Over time, Squire Wells's court book came to contain the names or autographs of most of the prominent citizens of Nauvoo, both Mormon and Gentile. Among those who appeared on its pages were the Prophet Joseph Smith; his brothers Hyrum Smith, Samuel H. Smith, William Smith and Don Carlos Smith; Sidney Rigdon and F. G. Williams, both counselors in the First Presidency; apostles Amasa Lyman, and Orson Pratt; John C. Bennett, William Marks, and Orrin Porter Rockwell.[26]

The worst as well as the best of the Saints were in court. John C. Bennett was involved in two cases. Joseph Smith made an affidavit against another church member charging him with "swindling"; he also testified in a possible persecution case where "certain citizens of this state had been unlawfully, illegally, and forcibly taken from this state into another." William and Wilson Law and Robert D. Foster had their share of troubles before they printed the *Nauvoo Expositor* that precipitated the murders of Joseph and Hyrum Smith. Foster's cases cover a dozen pages of the justice court ledger, as do the cases of William and Wilson Law. In one instance, the two brothers battled each other in court.

There was a non-Mormon resident of Nauvoo named Samuel Smith who must have frustrated the prophet's younger brother of the same name. He appeared in Daniel's court five times in as many years: in 1839 he was convicted of shooting a hog not belonging to him; a few months later Smith accused another citizen of threatening to kill him; he was charged with larceny in a third case; in a fourth, he was sued for a debt with William Smith; and in a fifth trial he was sued by one of the Pratts.

When Joseph Smith's friend John P. Greene (who was then a member of the Nauvoo City Council and later city marshal) was in court for a debt, Joseph demonstrated his characteristic loyalty by attending the trial in person. After hearing fellow Mormon leaders testify and feeling that the outcome looked unfavorable for Greene, the Prophet sent in $50 on behalf of his imperiled fellow Saint to settle the matter with the plaintiff. This was one of the cases in which Daniel had the litigants show their agreement to a settlement by signing the entry in his book.[27]

Daniel's county-wide role as a peacemaker and mediator sometimes extended even to physical intervention to cool down a heated dispute or minimize violence. He was a large and powerful man who had the courage to step between combatants, as noted in this August 1, 1843 entry from the journal of William Clayton. On that day Joseph rode in his buggy up to the temple lot where he began to discuss with Clayton and others the fact that some of his property was being sold for taxes.

> Suddenly Walter Bagby, the county assessor and collector, appeared and when Joseph confronted him with the issue, he denied all knowledge of it. As the discussion heated up, Joseph told Bagby that he was always abusing the citizens in

the area, and Bagby angrily called Joseph a liar. Obviously irritated, the church leader stepped down from his buggy, whereupon Bagby picked up a stone to throw at him. Enraged, Joseph went after him and struck him two or three times. Squire Daniel H. Wells stepped between them and succeeded in separating them. Joseph told the Esquire to assess the fine for the assault and he was willing to pay it.[28]

In August 1843, a group of anti-Mormon citizens held a rally at the Carthage courthouse and appointed a committee to draft resolutions enumerating the alleged offenses of the Mormons against their fellow citizens and describing what actions should be taken to rid the state of the Mormon menace. The committee accused church leaders, the city officials of Nauvoo, and Joseph Smith in particular, of all manner of crimes. None of the claims were new, but the resolutions that followed the recitation of supposed wrongs sounded a much more ominous note.

> Resolved, 1st. That inasmuch as we honestly believe that the combination of people calling themselves Mormons, or Latter-day Saints, have given strong indications, in their recent movements, that they are unwilling to submit to the ordinary restraints of law, we are therefore forced to the conclusion that the time is not far distant when the citizens of this country will be compelled to assert their rights in some way.
>
> Resolved, 2nd. That while we would deprecate anything like lawless violence, without justifiable cause, yet we pledge ourselves in the most solemn manner to resist all the wrongs which may be hereafter attempted to be imposed on this community by the Mormons, to the utmost of our ability,—peaceably, if we can, but forcibly, if we must.
>
> Resolved, 3rd. That in the event of our being forced into a collision with that people, we pledge ourselves that we will stand by and support each other in every emergency up to the death.
>
> Resolved, 4th. That we believe that it is also the interest of our friends in the neighboring counties and also neighboring states to begin to take a firm and decided stand against the high pretension and base designs of this Latter-day would-be Mahomet.[29]

Other resolutions called upon "all good and honest men . . . to come to the rescue," vowed to assist Missouri authorities in any future effort to arrest Joseph Smith, asked other counties to appoint like committees to adopt similar measures, and pledged not to support any man of either party who sought Mormon votes. The committee also vowed to, if necessary, "when the Government ceases to afford protection . . . fall back upon their original inherent right of self-defense" and take summary and signal vengeance upon the Mormons as a people.[30]

Far from being intimidated by this call to arms of their enemies, the Mormons responded by asserting in their newspaper, the Nauvoo Neighbor, that if the Carthginians came "to make war on Rome [Nauvoo] they might be destroyed like Hannibal of old."[31]

The Saints felt secure under the protection of the very instruments that their detractors accused them of debasing for their own purposes: the Nauvoo Charter, their votes, and the Nauvoo Legion. Confident that they had done nothing illegal and were entitled to use the Constitution, the courts, and their political power to serve their own interests, they did not recognize the intensity or the depth of the jealousy and animosity that their success had created among their foes. The Carthage resolutions marked the start of a storm that in less than a year became a deluge of hatred against the Mormons, one which neither they nor Daniel H. Wells foresaw accurately at its inception. When he wrote to his brother-in-law, Joseph Coombs, Daniel thought the citizens of Nauvoo had little to fear.

> Our city is still improving, emigrants begin to arrive and considerable preparations making for building. I expect the Temple will be enclosed this year. There was some excitement early in the winter. Those conventionists that met last fall and passed those resolutions . . . tried to raise an excitement in order to raise mobs and drive the Mormons away, but they found they had not influence to raise a tenth part of what would be necessary to do such a deed. I am only astonished that they should have influence enough to raise any for such a purpose. Men will let their prejudices lead them to do and perform things contrary to their own better judgment. They got so far carried away with their infamous plans, that they very gravely deliberated among themselves, whether they should drive and exterminate all the Mormons, men women and children, or only those more prominent men or leaders. They charged the Mormons with nothing that had any existence . . . they try to make believe that their liberties are in danger etc. etc. but since they have ascertained their strength they have been very quiet, the largest amount they could number under the greatest excitement they could possibly raise

was only two hundred and I am credibly informed that quite a large number even of these were so disgusted with the whole proceedings that they went home swearing they would never have anything more to do in the matter.[32]

In the fall of 1843, Daniel again visited his family in New York and Connecticut. This time he was accompanied by his wife Eliza and their son Albert, now six years old. Their stay was brief, probably no more than two weeks, because the press of Daniel's business and civic interests forbade him being away from Nauvoo for longer. Although she had corresponded with them for several years, this trip was Eliza's first opportunity to meet Daniel's older sisters, Pamela, Abigail, Lucy Ann, and Frank, in person. She got along well with all of them and was also introduced to Daniel's aged grandparents, David and Ruth Chapin, who were living in retirement in Montour, New York.

Abigail Rockwell, Lucy Ann Coombs, and Francis Raphel all had babies born in 1841 or 1842. Harriett Rockwell, Stephen Coombs, and Adelaide Josephine Raphel were too young to have much interaction with their cousin Albert, but he found a willing playmate in his cousin Henry Ross, age five, who was the ward of his Aunt Pamela since the death of his mother, Eliza Ross, in 1841.

The Wells family returned to Nauvoo in December. Daniel would not see any of his New York relatives again for forty years, by which time, among his immediate family, only Abigail Rockwell and her husband were still living. Eliza and Albert never saw any of their eastern relatives again. Both Harriett Rockwell and Stephen Coombs died within days of one another early in 1844. In June of the same year Frank Wells Raphel also died, leaving one child. Lucy Ann Coombs died in 1855, a few years after she and her husband Joseph moved to Wisconsin. Less than two years later Pamela, the only unmarried sister, died in January 1857.[33]

5

The Mormon Hegemony
Disaffection and Libel Lead to Mayhem and Murder

1843–1846

On August 12, 1843, Joseph Smith published the revelation defining the doctrine of plural marriage and commanding the Saints to practice it.[1]

The idea of polygamy was not new among the Mormons; it had been taught by the prophet for some time previously to some of the apostles and a few other church leaders, but its reading to the Nauvoo High Council and subsequent affirmation among church members was met with mixed reactions. Most Mormons were of Puritan descent and had been devoutly religious before their conversion to the restored gospel as taught by Joseph Smith. Nearly every Christian denomination taught the strict observance of monogamy, fidelity within marriage, and the complete abstinence from any sexual relationships outside marriage. While not always observed in practice, these standards were the universally acknowledged norm throughout the Christian world. Joseph's revelation on celestial marriage changed that norm for Mormons who accepted it, but not without great difficulty in adjusting their thinking and their actions.

Brigham Young later wrote that his reaction on hearing the doctrine of plural marriage "was the first time in my life that I desired the grave." Eventually, however, he accepted the revelation and lived it the remainder of his life.[2]

At least three members of the high council, William Marks, Austin Cowles, and Leonard Soby, opposed the new doctrine so strongly that they divided the council into pro- and anti-polygamous factions.[3]

Emma Smith, the prophet's wife, bitterly denounced polygamy to Hyrum Smith when he read the revelation to her. She had earlier accepted the doctrine and even participated in the marriage ceremonies of several of Joseph Smith's plural wives, but soon turned strongly against it and refused to allow Joseph's plural wives in her home.[4] After the revelation was made public in Nauvoo, she said that she "will have to submit" to it but, in fact, was never reconciled to it. Following her husband's death she again denounced polygamy and denied that he had advocated it.[5]

Heber C. Kimball also felt at first that he would as soon die as live in polygamy, but both he and his wife soon accepted it and were among the first to practice it.[6]

By the end of 1843 when Daniel and Eliza Wells returned to Nauvoo from their eastern trip, most leaders among the Mormons had accepted the celestial marriage principle, but it was still not widely known or understood by the general membership of the Church. Among most non-Mormons it had caused a huge increase in anti-Mormon agitation and vitriolic denunciations of the practice of "spiritual wifery."[7]

Daniel H. Wells was aware, at least since the affidavit made before him by John C. Bennett accusing Joseph Smith of immoral teachings and practices, of allegations that the Mormon leader was advocating and possibly practicing polygamy.[8] But there is no evidence that he personally knew of the teaching or practice of plural marriage in Nauvoo before the disclosure of Section 132 in August.[9]

His reaction upon learning of it was different than that of other non-Mormons. He did not speak openly against it as did other non-Mormons and even some Saints in the city. He did not make any recorded comment about it at all. His silence, in view of his own Puritan background and the outcry of others, is notable. He had already accepted Mormon doctrines relating to the eternal nature of marriage and the family, the salvation and resurrection of all persons through the atonement of Jesus Christ, and baptism by the living on behalf of the dead. This new (to him) revelation concerning plural marriage must have been a surprise and given him much cause for study, meditation, and prayer, but he did not reject it on first hearing.[10]

Daniel was a praying man, although his devotions were private and he seldom spoke openly of his personal religious practices. By 1843 he had been close friends with Joseph Smith for more than four years and had been in daily conversation with him during much of that time. Joseph rarely spoke, whether in the company of Saints or Gentiles, without teaching the restored gospel as he had received it. Over the years Daniel absorbed the prophet's ideas and merged them into his own belief system. He said that he found Mormon doctrines very appealing and easy to accept as truth and he cited the principle of celestial marriage as his main reason for joining the church and entering into polygamous marriages.[11]

Years later Daniel explained to members of his family the specific doctrines taught by Joseph Smith that he had ultimately concluded were true. The first of these was Joseph's personal testimony that he had been visited by heavenly messengers who had restored to him the priesthood and directed him to re-establish the Church of Jesus Christ. Daniel also embraced the concept that existence was infinite, extending back in time as well as forward, and that the organization of heaven was the family. And finally, he accepted the doctrine stated in the Mormon Article of Faith "that through the atonement of Christ, all mankind may be saved through obedience to the laws and ordinances of the Gospel."[12]

At some point of time, probably in 1844, but perhaps earlier, Daniel also concluded that Joseph Smith was God's prophet and not the devil's, as most non-Mormons believed. He thus became a Mormon in faith and testimony, although still not a church member. He delayed his formal baptism into the church a considerable time after he was fully converted to its principles. He did so for two reasons.

As an alderman, justice, and prominent land developer unaffiliated with the Mormons, Daniel felt he could do more to resolve conflicts between Mormons and their neighbors and to dispel prejudice against the Saints than if he were a church member. As long as he remained a non-Mormon, he could be an outside voice of reason who both sides in the growing confrontation would at least listen to.

Ironically, the Mormons were more willing to compromise their differences than were those combined against them. But if Daniel joined them, his influence with their adversaries would immediately end. In hopes that he could help keep the peace, he refrained from officially becoming a Mormon and did not speak openly of his conversion.[13]

His other reason for reticence was Eliza. She had rejected Mormon religious beliefs from the first time she heard them and the death of her minister father, who also opposed Mormon teachings, hardened her negative opinion of Joseph Smith and his restored gospel. The revelation concerning celestial marriage turned her vehement opposition to Mormon doctrine into absolute determination to never have any association with it, or any connection with those who accepted it.[14]

Daniel hoped to persuade Eliza to accept Mormonism and to be baptized into the new religion with him. He must have realized, from her attitude and that of her family, that there was little chance of her conversion, but he nevertheless refrained from joining the church alone. By holding back, he demonstrated his regard for his wife and his desire that they embrace the Mormon faith together. He also placed pressure on her to at least give Mormon doctrine a fair hearing so as not to be an obstacle to her husband's wishes.

But it was all in vain. Eliza would not look at anything Mormon except with loathing and her refusal to do so was set in stone by what she heard and readily accepted from non-Mormons regarding polygamy and other Mormon practices.

Daniel and Eliza's marriage was strained in one respect even before their conflict over religion took priority: Eliza had not conceived any more children after Albert. In March 1844 he turned six, but had no younger siblings. Catherine Woods had two additional children born after Nehemiah in 1837: William, born in 1841 and Eliza Jane, born in 1832. Daniel's older sisters had an additional five children among them and Eliza's married siblings at least six more during the same period. The reason for Daniel and Eliza's lack of offspring is puzzling. Neither said nor wrote anything about their marital relationship except Eliza's terse statement in her later divorce petition that she was "a good and lawful wife and never gave the said Wells any cause or provocation to desert [her]." There is another statement in the same document that states Daniel and Eliza lived together as man and wife from March 1837 "until May 184–." The last digit of the date is obscured by a large ink blot. The year is probably 1847, the year before Daniel went west, but it could be any other year back to 1840. If they stopped living as man and wife at a date prior to 1847, it would confirm an earlier serious rift in their relationship, but the ink blot leaves the mystery unresolved.[15]

Most non-Mormons were as antagonistic toward Mormon religious doctrines as Eliza and equally alarmed by the faith's continuing increase in numbers and its growing economic and political power. By late 1843 Nauvoo had risen out of swampland and vacant prairie to exceed Springfield and rival Chicago in size. Historian Donna Hill described the rapid growth of the city:

> That year, 374 missionaries were ordained and converts continued to pour into Nauvoo . . . [it] was the busiest city in the state . . . [and] could now boast of an iron foundry, two steam grist and saw mills, a water mill, two stone quarries, a match and powder factory, a pottery and a wagon shop, as well as numerous smaller enterprises, blacksmiths, tailors, milliners, tanners, cobblers and storekeepers.
>
> Two periodicals were published in the city, the semi-monthly Times and Seasons, which was both newspaper and official organ of the church, and the local gossip sheet, the Nauvoo Neighbor, which William Smith had first put out as The Wasp.
>
> Five riverboats docked on an average day at the landing at the bottom of Water Street, bringing freight and

passengers—converts to the church, tourists, journalists, politicians and businessmen. Passengers whose destination was somewhere farther up the Mississippi usually stopped over in Nauvoo . . .

Visitors liked to come too to take part in public holidays at Nauvoo, since there was nothing of Puritan solemnity among the Mormons . . . They loved music and dancing, and supported three bands: a brass band, a quadrille band with stringed instruments and the Nauvoo Legion Band . . . Singing groups often serenaded newlyweds or sang in the streets at Christmas and New Year's. Debating societies and amateur dramatics were popular, and the Mormons were always pleased to welcome a traveling circus or theatrical group.[16]

The Mormons' liberal social life was anathema to the conservative protestant ministers around them and the revelation on celestial marriage and polygamy gave them hard evidence with which to accuse Joseph Smith of plotting to overturn the economic, political, and social foundations of society and make himself an absolute monarch. The prospect of multiple wives producing a multitude of Mormon children, who would add to the burgeoning population of Nauvoo, and the economic strength and political clout of the church, created a strong revulsion in the minds of anti-Mormons. The reality that several women married to one man could produce no more children, and possibly less, than the same number married in monogamy seems never to have occurred to Mormon detractors.

The Mormons regarded their church (and preached about it) as a fulfillment of Daniel's interpretation of the king's dream in the Old Testament: a stone cut out of the mountains without hands that would roll forth destroying all other man-made institutions until it filled the whole earth with one true religion. The anti-Mormons saw themselves standing directly in front of the stone and about to be crushed by its momentum. The political actions of Mormon leaders in late 1843 and early 1844 did nothing to assuage their fears.

In October Joseph Smith wrote to the five announced candidates for the presidency, John C. Calhoun, Lewis Cass, Richard M. Johnson, Henry Clay, and Martin Van Buren asking "'What will be your rule of action relative to us as a people,' should fortune favor your ascension to the chief magistracy?" In a post script to Van Buren, he asked: "whether your views or feelings have changed since the subject matter of this communication was presented you in your then official capacity at Washington, in the year 1841."[17]

Van Buren and Johnson did not reply and the other candidates' responses gave no assurance that they would do anything to seek justice for or protect the rights of the Mormon people. Having thus confirmed national politicians' indifference or hostility to Mormon interests, Joseph Smith determined to give the Saints a candidate they could support with confidence: himself. He was nominated for president on a ticket proclaimed by the Twelve Apostles in January 1844.[18]

Anyone outside of Illinois who heard of the Mormon ticket undoubtedly considered it a minor party bid at most, but within the state its effect was profound. Many non-Mormons, who had observed the prophet's charisma, even on those who opposed him, and seen the thousands of converts who had gathered at Nauvoo, thought that his powers of persuasion might be sufficient to carry him into the highest office.

Daniel H. Wells did not think so, but even for him, it was a point of pride for the city of Nauvoo to field its own candidate for president. Although he had himself been heavily influenced by Joseph's proselyting, he did not think the prophet likely to become president, but viewed his attempt as further proof of the city's rising prominence. Revealing his own still dominant Whig leanings, as well as his sense of humor, he wrote to his brother-in-law Joseph Coombs in March:

> We still live and have our being, and not having anything very pressing on hand thought we would bring out a candidate for President as you will see by the papers I send you—not that we have anything particular against our own loved "Harry of West" [Henry Clay] but who would live in a city that could not have at least one candidate for President and then who knows what is in the future. Suppose we should elect our candidate, would there not be a new brood of "heaven born Amos's" [prophets] would not the Government Patronage fall like the "genial rays of the summer's sun" upon many an otherwise "luckless wight." [poor soul] with healing in its wings and blessings in its train? But not yet. Our own loved Harry must come first, and then the one term principal is a part of our creed you know, but enough of this.
>
> I do not yet quite despair of our place voting for Henry Clay. For Van [Buren] they most assuredly will not.[19]

The anti-Mormons did not think Joseph's candidacy a laughing matter. When combined with the confirmed rumors about polygamy, it caused a large increase in their denigration of him and the church in the press and in public meetings held in Carthage, Warsaw, and other nearby communities. Virulent denunciations appeared in newspapers, sermons, public meetings, and political speeches. But the greatest damage to the prophet's image came from some of his close friends who held high office in the church and the city.

William and Wilson Law were both members of the City Council and William was Joseph's counselor in the church's First Presidency. Wilson was a major general in the Nauvoo Legion and both brothers had profited handsomely in Nauvoo real estate trading and investments in construction, farming and lumber. When Joseph Smith sought to limit their personal gains in favor of greater contributions to temple building and the needs of poorer members, their enthusiasm for the restored gospel waned.

William Marks was also a City Council member and president of the Nauvoo Stake. He was a close confidant of Joseph Smith, but vehemently opposed polygamy. Dr. Robert D. Foster, who was elected school commissioner of Hancock County in 1843 with Mormon support, also strongly opposed polygamy, especially after an armed anti-Mormon band tried to persuade the county court to deny his office to him.

Two other brothers, Francis and Chauncey Higbee, were friends of Joseph, although no longer in good standing in the church due to their close association with John C. Bennett. The latter was still defaming the prophet and plotting to destroy his power.[20]

Aware that these men and others similarly disaffected posed a threat to his safety, Joseph Smith, as mayor of Nauvoo, appointed a police force of forty men to patrol the city day and night "to support the constitution of the U.S. & the State of Illinois and obey the ordinance[s] of this city and the Mayor according to the best of their ability" and to protect the mayor and other city officers. In December, the City Council, with Daniel H. Wells participating, approved the men selected and administered the oath of office to them.[21]

The police were instructed by the Mayor to enforce city ordinances and protect his life, if possible without violence. He also told them:

> I am exposed to far greater danger from traitors among ourselves than from enemies without . . . All the enemies upon the face of the earth may roar and exert all their power to bring about my death, but they can accomplish nothing, unless some who are among us and enjoy our society, have been with us in our councils, participated in our confidence, taken us by the hand, called us brother, saluted us with a kiss, join with our enemies . . . and we have a Judas in our midst.[22]

When the police patrols started, the dissenters in Nauvoo felt themselves threatened by a force they claimed would do Joseph Smith's bidding, even in defiance of the law. Beginning in March 1844, the Law brothers, Dr. Foster, and the Higbees began holding secret meetings with other ant-Mormons to discuss ways to bring about Joseph's downfall. By the end of April the Law brothers and Foster were excommunicated from the church "for unchristianlike conduct in general, for abusing my character privily, for throwing out slanderous insinuations against me, for conspiring against my peace and safety, for conspiring against my life, for conspiring against the peace of my family, and for lying."[23]

In early May, the Laws, Fosters, and Higbees established a printing house in Nauvoo from which they promised to publish the *Nauvoo Expositor*, a newspaper that would "advocate unmitigated Disobedience to Political Revelations, and to censure and decry gross moral imperfections wherever found, either in the plebeian, patrician or Self-Constituted Monarch."[24]

When the first and, as subsequent events assured, only issue of the Expositor was published on June 7, it caused such a reaction among all segments of Hancock County society that a response from Joseph Smith and city authorities was inevitable. Mormons were furious about the distortions and outright lies in the Expositor concerning the Prophet and polygamy; anti-Mormons immediately accepted the paper's inflammatory claims as fact and began organizing armed groups to drive the Mormons out of Nauvoo.

The next day, Saturday, Joseph called a meeting of the City Council to investigate the Expositor and determine what action should be taken concerning it. All but one of the Council members who were in the city (several were away on missions or other Church business) attended this day-long meeting, including Daniel H. Wells and another non-Mormon member, Benjamin Warrington. Sylvester Emmons was absent, to no one's surprise, as his name was listed on the Expositor's front page as its editor. The Council immediately ordered that Emmons, who was not Mormon, be suspended until he could be investigated for slandering the City Council. The heated session did not end until after six in the evening, but no action was decided upon. As the next day was the Sabbath and not to be profaned by politics, the Council agreed to consider the matter further at its regular Monday meeting.[25]

On Monday, June 10, the Council deliberated most of the day. Members heard many sworn witnesses testify to the immoral and criminal activities of those connected to the Expositor. The paper's prospectus and some of the first issue were read into the record, and Council members and citizens spoke at length about their personal knowledge of the Laws, Fosters, Higbees, and others who had turned against the Church. Daniel did not speak; he saw no need after listening to fourteen of his colleagues make points that he agreed with, but he voted with the majority (only Councilor Warrington dissented) when a resolution was finally passed.

> Resolved, by the City Council of the city of Nauvoo, that the printing-office from whence issues the Nauvoo Expositor is a public nuisance and also all of said Nauvoo Expositors which may be or exist in said establishment; and the Mayor is instructed to cause said printing establishment and papers to be removed without delay, in such manner as he shall direct.
>
> George W. Harris,
President, pro tem.
W. Richards, Recorder.[26]

An order was immediately issued by Mayor Joseph Smith that went well beyond what Daniel had in mind when voting that "said printing establishment and papers to be removed":

> State of Illinois,
> City of Nauvoo, ss.
> To the Marshal of said City, greeting.
>
> You are here commanded to destroy the printing press from whence issues the Nauvoo Expositor, and pi the type of said printing establishment in the street, and burn all the Expositors and libelous handbills found in said establishment; and if resistance be offered to your execution of this order by the owners or others, demolish the house; and if anyone threatens you or the Mayor or the officers of the city, arrest those who threaten you, and fail not to execute this order without delay, and make due return hereon.
>
> By order of the City Council,
Joseph Smith, Mayor.[27]

An order to the Nauvoo Legion Commander Jonathan Dunham was also issued directing him to assist the marshal in executing his order. A contingent of the legion accompanied the marshal to the Expositor office and destroyed the press, type, and all printed copies of the paper they could find. By nine the same evening, the marshal reported that he had completed the task assigned.

Marshal's return—The within-named press and type is destroyed and pied according to order, on this 10th day of June, 1844, at about 8 o'clock P.M.

       J. P. Greene, C. M.[28]

Six of the men identified as aldermen or councilors in the minutes of the June 10 meeting were not elected city officials as was Daniel. Some had been appointed to temporarily act for elected councilors who were away from Nauvoo and others were apparently members of the church High Council rather than the municipal government. Their participation as ex-officio city councilors indicates how much civil and church government had been blended together in Nauvoo by 1844.[29]

As a non-Mormon, Daniel should have recognized this mingling of religious and state authority and protested it. He should also have known that the order to destroy the Expositor printing press, libelous though it was, constituted a direct attack on the Constitution's guarantee of freedom of the press. His acquiescence to the resolution calling for removal of the press made him as guilty of the criminal act that followed from it as the mayor and others who voted for the action.

The destruction of the Expositor caused a storm of reaction against Joseph Smith and all Mormons. Once provided with an illegal act of violence ordered by the prophet, the anti-Mormons immediately agitated for a violent response, also illegal, that would expel or exterminate Joseph Smith and his followers from Illinois. Thomas Sharp, editor of the Warsaw Signal, editorialized on the first reports of the Expositor affair that he received from Robert Foster.

> War and extermination is inevitable! Citizens ARISE, ONE and ALL!!!—Can you stand by, and suffer such INFERNAL DEVILS!! to ROB men of their property and RIGHTS, without avenging them. We have no time for comment, every man will make his own. LET IT BE MADE WITH POWDER AND BALL!!![30]

At a mass meeting in Carthage held on June 13, among the resolutions adopted was the following:

> Resolved, that the time, in our opinion, has arrived, when the adherents of Smith, as a body, should be driven from the surrounding settlements into Nauvoo. That the prophet and his miscreant adherents should then he demanded at their hands; and, if not surrendered, a war of extermination

should be waged to the entire destruction, if necessary for our protection, of his adherents. And we hereby recommend this resolution to the consideration of the several townships, to the Mass Convention to be held at Carthage, hereby pledging ourselves to aid to the utmost the complete consummation of the object in view, that we may thereby be utterly relieved of the alarm, anxiety and trouble to which we are now subjected.

Resolved that every citizen arm himself to be prepared to sustain the resolutions herein contained.[31]

Hundreds of armed men gathered in various militia groups and mass meetings to hear diatribes against the Mormons and demands for retribution. The destruction of the Expositor was decried as a capital crime but none of the rhetoric called for prosecution of the perpetrators or any due process of law, only for their immediate expulsion or execution.

Nevertheless, Joseph Smith and fifteen other Mormons were indicted on a charge of riot at Carthage and the sheriff of that city was sent to arrest them. With unnumbered armed men waiting along the route to shoot him on sight, Joseph refused to surrender to the sheriff and instead secured a writ from the Nauvoo City Court, making the arrest warrant answerable before a judge in Nauvoo. That judge was Daniel H. Wells.[32]

It was an obvious conflict of interest for Daniel to judge a case brought under a city ordinance that he helped enact. All members of the Nauvoo City Council were authorized by the city charter to function as justices of the peace and nearly all the cases Daniel heard were for violations of city ordinances that he had voted on. This mingling of legislative and judicial functions was only one of many serious flaws in the charter, but none of them were ever addressed until the whole document was repealed in 1845.

The mayor and others were accused of riot in the destruction of the Expositor press rather than for enacting the ordinance that permitted the actions. If Daniel had been involved in the alleged riot, or been present when it occurred, he would have been precluded as a judge in the matter. Since he had no personal stake in the case and was charged by the charter to serve as a magistrate, he agreed to hear it.

Four members of the City Council and thirteen others were charged and of these at least two, Joseph and Hyrum Smith, were not present and did not participate in the destruction of the Expositor. But they were the ones whom the anti-Mormons wanted to get into court or within firing range and so their names headed the list of accused. Minutes of the trial in Daniel's justice court make interesting reading both for what was said and not said by both sides.

Twelve witnesses were called to testify and most of them were cross examined by opposing counsel. All agreed that the destruction of the press was carried out with little or no violence. Two of the proprietors of the Expositor Dr. Foster and Francis Higbee, were identified as being present during the incident. They objected to the proceedings, but handed over the key to the building at the marshal's demand and did not interfere with the execution of his orders. No one testified that any violence developed and no one identified Joseph or Hyrum Smith as being present when the order was carried out. It was soon evident to the prosecuting attorneys that they could not prove a case of riot against any of the defendants and, after recalling a few witnesses in an attempt to establish the value of property destroyed, the defense counsel, Edward Bonney and George P. Stiles, submitted the case without plea. Daniel H. Wells found no cause of action had been shown and the court discharged the prisoners.[33]

Daniel acquitted the accused because it was obvious that no riot had occurred, but he also realized that the actions of the mayor and City Council went well beyond their legal authority. After the trial, he told them so.

> The "Nauvoo Expositor" was destroyed in that riot. The Mayor and City Council has declared the paper a nuisance and they ordered it abated, therefore as such there was no riot about it . . . still, as I told the people, they were liable to damages for the destruction of the press &c., and that legally, it being an irregular proceeding.[34]

The anti-Mormons refused to accept the acquittal of those involved in the Expositor affair and agitated for an armed militia force to be assembled by the governor to bring Joseph Smith to trial on new charges in Carthage. Joseph responded by calling out the Nauvoo Legion to defend the city from any attack. During the next week meetings were held by the Mormons and their opponents, the apostles were called home from their missionary service, letters, and affidavits circulated around Hancock County, and newspaper articles and speeches fanned the conflict. By the time Governor Ford, who had been deluged with reports of the "Mormon conflict" by the Saints and their enemies, arrived in Carthage on June 21, an angry crowd was in full cry for the destruction of the Mormons.

At Ford's request, the Mormons sent delegates to present their side of the conflict, but the governor received them while surrounded by a group of their most bitter enemies who did not permit them to speak without interruption. After listening to the Saints' representations amid numerous contradictory remarks, Governor Ford concluded that the Nauvoo authorities had greatly exceeded their powers and told them so in a strongly-worded letter:

> I now express to you my opinion that your conduct in the destruction of the press was a very gross outrage upon the laws and the liberties of the people. It may have been full of libels, but this did not authorize you to destroy it.
>
> There are many newspapers in this state which have been wrongfully abusing me for more than a year, and yet such is my regard for the liberty of the press and the rights of a free people in a republican government that I would shed the last drop of my blood to protect those presses from any illegal violence.[35]

Ford's letter also told Joseph Smith that he and the others accused in the Expositor matter must surrender for trial at Carthage. His threat if they failed to comply was truly ominous:

> You are wrong in the first instance, and I can call out no portion of the militia for your defense until you submit to the law. You have made it necessary that a posse should be assembled to execute legal process; and that posse, as fast as it assembles is in danger of being imbued with the mobocratic spirit. If you, by refusing to submit, shall make it necessary to call out the militia, I have great fears that your city will be destroyed, and your people many of them exterminated.
>
> You know the excitement of the public mind. Do not tempt it too far. A very little matter may do a very great injury; and if you are disposed to continue the causes of excitement and render a force necessary to coerce submission, I would say that your city was built, as it were, upon a keg of powder which a very little spark may explode.
>
> . . . excitement is a matter which grows very fast upon men when assembled. The affair, I much fear, may assume a revolutionary character, and the men may disregard the authority of their officers.[36]

Almost as an afterthought, Ford added that he "will also guarantee the safety of all such persons as may thus be brought to this place from Nauvoo either for trial or as witnesses for the accused."

Joseph Smith did not believe Ford's assurance regarding his safety, but he realized that the threat of mob violence was all too real and, after failing to find any other means of avoiding a surrender that he knew would mean his death, he agreed to go to Carthage.

On Monday, June 24, Joseph and Hyrum Smith and all those charged with riot, along with several friends, started for Carthage on horseback. A number of family members and townspeople gathered at Joseph's home to see them off, but Daniel H. Wells was not among them. He had taken ill almost immediately after presiding at the trial on June 17 and was confined at home. After ten years in Nauvoo, he had finally been afflicted with the malaria that flourished on hot, humid summer days in the marshes along the waterfront.[37]

As the horsemen progressed up Mulholland Street to the top of the hill and passed the temple, Joseph turned aside on Woodruff Street to call on Daniel whose home stood a block north at the corner of Woodruff and Knight streets. Their meeting was brief and those who accompanied Joseph afterward recalled only his parting words: "Squire Wells, I want you to cherish my memory, and not think me the worst man in the world either."[38]

Later recalling this farewell to members of his family, Daniel said:

> I watched the caravan ride away with tears in my eyes and a choking sensation in my throat, for I knew I had touched the hand of a Prophet of God, a man above all other men; that he was riding to his martyrdom and I would never see his like again.[39]

Daniel returned to his sickbed but recovered sufficiently within a few days to resume his usual activities. He was again downcast, however, upon receiving word that his older sister Frank Wells Raphel had died on June 16, leaving her husband D'Ortigue to care for their only surviving child, three-year-old Adelaide.

On the night of June 27, the devastating news reached Nauvoo that Joseph Smith and his brother Hyrum were dead, murdered by a mob composed mainly of the Warsaw militia and the Carthage Greys, both units of the state militia that had been ostensibly protecting the Mormon leaders while they were confined in the Carthage jail awaiting trial on a newly manufactured charge of treason.[40]

6
The Decline of Nauvoo
Daniel Becomes a Mormon and Leads in the Battle of Nauvoo

1844–1846

In the months following the murder of Joseph and Hyrum Smith, a huge amount of sound and fury issued from the mouths of the anti-Mormons and from state and local authorities, but in the end it signified nothing. Immediately after the killings, the murderers dispersed and the majority of Carthage and Warsaw residents fled in fear that the Mormons would seek vengeance for the death of their prophet.[1] But the Saints never rose against those who had martyred Joseph and assured Governor Ford that they would keep the peace unless attacked again. Leaders of the assassination plot, as well as those who actually committed the crimes, were well known to many citizens of Carthage and Warsaw, but none were ever brought to justice for the murders or for their other depredations against the Mormons.[2]

Governor Ford, having failed in his pledge to protect the Smith brothers from lynching, failed again in his hesitant efforts to contain the anti-Mormons or to obtain justice for the slain. Many of those who participated in the violence openly justified the killings in articles and public speeches. Only nine of the sixty suspects in the murders who were brought before a grand jury were indicted and only five of them tried. The others, including those wounded by Joseph Smith in his own defense, crossed the river to Missouri and avoided arrest. When the five perpetrators were tried a year after the event, not a single witness testified against them and all were acquitted.[3]

The Mormon citizens of Nauvoo were more concerned with mourning the prophet's death than in avenging it. Joseph's and Hyrum's bodies were brought back to Nauvoo and, after a public viewing, funeral, and sham burial in the Nauvoo Cemetery, were secretly interred in the basement of the Nauvoo House to prevent their further desecration by their enemies. Months later, they were transferred to unmarked graves in the yard near the Mansion.[4]

Of more importance was the task of selecting a new leader for the church and multiple claims were made by his associates. Several of these, including Brigham Young and Sidney Rigdon, were not in Nauvoo at the time of Joseph's death. Sidney Rigdon arrived in the city on August 3 after a hurried trip from Pittsburgh; Brigham Young and four other apostles returned from their missionary and campaigning labors two days later. At a conference on August 8 church members voted to sustain Brigham Young, the senior member of the Twelve Apostles, as head of the church. Not all the Saints supported Young as their new leader and some, including Sidney Rigdon, James J. Strang, and William Smith, Joseph's younger brother, soon left the church to found splinter groups under their own leadership. But the vast majority sustained Brigham and stayed in Nauvoo.[5]

Daniel was pleased with the new leadership and equally pleased by the continuing growth and prosperity of the city. Unlike some, including Emma Smith, Joseph's widow, and Sidney Rigdon, his counselor, Daniel had no difficulty working with Brigham Young. The two men had established a firm friendship while serving together on the City Council after Brigham replaced Don Carlos Smith as a member in 1841. They had remained close even though Brigham was frequently absent from Nauvoo pursuing missionary labors or other church business.

Although a dozen years his senior, Brigham was much like Daniel in character. Both were from old New England Puritan families and had strong religious upbringing. Both were also self-made men who were not content to lead traditional lives in the homes and towns their families had occupied for generations. Each had struck out for new lands and built families and careers in frontier states where self-reliance and the ability to overcome hardships and primitive living conditions were paramount. Daniel had more formal education than Brigham, but both had a practical, no-nonsense mindset that enabled them to lead others effectively and to accomplish difficult tasks in the face of daunting obstacles. Neither was overly concerned about whether something could be done, only whether it should be done and, once having determined that, how to do it as efficiently as possible.

Unlike the charismatic but often impetuous visionary Joseph Smith, Brigham Young was a practical organizer and builder who could turn Joseph's revelations into a church organized on principles of personal sacrifice, missionary zeal, thrift, and Christian service. Daniel H. Wells, who within a few years would be first Brigham's aide and then his counselor, was well-qualified to help him develop the church into an empire of cities and towns in the western wilderness.

But at present they were still in Nauvoo; Brigham Young now the de-facto mayor as well as presiding apostle in the church, and Daniel an alderman and justice of the peace. The anti-Mormon faction was temporarily cowed by fear of inciting Mormon retribution, but they continued their campaign to reduce the Saints' political influence and economic power. In July, a delegation from Carthage and Warsaw asked Governor Ford to expel the Mormons from Illinois, presumably by issuing the same kind of order that Governor Boggs had in Missouri. Ford knew the law better than Boggs, however, and turned down the request, telling the anti-Mormon committee that he had no power to exile any citizen.[6]

With their presidential candidate dead, the Mormons' political activities diminished to almost nothing for a time, but revived quickly when they realized that, if state and county offices were won by anti-Mormon candidates, they would use these positions to further harass the Saints under color of law. In the elections of 1842 and 1843, the Mormons had managed to elect candidates to county offices who, if not favorable to their interests, were at least not strong enemies. By 1844, Hancock County was so politically polarized that any candidate who was not favorable to the Mormons was certain to be backed by those who hated them.

At a rally held in Nauvoo, the Saints put forth a slate of candidates who were not themselves Mormons, but who could be trusted to deal fairly with the Church and its adherents. General Minor Deming of Carthage was nominated for sheriff, Daniel H. Wells for coroner, and Jacob Backenstos, who had been elected sheriff in 1842, for state representative. So much had the Mormons' voting power grown in Nauvoo and the surrounding area that the candidates they favored swept every county office, all but one by a two-to-one margin or more. Daniel was elected coroner by 1838 votes to his opponent's 867. He continued to also serve as an alderman and justice of the peace in Nauvoo after he was sworn into his county office.[7]

The election results made abundantly clear that the Mormons were still gaining political strength and would soon be able to control state as well as county offices. The death of Joseph and Hyrum Smith had not affected the number of converts streaming into Illinois. On the contrary, church membership grew by more than 4,000 in each of the two years following the murders and the Saints' urge to gather to Nauvoo for mutual security and protection was made stronger by the attacks against them.[8]

Hancock County's new representative, Jacob Backenstos, with some help from Governor Ford, made a valiant defense of the Nauvoo Charter before the state legislature in January 1845, but their efforts were not enough to prevent the repeal of the city charter and that of the Nauvoo Legion. This action destroyed the city's government and disbanded its defensive force.

As soon as the repeal of the charter was known, Brigham Young met with city authorities, church leaders, and others to discuss what course to pursue in order to keep Nauvoo's city government functioning and maintain order in the community. Daniel H. Wells was a principal speaker at this meeting held in the Masonic Hall. Others included George Miller, George A. Smith, W. W. Phelps, and Brigham Young himself.[9]

With the approval of non-Mormon residents like Daniel, the church organization of wards presided over by bishops was adapted to also function as the civil government, thus completing the union of civil and religious authority among the Mormons that had been started by Joseph Smith. At the suggestion of Governor Ford, the center of Nauvoo was incorporated as a town in Hancock County. Under Illinois law, towns could not be larger than one square mile, so a dozen would have been needed to encompass the entire city, but the single township enabled residents both inside and outside the town boundaries to record deeds, maintain order, and transact official business with county officers. Daniel kept his duties as justice of the peace and county coroner and other former Nauvoo City officials continued to run the town as they had the city, receiving little or no pay for their services.[10]

Although it was no longer part of the state militia, Brigham Young also kept the Nauvoo Legion intact and continued its training schedule with members using their personal arms in place of the state weapons which were reclaimed by state officials and distributed among the anti-Mormon militias in the county. As former commissary general for the officially disbanded Legion, Daniel H. Wells protested vigorously against the state's actions on grounds that the Legion's members were still part of the state militia and were entitled to state arms and equipment on the same basis as other units in Hancock County, but his argument could not prevail against the anti-Mormon demands that the Legion be disarmed.[11]

Despite their increased arms, the anti-Mormon militia troops were no match in numbers or discipline for the Legion. They realized that the discipline developed by the Legion's training would be deadly if the Mormons ever decided to fight rather than forbear. These concerns proved well-founded in subsequent skirmishes. Recognizing their inferiority, the anti-Mormons made no attempt to confront the Saints militarily until they had changed the odds to be heavily in their favor.[12]

Despite losses due to death and disaffection, the church as a whole continued to grow in numbers and increase in religious commitment. Construction on the temple went forward through the summer and into the late fall. The last of the thirty capstones was set in place on the walls a few hours before the first heavy snow of the season in December. Fund raising went on through the winter while the roof timbers and interior woodwork were being prepared for installation.[13]

Sensing that they could not succeed in persecuting and driving away the Saints by democratic or legal means, the anti-Mormons soon returned to lawless tactics. Massive efforts were made to intimidate prosecution witnesses prior to the trial of the nine men charged with murdering Joseph and Hyrum Smith. So blatant were the threats made against Mormon witnesses that Governor Ford authorized the newly-elected Sheriff Deming, who had promised to bring the killers to justice in a fair trial, to call out units of the state militia, including the men of the Nauvoo Legion, to protect the court. Fearing a collision between Mormon and anti-Mormon companies that could result in open warfare, Deming declined to use the Nauvoo militia men and the trial, when it finally commenced in June 1845, was a raucous gathering of anti-Mormons, some of whom were members of the group that had stormed the Carthage jail.

None of the many Mormon witnesses who had been present in and around the Carthage jail on the day when the Smiths were murdered were called to testify. The verdict was predetermined.

> It was known to all concerned that the murders had been committed by members of the Warsaw militia, of whom the defendants were officers, and that Thomas Sharp had publicly urged the murders, and had justified them afterward. No alibis were possible, since the defendants had been seen in Carthage on the day and time in question.
> . . . The lawyers who spoke for the defense declared that the witnesses were incredible and the evidence inconclusive, but they also reminded the jury and the court how much the Smiths had been hated and feared by non-Mormons and they managed to imply that a verdict of guilty might well bring on a civil war.
> The trial had lasted for less than a week and the jury deliberated for less than three hours, including time for lunch. They filed back with a verdict that surprised no one—not guilty.[14]

Once the defendants were acquitted, the anti-Mormon faction resumed pursuit of its ultimate goal: to drive the Saints out of Illinois. Sheriff Deming was assaulted in the courthouse on June 24 by a well-known anti-Mormon and was forced in self-defense to shoot his assailant who died within a few minutes. Deming was indicted for murder, resigned his office to await trial, and died of a fever on September 10. His grieving widow afterward noted that sustained mob attacks on outlying Mormon settlements began the very day that Deming died.[15]

The burning of Morley Settlement, a small community about twenty-five miles south of Nauvoo, is graphically described by Daniel H. Wells.

> In the Fall of 1845 mobs commenced driving out the Mormons in the lower part of Hancock Co., and burning their houses and property. They set fire to the stacks of a man named Durfee who ran out of the house in the night to put out the fire, and they shot him by the light of the fire. The mob then took his family and set them outside, ordering them to leave immediately; helped them take the things out of the house into the street, and then set fire to the house burning it down.
>
> This burning was continued from settlement to settlement, where Mormons had settled, for 10 or 11 days without any resistance whatever. The Sheriff undertook to quell the mob and tried to raise a posse to stop them but was refused. President Young told him that it would be considered a Mormon War if they should raise a posse at Nauvoo to undertake to quell the mob, and he was determined no chance should be given to call that a Mormon War, so he refused the Sheriff a posse, telling him to go to Carthage or Warsaw and raise a posse. This the Sheriff tried to do, but the mob got after him and sought his life. The people at Nauvoo sent out wagons and teams to bring those people whom the mob had driven out of their homes and burned their property. The Sheriff finally raised a posse at near Camp Greek, south-east of Carthage, where they had a fight in which one or two men were killed; then the mob dispersed. After the mob was checked the old [non-Mormon] citizens of Nauvoo scattered in every direction, representing that the Mormons had driven them from their homes and were robbing them of their property; that they had left everything and fled for their lives.[16]

About 175 farms and homes were burned out in a week by the armed mob numbering some three hundred men. Sheriff Backenstos, who had replaced Minor Deming on the latter's death, could not raise a posse among the non-Mormons of Hancock County, even though many of them privately deplored the mob violence he was attempting to stop. As excuse, most said that Backenstos had gained his office through Mormon support and, if they assisted him in protecting the Mormons, they would be regarded as Jack-Mormons and attacked themselves by the anti-Mormons.

The posse Backenstos finally raised that fought the mob near Camp Creek, consisted largely of Mormons from settlements outside of Nauvoo who feared that their own homes would soon be torched unless the raiders were stopped.[17]

In November, Daniel's mother, Catherine Wells Robison, died in Nauvoo where she had returned to live after the death of her second husband Charles Robison. Her body was laid to rest in the Nauvoo Cemetery. Her death removed one impediment to Daniel's desire to be baptized into the LDS faith. Like her second husband Charles Robison, she was not favorably inclined toward the Mormons and was opposed to her son becoming affiliated with them. Daniel would not have refrained from joining the church due to his mother's opposition, but her passing relieved him of the conflict that might have resulted from going against her wishes. He was left, however, with even stronger opposition from his wife Eliza.[18]

Governor Ford concluded that the only way to end the conflict between the Mormons and their opponents was to persuade the Saints to leave Illinois. To effect this removal, he sent a four-man commission to meet with Brigham Young. Of this meeting and the agreement that resulted from it, Daniel says:

> Governor Ford of the State came up and brought a company or two of troops from the other side of Illinois River. General Harding then had charge of the military affairs of that state. He and Senator Douglass with one or two other leading officials came up with the Governor. They came with the soldiers to put a stop to this Mormon War as it was called.
>
> Then it was that the Mormons made an agreement to leave the country... The Mormons agreed to go out and it was stipulated that the old citizens should assist them in disposing of their property, so as to enable them to get outfits &c., but this they did not do; they did not fulfil that treaty, and the Mormons went up and down with their furniture &c., and traded for anything that could travel such as an animal or a wagon.[19]

The agreement made by the church council was brief and pointed:

> ... we propose to leave this country next spring for some points so remote that there will not need to be any difficulty with the

people and ourselves, provided certain propositions necessary for the accomplishment of our removal shall be observed, to wit:

That the citizens of this and surrounding counties and all men will use their influence and exertion to help us to sell or rent our property so as to get means enough that we can help the widow, the fatherless, and the destitute to remove with us; that all men will let us alone with their vexatious lawsuits, so that we may have time, for we have broken no law;

Help us to get dry goods, groceries, produce, beef, cattle, sheep, wagons, mules, horses, harnesses, etc., in exchange for our property at a fair price, and deed given at payments, that we may have means to accomplish a removal without the suffering of the destitute to an extent beyond the endurance of human nature . . .

That it is a mistaken idea that we have proposed to remove in six months, for that would be so early in the spring that grass might not grow, nor water run, both of which would be necessary for our removal, but we propose to use our influence to have no more seed time and harvest among our people in this country after gathering of present crops, and that all communications to us be made in writing.

> By order of the Council
> Brigham Young, President
> Willard Richards, Clerk[20]

Knowing that any of the Saints' property or possessions not essential for travel into the western wilderness would of necessity be abandoned when they left the state, the anti-Mormons refused to buy their homes or farms and discouraged others from doing so. Church leaders told members not to plant winter wheat or any other crop to be harvested in the spring, but to use their entire fall harvest to sell for needed equipment or to provide food on the journey west. A list of needed provisions and equipment was provided to each family and the Saints were organized into companies, each presided over by a captain. It was estimated that the cost of outfitting each family would be about $250.

Through the winter preparations for departure went on day and night, but the Mormons found few buyers for their property and most struggled to obtain the equipment and provisions they needed. Brigham Young even tried to sell the entire city of Nauvoo for one-half its appraised value, offering to include the temple as a gift to anyone who would agree to the $1 million discounted price. He got no takers.[21]

In December some of the temple rooms were placed in service as church leaders began administering ordinances to those who were planning to leave with the first contingent of Saints. All who passed through the sacred ceremonies within the temple knew that the edifice would not long survive the departure of its builders from Nauvoo. Nevertheless, while workmen continued to lay flooring, plaster walls, and install woodwork, more than five thousand persons received temple rites.[22]

By the end of February 1846, more than a thousand wagons crossed the Mississippi River into Iowa and headed west toward Council Bluffs more than four hundred miles distant. Many of these early departures were facilitated by the freezing over of the river during a bitter cold spell that began on February 25, but once across they suffered greatly from exposure to the elements. As the population of Nauvoo declined, anti-Mormon activity rose again. Daniel described the deteriorating situation in the city:

> In the Spring of 1846 the authorities of the Church went out as they agreed to, and another company went out in May, but they did not sell their property, leaving it in the hands of trustees to sell. In June they [anti-Mormons] raised a "hullaballoo" and gathered together menacing Nauvoo. But some new citizens had settled there by this time, and had bought property and were making homes; therefore not wishing to see their places destroyed and having a desire to induce immigration there, they combined with the remaining Mormons, and the mob got scared and dispersed . . . The Mormon people kept going out as fast as possible. The mob took Phinehas Young and Brigham H. Young prisoners and kept them for a time as kind of hostages. Some few who were harvesting their crops just outside [the city] were caught by the mob and whipped.[23]

Most of the Saints managed to get out of Nauvoo by the end of April, but those who remained behind felt the continued pressure of their enemies to hasten their departure. Daniel noted:

> During the preparations for the exodus, Major Warren had been stationed with a small military force in Hancock, to keep the peace; but about the middle of April he received orders to disband his force on the first of May, as that was adjudged by "the public expectation," to use a phrase of Major Warren's, when the last of the Mormons should have left the State. So soon as it was understood that there were still left in Nauvoo a number of Mormons who would likely remain through the

summer to continue their efforts to dispose of property, an uproar was raised in the surrounding counties, meetings were held and resolutions adopted, demanding that they leave at once, under threats of extermination. When the governor saw this new furore breaking out, he countermanded the order for Major Warren to disband his forces, and commanded him to hold his position and to preserve the peace until he received further orders.[24]

The exodus went on until by June more than fifteen thousand Mormons were strung out in wagon trains on the trail to Council Bluffs where they would remain through the coming winter. Meanwhile, about a thousand Saints, those too poor or too sick to join their fellows, remained in Nauvoo. Most were trying to recover their health or dispose of their property before leaving. A few had decided not to follow Brigham Young and were hoping to hold on until the anti-Mormon storm abated.

Daniel was also still in the city, and still not a Mormon, but he knew time was running out for him. He was fervently trying to persuade Eliza to accept the Mormon faith and be baptized with him; she was still adamantly refusing. By fall, the last of the Saints would be gone from Nauvoo and his decision would be forced: if he chose to stay with his wife and son, he would have to abandon the religion he knew was divinely inspired; if he chose to join the westward migration of the Saints, he would have to abandon Eliza and Albert and all his property in Illinois. There was no middle ground, no compromise position that would allow him to have both family and faith.

By August only a few hundred Mormons remained in Nauvoo along with a number of non-Mormons who had purchased property from those departing. The anti-Mormons, feeling confident that their strength had increased sufficiently that they could take the city by storm, began amassing weapons, ammunition, and artillery and planning their attack.

With the city he had helped build on the brink of destruction, its people driven into the wilderness, and the LDS Church at the most persecuted and embattled moment in its history, Daniel at last decided to become a Mormon. He afterward never said or wrote anything about why or even how he chose. He simply sought out Almon W. Babbitt, a Mormon lawyer and businessman, who had remained in Nauvoo at the request of Brigham Young to act as one of the three trustees for the church authorized to sell all of its remaining property. Daniel had been friends with Babbitt since the latter moved to Nauvoo from Kirtland, Ohio, in 1842. Babbitt accompanied Daniel down to the Mississippi River on a warm afternoon and baptized him by immersion. He then confirmed Daniel a member of the church. Years later, Daniel wrote of the event in the third person.

Daniel H. Wells was baptized for the remission of his sins and joined the Church of Jesus Christ of Latter-day Saints, called Mormon, August 9, 1846. He was ordained to the Priesthood and received his patriarchal blessing under the hands of Patriarch Father John Smith. in the Camp of Israel, on the south side of the Missouri River, near where Omaha now stands, September 27, 1846. Daniel Wells removed to the mountains since, Utah Territory in 1848, his family entirely refusing to accompany him, and now having left all for the Gospel's sake, and becoming lost in a manner to the world, his history from henceforth, and his acts and subsequent career are only found in the Church and Kingdom of God, where they will be kept in honorable remembrance.[25]

The anti-Mormon forces continued to increase in numbers and determination to force all the remaining Saints out of Nauvoo. William Clayton, a British convert, described the developing conflict on August 25:

> I learned today that the mob had made it known that they were coming to drive out the "Mormons." The Governor sent an officer to raise volunteers to disperse the mob, but the mob learning this they came sooner than they had calculated. The brethren being apprised of the intentions of the mob prepared to meet them as well as their circumstances would permit. Some of the new citizens also made preparations to join the brethren. They made five cannon shot of an old steam boat shaft. They also filled some barrels with powder, old iron, etc., which were buried in the pass to the city which could be fired by slow match but this was of no avail as some traitors informed the mob of it, hence they did not come into the settled part of the city.[26]

By the end of August, the threat of renewed violence against Nauvoo had become so great that Daniel temporarily moved his family out of the city for their own safety. Eliza and Albert went to Burlington for an extended visit with James and Catherine Woods while Daniel helped organize the defense of the city. Eliza was now aware of her husband's conversion to the Mormon faith and was doubtless concerned for his welfare in the event of hostilities, but she remained firm in her refusal to accept his new faith.[27]

Daniel went on with his business in Nauvoo, but his conversion to the Mormon faith had changed his economic objectives. He was no longer buying property in Nauvoo, but like other Mormons, was trying to sell at least some of his holdings for cash so that he could make his own preparations to leave. There were few buyers, however, and prices were almost in free fall as the anti-Mormons threatened daily to take the entire city by force.

Governor Ford sent a force of ten men from Fulton County, under the command of Major J. R. Parker, who was also authorized to take command of any volunteer forces in the city.

> He was also empowered "to pursue, and in aid of any peace officer with a proper warrant, arrest the rioters who may threaten or attempt such an attack, and bring them to trial . . ."
>
> Thus equipped, Major Parker went to Nauvoo and issued a proclamation calling upon the mobs then collecting, "in the name of the people of Illinois, and by virtue of the authority vested in him by the governor of the State to disperse . . ." The issue, then, was no longer between the mob forces and the Mormons; it was between the recognized authority of the State and this lawless banditti.[28]

Undeterred by the appearance of a legal force to protect the Saints, the leader of the anti-Mormons, John Carlin, issued a proclamation that he would consider Parker's men members of a mob and "proceed accordingly" if they interfered with his actions. Parker replied he would treat Carlin's troop as a mob if they tried to enter Nauvoo and also wrote to another mob leader, Major Singleton, expressing a desire to settle the conflict without bloodshed. His peacemaking efforts were rebuffed, however, when Singleton replied that he

> . . . saw nothing looking to the expulsion of the remnant of the Mormon people left in Nauvoo, and "that is," said he "a sine qua non with us." . . . now something more is demanded—the immediate removal of the Mormons, the surrender of Nauvoo, etc. Singleton concluded his terms to Parker, the representative of the governor of the State, in these words:
>
> "When I say to you, the Mormons must go, I speak the mind of the camp and the country. They can leave without force or injury to themselves or their property, but I say to you, sir, with all candor, they shall go—they may fix the time within sixty days, or I will fix it for them."[29]

A committee of citizens of Quincy, a river town south of Nauvoo, proposed terms for the peaceful surrender of Nauvoo, but these were rejected by the anti-Mormons and the command of their forces passed to Thomas S. Brockman a Campbellite preacher, known familiarly as "Old Tom," among his followers.

> He at once went into active preparations for bombarding the city; and with a force of more than one thousand men, and six pieces of cannon, took up a position about one mile east of the city, in a cornfield just at the head of Mulholland Street; and not far from the house of Squire D. H. Wells.[30]

During the first week of September, Daniel helped some of the remaining Mormon families get across the river. By mid-month Nauvoo was almost deserted with only about three hundred Mormon families and perhaps half that number of non-Mormon "new residents" in it. On September 10 the anti-Mormon forces gathered east of the city began to move. What followed is best described by the personal accounts of Daniel and others who fought beside him.

> At this time we were watching the mob outside Nauvoo. The Quincy committee came in to negotiate for peace upon the basis of the Mormons leaving immediately. The Mormons and new citizens were under orders from the Governor to defend themselves from the mob, having a regular militia. There were about 300 Mormons and new citizens who could then bear arms against the mob, but on the day of the fight no more than 100 could be found to go, as the Mormons were continually leaving.[31]
> Major Flood, of Quincy, in company with John Wood, Esq., Mayor of Quincy, Dr. Conyers and Mr. Joel Rice, visited the mob camp with the hope of dissuading them from their purpose, but without effect. Scarcely had their conference ended, and they on their way to the city, before a shower of six-pounders was sent among us and over our heads, but happily without injuring any one. This little exploit, with a few exchanges at long rifle distance between the respective guards, ended the hostilities for that day.[32]
> On Saturday the 12 inst., the mob made their appearance being about twelve hundred in number. The brethren and some of the new citizens in the whole about one hundred and

sixty went to give them battle, but many of the new citizens and some of the brethren when they saw the numbers of the mob fled and left about one hundred, nearly all brethren to fight the enemy. The mob had pieces of cannon. They met near Boscow's store on Winchester street. The cannon of the mob fired a number of times into Barlow's old barn expecting many of the brethren were concealed there but in this they were disappointed, the brethren chiefly lying down on the ground behind some shelter and fired in that position.[33]

No sooner, however, had [the anti-Mormons] opened their first fire, than they were answered with as good as they gave; and one round created a great sensation in their ranks, and drew from the defensive a loud and hearty cheer. A brisk cannonade was kept up on both sides during the whole of the engagement. Before the enemy came within full rifle range of our breast works, they began to flank, and sweep a compass to the south, with every prospect of an unchecked advance to the Temple square, which it was their object to get possession of.[34]

The cannon of the brethren was not of much service, they would not carry more than a quarter of a mile whereas those of the mob would hold well a half a mile. They shot nine balls through a small smith shop, one through Wells's barn and one at his house but the ball struck the ground in front of his house and glanced through the well curb.[35]

The mob-forces advanced in solid column, making a desperate effort to reach Mulholland street, the principal street leading into Nauvoo from the east. If the onset was desperate, the resistance was equally determined. The main shock of the conflict was sustained for a time by Gates's and Cutler's companies, and they must inevitably have been overpowered by the superior numbers of the mob, had not Squire Wells come up with Lamareux's company to reinforce them. The doughty squire had ridden across an open field exposed to the fire of the enemy, to where Lamareux's company lay behind their fortifications. He called upon them to advance at once to check the approach of the mob. There was one brave spirit who needed no second call to perform his duty. That was William Anderson, captain of what was known as the "Spartan Band." He leaped from behind the trenches and calling on his men to follow, started for the front. The rest of Lamareux's company did not so readily respond, and manifested a disposition to retreat rather than advance. Squire Wells, observing this, and seeing Anderson and his few brave followers rushing

Figure 6.1. The Battle of Nauvoo, detail from a painting by C. C. A. Christensen. The horseback rider is Daniel H. Wells.

headlong into the conflict, raised in his stirrups, and swinging his hat, shouted: "Hurrah for Anderson! Who wouldn't follow the brave Anderson!" This rallied their spirits, and they followed the squire to the front, where they were soon firing at the enemy as steadily as their comrades.[36]

This was an unexpected movement to them [the anti-Mormons], and our first fire brought them to a halt. We took position about a small brick shed, and along a slender picket railing; and being armed, many of us, with revolving rifles, we kept up such an incessant fire that portions of the enemy repeatedly fell back a little way into a slight hollow, but as often returned again to the attack. It was here that the brave Anderson fell, almost at the opening of our fire his eldest son [August L. Anderson], a lad about sixteen years of age, having fallen a few moments before, in another part of the field, by a cannon shot.[37]

The Mormon men stood firm behind the breastwork. I was by the side of young Anderson when he was shot and killed by a cannon ball. The ball almost cut my clothes. Anderson's father was killed by a musket ball ten minutes later. This happened in a blacksmith shop, and the cannon balls threw bricks all over me and bruised me quite bad. A musket ball hit me in the hand but [the wound] was slight. I was near [David] Morris when he was killed by a cannon ball and his head was nearly severed from his body.[38]

The mob forces by this time had nearly reached Mulholland Street, but now they recoiled from the rapid firing of the reinforcements and beat a retreat to the house of a Mr. Carmichael, but a short distance from Squire Wells's house. Here they waited until wagons came from their camp, and putting their dead and wounded into them, returned to where they were encamped in the morning.[39]

Three of the brethren were killed, viz. William Anderson, his son, and Norris, a blacksmith. Three others wounded. The mob would not own to any of their party being killed but one person saw them put sixteen men into one wagon and handled them more like dead persons than wounded. The ground where they stood was pretty much covered with blood, so that there is no doubt they had many slain or wounded. They had 150 baggage wagons. Squire Wells took command of the brethren and rode to and fro during the whole battle without receiving injury, although the balls whistled by him on every side.[40]

This last battle was fought on Saturday, and it exhausted the stock of ammunition that the mob brought with them. And although they were driven from the battle field, they were secure in their encampment . . . The idea now of forming a committee of mediation was acted upon; hence, what was called the Quincy Committee of one hundred, waited upon the belligerent parties, during the time that preparations were making for further hostilities. This committee did not mediate for the rights of man, but to spare the effusion of blood, which they represented would inevitably flow in case of failure to settle on some terms . . . We had been summoned, before the last engagement, to surrender at discretion, without terms; now, however, terms were again offered, and perhaps through the influence of the committee. The mob was also daily swelling in numbers, while the force in the city was materially diminishing. Several hundred men, who had been stationed on the west side of the river before the last battle, with red flags, denoting no quarter, and to cut off our retreat, still occupied that threatening position. Under these trying circumstances the Trustees of the Church were called upon to accept or reject the best and last proposition-the ultimatum of General Brockman.[41]

After receiving the anti-Mormons' terms of surrender from the Quincy Committee, the trustees felt they had no alternative and signed the agreement along with the committee chairman and the leaders of the attacking forces. The conditions imposed were harsh and the time allowed short, but both would soon be rendered even more draconian when enforced with inhuman cruelty.

1. The city of Nauvoo will surrender. The force of Colonel Brockman to enter and take possession of the city tomorrow, the seventeenth of September, at three o'clock p. m.
2. The arms to be delivered to the Quincy committee, to be returned on the crossing of the river.
3. The Quincy committee pledge themselves to use their influence for the protection of persons and property from all violence, and the officers of the camp and the men pledge themselves to protect all persons and property from violence.
4. The sick and helpless to be protected and treated with humanity.
5. The Mormon population of the city to leave the State or disperse as soon as they can cross the river.
6. Five men, including the Trustees of The Church, and five clerks, with their families (Wm. Pickett not one of the number) to be permitted to remain in the city, for the disposition of property, free from all molestation and personal violence.
7. Hostilities to cease immediately, and ten men of the Quincy committee to enter the city, in the execution of their duty as soon as they think proper.

These terms of, capitulation were signed on the part of the citizens of Nauvoo, by Almon W. Babbitt, Joseph L. Heywood and John S. Fullmer; and on the part of the mob by Thomas S. Brockman and John Carlin; and by Andrew Johnson on behalf of the Quincy committee.[42]

Upon hearing that the city would be abandoned and their arms surrendered, many of the defending volunteers were enraged and discussed whether to reject the agreement and continue the fighting. They would not hear the explanation of the trustees, but Daniel, who had led the defenders, was able to speak with them as a respected equal:

> There is no use of the small handful of volunteers trying to defend Nauvoo against such an overwhelming force. What interest have the Saints to expect from its defense? Our

interests are not identified with it, but in getting away from it. Who could urge the propriety of exposing life to defend a place for the purpose of vacating it? I have been in the councils of Joseph and Hyrum and the Twelve, and I know they were desirous that the Saints should leave the States and go westward. Have not the Twelve Apostles and most of the Church gone; and is not their counsel to us to follow? Have they not told us that our safety was not in Nauvoo, but in our removal westward?

The Trustees have no means with which to carry on the defense; they are already involved. Major Parker, who was sent by the Governor to aid us, when he left, promised to raise men and return immediately to our assistance, but he has forsaken us, and is it not well known that the Quincy Committee are prepared to join the mob, if a treaty was not effected?

Under these circumstances, I have thrown in my influence with the Trustees for the surrender of Nauvoo, upon the best terms we could get, and as being the best, the only wise policy for us to pursue.

Brethren, reflect. We have nothing to gain in defending Nauvoo, but everything to lose. Not only property, but life also is hourly in peril.[43]

Most of the volunteers accepted Daniel's reasoning and prepared to vacate the city immediately. A few swore they would never allow their enemies to enter Nauvoo while they had arms to defend it. Both groups concealed their arms from the committee, knowing full well that, if they were surrendered to the anti-Mormons, they would not be returned.

Daniel closed up his house, hid his important papers in a safe place, and made ready to leave Illinois. He was now a hunted man, the prime object of the anti-Mormons' wrath because he had led the successful defense of the city. He did not know how long he would be exiled, but planned for a lengthy stay in Iowa. He still had not begun preparations for his own departure to the west with the body of Latter-day Saints because he was still hoping that Eliza could be persuaded to join him. He doubtless felt that, after learning of the depredations of the men who attacked Nauvoo, her attitude might be softened enough for her to accompany him, if not to join the Mormons. Daniel H. Wells and Philo Johnson described the final evacuation of Nauvoo:

As soon as the treaty was made we commenced putting the people across the river. Many of the people then scattered, some went up the river and some down, and others into Iowa. After the people had crossed the river they lay on the banks for several days. Mayor Woods and others raised a subscription of provisions &c. in Quincy and sent them to our people while we were camping on the banks of the river. It was at this time that the visitation of quails took place, the people gathering them and being fed thereby. That was what was called the Poor Camp of Montrose.[44]

Now we had 3 days to vacate the city entirely; so we who were able, went to work with all our might day and night. We secured some flat boats and rowed those large flat boats across the Mississippi River and landed our people on the Iowa side as fast as possible. We worked until all our hands were blistered, but we got all the people across the river. Our stock was left in Nauvoo, and our three days were up that the mob gave us to get out of the state. We went back after our stock, but the mob had run most of it off and stolen them. We returned to the Iowa side of the river and our people were nearly all sick with the chills and fever, and but few of them had tents. They were all out in the open air and the hot sun and storms were pouring down upon them. We did not have teams enough to move the people out into the country, and they had nothing to eat. Truly the people exhibited a pitiful sight to behold.

We called upon God for assistance and truly he did hear us for at about eleven o'clock that day the whole air was darkened with tens of thousands of quails and they lighted all over the ground in our camp. When we all had caught as many as we wanted the balance of the quail flew away to the north, the same direction as they came. We all had enough meat to last us until we could move out into the countryside.[45]

The anti-Mormon army now some two thousand strong, marched into Nauvoo on September 17. As the anti-Mormons advanced up Mulholland Street, Daniel H. Wells and William Cutler, the last rearguard of the refugees, retreated ahead of them, keeping about two blocks' distance between themselves and their foes. At the river's edge they quickly boarded a flatboat and rowed across to the relative safety of Iowa.

On the other side of the river they were met by a patrol guard, who demanded their arms, which they refused to give up, this being in violation of the treaty which provided that the arms should be restored to the Mormons as soon as they reached the Iowa side of the river.

From the top of the Temple [lot] the enemy fired their cannon at the defenseless camp across the river. Gathering up the balls, Daniel Wells sent one of them, with his compliments, to the governor of Iowa, whose territory had been thus invaded.[46]

7
The Cost of Conversion
Travels to Winter Quarters and the Trail to Great Salt Lake City

1846–1848

The desperate condition of the refugees on the Iowa side of the river was exceeded only by those who had been unable to leave Nauvoo and fell into the hands of the mob. Governor Ford's agent, Mr. Brayman, who remained in Nauvoo to report to him on the final disposition of the Saints and their property described their pitiable state.

> I also learned that in addition to the duty General Brockman had assumed, under the treaty, of superintending the removal of the Mormons from the State, he had issued an order for the expulsion from the State, of all who had borne arms in defense of the city against his force, and all who were in any manner identified with the Mormons.
> It could scarcely be believed that such an order in such palpable and gross violation of the unanimous pledge which had been signed by the officers, agreed to by the whole force, and endorsed by the Quincy committee, had been given. But on applying to General Brockman, I learned that such an order had been given, and would be executed. This order was rigorously enforced throughout the day, with many circumstances of the utmost cruelty and injustice. Bands of armed men traversed the city, entering the houses of citizens, robbing them of arms, throwing their household goods out of doors, insulting them, and threatening their lives. Many were seized and marched to

the camp, and after military examination, set across the river, for the crime of sympathizing with the Mormons, or the still more heinous offense of fighting in the defense of the city, under command of officers commissioned by You, [Governor Ford], and instructed to make that defense.[1]

Even at the risk of his life, Daniel could do nothing for these people and so he immediately turned his attention to alleviating the suffering of those within his power to assist. He managed to rent or borrow a one-horse buggy and with William L. Cutler, one of the church trustees, drove day and night to reach the Missouri River at Cutler's Park where the Mormons had established their forward camp. They made the three hundred–mile journey across the open plains in seven days and reported to Brigham Young the events that had taken place in Nauvoo.

> I went to Winter Quarters and saw President Young who raised what teams could be spared and sent them to bring out the people who were on the banks of the river. About 19 wagons were sent.[2]

On hearing the plight of the refugees, the Mormon Council asked the two men to return to Nauvoo carrying a letter from the Council and instructions "that you will make use of this among the brethren on the way between Nauvoo and east of Keg Creek to raise all the teams you possibly can." The letter read:

> Camp of Israel, near Cutler's Park, Omaha Nation
> September 27, 1846
>
> To the High Council at Council Point:
>
> Beloved Brethren: Through our brothers William Cutler and Daniel H. Wells, we have been apprised of the fact that a bloody battle was fought in Nauvoo, on the 12th inst., 100 brethren against 1,000 mobbers, in which Captain Anderson and son, and Brother Morris fell, and died on the field . . .
>
> The Saints were victorious in the battle, but afterwards very wisely surrendered Nauvoo, on articles of capitulation, that their lives and property should be inviolate, till they could cross the river; and the mob of 1,500 strong marched into the city on Thursday following.
>
> The poor brethren and sisters, widows, and orphans, sick and destitute, are now lying on the west bank of the Mississippi,

waiting for teams to remove them, which Brothers Cutler and Wells have come to raise. Now is the time for labor. Let . . . every man . . . rise up with his team and go straightway, and bring a load of the poor from Nauvoo, or the river, to his own encampment, if they can be provided for there, or to some place in the intermediate country where they can get work, and find shelter for the winter . . .

The Trustees are making no sales, and have no ready means. The poor are crying for bread, and such is the condition of the sick and destitute as to draw tears from the mob. Then say to the rich, in the name of Israel's God, send some of your rusting dollars for the immediate purchase of bread.

There are many wagons at Nauvoo that have no teams, therefore it is best that wagons going should have four or six yoke of oxen, so as to divide with those who have none. Horses and mules will be the most effective, when they can be had . . .

Let copies of our epistle be furnished for your delegates to read to the brethren. This is a day of action and not of argument.

      Farewell.
      Done in behalf of the Council
      Brigham Young, President
      Willard Richards, Clerk.

P.S. Why we call on the brethren in your vicinity to send teams is because we had previously sent as many as we could spare of drivers, without producing too great suffering in our camp, and as yet we have not the first house, or hut erected.

      W. R. Clk.[3]

Before leaving Winter Quarters on September 27, Daniel received the Melchizedek Priesthood, the highest order of priesthood in the Mormon Church and was ordained to the office of elder in that priesthood by Patriarch John Smith, the uncle of Joseph Smith. He also received a patriarchal blessing from Patriarch Smith.[4]

Daniel returned to the Mormon camp at Montrose in early October and helped its inhabitants to move further west using the wagons sent from other camps. Within a short time, all of the Saints were cleared out of their temporary shelters and placed in better quarters where they could survive the coming winter and prepare to move on in the spring. The anti-Mormon force in Nauvoo, meanwhile, disbanded and most of its members departed from the city. From those remaining, most of whom had seized property that they hoped to obtain some form of legal title to, Daniel received a surprising invitation.

> I was requested by the mob to come back and settle my affairs with the promise that I should not be molested. After then I went back and forth. My family was in Burlington. Nauvoo was then deserted almost, a few still being there, but it was ultimately with the exception of some few of the "New citizens" as they were called. These new citizens tried to keep up the place after we were driven out, and they took possession of the town. The trustees stayed there as long as they could sell any thing, after which they came away and abandoned everything. The mob plundered anything valuable they could find in the deserted homes; they burned the Temple, and scattered the Temple rock which can now be seen for many miles around, utilized as foundations of houses, door steps &c.[5]

Descriptions of the "Mormon War" and the expulsion of the Saints from Illinois reached Daniel's sisters in the east soon after the events, but he was not able to write or mail any communication about his personal situation to them. His silence produced a panicked year-end plea from Lucy.

> Trenton, Dec. 29, 1846
>
> Dear Brother,
>
> Where are you? O where are you? Why do you not write to us and let us know of your welfare? Long and anxiously have we expected to hear from you. I most earnestly entreat of you to write to us immediately and relieve our suspense. We have indeed heard of the dreadful result of disturbances in your place and most sincerely do we sympathize with you and all the sufferers. We know nothing in particular of your own sufferings or your losses, we hope they have not been great.[6]

Part of Daniel's reticence in writing to his family may have been his wish to avoid responding to the nearly hysterical reaction in Lucy's letter, echoed by her sister Pamela, to the news that he had joined the Mormon Church and was planning to move west with the Saints the next spring.

Our dear sister Catherine and Eliza have written to us in the greatest affliction telling us that you are going to forsake them and us forever. O dearest brother, can it be so? We cannot believe it, we cannot believe that anything so dreadful can come upon us. We thought that we had drunk deep of the cup of affliction already. O dear brother, will you compel us to drain it to its very dregs in all its bitterness? You will not leave us all for an uncertain home. Who will love you so well? Who will watch over you like your dear wife and child, and sister? O for their sakes, for your own sake, for Catherine's sake, and for ours, do not leave us. You are dearer to us than words can tell. We have ever loved you with a depth of affection that few sisters feel for a brother, and the thought that you are about to sever the strongest ties that can bind us together on earth is too agonizing for us to endure.[7]

Daniel probably did not know how to respond to such an entreaty by long distance post. He was by now so far altered in his religious thinking from what he had been on his last visit to them that he could not explain in a letter what had precipitated the change or what had been revealed to him to assure him that his present course was right. His material losses resulting from the fall of Nauvoo into the hands of the anti-Mormons amounted to many thousands of dollars; he had gone within a few short days from the status of a moderately wealthy, respected city official to that of a baptized Mormon without property or position. He believed that what he had gained was more than what he had lost, but he could not explain his reasons for this conclusion to his New York relatives, any more than he had been able to explain it to Eliza or Catherine.

He kept trying through the winter and into the New Year. He stayed in Burlington with Eliza and Albert, first at the Woods home and then in rented quarters. He made frequent trips down river to Nauvoo to fulfil the office to which he had been elected, act as a Trustee in concluding the Church's business there, sell his own property and outfit his own wagon with the team and equipment he would need on the western journey.[8]

He also helped a few of the new citizens of Nauvoo to sell their property and move on to friendlier locations. Among these was Captain William E. Clifford who purchased land in the city and tried to defend it against damage or confiscation by the anti-Mormons. Judged by them to be sympathetic to the Saints, he was forced to sell his holdings and leave Hancock County. Daniel sent him to Winter Quarters with a letter of introduction to Brigham Young and requested the latter help him find work and a new home.[9]

Daniel told his wife and sister that he was going with the Saints in the spring and he pleaded with Eliza to go with him. From Daniel's point of view, it was not him but Eliza who was threatening to tear their marriage apart. In 1840s America, wives followed their husbands, whether the path led to a new home in the wilderness of the Omaha Nation, or to a new place of business in Connecticut or Ohio, as had been the case with his sisters Frank and Eliza when they married.

Wives followed their husbands, but his wife refused to do so. Daniel did not require that Eliza accept the Mormon faith or adhere to its doctrines. All that he insisted on was that she stay with him. But her answer was still no.

In the spring of 1847, Daniel was asked by Mormon leaders to serve as captain of a company of Saints as they journeyed from the temporary Iowa settlements along the Mississippi to Winter Quarters on the Missouri River. This was the same three hundred–mile trek he had taken the year before following the Battle of Nauvoo and he readily agreed to go. The trust in him developed by the Mormons in the years prior to his conversion gave him strong moral authority as a leader, in addition to the religious authority vested in him by the Council. The company arrived at Winter Quarters on July 14.[10]

For Daniel, the trip was an opportunity to sharpen the trail skills he had developed on his earlier journey and during his pioneering days in Ohio and Illinois. It was also a chance to separate for a time from Eliza so that she could evaluate what a permanent break in their relationship would mean. When he returned, as he planned to do, but apparently did not tell his wife prior to leaving, he hoped that she would see reason and agree to go with him the next year.

By the time Daniel's company arrived at Winter Quarters, the vanguard of Mormon pioneers with Brigham Young at their head had already departed for the Salt Lake Valley. Another five hundred young Mormon volunteers had been inducted into the US Army in July 1846 at the start of the Mexican War. They went first to Ft. Leavenworth, Kansas, in August and then started on a two thousand–mile march to San Diego the same month. The departure of the Mormon Battalion, followed by fifteen hundred of the best-prepared Saints headed for Zion, left the temporary Mormon settlements in Iowa short-handed for planting and harvesting crops. Daniel's company was instructed by the Council to remain in the Winter Quarters area for the year and help build up the Saints' supplies of food and equipment before starting for the Salt Lake Valley in the spring of 1848.

A few days after his arrival, a church member named Young claimed that Daniel had brought in a span of mules from Nauvoo that belonged to him. In the evening of July 25 a trial was held before the high council and Young's claim was disallowed. The council determined that he had abandoned or sold the mules prior to leaving Nauvoo and Daniel had purchased them from the new owner.[11]

Daniel stayed at Winter Quarters through the summer and returned to Eliza and Albert in the fall. They welcomed him, as did his sister Catherine and her family. All had been uncertain whether they would see him again. Pamela Wells, Abigail Rockwell, and Lucy Coombs were equally glad, when informed by Catherine that he had come back, as expressed in their joint letter to him.

Trenton, Feb 21st, 1848

My Dear Brother [written by Abigail]

We received a letter from Sister Catherine last week informing us of your return, oh I am so happy to hear that you are yet with your family and friends (when I have imagined you were suffering among the Rocky Mountains or some other dreary region if alive) had we known it you would have heard from us before this time, hope this will arrive before you leave, if you go this spring—but I do wish you would conclude to put it off another season and come and visit us next summer. We are all very anxious you should, for it seems to me that if you defer it until you go and return that we should never meet again . . .

Dear Brother. [written by Lucy]

I know it is unnecessary for me to tell you how truly I rejoiced when I heard you were with your family again for you know that I sympathize with you in all your happiness as well as all your sufferings and trials.[12]

This letter was sent to Daniel at Catherine's home in Burlington, but Daniel was not there to receive it. He had moved his family temporarily to Galesburg, Illinois, about fifty miles east of Burlington, late in 1847 and was still there in January of the following year. The reason for this move is uncertain, but it probably enabled him to more easily purchase a new team, wagon, and equipment. He had left his previous year's rig to aid the Saints at Winter Quarters and ridden back alone on horseback. The counties around Nauvoo and across the river in Iowa had been stripped of animals and wagons the previous two years by the departing Mormon population. But both were readily available at normal prices in

Galesburg and citizens of that community were not hostile to the Saints as were those in towns closer to Nauvoo.[13]

Daniel may also have moved to Galesburg to put some distance between Eliza and the rest of the Robison family in hopes that he could thereby more easily weaken her resolve to leave him. Her brother Lewis Robison had accepted the Mormon faith and had already reached the Salt Lake Valley with his family, but all the other Robison siblings opposed Joseph Smith's teachings and clung fiercely to their father's religion.

But the physical move had no more effect on Eliza's spiritual convictions than did Daniel's pleadings. She refused to go west with him either as a Mormon or a Gentile. At last accepting that her decision was as final as his own, Daniel wrote to Brigham Young (who had returned to Winter Quarters in late 1847 after leading the first pioneers west) in February 1848.

> President Young . . .
>
> In regard to my own affairs, they remain much as usual, whether for my own wickedness, unfaithfulness, or what I cannot tell, but I see no prospect short of a complete sacrifice of everything I hold dear on earth, as well in a pecuniary point of view, as the kindlier affections of the human heart.
>
> Please to remember me before the Lord that I may be sustained through the dark day and at least one ray of light may beam into my soul, to cheer me on the way. Think not that I am desponding or despairing, for though my soul is bowed down under a great weight of afflictions, yet my faith is placed upon the Lord of Hosts, and 'come weal come wo,' I will be with you by the 1st of April or sooner if possible.
>
> Excuse my troubling you with my puny affairs, for it is only that you may assist me by your faith that I have done so. I should be well pleased to have a line from you, if convenient. Remember me in love to the Council, and accept my sincerest wishes for the welfare of yourself and family.
>
> Your faithful brother in Christ,
> Daniel H. Wells[14]

Brigham Young's reply shows clearly that he understood the depth of Daniel's sacrifice and the faith required to make it. That was inspiration that Daniel sorely needed.

Winter Quarters
March 1, 1848

Dear Brother Wells:

I feel to sympathize with you in your afflictions, yet you are aware by this time that those who will serve the Lord will sacrifice everything, whether it be land or possessions, or pecuniary interest or the kindlier affections of the heart, and inasmuch as you do this to the glory of God, you will in no wise lose your reward in this world, and in the world to come you will receive eternal life, glory and immortality. Cheer up your heart, and rejoice in the day of your deliverance, and comfort your heart that my prayer is offered up in your behalf, and may the time soon arrive that we shall be able to strike hands and go on our way rejoicing to a land of peace, happiness and holiness, that we may all enjoy health and strength and do the will of Him that sent us.

Accept the assurance of
Your faithful brother in Christ,
Brigham Young.[15]

Daniel returned to Burlington with Eliza and Albert in February. From there, he sent a letter to Brigham Young enclosing a copy of the laws enacted by the recent session of the Iowa legislature and suggesting "the organization by our people of one or two counties, that they might be able to acquire and dispose of pre-emption claims and improvements according to law for outfits when they are able to start for the mountains, he having found by perusing the laws of said session that the way was prepared for such organization."[16] Brigham responded in March noting that "although ignorant of the provisions made at the last session by the Iowa legislature, the brethren had already petitioned for a county organization at Potawatomie."[17]

With the help of James Woods, Catherine's lawyer husband, Daniel transferred some of his property to the Woods family and the remainder to Eliza. He extracted a promise from Woods, just returned from a special session of the Iowa legislature to which he had been elected, that he would help Eliza manage and dispose of her holdings in a manner that would enable her to live comfortably for a long time. Eliza's later choices made this promise impossible for Woods to keep.[18]

Having done what he could to secure their welfare, Daniel bade a tearful farewell of his still youthful wife and eleven-year-old Albert. No matter how strong his personal conviction of resurrection and eternal family life in the hereafter, he knew that this parting was a mortal death. He would not see either Eliza or Albert again in life.

Figure 7.1. Winter Quarters in spring 1848 as the Saints were preparing to leave for Great Salt Lake City. Painting by C. C. A. Christensen.

At last "delivered" from all his worldly possessions and the association of every member of his family, Daniel started for Winter Quarters. Although he bore a heavy heart, he did not go sorrowing; he was now following the path that Christ had recommended to another young rich man: "Yet lackest thou one thing: sell all that thou hast, and distribute unto the poor, and thou shalt have treasure in heaven: and come, follow me."[19]

Daniel traveled west in company with a few other Saints, one or more of which he hired to help drive his wagon so that he could ride mostly on horseback. He brought more than one horse, in addition to his team of four oxen, but carried little in the way of personal possessions. Most of the space in his wagon was taken up by the tools, equipment, seeds, nails, gunpowder, rifles, and other supplies recommended for the journey by church leaders. He also brought an ample supply of basic foodstuffs, and some livestock that he would pay others to tend for him on the trail.[20]

The little group arrived at Winter Quarters just as the Saints who had wintered there, including Brigham Young and other members of the Council, were preparing to leave.

The wagon train formed up on the banks of the Elkhorn River west of Winter Quarters and by June 1 almost two thousand Saints were assembled in two divisions, one headed by Brigham Young and the other by Heber C. Kimball, with Brigham also presiding over the entire company.

At Brigham's request, Daniel joined his division and assisted him in organizing the camp into companies of a hundred wagons each, which were then subdivided into groups of fifty and finally into tens. Each group was presided over by a captain accepted by a vote of its members. On June 1 Daniel was sustained as Brigham's aide-de-camp.[21]

Brigham's division, when finally formed up and moving, numbered 397 wagons in four hundreds headed by Zera Pulzipher, Lorenzo Snow, William G. Perkins, and Allen Taylor. There were 1,229 people in the division and a total of 1,275 oxen, 74 horses, 699 cows, and 184 loose cattle. The statistics for the combined Young and Kimball divisions were impressive: 623 wagons, 1,891 souls, 131 horses, 44 mules, 2,012 oxen, 983 cows, 334 loose cattle, 654 sheep, 237 pigs, 904 chickens, 54 cats, 134 dogs, 3 goats, 10 geese, 5 beehives, 11 doves, 5 ducks, and 1 squirrel.[22]

President Young noted in his journal, "On the 26th I started on my journey to the mountains, leaving my houses, mills and the temporary furniture I had acquired during our sojourn there. This was the fifth time I had left my home and property since I embraced the gospel of Jesus Christ."[23]

Daniel's job as aide-de-camp was to carry messages from point to point within the miles-long wagon train, help any who fell behind to repair equipment or do whatever else was necessary to resume their places in the line, and resolve petty disputes and arguments that arose among the travelers. His previous long service as a justice and his reputation for fairness made him a trustworthy arbitrator whom all the Saints still referred to in speech and written journals as Squire Wells.

The trek was as uneventful as a thousand mile journey by wagon across untamed prairie could be, but Daniel had plenty of responsibilities to keep him busy. On June 14, a week and a day after the train began moving west, Brigham sent Daniel and a companion, Daniel Wood, back on the trail to deliver a letter to Heber C. Kimball whose second division was a day behind the vanguard. They delivered the letter that evening, stayed overnight with Heber's company, and returned the following day with a reply.[24]

> D.H. Wells. & Wood returned between 12 & 1 with a letter from Heber—the brethren were called together at Pres. Morley's Wagon & the letter read twice by T. Bullock. It appears they came in contact with a band of Indians on the 6th. Bros. Egan & Ricks were wounded—one ox was killed & taken away—& the Indians made signs (to some brethren who they had prisoners) that they had 4 killed 3 wounded. Heber's Camp was at Cedar Creek, will be here tomorrow—as soon as Meeting was dismissed it commenced a tremendous storm of rain, hail, thunder & vivid lightning which continued until night—it rained at intervals thro' the night.[25]

John D. Lee, who was one of the captains of fifty in the Perkins Company, wrote in his journal of several visits by Squire Wells to his camp and others, sometimes alone to deliver messages or discover the reason for a delay, and sometimes in company with Brigham Young and other leaders. The latter occasions were usually in the evening after the train had halted for the night and the men could gather around a fire to discuss organizational changes or plans for the next day's travel. Lee also noted that these gatherings frequently concluded with music and dancing. As the journey lengthened and the travelers became weary, enthusiasm for nighttime entertainment waned somewhat.[26]

On June 29, Daniel went buffalo hunting with four other members of the company who were good marksmen. They brought down some buffalo from a nearby herd, but found that their horses could not drag even one of the heavy animals back to the train where its meat would have been a welcome addition to the Saints' plain diet. Nor did they have the time or tools to field dress a carcass so that a quarter or smaller part could be brought away. They managed only to carve out a tongue and had to leave the rest to waste, "a wicked destruction of life" as Thomas Bullock noted.[27]

In early July, after an accidentally-set range fire threatened some of the advance wagons and burned off the grass needed to feed the teams and livestock of those following, Daniel rode to each company telling them:

> ... it was the wish of the Pres. that no more fires should be put out to burn up the rainge, that the cos. should be careful about fires & should they want any more coal, the ash hollow would be the best chance for Some distance to burn coal.[28]

A week later the Perkins Company was again delayed when some of the horses were bitten by rattlesnakes and were not fit to travel. After some dispute it was decided that the whole company would remain camped until the horses recovered or died, but Daniel was soon sent back from Brigham Young's moving company to ascertain the reason for the delay. When Young was informed of the cause, he replied that it would not do to stop a whole company because a horse was bitten by a snake. He recommended a treatment of "spirits of Turpentine with Tobacco" to wash the wound and a prayer for the recovery of the beast. He also told the company to move on as quickly as possible to get away from the snake-infested area and keep pace with the rest of the train.[29]

That same day after the train had stopped for the night, John D. Lee visited the camp of Absalom Pennington Free to see his son John B. Lee. The boy was traveling with his mother, Louisa Free, the eldest daughter of Absalom, who was driving one of her father's wagons on the trek. Louisa was an attractive twenty-three-year-old woman who had married Lee in

1845. Their son, John Brigham, was born a year later and the next year Louisa left Lee and returned to live with her parents. Some of Lee's seven other wives also left him about the same time and he was known as a man who was "hard on women."[30]

The specific reason for their breakup is unknown and, for a time, Louisa remained married to John D. Lee (a written divorce would not be agreed by both parties until May 12, 1849, months after they arrived in the Salt Lake Valley), but as far as she was concerned, her marriage was finished. She told Lee at their parting in March 1847 that she wished him to maintain contact with her and their young son, but she would not return to his bed. He accepted her decision in good grace.[31]

Daniel H. Wells became friends with Louisa Free, as well as her younger sister, Hannah Corilla Free, age 19, during the journey west. He was introduced to them by a third sister, Emeline Free Young, age 23, one of Brigham Young's wives whom he had married in Nauvoo in 1846. Emeline asked Daniel to check on the welfare of her parents and family and his friendship with the Free sisters quickly developed. As the women labored to drive their heavy wagon, nurse some of those who had fallen ill on the trail, and help mind their five younger siblings, Daniel often tied his horse to the rear of the vehicle and took over the reins to give Louisa and Hannah a break. The beauty of the Free sisters, as well as their bright, optimistic personalities and their commitment to the restored gospel in the face of severe hardships were qualities that made Daniel pursue his friendship with Louisa more ardently as the wagon train moved closer to the Salt Lake Valley and journey's end.[32]

Another young woman whom Daniel met during the trek was Martha Givens Harris, the sixteen-year-old daughter of McGee Harris and his wife Mary Givens. The Harris family were originally from Tennessee, but moved to Williamson County, Illinois, around 1837 when Martha was five years old. She described the family's conversion and later travels.

> We lived there until the spring of 1846, having joined the Church of Jesus Christ of Latter-day Saints a year or two previously. Father was preparing to dispose of his earthly possessions and move to Nauvoo. However, he was counseled not to go by Nauvoo, but to go straight to Council Bluffs and meet the Church members there in the fall of 1846. We left Illinois in the spring of 1846, and arrived in Council Bluffs in September, and crossed over the Missouri River to what was then called Winter Quarters. We stayed there until the spring of 1847.
>
> About fifty families were counseled to go up the river twenty-five miles and build a fort and raise a crop to help the

emigrants next spring. We did so, and in the spring of 1848, I was baptized in February in the Missouri River. The ice had to be broken, but I had recovered from a severe spell of sickness and felt that if my life were spared, I would be baptized as soon as possible.

In the spring of 1848 we left that place for our long journey across the plains. We came in Brigham Young's company. We left Elk Horn River June 1st, and arrived in the Valley September 28, 1848.[33]

Martha's granddaughter, Josephine Wells Lyman, later wrote that Daniel H. Wells met and fell in love with her grandmother during the crossing, but this seems unlikely. Daniel would probably not have actively pursued a teen girl half his age, especially one who had two older and more eligible sisters, while he was devoting considerable attention to Louisa Free. Eliza Robison was only sixteen and Daniel twenty-two when they married in 1837, but at thirty-four he was probably not seeking another teenage bride.

Martha, on the other hand, might very easily have set her sights from a distance on Brigham Young's dashing aide-de-camp and arranged an introduction to Daniel. Tall (five feet, seven inches), stately, and beautiful, she made a lasting first impression and Daniel would definitely have remembered her. There is no record of any close association between them during the journey west, but soon after their arrival, one of them, probably Martha, rekindled the spark of their early encounters and fanned it into something more.[34]

On July 16 Daniel's brother-in-law, Lewis Robison, who had gone to Great Salt Lake City in 1847, rode into the camp in company with O. P. Rockwell and two others. They brought mail from the Valley and news that the new settlements in the west were doing well. Daniel and Lewis shared information about their past year of separation and their respective families. Both wrote letters to be carried back to Winter Quarters and then to relatives in Nauvoo and other eastern cities. Lewis stayed only a day or two, then rode west again with Rockwell and others carrying letters and newspapers back to Utah.[35]

By late August the wagon train reached the Continental Divide and camped at the Sweetwater River. A number of the Saints were sick with Mountain Fever, and all were in need of a few days rest before pushing on the final miles to their destination. Riders from Great Salt Lake City brought letters and reports to Brigham Young and the President ordered all the captains of the company to gather at his fire for talks. Thomas Bullock wrote of this meeting and the following final days on the trail.

Figure 7.2. An 1866 Mormon wagon train descending through Echo Canyon toward the Salt Lake Valley on the same route pioneered in 1847. Photo by Charles R. Carter.

Prest. Young was well, gave me the letters from the Church in the Valley, & from P.P. Pratt which were read to the people. then conversation about the valley its prospects &c Prest. Young ordered me to bring my Wagons up to his Caral, to be on hand to do the writing.—Prest. Young, Squire Wells & many of the brethren come & visit me in 'Bullock's Settlement'—sit, chat, sing and enjoy ourselves through the evening—

Sunday 27 [August] . . . after making the necessary preparation for the Journey, Prest. Young, D.H. Wells, Fa[ther Horace] Gibbs & T Bullock start in the Carriage at 10.23 AM to go to Heber's Camp to ascertain what was wanting—. . . after crossing the two small Creeks met Wm. Clayton & Co. of about 8 Wagons, chatted a short time & resumed our journey, passed over the Rocky Ridges, descended to the Sweetwater, passed 4 Camps & arrived at H.C. Kimball's at ½ past 4 found him well, his daughter very sick indeed, & his Wife Sarah Ann confined of a fine boy last night about 10 o clock—

Monday 28 [August] Cold windy night, a shower of rain also—B. Young slept with H.C. Kimball. Squire Wells & T.B.

together in a Wagon—Fine Pleasant morning—B. Young & H.C. Kimball visiting . . .

Wednesday [August 30] Cold night—T.B. called up by break of day to continue writing—Finished copying list of return Cattle &c & gave same to Captn. Allen Taylor—Made up a Mail of 61 letters to send to Winter Quarters & U.S. Post Office 2 to go to England also given to Allen Taylor . . . after all my business was finished up—Prest. Young left Esq[ui]re. Wells with instructions what to do.[36]

On September 20, Daniel rode into the Salt Lake Valley with Brigham Young and the rest of his immediate company. The President's teams had fallen behind during the course of the journey, but the other companies who passed them pulled up and waited at the top of Emigration Canyon so that Brigham might have the honor of entering the valley first on his final trip. The company of Saints had traveled an average of twelve miles per day on each of the eighty-six days when the wagons moved forward on the trail. Another thirty-six days, including sixteen Sabbaths, had been still days when the majority of the camp's inhabitants rested while others made repairs, scouted the way ahead, and made plans to overcome newly encountered problems. During a total of 122 days they had covered 1032 miles from Winter Quarters to Great Salt Lake City.[37]

For Daniel, as for all those who had endured the thousand-mile trek, the Salt Lake Valley was a welcome conclusion of one task and a stark reminder that the Saints' efforts to master and tame the wilderness were only just beginning.

> I finally left there [Nauvoo] in the Spring of 1848 and arrived in Salt Lake City Sept. 20, 1848. The people were then living in the Fort. They had gone through the "Cricket War" and had got a little crop. The ground which had been cultivated around here that year in wheat had been eaten two or three times by crickets but finally some of it got to be about six inches high. I bought corn for $1.50 a bushel and scarce at that.[38]

8

Deseret Home and New Callings
THE SUPERINTENDENT, THE GENERAL, AND
THE ATTORNEY GENERAL

1848–1851

Less than a week after completing his calling as aide-de-camp to Brigham Young, Daniel received another from the Church President that would consume much of his time for the next twenty years. At a meeting held the Sunday following the arrival of the wagon train, Brigham announced that the first phase of the Salt Lake Temple construction would be the building of a wall around the entire temple block to protect the site from intruders. The wall, and a number of other projects, he said, would be built under the direction of the new superintendent of public works.[1]

> I was appointed Superintendent of Public Works in the Fall of 1848. The first house that was built was a little adobe place that was used for the Church office.
>
> We laid out the Temple and the Council House sites, and commenced to build the latter right away. The little office that was the first place built was one storey, about 18 x 12 feet, slanting roof which was covered with boards and dirt. This remained the Church office for about two years and a great amount of business was done in it. In the spring of 1849 we went out on the lots and commenced building. The foundation of the Council House was laid in the Spring of 1849, and then the first storey was put up. A great many temporary buildings went up in 1849.[2]

The wall around Temple Square was not actually commenced until 1852 and was not completed until 1854. It was built on a foundation of red sandstone about two feet high, to which were added thirty pilasters on each side of the block. The wall, constructed of adobe bricks plastered with hard cement, was then raised to a height of ten feet between each of the pilasters.

The Old Council House was the first public building completed under Daniel's direction. It was a square structure two stories high, forty-five feet on each side and was also built of red sandstone. It stood on the southwest corner of South Temple and Main Streets and was completed in December 1850. Several sessions of the Territorial Legislature were held in it, as were City Council meetings, meetings between Church leaders and visiting dignitaries, and other public events. Negotiations to end the Utah War were held in it and in later years it housed the University of Deseret until it was destroyed by fire in June 1883.[3]

As soon as the Council House was finished, Daniel began work on the Social Hall, which was completed in 1852 and formally opened in January 1853. It was a single story building with a basement, measuring seventy-three by thirty-three feet, and was intended for hosting celebrations, parties, plays, recitals, and other social events. It also served as the site of public events and the Territorial Legislature occasionally made use of it.[4]

The largest public building built in the territory prior to the Civil War was the old Tabernacle, which stood on the southwest corner of Temple Square where the Assembly Hall now is. It was built to house large Church meetings and conferences and measured 126 by 64 feet. Its arched roof had no supporting pillars and it could seat about 2,200 people tightly packed, but that number proved vastly inadequate even when the building was completed in 1852. An open Bowery was then constructed attached to the north end of the Tabernacle. This structure, which could only be used when weather favored its open-air seating, measured 156 feet long and 138 wide and could seat up to eight thousand on its wooden benches. Day-long summer conference sessions were made more comfortable in it by covering the interior with sagebrush laid on a wood lattice for shade.[5]

The small adobe Church office building was replaced in 1852 by a new and larger structure constructed on the same site. Daniel also supervised the construction of a public bathhouse at the warm springs north and west of the city. He was a frequent visitor to this facility as were many Saints in the days before indoor plumbing became common. An armory was built on north Main Street where the gunpowder and arms of the Nauvoo Legion were stored. These included the few artillery pieces that the Saints had brought with them across the plains.[6]

Figure 8.1. Public and religious buildings completed under supervision of Daniel H. Wells during the 1850s: (top to bottom) Council House, 1850; Deseret Store and Tithing Office, 1855; Old Tabernacle and Bowery, 1852; Endowment House, 1855; Territorial State House, 1855; Social Hall, 1853.

Recalling a similar assignment Daniel had received as an alderman in Nauvoo, Brigham also appointed him chairman of a committee tasked with locating and laying out a cemetery for Great Salt Lake City. In March 1849 he reported that the committee had selected twenty acres on the upland northeast of the city. The committee's recommendation was accepted and the old pioneer cemetery, on the west side of the settlement, which in less than a year had acquired over fifty graves, mostly young children, was closed. Future interments were made in the new Salt Lake City Cemetery, which eventually expanded to some 250 acres and more than 120,000 graves, including that of Daniel H. Wells and many of his family. It is today the largest city-operated cemetery in the United States.[7]

Daniel was asked to chair a second committee assigned to find a suitable location and build a bridge across the Jordan River that bisected the Salt Lake Valley from south to north. The site was quickly selected at North Temple Street, but years passed before a toll bridge was completed at a cost of about $800 in 1853.[8]

Even if his duties as superintendent had not occupied his time for the remainder of the year, Daniel arrived too late to build a cabin for himself before winter. Like most of the other Saints, he made do with a temporary shelter to live in until spring. Each family who came to Great Salt Lake City was given a city lot of two acres. Daniel drew a lot in the Eighth Ward near the public square on Fourth South Street that would later become Washington Square, the site of the present City and County Building. His lot was opposite one drawn by his brother-in-law, Lewis Robison, on which the latter had been living with his family since their arrival with the first pioneer company in 1847.

Daniel moved the wagon in which his goods had been transported across the plains onto this lot and slept in this shelter through the cold months. He took most of his meals with the Robison family in return for contributing to the family's provisions as he was able.[9]

With no harvest of his own and little grain or produce available to buy in the struggling city, Daniel's only real option for obtaining food was hunting. Deer, antelope, and elk were the preferred game, but these were also the prey of carnivores. They had already been hunted extensively by the Saints since their arrival in the Valley and by the Indians before them.

Finding these targets scarce and not wanting to venture into the deep mountain snows in search of them, Daniel and a number of other men organized a month-long hunt for other animals beginning in January 1849. Two groups of "picked marksmen, under the leadership of John Pyke and John D. Lee" were selected to compete with one another in hunting wolves, foxes, vultures, scavengers, and birds of prey. Whichever company had the smaller number of pelts at a count held in February was to furnish a dinner for both groups. Daniel was a member of

Pyke's company along with Brigham Young, John Taylor, Amasa Lyman, and John Smith. Lee's company included Heber C. Kimball, Williard Richards, Parley P. Pratt, and John Johnson. The contest was won by Lee's company and the victory prize was provided by Pyke's. The meat secured, though less desirable than deer or antelope, was still welcomed among the protein-starved settlers, as were the hides that could be made into clothing, footwear, and rugs. Feathers from the downed birds also provided a supply of writing quills.[10]

The day the hunt ended a petition was sent to the all the Great Basin settlements established by the Saints since their arrival in 1847 requesting that delegates be sent to establish a civil government for the Great Basin area. Under the Treaty of Gaudalupe Hidalgo signed on February 2, 1848, which ended the Mexican War, Mexico ceded to the United States a huge tract of territory that included all of the Great Basin and much more. Congress did not immediately act to organize the ceded territory or provide it with any form of government or laws. In the absence of any word from the federal government, the residents of the area met in a convention during February and drafted a constitution similar to those of existing states. Daniel participated in this convention and helped draft a memorial to Congress asking that the State of Deseret be admitted to the Union.[11]

Until Congress addressed the issue, a provisional government was established under the draft constitution to meet the needs of the territory. At an election held on March 12 in Great Salt Lake City, Brigham Young was elected governor; Willard Richards, secretary; Heber C. Kimball, chief justice; Daniel H. Wells, attorney general; Newell K. Whitney, treasurer; and Horace S. Eldredge, marshall of the provisional government of the State of Deseret.[12]

> During; the winter of 1849 and 50 the Provisional State Government of Deseret was organized and President Young elected Governor. We had a legislature, and I was elected General of the militia. of the state or the Nauvoo Legion as it was called. We also had a company of what was called Life Guards.
>
> Military districts were organized, one in each county. At first in most of the districts there was only sufficient for a company or battalion with a captain at their head. When a district had enough we would form a brigade and elect a Brigadier General, and when sufficiently increased in numbers a division was formed with a Major General at the head. Each district made returns direct to the Adjutant General's Office.[13]

Daniel's election as major general of the Nauvoo Legion with Jedediah M. Grant as brigadier general of the first (mounted) cohort and Horace S. Eldredge as brigadier general of the second (footmen) was recorded in Brigham Young's history on May 26, 1849. Thereafter, Brigham and most other church leaders referred to him as General Wells in written documents, although he was still Squire Wells in common discussions and when acting as attorney general for the State of Deseret. Daniel's legal knowledge and experience still exceeded his military expertise, but he continued to improve his skills in both areas through study and work in his elected offices.[14]

The militia organization was constituted as a means of maintaining peace with the Indians and preserving law and order in the event of any major disaster. The Saints policy toward the Ute, Goshute, Shoshone, Uintah, and San Pitch tribes who inhabited the northern Great Basin area was to befriend them, give them gifts of food and other necessities, make them welcome in the settlements, and maintain a peaceful relationship with them. They also frequently attempted to convert members of the tribes to Mormon teachings, though few were actually baptized. The pacific intentions of Mormon leaders were initially successful, but the ethical and moral differences between Native American and Mormon culture were so stark that conflicts inevitably developed within a short time. On relations with the Indians Daniel said:

> We always consider it cheaper to feed and clothe the Indians than to fight them, and so long as we can get access to them to feed them, &c. we have no trouble with them; but when they get out of the settlements into the mountains there is danger of depredations &c. by them.
>
> In 1848 some Indians came in here [Great Salt Lake City] with two Indian children offering them for sale. It appears that the tribes of Goshup [Goshute] and Wanship were at variance resulting in a fight between them in which Wanship was killed, and among other prisoners these two children were taken; and as they kill their prisoners unless they can sell them, these children were offered for sale. Charles Decker bought one of the prisoners which was a girl and President Young afterwards brought her up. She afterwards married an Indian chief named Kanosh.
>
> Our people fraternized with the Indians a good deal and got quite familiar with them; but they commenced their depredations, killing cattle, &c. They would also go to the houses and demand food and the women got frightened. They were

permitted in the Fort just the same as anybody else, and they got quite saucy and unbearable to the people who could no longer stand it.[15]

All the Deseret civil and military officers served without pay and functioned for the next two years as the government of the territory. At the general assembly held in July 1849, a second memorial to Congress requesting that a territorial government be organized was drafted and Almon W. Babbit was elected a delegate to carry the petition to Washington.

Daniel H. Wells, Parley P. Pratt, and Daniel Spencer as a committee wrote instructions to Babbitt and Dr. John M. Berhhisel, who had carried the first statehood petition to Congress. Their letter to the delegates stated how the second petition was to be presented, depending on whether Congress had already acted to create a territory in the Great Basin.

> Enclosed you will find the Resolutions of the Legislature of this State in relation to the Territorial Government, etc. Accordingly, we proceed to lay before you our reasons and feelings pertaining to governmental affairs.
>
> If Congress has passed at the present session [1849–1850] an act for the organization of a Territory called Utah Territory, which they designed for us, regardless of all our feelings in the matter, then we have only to yield our quiet acquiescence therein, for the time being, only urging the more strenuous the early adjustment of our boundaries and acceptance of our Constitution and admission. If on the contrary they have adjourned and no action had upon the subject, you will formally urge our claims for admission as a State . . .
>
> Necessity compelled us, for our safety and protection, to adopt some form of government; the people having the unquestionable right to choose their own form of government, have done so. They have formed a State, adopted a constitution, elected officers, passed laws, taxed themselves for the support of the government, repelled Indian invasions, established institutions of learning, laid out and improved roads, built public buildings, explored the country, etc., etc., all at their own expense.[16]

One of the government services most needed by the Saints was the coining of money that could be used in trade. Most settlers brought little cash west, having spent all their resources on their teams and wagons and the equipment and food they needed for the trip and after their arrival. Consequently, there was little hard currency in the territory in the first few years and most trade was carried on by barter.

Some gold came into Great Salt Lake City in 1848 in the form of gold dust brought back by members of the Mormon Battalion who had panned it during their homeward journey from San Diego. An estimated $17,000 in California gold arrived in 1848 and 1849 with returning members of the battalion. At least a tenth of this amount, and perhaps more, was given to the church as tithing.[17]

As dust, the gold was difficult to use as a medium of exchange because each transaction required it to be weighed with the resulting risk of loss or fraud. To simplify the process, gold dust was weighed into dollar-denominated packets that then served as currency. But this was a temporary solution and, when the California Gold Rush of 1849 brought thousands of people through Utah on their way to the gold fields, the demand for hard currency became intense. The need was met by minting gold coins in Great Salt Lake City. As superintendent of public works, Daniel helped establish the mint, which struck coins in four different denominations.[18]

Only 46 ten-dollar eagles were struck in 1848 and this denomination was never issued again. The following year as many as 1,000 twenty-dollar pieces were struck along with a larger number of two and a half- and five-dollar coins.[19]

Daniel described the process and its limitations.

> Robert Campbell engraved the stamp for the coin that was made here. President Young conceived the idea of coining the gold as currency was very scarce then. Gold dust from California was about the first currency we had. The gold was coined up into 2½, 5, 10, and 20 pieces. The dies and everything connected with the coining were made here. The coin was made of pure gold without alloy, which made it deficient in weight, therefore it was discounted and sold as bullion.[20]

Only the eagle coins, struck in 1848, were pure gold. Later issues in 1849 and 1850 were alloyed with silver and were more durable. Some, however, were struck from underweight blanks made of impure gold and were therefore worth less than their face value.[21]

In the spring of 1849, while Daniel was commencing public works, organizing the provisional government, and pursuing his personal affairs, an incident took place in Utah Valley that had far-reaching effects on future Indian-Mormon relations. Daniel was not personally involved in the matter and at the time did not consider it important. He says only that "The first Indian trouble was a little scrimmage between some sheepherders and some Indians in the county adjoining here, but was not a regular hostile movement. The place where it occurred was Battle Creek, now called Pleasant Grove."[22]

The "scrimmage" was actually between a company of Mormon militia sent south from Great Salt Lake City with instructions to "take such measures as would put a final end" to the Utes' practice of stealing stock from settlers in the area. One Indian leader named Little Chief, perhaps intimidated by encountering a large group of armed whites, ordered his son to lead them by night to a small camp of natives. The militia surrounded the Ute lodges before daylight and from this position of strength tried to negotiate with the Indians. The Mormon leader, Dimick Huntington, told them that they had not come to fight, but to investigate the thefts. With a dozen steer hides scattered through their camp proclaiming their guilt, the Utes concluded that they could not parlay the situation to a peaceful ending. Four warriors and their families ran to cover in the nearby creek bottom and opened fire on the much larger band of whites. Despite their "determined resolution to die rather than yield," the Indians did not succeed in killing or even wounding any of the militia men before they were themselves shot down. Although Huntington was trying, at least at the beginning, to pursue the peaceful Indian policy of Brigham Young, the one-sided result of this incident and the fact that the only reports of it were written by the victors leaves room for doubt about who was responsible for the start of hostilities.[23]

The Indian survivors, thirteen women and children, including one youth of about eighteen, were taken to Salt Lake and "cared for" until warm weather when they returned to their own people. The youth, who was the only Indian fighter not killed in the battle, was probably Black Hawk. Remembering his early defeat and humiliating captivity, he later became the most feared and revered Ute chief and led his people against the Mormons in the Black Hawk War.[24]

By the fall and winter of 1849, conflicts between the Indians and settlers of Utah Valley again increased. An escalating cycle developed: as the thefts increased in number and value, the settlers' defenses hardened and became more determined; the Indians responded with greater violence to secure the spoils they felt entitled to.

Many of the Saints did not agree with Brigham Young's policy of treating peacefully with the Indians. A number were Southerners and preferred the methods of Andrew Jackson who, as an army general, had defeated eastern Indian tribes in several battles and, as President, had presided over the "Trail of Tears" during which they were driven from their lands into western exile. Others were European converts who simply

Figure 8.2. Fort Utah in 1849, built on the site of present-day Provo. Unknown artist.

could not conceive of dealing with "savages and barbarians" with anything but force. Most accepted the pronouncements of Joseph Smith that the Indians were descended from the peoples of the Book of Mormon and would someday be converted to the restored gospel, but they were not ready to pursue that goal at the risk of their own lives or property.

In August 1849, an Indian nicknamed Bishop (because of his resemblance to the LDS Presiding Bishop Newell K. Whitney) was killed by Richard Ivie and two other Mormons in a fight over a stolen shirt. To hide their act from the Utes and from church leaders, the men gutted Bishop's body, filled it with rocks and dumped it in the Provo River. The Utes soon discovered it and sought revenge against Ivie and other Mormons by shooting at them and stealing more of their cattle.

The settlers holed up in their fort and fired a cannon they had mounted on a high platform over the wooden palisade to intimidate the Indians. It had little effect on the angry natives, however, and an accident while firing it caused the death of one man and the loss of another's arm. A party of settlers went to the Indians' camp to talk about the conflict, but by then the Utes were already on the warpath and preparing for battle. They war-whooped the whites out of their sight. The settlers then angrily appealed to Governor Young for approval to suppress the Indian depredations. Their request did not mention Bishop's death as a cause of the trouble and the Governor remained ignorant of that killing until much later.[25]

Brigham was aware, however, that the Saints had provoked the Indians in other ways and he adamantly refused permission for them to go on the offensive. He told them "there was no necessity for fighting and killing Indians if the brethren would act wisely in their intercourse with them." He also warned the settlers that "if they killed Indians for stealing, they would have to answer for it."[26]

Daniel H. Wells, President Young, and other Mormon leaders met with Captain Howard Stansbury and Lieutenant John W. Gunnison of the US Topographical Engineers who were engaged in surveying the Great Salt Lake and the surrounding country. Both the government officers were concerned that three of their party sent to deal with the Indians for horses might have been killed by them. They were familiar with the Indian problems of the Utah Valley settlers and strongly advised the Deseret State leaders to take whatever steps were needed to end the depredations.[27]

Brigham was still very reluctant to approve harsh measures against the Indians whom he felt were no more in the wrong than the Mormon settlers anxious to kill them. Although he later acknowledged acting against his own better judgment, he finally gave in to the settlers' demands and the importuning of Stansbury and Gunnison and ordered up a force of 150 men. At his request, Stansbury ordered Lieutenant George W. Howland to go with them to demonstrate that the US Army sanctioned the operation.[28]

Although he firmly supported Brigham's view that the Indians should be treated humanely and not killed for stealing, Daniel agreed to lead the Nauvoo Legion into Utah Valley "to co-operate with the inhabitants of said valley in quelling and staying the operations of all hostile Indians and . . . exterminating such as do not separate themselves from the hostile clans and sue for peace." He immediately sent a force of fifty men to give the Mormon settlers there some needed support. His orders to the advance group concluded with this admonition:

> In carrying out the above order you will keep in exercise every principle of humanity, compatible with the laws of war, and see that no violence is permitted to women and children unless the same shall be demanded by attendant circumstances.[29]

Before Daniel could assemble the rest of his force and lead them south, an engagement was fought on February 9, in which the Indians were driven away from the settlements. They then regrouped in the forest south of Utah Lake and, when the settlers attempted to dislodge them, killed and wounded several men by firing from their concealed positions. At the end of the day's fighting, another dispatch was sent to Salt Lake requesting General Wells to come at once and take personal charge of the campaign.[30]

Daniel arrived after a second day of fighting had caused additional losses on both sides. The next day was the Sabbath and he ordered a day of rest, in hopes that the Indians, having suffered heavy casualties, would sue for peace, surrender, or simply flee from the already bloody battleground. They did none of these, however, and the fighting commenced again the next day.[31]

Daniel's account of the battle is given here in its entirety as he related it from memory twenty-five years after the event.

> During that season this Indian trouble grew into hostilities and the people called on us for help, and Governor Young directed that I should send out assistance. I sent George D. Grant with about 50 men as quick as we could raise them, and John Scott stayed to raise other 50, but when the time came he declined to go.
>
> The Indians were camped on Provo Bottoms which was then covered with timber and brush, forming quite a hiding place for them; and they would shoot from under their cover. One man was killed and four or five others wounded. The people did not seem to be successful against the Indians, and they requested me to go down, which I did and took charge of the expedition. Colonel Stansbury was here at the time. Lieutenant Harland of the U.S. Army went out, but he got disgusted and came back about the time I went out.
>
> The Indians had guns as well as bows and arrows. Before I went down they [settlers] had improvised a battery and put it on truck wheels which could be shoved along before them to protect them from the Indians' fire, because the Indians would pick them off from under their cover. This battery done good service and had a good effect in frightening the Indians.
>
> The night that I got to Provo there was a great snowstorm. I had never been in Utah Valley before, and we got there about three o'clock in the morning. After having a little rest I organized the troops and declared martial law. Took all the men and brought them into service. As I was ordered not to leave

that valley until every Indian was out, I seized everything there in the shape of provisions &c to keep the men on.

We went out to search for these Indians and found that a portion of them had left this cover and gone into what is called Rock Canyon, and the others had gone south. Snow was then about two feet deep which made it very difficult to travel. With the majority of the troops I went out to Spanish Fork on the Indian trail and left a guard at the mouth of Rock Canyon to keep those Indians there, but some of them made their escape over the mountains. We encountered the Indians near the north end, on the west side of the mountain, east of the south end of Utah Lake, and completely defeated them.

During the whole expedition 27 warriors were killed. Their squaws, with their papooses and children, as is usual with them, threw themselves upon the victorious party for protection and support. We brought them to the city, fed and took care of them until spring when they ran back to their Indian camps. Many of them died, not being able to stand our way of living.

We cleaned all hostile Indians out of Utah Valley, but some escaped. There were settlements being formed in Sanpete [Valley], and I sent a detachment to notify the people in Manti that the Indians were hostile, and for them to be on their guard.

We had peace for some time after that. Our policy was to conciliate the Indiana all the time.—No trouble between 1850 and 52.[32]

The Indian casualties were much higher than Daniel recalled. Twenty-nine warriors were killed by the company he commanded. Thirteen more, including women, children and the Ute Chief Old Elk, were found dead of wounds or exposure by the company guarding Rock Canyon. The militia then fought several more small engagements in the canyon in which more Indians, male and female, were killed. A few, including Chief Stick-in-Head, escaped out of the box canyon on snowshoes. The Rock Canyon troop brought in twenty-three prisoners to add to the thirty or more, including a single warrior, An-kar-tewets, taken by Daniel's company.[33]

In all, at least seventy Ute warriors and some women were killed while Mormon losses were one dead and about eighteen wounded. It was by far the bloodiest Indian battle ever fought within the borders of present-day Utah and it left a lasting bitterness among the Utes against the Mormons whose leaders had preached peace, but permitted their people to wage unrestricted war. The Indians' desire for revenge would fuel additional conflicts during the next two decades.[34]

Following the battle in Utah Valley, Daniel sent a detachment of militia around the west side of Utah Lake to reconnoiter and deal with any other hostile Indians found there. They then moved north, crossed the lake eastward on the ice and rejoined the main militia troop at Provo. On February 19 the full group of militia returned to Salt Lake and were met and congratulated on their performance by the governor and the legislature.[35]

Soon after Daniel's militia force left Utah County, a barbaric atrocity was committed on the Indian bodies by two settlers at the request of Dr. James Blake, a government surgeon attached to the Stansbury expedition. Blake commissioned Abner Blackburn and James Or to return to the battlefield and behead all the corpses they could find frozen in the snow. Blake claimed he intended to send the severed heads to a medical institution in Washington for scientific study, but this was not credible as they could never have survived the four-month journey without complete decomposition. In fact, the gruesome trophies were put on display to the settlers and their Indian prisoners in Fort Utah for several weeks. When warming weather caused them to rot, they were disposed of as trash without ceremony. The impact on the Indians who saw this horrific desecration of their kinsmen can hardly be imagined. Among them was Black Hawk, who more than a dozen years later sought revenge against the white perpetrators.[36]

Black Hawk remained friendly to the Saints for the moment, however, so much so that Daniel arranged for him to be escorted to the April 1850 general conference of the church by two prominent settlers from Utah County. Black Hawk was probably baptized into the church either before or after the conference, although no record of this now exists.[37]

The troops brought back to Salt Lake a number of captured horses and these were returned, after a unanimous vote at the conference, to the Indians. Daniel arranged for the horses to be delivered to Black Hawk in Great Salt Lake City who could then distribute them "to the rightful owners, or nearest of kin."[38]

Daniel and other Mormon leaders hoped that this action would show that the Saints did not want to despoil the Indians of their property and that they received greater benefits from peaceful relationships with the Mormons. It may have helped build relations with some Northern Utes, but could hardly overcome the devastating effects of what had happened in the south.[39]

In a further attempt to reduce Indian hostility in Utah Valley, Daniel ordered Captain McBride of the Fort Utah militia to release the captured Ute warrior An-kar-tewets with instructions to "apprize the survivors of his nation" that they could now safely "return and dwell in peace if they ceased their depredations." The messenger was also to tell the Timpanogos Utes that the Saints did not want to continue to war with them and were anxious to again become their friends. Daniel also insisted that the Utes accept the friendly Indian Black Hawk as their chief in place of the slain Old Elk and the fugitive Stick-in-Head.[40]

How much of Daniel's message An-kar-tewets communicated is unknown, but the Utes did accept Black Hawk as their chief, an elevation of his status that the Saints bitterly regretted when he later turned against them. During the Utah Valley expedition, Daniel learned that the Indians there had many horses that they desired to trade for clothing and provisions. Some Salt Lake Valley Saints needed horses and a committee was set up to manage a trading session. Several wagon loads of goods were taken to Fort Utah (now Provo) where the Indians had gathered with their horses. At sunrise on May 23 the trading began and continued through the day. Both groups benefitted greatly from the exchange and peaceful relations were again established.[41]

In August 1850, Daniel joined Brigham Young, Heber C. Kimball, most of the apostles, and others on a journey to Weber County north of Great Salt Lake City. There he helped locate a site and lay out a plan for the city of Ogden, named after non-Mormon Peter Skene Ogden, an early fur trader in the area. Brigham and Daniel advised the local Saints to settle on city lots rather than on their farms in the countryside. The wisdom of this counsel was proved less than a month later by the occurrence of the final serious incident between Mormons and Indians during the year.[42]

On September 15 Chief Terikee of the Shoshone Tribe was shot and killed by Urban Stewart who lived at Four Mile Creek (now Harrisville) about four miles north of Farr's Fort in Ogden. Stewart thought that the Indian was stealing corn when in reality he was searching for his strayed horse in the settler's cornfield. Stewart, fearing for his life, fled south. Terikee's enraged band burned his house and set fire to his fields of grain.

When word of the killing reached Farr's Fort, Lorin Farr, fearing an Indian attack on other settlers, sent messengers to warn the people living in Ogden Hole (now North Ogden) to come to the Fort and gather their stock from the ranges for protection. They were pursued by a large band of Indians, but by the fleetness of their horses all but one arrived safely at the Fort. The exception was a Mr. Campbell, a millwright who worked for Loren Farr, who was overtaken and captured by the Indians. They disarmed him, used his own gun to kill him, and left his scalped body lying on the trail.[43]

Dr. David Moore immediately rode to Great Salt Lake City to notify Brigham Young. Moore rode back the same night with a note from Willard Richards on behalf of the Governor.

President Lorin Farr:

Your letter by Dr. Moore was received a few hours hence, and messengers with an interpreter will be ready to start with your express in a few minutes. As we were commencing to write, Judge Birch arrived with your letter at 2 p.m. General Wells is causing men to be raised as fast as possible to repair to your relief.[44]

Fortunately, Daniel was able to reach Ogden with a company of men in time to prevent any more bloodshed. The show of force made the Indians hesitate to attack a well-armed troop and Lorin Farr, who had maintained a good relationship with them, was able to calm the angry band of Shoshones. Once tempers had cooled, one death on each side was deemed an equal loss and neither whites nor Indians wanted to go to war. None of the nine Mormon forts in Weber County was ever attacked thereafter.[45]

An act creating the Territory of Utah was passed by Congress in September 1850, but word of it did not reach Great Salt Lake City until January 1851. President Millard Fillmore appointed Brigham Young as Governor of the new territory. With that appointment, the provisional State of Deseret ceased to exist and was superseded by the Territory of Utah. The territory, though smaller than the area claimed for Deseret, included all of present-day Utah, all but the southern tip of Nevada, the southwest sixth of Wyoming, and the third of Colorado west of the Continental Divide. The Saints, by resolution of the legislature, if not the acclamation of the populace, accepted the new government despite the Mormons' previous bad experiences with federal officials.[46]

In an unusually eloquent speech given at the 1851 Pioneer Day celebration in Salt Lake City, Daniel made clear his feelings about the US Constitution and the return of the Mormon people to citizenship under it after four years as outcasts.

> It has been thought by some that this people, abused, maltreated, insulted, robbed, plundered, murdered, and finally disfranchised and expatriated, would naturally feel repugnant to again unite their destiny with the American Republic . . . inasmuch as their superior intelligence appears to be exercised to devise the most wanton, cruel, and dastardly means for the accomplishment of our ruin, overthrow, and utter extermination. No wonder, then, that it was thought by some that we would not again submit ourselves . . .
>
> That country, that Constitution, whose institutions were all ours, they are still ours. Our fathers were heroes of the

Revolution. Under the master spirits of an Adams, a Jefferson, and a Washington they declared and maintained their independence. Under the guidance of the Spirit of Truth they fulfilled their mission whereunto they were sent from the presence of the Father.

Because demigods had arisen and seized the reins of power, should we relinquish our interest in that country made dear to us . . . Should we, for reasons such as these, seek the overthrow of that government, of that country, of those institutions whose only fault is the want of good and faithful administrators?

We have before us the widespread domain of public lands, rich in natural resources, flowing with cool clear rivulets, buoyant and life-inspiring, where health invigorates, and nature's sublimity exalts. We breathe the free pure air, drink of the free cool fountains, and cultivate the free earth in peace, and thank the Lord who has, in the abundance of His mercy, vouchsafed unto us so goodly an heritage.[47]

The same legislative resolution that welcomed the Utah Territory into the federal union also ordered that:

> . . . Union Square, Great Salt Lake City, be devoted for the use of public buildings of said Territory, that Governor Brigham Young be their agent to make drafts upon the treasury of the United States for the amount appropriated for said buildings, and to take such measures as he should deem proper for their immediate erection, that Truman O. Angell be architect of said buildings and Daniel H. Wells a committee of one to superintend their erection, that they proceed immediately to design and erect them.[48]

Daniel thus found himself, from 1851 onward, not only church superintendent of public works, but also territorial superintendent, charged with erecting the public buildings to be used by the territorial government.

In October Daniel joined Governor Brigham Young, Heber C. Kimball, George A. Smith and a dozen others on a trip south from the Salt Lake Valley for the purpose of locating and laying out the site of a new capital city for Utah Territory. The group traveled by carriage and wagon and was well armed as a precaution against the possibility of Indian attack. Daniel acted as captain of the guard and his men kept a constant watch both day and night. Five days were required to reach Chalk Creek in the Pauvant Valley, about one hundred fifty miles south of Great Salt Lake City. There, in almost the exact geographic center of the Territory, the commissioners laid out a town site for the seat of government and named it Fillmore in honor of the sitting President. They also drew out rough boundaries for a new county named Millard for which Fillmore, when built, would be the county seat.[49]

Daniel reconnoitered the area and found a good source of limestone for building, but determined also that the water supply was limited in summer and that timber would need to be hauled for miles from the eastern mountains. The town of Fillmore became a modest settlement and one wing of a statehouse was built in the public square at its center, but the territorial government only convened there for one year in 1855. The capital was then moved back to Great Salt Lake City, the population center of the Territory.

Daniel's multiple religious, military, and administrative duties increasingly consumed his time, but he fulfilled them all without complaint and, except for the territorial office of attorney general, without pay. For that office and other territorial appointments, Congress appropriated modest compensation. He never refused an appointment and never declined to accept a responsibility in church or public service. He became a reliable workhorse in the religious and secular structure of Utah, one who never sought credit for his labors and rarely mentioned any honors bestowed upon him as a result of his accomplishments. When one task was finished, he simply carried on to the next.

Daniel headed the committee, along with Jedediah M. Grant, that planned the 1851 Pioneer Day celebration and was asked to deliver the opening oration to the assembled crowd which included church leaders and three of the newly-appointed and recently-arrived non-Mormon officials of Utah Territory: Broughton D. Harris, secretary of Territory; Judge Lemuel Brandebury; and Indian sub-agent Steven B. Rose.[50]

Daniel spoke long (for him) and eloquently about the recent history of the Saints and described, among many other sufferings that they had endured, the extreme hardship that the enlistment of the members of the Mormon Battalion in 1846 to fight in the Mexican War had imposed on church members. He declared that the government's only motive in recruiting Mormon soldiers and marching them two thousand miles from their families while those same families were being driven destitute out of Illinois and across Iowa was to weaken and eventually destroy the church by dispersing its members and consuming its material resources.[51]

Daniel believed what he said regarding this episode in church history, but he had not been involved in the creation of the Mormon Battalion nor did he know the circumstances that brought it about and he was mistaken about both. The speakers who followed him said nothing to correct Daniel's remarks and, in the case of Brigham Young who spoke next, actually supported and reinforced his erroneous views, although he definitely knew better. The Battalion's march, far from being a drain or destabilizing influence on the church, strengthened it and provided many benefits to its members and those they left behind. Besides moving several hundred Saints west at public expense, battalion soldiers supplied more than $20,000 in cash from their advance pay and uniform allowances that helped their families and other church members get outfitted and prepared for their journey to Great Salt Lake City.[52]

But Daniel did not know any of this and his remarks were printed in the next *Deseret News* read by Saints and Gentiles alike as the official view of the church. Judge Perry E. Brocchus, who arrived in Utah to take up his federal appointment after the celebration, read Daniel's speech and the others given that day and felt strongly that the Mormon leaders were preaching subversion. When he was invited to speak at a conference soon after the account of the celebration appeared in print, he took the opportunity to answer them.

Brocchus's oration, which began with praise for Mormon industry and behavior that warmed his audience to him, progressed to advising the people not to contribute to the raising of the Washington Monument, then starting construction in the nation's capital, if they could not offer "in full fellowship with the United States." After questioning the Saints' patriotism at length, he then went on to lecture them about morality in an obvious attack on polygamy.[53]

Brocchus's speech was received with no applause and seething anger that he afterward said made him feel that his life was in danger as he sat down. Brigham Young, speaking after Bacchus, prevented any hostile action against the judge, but again inveighed against the government for failing to help the Mormons or redress many of the injustices they suffered. His remarks confirmed Daniel's wrong interpretation about the Mormon Battalion and helped elevate it to a myth that long persisted in Mormon thinking. Brocchus, and two other federal officers, Harris and Brandebury, felt so threatened by the Mormons' reaction to them that they resigned their positions and fled the territory within a few weeks. Arriving in the east, they spread extreme tales of Mormon rebellion by letters, speeches, and newspaper reports, inciting a major wave of anti-Mormon sentiment in government circles and among most of the populace.[54]

In October 1851, when the Federal District Court for Utah Territory was set up, Daniel was admitted to the bar. He was then legally qualified to perform his duties as attorney general, the office in which he had been serving for the previous two years. Although now free to do so, he never presented himself as a lawyer or practiced outside of his official responsibilities for making and enforcing the laws.[55]

The scope and complexity of Daniel's work in Utah Territory is revealed in an 1852 letter to Dr. John M. Bernhisel, the Territorial Delegate in Washington. It shows his frugality in avoiding unnecessary expenses and his broad understanding of the genuine needs of the Territory. The letter is long, but so was the list of problems and challenges addressed.

> Dear Brother:
>
> In addition to the letter upon the subject of appropriations to pay up arrearages, etc., I hope you will pardon me for making a few suggestions in relation to future appropriations, but first permit me to say to you in all confidence and although a petition has gone to the Department, and will probably be presented to Congress, praying for the increase of the salaries of the officers of this Territory, that there are plenty of men here, abundantly able to perform all the duties of said offices who would be glad to get the appointments at the present salaries . . .
>
> This brings me to the subject of appropriations. The Building Committee has taken the job of building the State House, of which you have the plan; the appropriation of twenty thousand will be expended by the end of the current fiscal year, and we shall have proceeded with the walls by that time. It is most earnestly hoped that an appropriation commensurate with the estimates will be made; if it is not possible to get it all at once, let us have at least twenty-five or thirty thousand, that we may be able to cover in the building the ensuing season and finish a part for immediate use.
>
> We shall go on with the building, I suppose, whether Congress makes any further appropriation or not. But they need not know that; they certainly do not expect that suitable public buildings can be erected and finished in this far-off country where there is little or no timber suitable for lumber, and where we have to pay such prices for every article that we cannot as yet manufacture, for the pitiful sum of twenty thousand dollars . . .
>
> We this ensuing year want $40,000 for a penitentiary, and $50,000 more for laying out and constructing a road from the east line of the Territory where the road intersects from the South Pass to this city, and west to Pilot Peak, and from the north side of Bear River on the road to Oregon and California (the northern route) to this city and south to where the southern California

road crosses the Rio Virgin or to the southern boundary of the Territory. These are two important roads, the roads upon which the mail routes principally run, and want bridging in many places . . .

East and north of this city, Bear River should be bridged, also the Weber and Green Rivers east, and the Sevier on the south, as also work done on the road in many places, East Canyon Creek, for instance, and many other places equally as bad.

In the immediate vicinity of the settlements the roads can ordinarily be made by the poll tax upon the citizens, but such bridges as I have alluded to, across the streams mentioned, should be constructed by the generosity of the Federal Government.

Perhaps Congress will sympathize with our forlorn situation sufficient to give us a few thousand on behalf of the University of Deseret. If she would, it would be gratefully received, and be of great benefit in promoting the cause of education in this Territory. And if Congress should see proper to go on with the triangulation [surveying] of this Territory, please give my respect to Captain Stansbury, and tell him I hope we shall see him again in these far distant vales . . .

It is proposed to hold treaties with all the Indians of the Territory the ensuing year and an appropriation of $40,000 or $50,000 should be placed to the disposal of the Superintendent of Indian Affairs for that purpose.

If other things should suggest themselves to my mind, I shall use my privilege of again communicating with you. In the meantime I hope that you will fully communicate with me in relation to any subject.

> I am, Sir, with high consideration,
> Respectfully yours,
> Daniel H. Wells[56]

9

Six Additional Wives, a Dozen Children, and Many Enterprises to Support the Family

1851–1855

In addition to fulfilling the multiple Church and civic functions he was called upon to perform, Daniel also wanted to re-establish the family life and restore the personal fortune that he had left behind in Illinois. Within a few months after his arrival in the Salt Lake Valley, he began a new family and set about developing the business and agricultural ventures that would enable him to support it.

Unlike many Saints, whose religious backgrounds made the concept of plural marriage very difficult to embrace and still more difficult to practice successfully, Daniel apparently accepted the idea of polygamy without strong objection when he was introduced to it in Nauvoo. The fact that he did so probably hardened his wife's opposition to Mormonism, although he might never have entered into any plural marriages if Eliza had come west with him and remained opposed.

Without her, his situation made plural marriage particularly appealing. He had no intention of divorcing Eliza, whom he still loved and whom he hoped would eventually repent her decision and join him in the Salt Lake Valley. But he was now thirty-four years old and had only one child whom he might never see again. A second wife offered the chance of more children and less of the loneliness he felt in Eliza's and Albert's absence. A large earthly family was one of Daniel's strongest desires, not least because he believed it would become an eternal family according to one of the main Mormon doctrines that had drawn him to the faith.

There were many single women in the valley and, although he was not handsome or smooth-tongued, Daniel was attractive in other ways and

Figure 9.1. Daniel H. Wells's first home in Great Salt Lake City, built of adobe on the north side of South Temple Street in the block east of Main Street.

could have his choice among the eligible females. He chose to expand his friendship with Louisa Free. After courting her within the limiting circumstances of the difficult winter of 1848, he proposed marriage to Louisa in the New Year. She accepted and they were married by Brigham Young on February 15, 1849.[1]

Although he performed Daniel and Louisa's marriage, Brigham made no mention of it in his writings, nor did he mention other weddings that he presided at before or after the Wells union. Although polygamy had been practiced in the church since the 1830s, and more or less openly after Joseph Smith announced the revelation on celestial marriage in 1843, the doctrine was still not publicly acknowledged until 1852.[2]

Louisa and Daniel were not at all hesitant to proclaim their union or live together openly as man and wife. The groom did not have any cabin of his own and so the newlyweds made their first home together in his covered wagon. Their quarters were made more crowded by the presence of Louisa's son John who turned three shortly after his mother's wedding. It is difficult to imagine today how even a small family could live with any degree of comfort in a four-by-ten-foot wooden box with a canvas cover too low to stand upright beneath, but such conditions were common, even for larger families, in early Great Salt Lake City.

After several months of living in the wagon, Daniel was ready to begin construction of a cabin on his lot. He had amassed materials and intended to do the construction work himself when he could spare time from his other responsibilities. Brigham Young, however, did not want him to be drawn away from his work as superintendent by the need to provide a home for his new wife. In order to have Daniel nearer the building sites he was supervising and more readily available for other assignments, Brigham offered Daniel the use of a small cabin that was already built on the president's property on the north side of South Temple Street. The couple immediately accepted and moved into the one room structure just east of the Eagle Gate.[3]

A short time later, and perhaps also at the instigation of Brigham Young, a divorce was formally written and approved by the president to dissolve the marriage of John D. Lee and Louisa Free. The document was signed on May 12, 1849 and "the union was dissolved in good feelings and the consent of both parties," as noted in Lee's journal. No one voiced any concern that Daniel's marriage to Louisa preceded her divorce from Lee by three months.[4]

Daniel soon adopted John Brigham Lee (with the consent of his biological father), changed his name to John Brigham Wells, and thereafter treated him as his own son until the day of his death.[5]

Martha Givens Harris, upon learning that Daniel now had one new wife and a roof over his head, increased her efforts to win his affections. Whether she was friends with Louisa prior to the latter's marriage to Daniel is unknown, but she must have become acquainted with her before pursuing him, as Louisa's consent was required before any additional plural marriage could occur. Martha and Daniel developed their relationship during the summer and were married on September 20, 1849. Louisa was present for the ceremony and was by then expecting her first child. Daniel Hanmer Wells Jr. was born in the cabin on South Temple Street in November.[6]

Daniel's cabin was large enough to accommodate another wife, but two marital beds in one room, or a single shared one, would have been awkward for all concerned. Consequently, he decided to provide separate apartments for each of his wives. He built a second adobe dwelling west of Brigham Young's home on South Temple. Until it was completed, Martha did not stay with Daniel and Louisa, but visited with her parents or slept in the wagon that he moved next to the cabin. By the end of 1851, Daniel had two finished dwellings and the wagon available for his enlarged family. Martha did not have her first child until April 1853, suggesting that she and Daniel may not have consummated their marriage until a year or more after the event.[7]

By that time Daniel had married four additional wives and had need for all the living space he could find. His fourth wife (he continued to regard Eliza as his first wife throughout his life, even though they never met again) was Lydia Ann Alley, the daughter of George Alley and Mary Symonds who were both descended from early New England families. Lydia's first American ancestors came over from England in 1634. Her father's family sailed from London and settled in Lynn, Massachusetts. Her mother's family was from Kent County and settled in Salem, Massachusetts.

Lydia was born in Lynn in 1828 and was converted with her parents to the Mormon Church by missionaries in 1842. The Alley family moved to Nauvoo the next year and Lydia was baptized there in the Mississippi River. Her older sister, Margaret Maria Alley, married Brigham Young in 1846. The entire family joined the Mormon exodus from Nauvoo, spent a year in western Iowa and then continued west in the spring of 1848.[8]

The Alley family were members of Brigham Young's company and Margaret traveled with the president in his wagons, along with Emeline Free and his other wives. As with Emeline Young, Daniel would certainly have become acquainted with Margaret and probably with her parents, but there is no record that he had any acquaintance with other members of the family during the trip. Lydia Alley was then twenty years old and her younger sister, Susan Hannah Alley, was eighteen.

After arriving in Great Salt Lake City, George Alley built a log cabin in the canyon north of the city (now City Creek Canyon) and moved his family into it for the winter. In the spring of 1849 they moved into the city and made their home in the Eighth Ward where Daniel had first resided and still had property. Although he moved away from his lot soon after the Alley's settled on their plot, he may have come to know the family better through that connection.[9]

It was Brigham Young and his wife Margaret Alley Young who were the matchmakers. Margaret had a child, Evelyn Louisa Young, the year after the family returned to the valley. By 1852, she was expecting a second child while her two younger sisters were still unmarried. Obviously happy in her own plural marriage, Margaret, with the approval and help of her husband, brought her pretty sisters to the attention of their new neighbor Daniel H. Wells. For the well-educated and refined Alley family, all of whom still spoke with the broad Massachusetts accent of their home state, Squire Wells was an ideal match.

By the spring of 1852, Daniel and Louisa were expecting their second child and living in improved comfort in one of his adobe homes. Martha, still childless, occupied the second home and had formed a close bond with Louisa. Because Daniel was rarely at home, they spent much more time with one another than either did with him, a fact of plural marriage that would sometimes help and sometimes hinder the harmony of home life. After more than two years together, Louisa and Martha had developed a friendship that enabled them to live and work with one another comfortably.[10]

Figure 9.2. The seven wives of Daniel H. Wells: (top row, from left) *Eliza Rebecca Robison, Louisa Free, and Martha Givens Harris;* (bottom row, from left) *Lydia Ann Alley, Susan Hannah Alley, Hannah Corilla Free, and Emmeline Belos Woodward.*

When Louisa's second child, Francis Louisa Wells, was born in March, Martha was there to attend her and help with the new baby. Daniel, though as usual deeply involved in Church, government, and personal duties, was also on hand. Family was very important to him and he made every effort to be present at births and other important events, although he was not always successful.

Margaret Young's efforts to bring her sisters into Daniel's family were by this time so successful that he had decided to ask both Lydia and Susan to marry him. He waited to do so, however, until after the birth of his first daughter before asking Louisa's and Martha's consent to add both of the Alley sisters to his growing family. They readily agreed and began preparing their homes to receive their husband's new wives.

Brigham Young presided at the wedding of Daniel H. Wells and Lydia Ann Alley on April 4, 1852 and two weeks later he again performed the ceremony as Daniel wed Susan Hannah Alley. All the members of the Wells, Alley, and Young families welcomed the joining of their clans in a relationship that they believed would last forever. The importance of being sealed to one another in a bond that transcended fragile mortal life was starkly emphasized a few months later when Lydia and Susan Alley's sister Margaret died following the birth of her second child, Mahonri M. Young in November 1852.[11]

Soon after his marriages to Lydia and Susan Alley, Daniel acquired a sixth wife. The bride was Hannah Corilla Free, younger sister of his wife Louisa Free Wells and Brigham's wife Emiline Free Young. Louisa and Emeline were the prime movers in bringing Daniel and Hannah together when the latter's need for a husband became suddenly acute through an unusual set of circumstances.

Like her sisters, Hannah had accompanied her parents to Utah in Brigham Young's 1848 company. She was then eighteen and eligible for marriage, but did not find a suitable partner until mid-1851 when she wed Dr. Lawrence Sterne Hotchkiss. Although he appeared to be an excellent match for the amiable and independent Hannah, the event proved otherwise. Soon after their marriage, as the personality and background of Dr. Hotchkiss was revealed, their relationship soured.[12]

Sterne, as he preferred to be called, was born in Connecticut in 1816. He received his medical training there and practiced herbal medicine and dentistry for several years. In 1842, he married Theresa G. Peyreferry in Philadelphia and they had a son named Thaddeus. The 1850 census shows that Dr. Hotchkiss was living in Pottawattamie, Iowa, with his sister Cordelia and son Thaddeus. Theresa was not living with the family, indicating that she had died previously or that the marriage had broken up. By 1851, Dr. Hotchkiss had arrived in Great Salt Lake City, been converted to the Mormon Church, and was advertising himself locally as a dental surgeon. He married Hannah Free and by the end of the year she was expecting their first child.

Whether it was disillusionment over Mormon doctrines, concern that his previous marriage would be revealed, or worry about the outcome of a court case in which he became involved that caused Hotchkiss's next action is unknown. But about May 1852, he suddenly abandoned Hannah and left Great Salt Lake City. No one in her family knew what had happened to him, although it was later learned that he returned to his native Connecticut, and in October 1852 married Esther R. Candee in New Haven.[13]

At a special Conference of Elders held on August 28, 1852, Brigham Young, apparently unaware that Sterne Hotchkiss had already departed from Utah Territory sometime earlier, called him on a mission to Siam (Thailand). Since he was not present at the conference to hear it, Sterne did not answer that call and at the following general conference in October, another missionary was called to serve in his place.[14]

Hannah, left pregnant and without a husband to support her, naturally turned to her family and to her older sisters Louisa Wells and Emeline Young in particular. By the end of July it was evident that Sterne Hotchkiss would not return to his wife or to Utah and Emeline talked with Brigham concerning what should be done about her situation. At the request of Hannah, and with the support of Daniel, Louisa, and

Emeline, Brigham Young granted her a divorce from the man who had abandoned her.

Daniel already knew Hannah and, given his gentle and accommodating nature toward his extended family and toward all women, he offered her his hand in marriage as soon as he was informed of her vulnerable position. On August 5, with Brigham presiding and all five of Squire Wells's wives in attendance, Hannah Corilla Free became his sixth wife. Her baby was born six weeks later on September 20 and was named Abby Corilla Wells. No adoption by Daniel was necessary as, according to Mormon doctrine, his daughter was born under the eternal covenant and was therefore a member of his family regardless of the origin of some of her genes.[15]

While Daniel was courting and marrying Lydia, Susan, and Hannah, he was also communicating with Emmeline Whitney, the young widow of one of his close friends, Newell K. Whitney, who died on September 23, 1850 at age fifty-five. At the time of his death, Bishop Whitney was the presiding bishop of the church, responsible for its temporal affairs under the direction of first Joseph Smith, who called him to the position, and then Brigham Young. Like Daniel, Brigham wanted Bishop Whitney close at hand and so had also asked him to live near the president's home and the church office, where he worked. After the bishop's death, his widow continued to reside in the family home with his other wives and married children. That home was on the same block in Great Salt Lake City as Daniel's two cabins.[16]

The youngest Widow Whitney (there were three others, two of Bishop Whitney's six wives having predeceased him) was Emmeline Belos Woodward, born April 29, 1828 in Petersham, Massachusetts, the daughter of David Woodward and his wife Deiadama Hare. Emmeline was, like the Alley sisters, a well-educated and refined lady who had joined the church in Massachusetts and had endured intense ridicule and pressure from non-Mormon family and friends to recant her new faith. To escape this persecution and have a safe means of moving west to Nauvoo, Emmeline agreed to marry James Harvey Harris, son of the presiding elder of the Mormon branch in New Salem, where the Woodward family also lived. The union was arranged by the young couple's parents and took place on July 29, 1843 when the teenagers were both fifteen.[17]

In 1844, the Harris family, including James and Emmeline, moved to Nauvoo, arriving a few weeks before the death of Joseph Smith. Emmeline's testimony of Mormonism was greatly strengthened by hearing the prophet's sermons and his personal witness of his visions. But his murder caused James's parents to apostatize from the church and leave Nauvoo when persecution there intensified. James and Emmeline stayed on and their son, Eugene Henri Harris, was born there in September

1844. Sadly, the baby lived only a few weeks before succumbing to malaria, the same fever that had killed many other Nauvoo residents. Emmeline also came down with it, but recovered without ill effects.

On November 16, James bade his wife farewell and took a steamer to St. Louis, promising to return in about two weeks. He did not come back, but instead sent her a letter asking her to join his parents at La Harpe where he would soon meet her. She refused to go (and probably had not the means), but remained in the city where she soon received a second letter saying that the marriage was over and that James would not return to her or to the LDS Church.[18]

Bereaved, abandoned, and destitute, Emmeline tutored young children entrusted to her teaching by other Mormon families. Among her students were the children of Elizabeth Ann Smith and Newell K. Whitney, who were both introduced to her by Miss Bishop, a friend of Elizabeth Whitney, who had traveled from Albany to Nauvoo with Emmeline and knew of her situation following James's departure. Elizabeth also became Emmeline's close friend, invited her to stay in her home, and eventually converted her to the doctrine of plural marriage.

On February 24, 1845, Emmeline, just turning eighteen, married Bishop Whitney, age fifty, and over the next five years had three children with him. Despite their age difference, she adored her new husband, who by almost all accounts was dearly loved by everyone who knew him.[19]

> Emmeline revered the man she had married, thirty-three years her senior. He was "as good a man as ever lived, a father to all within his reach and more than father to me," she recounted on the twenty-fourth anniversary of his death. "I looked to him almost as if he had been a God; my youth, my inexperience of life and its realities caused me to trust most implicitly in one who had power and integrity always at his command." An anchor of calm and security following her personal anguish in Nauvoo.[20]

Emmeline's son, Newell M. Whitney, was born at Winter Quarters in 1847 and died within a day. Her daughter, Isabel M. Whitney, was born in November 1848, soon after the family arrived in Utah. A second daughter, Melvina C. B. Whitney, was born in August 1850, a month before her father Newell K. Whitney died.[21]

Emmeline was stunned by the death of her second husband and, though she remained a member of the Whitney household, she longed for the love and support of a husband. While waiting for a prospect to appear, she resumed teaching to help support herself and her children.

Eighteen months later, she was still without a mate and decided to take matters into her own hands. She had known Daniel H. Wells since she arrived in Nauvoo in 1844 and the Whitney family had also traveled with him in Brigham Young's company on the trek west. Daniel had known Bishop Whitney even before his conversion and afterwards they became close friends as they worked together in ministering to the temporal needs of the Saints on the trail west and after their arrival in Utah. But he had only interacted with Emmeline, a dainty and beautiful girl, as the wife of Bishop Whitney. Following the latter's death he had barely had time to notice her in passing.

To compel him to see her as an individual worthy of his attention, Emmeline took the direct approach. In May 1850, just after Daniel's marriages to Lydia and Hannah Alley (which Emmeline may well have attended), she wrote him a note titled "A Letter from a True Friend" in which she reminded him of his friendship with Newell K. Whitney and asked him to

> " . . . consider the lonely state" of his friend's widow. She wrote that she had often hoped to be "united with a being noble as thyself" and requested him to "return to her a description of his feelings for her."[22]

Daniel responded favorably and over the next few months rekindled his friendship with Emmeline on a more personal level than it had previously been. It was easy for him to see the qualities that made her equally as desirable as his other wives and he soon asked her to marry him.

Daniel recognized that Emmeline, although she maintained an outward demeanor of tranquility, was a far more romantic, emotional, and dramatic personality than any of his other wives and he did his best to accommodate those differences. Either at her request or through his suggestion, they agreed that Emmeline would not share the homes of Daniel's other wives, but would have her own family residence nearby. Until he could provide that separate house, she and her children resided with the Whitney family. Also at her request, Daniel did not seek to adopt Emmeline's daughters, but supported them as part of his family while leaving their Whitney name and heritage intact.[23]

On October 10, 1852, Emmeline, now age twenty-four, entered into her third marriage and became Daniel's seventh wife in a ceremony again presided over by Brigham Young. Daniel quickly made good his promise to supply a separate home for her, and from that slightly distant base Emmeline, Isabel, and Melvina quickly became an integral part of the Wells family.[24]

By the end of 1852, when Daniel was thirty-eight, his family of seven wives was complete and he neither sought nor was offered the hand of any additional women during the remainder of his life. Six of his wives were in their early or mid-twenties, and over the next two years five of them bore him six children. In 1853, Catherine Wells was born to Lydia Alley Wells; Martha Deseret Wells was born to Martha Harris Wells; and Emeline Whitney Wells was born to Emmeline B. Wells. In 1854, Junius Free Wells was born to Hannah Free Wells; Rulon Seymour Wells was born to Louisa Free Wells; and Mary Minerva Wells was born to Lydia Alley Wells. At the close of that year, Daniel had a total of nine children (not counting the two Whitney girls), and others soon followed. Susan Alley Wells finally had her first child, Susan Annette Wells in 1857, during the Utah War crisis.[25]

Unknown to Daniel at the time, he actually had only two wives at the beginning of 1852 and six at year's end. On April 23, 1851, his first wife, Eliza Rebecca Robison, petitioned for a divorce in a Des Moines, Iowa, court. Her petition stated in part:

> Eliza R. Wells . . . was married to said Daniel H. Wells in the month of March 1837 and that they continued to live together as man and wife until May 184– and that said complainant has a child, Albert E. Wells, 13 years in March 1851. That the said Daniel H. Wells attached himself to the Mormon Church and emigrated to the valley of the Salt Lake in "California" where he has remained since May 1848. That during all the time the said complainant and the said Daniel H. Wells lived together, your complainant was a good and lawful wife and never gave the said Wells any cause or provocation to desert your complainant . . . yet said Daniel H. Wells has wholly abandoned and deserted your said complainant . . . since May 1848 . . . Hence to grant your complainant a divorce from the bonds of matrimony now existing between her and the said Daniel H. Wells.[26]

Daniel was not informed of the petition or that the divorce had been granted until after the event. His sister Catherine Woods, with whom Eliza and her son Albert maintained a close relationship after 1848, probably informed him of his wife's action within a year or two, but Daniel never considered himself divorced from Eliza nor relinquished hope that she would one day return to him. In the 1860 US Census, he listed Eliza and Albert as members of his household in Great Salt Lake City even though both were then living in Wisconsin.[27]

Before he arrived in the Salt Lake Valley, while still camped on the trail through the Wasatch Mountains, Daniel sent a letter back with the returning teams and drivers to tell his family in Illinois that he had arrived safely. That letter was not received until Christmas or later. Catherine Woods and her husband wrote back in March 1849, but their letter was not received by Daniel until July, delivered by a wagon train of forty-niners that passed through Great Salt Lake City on their way to California. The ten-month span of time between letters only made more evident the complete divergence of Daniel's life from the lives of those he left behind. Their letter is filled with remonstrance toward him for going west, pleadings for him to return east and abandon Mormonism, and complaints about their failing health. His reply describes the Salt Lake Valley, some of what he is doing to build a new home in the wilderness and the challenges he is facing.[28]

Daniel's next letter, sent in April 1850 did not materially improve communication with his family about important matters. In it he says nothing about his new wives, or the major responsibilities he has been given in the church and the new government. Pamela's response still shows her inability to accept his new situation.

> Trenton, August [1850]
>
> Dear Brother,
>
> We received your letter a few weeks since dated April. We are very glad indeed to hear from you again and that you are in good health after so much fatigue and danger. I am very glad you are resolved to write whether you hear from us or not, and be assured your letters are always acceptable. Still I cannot bear the idea of your being at such a distance from all your friends, we flattered ourselves that you would return last fall and that we should have the pleasure of seeing you here this summer, but the summer is almost gone—and we have heard from you, but you—you do not say one word about coming to see us, but we hope you are now making your arrangements to come and are going to take us by surprise. Oh! How happy we should all be to meet once more.[29]

James W. Woods, Daniel's brother-in-law, is much more direct in his criticism, but no better informed about the Mormons and Daniel's true situation among them.

> Burlington Iowa Sept 15th 1850
>
> Daniel
>
> I expect you will think that my letters are few and far between but not like angels' visits worth much when you get them but

the fact is you are so far removed both body and mind from all those for whom you ought to care and all those who have your true interests at heart that I suppose you don't care how things go along in this our country and amongst us heathens as the Mormons are pleased to term all who do not get with them—for I take it that it matters little what a man thinks is believable so that in his outward acts he conforms to their customs and again I have little encouragement to keep up a correspondence for the reason that I presume my letters undergo the same ordeal that those which you write which is that they are all opened and read before they are suffered to leave the Mormon settlements for fain something should be wrote that would not suit the leaders whose sole business I believe consists in deceiving their deluded followers and I shame to think that my beloved Brother is one. I would fain not say it but for the hope that it will not always be so.

Mrs. Woods writes and I presume will give you all the local news worth knowing and Joe Farly and Seth Robison will in this have told all and more than I could say in a letter. Eliza I presume will inform you that she did not receive the money you sent, and you can put that down as a fair sample of the confidence to be placed in a Mormon, and I will take occasion to say that I think you would be serving God in a much more acceptable manner if you would quit those deluded and deluding sons of the devil (for I am constrained to think them nothing better) and see after your own household. But perhaps I am to fast for I expect you have a household with you that you care more for than those whom you have declared before God and man to cherish and protect at this time I feel just as I write and I do hope that those who read this before you do will permit you to see it and if it should kindle one spark of that feeling I know you once had I shall be contented I am as ever your well wishing and

      Brother in heart
      James W. Woods[30]

  The money Daniel sent Eliza was probably California gold minted into Mormon eagles and double eagles, a temptation too great to resist for any poverty-stricken mail carrier, Mormon or non-Mormon. Woods's conjecture that mail to and from Mormon settlements was opened by Mormon leaders was prompted by the disappearance of Daniel's cash, but there is no evidence that censorship was ever practiced in Utah. That

Woods's opinion of the Mormons had greatly deteriorated since Daniel's departure can be attributed to the negative coverage of the Mormons generally, and the practice of polygamy in particular, in eastern newspapers.

Some of Daniel's relatives had joined in urging or even demanding him to forswear his Mormon faith, but by 1854 his sisters became reconciled to his convictions and to the fact that they would not see him again for many years. He still had not informed them about the extent of his new family and they did not ask questions that they did not want answered. While his cousins wrote long epistles explaining the error of his ways and citing scriptural references to prove their contentions, Pamela, Abigail, and Catherine contented themselves with giving him their family news and keeping him informed about the progress of Eliza and Albert who visited the Woods often. Daniel responded with as much information about himself and his activities as he thought they could bear. His letters were supplemented with copies of the *Deseret News* newspaper, now established in Great Salt Lake City, that often told more about him than he was able or willing to write.

In the five years after his arrival in Utah, Daniel's family grew from one to seventeen souls. Providing for such a large number of dependents in the unforgiving environment of the territory, while at the same time continuing to fulfill his church, civic, and military responsibilities, was a daunting prospect, but Daniel proved more than equal to the challenge. He brought to the Salt Lake Valley more hard currency than most of the Saints who came with him. Before leaving Nauvoo, he transferred most of his property to Eliza or to his sister Catharine and her husband. The latter paid him a modest sum for some city lots to help him on his way westward, and he was able to sell a few other parcels at heavily discounted prices. After purchasing his wagon, team, and other equipment, he brought the rest of his funds with him in coin. It was enough to see him through his first winter in the valley, but was mostly depleted at the end of it.

Throughout his life Daniel stated his occupation as farmer. This became a standing joke among his children because none of them ever saw him put his hands to a plow, but in the early Utah years he did. Beginning in 1849, he farmed his city lot in the Eighth Ward in partnership with his brother-in-law Lewis Robison who also had a lot in the same ward. Daniel and Lewis had become close friends as well as brothers-in-law in Illinois where they both operated farms on opposite sides of the Carthage Road next to the Nauvoo Cemetery a few miles south of the city. Their friendship was not adversely affected by Daniel's separation and later divorce from Eliza and they lived near one another and worked together in several enterprises during the remainder of their lives.[31]

Daniel also obtained a large farm tract a mile south of the Great Salt Lake City limits. This land, located at Twenty-first South Street and

Seventh East Street, would eventually be incorporated into the expanding city, but in 1850 it was open farmland on which he raised commercial crops for sale. On part of it he planted a large orchard of apple trees that, within a few years, provided fresh fruit for sale as well as for his family's use. A cider press was later installed to produce another commodity highly esteemed in the community.

Shortly after his first foray into Utah Valley in 1850, Daniel purchased a second farm there in the town of Pleasant Grove. He did not have time to work either of the farms himself, but hired others to run them for him, paying them with a portion of the harvested crop or in cash. One of his first employees was Stephen Taylor, a fifteen-year-old convert from England who by 1850 was already boarding with Daniel's family and working for him to help support his own family. Taylor was still employed by Daniel some twenty-five years later in 1875, and he had by then been joined by many others who found Squire Wells a fair and congenial employer.[32]

Daniel's business ventures outside of farming began with timber by way of road construction. On October 25, 1852, he was granted exclusive control of Emigration Canyon, including the privilege of harvesting wood, timber, lumber, poles, grass, stone, road, and water in it. In payment for this right, he was ordered to "make a good wagon road, and keep it in repair; also keep the same open to the public, for the purpose of hauling out wood and poles by paying him twenty-five cents per load for each load of wood and poles hauled out of said kanyon."[33]

Maintaining the Emigration Canyon road was important not only for the use of those hauling freight out of the canyon, but for the use of new arrivals who followed the same trail taken by the pioneers when they entered the Valley through it. After obtaining his contract for the canyon, Daniel published a notice stating that "arrangements are now making to construct a good road into the aforesaid kanyon, and that all persons are expected to desist from hauling out wood, poles or timber unless previous arrangements are made with John Killman, who is living in the kanyon." Killman (actually John Kilyon) was the first permanent resident in the canyon and was employed by Daniel to collect the tolls from those hauling freight on the road. Kilyon supplemented his income by hiring out as a laborer to those who cut timber and Daniel profited from the tolls they paid for the wood.[34]

In the summer of 1852, Daniel traveled back along the pioneer trail to the Green River crossing in the northeast corner of the Territory (now southwest Wyoming). There, with the help of some hired laborers and assistance from immigrants on the trail, he improved the primitive ferry that had been established in 1849 to take wagons across the stream. This was a difficult river crossing for wagons and animals and the ferry

Figure 9.3. This replica of the Green River Ferry was built in 1997 for the 150th anniversary celebration of the Mormon Pioneer National Historic Trail.

was used by everyone coming to Utah and California or turning northwest to Oregon. Daniel expanded the service by the addition of a second ferry about a mile above the original crossing point and by enlarging the barges to carry two wagons at a time across the hundred yards of swift-moving water. The ferries were rowed from east to west across the current and then towed back by mules pulling long ropes tied to the sterns.[35]

After completing the improvements, Daniel was granted a three year contract for operation of the ferry. The contract was approved by the territorial legislature in January 1853 and the term started on May 15. The legislature also set the rates of toll that could be charged: $3 for each vehicle not over 2,000 pounds, $4 for any vehicle between 2,000 and 3,000 pounds, $5 for those between 3,000 and 4,000 pounds, and $6 for those over 4,000 pounds; for each horse, mule, ox, or cow 50 cents, and for each sheep, goat, or swine 25 cents.[36]

Daniel was required to pay 10 percent of the ferry's gross income into the Perpetual Emigration Fund to assist new converts traveling to Utah from overseas. This fund helped bring more emigrants across the plains and so was actually an investment in promoting the business. As westward migration increased, the ferry was a lucrative source of income.

Despite the improvements Daniel made and the stable operation of the ferry he provided, his contract from the legislature caused howls of protest among non-Mormons, particularly Jim Bridger and other mountain men who did not want Mormon control of any part of the immigrant trail and correctly feared that it would reduce their profits from trading with travelers including Mormon immigrants. So great was the uproar over the ferry contract and Mormon control that the commander of Fort Laramie farther to the east wrote that he feared "bloodshed and disturbance" as a result. Bridger quarreled fiercely with the Saints both before and after they built Fort Supply in direct competition with him, forced him to flee Fort Bridger ahead of a posse Brigham Young sent to arrest him for selling guns to the Indians and bought the fort from his partner Louis Vasquez. The grumbling and complaints continued throughout the term of the contract, but no one was killed and the ferry continued to operate.[37]

When Daniel's contract expired in 1856, he helped Lewis Robison obtain a three year extension under the same terms and conditions, which commenced in May of that year. This contract did not prove as beneficial to Robison, however, as traffic on the trails was interrupted for almost a year during the Utah War crisis in 1857 and 1858.[38]

In 1854, Daniel went in to business with another brother-in-law, Brigham Young. Together they organized the Big Cottonwood Lumber Company and began logging trees and sawing lumber in the canyon southeast of Great Salt Lake City. The work began at the bottom of the canyon and gradually moved higher up as suitable trees in the lower canyon were depleted. Sawmills were constructed in the canyon to avoid the need for hauling heavy logs down the steep terrain into the valley. Trees were cut with axes and saws and dragged to the mills by ox teams. Additional mills were later built higher in the canyon as trees in the upper part were harvested. Mill A at the mouth was followed by Mill B farther up and the series eventually ended with Mill E, situated a short distance down-canyon from the town of Brighton and Mill F, located near the base of the present-day Solitude Ski Resort. The mills at first used water power to drive the main saws, but also employed pit saws and later steam engines to do the heavy work of cutting logs into lumber. Finished lumber was hauled on the road constructed in the canyon bottom. By the late 1850s the company, under Daniel's direction, was producing over a million board feet of lumber annually.[39]

The superintendent of sawmills was Archie Livingstone and his wife ran a boarding house nearby for the other mill employees. Rulon S. Wells, Daniel's son, described these workers as he knew them when he worked at the mills as a clerk filling orders for lumber, keeping workers' time records and making out payrolls.

Figure 9.4. Teamsters driving logging transports at the Big Cottonwood Lumber Company, ca. 1872.

There were sawyers and laborers—mill men—there were loggers or as we called them "bull-whackers," and Oh, my! how they did swear at those oxen. In all my life I have never heard such profanity as these men uttered, and when we protested they would defend themselves by saying the oxen understood no other language.[40]

Among the men who hauled lumber down the canyon into the city was William Stuart Brighton, for whom the town in the canyon is named. He arrived in the Salt Lake Valley with the Israel Evans Handcart Company in September 1857 and immediately went to work for Daniel as a teamster. He hauled lumber, coal, and other freight for Wells enterprises through the 1850s and in 1864 helped construct Mill F in Big Cottonwood Canyon. He continued hauling for the next several years and also filed a claim for which he received a federal land patent on eighty acres of land around Big Cottonwood Lake (now Silver Lake). This property became Brighton resort.[41]

With the same diligence that Daniel pursued his personal and business interests, he also continued his church and civic callings as superintendent of public works, as well as working with other leaders to found new settlements in the Salt Lake Valley and the Great Basin.

Congress refused to appropriate more funds for construction of a statehouse after the original amount of $20,000 was expended in 1852. That amount was not sufficient to finish even the first phase of the planned building, but Daniel carried on with construction using volunteer church labor and donated materials in order to complete the south wing as an independent structure. It was completed in 1855, but no other part of the building was built, and it was never used as a seat for the Territorial government except for a single session of the legislature that met there that year and decided to move the capital back to Great Salt Lake City.[42]

Much better used was the Endowment House that Daniel commenced work on in 1853. It stood on the northeast corner of Temple Square and was built of adobe. Its two-story central portion was flanked on either side by single-story wings. It was finished and dedicated in May 1855 and was the only building in which temple ceremonies and celestial marriages could be performed for the next twenty years until the St. George Temple was dedicated in 1877.[43]

Daniel also supervised the excavation and foundation work for the Salt Lake Temple. Ground was broken on February 14, 1853 with several thousand people observing the ceremony, including all of the non-Mormon civil and military authorities in the Territory. Two months later the cornerstones were laid; the southeast cornerstone by Brigham Young and his counselors, Heber C. Kimball and Willard Richards; and the other three cornerstones by the apostles and other general authorities of the church.

The temple was by far the grandest project undertaken by the Saints in Utah Territory. It was a huge endeavor for a community that numbered in 1853 less than six thousand souls in the Salt Lake Valley and less than twenty thousand in the entire Territory. The populace grew rapidly in the following decade, but thirty-nine years was still required to complete the massive edifice. The footprint of the building was 24,125 square feet, its five floors contained over 100,000 square feet of floor space, and its granite walls topped 107 feet in height. The highest of the six towers rose 210

Figure 9.5. Great Salt Lake City, looking south along East Temple Street (Main Street), 1853.

feet and each of the granite stones in the building was cut and shaped at the quarry in Little Cottonwood Canyon and hauled twenty miles to the temple site.[44]

Daniel, like many of the Saints who labored with him on the temple, did not live to see the temple completed or dedicated, but he directed its beginning phases of construction with his mind's eye as fixed on its building as that of Brigham Young, who said he saw its design in a vision. The walls were only about twenty-five feet high when Brigham died in 1877 and the towers were nearing completion when Daniel's life ended in 1891, but no other men labored more diligently to see the edifice reach its final state and its purpose fulfilled.[45]

In July 1849 Daniel journeyed with Brigham Young and others to the west side of the Salt Lake Valley and then around the Oquirrh Mountains into the Tooele Valley. They explored these areas, bathed in the briny waters of the Great Salt Lake and concluded that the western valleys were well-provided with grassland, antelope, wolves, quail, seagulls, and mosquitos. Based on their findings, Abraham Coon and others soon settled on the eastern foothills of the Oquirrhs and several communities were also established west of these mountains in the Tooele Valley.[46]

Other settlements were created wherever exploration indicated they could survive and prosper. By 1852 Daniel's travels with church leaders were less for the purpose of setting up new towns than for helping those already in existence to overcome problems and meet critical needs. With other leaders, he sought to encourage the settlers in their difficult tasks, buoy their spirits, and maintain their religious devotion through sermons and blessings. These multiple objectives required a larger and more diverse company. A trip to Sanpete County in April 1852 numbered sixty-four men, three boys, eleven women, and one girl; thirty wagons, sixty-seven horses, and twelve mules. Its purpose was for "visiting the southern settlements, exploring the country, ascertaining the situation of the Indians, making roads, building bridges, killing snakes, preaching the Gospel, and doing all other acts and things needed to be done as they may be led by the Good Spirit."[47]

Daniel was always captain of the camp on these ventures, charged with maintaining the safety of the travelers and the security and military preparedness of the settlements. As noted in his letter written on April 29 from Manti, Sanpete County, to Bishop Woolley in Salt Lake, he did not always feel that the Saints had done enough to back up their faith in the Lord's protection with practical defenses.

> The military here consists of two companies, one of horse, and one of footmen. Truly this is a people of great faith, for they rely on little else for protection. They settle out on their city lots and farms with all the freedom and apparent sense of security that the people of Illinois and Iowa do upon their prairies.
>
> I also am a believer in the principle of faith, but I like to see a proper exertion used on our part to insure its benefits . . . we should use the sense God has given us and the means which He has made us stewards over, according to the wisdom with which He has endowed us.
>
> Unquestionably, in time of great extremity He will interpose His mighty powers in behalf of His people. But a truce to sermonizing. I must conclude. It is now 4 o'clock and storming away—sometimes snow, then rain.[48]

In all these journeys, as in his other relationships with Brigham Young and other leaders of the church, Daniel was regarded as one of them. Although he held no high position in the Church hierarchy, his judgment was valued, his advice frequently sought and accepted, and his unstinting labor on behalf of the Saints appreciated. But he never assumed more than was offered by his brethren or sought a higher seat in their councils. He saw himself not as a ruler in the Kingdom of God, but a worker; one who had come late to the gospel of the restoration and was grateful just to be a member of the kingdom, a privilege for which he had sacrificed much. He felt that he should learn before he sought to teach, and should follow before he sought to lead. His humility about his own importance was chronicled in an anonymous newspaper article reporting on a trip to Davis County in 1855: "The Honorable Heber C. Kimball and the Honorable J. M. Grant [first and second counselors to

Brigham Young] took the carriage which was provided with a bed and suitable clothing. Lieutenant-General Daniel H. Wells took a quilt that he had been riding on, and a buffalo robe, and went out to the straw piles, where he made his lodging."[49]

10

Fighting Indians or Feeding Them, Family Matters, and Brigham's New Counselor

1855–1857

Three years after the Indian conflict in Utah County, Daniel's business labors were again interrupted by his duties as commander of the territorial militia, responding to another conflict between a group of Indians and Mormon settlers. "In 1852 there was trouble in Toolle [Tooele County] where settlements had been formed, between the settlers and Indians, and a company went out there; but I think the Indians got the best of it, and got away with the stock."[1]

The Indians' escape was accomplished before any militia troops arrived. Their tardiness may have been, in part, a reflection of Daniel's tolerant attitude toward stealing by Native Americans, a view that was shared by Brigham Young, but not by many other Mormons or Gentiles of that time.

> It was customary with the Indians to come to our camps while crossing the plains. We often hired them to herd our stock to make them feel friendly. We have found, if you trust an Indian when he comes to your camp he will not betray the trust; but if you act as if you were afraid to trust him and don't do it, he is very likely to steal, that is, if he can.
>
> In trusting Indians and treating them as human beings, we have never known them to fail to bring up our stock. If they see stock about not herded, they feel as though they had a right to take it as they would take any wild game. I don't think

Indians should be killed for stealing stock; they don't consider stealing a crime as we do.[2]

In late 1851 Brigham Young moved to abolish the slave trade in Utah Territory by ordering the Nauvoo Legion and all Mormons in the settlements to prevent the transportation of captives out of the Territory and to apprehend any persons, Indian or white, found engaged in this practice. The Northern Utes were the principal offenders, as much of their wealth and power was obtained by kidnapping Shoshone, Goshute, Paiute, Pahvant, and even other Ute children and teens and selling them in New Mexico Territory and Mexico where they were frequently worked to death in silver mines and other hazardous occupations. In addition to human traffic, the slave routes south to Taos and Santa Fe also carried stolen cattle, horses, and other contraband that was sold for cash or guns and ammunition. A young Indian brought $300 to $500 and Mexican traders sometimes came north to make purchases or to help the Utes increase their take of prisoners by planning more raids against weaker and less aggressive tribes.[3]

The slave trade was cruel and violent and debased the perpetrators of it almost as much as their victims. Daniel described one horrific incident he witnessed:

> They [the Utes] were in the habit of stealing children from the Piutes and selling them to Mexicans from New Mexico, who came up to trade. You could scarcely tell the difference between them and the Indians excepting the Mexicans wore hats. Slavery existed in Mexico at that time. Arapeen [brother of Chief Wakara] once had a stolen child that was sick; he could not sell it which made him cross and savage, and he took it by the heels, swung it around and dashed its brains out. Nothing but a fear of the consequences of an Indian war prevented our people from shooting him on the spot.[4]

Wakara [Walker], the Northern Utes' chief and his whole family, which included Black Hawk, the friendly Indian elevated to be a chief by Daniel H. Wells and the Mormons after the Fort Utah battle, were deeply involved in slave trading and refused to give it up. In the spring of 1853 Wakara and a group of his warriors held a group of Mormons from the Cedar City area at gunpoint long enough for the white and Hispanic slave traders whom the settlers were trying to capture to escape with their victims.[5]

Encouraged and assisted by Mexican slavers and white anti-Mormons, the Indians were spoiling for a fight over efforts to choke off the slave trade. Despite Brigham's continuing policy of non-violence, coupled with gifts and payments for peaceful coexistence, some Saints could not tolerate Indian customs and soon provided a provocation.

In July James Ivie, whose son Richard touched off the 1849 conflict by killing the Indian called Bishop, struck a Ute unconscious for beating his squaw over a bad trade he felt she had made. The victim was brought to Wakara's camp where he soon died of his injury. Days later a number of Indian braves visited Payson and were given a meal by the settlers there. As they were leaving, one of the Indians [said by Daniel H. Wells to be Arapeen] shot and killed Alexander Keele, the guard on duty, and the group then raced to tell Wakara that the killing at Fort Utah had been avenged. The Ute chief immediately broke camp and retreated into the mountains taking as much Mormon stock as his warriors could steal on the way. The war was on.[6]

Wakara and his men had learned from the heavy losses they suffered in 1850. They did not attack Mormon settlements or fortified positions, but struck at small groups in isolated areas and stole livestock not closely guarded. The *Deseret News* reported some early depredations:

> On the 19th of July the Indians attempted to surprise the settlement on Pleasant Creek [now Mount Pleasant] in the north part of Sanpete County, and stole horses and cattle at Manti and Nephi. On the 23rd, Clark Roberts and John Berry were wounded at Mount Pleasant while on their way to Provo in charge of an express. On the 23rd, Colonel Conover, who had been sent from Provo on the 19th with a command of 150 men in pursuit of the Indians, sent forth a scouting party, which encountered a band of 20 or 30 Indians near Pleasant Creek, and killed six of them. On the night of August 10 a party under Lieutenant Burns, encamped on Clover Creek, was attacked, and one of them was wounded, several animals being lost. On the 17th, four men who were hauling lumber near Parley's Park, east of Salt Lake City were fired upon and two of them were killed.[7]

As soon as news of the Utah Valley altercations reached them, Brigham Young and Daniel H. Wells, responded with a plan of action to contain the violence. They did not want another bloody battle like the 1849 conflict, and they did not order up any company of the Nauvoo Legion, but instead sought to nullify the Indians' hit and run tactics by issuing the ten-point General Order No. 1 to all the settlements to protect themselves and deny the Indians any opportunity to attack or rob them. This order was sent to every settlement and also published in the *Deseret News*.

> Headquarters Nauvoo Legion
> and the Militia of the Territory of Utah
>
> G.S.L. City, July 21, 1853
>
> General Orders, No.1
>
> 1. Owing to the present position of our Indian relations it has become apparent that the policy of constructing forts and occupying them, which has been so often urged by the General Authorities of this Territory upon the various settlements, should now be adopted and rigidly enforced.
> 2. The commandants of the various Military Districts in the Territory . . . will cause all of the forces under their commands respectively to repair immediately to their posts in their various settlements and locations . . .
> 3. All absentees, citizens, and residents of the various settlements and districts above mentioned are hereby requested and instructed to repair to their various locations without delay, and all are desired to remain at home in order to enable the various officers and authorities to carry into effect these orders and instructions.
> 4. The commandants of the several districts will, upon the receipt of these orders, proceed to put all the settlements within their respective districts in a state of efficient defense . . . [have] a good and substantial fort . . . the people should universally occupy them and reside in them . . . construct good and sufficient corrals for stock . . . be vigilant in preserving all the stock and grain from the Indians and in no case permit an Indian to commit any depredation upon the property in any of your districts . . .
> 5. They will also proceed to repair and put in complete order their arms, ordnance. and prepare ammunition suitable. that every possible means may be in readiness, and neglect no opportunity of procuring ammunition, guns, and means of defense, and see that all is kept in a perfect state for immediate use.
> 6. No person must be allowed to give, sell, or in any way dispose of to any Indian man, woman, or child, any gun, powder,

lead, caps, flints, or any other weapon or species of ammunition, or give them any aid or comfort whatever . . .

7. All stock should be strongly herded by armed herdsmen and strongly guarded and corralled at night.
8. It is understood that the Indians will continue to commit depredations as they shall have opportunity, which opportunity should be avoided as much as possible, but we wish it distinctly understood that no retaliation be made and no offense offered, but for all to act entirely on the defensive until further orders, but be particular in ascertaining the person, tribe, or name of every Indian and forward the same to this office, that it may be known who they are.
9. To all we wish to say that it is evident that the Indians intend to prey and subsist upon our stock and will shoot and kill whenever and wherever they can. It is therefore expected that these orders and instructions will be rigidly enforced and complied with . . . No excuses will justify any material variation, and we call upon all the citizens without exception to render their most extended aid and assistance in carrying them out to the very letter . . . whether it suits every individual circumstance or not, and the commandants of the various Military Districts and authorities of the various settlements are required to carry them into effect.
10. The commandants of the several districts are required as soon as these orders come to hand, to forthwith publish the same, and to cause copies to be forwarded to all the settlements in their respective districts, and the bearer of these dispatches is instructed to give notice, and publish them as he goes.

It is desirable in order to completely carry out the policy indicated in the foregoing that no threats or intimidations be made or exercised toward the Indians, no more than if nothing unusual had occurred to destroy peaceful relations heretofore existing.

                    Brigham Young
                    Governor, Ex~Officio Superintendent of Indian Affairs and Commander-in-Chief of the Militia.

                    Daniel H. Wells
                    Lieutenant General
                    Commanding Nauvoo Legion[8]

Before Order No. 1 could be fully implemented, additional attacks inflicted further casualties and damage on the Saints over a wide area. "On September 30, four men on their way to Manti with ox teams loaded with wheat were killed and mutilated at Uintah Springs. October 2, eight Indians were killed and others captured in a skirmish at Nephi. October 4, two Mormons named John E. Warner and William Mills were killed in the gristmill near Manti."[9]

The most tragic event of the war occurred on October 26 and those who died in it were as much victims of the stupidity of some white immigrants as of the Indians who shot them.

Lieut. John W. Gunnison first came to Utah Territory in 1849 as second-in-command of the Howard Stanbury expedition assigned by the government to explore and survey the Salt Lake Valley. In 1852 he published a book, outside the expedition's official report, describing his personal observations and interactions (generally favorable) with the Saints. Nearly all Mormons who met Gunnison regarded him as a friend and an objective observer of Utah Territory and its inhabitants.[10]

The Mormons sought advice from Gunnison in the earlier Indian troubles and he had helped mediate between the hostile parties, winning him praise and trust among the Mormons, but not so much among the Indians, as later events proved.[11]

In 1853 Gunnison, now promoted to captain, returned to Utah Territory as leader of an expedition charged with exploring for a railroad route west from the Kansas-Nebraska border to Utah and beyond. He entered the southern part of the Territory in October, stopped briefly at Provo, resupplied his group at Fillmore and divided them into two parties. At the head of the advance group, Gunnison camped on the Sevier River on October 25. He had been warned by Mormons of the Indian hostilities, but felt that he had a good relationship with the Utes and other tribes and could avoid any confrontation with them. He might have been correct, but was given no opportunity to negotiate or even to speak. Early the next morning his party was attacked by Indians who probably didn't know who he was.[12]

Daniel graphically described the incident and its immediate cause:

> Captain Gunnison was telegraphical engineer for the government. He and his party came in by way of the Spanish Fork trail; they landed [stopped] in Gunnison where they obtained an interpreter. They were warned about the hostile state of the Indians. Captain Gunnison knew we were friendly with the Indians, and he himself knew how to get along with them, and he thought he could get along without any difficulty. He went

from there to Fillmore where he got supplies. Before they got to Fillmore they divided; he took, I think, eight soldiers from Beckwith, and Beckwith camped on the Creek near Fillmore with the remainder of the men, while he detoured [to] Sevier Lake in Millard County. It was perhaps 40 miles west of the settlement from where Beckwith remained.

Anson Call, now of Bountiful, Davis County, had charge at Fillmore. Previous to Gunnison's going there some emigrants passed through, they went by the southern route thinking to escape hostile Indians. These Indians were exercised, but they had not committed much depredations up to that time. They had, however, shot two or three men and driven off some stock in Sanpete. Pavantee, the chief, acknowledged Kanash, as their chief. They were decidedly friendly, and they used their influence with Walker and others to quit their depredations . . . These emigrants declared at Fillmore to our people that they would shoot Indians at sight, if they came around their camp.

Mr. Call told them these Indians were friendly, and they would be sure to come to their camp, as was their custom, hoping to get something to eat or some little present . . . Brother Call warned them against shooting the Indians, telling them if they did so the Indians would surely seek revenge. This warning, however, was not heeded; they felt quite prepared to defend themselves and didn't care. When Indians are hostile they will withdraw to the hills; they won't come around your camp. But these Pahvant Indians came around the emigrants' camp as was their custom around ours. The result was, they killed one Indian and wounded one or two others. The Indians retaliated, shooting one of their number. I think his name was Hart. They returned to Fillmore.

Brother Call told them they had done wrong. They wanted Call then to furnish them an escort. He told them he could not spare any men as they themselves were not strong enough. They started on again. Call told them the Indians would follow them in all probability; and sure enough they did. Call said he heard from them; they went as far as Cedar Valley followed by the Indians; somewhere in this region they [the Indians] gave up the chase and started to return. They reached Sevier Lake at the time that Gunnison and party were there.

The Gunnison party consisted of himself, two engineers named Chrisfelt and Kerr, eight soldiers. a cook, and Potter, who was the guide and interpreter. They camped within a

Figure 10.1. Portrait of Daniel H. Wells, ca. 1856. This is the earliest known photograph of him.

hundred yards of the brush. In order to be safe they should have kept farther out. I don't know whether they had finished making their observations, but they calculated to move that day—the day they were killed. The Indians fired on the party out from the brush, while the party were at breakfast, sitting at table, killing Gunnison, Chrisfelt and Kerr, also the cook. Potter and the soldiers were [went] after the horses. Potter and four soldiers were killed, and four soldiers escaped.

Before Gunnison fell, he raised up his hands to the Indians, thinking he could get them to stop shooting. They were too mad, though, and Gunnison's was the first party of white men they met after the affair [with the emigrant train], and they avenged themselves, as is their wont to do. Gunnison had been warned about it, and our own people felt unsafe, at Fillmore, because of the hostile feeling, of the Indians. Walker at the time was away; he and others had made a raid and left. The emigrant company was said to be from Missouri; that is all we knew about them, as they were merely an ordinary train. They passed through Salt Lake, but there was no particular attention paid to them, as they were merely an ordinary train.[13]

Rumors circulated after the attack blamed the Mormons for either killing Gunnison and his men themselves or inciting the Indians to do so. But Lieut. E. G. Beckwith, second-in-command of the expedition, investigated the murders and in his official report concluded the opposite: the Mormons had no part in the attack and the Indians acted alone. He noted that the "statement which has from time to time appeared (or been copied) in various newspapers . . . charging the Mormons or Mormon authorities with instigating the Indians to, if not actually aiding them in, the murder of Captain Gunnison and his associates, is, I believe, not only entirely false, but there is no accidental circumstance connected with it affording the slightest foundation for such a charge."[14]

Anti-Mormon sentiment was not quieted by Beckwith's report and a second printing of Gunnison's book, ordered by his widow in 1857, contained a foreword by W. W. Drummond, who served a short time in Utah as a federal judge, that blamed the Mormons for this attack and others and called loudly on its first page for revenge against the "fiendish perpetrators of this cold-blooded murder." This remained the accepted view among non-Mormons for decades.[15]

Even in the face of the killings and property losses, Daniel continued to pursue a defensive strategy of fortifying settlements, guarding stock, and giving the Indians no opportunity to do harm to people or property. On July 25, he sent the Legion's Col. George A. Smith south to Utah County and placed him in charge of enforcing Order No. 1 among the Saints. He carried with him General Order No. 2, which stated his mission clearly and required all settlers to assist him.

Headquarters, Nauvoo Legion
Adjutant General's Office

G.S.L. City, July 25, 1853

General Orders, No.2

1. Colonel George A. Smith is hereby assigned to the command of all the Military Districts of this Territory south of G.S.L. County, and is strictly enjoined and commanded to enforce Orders No.1, of the 21st.

2. It is distinctly understood that all the people shall assemble into large and permanent forts, and no man is at liberty to refuse to obey this order without being dealt with as an enemy.

3. All surplus stock that is not particularly needed for teams and milk must be driven to this city and placed in the charge of the Presiding Bishop in this city until further orders.

4. Colonel Smith is fully authorized and required to carry out the instructions which have heretofore been universally given by the Governor and authorities of this Territory in regard to defense, and all the people are now required to obey these instructions as Colonel Smith shall direct.

5. Colonel G. A. Smith's instructions and counsel will be those of the Executive of the Territory; and he will be sustained by him in enforcing those which he has, or shall receive, and in doing all other necessary things, which in his judgment he may think proper.

>Brigham Young
>Governor, Ex-officio Superintendent of Indian Affairs and Commander-in-chief of the Militia.

>Daniel H. Wells
>Lieutenant~General, Commanding Nauvoo Legion.[16]

Many settlers still thought that they should retaliate for depredations by hunting down the raiders responsible and killing them, but Colonel Smith would not allow them to leave their families and stock to chase Indians through country the natives knew far better than the Saints. Though not entirely successful, the implementation of strong defensive measures and careful watches over stock and property reduced the targets of opportunity and left the Indians fewer chances to gain profit or revenge from attacks. The war quieted down into a tense stalemate that mostly kept the two sides separated through the end of the year. That separation left the Indians with little plunder from raids and no gifts or aid from the settlers or the government. By November some Indians had asked that peace be restored so that the benefits of good relations with the Mormons could again begin to flow.[17]

Black Hawk returned to Utah Valley by the summer of 1854 with about thirty warriors including Tintick, Peteteneat, Highforehead, Quieah, and Squash-Head. These were identified by the settlers as some "of the ones that done the most of the mischeaf last summer." They were still not overly friendly, but showed a willingness to at least "give peace a chance." Always ready to meet opponents more than halfway, Brigham and Daniel traveled to Chicken Creek in Juab County in May and there concluded a peace agreement with Wakara and the other chiefs.[18]

> When we approached them Walker was in his "Wickiup"; he had fastened it down to within about four feet of the ground and had to crawl to get in and out. I remember our having a good laugh at him because of this. He sat in this arrangement like a prince and never rose at all. He remarked, through our interpreter, that Brigham was a big Chief, and Walker was a big Chief. Suiting the action to the word, he put up his two thumbs to indicate that he was as big a chief as Brigham, and Brigham as big as he. In the treaty the Indians agreed to give up the stolen horses—at least, all they had of them then in their possession. Walker wouldn't talk, he had a child sick. If his child died, some one else, he thought, might die, and it was a long time before we got him to talk. He asked us to administer to the child (through prayer and laying on of hands) which we did. President Young asked him what he wanted in the way of presents. He said, "I don't know—you talk." I think he was afraid he would say something less than President Young would give him. After this treaty Walker became very friendly. He traveled with us that day to Cedar City and camped with us that night. He did this for our protection, fearing that some of his Indians, who did not know of the treaty, might make a raid on us. We enjoyed good peace after that for several years.[19]

Once the peace treaty was agreed, Daniel distributed the gifts that sealed the agreement in the minds of the Indians more than any other part of the talks. Among other presents, he tossed a plug of tobacco to each of the warriors, but Wakara took offense at his casual manner of distribution and let his gift fall to the ground. He refused to touch it saying he would not have a gift thrown to him like a bone to a dog. Though Daniel had not intended any insult, he quickly recognized the Ute's point of view, selected a new packet and presented it to Wakara with a formal bow. With his status duly recognized, the chief's anger evaporated and the meeting ended with good feelings on both sides.[20]

As Daniel stated, there was no further serious conflict with the Indians for a decade, but some of the native continued to steal stock and other items from the Saints and to frighten them by their aggressive behavior. Many settlers still thought Brigham and Daniel were wrong to deal with Native Americans through friendship, education, and gifts. Col. Peter Conover, a Nauvoo Legion officer who had led a company of men on a punitive foray against the Indians the previous summer, felt that a military response was called for. He wrote Daniel in September, months after the peace treaty was signed, that the Indians broke into houses, scared women and children, stole anything they get their hands on, and threatened to drive off stock. He asked pointedly whether the Saints should continue to bear such outrages, clearly hoping for permission to suppress them by force.[21]

Although Conover's letter was addressed to Daniel, the caustic response came from Brigham, the prophet calling one of his flock to repentance and telling him to adhere to the policy of peaceful coexistence as any good Christian must.

> Your letter by yesterdays express is received, from which I learn that the Indians in your vicinity are getting quite saucy, are pilfering &c. You very naturally inquire "shall we bear it?" Now what would you do if you did not bear it? Would you wrangle and quarrel with them when you know that that would only make matters worse, and lead on to even [further] hostilities? . . . I can scarce remember an instance where an Indian was civilly treated, that he abused a family. Tis true it sometimes becomes a little burdensome to comply with all of their requirements, but they are not generally very extensive, and it is much better to do so when a person can and do it with a good grace too, as tho' they were willing. I tell you the spirit of the [Latter-day Saint] people instead of holding them [up] by their faith, is against [the Indians], for the least aggravation or offense, damn them, kill them, is the first thing you hear, the boys set the dogs on them and threaten them; now until the people can get a better spirit in themselves toward them, how can you expect that the Indians will have a better.[22]

Daniel and other church leaders continued to urge that the Indians be treated as children in need of spiritual guidance and education rather than as enemies to be exterminated. For the next ten years this policy, though it required considerable forbearance on both sides, preserved the general peace and prevented violence against the whites as well as the killing of Indians. It was often expensive for the Mormons, who had to bear the cost of the stock and other supplies given to the tribes when the federal government refused to supply funds to the territorial authorities for this purpose, but the cost of preserving the peace was always less than the cost of war in both lives and property.[23]

While the Indians' hostility toward their Mormon neighbors was reduced to an often-strained but mostly peaceful co-existence, Mormon conflicts with Gentile settlers in Utah and with federal appointees to government positions in the territory caused intense friction between the two groups. About half of the officials appointed for Utah by President Fillmore in 1851 were Mormon, including Brigham Young as governor. The others, including Judge W. W. Drummond, who later falsely accused the Mormons of having murdered Captain Gunnison and his party, quickly revealed their anti-Mormon attitudes by the manner of their administration and the tenor of their court rulings. Their conduct roused an equal antagonism among the Mormons that soon caused the federal appointees to leave Utah, taking with them the money appropriated by Congress for administration of the Territory. Returning to the east, these officials claimed the Mormons were guilty of "malicious sedition" and had not received them properly.[24] How the Saints might have dealt more respectfully with Drummond, who left his wife and children in the east, presented his mistress as his wife in Utah, and then condemned Mormon polygamy in the harshest terms, was never explained, nor was the theft of the Territory's funds ever redressed. The officials' anti-Mormon rhetoric found a ready audience in Washington and other eastern cities and increased the hostility of the populace and the federal government toward the Saints and their leaders.[25]

Other federal officials were appointed, but the conflicts between Mormons and Gentiles continued in the communities, government offices, and courts of the territory. In Washington, anti-Mormons pressed strenuously for President Franklin Pierce to replace Governor Young with a non-Mormon appointee. A memorial from the mostly-Mormon Utah legislature, a petition signed by territorial officials and leading Mormon and Gentile businessmen, and the territory's congressional delegate, Dr. John M. Bernheisel, all urged that Brigham be reappointed for another term.[26]

Late in 1854 Lieut. Col. Edward J. Steptoe arrived in Utah at the head of a military engineering unit again surveying a route for a transcontinental railroad. Like Captain Gunnison before him, Colonel Steptoe got along well with the Mormons and, with the other officers in his command, he signed the petition urging Governor Young's reappointment. Colonel Steptoe was highly regarded in Washington, and President Pierce, bowing to the intense anti-Mormon sentiment around him, appointed him as Utah's new governor. The colonel, however, saw no reason to replace Brigham and declined the appointment. His refusal of the position left Brigham in office until another appointment was made, which did not occur until years later.[27]

While Colonel Steptoe was a gentleman of high moral character who respected the Mormon social order, even though he did not agree with it, many of the soldiers in his unit seduced women, both married and single, wherever they went in Utah. They found willing partners among those who were disaffected with the church, their spouses, or the living conditions in the territory. When Colonel Steptoe and his men departed to continue their work in California, as many as a hundred LDS women abandoned family and faith to go with them, joining a train of camp-followers similar to those that accompanied other army units in the field.[28]

The Saints were outraged by the defections and the manner in which they were accomplished. The immoral conduct of the soldiers and the non-military people with them was anathema to Daniel H. Wells and all the leaders of the church. The loss of so many Saints turned them against any army presence in the territory and made them determined to resist it, lest having soldiers in their midst again expose their people to what Daniel later called "the hell which follows after."[29]

For the moment, however, the army was out of the territory, Governor Young was retained in office, the other federal officials in Utah were tolerable to the Saints, and the Indian tribes were pledged to keep the peace (although not necessarily to refrain from stealing stock). The Saints were forbidden to chase or kill Indians for any infractions on the treaty and strongly encouraged to have few dealings with Gentiles, whether they were anti-Mormon or not. Daniel was able to concentrate his labors on supporting his family, supervising the growing number of public works, and fulfilling his territorial duties as attorney general.

The year 1855 was difficult for the people in Utah Territory. The harvest that year, adversely affected by hot dry weather and another attack of crickets and grasshoppers, brought in only about two-thirds the amount of grain and produce as the previous year. With hundreds of new arrivals coming into the settlements from the east and Europe, food became scarce and prices rose. A bitterly cold winter followed and delayed the spring planting of the following year, which impacted the next harvest as well.[30]

Daniel's family weathered the hard times better than many others. All of the ten children born to his wives during the years 1850 through 1854 survived infancy and eventually grew to adulthood. Not all of those born in later years were so fortunate; nor was Daniel's adopted son, John Brigham Wells. Louisa's first-born was a happy ten-year-old in the spring of 1856, but he fell ill in early June with a malady for which no treatment was then available. He died on June 9 and his body was buried in the Salt Lake City Cemetery.[31]

As Daniel and Louisa mourned the death of their child, they received word that Daniel's sister Lucy Ann Coombs had died the previous fall in Ripon, Wisconsin, where she had moved with her husband Joseph and their three surviving children in 1849. Lucy was the third of Daniel's older sisters to die at a relatively young age. Like the rest of his family in the east, he had not seen Lucy Ann since his last visit to New York in 1843. He had never met any of her children.[32]

In August, two months after John Brigham's death, Hannah Wells gave birth to Luna Pamela Wells, her third child and Daniel's twelfth. Their joy in their new daughter was short-lived, however, as Luna died shortly after her first birthday in November 1857.[33]

Another death that occurred in the final month of 1856 had a momentous impact on Daniel. Jedediah M. Grant, Brigham Young's second counselor in the First Presidency of the LDS Church, had held the position for less than three years. The youthful Grant, age thirty-eight, had replaced Willard Richards who died young in March 1854. Grant was a passionate orator who soon became known as "Brigham's Sledgehammer" because of his fiery condemnation of sin and his calls for repentance and a renewal of faith.[34]

Grant's preaching talents were well fitted to the "Mormon Reformation," which was then in progress throughout Utah, and for which he was sent to preach in the settlements during the fall of 1856. Beginning with a three-day sojourn in Davis County, Grant denounced smoking, drinking, profaning, Sabbath breaking, and immoral living, which, though proscribed, were common among church members. These practices and others, which had been tolerated during the early years of settlement in Utah Territory because the talents and labor of all the people were needed to build a civilization in the wilderness, were now to be stopped. Grant told the Saints to rededicate themselves to observing gospel principles more faithfully.

Hundreds of people presented themselves for rebaptism as a symbol of their determination to reform their lives. The reformation message quickly spread to other Mormon communities as other church leaders traveled around the territory, denouncing spiritual decay, and calling for repentance. All the First Presidency, as well as several apostles, gave fiery sermons in favor of greater orthodoxy and rebaptism in preparation for living on a celestial level prior to the second coming of Christ, which all the Saints thought would happen soon.

The strain of extensive speaking and traveling long hours exposed in a wagon to the intense winter cold injured Grant's health and in late November, at the conclusion of his speaking tour, he was stricken with pneumonia. His condition worsened rapidly and he died on December 1, nine days after the birth of his youngest son, Heber J. Grant. He was only forty years old at his passing but left seven wives and a dozen children in addition to Heber.[35]

On January 4, 1857, a month after Grant's funeral, Daniel H. Wells was ordained an apostle by Brigham Young who then set him apart the same day as second counselor in the First Presidency of the Church. He was formally sustained in the position by a vote of the people in the April general conference.[36]

Brigham's choice of his new counselor, which he made alone, was both logical and popular with the Saints, although perhaps not with all of the apostles and seventies from whose ranks all previous counselors had been chosen. Daniel had long been Brigham's advisor and, in his mind, of equal standing with the president's childhood friend and first counselor Heber C. Kimball. With Willard Richards and Jedediah M. Grant both gone too soon, Daniel was a natural choice to fill the large space left in the First Presidency. Moreover, Brigham trusted Daniel even though he had been a member of the Church for less time than any of the other apostles. Because he had joined when the church was at rock bottom and had done so at the cost of his family and all his worldly goods, Brigham knew that Daniel had a testimony gained through sacrifice, and no personal ambitions but the building of the kingdom. He was well-liked and well-respected among the Saints, many of whom knew the circumstances of his conversion and the services he had rendered to the Saints both before and after it.

In one respect, Daniel's elevation to the third position in the church hierarchy was a change in tone, if not substance, in leadership. He was not an archconservative in religious doctrine or practice. His conception of religion was as practical as Brigham's: men should do what was right because it was right; do it consistently, without ostentation; and help others to also do it while understanding and tolerating their weaknesses until they could overcome them. He had lived most of the precepts of Mormonism even before joining the church and had embraced the new doctrine of plural marriage and eternal family as a heaven-sent blessing.

Daniel was not equal as a public speaker to Brigham or Heber C. Kimball, to say nothing of the clever and entertaining Grant. His voice was pitched high for an orator and did not carry as well as those of his fellow apostles. He was not as comfortable speaking, as were many leading Mormons, although the requirements of his new calling soon made his remarks more practiced and more polished. He preached the message of repentance, rededication, and rebaptism, but his manner was always kind and his emphasis one of persuasion to do right rather than condemnation for past failure. He taught more by example than exhortation and continued to live after his call to the First Presidency much as he had before.[37]

In his first general conference address, delivered in the Bowery on the afternoon of April 6, 1857, Daniel acknowledged his limitations and stated clearly his priorities.

> Brothers and Sisters, I do not know that I shall be able to speak so that all of you can hear; neither do I feel that what I may say is of the greatest importance. I have never felt that confidence in addressing the people that perhaps I should, but I feel today as I always have felt, an interest for the welfare of the Church and Kingdom of God to which I belong, and to devote myself and all I possess or can control to its progress and building up.[38]

He then discussed the status of the numerous public works under development in the community and urged the Saints to contribute to their completion by donations of cash, materials, and labor. He asked for more men to work on the Big Cottonwood Canal, which was being constructed from the mouth of the canyon to Temple Square for the purpose of floating stone from the quarry to the temple site and for irrigation. He noted the need for stonecutters to quarry and shape the granite blocks to be used in the temple and offered to train unskilled men willing to contribute labor to these tasks. He implored the Saints to repay the loans many of them had received from the Perpetual Emigration Fund so that the fund could remain solvent and continue to assist other members in traveling to Utah and establishing themselves on their arrival. And he urged all the Saints to seek first for the Kingdom of God, saying,

> What is prosperity? According to my understanding it is not so much gaining the things of this world as it is progressing in the knowledge of God. What are true riches? They are not so much the obtaining of the things of this world, as they are in securing the principles and keys which unlock the treasures of heavenly wisdom, of the knowledge of God and the things that pertain to eternity. These are the riches we are seeking after; this is the progress we wish to make. In order to accomplish this, it is necessary that we should be faithful in all matters committed to our trust, honest before God and obedient to the counsels of his servants. I know that I have ever felt it to be so, and I have felt to do more than to talk . . .
>
> I feel more like receiving exhortation than giving it. I feel more like doing than talking; still I do not wish to withhold any good thing I may be in possession of. I feel to do what the Lord desires and will help me to do; I care not what it is, so it is the word and will of the Lord, I should strive to do it . . .
>
> If we have been faithful over a few things, let us try to be faithful in all, committed to our trust, and increase. Let us

seek for eternal riches, get hold of the principles and keys of knowledge which shall unlock the treasures of heaven to our understanding; that we may be better qualified for the performance of our duties, that we may go forward in the work of God and be faithful children; that we may seek unto him our Father with full purpose of heart, and work righteousness all the days of our lives with perfect hearts and willing hands.[39]

Speaking in a later conference address in the Old Tabernacle, Brigham Young said of his own calling and his counselors, "It is my calling and office to dictate in the affairs of the Church and Kingdom of God on earth; that is what you have chosen me to do for years, with Brother Heber and others for my Counselors, two of whom have passed behind the veil, and I now have a third, Brother Daniel H. Wells, who is as good a man as ever lived."[40]

One person who did not agree with that assessment was Heber C. Kimball. Heber was born June 14, 1801 in Vermont, the same month, year, and state as Brigham Young. He was ordained an apostle February 14, 1835, the same day as Brigham, and was, from 1839 onward, the senior member of the twelve after Brigham, the quorum's president. He was sustained as first counselor in the First Presidency on December 27, 1847, the same day Brigham was sustained as president of the church. Brigham's friendship with and regard for Heber placed him unequivocally as the most important leader in the church after the prophet himself.[41]

But Heber, who had worked effectively with Willard Richards and Jedediah M. Grant, the men who preceded Daniel as second counselor, felt his position among church members and his long-standing relationship with Brigham threatened by Squire Wells. Whether this was simply because Daniel was younger and better-educated than Heber, or because Brigham had developed such a high degree of trust in him and relied upon him to serve in so many capacities, is unclear. Because Daniel was not an apostle prior to his calling as second counselor and yet was chosen over older, long-standing members of the quorum, Heber may have felt his own position diminished.

Heber later noted privately that he was deeply offended by some action (or inaction) against him by Daniel and predicted that God would punish Daniel for this sleight and exalt Heber among the Saints. Two statements in Heber's private journals, made public only after his death, reveal the depth of his feeling against Daniel:

> G.S.L. City, March the [day missing, but
> between 1 and 10] 1862
>
> This night the Lord told me the time was near I Heber should be lifted up on high in favor of Israel and my [the Lord's] Servent Daniel Wells s[h]ould see Sorrow even as my Servent Heber had to his full becaus he, Daniel, had pressed my servent Heber and held him at a distance in stead of doing him good as he might, when he had the power in his hands.
>
> These words are true and shall come to pass in the Name of Jesus Christ, Amen.[42]

Again, some three to four week later, Heber wrote:

> G.S.L. City, March the 29, 1862
>
> It was told me the time was near when I Heber should be lifted up in the Eyes of Israel and Daniel H. Wells should see sorrow Even as he had caused sorrow to come on his servent HCK becaus he sat on me and oppressed me when he had power to do me good. Even so Amen. HCK.[43]

Why Heber felt oppressed or how he had been "sat on" by Daniel or what good the latter might have done him, he never revealed to anyone. Daniel never mentioned any conflict or distancing of himself from the first counselor and was unaware of Heber's feelings. But the fact remains that Daniel's influence with Brigham increased significantly after his calling as second counselor and the number and scope of his assignments grew from 1857 onward while Heber's duties remained static.

It is interesting to note that the discourses of noted LDS general authorities, published in twenty-six volumes dating from January 1853 to January 1886, include 111 talks by Heber C. Kimball over a period of fifteen years (1853–1868) and only forty-seven by Daniel H. Wells over a period of twenty-eight years. Heber preached more often to the general church population (7.4 times per year) than did Daniel (1.7 times per year), which indicates that, at least publicly, the former's position and influence remained intact, whatever Brigham's private feelings about their individual merits may have been.[44]

Speaking in the Bowery on a Sunday morning about the time Heber made his journal entries, Brigham Young remarked, "I have been obliged to ask Brother Wells to work like a slave to deal for me here and there and change property, and to keep him running until he was almost run out." The confidence that Brigham showed in Daniel's ability to handle whatever task he undertook may have been the source of Heber's feeling that he was being outperformed by the junior counselor.[45]

A week after Daniel's call, his sister Pamela Wells died in Trenton, New York, at age fifty-three. Pamela was the fourth of Daniel's older sisters to pass away at a young age and, like the previous three, he did not learn of her death until months after the event. Pamela, alone among the Wells sisters, had never married and left no children. She had for many years cared for Henry Wells Ross, the only child of her sister Eliza, who died in 1841. Both had been living since at least 1850 with Daniel's sister Abigail and her husband Stephen Rockwell. Henry was eighteen and still in school when Pamela died.[46]

The week after April conference, Daniel's life was brightened by the birth of Emeline Young Wells, Louisa's fifth child, and the next week by the birth of Emily Harris Wells, Martha's second child. Another daughter, Susan Annette Wells, first child of Susan Alley Wells, joined the family in November, three weeks after Hannah's daughter Luna died. Between the first Wells births of 1857 and the last, Daniel faced challenges greater than any that he or the Church had previously known.[47]

In April the First Presidency and a large group of church leaders, many with their wives, traveled north to visit Fort Lemhi, a missionary outpost that had been established in 1855. The company of 115 men, 22 ladies, and 5 boys traveled in a train of twenty-eight carriages and twenty-six wagons. Arapeen, the Ute chief, and his wife Wispit were among the group. To give greater speed on the trail, all the vehicles were pulled by horses rather than oxen. For the same reason the party brought no livestock with them. They arrived on May 8 bringing needed supplies and a strong moral boost to the Fort Lemhi settlers.

About thirty men had labored for two years to create a viable settlement in the Oregon Territory and teach the Shoshone Indians in the area. A few of the Mormons learned to speak Shoshoni, and preached to the Indians, but had little success converting them or in teaching them new ways of living. Having struggled to raise sufficient crops for their own needs, the Fort Lemhi pioneers welcomed the materials as well as the spiritual support brought by the Salt Lake visitors.[48]

President Young and Heber C. Kimball praised the accomplishments of the settlers and reminded them about the missionary objective of their work. Heber said that the men, who had no women living with them, should become one people with the Indians by marrying them. Following his instructions to "go now and take their daughters to wife," several men proposed to Indian women but none were accepted at that time. Brigham urged caution in social dealings with the Indians so as not to provoke resentment, but eventually several of the Fort Lemhi missionaries did marry Indians.[49]

Daniel H. Wells was silent on gospel doctrine and marriage and spent his time organizing and drilling the Fort Lemhi militia, to better prepare them for defense of the settlement and to demonstrate their readiness and discipline to the watching Indians, hundreds of whom visited Fort Lemhi to see the "Big Chiefs" of the Mormons.[50]

Impressed with the rich land, abundant water, and enormous tracts of timber in the Oregon Territory, the First Presidency selected a location for a second fort in the Salmon River valley. They also visited the Lewis and Clark Trail that led from the Missouri River into Oregon and a newly developed trail from the Fort Lemhi settlement north to the Bitterroot Valley in present-day Montana. With the help of Arapeen, they met with Indians from the Bitterroot and established a cordial relationship, marked with the presentation of blankets to them.

By the conclusion of their visit, the First Presidency felt that future Mormon settlements should be established to the north of Utah Territory, an area that had greater resources and potential than the southern settlements the Saints had earlier colonized. The group started for home on May 13, but diverted for further explorations on the way. They did not return to Great Salt Lake City until May 26, more than a month after leaving.[51]

By the end of the following month rumors were circulating in Utah that the newly elected president, Democrat James Buchanan, would appoint a new governor for Utah. The rumors also raised the possibility that another military force would be sent to install the new governor in office since it was widely believed by Washington officials, including the president, that "the civil government of Utah Territory are in a state of substantial rebellion against the laws and authority of the United States."[52]

No official communications from Washington reached Utah in May or June and the Saints were left to wonder what would happen next. The *Deseret News* reported a sermon delivered by Brigham Young on June 7 in which he stated that some informants had told him that the Mormon people might be forced to leave the Great Basin.[53]

In a sermon delivered on July 19, Brigham noted that an "expedition" might be sent to Utah and railed against the anti-Mormons who were encouraging such an action:

> They may shoot, and they will see Brigham a little to one side, and Heber in another place, and fire away—at what? At shadows. We shall live as long as the Lord wants us to. They may lie and write lies, and they may stay here, if they behave themselves; but if they do not stop their devilish conduct they will be over taken; for we will make their words true in regard

to their being in danger, if they persist in their efforts to bring destruction upon us.[54]

By reacting to the rumors, Brigham was trying to strengthen his people's resolve in the event they proved to be true. But he and his counselors did not want to decide on any course of action until they knew what was actually happening. Official word of the federal government's intentions regarding Utah Territory did not come, however, and the Saints were left to wonder into the summer what manner of beast might be headed their way.

11

The Utah Expedition, Causes and Consequences

A WAR OF LIES AND EGOS, BUT NO CASUALTIES

1857–1858

On July 23 a wagon train larger than any of those that had crossed the plains from Iowa to Utah Territory moved up Big Cottonwood Canyon to an encampment at the top of the canyon. It included 464 wagons, 1028 horses and mules, 332 oxen and cows, and 2,587 persons. The First Presidency, including Daniel, led the procession in carriages as it ascended the logging road and deployed across the large meadow that is now the town of Brighton. The purpose of this gathering was to celebrate on July 24 the tenth anniversary of the Saints' arrival in the Salt Lake Valley.[1]

The festivities proceeded enthusiastically and peacefully during the evening and throughout the next day. At sunset on July 24, all the participants assembled at the sound of a trumpet for evening prayers and an ominous announcement brought to the camp earlier in the day.

The news arrived with Abraham O. Smoot, the mayor of Great Salt Lake City. Smoot was also a mail conductor, one of several who was charged with carrying mail monthly from Independence Missouri to Great Salt Lake City under a contract secured the year before by Hiram Kimball, a Mormon businessman in Utah Territory. On winning the contract, Kimball had joined with Brigham Young in setting up the Brigham Young Express and Carrying Company (BYX), which was capitalized with enough assets to perform the required services over a thousand-mile distance. Nine stations were set up and manned along the route and mail service by BYX going east from Great Salt Lake City began in February 1857. BYX mail service coming west from Missouri commenced in May.[2]

When Mayor Smoot, who brought the eastbound mail shipment from Great Salt Lake City, went with another BYX conductor, Nicholas Groesbeck, to pick up the westbound June mail shipment in Independence, the postmaster refused to deliver it to them, saying that Kimball's contract had been annulled by the Post Office Department in Washington. They also learned that Brigham Young had been superseded as Governor of Utah Territory by Alfred Cumming of Georgia and that President Buchanan was sending with Cumming a force of army regulars supported by a large number of logistics personnel. Smoot had encountered some westbound heavy freight trains on his journey east whose drivers were reticent about their destination. He concluded that these were carrying part of the army's supplies.[3]

After confirming the information he had received with another postal official in Kansas City, Smoot immediately started back to Utah in company with Judson Stoddard, another BYX employee, at the best speed they could attain. On their way, they closed up the BYX stations and instructed the employees at each of them to return as many company assets as possible to Utah.[4]

Smoot and Stoddard picked up Orrin Porter Rockwell at Fort Laramie and bolted into Great Salt Lake City on the evening of July 23 after a five-day wagon run of five hundred miles. They raced on to Big Cottonwood Canyon the following day, arriving about noon, and informed the First Presidency of the threat. A brief meeting was quietly held to deliver the news to other leaders and a general announcement was made at evening prayers.[5]

Governor Young, after first informing the entire assembly of the facts brought from the east by the mayor and his companions, asked Daniel to speak.

> President Daniel H. Wells stood upon an isolated rock of immense size and about eight feet high and read some letters from the United States stating the reasons why the mail was stopped and information in relation to the army. Brother Wells then spoke a few moments full of the spirit of prophecy and predicted many things in relation to the United States, and these troops that are coming toward Utah. He then made a prayer so solemn and powerful that all were effected. Many tears were shed.[6]

Daniel, who as usual was serving as captain of the camp, also gave instructions on the order for breaking camp in the morning for the return to Great Salt Lake City and reminded those driving wagons to follow the directions of the Nauvoo Legion company whom were serving as escorts and guides for the occasion.[7]

Despite the somber tone of the announcement, those who received it were not downcast, but reassured by Daniel's remarks. Some retired early to consider what they had heard, but for most the Pioneer Day singing, dancing, and "general hilarity" continued far into the night, while response planning to the crisis began immediately among the leaders present.[8]

Brigham Young had known since 1855, when Edward Steptoe was offered and declined the governorship of Utah, that he would not be reappointed to the position. He also knew that his successor would be a non-Mormon from the east who would know nothing about the territory except the inflammatory (and often false) stories published in the eastern press. But he did not expect that the president would declare Utah Territory to be "substantially in rebellion" against the US Government and dispatch a military force to subdue the revolt and install the new governor. Such an action had never been undertaken in any US territory, nor ever would be again. It soon became known as "Buchanan's blunder" and the reasoning behind his decision to do it merits some explanation.[9]

After the surge of anti-Mormon sentiment that followed the departure of the federal officials who became known as the "Runaways" in 1851 and their subsequent campaign to defame the Saints, the citizens of Utah Territory had a few years of comparatively cordial relations with the new group of appointees sent to replace them. Governor Brigham Young appointed Willard Richards, a prominent and well-liked Mormon, as temporary secretary of territory to replace Harris and asked the one remaining judge, Zerubbabel Snow, also a Mormon, to take charge of all three judicial districts. These actions, though popular with the Saints in Utah, confirmed again to the government in Washington that church and territorial government in Utah were absolutely and unconstitutionally combined.[10]

Secretary Harris was advised by Daniel Webster to return to his duties in Utah or resign. He chose the latter course and President Fillmore appointed Benjamin G. Ferris to replace him in mid-1852. Ferris was from New York and an adherent of Swedenborgianism. He and his wife were so opposed to Mormonism that they could not tolerate living among the Saints and departed Utah after only six months' residence there.[11]

Ferris's replacement was Almon W. Babbitt, the Mormon elder who baptized Daniel H. Wells and served in several church positions as well as a term as Utah Territorial delegate. Babbitt had some conflicts with Brigham Young, who consequently came to doubt his full commitment to the faith, but he was not anti-Mormon in action or speech and proved far easier for LDS leaders to work with than his predecessor. Babbitt served longer than any other territorial secretary and was still in office when he disappeared in 1856 while traveling east from Utah. He was later presumed killed by Indians, but his body was never found.[12]

Judge Lazarus Reid and Judge Leonidas Shaver replaced the two "runaway" judges in 1853 and both served without serious conflict in Utah. They were tolerant of the Mormons' religious and social practices, including polygamy which since 1852 was publicly preached, and got along so well with Brigham Young that he requested they both remain in Utah. Chief Justice Reid said of Brigham "that no man has been more grossly misrepresented . . . he is a man who will reciprocate kindness and good intentions as freely as any one, but if abused, or crowded hard, I think he may be found exceedingly hard to handle."[13]

Unfortunately for the Saints, Judge Reid fell ill in 1855 and returned to his New York home where he died in April. Soon afterward, Judge Shaver was found dead in his home after retiring the previous evening in seeming good health. The cause of his death was unknown, although some anti-Mormons claimed he was poisoned at the behest of church leaders. Judge Reid was replaced by Chief Justice John F. Kinney and Judge Shaver by Judge William W. Drummond, both of whom proved to be fanatically opposed to Mormonism and determined to use their appointments to suppress it to the maximum extent possible.[14]

Soon after his arrival in Utah in July 1855, Judge Drummond lost credibility with LDS leaders by introducing the prostitute Ada Carroll, whom he had picked up in Washington and brought west with him, as his wife and later inviting her to sit on the bench with him and advise on his decisions. After the real Mrs. Drummond's existence at her home in Oquaka, Illinois, became known, revealing the judge's abandonment of his wife and children and "his general perfidy," his standing among the Saints fell to zero and then descended lower when he purported to lecture them on the immorality of polygamy.[15]

Along with Judge Stiles, a former Mormon excommunicated for adultery, Drummond refused to recognize the extended jurisdiction of the territorial courts and sought to abrogate the decisions they had made in the absence of federal judges after the "Runaways" departure. Judge Drummond stayed longer in Utah than had the "Runaways," but Mormons and Gentiles alike detested his immorality and his attempts to alter the Utah court system were not well received. Claiming that his life had been threatened, he left Great Salt Lake City in 1856 and spent some time unsuccessfully trying to operate his court at a new site near Carson City. From there he and his lady Ada went back to Washington by way of San Francisco and Panama. Judge Stiles also left Utah after his office was ransacked. He too claimed that his personal safety could not be assured there.[16]

After leaving Utah both Drummond and Stiles resigned their positions and, when they reached Washington, they quickly increased their anti-Mormon propaganda assaults against the Saints. As was the case with the string of federal officials who preceded them on the trail to Utah and then east again after abandoning their appointed posts, most of the claims they made and the crimes they accused the Mormons of were either exaggerated or complete fabrications, but enough had a basis in fact that government officials and the general public, both already predisposed to believe the worst of all Latter-day Saints, willingly concluded that they were in rebellion against the laws of civilized society and the Constitution. As one historian later noted about some of the anti-Mormon diatribes, it was "unclear whether the [Mormons] habitually kicked their dogs; otherwise their calendar of infamy in Utah was complete."[17]

The public could do little to reduce the supposed menace of Mormonism beyond buying more newspapers filled with stories and letters that vilified them, but this they did with enthusiasm. Writers and editors, with few exceptions, fed their readers a steady stream of immorality, lawlessness, rebellion, atrocities, and murders all imputed to Brigham Young personally or to his subservient flock of deluded followers acting under his direction. Daniel H. Wells was featured in at least three New York newspapers as having a "seraglio" comparable to an Islamic harem. All the stories were written by reporters who had never been in Utah and who had never visited Daniel's adobe homes.[18]

Federal officials read this torrent of abuse, starting in 1851 and rising in quantity and intensity each year, and agonized over what, if anything, to do about it. Whig President Millard Fillmore, who served from July 1850 to March 1853, and Democratic President Franklin Pierce, who succeeded him until March 1857, both contented themselves with appointing federal officials to administer Utah Territory and allowing them to function on their own. Neither provided much guidance about how to govern in the unique Utah situation; neither recalled any official from his Utah post (although several resigned) and neither sent any investigative body to obtain an objective view of life and government in Utah despite the wild claims and reports that continually filtered back from Great Salt Lake City.

This benign neglect was exacerbated by the fact that one-way communication to or from Utah required from forty-five days (in summer) to seventy-five days (in winter). As a result, by the time President James Buchanan took office in March 1857, he and his advisors were badly misinformed about conditions in Utah; lacked understanding of any of its citizens, Mormon, Gentile, or Indian; and were being urged to suppress with military force a non-existent rebellion there.

About two months after being sworn in, President Buchanan decided to appoint a new governor and other officials for Utah and to send a military force of 2,500 men to Utah. Their mission was to "restore the supremacy of the Constitution and laws within its limits," and to "insure the success" of the governor and his associates who are "charged with the establishment and maintenance of law and order." The troops were also to "aid as a *posse comitatus,* in case of need, in the execution of the laws."[19]

Buchanan's decision to order troops to Utah was based on at least four considerations, about all of which he had inadequate or inaccurate information. Having come into office on March 20, 1857, he made his decision regarding the Mormon situation in May, leaving no time for any on site investigation of the situation and very little for objective analysis of an effective solution. Buchanan believed what he was told and what he read and his decision was as flawed as his information.

The major factor was the flood of anti-Mormon letters and writings of federal officials and others who had been in Utah and claimed that the Saints were in rebellion, persecuting and even killing Gentiles who dared to come among them, and conspiring with the Indians in a dark conspiracy to control the Great Basin and surrounding territories for themselves and their Native American allies. Buchanan could not be faulted for believing at least most of what he received from Brocchus, Harris, Brandebury, Stiles, Kinney, Drummond, Burr, Steptoe, and some of their wives or mistresses. There were no countering arguments except the lonely voices of Dr. Bernhisel and Col. Thomas L. Kane, which were lost in the clamor.

Buchanan was also influenced by the public outcry against Mormon polygamy sensationalized in the eastern press and preached against by ministers and pastors across the country. The anti-polygamy sentiment grew into a demand for a crusade to stamp it out after the public announcement of plural marriage in Utah.

The third factor figuring in Buchanan's decision was national politics. After the Kansas-Nebraska Act in 1854 granted popular sovereignty on the question of slavery in those two territories, men who opposed the act formed the new Republican Party to work against the extension of popular sovereignty and slavery into other territories. Republican orators used Utah to show how wrong the principle of popular sovereignty in the territories was. If it was adopted, they pointed out, Utah citizens would surely vote in support of polygamy, an abhorrent practice that no civilized society would tolerate. Buchanan reasoned that suppressing an alleged Mormon rebellion in Utah would show that he and the Democrats in Congress, who supported him by appropriating funds for the expedition, were as determined as their Republican opponents to "prohibit in the Territories those twin relics of barbarism—Polygamy and Slavery."[20]

Brigham Young, Daniel H. Wells, and other church leaders were well aware that a new administration in Washington meant a new one would also be appointed for Utah, but they did not expect the new appointees to come with a military invasion force or without any notification to the incumbent governor that he was being replaced. Until Smoot's and Stoddard's arrival, no one in Utah knew with certainty of the new appointments or that the army expedition was actually on the march. By that date the soldiers, although still in Kansas, had been moving west for almost a week.[21]

The seven-week delay between Buchanan's decision to send the expedition and the departure of its advance contingent was the result of several problems. A month was spent finding a candidate who would agree to replace Brigham Young and Alfred Cumming, the eventual choice, accepted only after journeying to Fort Leavenworth to inspect the military force that was to accompany him. With a new governor selected the expedition could start, but three more months were required to find three new federal judges and the men chosen, Delana Eckels, Charles E. Sinclair, and John Cradlebaugh, joined the soldiers on route.[22]

Assembling the military units for the expedition also took time, not least because the commander selected, Gen. William S. Harney, was reluctant to accept. Both he and the army commander in chief, Gen. Winfield Scott, thought the season was already too far advanced to send the expedition in 1856 and suggested waiting a year to better prepare.[23]

The administration pressed on, and by early July had assembled the logistical support needed to feed the army on its way across the plains, although not enough to supply it for a winter in the western mountains. The commercial freight company Russell, Majors, and Waddell was hired to recruit teamsters and organize more than two hundred wagons loaded with food, clothing, ammunition, and other equipment into transport trains. The contract called for the movement of 2.5 million pounds of freight to Great Salt Lake City. The firm also provided additional riders and herders to manage large numbers of cattle, horses, mules, and other animals to be used as food or as replacements for fallen cavalry mounts and draft animals.[24]

The military force that eventually gathered at Fort Leavenworth was composed of the Fifth and the Tenth Infantry Regiments, two companies of the Fourth Artillery Regiment and elements of the Second Dragoons. All the units were in less than prime condition and all were below full strength, the Tenth Infantry being the worst at about half its manpower. The Fifth Infantry was weary from its campaign against the Seminoles in Florida's swamps and had many men recovering from wounds and scurvy, a disease that also afflicted the Second Dragoons. Desertions further sapped the strength of the units with more than two hundred occurring

Figure 11.1. The Utah Expedition crossing the plains. From an engraving in Harper's Weekly, April 14, 1858.

in the Fifth, along with several officers' resignations, when the unit was ordered to join the Utah expedition.[25]

Despite the formidable obstacles, some resolved and some remaining, on June 29 Buchanan ordered Gen. William S. Harney to Fort Leavenworth to take command of the military force and accompany the new governor to Utah. The order read in part:

> The community and, in part, the civil government of Utah Territory are in a state of substantial rebellion against the laws and authority of the United States . . .
>
> As Chief Executive Magistrate, I [am] bound to restore the supremacy of the Constitution and laws within its limits. A new civil governor is about to be designated, and to be charged with the establishment and maintenance of law and order. Your able and energetic aid, with that of the troops to be placed under your command, is relied upon to insure the success of his mission . . . to aid as *a posse comitatus*, in case of need, in the execution of the laws.[26]

The first unit to march was the Tenth Regiment, which moved out on July 18 followed a day later by one of the artillery batteries. The Fifth Infantry marched in their dust a short time later. The expedition moved north and west until it reached the Platte River, which it followed west along the Mormon Trail toward Great Salt Lake City.[27]

The reaction of the Saints to the prospect of being subjected to the violence of a mob, as Brigham described the armed force coming against them to be, was swift and predictable. It began as fiery rhetoric and progressed rapidly to determined resistance. Heber C. Kimball's statement was typical: "Send 2,500 troops here, our brethren, to make a desolation of this people! God Almighty helping me, I will fight until there is not a drop of blood in my veins." And Brigham confirmed: "God Almighty being my helper, they cannot come here."[28]

By August 5 Brigham had conferred with his counselors, received additional intelligence from the east, and decided on a plan for resisting the army's advance. He began its implementation with a public proclamation.

> We are invaded by a hostile force who are evidently assailing us to accomplish our overthrow and destruction . . . Our opponents have availed themselves of prejudice existing against us because of our religious faith, to send out a formidable host to accomplish our destruction . . .
>
> The issue which has been thus forced upon us compels us to resort to the great first law of self preservation and stand in our own defense . . . Our duty to our country, our holy religion, our God, to freedom and liberty, requires that we should not quietly stand still and see those fetters forging around, which are calculated to enslave and bring us in subjection to an unlawful military despotism . . . This is, therefore,
>
>> 1st:-To forbid, in the name of the People of the United States in the Territory of Utah, all armed forces, of every description, from coming into this Territory under any pretence whatever.
>>
>> 2nd:-That all the forces in said Territory hold themselves in readiness to march, at a moment's notice, to repel any and all such threatened invasion.
>>
>> 3d:-Martial law is hereby declared to exist in this Territory . . . and no person shall be allowed to pass or repass into, or through, or from this Territory, without a permit from the proper officer.[29]

At the same time the broadside was being distributed throughout the Salt Lake Valley, Gen. Daniel H. Wells was writing orders to the Nauvoo Legion companies under his command. On August 1 George A. Smith and a company of men departed Great Salt Lake City for the southern settlements carrying orders from Daniel and letters of instruction from Brigham and other church leaders. The orders reported that "an army from the Eastern States is now en route to invade this Territory" and officers were ordered to prepare their men "to march at the shortest possible notice to any part of the Territory" to defend against aggression. Daniel recalled the repeated outrages against the unoffending Saints who had seen "their leaders arrested, incarcerated, and slain; and themselves driven to cull life from the hospitality of the desert and the Savage." If an exterminating war was planned against them, he said "and blows alone can cleanse the pollution from the nation's bulwarks, to the God of our fathers let the appeal be made." Militia officers were to enforce laws regulating arms and ammunition and "report without delay any person from [their] district(s) that disposes of a kernel of grain to any Gentile merchant or temporary sojourner, or suffers it to go to waste."[30]

President Young sent similar instructions to the bishops: "Save your ammunition, keep your Guns and Pistols in order, and prepare yourselves in all things—particularly by living your religion—for that which may hereafter come to pass." The prophet directed Stake President Isaac Haight at Cedar City, "Save all . . . grain, nor let a kernal go to waste or be sold to our enemies. And those who persist in selling grain to the gentiles, or suffer their stock to trample it into the earth I wish you to note as such." Despite an abundant harvest in 1857, Mormon leaders wanted to retain all of it in preparation for a protracted war. Brigham prohibited the Saints from trading in grain even though he noted that sufficient supplies for several years were available to them and that generally "all things are prospering with this people."[31]

Smith delivered these orders to Col. James Pace at Provo on August 3; to Gen. Aaron Johnson at Springville on August 4; to Major Bradley at Nephi on August 5; to Major McCullough at Fillmore on August 6; and to Col. William Dame at Parowan on August 8.[32]

On August 18 Colonel Dame received additional orders from General Wells by an express rider. He was directed to send scouts into the mountain passes in the southern part of the territory to give warning if any military forces approached Utah from the south or west. This precaution was ordered because of fears, fueled by rumors and correspondence from other settlements, that armed volunteers might be coming from Texas or the west coast to join in the federal government's war on the Mormons. Dame was also ordered to have his men find safe havens in the mountains where women, children, and grain could be hidden in case an evacuation was ordered. Finally, he was instructed to keep good relations with the Indians and to remind them that the enemies of the Mormons were their enemies as well.[33]

Similar orders from Daniel, supplemented by spiritual instructions from Brigham to church leaders, went to militia officers in settlements north, east, and west of the Salt Lake Valley. Some of the eastern dispatch carriers proceeded further than those going in other directions. They obtained intelligence on the organization and progress of the army as it began moving west. Reports were sent to Great Salt Lake City detailing the movements of the soldiers and, more important, those of its supply trains.

These communications, besides keeping Utah authorities informed about the army's march, confirmed their worst fears about what would happen if regular soldiers were allowed to quarter among the Saints. Samuel W. Richards, who traveled east in August on a mission to brief Col. Thomas L. Kane in Philadelphia and LDS British Mission leaders in Liverpool concerning Mormon war plans, wrote after passing through the US Army garrison at Fort Kearny, Nebraska:

> The soldiers were in very high glee at the idea of wintering sumptuously in Utah, where, as the Paddy [Irish soldier] said, "the women are as thick as blackberries," and it was a great wonder to them what Brigham Young would say to them with his wives parading the streets of Great Salt Lake City. Every dirty, foul-mouthed Dutchman and Irishman, of which many of the troops were composed, fully expected some "Mormon" woman would jump into his arms upon his arrival in Utah . . . the information we received at this point was of the most interesting character to such as have families in Utah.[34]

Having managed large bodies of emigrants moving across open country themselves, Daniel and Brigham knew well that military expeditions, like civilian migrations, travel on their stomachs. They did not plan to mount a pitched battle to stop the army by force of arms, but rather a prolonged disruption of its food supply and the destruction of its ability to move and fight through the winter in wilderness conditions. They knew that this logistical war was the surest way to block the army from reaching Utah until 1858 and thus provide time for negotiation to settle the conflict without bloodshed.

Belatedly recognizing after the army's start for Utah that it would have inadequate supplies for winter, the Adjutant General's office ordered General Harney, who was still in Kansas to send "a discreet staff officer" to Great Salt Lake City to determine whether winter supplies for the soldiers could be purchased there. He sent Capt. Stewart Van Vliet of the quartermaster corps to Great Salt Lake City to negotiate for supplies. Van Vliet had established many friendships with Mormons whom he hired when serving as quartermaster at Fort Kearny on the Oregon Trail, and had a high regard for the Saints. His small party left Fort Leavenworth on July 28, only a week or so after the expedition started west, but did not arrive at his destination until September 8 by which time the army's advance units had reached Camp Winfield, only about 150 miles from the Mormon capital.[35]

Van Vliet was welcomed in Utah and spent a week among the Saints. He met with the First Presidency and told them that he did not think the army supply trains would be able to reach the Salt Lake Valley in the fall. This was the first good news the Saints had received from the east since they learned of the impending invasion. Van Vliet delivered a letter to Brigham Young officially informing him for the first time, more than four months after the fact, that he was being replaced as governor. Another letter stated that the captain's mission was to obtain fuel, forage, lumber, food, and other supplies for the army. Daniel read this letter to the others in the room twice to be sure it was clearly understood by all and a question-and-answer session followed. Van Vliet was assured that the supplies he wanted were available in Utah, but the Saints would sell nothing to the army if it advanced further west than Fort Bridger before going into winter quarters.[36]

During the next few days, Van Vliet was feted as an honored guest by the Saints. He attended public meetings in the Old Tabernacle and Bowery, met several times with church leaders, toured Brigham Young's homes, met all of his wives and children, visited the military reservation established by the Nauvoo Legion in Rush Valley, and was well fed and entertained at several dinners and social gatherings. During one of these, he was left alone with some of Daniel's and Brigham's wives while the Mormon men went out to greet an incoming wagon train. He had a spirited discussion with them concerning polygamy, in which he acknowledged defeat in that he could not find one who expressed dissatisfaction with the practice or who desired to leave it.

By the end of his stay, Van Vliet felt that the Mormons had been misrepresented to the president and those in Washington who had pushed for military intervention in Utah. He expressed regret that some responsible men had not been sent to investigate the situation before the military orders were given.[37]

On September 20, while Van Vliet was still in Great Salt Lake City, Capt. James Haslam of the Iron County Militia rode into the city at the end of a three-day, 250-mile ride with an express message for Brigham Young. The letter, from Cedar City Stake President Isaac Haight, stated that a wagon train of California-bound emigrants had gotten into trouble with Paiute Indians who had surrounded them and forced them into a defensive circle behind which they were sheltering. Haslam, who read the letter he carried before starting his journey, said it stated, "The Indians had got the emigrants corralled at Mountain Meadows, and [John D.] Lee wanted to know what should be done."[38]

Brigham knew that other wagon trains passing through Utah had encountered difficulties with the Indians because of their hostile treatment of them. He also knew that the Mormons' relations with the tribes, though marred by several tragic events, were generally better than those of other whites and that many Saints harbored strong resentment against all Gentiles because some had supported or participated in their persecution. Finally, he was aware that most Americans falsely believed that the Saints were in league with the Indians of Utah and encouraged them to prey upon and kill any Gentiles they encountered in the Territory. These factors, added to what he knew about the danger posed by the advancing army expedition, and the added hostility any attack on non-Mormons in Utah would provoke, made him reply unequivocally and in haste to Haight's request for instructions.

> President's Office
> Great Salt Lake City Sept. 10, 1857
>
> Elder Isaac C. Haight:
>
> Dear Brother: Your note of the 7th inst. is to hand. Capt. Van Vliet, Acting Commissary, is here, having come in advance of the army to procure necessaries for them. We do not expect that any part of the army will be able to reach here this fall . . . So you see that the Lord has answered our prayers and again averted the blow designed for our heads.
>
> In regard to the emigration trains passing through our settlements, we must not interfere with them until they are first notified to keep away. You must not meddle with them. The Indians we expect will do as they please but you should try and preserve good feelings with them. There are no other trains going south that I know of. If those that are there will leave, let them go in peace. While we should be on the alert, on hand, and always ready, we should also possess ourselves in patience, preserving ourselves and property, ever remembering that God rules. He has overruled for our deliverance thus once again, and He will always do so if we live our religion and be united in our faith and good works.
>
> All is well with us. May the Lord bless you all the Saints forever.
>
> Your Brother in the gospel of Christ.
> Brigham Young[39]

Captain Haslam started back to Cedar City with Brigham's directive four hours after arriving in the Salt Lake Valley. He arrived on the morning of September 13, but he was too late to prevent the disaster that occurred two days earlier.[40]

Contrary to what Haight had written to Brigham, the attack on the wagon train was planned and organized by Mormons who then drew some Paiute Indians into the scheme to strengthen their numbers and provide a plausible scapegoat on whom to blame it. The principal leaders in the plot were John D. Lee, major of the fourth battalion of the territorial militia and southern Utah Indian agent, and Isaac Haight, major of the fourth battalion, mayor of Cedar City and stake president of the Cedar City LDS Stake, but there were many other Mormon participants.[41] At least sixty-nine Saints were identified later as having been present at Mountain Meadows and there were probably others who remained unknown. In addition, twenty-five Indians, principally chiefs and those who were killed or wounded in the early phase of the massacre, were identified by the whites as participants, but most of the ordinary Paiute warriors were not known by name to them.[42]

Many of the Mormons who took part in the massacre later blamed their willingness to kill innocents on the fiery preaching of Mormon leaders during the "Restoration" and the exhortations of Brigham Young, Daniel H. Wells, George A. Smith, and others, after they learned of the approaching army expedition, to prepare for war with hostile Americans. There is no doubt that the anti-Gentile rhetoric of many LDS leaders, all of whom talked too much and often said more than they intended or could afterward justify, contributed to the highly charged emotional state of many Utah Saints in 1857. But neither Brigham nor Daniel ordered the attack at Mountain Meadows or on any other Gentile party in Utah, although both were tarred with accusations for decades.

At Mountain Meadows, a group composed of Mormon militiamen and some Indians attacked the wagon train on September 7, the same day Captain Haslam left southern Utah with Haight's letter to Brigham Young. This initial attack, while the train was stopped at the much-used campground, forced the emigrants to defend themselves by circling their wagons and digging hasty entrenchments. In the first day's assault, seven emigrants were killed and sixteen more were wounded.[43]

The attackers kept the emigrants pinned down in their defensive position for the next four days until their supplies of water and ammunition were nearly exhausted. On September 11, the besieged wagons were approached under a white flag by John D. Lee who told the battle-weary emigrants that he had negotiated a truce with the attacking Paiutes. Lee promised that the whites would all be escorted safely back to Cedar

City under Mormon protection if they agreed to surrender all of their livestock and supplies to the Indians. With no alternatives except death by thirst or continued attack, the emigrants accepted these terms. The women and children were separated from the men and the latter were each paired with a militiaman as escort. As the emigrants marched out of the fortified wagon circle, a signal was given and each militiaman turned and shot the emigrant male walking beside him. Some men failed to kill their victim immediately, but others more willing soon completed the executions. The women and older children, following behind the men, were then killed by more militia and Indians.[44]

Only seventeen small children, who were deemed too young to relate the atrocity, were spared. They were taken in by local Mormon families after the massacre. The Mormons were sworn to secrecy and in their official reports the killings were attributed exclusively to an Indian attack. The stock, equipment and supplies of the emigrants were divided among the participants in the murders and some were later auctioned to other Mormons in Cedar City. The bodies, many mutilated by trophy hunters, were stripped naked and mostly left where they fell to be eaten by wild animals.[45]

When Brigham heard the sanitized report of the massacre at Mountain Meadows, he wept. He knew the story would be spread as a Mormon atrocity, although he didn't know until later that it actually was. He also knew that news of the massacre would stiffen the resolve of the army to enter Utah as soon as possible to prevent additional tragedies. Nothing that could be said or done after the fact would mitigate the government's hostility or its determination to bring the Mormons under control by whatever means necessary. Time was the Saints' only remaining ally. Daniel H. Wells and the Nauvoo Legion had to provide that time by delaying the army's arrival in Utah until a compromise could be found to reduce or eliminate its threat.[46]

By the time news of the Mountain Meadows Massacre reached Great Salt Lake City, the army expedition's advance units were at the Sweetwater River, having topped South Pass and begun their downward trek toward Great Salt Lake City. The rest of the military force and its supply trains were strung out a hundred or more miles behind, but had mostly caught up by the end of September.[47] The expedition's commander, General Harney, who had never actually marched with the expedition since being appointed its leader, was relieved by Col. Albert Sydney Johnston on August 28.[48] Johnston left Washington, DC, immediately by train for Fort Leavenworth and from there started west to join his command. But by the end of September he was only nearing Fort Laramie, several hundred miles behind the advance units. Until Johnston could join his troops, Col. Edmund B. Alexander was acting commander and the Saints hoped to

Figure 11.2. Nauvoo Legion company of fifty men (only forty-five are present here) mustered in 1865 with tents in background. This troop is better outfitted than were those who served in the Utah War of 1857–1858.

convince him and his officers that the expedition should not advance beyond Fort Bridger.[49]

To stop the army, Gen. Daniel H. Wells and the Nauvoo Legion had to win what would later be called the "Utah War" without killing or seriously injuring anyone in the opposing force. Neither Daniel nor other LDS leaders wanted a shooting war with the US Army. Although the undermanned expedition numbered only about 1,750 soldiers, rather than the 2,500 that Buchanan authorized, that was enough to heavily damage or even destroy the Nauvoo Legion in a pitched battle. The soldiers were better armed, better trained, better equipped with artillery batteries, and better supplied with ammunition and replacement hardware, than the Saints. When well led, as they were after General Johnston took command, they were a fighting force equal to any that the Mormons could muster.[50]

In April 1857, before the decision to send the army expedition was made, Gen. Daniel H. Wells organized Utah Territory into military districts and placed the Nauvoo Legion in each district under a local commandant. He also ordered a new election of officers by the militiamen. With the exception of Daniel and a few others, most of the officers chosen were not high church officials, but men who had the confidence of those who served under them in military duties. Those officers, such as Lot Smith, Robert T. Burton, and Orrin Porter Rockwell, were men who were more at ease on horseback with rifle in hand than at a pulpit with scripture in hand.[51]

The Saints could field a larger force of men than the army expedition, but they were not as well armed or equipped. The Legion's adjutant James Ferguson reported in July that the militia numbered 6,100 men in all districts, but had only 2,364 rifles, 1,169 muskets, 295 revolvers, and 99 pistols, leaving a third of its force unarmed and a quarter with short range or obsolete weapons. The Saints also lacked artillery and were chronically under-supplied with ammunition. They exerted great effort to buy these items or to trade for them from passing emigrants, but the army expedition intercepted the arms they purchased and shipped west by freight wagon and few travelers were willing to part with their weapons or ammunition at any price. The San Bernardino Saints that Brigham Young called back to Great Salt Lake City brought some military supplies with them, but the church's costly efforts to manufacture arms and ammunition were not successful before or during the war period.[52]

The militia also lacked adequate clothing, shoes, tents, and other equipment for a winter campaign in the mountains and the men suffered severely from illness and frostbite because of the shortages. Except for a few who had basic uniforms made by family members, the men each outfitted themselves and the overall scarcity of everything in the territory resulted in some ragged and outworn attire. A teamster from one of the expedition's supply trains who was captured by the Mormons wrote of his captors' dress: "And such clothing! It was impossible to tell what the original goods were. Remnants of old bed quilts and blankets served as overcoats."[53]

Captain Van Vliet told the First Presidency before leaving Utah on September 15 that he did not think he could convince General Harney, who he thought might have been replaced, to delay his march into Utah until spring. When he reported to Colonel Alexander, that he had been unable to contract for any supplies or provisions for the army, if it moved west of Fort Bridger, the colonel realized the exposed condition of the expedition and moved to consolidate his forces at Ham's Fork where the soldiers could guard the supply trains and animal herds that were their life support. The news of Indian trouble at Mountain Meadows that Van Vliet also brought reinforced the conviction of Alexander and his officers that the Mormons were in league with the tribes and that only the army could restore order to the Territory. It also convinced them that the Saints were prepared to fight and that the soldiers were vulnerable to attack on their supply trains and could not force their way into Great Salt Lake City against determined Mormon resistance.[54]

On the strength of Van Vliet's report, Colonel Alexander determined to move the army expedition into winter quarters, either in the

Bear River Valley or the Wind River Valley, where he thought he could get sufficient feed for animals. Both of these locations were west of Fort Bridger, but Alexander did not think the Saints would attack if they observed that the army was not moving further before spring.[55]

Captain Van Vliet, convinced that the whole expedition was a blunder on the part of the government, continued east to Washington, DC, in company with John Bernhisel, the Utah Territory delegate to Congress. While Bernhisel delivered letters from Brigham Young to Col. Thomas L. Kane in Philadelphia, Van Vliet advocated in Washington for an investigation of the alleged Mormon rebellion and sought to promote a peaceful resolution to the crisis.[56]

Soon after Van Vliet had departed, Gen. Daniel H. Wells also left Great Salt Lake City with a company of Nauvoo Legion militia and took up positions in Echo Canyon about fifty miles northeast of the city. The only road into the valley ran through this narrow canyon, which is dominated for several miles on the north side by cliffs about six hundred feet high and on the south side by alternating steep slopes and ravines impassable to vehicles or horses. Daniel made his headquarters first at Weber Station about a mile below the mouth of the canyon. From there he issued orders to Col. Nathaniel V. Jones take his men into the canyon and do all that they could to render it impassable to the oncoming army. He directed them to dig trenches, construct breastworks on top of the cliffs from which marksmen could fire down on the roadway, pile boulders on strategic high points from which they could be tumbled into the canyon bottom, and build dams across ravines that could hold snow melt to be released in icy torrents on those passing below.[57]

Daniel and a small escort traveled on to Fort Bridger about seventy miles from Weber Station. The fort was owned by Daniel's brother-in-law Lewis Robison, who had purchased it in 1855 from Jim Bridger and his partner Louis Vasquez for $8,000. It had served since then as a successful trading post and supply base for emigrants on the Overland Trail. As soon as word of the US Army's movement toward Utah was received in Salt Lake, Daniel instructed Robison to improve the fortifications of the settlement in anticipation of resisting the advance of the troops. These fortifications, consisting mainly of an adobe and timber wall around the post, were completed in late August, a few weeks prior to Daniel's arrival at the end of September.[58]

At Fort Bridger Daniel met with Capt. Robert T. Burton, a Legion officer who he had previously sent there in mid-August with a group of mounted militia to reconnoiter the oncoming soldiers' movements. Burton reported that the army had established Camp Winfield about thirty-five miles east of Fort Bridger on September 28 and that the government supply trains were still some miles east of that point. With this intelligence

Figure 11.3. Fort Bridger from the northeast with the army camp beyond. Drawing from the "Journal of Captain Albert Tracy, 1858–1860."

as a guide, Daniel, his officers, and church leaders planned their strategy to stop the advancing troops. Included in the sessions were Majors Robert Burton, John McAllister, Lot Smith, and Adjutant General James Ferguson. Apostles George A. Smith and John Taylor were also present.[59]

On September 30 Daniel sent Lewis Robison with a letter to Colonel Alexander, notifying him that he had disregarded the proclamation issued by Governor Young forbidding armed forces to enter Utah Territory. Daniel directed the colonel to retire out of the Territory immediately or else disarm his force and deposit their weapons with Robison, the quartermaster general of the territory, at Fort Bridger.[60]

Enclosed with Daniel's letter was a copy of the Proclamation dated September 15 declaring martial law in Utah Territory issued by Governor Young and a letter from him directing the US military forces to leave the territory or go into Winter Quarters until the spring and then leave. The Governor also advised that, if the troops were short of provisions, they would be supplied by General Wells and his men upon request.[61]

Colonel Alexander replied that he would submit Daniel's communication to the commanding officer, Gen. Albert Sidney Johnston, as soon as he arrived at Camp Winfield. In the meantime, he added, "the troops are here by order of the President of the United States, and their future movements will depend entirely upon orders issued by competent military authority."[62]

Daniel took Alexander's response as a refusal to halt the army's advance and issued orders to Lewis Robison to burn Fort Bridger in order to deny the army the benefit of any supplies or accommodations to be found there. Robison immediately carried out those instructions and destroyed his own property. The next day, he and the other settlers at the fort returned to Salt Lake City. Daniel and his staff accompanied them as far as their headquarters camp in Echo Canyon. On the way, he also ordered that Fort Supply, some ten miles west of Fort Bridger be burned and this order was immediately carried out.[63]

Before leaving Fort Bridger, Daniel issued orders to Maj. Lot Smith and his men, soon known as the Mormon Raiders, to delay the army by every means at their disposal short of taking any life. He issued similar orders to four other mounted militia units under the command of Majors Smith, Burton, Rockwell, and McAllister.[64]

The next day Daniel issued orders to another group of Mormon Raiders under the command of Maj. Joseph Taylor of Weber County. These very detailed orders, issued after Daniel had moved his headquarters from the mouth to the head of Echo Canyon, read:

> Headquarters Eastern Expedition,
> Camp near Cache Cave, Oct. 4, 1857.
>
> You will proceed with all possible dispatch without injuring your animals, to the Oregon road, near the bend of Bear River, north by east of this place. Take close and correct observations of the country on your route. When you approach the road, send scouts ahead, to ascertain if the invading troops have passed that way . . . On ascertaining the locality or route of the troops, proceed at once to annoy them in every possible way. Use every exertion to stampede their animals and, set fire to their trains. Burn the whole country before them and on their flanks. Keep them from sleeping by night surprises; blockade the roads by falling trees and destroying river fords where you can. Watch for opportunities to set fire to the grass on their windward, so as if possible to envelop their trains. Leave no grass before them that can be burned. Keep your men concealed as much as possible, and guard against surprise. Keep scouts out at all times, and communications open with Colonel Burton. Major McAllister, and O. P. Rockwell, who are operating the same way. Keep me advised daily of your movements, and every step the troops take, and in what direction.
>
> God bless you and give you success.
>
> Your brother in Christ,
> Daniel H. Wells.
>
> P. S.—If the troops have not passed, or have turned in that direction, follow in their rear, and continue to annoy them,

burning any trains they may leave. Take no life, but destroy their trains, and stampede or drive away their animals, at every opportunity. D. H. W.[65]

By the time Major Taylor received these orders, Major Smith was already executing his. With a force of about forty men including Capt. H. D. Haight, Lieutenants Thomas Abbott and John Vance, he intercepted a supply train early in the morning of October 4. This train was temporarily turned back, but eventually overtaken by federal troops who relieved it of its cargo. Smith then divided his command, sending Captain Haight with twenty men to "see if he could get the mules of the Tenth regiment on any terms." Major Smith and the remaining men then moved up the river until they encountered two government supply trains camped together. When Smith announced his intention to destroy the supplies, the train master, Captain Dawson, cried, "For God's sake don't burn the trains." Smith replied "It's for His sake that I'm going to burn them." After replenishing their own supplies from the government stocks, Smith's men burned fifty-two wagons, leaving the government men with two wagons intact in which to return east.[66]

The Raiders then proceeded to the Green River bluffs, and sent a single horseman with an express to Daniel advising him of their actions. The next morning Major Smith's force met another train at a place that ever since has been known as Simpson's Hollow. Simpson was the train master and wanted to fight the Raiders, but his drivers refused to join him, saying, " . . . not by a damn sight. We came out here to whack bulls, not to fight." This train was also set on fire and destroyed, except for two wagons that were left to transport the men east again.[67]

Major Smith's company moved off from the burning wagons and reassembled a short distance away. The men dismounted and, while resting on the ground, two of them were wounded when a large bore gun accidentally discharged. One injury was slight, but the other was very serious and the man, Orson P. Arnold, had to be carried by his comrades on a litter roped between two horses some thirty miles to Green River. From there a dispatch was sent to inform General Wells of the accident and he sent a wagon to convey home the only casualty suffered by the Raiders.[68]

Maj. Joseph Taylor and his men also attempted to destroy army supply trains but were surprised by a mounted company of soldiers sent ahead of the main army to seek out the Mormon Raiders. Most of the men escaped, but Taylor was captured and taken into Fort Winfield, the camp established by the army east of the burned-out Fort Bridger on Ham's Fork. He was held there for several days, but was able to escape during the confusion of the army's march toward Fort Bridger. While a prisoner, he sowed doubt about the federal expedition's prospects for success by exaggerating to his captors the strength and armament of the Nauvoo Legion.[69]

Only three of the forty-one supply trains sent in support of the army during 1857 and 1858 were burned by the Mormon Raiders under Daniel's command, but the frugal Saints mourned the seventy-four large wagons they destroyed. The lost supplies were enough to feed the entire army for three months and included seventy thousand rations of desiccated vegetables, eighty-four tons of flour, forty-six tons of bacon, four tons of bread, four tons of coffee, three thousand gallons of vinegar, and seven tons of soap. The Raiders also captured fourteen hundred of the two thousand head of cattle that were sent with the federal expedition, but most of these animals were returned to the army the following year after the soldiers had passed through the Salt Lake Valley and established Camp Floyd.[70]

Daniel ordered his forces not to harm any supply trains of Livingston & Kinkead and Gilbert & Gerrish, two merchants who were doing business in Great Salt Lake City. The Raiders allowed their trains to pass unmolested, but they were detained in the camp of the US troops in response to the Mormon destruction of the army's supplies.[71]

After reading Van Vliet's report of the Mormon forces entrenched in Echo Canyon, and considering their numbers, as inflated by the captured Major Taylor, Colonel Alexander decided not to attempt to force passage through the canyon. Instead, he turned north in an effort to circle around the Mormon defenses and enter the Salt Lake Valley by following the Bear River's large horseshoe bend around the Wasatch Mountains. Starting on October 13, the army spent a week traveling just thirty-five miles north from Camp Winfield toward the Bear River in winter weather that became a blizzard. Without food other than sagebrush, the army's animals became exhausted and could barely move forward through the snow. Finally, Colonel Alexander, after conferring again with his officers, decided to turn the army back the way it had come and retreat to Camp Winfield. But having decided, Alexander failed to act, and the army stayed in its exposed forward position for another eight days.[72]

On October 19, General Wells sent an order by express rider to Major Smith to take fifty men north into the Bear River Valley and watch the enemy camp there. The order was received in the midst of a snowstorm, but Major Smith immediately sent a detachment under Captain Rich. Daniel's first directive was countermanded by another order to Smith that he received the following day. It stated that the army had turned back and its movement was confirmed to Major Smith by Captain Rich and his men who returned to Smith's camp after observing the army's retreat.[73]

Figure 11.4. The Utah Expedition marching in a snowstorm near Fort Bridger, November 1857. From an engraving in Harper's Weekly, *April 14, 1858.*

The army's end-around tactic would have meant extending its march to Great Salt Lake City by over two hundred miles, but before the soldiers had covered even a tenth of that distance, they were overtaken by the same blizzard, which Major Smith and his raiders also experienced, that made the less-traveled Bear River route impassable for the rest of the winter. The army returned to Camp Winfield on November 2 where Colonel Alexander was relieved and the command was assumed by General Johnston.[74]

By the time Colonel Alexander's foray north had been abandoned and the army reassembled at Camp Winfield, it was not able to advance to Fort Bridger until November 6. That advance, in the teeth of worsening winter weather and continual harassment by the Mormon Raiders under Daniel's command, took fifteen days to cover thirty-five miles and exacted a heavy toll on men and animals. The whole command suffered severely from the extreme cold, as did the Mormon militia who harassed them. The expedition lost at least three thousand pack animals, cavalry mounts, and wagon teams (in addition to the cattle stolen by Mormon Raiders) in the foray up and back along Ham's Fork and the subsequent march from Fort Winfield to Fort Bridger. By the time the dragoons reached winter camp, two-thirds were on foot with no mounts at all and the remaining mules and oxen had to make multiple trips back and forth to pull the expedition's wagons the last miles.[75]

When the soldiers reached Fort Bridger, they found only the burned out hulks of buildings that offered no shelter from the storms and no supplies to augment their reduced stores. Faced with the prospect of more extreme hardships to come, General Johnston issued orders for a winter camp to be built and instituted rationing to extend the range of the army's remaining supplies, now diminished by the loss of some 145 tons of food and supplies, and over four thousand food animals, horses, and mules.[76]

When Daniel was informed that the army had stopped its advance and had not passed Fort Bridger, he returned briefly to Great Salt Lake City with his staff to confer with Governor Young and other leaders about the progress of the conflict. Several units of the Nauvoo Legion also rotated back to the city and other settlements in order to resupply themselves for an extended winter campaign. Daniel left the camps in Echo Canyon and the men watching and reporting troop movements on Ham's Fork under the direction of Gen. George D. Grant and Col. Robert T. Burton.[77]

Daniel told Governor Young that he thought the army would yet try to force its way into the Salt Lake Valley despite the loss of supplies inflicted on it by his militia and the increasingly hostile weather. To this Brigham responded,

> If any officers come to the army, the governor or judges, just inform them that they are as near as they can come. Had they come without a military array, they could have come and not been molested; but now they cannot come. We will not have any cursed scoundrels forced upon us to judge or rule over us, and they shall not come among us. If Johnston comes with troops and intends to come in I expect they will leave their baggage, battery, and a company to guard them and come in on a forced march. Then we must not let them sleep, but use them up as soon as we can—work night and day, and not let them sleep. Brother Wells thinks that they are determined to try to come in. You will find that when the Lord sees that we are willing to fight and get ready to shoot, he will fight our battles.[78]

Daniel's judgment was confirmed when word was received that General Johnston was again on the march with some troops west of Fort Bridger and that all their laggard supply trains had arrived in the vicinity of Ham's Fork. The Governor immediately directed General Wells to return to Echo Canyon and assemble all available units of the Nauvoo Legion there to meet the advancing army. Daniel and his staff reached Echo the next day and he resumed command of the Legion troops.

Still believing the army would attack through Echo Canyon rather than winter at the burned out Fort Bridger or Fort Supply, Daniel left his Cache Cave headquarters and retired back to Echo Camp at the mouth of the canyon. He ordered preparations made for the rapid movement of the main Nauvoo Legion forces, consisting of about 1,950 men, to forward positions in the canyon where they could intercept the army if it attempted to force passage. The full call-up of the Legion, which was completed by November 19, gave Daniel a total command of almost 2,500 men in the field. This number exceeded by hundreds the strength of General Johnston's military command, although the latter were still better trained and better armed.[79]

Even though they were directing a military campaign, both Daniel and Governor Young felt their actions were being guided by a higher Power. Brigham said as much in a discourse delivered in the Bowery on November 15, "I will tell you my faith in regard to the brethren now in the mountains. General Wells takes charge, and when I write to him I counsel him to do as the Holy Ghost shall dictate to him, and inform him that whatever he may order and perform, he has my faith and influence to sustain him."[80]

Writing seventy-five years later, Bryant S. Hinckley wrote of these events, "General Daniel H. Wells had conducted this campaign with signal courage and ability. This was a crisis and called for wisdom and unerring judgment, both of which he possessed in an eminent degree . . . One mistake might have proved disastrous. He made no mistakes. He proved his leadership. He enjoyed to the full the confidence not only of his great leader and associate, Brigham Young, but of his fellow officers and men, and the inspiration of the Almighty."[81]

Daniel ordered Colonel Burton with a rear guard of two hundred mounted men to remain at the Muddy River for a few days and then retire slowly through the snow to Echo Camp. In the meantime, Maj. Lot Smith and Colonel Callister were out upon the flanks of the army, each with a small detachment of men. They were supplied in the field with food for themselves and their mounts by other militiamen who led pack animals to them through the deep snow and bitter cold. Their orders from Daniel were to attack the soldiers only if they pushed beyond Fort Bridger or tried again to enter the Salt Lake Valley from the north.[82]

General Johnston drove his troops forward for a few days, still convinced that they could enter the Salt Lake Valley in a week of forced marches. But snow again began to fall and its accumulating depth soon convinced even the aggressive commander that his soldiers could not fight their way through Echo Canyon in such conditions against entrenched opposition. To their great relief, the troops were finally ordered to return to Fort Bridger, after having spent a week covering an

Figure 11.5. Camp Scott near Fort Bridger, January 1858. From an engraving in Harper's Weekly, *January 30, 1858.*

ordinary day's march. General Johnston garrisoned what remained of Fort Bridger and his men repaired the damaged stone fortifications there enough that stock could be corralled within the perimeter. The main army force moved two miles south of Fort Bridger where they established Camp Scott. Having determined on their last westward foray that Fort Supply was also in ashes, the army did not attempt to occupy it, but ended all forward movement and went into Winter Quarters at Camp Scott.[83]

By mid-November it was evident that the army would not proceed beyond Camp Scott until spring. Mormon scouts reported to Daniel that the army was hastily constructing shelters and corralling its livestock. On November 25, several soldiers captured by Colonel Callister's command were brought to Daniel at his camp in Echo. They were immediately released by order of the Governor. A few days later, Capt. William Maxwell and his detachment returned with information that the army had definitely settled into winter quarters.

The last contingent of General Johnston's forces finally joined the main body on November 21. They were the 2nd Dragoons, commanded by Lieut. Col. Philip St. George Cooke, who were accompanying Alfred Cumming, Utah's new governor, and a roster of other newly-appointed federal officials headed to Utah. Since the civilians, like the army, could not proceed further, Johnston established the civilian community of Ecklesville near Fort Scott to house the territorial officials. The federal appointees were obliged, along with the US military force, to winter in crude accommodations.[84]

Major Callister proposed that the Mormon Raiders make an effort to capture the horses of the dragoons, but General Wells forbade this attempt and issued orders to legion units to cease all further actions against the army unless the soldiers again showed an intention to advance. He did suggest that it would be advisable to capture Jim Baker, Mr. Martin, or others of General Johnston's guides, and to intercept the military and civilian dispatches sent from Camp Scott to the east. Neither of these objectives proved possible to achieve, however, and the Saints were denied the intelligence they might have produced.

Daniel was also informed about the progress of Captain Marcy's expedition to New Mexico. The Saints thought he had been assigned to raise a force of volunteer Indians to come against the Mormons from the south, but he had actually only been ordered to obtain horses and other animals to replace those lost in the expedition's march. Even though they were mistaken about Marcy's mission, no action was taken to delay or stop his small detachment as Daniel had already issued orders to the Saints' in southern settlements to guard against any incursion there. The Mormons had little to fear from any thrust from the south because they had detailed knowledge about the extreme difficulty of traversing the southern wilderness from reports of the Mormon Battalion and from their own explorations since their arrival in Utah. Captain Marcy and his men were able to bring about fifteen hundred replacement animals to Fort Scott, which enabled the army to enter Great Salt Lake City in 1858 on fresh mounts and with their supply trains intact.[85]

With the planned invasion of the Territory stopped for the winter, Daniel wrote Governor Young on November 21 that the situation was for the moment stable, but that he and the Legion were ready to meet any eventuality:

> We trust therefore if it comes to a crisis to give a good account of it, but withal our trust is in the Lord of Hosts . . . I would rather lie in their [the army's] path ten or twenty years, thereby blocking up their way than let them enter our peaceful city, or settlements with the train of Hell which follows after and is already in their midst.[86]

On the same day, Governor Alfred Cumming sent a proclamation to the citizens of Utah declaring them to be in rebellion and soon after, Utah Territory's newly-appointed Chief Justice Eckels empaneled a grand jury at Camp Scott. This body was composed of the civilian contractors and camp followers of General Johnston's army and it proceeded, with the encouragement of Justice Eckels, to indict Brigham Young, Daniel H. Wells, Heber C. Kimball, and every member of the Utah Territorial legislature who had signed the 1857 appeal to President Buchanan regarding the appointment of federal officers for Utah, on charges of treason. Unlike the Governor's edict, which was forwarded to the Saints in Great Salt Lake City by Mormon messengers, the indictments did not advance further than the snowfields that surrounded Camp Scott, where the jury was convened, and none of the accused chose to place themselves voluntarily in the custody of the court.[87]

On November 26, Daniel, in company with Lewis Robison and several others, rode out to the head of the Bear River Valley and then north to find a station site where watchmen could be posted through the winter to detect any movement by the army along the Bear River. A day's search produced no suitable location and they then determined that it was best to watch the army at Fort Scott and observe its route if and when it started to move. Daniel stayed on at the Bear River camp for a few days receiving reports from those watching the army's winter camp and arranging for the Mormon Raiders to pull back to the Echo camp. On the evening of November 30 he rode back down to the mouth of Echo Canyon, leaving only a few men at the Bear River camp to facilitate the return of the last Mormon Raiders coming in from the east.[88]

On learning from the watchers around Camp Scott that those camped there, both military men and civilians, were much in need of salt, Governor Young sent Henry Woodward and Jesse J. Earl with a wagonload of eight hundred pounds to Daniel. In a letter to General Johnston accompanying the gift, the Governor offered it free saying, "You are perfectly welcome to the salt now sent, but should you prefer making any compensation therefor, I have to request that you inform me, under sealed envelope, of weight received, and the amount and kind of compensation returned." Brigham suggested Johnston might pay for the salt as a means by which he could obtain it without placing himself under obligation to the sender, who the general regarded as an enemy.

Daniel augmented the outfit of Woodward and Earl and sent the salt on to Fort Scott with his own letter to General Johnston: "With a view of gratifying the wishes of the governor, I have taken pleasure, although in a furious snowstorm, in fitting up Messrs. Earl and Woodward with packs and additional men and animals in order to insure its safe delivery." Daniel asked the same consideration and safe passage for the additional men as Governor Young asked in his letter for Earl and Woodward and ended with another enclosure: "I also send you one copy of the *Deseret News*, which though somewhat worn, is the last received by me."[89]

General Johnston refused the salt and made no reply to the letters accompanying it, although he did retain the newspaper. He dismissed Earl and Woodward with the remark that he could accept "no favors from traitors and rebels and that any communication which they might in future hold with the army must be under a flag of truce." While he conferred with them, the other Mormon men had an opportunity to observe Camp Scott and its inhabitants closely and confirm to Daniel on their return that the army men and civilians were firmly, but uncomfortably, settled in for the winter.

Rather than haul the salt back down Echo Canyon, as General Wells had instructed, Earl and Woodward turned it over to a group of Indians camped between Fort Scott and Echo. They accepted the gift without hesitation and, finding that the amount vastly exceeded their own needs, promptly broke it down into smaller bags and smuggled it into the army camp when they went there to trade. The enlisted men, not nearly as haughty as their commander and the new federal officials, willingly paid $2.50 per pound for the salt in transactions that benefitted them as well as the Indians. Johnston's officers, not daring to defy the general, went on a salt-free diet until after the end of the year when part of a thousand pound shipment of salt reached Camp Scott from Fort Laramie; thirty of the forty-six mules carrying it having died on the way.[90]

By early December, Daniel was satisfied that the army would not move until spring and he issued orders forbidding any further interference with the troops. He also released the majority of legion men to return home. The Nephi and Utah County troops left Camp Echo on December 1, in the morning. Weber and Box Elder County troops moved out the next day and Daniel departed two days later, leaving Colonel Burton for one more day to make final disposition of property. Daniel also left orders for Capt. John R. Winder and the detachment of fifty men (soon reduced to ten) who were to remain at Echo as an outpost to watch the Echo Canyon road. Three men were constantly kept at Yellow Creek, three or four at Weber Station, at the mouth of Echo, and the others riding patrol on the road itself. After Christmas, Captain Winder and his men were replaced by Maj. H. S. Beatie with a new detachment of ten, and two months later Brigham Young Jr. and another contingent replaced them.[91]

Daniel reached his home in Great Salt Lake City on December 5, just in time to arrange a welcome for the returning Legion troops. They were met as they marched out of Emigration Canyon by a band, which escorted them into the city. The men marched down South Temple Street to the front of Brigham Young's home where General Wells dismissed them and Brigham Young blessed them for their service.[92]

The Saints rejoiced at the return of the Legion and the news that the army had halted for the winter. In a Sunday sermon delivered the next day in the bowery, Elder Wilford Woodruff observed: "I do not believe that any general since the Lord made the world has been the subject of more earnest prayers than General Wells has since he has been out in the mountains. He has been well sustained."[93]

12

The Peace Commission and War by Other Means

CHURCH, TERRITORIAL, AND FEDERAL
POLITICS IN UTAH

1858–1859

The Nauvoo Legion, under Daniel's leadership and with considerable help from the weather (which the Saints attributed to divine intervention), won a significant victory by compelling the army expedition to halt at Fort Scott and winter there until the following spring. The Mormon Raiders also humiliated the soldiers by burning some of their supply trains and stealing their cattle, leaving them to survive for months in very harsh conditions with less-than-adequate food and shelter. The advance of the army was halted without any loss of life (except thousands of animals), a remarkable feat in view of the fact that most of the armed men on both sides were willing and even determined to shoot one another, being only restrained by their officers' firm orders.

But despite their victory, the Mormons had by no means won the war. They had only secured some time to allow reasonable men to work out a rational solution to the conflict. The time was short, however, and by the New Year the necessary intelligence and attitude of compromise necessary to find a peaceful way out of the impasse was not yet evident among the Saints or their adversaries. Brigham Young, Daniel H. Wells, and other LDS leaders, although willing to accept the new governor and other officials, remained adamantly opposed to the army expedition entering the Salt Lake Valley. The Buchanan administration remained equally determined to end the Mormon rebellion using the army expedition to subdue the Saints in the field and establish constitutional government at bayonet point, if necessary, in Great Salt Lake City.[1]

The army expedition's officers and men, having suffered privations and indignities at the hands of the Saints, were consequently the most hardened against them. General Johnston's orders to his men, after going into winter quarters, instructed them to "treat all men as enemies who interfere with your movements or threaten your charge," to "pursue, capture, or rout them," and never "to relax the vigilance which should be exercised in an enemy's country." To a man, his subordinates continued to believe that the Mormons were in open rebellion against the United States and hungered for a chance to open fire and take revenge upon them.[2]

Despite the frozen animosity evident on the surface in Washington, Camp Scott, Eckelsville, and Great Salt Lake City, a thaw was beginning in the hearts of a few men in each of these communities that by early spring began to melt a little of the accumulated ice in Utah Territory. To the Gentiles involved, this trickle of common sense was a matter of practical politics, recession economics, and changing public opinion. To the Saints it was the Lord's hand gently turning away the wrath of their enemies and pointing the way toward deliverance. Regardless of its source, the trickle had to flow uphill for a time and the fact that it did so played well to the believers in prayer.

By December, the army expedition and its associated federal officials and their wives, teamsters and herders from the supply trains, and camp followers that served the troops, numbered almost twenty-four hundred souls at Camp Scott and Eckelsville. They had shelter and enough to eat, but the accommodations were primitive and the food poor: no milk, no eggs, no butter; sugar and tobacco only at up to 400 percent above St. Louis prices; salt at $5 a pound; rotgut whisky at $12 a gallon. Flour rations for the soldiers started at eighteen ounces per day, went to fourteen and then ten. Civilians got eight. The beef, allotted at two pounds daily for soldiers, less for civilians, came from cattle driven over a thousand miles or oxen that had pulled freight wagons the same distance. It was, one officer complained, "all bone . . . nearly dead when it got here." By spring it was almost gone and soldiers were buying dog meat (dignified as mountain sheep) from Indian traders.[3]

General Johnston saw the peril of his forces clearly and made enormous efforts to get supplies over the winter. He sent Captain Marcy south to Taos to buy animals and bought hundreds of cattle from mountain men to the east of his camp. He repeatedly dunned officers at Fort Laramie, Fort Leavenworth, and Washington for more supplies and more soldiers. He eventually received both, but it was June 1858 before he felt his forces were well-prepared to move forward again. When they were ready, he marched on the same orders he had received the previous year, in complete disregard of the negotiations and changes that had occurred meanwhile all around him.

As the watchmen in Echo Canyon guarded against any surprise by the military, the Utah War progressed simultaneously on two other fronts far removed from the territory. In December, Col. Thomas L. Kane, the long-time friend of Brigham Young who had previously assisted the Mormon people, requested and received an interview with President Buchanan. He offered to travel to Utah at his own expense, and without any official position, to mediate the Mormons' dispute with the federal government. He told the president that he would have Governor Cumming installed in office and arrange for the army to establish a camp in Utah Territory. Buchanan, by now feeling that his actions in sending the army were ill-advised, gave Kane a letter stating that Kane had the President's confidence and was "recommended to the favorable regard of all the officers of the United States whom he should meet as he traveled."[4]

Kane knew that Brigham Young and other church leaders would hear his proposals, but he had to get to Utah in order to present them. Realizing that General Johnston would not allow him to proceed beyond Fort Scott, he set out to reach Great Salt Lake City from the west. Traveling with one servant under the name Dr. A. Osborne, Kane took a steamer from New York to Panama, crossed the isthmus on the newly-constructed railroad there, and sailed up the California coast. On his arrival in San Francisco, he learned that the Sierra Nevada passes east of the city were closed by snow. Kane sailed south again to San Pedro, made his way to the Mormon settlement of San Bernardino in southern California and there was provided with equipment and provisions for the final leg of his journey to Utah.[5]

He arrived on February 25, 1858 and immediately met with Governor Young, General Wells, and other Mormon leaders. He was at first discouraged to learn that they were determined not to permit the new governor to come into the Territory at the head of the army and were determined to block the soldiers and "the train of Hell which follows after," as Daniel had described in his letter to Brigham, from entering any of the settlements in Utah. Kane then asked what the church leaders would have him do and accepted, apparently by the same spirit in which it was offered, Brigham's proposal:

> Then he [Kane] said, I could dictate and he would execute. I told him that as he had been inspired to come here, he should go to the army and do as the Spirit of the Lord led him, and all should be right.[6]

After resting a few days to recover some measure of his health, Kane traveled with a Mormon escort to Fort Scott. He entered the fort exhausted and alone but for his servant, rode his horse too close to General Johnston's tent, and spoke with him while still in the saddle because he feared collapse if he tried to dismount. Johnston grudgingly granted Kane permission to visit with Governor Cumming, but he and his officers were offended by Kane's manner and his attempt to make peace when they preferred war. The rider was taken to the tent of Governor Cumming in the adjacent Eckelsville settlement where soldiers helped him from his horse and introduced him to the Governor. General Johnston and his men maintained a hostile attitude toward him and freely circulated the rumor that Kane was a Mormon spy come to ferret out weaknesses in their camp.[7]

Kane was a close friend of Brigham, Daniel, and other church members, but he was not a Mormon. This fact, along with his letter from President Buchanan, Cumming's boss, made him an objective observer in the governor's eyes. Although not as fanatically anti-Mormon as the embittered Judge Eckels, Cumming was still strong in his belief that the Mormons were in rebellion and that the only cure for their refusal to accept constitutional law and federal officials was military force. Kane had no authority to negotiate and did not attempt to forge a treaty between the Saints and federal officials. He simply assured Cumming that he had seen that the Mormons were not in rebellion and would welcome him to his office when he chose to occupy it, without the need for any military force to back him up. Over time, Kane was able to convince the governor who, unlike some of the other federal appointees, was an intelligent and reasonable man, that he would be accepted as governor in Utah Territory if he entered the Salt Lake Valley on his own without the army.[8]

What Kane promised Cumming was exactly what the latter wanted: to take his position as the supreme federal officer of Utah with control over the military when the army expedition entered the Territory. If the governor went in with the soldiers, he felt General Johnston would be the real power and his own civilian office would be permanently diminished. In early April, Cumming decided to risk acting on Kane's advice and travel to Great Salt Lake City with him.[9]

When this proposal was placed before the military officers, however, it was met with heated rejection, as had all of Kane's efforts to have a constructive discussion with the military since his arrival at Fort Scott. General Johnston dismissed an offer of fifteen to twenty thousand pounds of provisions from Brigham Young that Kane brought him. Nearly all subsequent communication between Johnston and the Mormon envoy was done in writing, although they were usually within shouting distance of one another. Johnston did not deviate from his position that the Saints were enemies of the United States and must be conquered by force. None of his officers, even had they wished to do so, dared disagree with him and Kane made no progress persuading any of them that an invasion of Utah was unnecessary. One soldier actually fired a shot that narrowly missed Kane and another placed him under arrest, allegedly on Johnston's orders. Kane was so offended that he challenged Johnston to a duel. Governor Cumming was able to dispel the worst of the bad feelings after Johnston told him that he had not ordered Kane's arrest, but had intended to invite him to dinner.[10]

While Johnston refused to alter his views of Mormon treason in his communications with Kane, the Buchanan administration still held a similar outlook, but it was being undermined in several ways. The Panic of 1857 significantly reduced the revenue of the federal government for the year and obliged the president to ask Congress for a deficiency appropriation of $6.7 million to pay for the Utah Expedition's expenses. Buchanan also sought authorization for four additional regiments to be sent west to strengthen Johnston's forces sufficiently to defeat the resilient Mormons. Congress considered the previous and continuing expense of both requests and rejected them. Turned down by members of his own Democratic party, which controlled the House and Senate chambers, Buchanan began to feel that a peaceful solution to the Mormon problem was preferable to military action in Utah and an ongoing political fight in Washington.[11]

Public opinion, as expressed by some eastern newspapers, also became less strident against the Mormons and a few articles even suggested that the Saints might be victims of an overreaching government. Once the Utah Expedition bogged down in Winter Quarters beyond the reach of easy communication, it ceased to provide any press copy upon which reporters could base their often fanciful stories. The failure of the troops to reach their objective and the wasted millions expended for their mission became common themes after the New Year.[12]

But Buchanan persevered for a time in support of his original decision and pressed Congress to supply the necessary funds to implement it. The War Department ordered another year's supplies for the expedition and prepared the four regiments of reinforcements the president requested. The first detachment left Fort Leavenworth in March and others followed in the succeeding months, but by then the administration had also decided to send an investigation commission to Utah.[13]

While Kane was meeting with Cumming at Fort Scott, Mormon leaders met in a "Council of War" on March 18 to decide how best to meet the coming of the army. They recognized that the Saints could not win a protracted conflict with the US Army and that the losses sustained in any attempt to do so would devastate the church. All reluctantly agreed that the best course was to retreat from confrontation and seek an objective investigation and recall of the army from Washington. Daniel still felt that the Nauvoo Legion could prevent the army from passing through Echo Canyon, but only with heavy losses in lives and the labor of men needed to produce the year's harvest. Everyone concluded that the sacrifice required was too great and opted for another plan that relied on divine assistance or at least influence to succeed.

Three days later at the regular Sunday meeting in the Bowery, Brigham called for the evacuation of the Salt Lake Valley ahead of the army's arrival. If the soldiers showed any intention of setting up camp in or near the city, the Saints themselves would burn it to the ground along with all the surrounding crops and pasture, leaving only ashes for the invading military as they had done at Fort Bridger and Fort Supply. This proposal was approved by the congregation.[14]

The next day a courier was sent to inform Kane of the decision to leave Great Salt Lake City and to destroy it, if necessary.

> We are now preparing to remove our men, women and children to the deserts and mountains, that our enemies may come in and complete their instructions to establish a military post at or near Salt Lake City, if that is their only alternative . . . Will our enemies keep off and let us alone while we are removing, or are they so bloodthirsty that they will not be satisfied short of doing their utmost to destroy our lives?
>
> So far as we have information, their present instructions only reach to establish a "post" in this city and act as a 'posse' if called upon. If they come here and find neither people nor city, what will be their next move?[15]

When the "Sebastopol Plan," as it was called in reference to the similar Russian evacuation and destruction of that town during the Crimean War two years earlier, was first considered, the Saints' intention was to move north into the Cache Valley of Utah and beyond into the Salmon River and Bitterroot valleys of the Oregon Territory. This country, which Brigham, Daniel, and other church leaders had visited the previous year, was thought capable of supporting a large population and was far enough off the Oregon Trail to allow the Mormons to remain isolated and, if necessary, defend themselves. But this destination was rejected after word reached the Salt Lake Valley of an Indian raid on Fort Lemhi in which at least two Mormons were killed and others wounded. Conflicts with the Shoshone and Bannock tribes continued after the raid and the First Presidency determined not to risk taking large numbers of settlers into hostile Indian country while another hostile force of soldiers behind them closed off their retreat. Consequently, the original move north, as approved by church members, became known as the "Move South" and its implementation began immediately.[16]

The organization for the move divided church members into three groups; those living south of the Salt lake Valley who would not move from their homes, but would send wagons, teams, and teamsters to help move others in the northern part of the territory; those living north of South Point Mountain in Salt Lake County, some thirty-five thousand of whom would participate in the move; and a contingent of about a thousand men and boys, young, strong, and brave, who would stay behind in the evacuated settlements to irrigate crops, guard property, monitor the army's movements, and if ordered to do so, set fire to everything to complete the final phase of the Sebastopol Plan.[17]

Daniel H. Wells, put down for the moment his military hat and took up again his duties as superintendent of public works to direct the work of the second and third groups. Bishops were given charge of moving the people and their belongings in wagon trains set up in strict Mormon military fashion with captains of hundreds, fifties, and tens. Daniel ordered the stay-behind group to prepare for transporting all church property, records, equipment, and supplies to Fillmore, a destination that was later judged too distant and was changed to Provo. All of the tithing grain was placed in bins holding about seventy-five bushels each, loaded on wagons and driven to Provo where it was off-loaded into granaries there. Some twenty thousand bushels were moved to safe storage in Utah Valley. Equipment and machinery, including the public machine shop, the *Deseret News* print shop, gun and ammunition manufacturing tools, and wagon loads of farm implements, grindstones, and tools were hauled to Fillmore, Parowan, and other southern settlements. Many were set up in temporary quarters so that their services would continue to be available to the Saints.[18]

Work on the Salt Lake Temple stopped as all the volunteers went home to prepare their own families for the Move South. The foundation of the temple was almost complete and a few of the granite blocks for the walls had been transported to the building site from the quarry in Little Cottonwood Canyon. Daniel supervised another group of young men as they dug a cache on Temple Square for the granite stones and buried them. The remaining sandstone blocks not used in the foundation were moved off the site. The men then covered the entire sixteen-foot wide, eight-foot deep foundation, whose top surface was eight feet below ground level, with dirt, leveled the site and plowed the ground so that it would appear to be a field ready for spring planting. The Tabernacle, the Bowery, and the Endowment House, three buildings occupying other plots of ground inside the walls of Temple Square, were prepared for destruction in the same manner as other buildings in the city.[19]

Despite the military's continued opposition, Thomas Kane and Governor Cumming left Fort Scott for Great Salt Lake City in early April. They took only two personal servants with them and went without military escort. Governor Cumming asked General Johnston not to advance his forces until he received word from the Governor to do so.[20]

Daniel, who was still not reconciled to having Cumming become governor, was forewarned by Kane of the date that he and the Governor would travel to the Salt Lake Valley, and sent a detachment of the Nauvoo Legion to provide a suitable welcome. The militia arrived in Echo Canyon in time to join the watchers already on duty there and with them stage an impressive display for the governor.[21]

The men prepared campsites with tents and fires ready to be lighted at high points on the cliffs that ran the length of the canyon. They also set wooden poles that looked like musket and rifle barrels protruding over the crude breastworks built to deter the army's progress. As Governor Cumming and Colonel Kane came down the canyon after dark, the militia divided into two groups, one of which manned the first fortification that came into view from the roadway. Every man made himself conspicuously visible to give the impression of a well-manned emplacement to those passing below. Meanwhile, the second group rode to the next fortification point and repeated the display of firepower shown at the first. The two groups leapfrogged one another along the cliffs, showing themselves at every opportunity as if each breastwork were manned by a different company. When Kane and Cumming stopped for the night at Echo Station, the militia men rode from camp to camp in the surrounding hills lighting and refueling fires, showing themselves silhouetted with the flames behind them, and shouting watchwords from one to another across the canyon until late into the night.[22]

Cumming was impressed by what he observed, especially when his exaggerated estimate of Mormon militia strength was reinforced by Kane, who told him that the Nauvoo Legion far outnumbered the army's Utah Expedition. That statement was true, but Cumming did not realize until weeks later that he had been convinced of it by seeing less than a hundred men while the rest of the Mormon militia remained in the Salt Lake Valley preparing for the Move South. Cumming sent word back to General Johnston that the Mormons were numerically superior to the army forces and again urged him not to advance on the Salt Lake Valley until negotiations for a peaceful entrance were completed.[23]

When Kane and Cumming arrived in Great Salt Lake City, they met at once with Governor Young, Daniel H. Wells, and other church leaders. Daniel was opposed to accepting Cumming as governor of Utah Territory and expressed his view openly. Brigham, however, relinquished his official responsibilities to Cumming with good grace and offered him whatever assistance he needed. The only exception to Brigham's generosity was his physical office, which he refused to turn over to Cumming's occupation. When Kane explained that the governor's office (as well as his church office) was a room in the president's private residence, Cumming agreed to accept an office space in the Council building.[24]

With that difficulty resolved, Brigham delivered the records and seals of the governor to Cumming and from that point on he was accepted by all the Mormon leaders, Daniel included, as governor. A few days later Governor Cumming wrote to General Johnston that he had been recognized as governor throughout the territory and had suffered no indignities or insults. He stated that Brigham Young and his associates "evinced a willingness to afford me every facility which I may require for the efficient performance of my administrative duties."[25]

Cumming's recognition as governor, however, did not halt or even delay the Move South. The First Presidency did not, under any circumstances, want the US Army to occupy Great Salt Lake City or any other Mormon settlement. They also did not want the soldiers or their community of camp followers to have any contact with church members. Since the army had not left the territory and still showed indications of marching in, despite the Governor's assurances that it was not needed, the Move South continued. Hundreds of wagons moved out of the northern valleys each day through April and the first half of May.[26]

Governor Cumming observed the wagon trains moving south and was understandably distressed to see that his jurisdiction was being depopulated before his eyes. He made several journeys along the caravans pleading with the drivers of each team to turn back and assuring them that they had nothing to fear from federal authorities or troops. He soon found, however, that he did not possess even a fraction of the influence that his predecessor exercised over the people and he finally appealed directly to Brigham, "Is there not some way to stop the moving?" to which the church leader replied, "if the troops were withdrawn from the Territory, the people would stop moving, but that 99 out of every hundred of the people would rather live out their lives in the mountains than endure the oppression the Federal Government was now heaping upon them."[27]

Despite Cumming's successful installation as governor of Utah Territory, which President Buchanan, did not learn of until weeks after it happened, he continued to urge Congress to increase the size of the nation's standing army and appropriate more money for the Utah Expedition to support its spring advance. The army bill passed the House of Representatives with ease, but was defeated in the Senate, primarily due to the efforts of Texas Senator Sam Houston. While he was President of the Republic of Texas, Houston had known and dealt with Mormons as far back as 1844 when Joseph Smith sent a delegation to negotiate with him about moving the Saints there from Illinois. Some Mormons had settled in central Texas and become prosperous and well-regarded citizens in the succeeding years.[28]

Houston opposed increasing the size and expense of a standing army, in part because he foresaw its use against southern states in the event of their secession, but also because he strongly opposed the whole purpose and function of the Utah Expedition. In several speeches on the Senate floor, he detailed, as effectively as Brigham or Daniel could have done, why he thought the army's mission ill-advised:

> I received the other day from a very intelligent Mormon whom I knew in Texas, and a very respectable man he was, once I believe the United States District attorney for Utah, a letter of seven pages. In that letter he takes a comprehensive view of this subject. He protests most solemnly that there never would have been the least hostility to the authorities of the United States if the President had sent respectable men there. He says that Governor Brigham Young has been anxious to get rid of the cares of office, and would freely have surrendered it and acknowledged the authority of the United States . . .
>
> I am satisfied that the Executive has not had the information he ought to have had on this subject before making such a movement as he has directed to be made. I am convinced that facts have been concealed from him. I think his wisdom and patriotism should have dictated the propriety of ascertaining, in the first place, whether the people of Utah were willing to submit to the authority of the United States. Why not send to them men to whom they could unbosom themselves, and see whether they would say, "we are ready to submit to the authorities of the United States . . . "[29]

Houston also predicted that an army led by General Johnston, whom he knew well and whose military abilities he thought very limited, would be no match for the Mormons' determined resistance.

> They [the army] will find Salt Lake, if they ever reach it, a heap of ashes . . . Just as sure as we are now standing in the Senate, these people, if they fight at all, will fight desperately. They are defending their homes. They are fighting to prevent the execution of threats that have been made, which touch their hearths and their families; and depend upon it they will

fight until every man perishes before he surrenders . . . I say your men will never return, but their bones will whiten the valley of Salt Lake. If war begins, the very moment one single drop of blood is drawn, it will be the signal of extermination.[30]

Houston was joined by other senators in opposing the expanded army and the bill to authorize it failed to pass the Senate. Another bill authorizing an increase in volunteers for the army eventually did pass, but President Buchanan was left for the moment with an army in the field on a mission that his own majority party did not support. The Utah War had now become established as "Buchanan's Blunder" and in an effort to support the action he had taken and regain some of his lost prestige, the president issued a proclamation on the Utah Expedition. In it, he justified his policy by restating the same accusations made by the Saints' enemies, but also offered a full pardon for their participation in any anti-government activities.

> Proclamation on the Rebellion in Utah
>
> . . . Now, therefore I, James Buchanan, President of the United States of America, have thought proper to issue this, my Proclamation, enjoining upon all public officers in the Territory of Utah to be diligent and faithful, to the full extent of the power, in the execution of the laws; commanding all citizens of the United States in the said Territory to aid and assist the officers in the performance of their duties; offering the inhabitants of Utah, who shall submit to the laws, a free pardon for seditions and treasons heretofore by them committed; warning those who shall persist, after notice of this proclamation, in the present rebellion against the United States, that they must expect no further leniency, but look to be rigorously dealt with according to their desserts; and declaring that the military forces now in Utah, and hereafter to be sent there, will not be withdrawn until the inhabitants of that Territory shall manifest a proper sense of the duty which they owe to this government.
>
> James Buchanan April 6, 1858.[31]

The proclamation was distributed the same week that Governor Cumming was installed in office in Great Salt Lake City, but he and the Saints did not learn of it until weeks later.

Shortly after he issued the proclamation, Buchanan also appointed Sen. Lazarus W. Powell of Kentucky and Maj. Ben McCulloch, a Texas legislator and militia officer whom he had considered for appointment to the Utah governorship, as peace commissioners to bring the expensive and now unpopular Utah War to an end. The commissioners started west immediately and Kane, having accomplished in fact what they had been designated to do on paper, left Salt Lake City and traveled back to Fort Scott with Governor Cumming. They did not encounter the same Mormon military maneuvers in Echo Canyon as on their first passage and, when Cumming realized the former deception, he complained about it, but more because the ruse offended his dignity than because it had damaged negotiations with the Saints.[32]

About the middle of May, when the Move South was nearly completed, Governor Cumming, who had remained at Fort Scott trying unsuccessfully to persuade the other federal officials still living in the primitive Eckelsville that they could come safely to Great Salt Lake City and assume their posts, brought his wife back with him to the city. They arrived at the same time that Daniel H. Wells was leaving the valley with his wives and children, two of whom were less than a month old. There were now twenty souls in Daniel's family and a dozen wagons were needed to carry them and their essential goods to Provo where they would reside temporarily with the families of Brigham Young, Heber C. Kimball, and other church leaders.

Finding the city almost deserted and huge bundles of straw and other combustibles in every yard in preparation for burning it down, Mrs. Cumming was so affected by the sight that she burst into tears. She entreated her husband not to allow the army to remain in the city and begged him to do something to bring the people back to their homes. "Rest assured, Madam," said the kindhearted Governor, "I shall do all I can. I only wish I could be in Washington for two hours. I am sure I could convince the government that we have no need for troops."[33]

Governor Cumming and his wife waited in Great Salt Lake City for the arrival of the peace commissioners. They were almost the only non-Mormons to stay with the young Mormon militiamen who had been left behind with orders to fire the city in the event of the army's occupation. The empty city clearly displayed the huge economic impact of the army's Utah Expedition and the Saints' Move South in response to it. Non-Mormon merchants had fled because there was no business left in northern Utah and they feared losing their possessions in the event of a fight or a fire. No wagon trains could cross Utah Territory during the crisis and the cash economy had come to an almost complete standstill. Despite the governor's request and later warnings, General Johnston was still preparing to move his men forward. When news of the approaching peace commissioners reached him, however, he was ordered to hold his position and await their arrival.[34]

The commissioners, Powell and McColloch, reached the deserted Great Salt Lake City in early June. After conferring briefly with Governor Cumming, they sent a letter to Brigham Young inviting him to meet with them about the "unfortunate difficulties" in Utah Territory. On June 10, Brigham, Daniel H. Wells, Heber C. Kimball, nine apostles, and several other Mormon leaders left their families in Provo and returned to the Salt Lake Valley. That evening Brigham and Daniel met with Governor Cumming at the home of William C. Staine where he and his wife were staying. There were no other accommodations in the boarded up city and the commissioners were left to fend for themselves living in the wagon they traveled in. The governor told Brigham and Daniel that the commissioners would take a hard line to begin with, but he felt they could be persuaded to see reason.[35]

The next morning, at the invitation of Brigham Young, the commissioners met in the Council House with the church leaders. Governor Cumming, and Jacob Forney, the new Indian Agent who had replaced Brigham in that capacity, were present as observers. Lazarus Powell opened the session by stating the firm position that Cumming had forewarned the Mormon leaders to expect. He said that his message was not hard to understand. He and Major McCulloch had been sent by the president to Utah to see that law and order were established and to insist that the Mormons obey the constitution and laws and officers of the United States. The army would enter the territory as ordered by the president, but would not injure the inhabitants. The commissioners officially proffered the presidential pardon that Buchanan had proclaimed in April and he urged the Mormons to accept it.[36]

Brigham responded that he was greatly disturbed that the commissioners, who knew nothing of the true situation in the Territory, were to determine the future of the Mormon people on the basis of lies told against them in Washington. Daniel then spoke with feeling about the Mormons' experiences in Missouri and Illinois, where they were robbed of their property and possessions and many of them were killed while the government did nothing to help them. It had done nothing since to redress these previous wrongs, he said, and was now imposing an army on a civilian population that had done nothing wrong. He pointed out that Governor Cumming was an objective witness that the charges of rebellion and sedition made against the Saints by the Buchanan administration were false.

Daniel further stated that the pardon offered by the commissioners did not apply to the Mormons or their leaders because they had not committed any of the alleged acts that would have required a pardon. They were, he added, determined to defend their rights under the Constitution and insisted that these not be infringed by the imposition of military rule.[37]

Other Mormon observers, including Erasmus Snow and Gilbert Clements, backed up Daniel's words with experiences and observations of their own. The meeting adjourned so that each side could review its position privately. Brigham, Daniel and Heber Kimball conferred about how far they would go in meeting the peace requirements set by Powell and McCulloch. While they determined their final position, Governor Cumming met with the commissioners and tried to convince them to accept his view that the Mormons were not then and had never been in rebellion.[38]

None of the First Presidency felt inclined to trust government officials or the military to implement any peace plan they negotiated. Consequently they determined to keep the option of destroying their settlements or armed resistance open until the army and the administration had proved its good faith. Daniel again told Brigham that the Nauvoo Legion could defeat the present army, if necessary, but only at a high cost. Their threat to destroy Great Salt Lake City and the northern settlements remained the Saints' best means of pressuring the commissioners to restrain the army.

In the evening the commissioners met privately with Brigham, Daniel, and Heber who agreed to allow the army to enter Utah Territory, but only if the soldiers did not remain in Great Salt Lake City or any other Mormon settlement. They said this concession would prove the Saints' peaceful intentions and their willingness to obey federal law. They insisted, however, that the army, once established in Utah, be subject to Governor Cumming's orders regarding its actions in the territory and not to contrary commands received from the War Department in Washington. Although they maintained that the charges of treason and sedition made against them and other Mormon leaders were false, they agreed to accept the pardon offered by the president in order to save the lives of innocent men and women and prevent any future hostile action against them. This acceptance later proved provident when a federal judge attempted to again file charges against the church leaders.[39]

The commissioners accepted the Saints conditions for ending the confrontation at this meeting and Powell announced at a public assembly the following day that all the difficulties between the US government and Utah were happily settled. They sent a letter to John B. Floyd, the secretary of war, confirming the peace accord and communicated the same news to General Johnston. They also asked the general to issue a statement assuring the people of Utah that he would not violate their property rights. Johnston was furious at the prospect of a peace that would deny him any opportunity to wreak vengeance on the Mormons for having blocked his march the previous year, but he could not defy the order of the commissioners who spoke for the commander-in-chief. His letter promised that the Saints would not be molested and stated that the army was "as ready now to assist and protect as it was to oppose them [the Mormons] while it was believed they were resisting the laws of their government."[40]

The courier that brought Johnston's letter to Great Salt Lake City confirmed that the general could not be trusted and noted that his troops were already on the march to the Salt Lake Valley. He had started the same day the commissioners first met with Brigham and Daniel, despite their insistence that he remain at Fort Scott until negotiations were completed. The Mormon leaders were angry at Johnston's immediate breach of the peace agreement. They correctly foresaw that he was seeking to provoke an incident with the Saints that would justify him in ordering an attack on them, but they did not repudiate the agreement nor respond negatively to the general's breach. Daniel ordered the militiamen watching the army's progress not to interfere with it and did not call up any additional units of the Nauvoo Legion. Despite Governor Cumming's assurance that they could safely return to their homes, Brigham told all church members to hold their places in the Move South until after the army had passed through the city and reached its final destination. The First Presidency and apostles then returned to Provo to await the army's coming and see what General Johnston would do.[41]

On June 26, General Johnston led his troops out of the mouth of Emigration Canyon and down the road used by thousands of wagons into Great Salt Lake City. The first company arrived in the almost deserted city about ten in the morning and the last departed over the Jordan River bridge constructed by the Saints about five in the afternoon. The Mormons left in the city stayed out of sight, as ordered by Brigham and Daniel, and observed the troops march through in mostly silent formation. No soldier broke ranks and no Saint showed himself or spoke to the troops. Some of the officers displayed their different attitudes toward the Saints and the Utah War: Col. Phillip St. George Cooke, in command of the Second Dragoons cavalry unit, doffed his hat through the city as a token of respect for the Mormon Battalion he had commanded during the Mexican War. As he passed Brigham Young's home, General Johnston ordered his adjutant, Fitz-John Porter, to have the band play "One Eye Riley," an obscene marching song, so his men could sing its vilest verses to the Mormon prophet who was not there to hear them.[42]

The troops camped about two miles beyond the river resting and feeding their animals and renewing their water supply. They found no adequate food or supplies could be had in the valley and so, three days after their arrival, the army pulled out of camp and marched south to Cedar Valley, an uninhabited area some forty miles southwest of Great Salt Lake City. There they established Camp Floyd, named for the secretary of war. When Brigham received word that they had passed out of

Figure 12.1. The US Army Utah Expedition marching through the deserted streets of Great Salt Lake City, June 26, 1858.

the Salt Lake Valley, he breathed a sigh of relief and announced that he and his family were returning to their home. He invited all the Saints to begin their return journey as soon as they were ready. Within thirty days, most families were back in their communities and working their farms and businesses. For them, the Utah War was finally over.[43]

The formal conclusion came a few days later when the First Presidency signed their agreement to the report of Commissioners McCulloch and Powell to Secretary of War Floyd. The report summarized the results of the June meetings and subsequent actions of the Saints, the Utah Expedition, and federal officers in Utah Territory. Its final sentence noted "it was agreed that the officers, civil and military, of the United States should peaceably and without resistance enter the Territory of Utah, and discharge, unmolested, all their official duties."[44]

But the conflicts that had caused the Utah War were not resolved for Daniel and other church leaders. Governor Cumming quickly learned to appreciate the Mormons' grievances and the attitude of suspicion and resistance to government authority that they produced. He worked to rebuild trust within the community, but his efforts were continually hindered by the other federal appointees whose terms began at the same time. These officials included Chief Justice Delano R. Eckels, who established his court at Camp Floyd; Judge Charles E. Sinclair, who arrived near the end of July and opened his court in Salt Lake City; and Judge John Cradlebaugh, who did not reach Utah until November and established his court in Provo although his district seat was designated as Fillmore. All of these men, with the support and help of the virulently anti-Mormon General Johnston, worked to rekindle the conflict between the Saints and the government.[45]

Judge Sinclair, in the opening session of his court, impaneled a grand jury and instructed its members to indict Brigham Young and Daniel H. Wells on charges of treason for their parts in the Utah War. He claimed that the pardon issued by President Buchanan to all Mormons who had participated in the conflict "while a public act in the history of the country," was a thing of which his court could not "take judicial cognizance" and he asked that all those charged in the two indictments issued at Eckelsville in December 1857 and April 1858 be indicted again.[46]

The US Attorney Alexander Wilson felt strongly that the president's pardon was absolute, as defined in the Constitution, and could not be set aside by any judge. He refused to seek a bill of indictment, as requested by Judge Sinclair, and went so far as to block the judge's effort by filing a *nolle prosequi* with federal officials in Washington stating that he would not bring any charges against any of the twenty or more persons charged in the original indictments.[47]

Judge Cradlebaugh tried to foment discord by requesting General Johnston to send troops to his court in Provo to protect him, guard prisoners and prevent the intimidation of witnesses and jurors. General Johnston promptly provided a company of infantry and, when city officials increased the local police force to maintain order and prevent conflict between the populace and the soldiers, he reinforced the military presence with eight more infantry companies, a cavalry company, and an artillery company. Judge Cradlebaugh then began conducting investigations into alleged atrocities committed by Mormons, principally "what was known as the Springville murders, the killing in March 1857, of William R. Parrish, his son Beason, and E. T. Potters, by persons unknown. He deemed the presence of the troops necessary for his protection and for the protection of the jurors and witnesses. In charging the grand jury he accused the church authorities of directing those crimes and the Utah Legislature with having enacted laws to prevent the judiciary from bringing such offenders to justice."[48]

The judge dismissed the grand jury he had impaneled when its members refused to bring indictments against accused persons without sufficient evidence. He continued to hold court without a jury and had several persons arrested including the mayor of Provo. He disregarded complaints by Provo City officials about the presence of almost a thousand soldiers and the citizens then appealed to Governor Cumming to have the troops withdrawn. The governor visited Provo and assessed the situation himself, then returned to Great Salt Lake City where he met with Daniel H. Wells.[49]

> The Governor came in on the stage last night. Daniel H. Wells had an interview with him this morning, and asked him what he was going to do in this disturbance. He seemed a little troubled about it. He had reported to the government that he could not be responsible for the peace of the country unless he had control of the military, and they be out of the control of the judges, and that he will make the same report by the next mail. He said there was no necessity for calling out the military in Provo. He was asked if he would require the citizens to be taken to Camp Floyd for trial. He said he should not say that he would require it . . .
> Governor Cumming told General Wells that there appeared to be a shrinking on the part of Judge Cradlebaugh. He wished to shift the responsibility of sending the 800 troops to Provo onto General Johnston. The judge denied making a requisition for them.[50]

The governor requested General Johnston to recall his troops, but Johnston refused saying, "I am under no obligation whatever to conform to your suggestions with regard to the disposition of the troops in this department, except only when it may be expedient to employ them in their civil capacity as a posse."[51]

Governor Cumming's instructions from Secretary of State Cass (acting for President Buchanan) stated that he was empowered to use federal troops as a *posse comitatus* in the event of need to "uphold the supremacy of the law." He correctly interpreted these orders to mean that, as governor, he had full authority over the army in Utah Territory. General Johnston, also correctly, claimed that his orders from the War Department allowed his forces to act as a *posse comitatus* at his discretion or when requested by a federal judge and he chose to disregard the section of those orders that called for "a zealous, harmonious, and thorough cooperation with [Cumming], on frequent and full consultations." Governor Cumming wrote a proclamation protesting Johnston's actions and forwarded it to Washington with a request that the role of the military in Utah be clarified.[52]

> The following day General Wells visited Governor Cumming. His Excellency showed him a dispatch from General Johnston at which the Governor was very much

annoyed. It appears that the General does not recognize the Governor's authority, and sent his troops to interfere with the civil authority on his own responsibility.[53]

When Daniel asked the governor what he planned to do about the illegal military actions, Cumming's response indicated that he felt the peace of the Territory and his own authority severely threatened by the army's tactics, but he could not do more until he received clarification of the conflict of orders from Washington. His request required two months to travel to the capital and back, but the President, after meeting with his cabinet officers, came down squarely on Cumming's side, much to Johnston's annoyance. The general was told that "Peace now being restored to the Territory, the judicial administration of the laws will require no help from the army under your command . . . You will therefore only order the troops under your command to assist as a *posse comitatus* in the execution of the laws, upon the written application of the Governor of the Territory, and not otherwise."[54]

Mormon leaders managed to prevent any major conflict between citizens and the troops and persuaded their people to endure the soldiers' taunts and insults without response. Cradlebaugh could not convince the grand jury he impaneled to issue the indictments he requested of them and, after a stormy argument with jury members, the grand jury was dismissed by the judge with the statement entered on the court record that "The whole [Mormon] community presents a united and organized opposition to the administration of justice."[55]

The grand jury published a protest against its discharge, stating that they were surrounded, during their deliberations, by a detachment of the army, and that army officers were quartered within hearing of the evidence of witnesses who were being examined in the jury room. Their lawful indictments, they added, had been treated with contempt and the accused liberated without trial. Subpoenaed witnesses had been arrested and the jury deprived of their evidence. Despite the court's failure to support their work, they were endeavoring to faithfully discharge their duties when they "were dismissed by his honor with a slanderous and insulting harangue."[56]

Judge Cradlebaugh was eventually ordered by US Attorney General J. S. Black to cease his efforts to subvert justice by military intimidation. Black's letter to Governor Cumming, Judge Sinclair, and Judge Cardlebaugh concluded with strong points:

On the whole, the President is very decidedly of opinion:

1. That the governor of the Territory alone has power to issue a requisition upon the commanding general for the whole or a part of the army.

2. That there was no apparent occasion for the presence of the troops at Provo.
3. That if a rescue of the prisoners in custody had been attempted, it was the duty of the marshal, and not of the judges, to summon the force which might be necessary to prevent it.
4. That the troops ought not to have been sent to Provo without the concurrence of the governor, nor kept there against his remonstrance.
5. That the disregard of these principles and rules of action has been, in many ways, extremely unfortunate.

I am, very respectfully, yours, &c.,
J. S. BLACK.[57]

Army officers stationed at Camp Floyd next tried to implicate Brigham Young in a counterfeiting scheme that was uncovered among some Gentiles living at the camp. The officers accused Brigham of complicity in the crime because the paper for the counterfeiting had been obtained from someone in his employ, but when they presented this flimsy evidence to Governor Cumming and requested his help in arresting Brigham, he strongly rebuffed them.

> They rubbed their hands and were jubilant; they had got the dead wood on Brigham Young. I was indignant, sir, and told them, By——, gentlemen, you can't do it! When you have a right to take Brigham Young, gentlemen, you shall have him without creeping through walls. You shall enter by his door with heads erect as becomes representatives of your government. But till that time, gentlemen, you can't touch Brigham Young.[58]

Having failed to win the governor's help, the army officers were thought by Daniel and other church leaders to be plotting Brigham's arrest by military force. Two regiments backed with artillery were rumored to be preparing an attack on his home. Governor Cumming informed Daniel of the plot, which the officers had revealed in their interview seeking his help.[59]

> General Wells asked the Governor what should be done if that army moved into this city, as from threats made by military officers and others it was evident that their intention

was to try and harass and arrest Brigham Young, and it was also evident that were he in their hands he would be massacred, and that the people would not submit to have President Young dragged into a military court and murdered. The Governor replied that he was not prepared to give an answer to that question, but if such emergency occurred, he would then decide what to do. Wells told him that the emergency was likely to occur before tomorrow morning and we should be obliged to decide, and we may as well decide the matter at once, and that the people had submitted to have Joseph Smith and Hyrum Smith treacherously murdered in the same way they were trying to get up now. He also told the Governor that Captain Furnley and Colonel Crossman had declared that Brigham Young should be hung, and many other officers had made similar declarations.[60]

Weeks passed without any military movement being detected at Camp Floyd, but tension remained extremely high in Great Salt Lake City because several soldiers were seen reconnoitering there. On April 24, the First Presidency, still guarded by hidden sentries, met with Governor Cumming at his home regarding the continuing threat.

> His Excellency received them very courteously and soon he began to make inquiries in relation to the progress of events and the probability that the army would come to Salt Lake City, and said he had under-stood some time since that that was their intention, but he was in hopes they had given it up . . .
> The Governor inquired if they had any late news of their movements.
> General Wells said that some "gentlemen in stripes" had been examining the points above President Young's house, apparently looking out positions for artillery encampments. Governor Cumming said he had understood that some civil engineers were making observations to obtain the longitude of the city. General Wells replied that if that was their business they seemed very much interested in the high grounds that commanded President Young's mansion and the city and the paths and roads that led to them . . .
> Governor Cumming said, "I presume, General Wells, you have arrangements so made that if any army starts from Camp Floyd that you will soon know of it."

The General replied, "I presume I should learn about it in a short time." Governor Cumming said: "In case such a thing takes place I wish you would let me know." General Wells replied, "I will do so, and make you acquainted with our movements immediately."

General Wells told the Governor that we had some cannon, and that last year when we left the city they were cached, as they were too heavy for mountain use and that they had been raised and would be used if necessary.[61]

Because the Saints were expecting trouble and were prepared to defend against it, no attack came. Despite his broad interpretation of his orders, General Johnston would not risk his career on open defiance of the governor's authority nor the possibility of a defeat at the hands of Mormon volunteer militia. While he vacillated, seeking other means of apprehending Brigham, Governor Cumming's communications reached Washington and Attorney General Black's response soon followed placing the general firmly under the civilian authority of the governor.

> The Governor as the supreme executive of the Territory is responsible for the public peace. From the general law of the land and the nature of his office and the instructions he received from the State Department, it ought to have been understood [by General Johnston] that he alone had power to issue a requisition for the movement of troops from one part of the Territory to another, that he alone could put the military forces of the Union and the people of the Territory into a relation of general hostility with one another. The instructions given to the commanding general by the War Department are to the same effect.[62]

With this admonition in his hands, the general was obliged to give up the open pursuit of his anti-Mormon crusade, although his opinion of the Saints and their religion remained unchanged.

13

Family, Business, Church, and Politics in Utah while the Civil War Ravages the Nation

1860–1864

The Utah War, the Move South, and their rancorous aftermath brought Daniel's personal and business life almost to a standstill. He was away from home almost constantly during the second half of 1857 and the first half of 1858, and his family was on the road or in hiding for a good part of that time as well. No children were added to the Wells family during 1858 until December when Lydia gave birth to Lucy Ann Wells, Daniel's sixteenth child. Lucy was a frail child who lived less than a year and died in October 1859. By then, however, two more sons and a daughter had been born: in April Louisa's sister Hannah gave birth to Brigham Wells; in August, Heber Manning Wells was born to Martha; and in October Eliza Free Wells was born to Louisa. Soon after little Lucy's death, Emmeline gave birth to Elizabeth Ann Wells in December and Lydia's sister Susan gave birth to George Alley Wells on December 18. By the end of the year, Daniel had celebrated his forty-fifth birthday and was the father of twenty-one children, eighteen of whom were still living.[1]

With a family of over thirty souls (counting Emmeline's two daughters from her second marriage) to provide for and numerous employees and servants to maintain, Daniel rapidly expanded his existing business enterprises and developed new ones. He increased the operation of the Big Cottonwood Lumber Company by adding a new mill further up the canyon than the first two, which were built near the mouth. Timber on the lower slopes of the canyon within easy hauling distance of the first mills was already being depleted and in 1859 there was still no steam engine available in Utah to power a winch capable of pulling logs. All the felled trees had to be dragged by oxen to the mill and, as the distance increased, the time and labor required also multiplied, raising the cost of the lumber. A new mill built nearer to untouched stands of timber higher up the canyon renewed the available supply of logs and helped keep prices down for cash-strapped purchasers.

Daniel and other leaders in Utah recognized early that the supply of timber in the Territory that was suitable for lumber was limited and should not be burned as firewood for cooking, home heating, or industrial purposes. For the first few years after the pioneers' arrival, they burned scrub oak, sagebrush, mesquite, and other small trees and bushes, but the supply of these was also limited and the need for another fuel source quickly became apparent. The 1854 Utah Territorial legislature posted a one-thousand-dollar reward payable to the first person who discovered a coal vein not less than eighteen inches thick that was located within forty miles of Salt Lake City.[2]

Steven W. Taylor, the young English convert who boarded with Daniel H. Wells's family and was first employed by him at age fifteen in 1850, was one of many men who prospected for coal in the mountains east of Great Salt Lake City. Summit County records credit Taylor with the discovery in Chalk Creek Canyon of what became known as the Old Church Mine in 1856, although Thomas Rhodes, John Muir, and Samuel Fletcher also are known to have explored in the same area in the late 1850s. No one was able to claim the reward, however, because the coal was located five miles beyond the qualifying distance. The Utah War and subsequent events delayed efforts to develop the discovery until 1859.[3]

In the summer of that year Daniel, in company with Steven Taylor, Briant Stringham, and Robert T. Burton, started the first coal mine in Chalk Creek Canyon and established a shipping concern to transport coal to the Salt Lake Valley by wagon. After opening the Old Church Mine as a church-owned enterprise, Daniel and Steven Taylor also established their own company and began another coal shaft nearby. This became known as the Wells and Taylor Mine and was owned and operated by the two men until 1880. The Church Mine operated simultaneously under management of the Wells and Taylor company with volunteer laborers working the Church Mine and paid miners digging in the Wells and Taylor Mine.[4]

Within ten years at least twenty additional mines were opened in the Chalk Creek and Grass Valley areas of Summit County and more than a thousand miners were at work there. Chalk Creek's name was changed to Coalville and Wells and Taylor company coal shipments were a daily feature on the road from the town to Great Salt Lake City. The Wells and Taylor Mine was an excellent source of income for Daniel and for Steven Taylor who remained a partner in the venture for more than twenty years.[5]

Daniel also founded a nail factory to alleviate the chronic scarcity of this commodity in the territory. The factory was built on his farm in the Sugar House Ward of Great Salt Lake City in the fall of 1859. He hired James Finlayson, a Scottish convert who arrived in Utah in August, as the principle builder. A small nail factory had operated briefly in Payson prior to Daniel's endeavor, but his nail factory was the first commercially viable venture of its kind in Utah. It became an important factor in the growth of the whole Territory, because, until its opening, nearly all the nails used locally had to be imported from the east by freight wagon at high cost because of their weight.[6]

Brigham Young was particularly pleased by the development of the nail factory as George A. Smith noted when he visited with Brigham shortly after the factory opened. "The President was in pretty good humor and was exhibiting some nails made by Daniel H. Wells' factory, where six hundred pounds of nails can be made per day. They were of good quality. President Wells in his late journey to the Weber Coal Mines discovered a new place for digging coal, a little below Chalk Creek, a better place than the one now being worked."[7]

Iron was also scarce in Utah Territory and so the nail factory was initially reliant on scrap metal for its supply of raw material. Coal from the Wells and Taylor Mine was used to fire the furnace that melted the iron so it could be recast as long strands that were then cut to length and hammer-finished in final form. Some of the first iron fed into the nail forge was salvaged from the army wagons burned by the Mormon Raiders under Daniel's command in the Utah War. The warped iron tires from the wheels of these vehicles were brought from the Green River area where they had been destroyed and found new life as a critical component in buildings throughout the territory.[8]

As with Daniel's timber, mining, and other business enterprises, the nail factory provided employment for newly-arrived Mormon converts. In addition to Finlayson, who left the factory after its completion, Daniel hired several others to operate it. Among them was Thomas Griffen, of Birmingham, England, who was trained as a machinist, James Henry Hart of Hemingford, Huntingdonshire, England, David William Leaker and William Tonks, both blacksmiths, and Adolphus R. Whitehead, who operated a nail-cutting machine at age eighteen. Brigham Jarvis Sr. was only nine years of age when he spent the winter of 1860 firing the furnace of the nail factory, a job he was glad to relinquish the following year in favor of farming with his father.[9]

Before the factory was built, nails sold in Great Salt Lake City at 50 cents per pound. The price declined by half after local production began, and the supply became more abundant and stable. Daniel offered nails at $25 per hundred pounds and the money he received from buyers stayed in the local economy rather than moving east out of the territory.[10]

By the close of 1859, the nation's political parties, as well as the elected officials and population of each state, were bitterly divided over the continuance and expansion of slavery, which promised to be the decisive issue in the election of 1860. In Utah Territory, however, this issue created scarcely a ripple. The Compromise of 1850 that organized Utah and New Mexico as US government entities, put no restriction on slavery in these territories and allowed their inhabitants to choose by vote (popular sovereignty) whether slavery would be permitted. A few southern converts to Mormonism brought some black slaves with them to Utah, but the number of African-ancestry slaves in the territory never exceeded a hundred and was probably less. Although slavery was permitted in Utah, the vast majority of its residents, including Daniel and his wives, were opposed to slavery. The Utah legislature authorized the purchase of Indians as indentured servants, both as a method of ransoming prisoners held by other Indians and as a means of providing labor for Mormon settlers. Those purchased were mostly captured women and children who would otherwise have been killed and their indenture lasted until their purchase price was repaid in labor. Brigham Young's campaign against the selling of Indian or Hispanic human beings virtually eliminated the slave trade by 1855 in areas where the Mormons were dominant.

Citizens living in the territories could not vote for president, nor for any voting members of Congress (Utah and other territories each had one non-voting, elected delegate in the House of Representatives) and so were less involved or concerned about the developing national crisis that led to the southern states' secession.[11]

For the Saints, the critical issues of the day were recovering from the economic disruption caused by the Utah War and the Move South, dealing with the federal officials who now controlled the territorial government, and accommodating the permanent presence of the army regiments now stationed in Utah with its "train of Hell which follows after and is already in their midst," as described by Daniel, that had arrived with them.

There were Gentiles in Utah prior to the arrival of the army expedition, but they were a tiny fraction of the total population. Those who found the theocratic government, strict moral code, law-abiding habits, and non-alcoholic lifestyle of the Saints not to their liking usually moved on to more compatible settlements in other territories or in California. Similarly, some disaffected church members, such as Hannah Wells's first husband, Dr. Hotchkiss, severed their ties with the church and left the territory rather than continue to live in the conservative community they had rejected. Thus, during its first decade, most of Utah's population was composed of two groups: observant Mormons who followed Brigham Young's leadership and adhered generally to church teachings, and friendly or at least accommodating Gentiles who were comfortable doing business with the Saints and living among them in their tightly-controlled society. The Indian tribes were part of the second category and the Mormons actually made greater allowances for their cultural differences than they did for whites who were unwilling to accept the standards of their religion.

General Johnston's soldiers had the average moral and ethical level of a professional army, but most were strongly anti-Mormon and were led by officers who were, almost to a man, even more hostile toward the Saints. The twenty-four hundred military men and civilian camp followers at least tripled the number of unfriendly Gentiles living in Utah; people who were obliged to stay in the Territory and yet were unwilling to live among the Mormons without conflict.

Behind the army and its camp followers came more non-Mormons who felt that Utah, with its government now under Gentile control, offered good opportunities. These included merchants, bankers, entrepreneurs, freighters, cattlemen, prospectors, as well as a number of gamblers, scam artists, whiskey dealers, barmen, and prostitutes. All these professions moved to Utah in increasing numbers following the restoration of peace. Most were comfortable in a frontier community, but were accustomed to much looser and open social customs than the highly organized and closed-to-outsiders Mormon civic structure. They were generally law-abiding, unless legal boundaries threatened their self-interests, but were also used to fending for themselves, doing whatever was necessary to survive and prosper.

Church leaders did not want unfriendly Gentiles living among the Saints. They also didn't want even friendly Gentiles to prosper too much doing business with their Mormon neighbors, lest the latter be tempted to seek for treasure on earth rather than that promised by their faith in heaven. That prejudiced attitude was born of bitter experience over twenty years of building Zion in hostile environments only to have their communities overthrown or seized by their enemies.

Daniel had opposed allowing the army to even enter the Salt Lake Valley, but Brigham concluded that the policy would be unsustainable in the long run and settled for isolating the military and its entourage at Camp Floyd, forty miles away from the church's center. This distance between the Saints and the Gentile temptations in Cedar Valley proved sufficient to keep most Mormons from visiting the vices of the army camp, but wholly inadequate to keep the Gentiles from bringing their businesses to Great Salt Lake City. Many new Gentile-operated establishments, some offering goods and services prohibited by the church, soon sprang up in the capital city and law enforcement became a greater challenge.

An additional influx of Gentiles occurred in late 1859 following the discovery and public announcement of the Comstock Lode in the far western part of Utah Territory near the California border. Just as the California gold rush had brought thousands of Forty-Niners through Utah a decade earlier, the gold and silver strike near the Carson River caused a rush to the new mining camps that became Gold Hill, Virginia City, and other towns. Mormons were not significantly involved in the Comstock mining operations, but they fed, outfitted, and supplied those who were. The resulting income helped revive the damaged economy of Utah in 1859 and after, but the newcomers, like every wave of riches-seeking migrants before them, included criminals, fugitives, and miscreants of every variety who often preferred their own brand of lawless freedom to the orderly communities established by the Saints. As with the Gentiles who arrived behind the army, a continuing clash of cultures was inevitable.[12]

The Mormon majority was maintained and even increased in Utah during the 1860–1870 decade by the arrival of at least three thousand converts each year, mostly from Europe. These people were imported into the territory mainly in Church Trains, wagon companies that set out from Great Salt Lake City during the last week in April carrying Utah-made goods for sale or trade in the Midwest. In Nebraska Territory, the trains, often consisting of over two hundred wagons and teams, unloaded their cargos, picked up immigrants who had arrived from eastern ports and transported them back to Utah.

Daniel helped organize the Church Trains, which were made up of elements drawn from all the communities in the Territory, but he did not make the trip east himself until 1864 and then not as part of the returning Train, but as a mission president heading to Europe.[13]

Church membership, which had declined by more than eight thousand during the time of the Mormon Reformation and the Utah War, rebounded strongly beginning in 1860. In the following decade more than thirty-three thousand new Saints were baptized and most of them made their way to Utah Territory. As a result of this growth, more than 130 new settlements were established in Utah, Idaho, and Nevada, which was partitioned from the western part of Utah Territory in 1863.[14]

Daniel served as the president of the Constitutional Convention of 1856, which drafted a state constitution for Utah Territory and a petition to Congress for admission to the Union. George A. Smith and John Taylor took these documents to Washington, but Utah's delegate to Congress, Dr. John M. Bernhisel, told them that a statehood attempt would be futile at that time because anti-Mormon feeling was too high. The petition was further delayed by the Utah War and succeeding events, but in December

1860, the month following Lincoln's election and the same month that South Carolina seceded from the Union, it was presented in Congress by the new Utah Delegate, William Hooper. This effort to gain statehood again failed, as had the previous one in 1850, despite Hooper's effort to contrast Utah's actions with those of the rebellious South.

> I think three-quarters of the Republicans of the House would vote for our admission; but I may be mistaken. Many say they would gladly "swap" the Gulf States for Utah. I tell them that we show our loyalty by trying to get in, while others are trying to get out, notwithstanding our grievances, which are far greater than those of any of the seceding states; but that I consider we can redress our grievances better in the Union than out of it; at least we'll give our worthy "Uncle" an opportunity in engrafting us into his family; and if he doesn't want us, we must then carve out our own future.[15]

Congress passed the Pacific Telegraph Act in 1860 authorizing funds for construction of a transcontinental telegraph line from Missouri to San Francisco. Two companies were organized to build large portions of the line: the Pacific Telegraph Company for the segment from Omaha, Nebraska, to Salt Lake City, and the Overland Telegraph Company for the segment from Carson City, Nevada, east to Salt Lake City. Both companies contracted with the LDS Church through President Young to provide timber, transportation, livestock feed, food, and other supplies for the project.[16]

Daniel's Big Cottonwood Lumber Company sawmills provided a large number of the poles for a thousand miles of telegraph line running east and west from Salt Lake City. In his capacity as superintendent of public works, he also directed the organization, outfitting, loading, and manning of the supply trains that hauled needed materials and supplies to the work head of each company as its line progressed. When the project was completed in October 1861, the church received $11,000 in gold and $10,000 in stock in the overland Telegraph Company in payment for the assistance the Saints had rendered. These payments were in addition to those made for purchases from Daniel and other Mormon suppliers.[17]

By the time the telegraph line was completed the Civil War was well underway in the eastern part of the country. Utah Territory was less affected than states where fighting occurred and large armies were being recruited, but the war brought several significant changes. General Johnston, who still commanded the US Army forces at Camp Floyd, was a southerner and was determined to join the Confederacy. In February 1860 he left his command in Utah and traveled to California to take command of the Pacific Department. He resigned his commission in April 1861 and journeyed east to Richmond where he joined the Confederate States Army. He was given the rank of general in the southern army in which he served until he was killed while leading troops at the Battle of Shiloh in 1862. Johnston was the highest ranking officer killed in the Civil War on either side.

The US Army renamed Camp Floyd as Camp Crittenden and then abandoned it about April 1861. The soldiers of the Utah Expedition returned to the eastern states to become part of the Union forces that fought against the Confederate States.[18]

On April 17, 1861, Governor Cumming also left Utah, officially on leave, but actually to return to his native Georgia to support the Confederacy. A series of less-than-competent officials followed during the Civil War years. Since the president had appointed no successor, Cumming was temporarily replaced by the Territorial Secretary, Frank Fuller, as acting governor. Fuller was appointed secretary by Lincoln shortly after his election to replace Francis Wooton, whose constant drunkenness the new president would not tolerate. John W. Dawson was appointed governor by Lincoln in 1861, but he stayed only a month in Utah Territory before his conflicts with LDS leaders caused him to resign his office and return east. Secretary Fuller again became acting governor. In 1862, Lincoln appointed Stephen S. Harding as governor for Utah, but he so antagonized his Mormon constituents that they successfully petitioned the president to dismiss him in 1863. Again Secretary Fuller served as acting governor until the appointment of James D. Doty later that year.[19]

During the Civil War, President Young decided that Utah Territory needed a grand theater to provide a performance venue for the Deseret Dramatic Association that had produced plays and other presentations since it was organized in 1850. He directed that the Salt Lake Theater be patterned after the Drury Lane model in London, and he asked Daniel H. Wells, in his continuing capacity as superintendent of public works, to oversee its construction.

Although by comparison with modern venues, the theater was not large, it was by far the largest public works project completed in Utah since the arrival of the pioneers. Its outer dimensions measured eighty by one hundred forty-four feet and its seating capacity was estimated at fifteen hundred. Two Doric columns dominated the entrance of the three story structure and its exterior was finished in white plaster. The interior was more elegant, being fashioned in the style of a European opera house with four ascending circles of seats and two side boxes that overlooked the spacious sloping stage. Offstage and behind, the theater had ample dressing, rehearsal, and storage rooms that few American or European playhouses of the time could equal.[20]

Daniel called upon many resources, including his own Big Cottonwood Lumber Company sawmills, to build the theater. Some materials were supplied from government surplus property that he had purchased for the church from the army when the soldiers were recalled east. Cash purchases were also made using funds that had previously been collected for the construction of a hall of science. Total cost for the theater was estimated at $100,000.[21]

Skilled labor for all phases of the framing and finishing was available among the immigrant converts who were continually arriving from the eastern states and from Europe. Brigham Young's creative ingenuity was also evident in the theater and he described part of his contribution to an 1870 visitor with enthusiasm.

> I was greatly astonished to find in the desert heart of the continent a place of public amusement, which regarding comfort, capacity, and beauty has but two or three superiors in the United States . . . My greatest surprise was excited by the remarkable artistic beauty of the gilt and painted decorations on the great arch over the stage, the cornices, and the moulding about the proscenium boxes, President Young, with a proper pride, assured me that every particle of the ornamental work was done by indigenous and Saintly hands.
>
> "But you don't know yet," he added, "how independent we are of you at the East. Where do you think we got that central chandelier, and how much d'ye suppose we paid for it?"
>
> It was a piece of work which would have been creditable to any New York firm, apparently a richly carven circle, twined with gilt vines, leaves and tendrils, blossoming allover with flaming wax-lights, and suspended by a massive chain of golden lustre. So I replied that he probably paid a thousand dollars for it in New York. "Capital!" exclaimed Brigham; "I made it myself! That circle is a cart wheel, the wheel of one of our common Utah oxcarts. I had it waxed, and gilded it with my own hands. It hangs by a pair of ox-chains which I also gilded; and the gilt ornaments of the candlesticks were all cut after my patterns out of sheet tin."[22]

On March 6, 1862, Daniel offered the dedicatory prayer at the formal opening of the Salt Lake Theatre. As indicated in the following brief excerpt, it was an eloquent prayer, particularly for Daniel who was not an accomplished preacher.

> All and every part of this building we consecrate and dedicate unto Thee, our Father, that it may be pure and holy unto the Lord our God, for a safe and righteous habitation for the assemblages of Thy people, for pastime, amusement and recreation; for plays, theatrical performances, for lectures, conventions, or celebrations, or for whatever purpose it may be used for the benefit of Thy Saints.
>
> . . . may order, virtue, cleanliness, sobriety and excellence obtain and hold fast possession herein, the righteous possess it, and 'Holiness to the Lord' forever be inscribed therein.[23]

Daniel's ever-practical wife Louisa thought the prayer too long. Brother Wells, she opined dryly, should have left out the blessing of some of the lath and plaster.[24]

Daniel not only helped build the Salt Lake Theatre; he was also an enthusiastic patron of it. His daughter, Annie Wells Cannon, said of him: "He was himself most fond of reading and the theatre, and encouraged us all along these lines. We were almost as much at home in the historic Salt Lake Theatre as in our mothers' apartments, and so familiar with the great plays presented there that we could easily repeat them on our own improvised stage."[25]

Rulon S. Wells also described the extent of his father's commitment to the dramatic arts:

> In order to enjoy the advantages offered by the theater, father secured nine reserved seats, later increased to thirteen, buying season tickets good for the whole year round, thus providing not only for his own accommodation, but also for all the members of the family. The great actors of the world filled frequent engagements in our theater, and we had the privilege and pleasure of witnessing the Shakespearian and other great plays rendered by the leading performers of the world . . . In between the engagements with these world celebrities we had our stock company who, in addition to assisting the visitors, continued throughout the year, excepting a short vacation in the heat of summer.[26]

The Salt Lake Theatre was built at the same time that Daniel was supervising work on the Salt Lake Temple. Work on the temple was stopped in early 1858 when the Utah Expedition was poised to enter Salt Lake City and the foundation of the building was concealed. Draftsmen continued producing detailed specification drawings for each of the stones that would be used in the temple and quarrying continued in Little Cottonwood Canyon, but no further progress was made at the site while the army remained in Utah.[27]

When the army left for the eastern states in 1861, Daniel immediately set a work force to uncovering the buried temple foundation. By December the entire footprint of the building was exposed and ready for new stone courses to be placed. Before this work commenced, however, the sandstone foundation was inspected by Daniel, President Young, and others and was found to be defective. The mortar joining the relatively small stones in it had cracked in numerous places and tests showed that neither the sandstone nor the mortar was capable of bearing the massive weight of granite walls. Consequently, the entire foundation constructed before 1858 was removed and the stones in it used for other less demanding purposes. The work of replacing the old foundation with a new one made of solid granite blocks was begun in January 1862 and six years of labor was required to again raise the walls to ground level at the end of 1867.[28]

Daniel was chosen president of a third State Constitutional Convention held in January 1862 in accordance with a memorial to Congress that was passed by the Territorial Legislature and sanctioned by Acting Governor Fuller, who was again serving as chief executive of the Territory after the departure of Governor Dawson, asking that Utah Territory be admitted to the Union. The Convention framed a state constitution, nominated candidates for state offices, and scheduled a March election to determine who would occupy the positions.[29]

> On that day the Constitution of the State of Deseret, with a memorial to Congress praying for the admission of said state into the Union, was unanimously adopted. The first general election under the constitution was set to take place on the first Monday in March. The convention closed on the 23rd of January, after nominating for the coming election Brigham Young as Governor, Heber C. Kimball as Lieutenant-Governor, and John M. Bernhisel as Representative to Congress for the proposed State of Deseret.
>
> The election was held on the day appointed March 3rd the constitution was unanimously adopted by the people, and the officers named elected without a dissenting vote. An election for Senators and Representatives of Deseret occurred simultaneously, and on the 14th of April, pursuant to proclamation by the Governor elect, the first General Assembly of the State convened at the Council House in Salt Lake City . . .

An adjourned session of the Assembly was held on April 16th, when other State officers were chosen as follows: Senators to Congress, William H. Hooper and George Q. Cannon; Secretary of State, Daniel H. Wells; Treasurer, David O. Calder; Auditor of Public Accounts, William Clayton; Attorney General, Aurelius Miner; Chief Justice, Elias Smith; Associate Justices, Zerubabbel Snow and Seth M. Blair.[30]

This third memorial for statehood was again rejected by Congress as was a fourth sent in 1872. Daniel was again an officer of the Territorial Legislature and the State Constitutional Convention that year. He helped draft the documents and elect the candidates and officers of the proposed state, but the petition was once more rejected by the Republican-dominated House of Representatives whose members were determined not to admit a Mormon-dominated state into the Union.[31]

In April 1862, six months after the transcontinental telegraph was completed, Acting Governor Frank Fuller ordered that a volunteer company of Territorial militia be raised and sent to patrol the trail eastward from Salt Lake City, "for military protection of mails, passengers, and the property of the mail company from the depredations of hostile Indians." Daniel immediately called up "twenty mounted men duly officered and properly armed and equipped, carrying sufficient ammunition for thirty days' service in the field," and placed them under the command of Col. Robert T. Burton. He also arranged for the company to be "furnished with the necessary commissary, stores and forage with proper means of transportation for the same." Colonel Burton's command, supplemented by teamsters and supply wagons, left Salt Lake City on April 26 and fought their way through deep snow and difficult conditions to reach Devil's gate on May 16. On the journey they found some mail company employees dead or wounded, mail stations abandoned and damaged or destroyed, stock run off, and mail scattered. Much of the destruction was done by marauding Indians, but evidence showed some was the work of white immigrants moving east or west on the trail.[32]

From Devil's Gate, William H. Hooper, Utah's Territorial Delegate to Congress, and Chauncey West, who had traveled with the command, continued east with a reduced escort of eight men. Colonel Burton and the remainder of his company, after a few days' rest, headed back to Salt Lake City.[33]

Two days after Colonel Burton's detachment left Salt Lake City, Army Adjutant General Lorenzo Thomas telegraphed Brigham Young, "By express direction of the President of the United States, you are hereby authorized to raise, arm, and equip one Company of Cavalry for 90 days' service . . . to protect the property of the telegraph and overland mail companies in or about Independence Rock, where depredations have been committed, and will be continued in service only till the U.S. troops can reach the point where they are so much needed."[34]

The authorization for troops should have been sent to the governor of Utah, who was not Brigham Young, but the church leader nevertheless immediately forwarded it to Gen. Daniel H. Wells, commander of the territorial militia. General Wells promptly organized one hundred and five men under the command of Capt. Lot Smith. They were mustered into the service of the US Army and became known as "Captain Lot Smith's Company of Utah Cavalry." In another bit of irony, Daniel H. Wells, Robert T. Burton, and Lot Smith, three of the foremost leaders of the Nauvoo Legion in the Utah War, now found themselves mustered as officers into the same army they had once opposed. Many of the men in the two companies, which together constituted the only direct participation of Utah military forces in the Civil War, were also veterans of the Utah War on the Mormon side.[35]

Before the company, which was the only military force organized by a religious body during the war, rode out of Great Salt Lake City on May 1, Brigham counseled them to have daily prayers, avoid liquor, bad men, and lewd women, and to "conduct themselves as gentlemen, remembering their allegiance and loyalty to our government, and also not forgetting that they are members of the organization to which they belong." They were also to "Aim never to take the life of an Indian or white man, unless compelled to do so in the discharge of duty, or in defense of your own lives, or that of your comrades . . . always give ready obedience to the orders of your commanding officers. If you do this, I promise you, as a servant of the Lord, that not one of you shall fall by the hand of an enemy."[36]

Daniel's instructions to the troops, though he also spoke in favor of prayer and against profane language, were mostly practical advice: do not camp near the mail stations so as not to provoke conflict by crowding their inhabitants; stay sufficiently close "to render prompt and ready aid when required"; take care of the company's mules and horses; cultivate as far as practicable friendly and peaceful relations with the Indians; be vigilant in guarding against surprises and use "the greatest economy . . . with ammunition; none should be needlessly wasted."[37]

Captain Smith's company met Colonel Burton's returning troop of Utah militia near Independence Rock. Burton's men passed several dozen recovered mail bags to government mail agents there who forwarded them east or west to their intended destinations. The two militia companies then parted and Burton's force continued their journey home, arriving in Salt Lake City on May 31.[38]

Lot Smith's company served as a unit in a regiment of Ohio Volunteers under the overall command of Brig. Gen. James Craig and the line command of Lieut. Col. William O. Collins. They were issued regular army uniforms, but at the instruction of Daniel and President Young, did not wear the Union blue on patrol. This practice marked them to the Indians as Mormon volunteers and may have protected them from at least one attack that would otherwise have been made against them. General Craig sent Smith's unit back from Fort Laramie to Fort Bridger with orders to guard the mail route from there to Great Salt Lake City. The company had enough manpower to chase down the marauding Indians and retrieve stolen livestock. They also pursued, but did not catch, some of the Indians and white men who had attacked the mail line and nearby ranches.[39]

Captain Smith and his men were highly regarded by the regular army officers and men with whom they served. Because of their extensive knowledge of the mail route and the terrain over which it passed, the army officers all felt that the Utah militiamen were better-suited for guarding the mail and telegraph than were the professional soldiers. In a dispatch to Brigham Young sent June 27, 1862, Major Smith noted that the army might seek to extend the original ninety-day service time of the Mormon cavalry.

> I have had frequent interviews with Col. Collins and officers; they have behaved very gentlemanly, and express themselves much pleased with our exertions, and seemed disposed to render us every assistance to contribute to our comfort . . .
>
> Col. Collins and officers all allow we are best suited to guard this road, both men and horses; they are anxious to return, and if they have any influence, I imagine they will try to get recalled and recommend to Utah to furnish the necessary guard. The Colonel has just left our camp, he has sent for Washakie, chief of the Snakes, with a view to make treaty or obtain information. No sickness at all in camp at present. We are attached to Col. Collin's regiment, Gen. Craig's division, and furnish our muster, descriptive and other returns to that command. Should General Wells require duplicates we will forward them.
>
> I am sir, yours respectfully,
Lot Smith.[40]

The Ohio regiment was recalled, but the service of Capt. Lot Smith's Utah Cavalry was not extended. The task of guarding the mail and telegraph was assigned instead to the command of Col. Patrick Conner's Third California Infantry, whose members had been recruited

Figure 13.1. Camp Douglas in 1866, looking southwest over the Salt Lake Valley, which is mostly obscured by coal smoke pollution in the air. Unknown photographer.

there the previous year for service in the Union Army. Colonel Conner and his men were disappointed to be assigned to guard duty in the western territories rather than as a fighting unit in the eastern states where the war's major battles were fought. Their orders to this mundane duty deepened their existing antagonism toward the Saints among whom they labored and Colonel Conner lost no time in making his anti-Mormon bias evident by establishing his headquarters at Camp Douglas on high ground above Great Salt Lake City, from which vantage point his forces were poorly positioned to protect any part of the mail route. His artillery was well-situated to fire at Brigham's and Daniel's homes, but like most of the downtown area, they were well out of cannon-range.[41]

In May 1862, while both Burton's and Smith's militia companies were still on patrol in the east, five leaders of the Morrisite sect ignored a writ of *habeas corpus* issued by Chief Justice John Kinney. The Morrisites were a dissident group of Mormons who had been excommunicated from the church in 1860 on grounds of apostasy for following the purported revelations of their self-styled prophet, Joseph Morris. Leaders of the group were fanatical, disciplined, well-armed, and adamant in their refusal to allow several of their number who wanted to leave the sect to come before Justice Kinney. After the writ was served by Deputy Marshall John L. Stoddard, two weeks passed without any action on the part of the Morrisite leaders to comply. On June 10, another writ was issued for the arrest of Joseph Morris, John Banks, Richard Crooks, John Parsons, and

Peter Klemgaard on charges of contempt of court and unlawful imprisonment of the seceding members of their sect.[42]

Marshall Lawrence, to whom the second writ was issued, was out of the Territory and service of it therefore devolved on his chief deputy Col. Robert T. Burton, who had just returned with his volunteer detachment from Fort Laramie. Fearing that the Morrisites would resist violently, Burton requested Gen. Daniel H. Wells to furnish a militia posse of sufficient strength to overcome any opposition. Daniel called up a force of 250 men who arrived at Kington Fort, the Morrisite settlement near Ogden on June 14. An order to surrender was sent in by Deputy Burton, but went unheeded by Morris who encouraged his followers to resist. After an hour's wait, two cannon shots were fired over the settlement from the bluff on which the posse was deployed. One ball passed harmlessly over the settlement, but the second was either badly aimed or, more likely, undercharged with powder to carry its intended distance. It struck the ground between the bluff and the fort and ricocheted straight into the gathered Morrisite crowd, killing two women and wounding a young girl.[43]

The Morrisites immediately took shelter in their entrenchments and returned fire against the posse. During the three-day battle and siege that followed, two members of the posse, Jared Smith and J. P. Whiplin, were killed by fire from the fort. After the fighting on the first day, Colonel Burton sent a written report to Acting Governor Fuller, who answered him in these words: "The shedding of blood in resistance to civil authority renders execution of the law imperative . . . Let your acts be tempered with mercy, but see that the laws are vindicated."[44]

About sunset of the third day, after some of Burton's men had advanced to the gate of the fort under cover of a moveable barricade, a white flag was hoisted by those within the fort and the gate was opened. Deputy Marshall Burton and a few men rode in to receive the surrender. He told the assembled Morrisites that all men who had born arms against the posse were under arrest. While the Morrisites were stacking their weapons, some asked permission for their leader to address them. Burton granted the request on condition that he would say nothing to cause further excitement. Morris, who was probably insane, disregarded this caution. Lifting his hands above his head, he shouted: "All who are willing to follow me through life and death, come on!" Many of his followers shouted their approval, and made a dash for the firearms. Over a hundred fanatics confronted the deputy marshal and his outnumbered escort. Burton twice commanded the leaders to halt and, when the commands were ignored, he seized the pistol in his holster and fired. Several of the posse also fired and in the brief but deadly melee, Morris was killed, John Banks was mortally wounded, and two more women, who may have thrown themselves in front of the men to protect them, were accidentally slain.⁴⁵

The shooting ended in less than a minute, but five of the Morrisites lay dead as well as two members of the posse who had accompanied Colonel Burton into Kington Fort. The surviving Morrisite men laid down their arms, were arrested and marched to Salt Lake City where they were placed under bonds to appear at the next session of the District Court.⁴⁶

Steven S. Harding was appointed governor of Utah by President Lincoln in March 1862. When he spoke to the assembled citizens of the territory at the Pioneer Day celebration in July, he related a very accommodating and peaceful view of his duties and assured the Saints that he had no interest in interfering with their religious practices. But this speech was a deliberate deception that masked the governor's true attitude, as well as that of the two new federal judges, Charles B. Waite and Thomas J. Drake, who came to the territory with him. All three soon revealed that their anti-Mormon feelings were similar to those of Colonel Conner and his officers: they believed that most Mormons did not support the federal government and would be glad to see its demise. At a December session of the legislature, over which Daniel presided as president, the governor stated his feelings that the Saints were disloyal and inveighed against the practice of polygamy.⁴⁷

> I am sorry to say that since my sojourn amongst you I have heard no sentiments, either publicly or privately expressed, that would lead me to believe that much sympathy is felt by any considerable number of your people in favor of the Government of the United States, now struggling for its very existence . . .
>
> It would be disingenuous if I were not to advert to a question . . . I mean polygamy, or, if you please, plural wives . . . I will not be drawn into a discussion either of its morality or its Biblical authority . . .
>
> I lay it down as a sound proposition that no community can happily exist with an institution as important as that of marriage wanting in all those qualities that make it homogeneal with institutions and laws of neighboring civilized communities.⁴⁸

After he publicly attacked Mormons' polygamy, the governor secretly drafted a bill, with the help of Judges Waite and Drake, to limit the jurisdiction of probate courts, allow the federal marshal to exclude Mormons or anyone he deemed unfit from juries, and change the election of territorial militia officers to appointment by the governor. The

Saints responded with a resolution of censure passed at a public meeting in the Tabernacle. This document was delivered to the governor and the two judges and all three were requested to resign their offices and leave Utah. They refused and Judge Drake expressed the feelings of the three officials to the delegation who brought it.[49]

> Go back to Brigham Young, your master—the embodiment of sin and shame and disgust—and tell him that I neither fear him, nor love him, nor hate him—that I utterly despise him. Tell him, whose tools and tricksters you are, that I did not come here by his permission, and that I will not go away at his desire or by his direction.[50]

Colonel Conner and his officers allied themselves with the governor and his anti-Mormon stance by signing a counter-petition to President Lincoln asking that the federal officials be retained in office. Chief Justice John Kinney, Territory Secretary Frank Fuller, and other Utah Gentiles refused to sign this petition and were thereafter accused of being "subservient to Brigham Young."[51]

With a federal anti-polygamy law now in place[52] and military and federal officials aligned against leaders of the LDS Church, rumors circulated that some of Colonel Connor's men planned to surround President Young's home, arrest him by force, and carry him out of Utah Territory for trial on the charge of polygamy. Colonel Conner denied that any plot was in the making, but his assurances did not quiet the fears of the Saints, who had seen the reality of several previous military actions to their great loss. To forestall any arrest or kidnapping, Daniel ordered a militia guard placed night and day around Brigham's home as well as Heber C. Kimball's and his own. The guards were instructed, in the event of an attack, to give a signal that would bring hundreds of armed volunteers running to protect the church leaders.[53]

Daniel, who took personal charge of the matter, directed Heber C. Kimball, with a guard of ten men, to occupy the Historian's Office. Franklin D. Richards also remained in the office during the night. Daniel had another fifty men under John Pugmire distributed in the Tithing Office and the barn next to it. The Legion's cannons, which were stored on Brigham's property, were all put in a state of readiness.

On the afternoon of March 10, 1863, the US flag was unfurled from the top of President Young's Beehive House due to a report that a warrant had been issued to arrest Brigham Young and had been put into Colonel Connor's hands to serve using military force. At this previously arranged signal, a large crowd of citizens, all with their arms, found their way to Brigham's home and surrounded it. By evening the President's Office and yard, Daniel H. Wells's yard, the Historian's Office, and the Tithing Office were full of armed volunteers, all determined to prevent any surprise arrest of Brigham, Daniel, or any church leaders.[54]

In an effort to forestall any violence, Brigham submitted to arrest by Marshal Gibbs, who served the warrant without the aid of any troops. He appeared before Chief Justice Kinney the same day and, after a hearing, was released on $2,000 bond until the next term of court.

By the following day, news of the threatened Mormon confrontation with the military was telegraphed to both coasts and appeared in newspapers.

> It seems that matters at Salt Lake are in an unsettled and uncertain state. Some difficulty has grown up between the Governor, the United States Judges, and the head of the Mormon Church, which may—though we hope not—terminate in a collision. We never deemed it particularly an act of wisdom to order a single regiment to Salt Lake. It was not needed there for protection. We fear, too, that the Governor has been imprudent. The Mormons should, of course, submit to the laws, but laws ought not be forced upon them which are repugnant to a very large majority of that singular people. A conflict at this time would prove a great misfortune to California. It would also prove fatal to the Mormons, and hence we reason that they will avoid any hostile demonstrations except in self-defense. The pretty-much let-alone policy is the one which should be adopted toward the Mormons.[55]

Because it was evident that the Mormons would resist any use of force, the planned assault did not take place and tempers gradually cooled down on both sides. General Connor obeyed his orders to leave the Mormons alone, but some of his officers and men continued in their off-duty time to seek some means of getting the Mormon leaders into custody. Consequently, Daniel kept a reduced guard force on duty throughout the winter and spring months and the signal system to summon additional help remained in place.[56]

The first case in Justice Kinney's next court session was the trial of the men charged in the Morrisite conflict. Seven of the ten men who had been indicted for killing two members of the Marshal's posse were convicted of murder in the second degree and sentenced to prison terms of ten to fifteen years. Two were acquitted and the remaining one was released without prosecution. Sixty-nine other Morrisites were fined for resisting an officer of the law and ordered held until their fines of one hundred dollars each were paid.[57]

Within three days after the verdicts were announced however, Governor Harding, in response to a petition from some federal officials and Camp Douglas officers, pardoned all the convicted men and set them at liberty. One of those freed by the governor later swore in an affidavit that the killing of Joseph Morris and the other Morrisites at Fort Kington had been ordered by Brigham Young and Daniel H. Wells. No action was taken against either of them, but Deputy Marshall Burton, who led the posse, was later charged with murder by anti-Mormon officials. He was acquitted, but the handling of the Morrisite affair, in which murderers were pardoned and officials performing their duties falsely charged, left a lasting bitterness among Mormons against the federal officials responsible for the miscarriage of justice.[58]

Brigham Young fared better in Judge Kinney's court. The grand jury refused to indict him for polygamy and he was released from his bond.

14

The Wells Family Grows and Prospers during the Civil War

1860–1864

The Wells family added no new members in 1860. In 1861 one child, Preston Strait Wells, was born in May to Hannah Free Wells, but little Preston lived less than a month before dying in early June. He was the second of Hannah Free Wells's children to die in infancy and his passing left the Wells family saddened and no larger than it was at the close of 1859.

1862 was a better year for Daniel and his wives. In May Joseph Smith Wells was born to Martha Harris Wells and in September Ephraim Willard Wells was born to Susan Alley Wells. Louisa Free Wells gave birth to Clara Ellen Wells in October, and Lydia Alley Wells gave birth to Louis Robison Wells in December.[1]

These four children brought the Wells household to thirty-three living people, not counting Daniel's first wife, Eliza Robison, and their son Albert, who by 1860 were living in Summit, Wisconsin. Albert, who turned twenty-one that year, attended the Nashotah Theological Seminary and planned to enter the ministry; his mother was also employed at the seminary.[2]

Although he had not seen either of them since 1846 and was by now aware that Eliza had divorced him, Daniel still considered her and Albert to be part of his family. The pain of his separation from them remained with him and he still hoped that Eliza and Albert would eventually accept the restored gospel and return to him. Daniel's daughter Annie Wells Cannon, wrote of this hope and his sorrow that it was not fulfilled.

Of this home life in Nauvoo, and the separation, father seldom spoke in his family conversations. His family respected this silence and forbore questioning. That the separation was a great trial and sorrow to both of them is beyond doubt. That father at first and for some years afterwards believed his wife would change and come west, we know; that she chose otherwise, was to him and to her the beginning of two rather remarkable careers.[3]

Daniel was kept informed of Eliza's and Albert's whereabouts by his sister, Catherine Woods, with whom they corresponded regularly and sometimes visited. Despite his knowledge of their actual residence, Daniel gave their names as members of his family to the census enumerator in 1860 and they are listed in the census as living in Salt Lake City as well as in Wisconsin.[4]

In addition to family and relatives, the Wells residences were now home to a dozen or more other relatives, servants, and employees. Included among these in 1860 were Elizabeth Hyner and Mary Hyner Whitney from Pennsylvania; Anna Yenson and Clara Hansen from Denmark; Maria Taylor from England; Catherine Smith and Emily Harness from Illinois; Huldah Duncan from Iowa; and John Gibson from South Carolina.[5]

The oldest of Daniel's Utah children reached their teens in 1862 and the adobe homes in which they had lived for more than ten years were now too small to accommodate the multitude of siblings, let alone provide individual apartments for each of Daniel's wives. His first response to the housing crisis was to build, or rather have built, a large home on First East Street, now State Street. Daniel was too busy with church duties, public works, and business matters to supervise the construction of his own house, but he was once again prosperous enough that he could hire the work done, provide much of the interior materials required from his own sawmills and nail factory, and pay cash for the whole building when it was completed.[6]

Into this home between Second and Third South Emmeline Wells moved with her four children (two named Wells and two Whitney), along with a cousin Mary Hyner Whitney and three or four servants. Before Daniel could move further in his quest for better housing, President Young intervened with a plan designed to keep his second counselor in close proximity to his own home. Brigham's plan was characterized as a "mean trick" by Heber J. Grant when he jokingly described it many years later to Ezra Taft Benson, who related it in an address at the centennial celebration of the Logan Temple.

I walked over to him, and President Grant said, "Did I ever tell you about the mean trick Brigham Young played on your great-grandfather?"

I said, "No, President. I didn't know Brigham Young ever played a mean trick on anyone."

He responded, "Oh, yes, he did. I'll tell you about it . . . You know where Zion's Bank and ZCMI are over on the corner?"

I said, "Yes."

He continued, "Your great-grandfather built the finest home in Salt Lake City on that corner, with the exception of Brigham Young's home (which, of course, was the Lion House). He had it all finished. It was a beautiful home—two stories with a porch at both levels on both sides of the house. It had a white picket fence around it with fruit trees and ornamental trees and with a little stream running through the yard. He was all ready to move his families in from their log cabins when President Young called him into the office one day. "Brother Benson," he said, "we would like you to go to Cache Valley and pioneer that area and preside over the Saints. We suggest you sell your home to Daniel H. Wells."

"Now," President Grant said, "Daniel H. Wells was Brigham Young's counselor. Wasn't that a mean trick?"[7]

The story related by Grant is accurate except for a few details: the home was begun in 1856 and finished in 1859. During those years, Apostle Ezra T. Benson was on a mission in Europe and his family lived in Tooele County. In 1860 Benson was called to preside over the settlements in Cache Valley and he sold his newly-completed home to Daniel H. Wells for the mutually agreed sum of $12,000, the amount that it cost to build. The transaction gave Benson the funds he needed to outfit his family for pioneering in the north and provided Daniel with a home large enough to accommodate his family. Neither man regarded the sale as a "mean trick," although it did, as Brigham wished, keep his counselor's residence a short walk across South Temple Street from his own.[8]

Their new homes brought all the Wells wives and children into full prominence as one of the first families in the territory. Daniel was not wealthy by national standards, but his assets and income were definitely in the top two percent of men in pre-mining era Utah. The "Big House," as it came to be known among family members, soon became a landmark in Salt Lake society and a cherished and happy home to those who dwelt in it. Annie Wells Cannon speaks glowingly of it as well and of her own home on State Street.

The Wells Family Grows and Prospers during the Civil War 249

Figure 14.1. Daniel H. Wells's home at No. 8 East South Temple Street, Salt Lake City, ca. 1884. The one-story L-shaped extension added at the back can be seen under the sign atop the ZCMI Main Street Store.

In 1862 father acquired the large commodious house and surrounding property on the corner of Main and South Temple Streets. This home was known far and wide as the "Wells Mansion," and was the scene of many historic and interesting events. It was colonial in architecture, with wide porches, large rooms with high ceilings, and deep windows with green shutters. Its wide outside doors, never locked, swung into a spacious hall with a long artistic staircase, where guests from near and far were ever welcome to enter and enjoy the proverbial hospitality of the gracious occupants . . .

Each wife had her own separate apartment—sitting room, bedrooms, dining room and kitchen. Aunt Louisa occupied the lower west side, in which was the large family parlor with its open fireplace, comfortable chairs and family piano . . .

For many years my mother, Aunt Emmeline, was the only one of the wives who had a home elsewhere, but we were quite as much at home in the "Big House" as any of the rest, and almost always were present at family prayers. Likewise, our home, only three blocks distant, was just as open and free to other members of the family.[9]

Polygamy was an extremely difficult lifestyle for anyone to live comfortably. Daniel and his wives, like others who accepted the challenge of living in plural marriages, had to overcome many of the individualistic ideas that they had all been raised with and learn to accept and to love all the members of the communal family in their various roles. That the Wells family was able to do this for over forty years until Daniel's death and his widows for another thirty thereafter without any estrangement or even serious dispute among any of the members, marks them as one of the most successful plural families in LDS history.

Four of Daniel's wives were from New England Puritan families and three were from southern backgrounds. All except Eliza became Mormons as children or teens and, prior to their conversions, the concept of plural marriage, had it even entered their minds, would have been anathema to all of them. Likewise, had any been invited into any sexual relationship outside traditional marriage, they would have rejected it out of hand. Eliza never accepted Mormonism and vehemently opposed polygamy. Her rejection of both led her to finally also reject Daniel, who was baptized into the church before their separation, but did not then embrace polygamy. He might never have done so had his wife joined him in the LDS faith but remained opposed to plural marriage.

Unlike some Mormons, Daniel and all six of his later wives were introduced to plural marriage after their conversion to the faith and all had accepted it as an integral part of their religion prior to entering into the practice. All the wives accepted Daniel as a husband knowing he was already married and were willing to join the communal family life that polygamy required. They became friends with one another as well as spouses of the same husband and those bonds helped as much as marriage vows in making the family successful.

Daniel's personality was also well-fitted to a family with many women. He had grown up as the only male in a home with six sisters; the coincidence that his later life included six wives probably felt entirely natural to him. His gentle attitude toward all of his wives and children communicated the affection and regard he had for each of them. He was a family man to the core and had accepted Mormonism largely because of its emphasis of family importance, both in mortality and in eternity. He frequently explained to his wives and children the LDS teachings of which he was most certain:

> ... the divine authority of the living Priesthood, the authority and unchangeableness of fundamental principles—that of celestial marriage, the baptism for the dead ... the fact that

eternity reaches as far back as it does forward, and that all the children of men may become partakers of salvation through the laws of God. These he said were the reasons he had accepted Mormonism. For this purpose he married his wives, soon after coming into the new land, and established his patriarchal family . . .

Father's wives, the mothers of the family, were held in great respect and affection by all the children. We addressed each of them, except our own mother, in the relationship of aunt. Each of these mothers held the same sacred views of the faith [he] had espoused, and a perfect understanding of the responsibilities and obligations pertaining to the system of celestial—plural marriage. This large family lived as peacefully and harmoniously as families anywhere. The mothers were helpful to each other, and united in reverent and loyal affection to their husband.[10]

Daniel's wives were often completely engrossed in bearing and raising their children, assisting other family members, training new immigrants to cope with pioneer life, and helping needy families and those with sickness or other afflictions, but they each managed to retain and express their independence within the family structure.

Aunt Louisa was a natural nurse and with study and experience had acquired some knowledge of medicine. Her services were often sought by friends and neighbors, and in many emergency calls by her quick attention, life was saved. "Send for Aunt Louisa" was the first thought in cases of accident or sudden illness, and she never failed them.

Aunt Martha, tall, of fair complexion and a comforting, sympathetic manner, was born in Tennessee and had the natural southern gift of delightful story telling, while, in her complacent way, she pursued her domestic tasks. A genial atmosphere pervaded her rooms and her very presence invited confidences.

Aunt Lydia Ann, short of stature with dark hair and eyes, was typical New England–thrifty (must have been shocked many times at the family extravagance), had an attractive eastern accent, broad "a" and short "r," which we all would have liked to acquire. She was quite reserved with a deep sense of values. She had charge of father's choicest books and prized all her possessions.

Aunt Susan was short like her sister, Aunt Lydia Ann, but of fair complexion, possessing also the New England traits. Both were fine needlewomen and expert with the spinning wheel, using it long after others had discarded it.

Aunt Hannah was tall and dignified, with kindly, motherly ways. All were thoroughly acquainted with the arts of homemaking, and were devoted mothers and sincere Latter-day Saints.

Aunt Emmeline, my mother, whose home was on State Street, a few blocks distant from the "Big House," possessed also these qualifications of homemaking, homeloving tenderness. Her natural talents and early education, however, were along literary lines and her home became almost a mecca for others of like tendencies . . . She had artistic talents, was a sweet singer, a progressive thinker, and a poet. It was in her home that the Wasatch Literary Association was organized in 1872.[11]

Because, by her own choice, she lived separately from Daniel's other wives and consequently saw him less frequently than they did, Emmeline Wells often felt lonely and deprived of the intimate one-to-one relationship she wanted with her husband. Several entries in her diaries express this longing for a more exclusive closeness that even she recognized was impossible in a polygamous family.

> This evening I fully expected my husband here but was again disappointed . . . He is not in want of me for a companion or in any sense, he does not need me at all, there are plenty ready and willing to administer to every wish caprice or whim of his, indeed they anticipate them, they are near him always, while I am shut out of his life . . . It is impossible for me to make myself useful to him in any way while I am held at such a distance.[12]

Emmeline's love for Daniel was strong and heartfelt, but she felt he did not express the same depth of romantic affection, even on the occasions when they were together.

> My husband came, my heart gave one great bound towards him; O how enthusiastically I love him; truly and devotedly if he could only feel towards me in any degree as I do towards him how happy it would make me.[13]

The other wives may have also felt the desire for a greater share of Daniel's time and a more intimate personal relationship with him, but as none of them kept a diary or wrote of her personal feelings, we cannot know this with any certainty. Not so with Emmiline: her unfulfilled romantic longings eventually turned her toward an independent career as a prolific writer, poet, and feminist that spanned more than fifty years and extended for a quarter-century after Daniel's death. During his lifetime, he always gave her the independence she requested, if not the exclusivity of his affections that she craved.

Daniel's church responsibilities, business affairs, and territorial duties were at their peak during the 1860s and he was obliged to leave much of the care and direction of his children to his wives who proved more than adequate to the task. He presided as the patriarch in his homes, but with an intermittent, almost casual presence. He trusted all of his wives, assumed that they would do right according to gospel principles and felt them all competent to teach their children to do likewise. He never struck any member of his family and rarely ever raised his voice. He felt that, given the understanding of right and the opportunity to do it, most people would. He was rarely disappointed by his family or by those who worked for him. Rulon S. Wells describes his own mother's efforts to instill correct social skills into the behavior of her own children as well as those of the other wives.

> And, then, there was my own dear mother who had also taught school before the exodus from Nauvoo, and who was an adept in quoting the scriptures . . . During father's absence in England, while filling his first mission as President of the European Mission in 1864–65, she organized what was known as the Manner Meeting. I suppose we children were a lot of little savages at that time and she saw to it that we learned how to behave in company, at the table, and in our plays . . . All the children were brought into this school the fame of which spread outside the family, and our neighbors sent their children as well to Aunt Louisa's Manner Meeting.[14]

Daniel did not believe in the accumulation of wealth for its own sake and felt an obligation to help those who were struggling to improve their situation. His notion of spreading and increasing prosperity by spending generously on his family and hiring as many as he could of those who needed work was reinforced by the covenant that he had made soon after joining the Church to consecrate all that he owned or would ever acquire to the "building up of the Kingdom of God on the earth." He had made a complete sacrifice of all his personal wealth when he joined the church and through the remainder of his life he regarded his assets as a stewardship over property that actually belonged to God and was to be used to further the Lord's purposes as he understood them. As Annie Wells Cannon explained:

> It was a part of father's philosophy that men who could should provide work for those who were in need of work. Accordingly, he obeyed his own ideas and employed a large number of men and women. Prominent among these was a family steward, Brother James Snarr, who remained as purchasing agent for the family for a number of years. There were also gardeners, teamsters, superintendents of the big lumber mills (one of the numerous industries father promoted), and, in the homes, women for the various branches of housework. He was known as one of the kindest and most considerate of employers, never distrusted anyone, and his kindly ways generally brought a like return.[15]

Among the other employees who labored in the Wells industries during this prosperous period, one of Daniel's sons, Rulon S. Wells, remembered a number who worked under the direction of James Snarr or in other enterprises.

> Brother Snarr also had charge of the cows and pigs, and the force of men to help—Walter Hawks, Mark Barnes, Steve Parsons, and Brother Bawden—in the lumber yard. There was Arza Hinckley who had charge of the stables, the horses and mules, the teams and the teamsters, the wagons and carriages, of which there were a goodly number. There were Ike Neibauer, Matt Luce, Sandy and Jim Bullock, George Naylor, and George F. Brooks, Stephen Taylor, and others whose names I do not now recall.
> We also had a very congenial gardener, James T. Wilson; I think he was a Frenchman from Tipperary or somewhere on the Emerald Isle. He it was who saw to it that fresh vegetables were supplied on every table.[16]

Others who worked for Daniel included Daniel Smith, who was employed on the Pleasant Grove farm; Henry Dittmore, who worked the Salt Lake City farm beginning in 1861; and Walter Henry Brown, who hauled coal from Coalville and lumber out of Cottonwood Canyon for his employer.

At the end of 1864, Brigham Young compiled a list of 183 persons who were employed by him at that time and the number of family members in the household of each employee. The total came to 1,079 persons supported financially by Brigham and his various business enterprises. People working for Daniel H. Wells were not as numerous, but definitely numbered near a hundred. Many of Daniel's workers and business partners were long term associates, such as Steven Taylor and Sandy Bullock, both of whom stayed with him for more than twenty-five years.[17]

For all the improvement the Big House made in the family's comfort, educational opportunities, and cultural refinement, it almost didn't survive the first anniversary of their occupying it. Rulon S. Wells graphically describes the near-disaster that could easily have become a catastrophe.

> We had a fire—the biggest fire that had ever occurred in Great Salt Lake City (that was the right name then) and no fire department. Just a volunteer bucket brigade. The fire happened in 1863, during the Civil War, but it bore no relation to it. We were celebrating the Fourth. It was our regular custom to celebrate both the Fourth and the Twenty-fourth of July in the true fireworks fashion, and the boys of our neighborhood, including ourselves, although we were quite young, were having a little celebration of our own on the sidewalk just north of the corral, and I was delegated to go after the matches.
>
> We had the barrel of an old blunderbuss (gun) which the bigger boys were loading with powder and wadding and priming the touch-hole with powder. This was all before we ever heard of caps or cartridges, and matches were needed to touch it off. Having secured a box of matches I took what I thought was the nearest route to where the boys were waiting and climbed up an old shack on the west side of the corral wall, up onto the haystack, leaving considerable hay behind me, and then ran along the top of the haystack to the South Temple Street sidewalk. I took the box of matches, now on fire [phosphorous matches could ignite when shaken in their metal box] through my climbing operations, and threw it down to the boys. After several futile attempts at picking up the burning matches and touching off the miniature cannon, Aunt Susan, one of father's wives (we always called them "Aunt") came down the sidewalk from the east and said: "Boys, what's that smoke over in the garden?" We all ran to see, and found the shack and haystack afire right where I had climbed up. My conscience was burning in my bosom where the matches had

been doing the same thing a few minutes before as I clattered my way up to the top of the haystack. But I said nothing.

Everybody was too busy to ask any questions for the next several hours. The fire spread rapidly along the haystacks in every direction. The barn took fire and burned to the ground. The barn doors, however, were first opened and the horses liberated, and the pens were opened and the cows went out into the street; but the stubborn and frightened pigs perished in the flames. One of the horses, however, was held in his stall long enough to get one side badly burned, but he survived and was ever after called "General Burnsides," in honor of the U.S. General then fighting in the War of the Rebellion. Water was carried from the ditches and from our forty-foot well. Everybody turned out to help and worked hard, but they might just as well have stayed home, for the fire went on until everything was destroyed. Our home, however, at the western end of the lot—where Zion's Savings Bank Building now stands—was saved from the flying and blazing embers by spreading the roof with wet blankets and pouring water drawn from the deep well over the windlass in oaken buckets.

The soldiers, or a goodly number of them, from Fort Douglas, also came to our aid and formed themselves into a bucket brigade. The way and the rapidity with which they emptied the oaken buckets at the well into other moveable buckets and practically tossed them from one to another along the long line to the fire and also from one porch to the other and onto the roof of the home and to the wet blankets, was indeed a marvel and made us stare with amazement and wonder . . .

Father had climbed up on the shed and endeavored to break it down in order to prevent the spread of the fire, but all to no effect; and then he went to the roof of the home where through hard work he continued until the fire subsided and the safety of the home was assured. The apple trees between the corral and the home were loaded with delicious apples and for weeks after we were well supplied with baked apples—all we had to do was to pick them off the trees already baked.

Well, the fire was out and everything was quieted down and people went about their business and, I suppose, talking about the big fire and wondering how it started. Nobody knew, and even I only suspected it, but these suspicions grew on me so heavily that I hunted up father and found him sitting in the front room just on the east side of the hall all alone by himself, tired out from the arduous and perilous labors of the day.

The room was rather dark and all was perfectly still, but father, seeing me standing sheepishly at the door, said: "Rulon, do you know how the fire started?" To this I replied, "I think I do, father." Then I related all the circumstances just as they occurred and he looked at me and said: "Well, always be careful when playing with matches." After this scathing rebuke my conscience was greatly eased, but ever since I have been extremely careful "when playing with matches."[18]

In August 1863, Louisa Martha Wells, Daniel's twenty-seventh child was born to Emmeline Wells. The family's joy at that event turned to sadness in October when Ephraim Willard Wells died at age one and his brother Brigham Wells died at age four a week later. Hannah Free Wells was the mother of both of these children. They were the third and fourth of her children to die before age five and she was deeply saddened by their loss. She was left at the end of the year with only two living children, Abby and Junius. None of Daniel's other wives had lost more than one child and all except Eliza had from three to seven surviving children.[19]

Although the Civil War had not greatly affected the Wells family in Utah, the few members of Daniel's family remaining in the east were more involved in the conflict. A letter from Catherine Woods gave family news and told how she saw the war, then in its second year, from a Midwestern viewpoint.

September 8th [1862]

My Dear brother

I know you must feel anxious to hear from us thru stirring war times. It is dreadful to think that our country has come to this. I fear we will never have peace and [unreadable] again, as yet we have not personally been much affected except that Willy [William Wells Woods] has joined the 3rd Lancer Regiment. He is receiving pay as quartermaster sergeant but will be a lieut.—if it [the regiment] is got up. I feel very bad to have him [there] and sincerely wish we had all gone to Utah or California this last spring . . . for my part I cannot see any hope for the country—let either party win there can be nothing but bitterness of feeling— I am afraid it will be a long disastrous struggle and in the end no good results . . .

James [Catherine's husband] is at home and [his] Br Park Woods is still here and the boys are all at home at present. Lily [Eliza Jane Woods] taught school through the summer—her first experiment succeeded very well . . . Park received a letter from

Albert [Wells] a day or two since—he is settled as clergyman over a parish and appears to be in good spirits and interested in his work. I received a letter from Eliza [Wells] not long since. She was well— also from Br Joseph Coombs. They were all well but he says hard work is his portion. My dear br. do write as often as you can and believe me ever your aff. sister,

C.C.Woods

Give my love to Lewis [Robison] and wife when you see them, yours with much love, C.C.W.[20]

The next year Daniel received a letter from Catherine's oldest son, Park Woods, giving further information about the family, including the news that Catherine was gone.

Burlington
Sunday September 20th 1863

My Dear Uncle,

I have the sad duty to perform of apprizing you of poor dear Mother's death . . . on the 25th of August after many years of suffering . . . Brother William was at home on a short leave of absence from the Army for the first time since he entered the service. I had come home to see him and then Aunt Eliza [Wells] and cousin Albert [Wells] were both with us. Poor Jimmie boy [James Dan Woods] being the only absent one; he having gone to Denver last April. I enclose a letter to you for him as the last letter he wrote stated that he was going to Salmon River by way of Great Salt Lake City . . . I am working for the Burlington & Missouri River R R [Railroad] Co. as land agent and have a very pleasant berth did it not take me away from home so much. Father is away from home just at the present time. When he returns he will write you. Will we have not heard from since he rejoined his Regiment. He left it at Vicksburg. He likes the service very well—is Capt. of a cavalry company. Sister Lile [Eliza Jane Woods] has a lonely sad time of it—she had been mother's constant companion and will miss her so much more. I write with much love. I am your afft. nephew

Park Woods

. . . It is unnecessary for me to ask you to give brother Dan good advice if he passes through your place as I know you will do so anyway. He is young to depend upon himself but I am in hopes that his love for his mother and her good council will mold a useful and good man of him—will you, if they take them there, have the picture you have of dear mother photographed and send us two or three. Your nephew Park.[21]

The Battle of Gettysburg in early July 1863 marked the turning point of the Civil War and the largest number of casualties of any battle fought during the conflict, but neither the outcome of the engagement nor the horrendous loss of life it caused produced more than a ripple in Utah. In the territory, the continuing hostility of Governor Harding and other federal officials toward Brigham Young, Daniel H. Wells, and other Latter-day Saint leaders was the major ongoing conflict. Daniel felt obliged to keep militia forces at his own home, as well as Brigham's and Heber C. Kimball's to guard against a surprise arrest raid by some of Colonel Conner's troops, who were still denied the chance to fight in the national conflict and were still determined to vent their frustration on the Mormons.

Governor Harding wanted a confrontation between the military forces and the people of Utah in order to justify his request that additional troops be sent to Utah Territory. Judges Waite and Drake supported this policy and Colonel Conner was asked to carry it into action by having his men arrest the First Presidency and hold them for trial on charges of treason. In March D. O. Calder reported to George Q. Cannon an overheard conversation between Judge Waite and Colonel Conner that confirmed their intentions. "The Colonel said: 'These three men must be surprised.' The Judge replied: 'Colonel, you know your duty.'"[22]

While Daniel maintained the round-the-clock guard in plain view of Colonel Conner's observers, non-Mormon businessmen in Great Salt Lake City, telegraphed friends in the east that "they must work for the removal of the troops, Governor Harding, and Judges Waite and Drake, else there would be difficulty and the mail and telegraph lines would be destroyed. Their moneyed interests had given them great energy in our behalf. They have placed their line at the disposal of President Young to be used to Washington or New York. We fully expect the Colonel, Governor, and judges will be recalled."[23]

Governor Harding was removed from office by President Lincoln in June. This action was possibly the result of the pardons he had issued to the convicted Morrisite murderers, but more likely a reaction to the very bitter antagonism he expressed toward his Utah constituents and the complaints that church members and non-Mormons alike made about him. He was then appointed as chief justice of the Colorado Supreme Court but was also removed from that office in 1865 for alleged incompetence and immorality.[24]

Harding's successor was the former Utah Territorial Indian Superintendent James D. Doty, a man who had done good work in his former position and was well-regarded as a gentleman and competent administrator by Mormons and non-Mormons alike. Doty would not countenance any effort to arrest members of the First Presidency and Colonel Conner was obliged to abandon his plan. His antagonism toward the church and its leaders was undiminished, however, and his men took every opportunity to demonstrate it as revealed in a letter written by Brigham Young Jr.:

> A little circumstance occurred yesterday at the mouth of Parley's Canyon, which shows that the feeling entertained toward us by our friends (?) is as bitter as ever. Brother Arza Hinckley [an employee of Daniel H. Wells], with whom you are very well acquainted, was coming out of the canyon with some sheep. He had a boy with him named Smith, about 14 years of age, who was a little in advance, when they met a wagonload of troops who were going up the canyon to get some wood. As they met, one of the soldiers jumped out, and, approaching the boy, said: "You are the first wild man I have seen," at the same time striking him and knocking him clear off the dugway. The boy had scarcely struck the ground before he was joined by the soldier, sent after him by a well-directed blow from Arza.
>
> Ten of these northern braves then rushed upon him. Three of them he knocked down, but they were too many for him and they beat him in a most shocking manner. He is now at Brother Wells', and there is no apprehension but what he will recover soon. I know not what steps will be taken by our brethren in this affair, but I think they (the soldiers) will not get another opportunity at an unarmed man.[25]

In January 1864, Daniel H. Wells, acting as president of the Utah Territorial Council, and John Taylor, acting as speaker of the House of Representatives, signed a memorial to President Lincoln in response to an act unanimously passed by both houses of the Utah Legislature. It asked that an Indian reservation be created in the Uintah Basin and that the government move the Indian tribes of Utah onto the reservation, provide continuing compensation to them for the loss of other lands they occupied, and extinguish their title to all lands outside the proposed reservation so that title to these lands could be transferred by the government to the white settlers who claimed them.[26]

Daniel, who was commander of the territorial militia as well as president of the Territorial Council would, under normal circumstances, have been deeply involved in the treaty negotiations with the Utah tribes, but soon after the memorial was sent to President Lincoln, he temporarily left his military position and did not resume his duties as lieutenant general until July 1865. He also laid aside his responsibilities as superintendent of public works and his work as a private businessman directing his several companies. Daniel charged his employees to manage his business affairs and secured others to take over his military and public works responsibilities while he accepted a new church calling and departed on a mission to Europe.

15

Daniel's First (Incomplete) Term as European Mission President

1864–1865

Daniel H. Wells was called during General Conference of April 1864 to preside over the European Mission, headquartered in Liverpool, England. Brigham Young's son Brigham Jr. was called to go with him as his assistant. Mission calls were then usually open-ended, but commonly lasted for two to three years. Daniel made his preparations accordingly, arranging for his businesses to be managed by trusted employees and taking leave of his other responsibilities with the promise that he would resume them on his return. The prospect of being absent from most of his family for such a long period was difficult, but his wives and children pulled together to send him off with the best of feelings.[1]

> In 1864 father was called to preside over the European Mission. Aunt Hannah was selected to accompany him. She had recently had a great bereavement, two of her little ones having died of diphtheria. This was before the days of antitoxin, and few cases survived an attack of this dread disease. Because of her sorrow the family united in desiring her to have this opportunity.
>
> Great preparations were made for their departure, the first long journey after coming to the Valley, and this time not in a covered wagon, but by stagecoach across the country to St. Louis. A farewell party by the family was given in the "Big House," and a sumptuous dinner served . . .

Some weeks after this event our first piano arrived. Father had purchased it in St. Louis, and had it freighted home with a party of emigrants. The unpacking of the instrument and setting it up in the large parlor was a most exciting occasion for which all the family gathered. In the evening Sister Widerburg, a cultured Scandinavian lady, was invited to come in and play for our entertainment. She was later engaged to give lessons to the older girls, so that when father returned he might see how profitable his gift had been. She continued to be our music teacher for some years, but few of us ever showed much musical talent.[2]

Unlike the church's present policy, which is to pay the transportation expenses of its missionaries, Daniel was expected to provide the funds for his own and his wife's travel to England and back and to pay their living expenses while there. To do this, he sold a farm and purchased a carriage and four mules. These animals were preferred over oxen or horses because they could pull as heavy a load, but required less food. They were also not as likely to be seized by soldiers of the Union Army for service as cavalry mounts or artillery teams, a practice that by 1864 had become common among units desperate for replacement animals.

Daniel and Brigham Jr. with their wives, joined the eastbound church wagon train that departed Great Salt Lake City in early May. Their company, one of six assembled that year for the eastward journey, was captained by John R. Murdock. Alexander (Sandy) Bullock, Daniel's employee who had by then also become his brother-in-law through his marriage to Emily Caroline Harris, the sister of Martha Givens Harris, drove the Wells carriage. Sandy was a teamster who started working for Daniel at age fifteen in 1854 and stayed in his employ for thirty-three years.[3]

John Murdock's mule and horse train of about seventy-five wagons was the first church train of the season to reach Wyoming, Nebraska Territory, on June 6. Wyoming, about twenty-five miles south of Omaha, was the eastern termination point for the church trains, which waited there until they were filled with immigrant Mormons arriving from the east and then returned with them to Great Salt Lake City. Daniel and Brigham Jr. and their party left Wyoming and journeyed north to Omaha where they crossed the Missouri River and traveled on by train to New York City. Sandy Bullock loaded the carriage in which they had traveled with goods for the Wells family, including the piano mentioned by Annie Wells Cannon, and other items for sale in Utah. He then returned to Wyoming, rejoined the westbound Murdock Company, now loaded with immigrants from Europe, their baggage, and additional goods for sale in the territory, and returned with it to Utah.[4]

Travel was slow due to the continuing demands placed on the railroads by the Army, but the missionary group was able to reach New York without incident. Although Daniel was then within 150 miles of Trenton, closer than he had been in more than twenty years, there is no evidence that he visited Abigail Rockwell, his only surviving sister, or any other family members who still lived there.

Abram Hatch, W. W. Raymond, Harrison Shurtliff, and George Boardman Spencer also traveled with the company on their way to missions in Europe. Hatch briefly described the voyage to England.

> I sailed for Europe in company with President Daniel H. Wells, his wife Hannah, Apostle Brigham Young, Jr., and his wife Kate. Harrison Shurtliff also went with us on this mission. We crossed the ocean on a steamer of the Anchor Line, and landed in Glasgow without any incident of unusual interest of a sea voyage, except coming in close proximity to a mountain iceberg. From Glasgow we took rail to Liverpool, and arrived the same day in that great, smokey seaport city.[5]

The *Britainnia*, which sailed from New York on July 11, arrived in mid-August, and Daniel assumed his duties as president on September 1, replacing George Q. Cannon.[6]

Daniel's labors as president consisted of presiding over the work of the various missions in Europe and South Africa. He organized, attended, and spoke at conferences, assigned missionaries to the various areas within each country (missionaries were called by the First Presidency to the country where they would labor), trained new missionaries for their ministry work, ordained priesthood holders, called and released branch officers, wrote and answered correspondence to and from the missions as well as from Great Salt Lake City. He also organized the travel of Saints immigrating to Utah, a responsibility that included arranging berths on ships making the Atlantic crossing or leasing an entire ship, if a large enough number of Mormons were making the journey at the same time. He was also the publisher of the weekly *Millennial Star*, the church newspaper in the United Kingdom.[7]

Daniel spoke at the district conference held in Cheltenham on August 21, about three days after he arrived in the country. With him at the conference were Orson Pratt Sr. and George Q. Cannon of the Quorum of the Twelve Apostles, Brigham Young Jr., John G. Holman, president of the Cheltenham District, Miles P. Romney, president of the

Figure 15.1. Side-wheel steamship similar to City of New York, *on which Daniel H. Wells traveled from Liverpool, England, to New York City in 1865.*

Cheltenham Conference, and several other district and conference presidents and officers. From that day onward, scarcely a week passed when he did not preside and speak at a conference meeting.[8]

In addition to his work in the United Kingdom, Daniel was also responsible for supervising the other missions on the continent, mainly the Swiss and German Mission and the Scandinavian Mission. Beginning in 1861, missionaries from the Swiss and German Mission also began proselyting in the Netherlands and were so successful that within three years branches were established in Rotterdam, Amsterdam, and Gorinchem. The first group of converts from the Netherlands, numbering sixty-one souls, immigrated to Utah in the summer of 1864 just as Daniel arrived in Liverpool. Following the departure of these Saints, Daniel ordered the organization of a new Netherlands Mission to direct missionary work there and shepherd the remaining members. After the mission was established, organized opposition and a lack of published tracts in the Dutch language slowed the growth of the church for several years.[9]

Daniel's wife Hannah had conceived another child early in 1864, shortly after the deaths of her two sons Ephraim and Preston. The three-month, four thousand–mile trip across land and sea to England must have been difficult for her, but she survived without ill effect and on November 19 gave birth to Gershom Britain Finley Wells. His name was chosen by Daniel over the objection of Hannah, who wrote home that she preferred another. Daniel soothed her feelings somewhat with his explanation that Gershom was a Biblical name meaning "born in a foreign land," and the family soon shortened it to "Gersh," by which he was known throughout his life.[10]

In January 1865, Daniel dispatched Apostle Orson Pratt from England and Elder William W. Riter from the Swiss and German Mission to Vienna with instructions to open a mission in the Austrian Empire. Orson Pratt had arrived in England the previous July, having come from Utah by way of California, Panama, and New York, and labored there for several months before being called to go to Austria. Elder Riter had been leading the Swiss and German Mission, which included Italy and France, since May of the previous year. Because he had learned German well in that assignment, he was called back to Liverpool in January and assigned to accompany Pratt.[11]

The two arrived in the capital city on January 25 and labored for a full six months without baptizing a single convert. The Austrian government proved to be very hostile to the Mormons and, after interrogating them at length, banished them from the Empire. They returned to Liverpool in September, by which time Daniel had departed for home, and continued their missionary work there for a time.[12]

In addition to his other church duties, Daniel spent a great deal of time negotiating for and contracting with the shipping companies from which the church chartered ships to carry immigrating Saints across the Atlantic. He arrived in Liverpool after the last immigrant ship for the 1864 season had sailed, but after the first of the year he was engaged in securing berths for another large group of Saints who wanted to make the journey to Zion.

The first ship to sail for New York City in 1865 with a company of Mormon converts aboard was a small sailing vessel of only 276 tons named the *Mexicana*. Daniel was informed of this ship's planned voyage by Miner Grant Atwood, one of the elders presiding over the Saints in South Africa. Atwood was appointed by President Cannon, Daniel's predecessor, to lead the Mormons there in their preparations to go to Utah. He made arrangements with Captain Sanderson of the *Mexicana* to have it fitted to accommodate the company of emigrants who wished to go. The ship sailed on April 12 from Port Elizabeth carrying forty-seven Saints. One man, George Fredrick Kershaw, who served as cook for the company, died on June 6 when the vessel was 980 miles from New York, and was buried at sea. He was the only fatality on the trip, and the *Mexicana* arrived safely in New York on June 18 after a voyage lasting sixty-eight days.[13]

Less than a month after the *Mexicana*'s voyage began, the twelve hundred-ton B. S. *Kimball*, under command of Capt. Henry C. Dearborn sailed from Hamburg with 558 Saints aboard, most of them from Scandinavia. This was the second voyage of the B. S. *Kimball* under Captain Dearborn carrying Mormons to America. The first trip was arranged by President Cannon in 1863 and sailed from Liverpool carrying 657 Scandinavian and British immigrants. The ship made a successful thirty-eight-day voyage during which there were four deaths, two births, and eleven marriages, a record which Daniel felt merited engaging the vessel for another voyage in 1865.[14]

Daniel signed the charter for the B. S. *Kimball* in Liverpool, but the ship called at Hamburg where the company of Saints, led by Elder Anders W. Winberg and his counselors John Swensen and Hans C. Hogsted, boarded the ship. Soon after it sailed on May 8, disaster struck when measles and scarlet fever broke out among the passengers. During the thirty-seven-day passage, three adults and twenty-five children died, one of the highest death tolls among an LDS emigrant company. The ship arrived at New York on June 14 and the surviving passengers quickly left. The vessel was never used by the Saints again and was lost at sea in 1868.[15]

Daniel directed the chartering of three more ships to bring British emigrants to America during 1865. The first of these was the *Belle Wood*, an American-built clipper ship of fourteen hundred tons that was sold to British owners at the start of the Civil War so that it could sail under a neutral flag and not be threatened by Confederate raiders or Union blockaders. Six hundred thirty-six Mormon passengers boarded the *Belle Wood*, and Daniel organized the company into wards under the overall leadership of Elder William H. Shearman and his counselors, Elders Charles B. Taylor and William S. S. Willes. They were among the nine returning missionaries who had completed their service in Europe and were going home. Capt. Thomas William Freeman cleared the *Belle Wood* from Liverpool harbor on the afternoon of April 29. The crossing to America under sail alone required only thirty-three days and the ship arrived at New York on May 31, a week before the disease-stricken B. S. *Kimball*, which was steam-powered.[16]

The *Belle Wood* was followed a month later by the *David Hoadley* with twenty-four Saints on board led by Elder William Underwood. This ship, which sailed for New York from Liverpool on May 10, was smaller by a third than the *Belle Wood* and had less passenger capacity. The Mormon company constituted only a small portion of the immigrants on board, in marked contrast to the *Belle Wood*, which was chartered exclusively by Daniel for church use.[17]

The last Saints to depart from Liverpool in 1865 were a Welsh family named Price and a single sister named Ruth Williams. They took passage on the *Bridgewater*, captained by Charles Sisson. Daniel arranged for their late departure on this ship, despite Captain Sisson's reputation as a hard master who did not like Mormons, because they had missed the earlier ships and did not have the resources to stay in England until the following season. They arrived safely on July 14 after a voyage of thirty-four days and were still able to reach Wyoming, Nebraska Territory, in time to join the last church train going west that year.[18]

Only about 1,250 Saints reached Utah from Europe in 1865, a number considerably less than the three thousand average for the decade of the 1860s. The slowdown in immigration was mainly the result of fewer converts being baptized in both 1864 and 1865 than in the previous and following years. Relatively few missionaries were called during the Civil War years and the number of persons they were able to teach and baptize was consequently less.[19]

With the end of the war and the assassination of President Lincoln in April 1865, President Young recognized that the situation in America had changed drastically and that the Mormon Church's survival might be again in jeopardy. With Lincoln's death, his policy of "plowing around" the Mormon problem of polygamy was no longer valid and the radical Republican majority in Congress again demanded an end to the other "twin evil" that its members had railed against in the 1850s. With a million-man army now released from service on the battlefields of the Civil War and some congressmen openly speaking about other objectives the army could be used to achieve by force in the defeated South, in Canada, and in the western United States, Brigham perceived a real danger that another military expedition might be dispatched to overpower and destroy the Saints in Utah.[20]

He wrote Daniel about his concerns that federal officials were planning an attack:

> The workers of wickedness . . . would really like, now that the war east appears to be off the hands of the Government, to have attention drawn to us here, and troops to be sent to break us up. They openly avow their intention to break the power of the priesthood and to destroy our organization, and since the receipt of the news of the surrender of Generals Lee and Johnston and the capture of Jeff. Davis, they have been very exultant and their tone is more arrogant and defiant than it has been. But the Lord Almighty has not surrendered, if Lee and Johnston have, and . . . He still reigns and He has the power in heaven and on the earth to accomplish His purposes and fulfil His word.[21]

Brigham also worried about the progress of the Indian war that the territorial militia was fighting, without any assistance from the federal troops at Fort Douglas, against a large band of Ute Indians led by the very able Chief Black Hawk.

In response to the memorial to President Lincoln authored by Daniel before he left for Europe, Congress passed an act in February 1864 authorizing treaty negotiations with the Northern Ute Confederation of tribes to accomplish the objectives set forth in the memorial. The orders implementing this act from the secretary of the Interior to the Commissioner of Indian Affairs were forwarded to Utah Indian Superintendent Orsemus H. Irish with a recommendation that Brigham Young be asked to use his influence with the Indians to persuade them to sign the treaty.[22]

Colonel Connor thought it outrageous that "the arch traitor" Brigham Young was to be part of the negotiations, but was informed by Superintendent Irish "the fact exists, however much some might prefer it should be otherwise, that he has pursued so kind and conciliatory a policy with the Indians, that it has given him great influence over them." The same could not be said of the colonel whose troops had killed dozens of non-combatant Indian women and children at the Battle of Bear River the previous year.[23]

When Brigham's participation was confirmed to them, most of Utah's federal officials also refused to attend the treaty negotiations saying they would prefer that the negotiations fail and that the Indians keep their land in preference to any of it going to the Mormon settlers. Governor Doty alone promised to attend, but was prevented from doing so by an illness that eventually proved fatal.

In addition to Brigham Young, the council was attended by at least five apostles, some Nauvoo Legion officers (not including Daniel who by then was out of the Territory) and Indian interpreters Huntington and Bean. Superintendent Irish was the only white non-Mormon person present.[24]

After days of talks, the treaty was finally signed by fifteen of the Ute Chiefs. Superintendent Irish alone signed as representative of the US government, but at the request of the chiefs, Brigham Young also signed as a witness to the treaty. Council President George A. Smith (who replaced Daniel H. Wells after the 1863 session) and House Speaker John Taylor, both Mormons, signed as representatives of Utah Territory. The treaty became known as the Spanish Fork Treaty after the place where it was signed.[25]

One Ute chief who did not attend the Council or sign the treaty was Black Hawk. During the years after the 1850 Indian massacre in Utah County and his captivity in Fort Provo the following winter he had at first accepted the Mormon presence in Utah and maintained peaceful relations with the whites. But as the attitude of many settlers hardened from peaceful coexistence to "the only good Indian is a dead one," Black Hawk also changed his view to one of defiant opposition to the presence of all white men on Indian lands and a determination to drive them out or kill them. Beginning in 1864 he led his band of Utes on raids against settlers to steal their stock and destroy their farms. These raids continued the following year and, within weeks after the signing of the Spanish Fork Treaty, more settlers were killed and hundreds of cattle were driven off to mountain hideouts by Black Hawk and his warriors. Territorial Indian Superintendent O. H. Irish soon faced an Indian uprising more serious than any that had previously occurred in Utah: the Black Hawk War.[26]

The conflict spread from localized raids in central Utah to involve members of other tribes who were recruited by Black Hawk and his men. By the end of 1864 the territorial militia was unable to capture or kill the Indian raiders who preyed upon Mormon and Gentile settlers alike. The range of their attacks also expanded into southern Utah, Colorado, Idaho, and Nevada. Despite their lack of success, church leaders still felt strongly that the Nauvoo Legion was best suited to fight the Indians and preferred them to do so without any help from federal troops.[27]

During the war, Union troops stationed at Fort Douglas confined their actions to guarding the Overland Trail, the mail routes, and the telegraph lines that tied the nation together. But with the war now ended, Brigham feared that the Indian hostilities would provide an excuse for the federal government to send a major military force into Utah Territory.

Following the ambush of a Nauvoo Legion troop by Black Hawk's band in Salina Canyon on April 12, 1865, a request was made to the acting commander at Fort Douglas, Col. William M. Johns for troops to chastise the Indians. Colonel Johns forwarded the request to the recently-promoted General Conner, who was campaigning against Indians on the Powder River in Wyoming and Montana. General Conner refused the request by saying that the Mormon-Indian conflict was not under his jurisdiction as it did not involve the mail route or telegraph lines. His anti-Mormon feelings influenced the general's response, but his decision pleased Brigham Young who wanted no federal troops active in Utah who could request reinforcements from the east on any pretext.[28]

More Indian attacks occurred as the summer progressed, while a visit to Great Salt Lake City in June by Speaker of the House Schuyler Colfax, editor Samuel Bowles of the *Springfield Republican*, and reporter Albert Richardson of the *New York Tribune* failed to calm any of the anti-Mormon agitation in the east. Their reports on Utah called for the removal of polygamy, the "foul and filthy ulcer upon the body politic" by means of the government exercising a "wise guardianship, a tender nursing, a firm principle," exactly the kind of federal interference the Saints feared.[29]

By July Brigham felt the situation would get worse before it got better and he wrote Daniel, his trusted counselor, requesting that he return to Utah immediately to resume command of the Nauvoo Legion and his other responsibilities. Daniel responded at once and booked passage home for himself, Hannah, and Gershom on the *City of New York*. He summarized the accomplishments of his curtailed missionary service in a valedictory published after his departure:

> By the time that this number of the Star reaches the hands of the Saints, I expect I shall be on the bosom of the Atlantic on my return home to the valleys of the mountains . . . I was not decided myself as to whether I should return before spring or not, but . . . as the servants of the Lord have seen fit to recall me to the scene of my former duties and associations, I gladly embrace the opportunity.
>
> On entering upon the presidency of the European Mission I found that through the faithfulness and energy of my predecessor, matters were in a prosperous condition . . . and the experience of the past year has fully borne me out in this belief . . .
>
> To the Elders laboring in the ministry I need not say much. The knowledge they have received through their obedience, teaches them the path they ought to walk in . . . and I heartily wish them Godspeed . . .
>
> To the brethren and sisters . . . be faithful be prayerful; remember that this is the Dispensation of the Fulness of Times, and that the hour of God's judgment is come . . . We see that the whole earth is in confusion and distress, and that men's hearts are failing them for fear of those things which are coming upon them. Seek, then, diligently to the Lord for strength, and it shall be given unto you according to your day, and through this means you will not only escape temporal misery and sorrow, but at last sit down in peace in our Heavenly Father's kingdom.
>
> May the Lord bless you continually, so that you can gather to the land of Zion, receive there the blessings promised to the faithful and come forth in the morning of the First Resurrection, purified, redeemed, and sanctified, sons and daughters of God. Amen.
>
> President Brigham Young, Jr., will, upon my departure, assume the presidency of the mission, and all communications on business and other matters should be addressed to him, instead of
>
> Daniel H. Wells[30]

Daniel, Hannah, and their baby sailed in August and arrived in New York on September 11. The trip was uneventful, but they encountered some delay passing through customs in New York, possibly because agents there were trying to apprehend fugitive southerners and contraband goods arriving in northern ports after the war. Daniel's haste to be home is evident in his letter sent back to Brigham Young Jr.:

> We arrived in New York, on Monday, the 11th inst. All well. We were a little troubled by the customs officers; had to go to the customs house the next day to pass an examination, but they finally let us have all—very reluctantly, however,—without paying anything. They were very strict, but on the whole we got through very well, although very annoying at times.
>
> All things are working favorably so far, and we expect to leave Atchison about the 24th inst. Mr. Halliday says that there are no Indians on the road at present.
>
> We all stood the trip across the sea very well. We had prevailing head winds or should have made a quicker passage. The City of New York is a good steamer, but she was too overcrowded with passengers to make it very pleasant crossing.
>
> Remember me kindly to all the brethren. God bless you.
>
> I am your brother,
> Daniel H. Wells.[31]

From Atchison, Kansas, which was now the western rail head and the terminus of the overland stage, the party headed west, preceded by a telegram published the day of its arrival in the *Deseret News*.

> To President Young:
>
> We learn that President Wells and party left Atchison on Monday morning, the 25th inst., by stage for this city. We wish them a pleasant and a speedy trip across the plains, and will be pleased to greet them again in their mountain home.[32]

Daniel described the last leg of the trip home as a pleasant trip. "We had a very successful journey through the States and across the plains, only turned over once in the stage, injuring no one but slightly; seeing no Indians, and escaping rather remarkably cold weather and storms . . . We did not see an Indian all the way, and crossed the plains from Atchison, 1,253 miles, in eleven traveling days. We laid over one day at Denver to rest."[33]

Figure 15.2. Stagecoach on Main Street, similar to the one in which Daniel and Hannah Wells and their baby Gershom traveled on their return to Great Salt Lake City in 1865. Charles W. Carter photograph.

Although Daniel may have considered a journey very successful that included only one rollover, his wife Hannah probably differed in that assessment. The mission to England was far more physically demanding for her than for her husband. In the fifteen months she and Daniel were away from the Big House, Hannah endured a thousand-mile wagon trip followed by a thousand-mile train trip, all in the second trimester of her pregnancy; a two-thousand mile sea voyage in the third trimester, the birth and nurturing of her baby in a foreign environment; and the return voyage and overland travel with a nine-month-old infant. The passenger list of the *City of New York* notes that she had the help of a servant woman to assist her on the way home, but even so, the opportunity to accompany Daniel to England was a daunting venture for her. Hannah uttered no word of complaint, although she was doubtless very grateful to be back in her own apartment with a healthy child. Her son Gershom would outlive all of his siblings; he died in his eightieth year in 1944.[34]

The Wells family welcomed their patriarch home with enthusiasm. "When father returned from this mission there was great rejoicing. The mothers were particularly interested in the new baby that had been born in Liverpool . . . The day following the arrival home the excitement in the family was enhanced when again we assembled to witness the unpacking of the trunks which we knew contained a gift for each of us. We were made very happy by the little remembrances from overseas, and greatly enjoyed comparing and measuring our ribbons and pieces of dress goods."[35]

Daniel arrived home during the annual October General Conference and Brigham "received me with open arms, and pressed me to his bosom with a paternal kiss. It was the second day of Conference, and the President took me with him to meeting without giving me a chance to even change my dusty traveling apparel. His health is good, as is also that of Brother Heber, who also kindly greeted and welcomed me back."[36]

President Kimball's welcome apparently concealed the continuing animosity against Daniel and other church leaders that he expressed again in a journal entry a few months earlier while Daniel still was in England. "I was told by the Lord that those that had Saught my hurt and had caused me to be cast off by His Servent Brigham should see sorrow and be removed out of their place. Daniel H. Wells, Albert Carrington, Joseph A. Young and others and they should be spoiled in all there Evil designs." As in his earlier journal entries regarding Daniel, Kimball made no mention of what the "evil designs" of his perceived enemies were and again, there is no indication that Daniel was aware of any estrangement between himself and the First Counselor.[37]

Brigham was not the only Saint who was glad to see Daniel back in Great Salt Lake City. The *Deseret News* published a notice of the family's arrival in early October.

Welcome Home

President Daniel H. Wells, lady and child, and Elder F. B. Free, arrived on the 7th inst., by stage, having reached Denver on the 30th ult., and left there on the 2nd inst. Friends of President Wells—and their name is Legion—will be pleased to learn that he is well and come home in the enjoyment of excellent spirits.

Professor Thomas of the Ogden Brass Band was serenading him as the people were assembling for morning meeting in the Bowery.[38]

16

Years of Defending Against Patient, Tenacious Raiders

UTAH'S BLACK HAWK WAR

1865–1868

As soon as he rested a few days and reconnected with each member of his family, Daniel resumed command of the Nauvoo Legion and set about finding a solution to the Black Hawk War that continued to cause loss of life and property throughout Utah Territory. Chief Black Hawk's raiders were masters of hit and run tactics that enabled them to drive off cattle and attack small groups of settlers in one place, then melt away into the surrounding wilderness before any pursuit could be assembled, only to strike again later a hundred miles away on another undefended hamlet or herd. Against this type of guerrilla warfare, the use of large companies of troops mustered to seek out and destroy the Indians was completely ineffective. The raiders were too well-armed (often better than the settlers they attacked), too mobile and swift in their movements, and too knowledgeable of the terrain in which they operated to ever be surprised or trapped by a slower-moving military force.[1]

The only strategy that held promise of stopping the Indians' depredations was the defensive policy that Daniel and Brigham had counseled the Saints for years to adopt: every settlement needed to be armed and prepared to defend itself and every herd of animals needed to be so well-guarded that any attempt to rustle it would be too costly for the attackers to warrant their efforts. When the Black Hawk War commenced in April 1865, Daniel was in England but General Orders No. 1, issued over his name that month, reminded all Saints that "eternal vigilance is the price of safety."[2]

Although it was effective, a strong defense in all the settlements was also expensive and time consuming. Constructing walled compounds and homes with built-in fortifications required more money and material than a simple log cabin; armed cowboys to watch herds had to be paid wages that detracted from the profits of the cattle ranchers. And even when these measures were faithfully adopted when the first alarm of trouble was sounded, they suffered from the inevitable axiom of all defenses against siege: time erodes security. Months of careful management and unending guard duty seemed pointless when no sign of hostile forces appeared. Vigilance slackened, night patrols were shortened, and strict adherence to other security measures was relaxed. The watchful Indians, always more patient than their white adversaries, waited until peace and boredom wore down the alertness of their target and then struck.

Daniel moved quickly to re-ignite the fervor of the Saints to defend their lives and their property by holding training camps in various settlements. He did not attend all of these events personally, but directed local officers to practice their marksmanship, improve their defensive plans, assist one another in guarding property, and renew their enthusiasm for preventing attacks instead of seeking revenge after the fact. In October 1865, two weeks after his return home, he wrote to Brigham Young Jr. about his new duties: "We are going to have a three-day muster camp in Provo next week, and of this [Salt Lake County] military district, commencing on the 1st of November. There has been great talk of a large number of troops being sent here this fall, but as usual their plans have failed, and they are left to chew the cud of bitter disappointment and chagrin. Praise be to the Lord of Hosts, the Saints yet possess the land in peace and quietness."[3]

The talk Daniel mentioned of a large military presence in Utah was partly prompted by the incorporation of the Military District of Utah, which General Connor had commanded with his California volunteers since 1862 as part of the Department of the Pacific, into the Department of the Plains. The new department was created in April 1865 with Connor as its commander and included the districts of Colorado, Nebraska, and Idaho as well as Utah. General Connor took command of a larger volunteer force, but in July 1865 led most of his troops to Wyoming for the punitive Powder River Expedition, leaving only a token force in Utah. The Expedition ended with only slight success in October and General Connor returned to Utah where he and his volunteer soldiers were mustered out of service in 1866. Regular army troops were sent that year from the east to garrison Camp Douglas, but their numbers were fewer than in the war years.

With the US military fighting Indians only outside Utah, the Mormon settlers in the territory continued to rely on their own militia for protection. The wisdom of a strong defensive stance was again proved in early 1866 when the Peter Shirts family withstood a three-month siege by

Indians in their well-built rock home with no loss of life.[4] Another attack on Kanab ranchers yielded the Indians only a few horses because the rest of the settlers' stock was corralled and guarded.[5] At the same time, however, James Whitmore, a prosperous Mormon rancher in the Pipe Springs area lost four hundred cattle, a thousand sheep, and his life when he left his herds on open range unguarded and then went unarmed to round them up with his ranch hand Robert McIntyre. Both men were killed by raiders who then also burned the Whitmore ranch. Whitmore's nine-year-old son survived by hiding in a rock dugout during the ranch attack.[6]

A militia detachment found the bodies of the slain men and then killed several Indians in reprisal when they found some of Whitmore's and McIntyre's clothes and paper money in their possession. But the slain Indians were mostly old men and women and not the warriors responsible for the raid. They claimed they had received Whitmore's belongings as gifts from the raiders. Some of the militia believed the Indians, but others expressed a lust for killing with such comments as "Damned if I wouldn't like to kill an Indian before I go." The result was at least six noncombatant Indians executed without trial after being captured by the Legion troop. Edwin D. Woolley, one who opposed the killings, declared "I never was so ashamed of anything in all my life—the whole thing was so unnecessary." Apostles George A. Smith and Erastus Snow wrote a similar appraisal of the events to Daniel H. Wells.[7]

This was exactly the wrong sequence of events that Daniel and other leaders wanted to happen: Indians killing innocent whites followed by whites killing innocent Indians. Just before the Pipe Springs raid and reprisal, Daniel sent Erastus Snow and George A. Smith on a tour of southern settlements to promote strong measures that would discourage further Indian attacks. He told the two men, who were also Nauvoo Legion officers, to reorganize military districts, and strongly counsel the Saints to buy more weapons and ammunition, build more and stronger forts, move herds to more secure locations and strengthen guard procedures. They traveled eight hundred miles in two months and succeeded in raising the level of preparedness in most towns they visited. They also advised the militia in each area to watch friendly Indians carefully to be certain they did not pass intelligence to Black Hawk's raiders, as some were suspected of doing.[8]

Daniel wrote to Snow and Smith during their journey cautioning them to be circumspect in their work and go about it as quietly as possible so as not to attract any attention from federal authorities that would make the already tense political situation in Utah worse. At that time bills were introduced in Congress to dismantle Utah Territory and Utah's Gentile chief justice appeared before the House Committee on Territories to plead for five thousand soldiers to be sent to enforce anti-polygamy laws.

The bitterly anti-Mormon Colonel Conner was summoned to testify to the necessity of such an action and church authorities did not want hostile Indian actions to give further excuse for a military invasion.[9]

In order to bring the Black Hawk War to a conclusion and preclude additional Indian raids from being used to justify intervention by federal troops, Brigham Young and Daniel H. Wells devised a plan to capture and hold hostage friendly Indians and chiefs who had signed the Spanish Fork Treaty until they fulfilled their pledge made in that treaty to tell the white settlers where renegade Indians were hiding so that they could be apprehended. In March 1866, a Nauvoo Legion detachment from Utah County, led by Warren Snow, surrounded a Ute camp near Nephi and took two chiefs, Sanpitch and Ankawakits, prisoner with half a dozen other Indians. Daniel approved this action and ordered Snow to provide "the chiefs and principle men of the Indians . . . comfortable quarters in your settlement until they can have a visit from Black Hawk." He added that "Should they see that you are so very pressing, and determined that they shall share your hospitality, they may be induced to send for Black Hawk and Jake and their distinguished friends to come and visit and have all differences adjusted so that we can live together in peace."[10]

After being put in irons and threatened with continued confinement, Sanpitch ordered Chief Kanosh and "all the men of the nation" to unite and capture Black Hawk so that he and the other prisoners could be released. But when Kanosh gathered a large group of Indians for the purpose of taking Black Hawk, Snow and other Mormon leaders feared that the powerful force of Utes could just as easily turn on the settlers and rescue the hostages by force, or stage an attack in retaliation for their capture. Snow sent a troop of militia to Sanpitch's camp where they killed one Indian and captured three others who were identified by friendly Indians as raiders. These prisoners were immediately taken to Nephi, tried by court-martial, and executed the same day.[11]

When the other captured Indians learned the fate of the raiders, they understandably feared for their own lives and attempted to escape. At least a dozen more Indians were killed in several unsuccessful breaks for freedom and other incidents, and most Utes then fled from Utah and Sanpete Counties, leaving Sanpitch and the other captives still jailed in Manti. Realizing that execution at the hands of Snow and his men was likely for the remaining prisoners, Sanpitch communicated secretly with Black Hawk and together they devised a plan for the Indians to escape. The captives also turned silent and provided no more information about the raiders while they patiently sawed through their shackles using files smuggled in by friendly relatives and other Indians.[12]

In an attempt to draw the Nauvoo Legion troops guarding Sanpitch and the other hostages away from Manti, Black Hawk and his men launched a raid on Salina, killing two persons, wounding others and making off with more than a hundred cattle. After securing the animals and forcing the settlers to retreat into fortified cabins, Black Hawk stood with his raiders on high ground outside the town and, speaking in English, dared the whites to come to them.[13]

When word of the Salina attack reached Manti on the evening of April 13, Warren Snow sent a dispatch to Daniel stating his belief that Black Hawk had made "this move so as to draw our forces from this Point so as to make a Break on Manti and if Possible obtain those in charge from their confinement." Although angry at the loss of life and property, Snow said he would keep his forces in Manti and also suggested that if the Indians "still commit their deprations [*sic*] we head better get [rid] of what we have on hand [kill the hostages] and prepare for the worst." His latter concluded, "I have sent to Kanosh if he is our friend to send some of his men and Bring back the stoke [cattle herd] taken from Salina and then we shall Know that he wants to live in Peace."[14]

The next evening Sanpitch and the other Indian hostages slipped out of the jail and fled the town despite the presence of the large guarding force. Ankawakits and two others were killed and Sanpitch was wounded during the chase to recapture the escapees. Snows's letter to Daniel describing the event reveals his frustration. "I cannot express my feelings of Regret at the affair . . . [that] the guard should be so careless as to let them escape." He told Daniel further that "San Pich, will doubtless make war with a vengence" and that he was sending men to guard the trails to Spanish Fork Canyon, which he was certain would be Sanpitch's natural escape route and where he hoped to recapture the prisoners.[15]

None of the Indians were recaptured, but the injured Sanpitch and the others were killed the next day by the Nauvoo Legion troops Snow had sent to pursue them. Snow was not with the men who brought the Indians down, but he justified their actions by noting that the Utes "would not be retaken alive" and that it was far better to have killed all of them than "to let them go into the Indian camp." Killing Indians who were fleeing for their lives was a practice followed by Snow and many Mormon settlers in defiance of Daniel and Brigham's long-standing policy that Indians should not be killed except in self-defense when under actual attack. Although Snow did not personally participate in the executions, they were in keeping with his own oft-expressed view that good Indians were dead Indians.[16]

The cycle of Indian reprisals followed by additional killings by whites continued a week later when Mormon militiamen looking for stolen stock were ambushed near Marysvale. Two men were killed and two others wounded and the Indian raiders escaped with their plundered animals. The next day a Nauvoo Legion troop attempted to take another group of Indians prisoner. When the natives, who had heard of the death of Sanpitch and feared for their own safety, resisted and shot one white man, the others responded by killing one Indian and wounding another who nevertheless managed to escape.[17]

At Circleville, another group of militiamen rounded up an entire camp of twenty Piede Indians at gunpoint and marched them into town. These Indians were not part of Black Hawk's band, although they confessed that they had previously carried supplies and ammunition to him. Also aware of the previous killings, the Piedes tried to escape the next day, but they were discovered and six of the men, all unarmed, were killed in a singularly one-sided fight with their guards.[18]

The killing of six unarmed non-combatants was a tragic event, which the settlers justified because it occurred during an escape attempt, but what followed later in Circleville could not be described as anything but murder. The three remaining Indian men, together with five women and the two oldest of six children were led one at a time out of confinement and executed by having their throats slit. The remaining four children, thought too young to tell of what had taken place, were spared and sent singly to live as virtual slaves in white homes. When the bloodlust had subsided and the bodies were disposed of, those Saints who perpetrated the atrocity tried to cover up their participation by claiming that most of the Indians were killed while attacking their guards. When Daniel was given this patently false version of the killings, he wrote that the circumstances (as described to him by the settlers) appeared to justify what had happened, but Brigham Young publicly deplored the murders and later said that the curse of God rested upon the Circle Valley and its inhabitants because of it.[19]

Both Daniel and Brigham were deeply frustrated that the Saints continued to kill friendly Indians while refusing to assemble and man the defenses that would protect them from the hostiles. Even Orson Hyde, an apostle who lived in Sanpete County and had lost some of his own cattle to Indian depredations, supported the killings, telling George A. Smith, "Sanpitch and his Braves and the Piutes of Circleville have received the kind of gospel which they merit." Hyde was absolutely convinced that the loss of Mormon lives and property justified killing all Indians, a view absolutely contrary to the vigilant coexistence consistently taught and practiced by Brigham and Daniel. "I do not know but that there are friendly Indians in Utah," Hyde wrote, "but I must confess I know not where they are."[20]

There were, in fact, far fewer friendly Indians in the territory after the Circleville Massacre than before it. Indians that had moved to the Uintah Reservation after their chiefs signed the Spanish Fork Treaty, were angered by the killings and by the federal government's failure to deliver the food and supplies promised under the terms of the treaty. The peaceful but aged Chief Sowiette was replaced by Chief Tabby who led his warriors against the reservation's Indian Agent, F. H. Head, his employees, and a troop of US Army soldiers, driving them off the reservation to seek shelter with Mormon settlers. Brigham tried to placate Tabby and Toquana, another chief who joined forces with him, by promising to provide the needed supplies and declaring again that the Mormons wished to live in peace with the Indians, but it was too late. The messenger who carried Brigham's letter only escaped with his life through the intervention of Sowiette, and the Indians remained poised on the warpath.[21]

Superintendent Head asked for one or two companies of federal troops to put down the uprising, but Maj. General Pope, in the middle of downsizing the army after the Civil War, replied that there were no troops available for Utah. Soldiers were sent to fight Indians in Colorado and New Mexico in response to a request made by Kit Carson at the same time as Head's, but Utah's settlers were advised in a telegram from General Pope, acting on instructions from General Sherman, "to help themselves." When Daniel heard of Head's request for troops he brushed it off with a sarcastic reference to the usual duties of soldiers in Utah. "I don't think they have time for such matters, and very much doubt if any will go. The regeneration business [trying to reform Mormon society to a Gentile mold] keeps them all busy."[22]

Daniel and Brigham were glad that federal troops were not dispatched to Utah, but less pleased when the territory's Governor, Charles Durkee, was authorized in May to mobilize the local militia to combat the Indian uprising. The First Presidency had been controlling and directing the Nauvoo Legion since the pioneers first arrived in Utah. Brigham had used them against Black Hawk's band since early 1865 and had called Daniel back from England to resume command of the Legion, even though by law only the governor was empowered to use the militia. Neither Brigham nor Daniel was about to relinquish command of the Saints' only defensive force, which had protected them equally against invasion by the US Army and depredations by Indians, to a Gentile, anti-Mormon governor who regarded the legion as "a standing menace to [US] authority in Utah." Durkee tried to get control of the Nauvoo Legion turned over to him, but his efforts, like those of other Gentile governors before him, proved futile. Brigham Young remained the de facto governor of Utah and Daniel H. Wells remained in command of the Nauvoo Legion.[23]

Over the next month, Brigham and Daniel, working sometimes with Governor Durkee and Superintendent Head and sometimes without their knowledge or assistance, managed to pacify the Uintah Reservation Utes and prevent Tabby, Toquana, and the three hundred or so warriors they commanded from going to war on their own or joining with Black Hawk's band in a widened conflict. Brigham loaned flour and other supplies to Head for delivery to the Indians and Daniel sent a detachment of twenty-five Mormon militiamen with a herd of seventy cattle to the reservation. The gifts were at first rejected and the Indians refused to listen to the reading of a letter arguing for peace that Brigham sent with the cattle. The militiamen quarreled with Head and commandeered a government building to use for defense against a possible siege by the Indians. Careful negotiations and the Indians' hunger eventually combined to make compromise possible.[24]

Tabby and other Indian chiefs demanded the life of Warren Snow as retribution for the death of Sanpitch. Snow, who had become the Utes' principal Mormon enemy and the man they held responsible for most of the deaths among them, was described as the white equivalent of Black Hawk: a killer of the innocent. Brigham and Daniel pointed out that Sanpitch had not helped to apprehend Black Hawk, but had aided him contrary to the requirement of the treaty he signed. They also said that war did not benefit whites or Indians and again stated that peace was the better way. After hours of venting about the wrongs done to them by the whites, the Indians calmed enough to accept the offered gifts and agree to remain on the reservation. At the same time Tabby insisted he could not prevent some of his warriors from going to join Black Hawk or from killing Mormons. In the event, however, the young men expressed their wrath by shooting the entire herd of cattle brought by the Mormons as soon as they were delivered to the Utes and then cutting pieces from the dead steers to eat raw and dripping with blood. Superintendent Head then held further talks and distributed more gifts until he was able to report that all the Indians were pacified except Black Hawk's band who continued to fight.[25]

The failure of the hostage plan and the resulting death of so many non-combatant Indians convinced Mormon leaders that a change in strategy was needed to end the Black Hawk War. Brigham and Daniel were still certain that the vigilance policy denoted in General Order No. 1 in April 1865 and restated again in April 1866 was the surest way of stopping the Indian attacks and preventing more loss of life on both sides. They were also sure that this policy had been neglected in favor of retaliation by Mormon settlers following each Indian depredation. On most occasions, the perpetrators of a raid escaped with their stolen property and could not be overtaken by the pursuing militia. The whites then turned for vengeance on the first Indian camp they encountered, frequently killing women and children as well as men who had no connection to the raiders except that they belonged to the same race. This response actually prolonged the war by giving the Indians new grievances against whites for which they, in turn, sought vengeance.[26]

When Mormon scouts learned in May 1866 that Black Hawk's band was returning to Utah along the Old Spanish Trail from their winter hideout in Colorado, Daniel and Brigham warned Orson Hyde, Erastus Snow, and other church leaders in the area that the Indian chief would likely attack Manti, to avenge the death of Sanpitch and his group and to kill their mortal enemy Warren Snow. The Sanpete Nauvoo Legion was put on alert and Daniel ordered a troop of one hundred men from Salt Lake and Utah Counties south to reinforce them. He also called up a second group of reinforcements to be ready to march in June and prepared to lead this detachment himself. Meanwhile, the inhabitants of Manti and the surrounding communities worked in deadly earnest to prepare their defenses.[27]

Black Hawk also had scouts who provided him with intelligence and, when these informed him that the communities of Sevier and Sanpete valleys were well prepared to defend themselves, he turned his attention to a weaker target, the small town of Scipio. Despite Daniel's directives, the Saints in Round Valley refused to build a fort or to concentrate their numbers in communities of at least 150 persons. Their large herds of cattle were also scattered on rich grazing land and were not corralled under guard at night. Scipio's population numbered only twenty-five men and boys and almost half of these had no guns. They presented an ideal target that the Indians' scouts could not fail to discern and inform their chief about.[28]

The raiders struck quietly in daylight on Sunday, June 10, first killing James R. Ivie and a fourteen-year-old herd boy and then rounding up 350 cattle and 75 horses. When a group of settlers moved toward them, the Indians forced them to retreat by threatening to attack the poorly defended town. They drove the stock away to the southeast, heading toward their well-used escape route through Castle Valley to the Old Spanish Trail. A band of fifty raiders remained behind near Scipio Lake to ambush any pursuing whites and another sixty were posted ahead to guard the Gravely Ford crossing of the Sevier River that required a full day's travel for the raiders to drive their stolen animals.[29]

Quickly informed by couriers of the Scipio attack, a small troop of Nauvoo Legion militiamen traveled through the night and reached Gravelly Ford about the same time that the Indians arrived with their stolen herd. Although outnumbered three to one, the militiamen opened fire on the Indian force holding the crossing and a two-hour gun battle ensued during which several Indians were killed and wounded along with one white. Maj. William B. Pace, commanding the Legion troops, then realized that their ammunition was running out and ordered a retreat out of range of the Indians. When the Indians then tried to force their way across the river, a Mormon sharpshooter seriously wounded a warrior named Tamaritz, who survived his injury and later became a chief in Black Hawk's band in recognition of his bravery. But the militia left Gravelly Ford in possession of the raiders, who secured their victory and their spoils as they crossed the river with the stolen herd and escaped into the mountains.[30]

Major Pace decided to abandon the fight in part because he mistakenly believed that another group of raiders were coming up behind his troops. They were, in fact, militia reinforcements from Fillmore riding to the aid of the embattled Legion force, but the opportunity to defeat Black Hawk's band was lost. Daniel, who arrived at Scipio with his troops a few days after the battle, lamented the Indians' victory and the substantial loss of property that he felt certain would encourage the raiders to make further attacks. The Nauvoo Legion leaders noted that Black Hawk's band was "gaining strength [with] every raid" and their "every move . . . indicates smartness and ability to carry on a long war in these rough and rugged mountains."[31]

Unknown to Daniel or other leaders at the time, Black Hawk himself was also wounded at Gravelly Ford. While trying to rescue one of his warriors, the chief was hit by a ball that passed through his horse and struck him low in his abdomen. The horse fell dead, but Black Hawk was picked up by another of his braves and carried away. He recovered from the wound sufficiently to lead his band for another year, but the bullet remained in his body. It left him crippled and eventually ruined his health with lead poisoning. As his strength declined, much of his charisma and leadership duties were taken over by Tamaritz who, after recovering fully, changed his name to Shenavegan meaning "Saved by Almighty Power" and continued to fight long after the older chief had made peace.[32]

On learning of the Scipio raid, Daniel H. Wells had drafted another hundred men into Legion service as he passed through Utah County on his way south. This brought the total number of militiamen from northern Utah to over three hundred and, combined with those already mobilized in the southern counties, put at least six hundred armed men in the field against Black Hawk and his raiders. Gen. Warren Snow started again after the Indian raiders with a hundred riders, but proceeded so slowly and cautiously that his own men complained that he had already "delayed too long to be successful." Daniel also confided to Brigham that he had "but little confidence" in Snow's "overtaking the Indians on account of their late start," and General Snow soon confirmed his superior's assessment when he turned back with his men after only two days. They thus missed another opportunity to recapture the lost Scipio herd and defeat the raiders who were out of sight, but only a few miles ahead of them when the pursuit was abandoned.[33]

Daniel and his troop met Snow's detachment as they returned to Salina and his disappointment at the latter's retreat must have been evident in his expression, as noted by one of Snow's equally frustrated volunteers who wrote, "You should of seen the Genral [Wells] when he met us. When he met us he said nothing but he cept a thinking I know not what. But I know what he had ought of thought, 'Boys you have showed your asses.'"[34]

Daniel could do nothing about the lost opportunities to strike a significant blow against Black Hawk's band, nor could he prevent the revenge murder of another friendly Indian by James A. Ivie, the son of one of the Mormon settlers killed in the Scipio raid. Daniel agreed wholeheartedly with Brigham's assessment that Ivie, who killed the inoffensive Panikrey in cold blood, was "as much guilty of murder as if he had stepped up and killed a white man," and declared that he must be "arrested and tried for murder." Ivie was later tried for the murder of Panikrey, but the jury impaneled in Scipio still held the opinion that all Indians were hostile and acquitted him. Ivie was excommunicated by Brigham, but he was never otherwise punished for his crime.[35]

Faced with the reality that fear of additional attacks and a desire to avenge previous ones were the principal emotions governing the behavior of the Saints in southern Utah, Daniel used these feelings to motivate the settlers to further strengthen their defenses and guard their property. In this effort he was markedly more successful. He dispersed the 350 men from Salt Lake, Davis, and Utah counties under his command among the towns with orders to help their residents build forts and corrals as stipulated in General Order No. 1. Now the settlers responded with a furious effort to prevent any repeat of the Scipio attack on their own villages. Some forts and walls had been built prior to the summer of 1866, but a boom in construction ensued after the arrival of Daniel and his troops. He personally visited each settlement to ensure that the defensive measures were implemented fully. He deployed groups of ten to fifty men in each town to work with local settlers and positioned detachments along known Indian trails to guard against surprise attack while work in the towns was progressing. He also sent scouts far afield to discover the location and movements of the Indians. By the fall of 1866 most Sanpete and Sevier settlements had completed forts and were building "Spanish walls" to enclose larger areas for protection of cattle and people.[36]

Many of the Nauvoo Legion volunteers from the north under Daniel's command were young men who came south poorly outfitted and ill fed, only too glad to receive the $15-per-month pay of a new recruit. Many others were transients or idlers who joined the Legion for a summer adventure and the chance of more and better food than they were used to. They were required to provide their own horses, saddles, weapons, and ammunition, which for many meant borrowing these items from relatives or procuring some of the poorest quality at the cheapest possible price. Few had uniforms and most were badly clothed, even for summer weather, often lacking "shoes shirts or hats" as one of Daniel's officers noted.[37]

As the summer passed, Daniel quietly transformed the military nature of the Legion's labors into a mission calling, telling his men that the work they were doing to protect Utah communities was "as honorable as if we had been called to go forth Amongst the nations of the earth to preach the gospel." Many were actually "set apart" for their callings and the length of their service was increased from the original forty-five day enlistment period. Finding themselves working under the personal direction of a member of the First Presidency and well-provided with good food and companionship among the southern Saints, many volunteers stayed on through the end of the year and even into 1867 to continue their labors. A number of the militiamen were disaffected Church members, some of whom found their way back into the fold through their service.[38]

Among the Utah communities where fort-building commenced or expanded in 1866 were the central Utah towns of Lehi, Springville, Spanish Fork, Payson, Santaquin, Nephi, Scipio, Fillmore, Deseret, Moroni, Mt. Pleasant, Ephraim, Manti, and Richfield. Forts designed to be permanently garrisoned by Nauvoo Legion troops were also built at Gunnison and Sanford. Lesser fortifications were constructed in Marysvale, Spring Lake, Fairview, Spring City, Glenwood, Monroe, and Salina. Further south, the settlements of Beaver, Parowan, Panguitch, Cedar City, St. George, Glendale, and Kanab also built forts.[39]

Daniel ordered another garrisoned fort to be built at Thistle Valley at the intersection of the Old Spanish Trail and the route from Sanpete Valley east to the Uintah Reservation and he directed a force of 57 militiamen, both foot soldiers and mounted cavalry, under the command of Captain Albert Dewey into action there on June 20. Four days later, before they had done more than commence construction, they were surprised by a band of about thirty Indians who killed one man, drove off most of their horses, and forced the troops into a makeshift circle barricade of baggage wagons and equipment. Captain Dewey, fearing a long battle with his force surrounded, took advantage of a lull in the action following the first attack to send couriers for reinforcements.[40]

The original group of Indians was soon reinforced to a total of more than seventy warriors. They were also better armed than the now outnumbered militiamen and rode in circles around their wagons firing from under their horses. Over the next few hours the Indians attacked three times and were driven off with losses on each occasion. Several warriors were brought down, but the militia suffered only one man seriously wounded. Finally, an hour before sundown, a force of thirty men from

Fairview and Mount Pleasant rode into the circle of wagons. The Indians immediately attacked again, but the strengthened defenders once more drove them off with more casualties. Another Nauvoo Legion troop arrived next morning and a third on the following day. With about three hundred Mormon men now holding the Thistle camp, the Indians broke off the engagement. Legion officers surveyed the battlefield to confirm casualties and then followed the retreating raiders until they separated into smaller groups and fled into the mountains.[41]

Several Mormons thought that Chief Tabby, who had made peace the month before, led the Thistle attack, but Daniel, who knew the chief and trusted his word, felt certain that Tabby's renegade brother Jim was responsible.[42]

Another attack, led by Chief Mountain, occurred on June 26 near Spanish Fork when Indians rustled about forty cattle and fifteen horses from the pastures of William Berry, but failed to take any of the more than three thousand head under guard in corrals west of the Spanish Fork River. The raiders barely escaped capture by nearby militia troops and were forced by another force guarding their usual escape route through Hobble Creek and Spanish Fork canyons to drive their stolen stock into the steep Maple Canyon, which was undefended by the Legion because it was considered impassable for stock.

The Indians were able to get over the top of the canyon and descend another on the eastern slope of the mountains. At the Diamond Fork River pursuing militia overtook and surprised them in their camp. The Mormon riders rushed past the Indians and blocked their path down the steep canyon. Although outnumbered and outgunned, they took cover and opened fire in an effort to hold the raiders in place until reinforcements could arrive and trap them in crossfire. After about two hours of shooting, during which one Mormon and two or three Indians were killed, another group of militia joined the battle from behind the Indians. They were only eight men, but the two groups pinned the Indians down between them and, after another hour of firing, managed to shoot their leader off his horse as he was rallying his warriors. At that, the Indians abandoned the stolen cattle, their camp equipment, and even a few of their horses and escaped up the sides of the canyon, carrying their dead and wounded with them.[43]

These Mormon victories at Thistle Valley and Diamond Fork proved to be decisive points in the Black Hawk War. The militia suffered three dead and several wounded in the two battles, but Indian casualties were more than a dozen dead and twice as many seriously wounded. More importantly, the Indians gained nothing in the raids, thereby showing that Brigham and Daniel's policy of vigilant defense could work and causing the Saints to implement it more effectively. The

Indians soon realized that they had "no chance of getting a single hoof without first getting a bullet" and their enthusiasm for raiding waned. Black Hawk and his band remained on the warpath, but the reservation Indians who had participated in the raids returned home, convinced that they had had enough fighting.

Daniel's faith in Chief Tabby was vindicated when he met his returning warriors and berated them in disgust, telling them "that he was glad that [they] got wounded for they had no business to goe and fight." In a clever twist, he then consoled them by saying that the blood of the three whites killed at Diamond Fork and Thistle Valley was enough "to pay for the killing of Sandpitch," and reclaim Ute honor lost due to the manner of that chief's death. Tabby and Sowiette also sent a delegation to Great Salt Lake City to reassure Brigham and Daniel that they were anxious to maintain peace with the Saints.[44]

As the momentum of the conflict turned in favor of the settlers, Daniel returned home to take up other duties. The work of strengthening defenses in the settlements, which he had championed, went on throughout the remainder of the summer and the last of the Nauvoo Legion units that he led south was not released from service until October. There were more skirmishes with Indian raiders, including one in late December at Pine valley in the southwest corner of Utah. Indian raiders stole thirty horses and fifteen cattle, but were overtaken and defeated with twelve dead and all the lost animals were recovered. Black Hawk and his men retreated again to Colorado and New Mexico for the winter and peace reigned into the next year.

Black Hawk finally came to a peace conference at Mount Pleasant in June 1868 and signed a treaty for himself and his band of Utes. He rode away on a new saddle, a gift from Brigham Young, having promised to seek peace among the remaining bands of Utes still fighting. On August 19, he proved his stature as the leading Ute chief in peace as well as war by leading a delegation of other chiefs, including Tamaritz, Augavorum, and Sowahpoint to Strawberry Valley where they finally agreed to peace in a treaty with Indian Superintendent Franklin Head.[45]

17

Mayor of Salt Lake City
Defending the Faith, Fighting Crime, and Obtaining the Deed to the City

1868–1870

Daniel H. Wells was a strong supporter of the Perpetual Emigration Fund, set up to help overseas converts to the church to gather to Zion, since 1852 when he pledged a percentage of his income from the Green River ferries to the fund. As noted previously, he was also deeply involved in organizing and funding the church trains that, beginning in 1860, traveled east each spring from Great Salt Lake City to Wyoming, Nebraska Territory, to bring back to Utah those who had voyaged across the Atlantic from Europe earlier in the year.

Having observed firsthand, during his mission presidency, the dedication and the need of the Saints in Europe for adequate travel accommodations, he increased his personal commitment to help finance the Perpetual Emigration Fund and increase the number and capacity of the church trains that brought converts across the plains. Prior to his departure to central and southern Utah with the troops called up for the Black Hawk War, he wrote Brigham Young Jr. telling him about the increased efforts being made to transport the emigrants and encouraging the European Saints not to delay their departure from Babylon.

> My heart was made glad by the President proposing in Council that we send down 500 teams to the Missouri River for the emigration next season [1866]. I trust the Saints will avail themselves of the opportunity thus afforded to deliver themselves . . . let them begin early to prepare and save their

earnings, and make their deposits for this object, for I have no assurance how long such an opportunity will be afforded, or whether it will ever offer again. It is bad business for the Saints to procrastinate, thinking that some other time will do just as well; the present is all that they are certain of, and by neglecting to improve present opportunities we often fail in obtaining those blessings which otherwise might have been ours to possess and enjoy.[1]

Daniel also resumed his position as superintendent of public works and, in that capacity, took over supervision of the new tabernacle construction project. The Tabernacle was announced in 1862, but ground was not broken on the project until July 1864 while Daniel was crossing the Atlantic on his way to England. The huge building was designed as an oval structure 150 feet wide and 250 long. Its roof, shaped like a turtle shell, rested on forty-four sandstone pillars set around the perimeter of the oval. By the time Daniel returned from Europe in September 1865, the stonework on the building was almost complete. As he noted when he returned to the project, "The new Tabernacle is considerably advanced, and seems to occupy the chief attention at present; all the pillars are up, and they are about ready to raise three or four of the bents. It is the design to have it ready for the next October Conference."[2]

The "bents" as Daniel called them were actually wooden arch trusses that spanned the entire width of the Tabernacle. The arches were formed of latticed planks set between outer stringers nine feet apart. They were each constructed flat on the ground and then raised into position with a crane. Much of the 1.5 million board feet of lumber used to build the Tabernacle went into these arches, and a large portion of that lumber came from Daniel's Big Cottonwood Lumber Company sawmills. Most of these materials, like those used in other church projects that he supervised, Daniel donated. His contributions to the church exceeded the ten percent of his income called for by the tithing commandment, but he regarded the excess as a free offering and always supplied without charge whatever items he could to build the Saints' community.[3]

Daniel's estimate that the Tabernacle would be finished in time for October conference in 1866 proved optimistic. Construction was delayed by the diversion of labor, including Daniel's, into other critical areas. The hundreds of northern Utah men called into service for the Black Hawk War drew workers away from local projects and from the mills, quarries, and manufacturing firms that supplied materials for them. Henry Grow, the civil engineer who designed the Tabernacle, also encountered difficulty in forming the semi-circular ends of the Tabernacle's roof structure

Figure 17.1. Public and religious buildings constructed under supervision of Daniel H. Wells in the 1860s: (top to bottom) Salt Lake Theater, 1862; Salt Lake Tabernacle, 1867; and Salt Lake Temple, under construction ca. 1875 and completed in 1893, after Daniel H. Wells's death.

to be as strong as the central vault. Work on the roof started by placing the center trusses and progressed in both directions toward the ends. By the time the ends were fully framed, many of the three hundred thousand shingles from Daniel's sawmills were already in place on the central roof section. The entire roof was not competed until the spring of 1867.[4]

Much of the labor on the building, especially after Daniel resumed supervision of the project, was performed by newly arrived immigrants who were paid two to $3½ per day in cash or credits redeemable in food and other supplies from church storehouses.[5]

In a meeting held in the Bowery, which the Tabernacle would replace, Daniel called for more skilled laborers to do the interior finishing work on the building. He also asked for teams to haul wood laths from the canyon sawmills and reminded those whose service had not been required earlier that they had voted at the last conference to contribute when called. The response was generous and by the end of the summer as many as seventy plasterers were at work on the vast ceiling.[6]

Although the Tabernacle was still unfinished in October, the building was used for general conference that year. The interior work, including benches, the original seven hundred–pipe organ, and a freestanding gallery to increase seating capacity by two thousand, continued through 1870. Additional improvements delayed the formal dedication of the building until October 1875.[7]

Another construction project that Daniel supervised was the Deseret Telegraph Company. The transcontinental telegraph line that connected Great Salt Lake City to California and the east coast was completed in 1861. More than five hundred miles of it was built by Mormon workers employed to fulfill contracts Brigham Young negotiated with the two telegraph companies. Utah benefitted from the telegraph and, when the Civil War ended and materials became available, Brigham determined to connect all the Mormon settlements by wire. The value of coordinating defenses again Indian raids, keeping church members informed of news, and allowing them to order supplies and report developments in their areas was obvious.[8]

During the winter of 1865, the First Presidency organized Mormon communities north and south of Great Salt Lake City to construct a five hundred–mile regional telegraph line to connect the various settlements with one another. Workers from each community were assigned to cut and install the poles within their boundaries and halfway to the next towns up and down the line. Each settlement was also asked to send one or two young men or women to a school in Great Salt Lake City to learn telegraphy from those Mormons who were experienced in the technology from their work during the building of the transcontinental line. Both the line crews and the telegraphy students regarded their work as a mission call and were supported on the job or in training by their families or communities.⁹

To purchase the wire, insulators, and telegraphy equipment for the line, articles that could not be locally produced, $56,000 in cash was collected throughout the territory. Communities that would be connected to the telegraph line also furnished a total of sixty-five heavy wagons with teams, drivers, and provisions for the 1866 church train that brought the eighty-four tons of materials purchased to Utah. The poles were already up by October and the wire was quickly strung on its arrival. By December, the line from Ogden to Great Salt Lake City was in operation and by February 1867, the full five hundred miles of line was up and operating from Logan to St. George.¹⁰

After the telegraph line was built by church labor and donations, the Deseret Telegraph Company was organized in January 1867 to hold ownership of the line and operate the service. Most of the five thousand shares of stock in the company were issued to the LDS Church, whose members had built the line. Brigham Young served as president of the company and Daniel was elected vice president and a director. He and a few other investors who had put up some of the funds for the telegraph were also given shares in the new company, but none of them or the church itself profited much from the enterprise. Rates were set low so that small towns and individuals in remote places could use the telegraph economically. Additional lines were eventually extended north into Idaho and south to Pipe Springs in Arizona. The Deseret Telegraph Company remained the only church-owned public utility in America until it was sold to Western Union Company in 1900.¹¹

In the municipal elections held in February 1866, Daniel H. Wells was elected mayor of Great Salt Lake City. As with other civic positions to which he was elected, Daniel did not actively seek the job of mayor. But when Abraham O. Smoot, who had been the city's mayor for more than nine years, declined to run again and indicated his intention to move to Provo, Brigham Young requested Daniel to stand for the office. He agreed and was elected by a large majority.¹²

During his term as mayor, Daniel felt it his responsibility to be always alert to events in other parts of Utah Territory and in the nation so that he could respond to any request made upon the city or its citizens. He also wanted to be aware of any problems or controversies that developed outside the territory that might have an impact on the people and the city he had grown to love. After the completion of the Deseret Telegraph line, he kept informed on all Utah, national, and world events by going to the telegraph office every night and reading the latest dispatches. No event of importance passed unnoticed, and he was often able to counter misinformation sent east by anti-Mormons in Great Salt Lake City or take quick action regarding controversial issues that came over the wires from the east or west coast.[13]

Daniel was the third mayor of Great Salt Lake City and was well qualified by temperament and personal integrity to preside over the fast-growing, dynamic city. Bryant S. Hinckley, who was born during the time that Daniel served as mayor, described the requirements of the job and the men who filled it:

> The two men who had preceded him [Daniel] in this office, Jedediah M. Grant and Abraham O. Smoot, were strong, positive characters. The times required men of that type, for those were frontier days demanding leaders who could meet dangerous situations without hesitation. Ruffians and criminals made up a lawless element that was difficult to deal with. The police force in Salt Lake City was a small one, but every man had proved his mettle in situations that measured his courage and his willingness to do his duty. General Wells, as Mayor, conducted a warfare against liquor selling, gambling and kindred evils, and he lacked neither the physical stamina nor the moral courage to see that the city ordinances were respected and obeyed. Much to his credit, it was said that while he was Mayor peace was so well maintained that a woman could walk through the streets of Salt Lake City as safely at midnight as she could at midday.[14]

During the time that Daniel served as mayor, anti-Mormon Gentiles tried relentlessly to wrest political power away from the municipal officials who had been elected by the people. Nearly all of these officials were Mormons because the majority of citizens were also Mormons who voted as a group for Mormon candidates. This practice of voting for men endorsed by church authorities dated from the Saints' days in Nauvoo and Daniel's election as a non-Mormon to the first city council there in 1841. It had caused serious problems for the Mormons from its inception and, while legal, was seen by Gentiles as an unacceptable mixing of church and state. It especially infuriated anti-Mormons who wanted to take control of local governments in the territory, but were not numerous enough in any municipality to do so when running against Mormon candidates.

The majority of non-Mormon federal officials also objected to the Mormons' domination of territorial and municipal offices. They frequently used their official positions to assist the anti-Mormons in reducing the political power of Mormon political figures, particularly those who, like Daniel, were also church leaders.

Almost as soon as he was elected mayor, Daniel was thrust into conflicts over law enforcement and the administration of justice in the city by two sensational murder cases, neither of which was ever solved.

In April 1866, S. Newton Brassfield, a freighter from Nevada who was doing business in Great Salt Lake City, induced Mrs. Mary Emma Hill, the plural wife of Archibald N. Hill, a Mormon missionary then in Europe, to abandon her spouse and accept Brassfield as her husband. Judge Solomon P. McCurdy, associate justice of Utah, who was from Missouri and strongly anti-Mormon, married the couple without any consideration of the fact that Mary Emma was already married. No attempt was made to secure a divorce since Brassfield felt her existing marriage was invalid.[15]

A few days later, Brassfield was arrested after a dispute with friends of Elder Hill and the police over his attempt to remove his new wife's possessions from the Hill home. Brassfield was released after posting bail and while his case was pending, along with his wife's effort to secure custody of her children, he was fatally shot by an unknown assailant as he was about to enter his hotel in company with a US marshal. There were no witnesses and no clues as to who had committed the crime, although suspicion centered on relatives or friends of the absent husband. Despite the presence of the marshal during the crime, the later posting of a $4,500 reward, and the efforts of a grand jury and police, the killer was never identified or apprehended.[16]

Dr. J. King Robinson was an assistant surgeon at Camp Douglas who stayed in Great Salt Lake City after resigning his commission in 1865 and married a Utah girl. Dr. Robinson filed a claim on some property in the northwest part of the city where the Wasatch Hot Springs was located. He intended to build a hospital there, using the hot springs to treat his patients. He also became Sunday school superintendent of the First Congregational Church, the first non-Mormon church organized in Utah Territory. The church's minister, Norman McLeod, was strongly anti-Mormon and delivered sermons and lectures critical of the LDS church in Utah and in Washington, DC.[17]

On the night of October 22, responding to a young man who told the doctor he was needed and to come right away, Dr. Robinson rushed out of his home. Within blocks of his house he was ambushed by a group of about seven men who struck him down, shot him in the head, and disappeared before anyone else arrived on the scene.[18]

Both of these crimes were attributed to the Mormon people by some anti-Mormons, including a few federal officials. A relative of Dr. Robinson accused Mayor Daniel H. Wells of being complicit in his murder because he presided over the city council, which had ejected Robinson from city-owned property that he had jump-claimed at Wasatch Hot Springs. Robinson appealed his case to the Territorial Supreme Court, but Chief Justice John Titus ruled against him. The non-Mormons' feeling that church members were involved in his death was not helped by Brigham Young's statement about claim-jumping: "If they jump my claims here, I shall be very apt to give them a preemption right that will last them to the last resurrection. I hope no man will ever venture so far as to tempt me to do such a thing."[19]

A reward was offered for the killers and Mayor Wells was vigilant in his efforts to apprehend them, but no proof was found against any individual and no arrests were made. The lack of justice in these cases left the anti-Mormon faction free to blame Mormons generally for lawlessness in the city, thus further poisoning the relationship between Saints and Gentiles in the territory.[20]

Before Daniel became mayor, the city council had passed an ordinance to control the manufacture and distribution of alcohol, which, until the end of the Civil War, had been openly available in saloons and other establishments. The ordinance prohibited anyone except city agents from manufacturing, buying, or selling alcohol. It created a liquor monopoly in the city, the profits of which went to the city treasury. The ordinance also barred private billiard and gaming establishments and in their place allowed only city-operated businesses. Existing licenses were allowed to run out and no new ones were issued. This greatly suppressed the liquor trade since the city government was not keen to operate saloons or gambling parlors. Brigham, who lobbied to get the ordinance passed, thought it did "a great deal of good," but the non-Mormon citizens, and the businessmen whose shops had to close, were enraged and sought ways to circumvent the law.

A few months after his election, Daniel presided at a city council meeting that amended the liquor ordinance by adding a new enforcement clause to control "nuisances." Under this clause, any public nuisance [private saloon or gambling parlor] found to be operating in the city could be closed by the city marshal, who could also "take possession of such house or place, with the gaming tables, and all other instruments or devices used for the purpose of gaming and may demolish such instruments or devices or hold the same, including liquors and bar fixtures."[21]

Daniel must have had conflicted thoughts about this ordinance. The suppression of drinking and gambling were priority church objectives that he supported as a member of the First Presidency. But the ordinance bore a striking resemblance to the "abatement of nuisances" ordinance passed at the behest of Joseph Smith by the Nauvoo City Council some twenty-two years before. Daniel thought that ordinance unwise and warned Joseph Smith that the city council was liable for damages to property seized under the ordinance. Most disturbing, the Nauvoo ordinance had incited anti-Mormons there to violent persecution of the Saints and the murder of Joseph and Hyrum Smith.

Gentiles in Great Salt Lake City, who had organized private clubs that sold liquor now also feared their property would be "seized and destroyed" and sent a petition to Col. Carroll E. Potter, the new commanding officer at Camp Douglas, and a telegram to his superior in Washington, DC, Gen. Grenville M. Dodge, which claimed that the ordinance could cause the destruction of property "without due course of law."[22]

General William T. Sherman replied to Colonel Potter in a belligerent telegram:

> In the month of April a telegram was received from American Citizens that their lives and property are in danger, received by General Dodge. Let the troops at Ft. Bridger and Camp Douglas be employed to protect the Gentiles [Sherman's term], and let the Mormons know that if they injure the Gentiles they shall have to pay the penalty. Give them to understand that the people of the United States are only waiting for some pretext to destroy them root and branch.[23]

After receiving the telegram, Colonel Potter asked for a meeting with Mayor Wells, Brigham Young, former Mayor Abraham Smoot, and other city leaders. In a long and sometimes acrimonious discussion Potter declared, "I do not want the policemen to go and seize on property under this ordinance and destroy it, until it is tried in the proper courts of law." Daniel promised that the law would be enforced judiciously and nothing would be destroyed unless ordered by a court. Brigham reinforced that commitment by assuring Potter that "If private property is infringed upon illegally or unjustly, you will have my assistance, as an individual, to the utmost."[24]

The anti-liquor and gambling ordinance remained in effect, but Mayor Wells found it difficult to enforce. Some illegal establishments were closed, but many more continued to operate and the city authorities lacked the resources to discover and suppress them. As non-Mormon numbers and influence continued to grow, the city abandoned its liquor monopoly and again began issuing licenses for saloons and places of amusement.

Other Gentile merchants, not connected to the "sin" businesses also feared that their livelihoods were threatened by the Mormons' absolute grip on city government and Brigham's denunciations of those who he claimed charged "exorbitant prices," and used their money and influence

Figure 17.2. Salt Lake City business district, ca. 1869. Photo by William H. Jackson.

to oppose the Saints. When President Young, his Counselor Mayor Wells, and other leading Mormons sponsored a boycott against unfriendly Gentile merchants (some of whom were Jews), many of them sent an open letter to Brigham and "Leaders of the Mormon Church" in which they offered to sell out their businesses to the church and leave the territory. Brigham rejected the offer, which stipulated a price of retail "cash valuation" less 25 percent, as exorbitant and told the Gentile merchants they were free to stay or go as they pleased.[25]

Brigham firmly maintained that the Saints had every right to refuse their patronage to any business whose owners were actively anti-Mormon:

> The wealth that has been accumulated in this Territory from the earliest years of our settlement by men who were not connected with us religiously, and the success which has attended their business operations prove . . . [that] in business we have not been exclusive in our dealings, or confined our patronage to those of our own faith . . .
>
> There is a class, however, who are doing business in the Territory, who for years have been the avowed enemies of this community. The disrupture and overthrow of the community have been the objective which they have pertinaciously sought to accomplish. They have used every energy and all the means at their command to put into circulation the foulest slanders about old citizens . . .

What claims can such persons have upon the patronage of this community, and what community would be so besotted as to uphold and foster men whose aim is to destroy them? Have we not the right to trade at whatever we please, or does the Constitution of the United States bind us to enter the stores of our deadliest enemies and purchase of them?[26]

Brigham's counsel to "Sustain those who sustain this kingdom, and those that fight against it, cease to sustain them" was effective enough that a few of the most vociferous anti-Mormon merchants left the territory, taking their merchandise with them. Most, however, remained and moderated their opposition to the Mormons so as not to be singled out for economic punishment.[27]

Mormon competition with Gentile merchants increased significantly with the founding of Zions Cooperative Mercantile Institution (ZCMI), a cooperative organization designed to import goods to Utah at the lowest possible freight rates and wholesale them to member retail stores at a common fixed price. The cooperative organization was set up under the direction of church leaders and more than a hundred and fifty stores in Great Salt Lake City and other Mormon communities joined ZCMI. The large buying volume of goods purchased and shipped enabled these Mormon firms to compete more successfully with large Gentile establishments. The Saints were encouraged to buy whenever possible from ZCMI-connected stores and thus keep their trade away from the anti-Mormon Gentile merchants.[28]

ZCMI helped level the competitive playing field for merchandising in Utah and the economic conflict between Mormons and Gentiles subsequently waned. Since the vast majority of the population was Mormon, the Gentile merchants needed some of the Saints' patronage to remain profitable. Most of them continued to prosper in competition with Mormon firms, and the strongly anti-Mormon group among them shifted their emphasis from economic conflict to political confrontation and opposition to the Mormon doctrines of polygamy and the control of alcohol and other vices within Utah Territory. As a strongly anti-Mormon writer noted about Utah and Great Salt Lake City during Daniel's first term as mayor:

> The amount of travel increased, and with it the amount of money; trade was free, with no distinction between Mormon and Gentiles; contracts on the railroad were taken by both, and little distinction made in giving employment, and in July, 1868, at a great railroad meeting, Mormon, Jew and Christian

fraternized in the Tabernacle, and seemed to feel they had a common interest in the country's prosperity.[29]

After the inauguration of U. S. Grant as president of the United States, the anti-Mormon faction in Salt Lake City (the word "Great" had been officially dropped from the city's name in 1868 to conform to common usage) became more extreme in its efforts to seize political control from the LDS populace and their elected officials. Their efforts were aided by Grant's appointment of Judge James B. McKean as chief justice of Utah. Before leaving Washington to take up his new position, Judge McKean stated openly that he had been divinely commissioned to overthrow the Mormon-dominated government in Utah: "The mission which God has called upon me to perform in Utah is as much above the duties of other courts and judges as the heavens are above the earth, and whenever or wherever I find the local or Federal laws obstructing therewith, by God's blessings, I shall trample them under my foot."[30]

Judge McKean arrived in Salt Lake City on the last day of August 1870. He began his attack against Mormon power by ignoring the statute that created territorial offices in Utah. This law, passed in 1852, specified that the Utah attorney general attend to all legal business in which the territory was a party and that the Utah marshal execute all orders and processes of the supreme court and the district court in cases that arose under the laws of Utah. This arrangement left to the US district attorney and the US marshal all cases and legal business arising from acts of Congress in Utah. The federal government paid all expenses incurred by US officials and Utah Territory assumed the costs of its own marshal and attorney. This law, supplemented by others that gave the local probate court general civil and criminal jurisdiction, had been in operation for eighteen years when Judge McKean set its provisions aside.[31]

To do so, he used the case of Paul Engelbrecht, who violated an ordinance of Salt Lake City prohibiting the sale of liquor and was fined, but afterward continued to operate his unlawful business. A warrant was issued and Engelbrecht's establishment was closed by the police in August 1870. All the liquor and equipment he had in his business were confiscated. He then filed a complaint against the city officials who had helped execute the warrant. These officials were arrested by the US marshal and, after a hearing before Judge McKean, were placed under bond to await the action of the grand jury.[32]

In an effort to get indictments against the Mormon city officials, Judge McKean impaneled the grand jury in an illegal manner. Instead of allowing the county clerk, in the presence of the territorial marshal or the sheriff, to draw jurors by lot from the names of taxpayers on the county rolls, he ordered the grand jurors to be selected by the US marshal, using a process by which Mormons were challenged and excluded. The grand jury, consisting entirely of non-Mormons, then indicted the city officials, but those accused appealed to the US Supreme Court. There Judge McKean's action was ruled invalid and, because his method of choosing grand jurors was followed by the other judges in Utah Territory, all the proceedings of the territorial court done using improper jurors were invalidated. The charges against Salt Lake City officials and more than a hundred other cases were dismissed.[33]

Following the *Engelbrecht* case, Mayor Wells made a brief address before a political convention about continuing anti-Mormon efforts to pressure Congress into enacting laws against the Saints. He said he did not think reasonable men would disenfranchise a whole community at the behest of a clique that aimed at destroying republican liberty in Utah. When the assessor went to assess property, the mayor said, he did not inquire whether the owner was a Methodist, a Baptist, a Mormon, or a Roman Catholic; he assessed the property, not the man.[34]

In a letter to President Horace S. Eldredge, then presiding over the European Mission, Daniel described more of the continuing anti-Mormon efforts to damage the LDS Church's reputation, tax its financial resources, and reduce its political influence in Utah. He was personally involved, as an attorney representing the LDS Church, in combating efforts to tax the organization out of existence.

> Never were the emissaries and agents of the Evil One more thoroughly awake and restlessly active than now. They can scarcely eat, sleep, or do anything except plan and plot for the overthrow of the kingdom of God; and by the influx of many strangers, drawn hither by fabulous reports of great mineral wealth in the mountains around Salt Lake City, they hope to accomplish much this coming summer [1871]. But if we may judge from their herculean labors during the year just past and the infinitesimal results following, we have little to fear, if we do our duty . . .
>
> Amongst other despicable attempts to rob us of our means has been that made by Dr. Taggart, Assessor of Internal Revenue, to compel the Church to pay an enormous tax on the tithing donated by the Saints. This was considered virtually settled during the last session of Congress, by the passage of a law affecting the collection of the income tax, in which a clause was inserted to meet the wants of our case. But Dr. Taggart

would not let the matter drop; he insisted that the law did not apply to us, obtained the legal opinion of Major Hempstead, the U. S. Attorney for the District of Utah, to the same effect, and carried the case back to Washington. Mr. Delano, the Commissioner of Internal Revenue, having been appointed Secretary of the Interior by President Grant, Mr. Douglas, his assistant, who acted in his place for a short time, decided that the tithing should be taxed, but abated the penalty of fifty per-cent, added by Assessor Taggart. Mr. Hollister, the Collector, proceeded to take steps to collect the same and to levy on Church property, if necessary, to secure the payment.[35]

Daniel noted that the new Commissioner of Internal Revenue, General Pleasonton, reversed Douglas's decision and decided that tithing was not taxable, but Taggart objected, assessed another tax of $50,000 for the year 1869, again with the threat of a 50 percent penalty for non-payment, and journeyed to Washington to press his view, unsuccessfully, on the new commissioner. Obviously disgusted with the government's effort to tax church donations, Daniel continued:

> If there is anything more absurd than taxing the gifts of a people who pay taxes on their income, and which has all, consequently, been taxed before given, I have failed to hear of it . . . it is an embittered spirit of persecution that has actuated the assessment, which, if collected, would be an outrageous act of spoilation and legal robbery.[36]

The new Commissioner's ruling stood, however, and the tax was not collected. But another way of restricting Mormon influence in the Great Basin was more successful. Following the Comstock discovery in far-western Utah, Nevada Territory was created from the western third of Utah with the Utah-Nevada boundary at the 116th meridian, in 1861. Congress moved the boundary east to the 115th meridian in 1862 and Nevada was admitted as a state in 1863, even though its population was smaller than Utah's. Mormon settlers in Nevada, once a majority of the population there, became a minority as the mining boom commenced and non-Mormons flooded in. In 1866, Congress again moved the Utah-Nevada border east to the 114th meridian, thus placing more of the area's Mormon residents under the rule of Nevada's Gentile and often anti-Mormon government. In the same letter to Horace Eldredge, Daniel describes the reaction of many of these new Nevada residents.

You are aware that the boundary line between Utah and Nevada has lately been determined by Government surveys. It was then found that our settlements on the Muddy, and others further north, were in the State of Nevada; this being ascertained, the people as a general thing were anxious to leave, the taxes in that State being high and the majority of the people unfriendly. This move will greatly help the settlement of the new "land of Canaan," as many of those leaving the Nevada settlements will locate at Kanab and in the surrounding regions.[37]

Fort Kanab had been established a few years previously and was connected by a Deseret Telegraph wire to the main line at Toker (now Toquerville). In anticipation of the influx of new settlers Daniel referred to in his letter, he and Brigham Young visited Fort Kanab in September 1870. They located a town site and laid out the cardinal lines for its main streets. They also called Levi Stewart, who was already residing at the fort, as the first bishop of the LDS branch there. Kanab at that time had few permanent residents, but the calling of Bishop Stewart indicated the belief of church leaders that it would grow rapidly.[38]

One of the federal officers whose actions plagued Mayor Wells from the early days of his administration was George R. Maxwell, the US Land Office Registrar. The US Land Office was opened in Salt Lake City in March 1869, more than twenty years after the US government obtained title to the land of Utah Territory from Mexico. Maxwell, a Civil War veteran, was appointed registrar by President Grant and soon allied himself with the anti-Mormon faction, whose members were eager to get control of as much property in the city as possible.[39]

Registrar Maxwell favored Gentile efforts to obtain property in Salt Lake City by repeatedly accepting "jumped" claims to ownership of city lots that he filed over the legitimate claims of the Mormon pioneer owners. These spurious claims each had to be adjudicated before the rightful owners could receive legal title to the land they occupied. These owners included the LDS Church, which claimed Temple Square and other properties, and Salt Lake City, which claimed City Hall, parks, and public squares. A few nervous property owners committed violent crimes to get "claim jumpers" off their land, but the intruders could still press their claims in court. Some non-Mormons asserted that Dr. Robinson's murder was the result of his claim jumping the Wasatch Hot Springs land that belonged to Salt Lake City and a few even implicated Daniel H. Wells in the crime.[40]

Maxwell's obstruction was possible because all land in Utah came into the possession of the federal government when the United States signed the Treaty of Guadalupe Hidalgo with Mexico in February 1848. No private rights had been established while Utah lands were part of Mexico and the treaty ceded all the land to the United States government, leaving it to adjudicate Indian claims and transfer property to new settlers. Thereafter, every land title in Utah had to be granted by a patent or other document that transferred it from the federal government to the new owner. This process should have been easy as Congress had already established laws governing the transfer of land from the government to private ownership, but Utah proved to be a more difficult case.[41]

Great Salt Lake City was laid out in the summer of 1847. The plan of the city was a square of eighty-one blocks, each block containing ten acres of land. The streets were eight rods wide, with walks twenty feet in width on either side. Four blocks were reserved for public squares. On the outskirts, fields of five, ten, and twenty acres were laid out, the smaller ones nearest to the city and larger ones further out. The pioneers distributed these lots and fields by lot. Each household received a city property of one and one-quarter acres and a larger farm field with a water right sufficient to irrigate it. Each city lot cost its holder $1.50 plus a small fee for surveying and recording. Under the provisional government of 1847 and the territorial government organized in 1851, "right of occupancy" permits were issued by the territory to serve as valid proof of ownership until the federal government surveyed the lands and issued patents to the owners. But twenty years passed and no patents were issued to Utah landowners.[42]

In March 1867 Congress finally passed an "Act for the relief for the inhabitants of cities and towns on the public domain." This act provided that a mayor (for incorporated towns) or the county probate judge (for unincorporated towns) should register town site lands at the land office and purchase them for the benefit of all the inhabitants. Pursuant to this law, the Utah Territorial Legislature established regulations for disposing of town site lands. Within thirty days after making the land office entry, the judge or mayor was to give public notice and advertise the land he had entered. Every person, association, or corporation claiming to be a rightful owner of any part of this land was required within six months to present a claim to the probate court. In case of adverse claims the probate judge was required to "decide according to justice in the case" and when a claim was undisputed, to determine its validity. The probate judge or mayor could then issue a deed to be recorded.[43]

Most of Great Salt Lake City had been claimed and occupied by pioneer settlers prior to 1865. Nearly all of these settlers were Mormon, although a few original claimants were Gentiles and some non-Mormons had purchased claims from the original settlers. On behalf of city residents, Mayor Wells entered a claim for a patent to all the land in the city so he could deed each parcel to the rightful claimant. Registrar

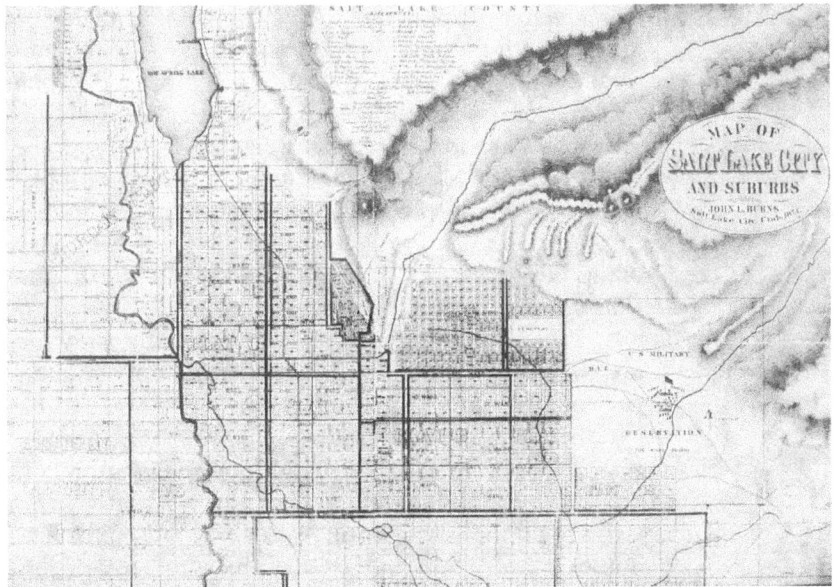

Figure 17.3. An 1871 map of Salt Lake City by John L. Burns showing the 5,700 acres included in US Land Patent No. 710, issued to Mayor Daniel H. Wells for the city.

Maxwell accepted the mayor's entry, but immediately began also accepting "jumped" adverse claims for various city lots from non-Mormons who wanted these properties. Each adverse claim had to be adjudicated and more than five years after his original entry was made, Daniel was still arguing in court to dispose of spurious claims.[44]

His frustration was evident in an interview that he gave to John H. Beadle, a reporter for the Cincinnati Commercial, in 1870.

[Mayor Wells]   It is no fault of the United States Government that we are not now peacefully possessing titles to the ground we have redeemed, and which Congress wishes us to retain. It is the fault of the unrelenting Land Registrar here, Maxwell, who has entertained and abetted every petty and malicious claim contesting our right to the site, and who hindered the entry of our city.

[Beadle]   How much do you claim as the proper area of Salt Lake City?

[Mayor Wells]   About 5,700 acres, sufficient to give us water front on the Jordan and control of the irrigation reservoirs. The law is general upon the subject of municipal sites. It gives three hundred and twenty acres to every one hundred people in a town. A town of five thousand people receives four sections of the public lands. Salt Lake has grown far beyond all precedent that we had to get a special relief bill passed applying to our city, and we took a census for the purpose. The Land Office in Washington recommended, and Congress promptly passed, a special bill, under the terms of which we added to our original charter other essential bits of ground.

What I wish to make plain to you is the nasty pretexts on which we are retarded in the matter of our entry.

[Beadle] Give me the names of all the claims which Maxwell has entertained against the city.

[Mayor Wells] Well, there are the Robinson, Slasson, Williamson, and Orr cases. Robinson was a retired surgeon to the army. He jumped the Warm Springs property and public bath houses on the outskirts of town, with eighty acres of environing land. He put a tent and a guard by the Springs, built a fence within our fence. We removed these obstructions, and he embarrassed us at law until his death, and his widow continued the suit. The land agent actually permitted her to make a cash entry of the place. Very differently did the Washington authorities behave. The commissioner of the Land Office decided without hesitation in our favor; and the Secretary of the Interior confirmed it.

[Beadle] What was the *Slasson* claim?

[Mayor Wells] Slasson was a fellow who first rented a quarter section of ground from the city on the road leading to Camp Douglas. And when he undertook to keep a rum shop on it in violation of law, we ejected him. He was then abetted by Maxwell in a bare-faced attempt to claim it, and entered it. And Maxwell's decision was reversed by the heads of the Department at Washington.

The other two claims are even more preposterous, yet they are received and considered and, instead of disposing of them, Maxwell spends his time acting as volunteer counsel against us in criminal cases before the United States Court. Williamson 'jumped' a bit of ground, claiming the preemption laws, and put a shanty upon it. It was a spot we had long previously reserved for a parade ground. J.M. Orr, a lawyer here, filed also Chippewa scrip

	[paper money] for eighty acres between Ensign Peak and Arsenal Hill, half a mile from the heart of the city. Now scrip can only take up land for agricultural purposes and this claim is impudent beyond degree, but this land registrar entertains it, refuses to decide it, and so keeps back our entry. We are nearly or quite twenty thousand people; our city is as old as many great towns in the Mississippi Valley, but here men are allowed to preempt farms right in the midst of us as if they meant to plow us under.
[Beadle]	What should I suggest, General Wells?
[Mayor Wells]	Why, the General Land Office ought to instruct this devilish Maxwell not to entertain these paltry claims, each of which is a paltry reproduction of claims already thrown out. The government means to encourage the formation and building of towns, but this agent vetoes the law in the case of the largest town ever established on the public lands.
[Beadle]	Here General Wells left me and went over to the city hall, returning in a few minutes with copies of the land office decisions in the two cases decided, signed by Willis Brummond and affirmed by the Secretary of the Interior. These decisions state that "parties taking up land in the environs of town sites like Salt Lake City must take the risk of the lands falling within the town site" and that "where churches, schoolhouses, public buildings and places of trade and commerce are established in the form of a town, the land is already selected and held in reserve under the act and can not be infringed upon."
[Mayor Wells]	We have no complaint to make of Congress or the Land Office in respect to our rights under the act. They have treated us well.[45]

In November 1871, after five years of contending with conflicting claims, fighting some through to successful resolution in the courts, and encountering months or years of delay in others that Registrar Maxwell held in abeyance, Daniel finally submitted the city's application for the full 5,730 acres of land covered by the original entry made in 1866. In doing so, he bypassed some conflicting claims still held by Maxwell, who continued his delaying tactics by refusing to decide whether these claims should be submitted to court proceedings for decision. Daniel informed Maxwell's superiors in Washington that the application had been submitted so that the Registrar could not refuse to forward it. He felt confident that the Secretary of the Interior would recognize Maxwell's dereliction in failing to resolve the conflicting claims quickly and conclude that they had no merit.[46]

He was right. On June 11, 1872, federal patent certificate number 710 was issued to Daniel H. Wells, mayor of Salt Lake City, in trust for the personal use and benefit of the inhabitants of the city. The patent included all the land in Salt Lake City and was granted on payment of $1.25 per acre. It transferred clear title to the land from the federal government and quashed every conflicting claim.

As soon as the patent was received, Mayor Wells announced that deeds to all city lots would be issued to claimants for a transfer fee of $3.25 per lot. Title to public properties such as City Hall, Washington Square, Liberty Park, Salt Lake City Cemetery, and the city streets and infrastructure was retained by the city.[47]

As his final duty in the long quest to confer legal ownership of their property on the city's residents, Daniel personally signed each deed before it was delivered. Among the deeds were those given to Brigham Young for the Lion House and Beehive House, to the LDS Church for Temple Square, to the Episcopal Church for St. Mark's Cathedral, to the Catholic Church for the future Cathedral of the Madeline, and to Daniel himself for the Big House and Aunt Em's home on State Street. Property owners received their deeds almost twenty-five years after the pioneers entered Utah. Salt Lake City was the largest city in America for which deeds were issued directly from a federal patent on public lands.

Despite his ever-increased workload, which often kept him absent from home for weeks at a time, Daniel's family continued to grow. Two years after the birth of Gershom Wells in England, Stephen Franklin Wells was born to Susan Wells in January 1867. His arrival was followed in February by the birth of Herman Chapin Wells to Martha Wells and in July by the birth of Melvin Dickenson Wells to Louisa Wells. In May 1868, Hannah Wells gave birth to Victor Pennington Wells, and in June Wilford Woodruff Wells was born to Lydia Wells. Two of these children did not survive infancy due to the continuing scourge of diphtheria and other childhood illnesses among the Saints and the lack of effective medicines to prevent or treat them. Herman Chapin Wells died six months after his first birthday in September 1868 and Wilford Woodruff Wells died a month later at age three months.[48]

Only a single child was born into the Wells family in each of the next two years: Martha Wells gave birth to Edna Margaret Wells in July 1869, and Susan Wells gave birth to Charles Henry Wells in August 1870. Arthur Deming Wells was born to Lydia Wells in September 1871, but lived only three months before dying in December the same year. That same month, Briant Harris Wells was born to Martha Wells. Bryant was

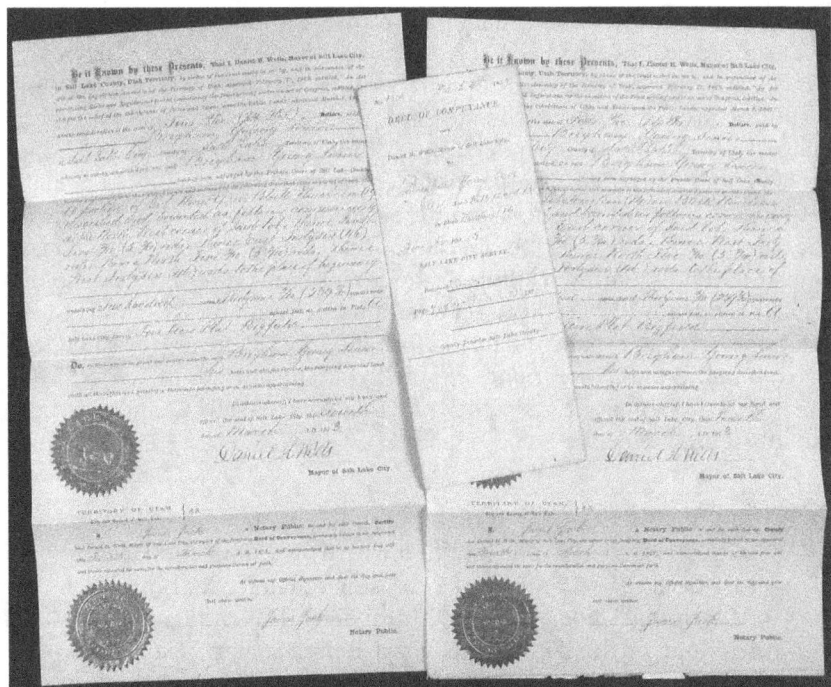

Figure 17.4. Deeds signed by Mayor Daniel H. Wells, transferring parcels of Salt Lake City property to LDS president Brigham Young.

the last-born of Daniel's thirty-seven children and he was fifty-seven years old at the time of his youngest son's birth. The Wells family was then at its greatest numerical strength and consisted of thirty-six living persons. Nine of the children born to Daniel's seven wives died prior to the birth of Briant Wells and four more succumbed afterward before reaching adulthood. Photographs of family members taken in later years show thirteen daughters and thirteen sons.[49]

In the spring of 1868, Heber C. Kimball, first counselor to President Brigham Young was thrown from his buggy while visiting in Provo. He did not appear seriously hurt and resumed his duties within a day or two, but his family and friends noticed that his health and vigor seemed weakened after the accident. He may have suffered a concealed head injury that worsened until, in early June, he complained of dizziness and paralysis gradually developed on his right side. Within a few days he was confined to his bed and able to speak only a few words occasionally. On June 22, Heber C. Kimball died without regaining consciousness from the previous day's coma.[50]

Kimball's funeral was scheduled in the new Tabernacle, which was not completed but had been put in service the year before. The acoustical properties of the building were so sensitive that it was impossible to understand a sermon from the pulpit because the speaker's words echoed repeatedly from the ceiling. Although the design of the building was not his, Daniel, as superintendent of public works, felt personally responsible for this flaw and undertook to provide a temporary remedy for the defective acoustics before the funeral. He decided to hang a heavy canvas curtain from the ceiling to the floor, about two-thirds of the distance back from the pulpit to serve as a baffle and absorb sound. Given the very short time span available before the funeral, he also decided that his own family and close friends should make the curtain.[51]

This was a major project, but one that Annie Wells Cannon said the family willingly accepted:

> All the women folk of the household, young and old, were set to work to sew the long seams. In two days the curtain must be finished and in place. Sister Rachel Grant, mother of President Heber J. Grant, a dear friend of the family and president of the Thirteenth Ward Relief Society, seeing the dilemma, offered to supervise the project. The big parlor, long halls and wide porches were covered with sewers and yards of canvas. The curtain was completed in time and was a success. We children were all very proud to have a part in this gigantic sewing bee.[52]

The canvas baffle remained in the Tabernacle for a few years until the freestanding gallery was built around the perimeter of the building to increase its seating capacity. The gallery served equally well to damp the ceiling echoes and the curtain was taken down.

At the time of his death and for several years previously, Heber C. Kimball served as president of the Endowment House, conducting the ceremonies there and performing marriages, sealings, and other ordinances. A short time after Kimball's funeral, Brigham Young called Daniel H. Wells to preside as president in the Endowment House. This calling, in which Daniel continued to serve for nine years, consumed much of his time and, more than any other position he held, brought him face-to-face with the bitter persecution of the anti-Mormon clique in Utah and the anti-polygamy federal government in Washington.[53]

Daniel's calling as second counselor in the First Presidency was not changed, nor was he released from any of his other church responsibilities. In the October 1868 conference, he was again sustained in the positions he had held for ten years and George A. Smith was sustained as first counselor to President Young.

Over the next nine years, Daniel sealed hundreds of couples in marriage. Most of these unions were monogamous, but as the church still had more single females than males and the doctrine of celestial marriage was an integral part of the restored Gospel, some were polygamous. One of the latter would eventually lead him to court and to prison.[54]

About the time of Heber C. Kimball's death, N. Park Woods, the eldest son of Daniel's sister Catherine Chapin Woods, arrived in Salt Lake City with his wife, Clayanna. Park's youngest brother, James Dan Woods, had preceded him to Utah by a few months and was working in the city as a teamster. A third brother, William W. Woods, who was a former Union Army captain, would arrive a few years later. William became the husband of Melvina Whitney, the daughter of Daniel's seventh wife Emmeline by her second husband, Newel K. Whitney. All three of the Woods brothers prospered in Utah through the generosity and influence of their uncle, who helped them secure employment, social contacts, and lodging.[55]

In Park's case, the rooms that Daniel insisted he and his wife occupy benefitted not only the young couple but the family of Rachel Grant with whom they boarded. As Rachel's son Heber, later the seventh President of the LDS Church, explained:

> One day President Daniel H. Wells came to mother's home and informed her that his nephew, Park Woods, was coming to Utah with his wife to represent the New York Life Insurance Company, and he said: "As you are a fine cook, I would like you to take them as boarders, and he will pay you twenty dollars a week for board and lodging for himself and wife."
>
> This seemed like a fortune to mother. It was a change from real poverty to what we considered almost affluence.
>
> Some months later Park Woods said, "Mrs. Grant, the man for whom I work, Colonel Alexander G. Hawes, the general agent of this company, is coming on the Overland Stage, and I would like to invite him to dinner here next Sunday."
>
> Mother said she would be pleased to have the Colonel to Sunday dinner.
>
> After dinner the Colonel said, "Madam, I like your face and I like your cooking very much. I will be here tomorrow with my valise to board with you."[56]

Rachel Grant insisted that she had no room for Hawes to stay in and could not take him, but notwithstanding her protest, he came and a large closet was converted into a bedroom in which the colonel slept for the duration of his stay. Later, after the colonel married, he and his wife came west again and lived with the Grants for six months. His first child was born in the Grant home.

Colonel Hawes became not only a friend to the widow Grant and her son, but an influential and powerful patron as well. Before Heber J. Grant was twenty years of age he entered the insurance business at Hawes's urging. The colonel secured for him the agency for a number of insurance companies, and Heber was soon on his way to prosperity.[57]

18
Mormon versus Gentile in Railroads, Business, Government, and Religion

1870–1878

As early as 1852 and 1854, memorials were sent from the Utah Territorial Legislature, in which Daniel was council president, to Congress requesting that a railroad be constructed across the country through Utah Territory. The benefits of such a transportation link to the east and west coasts were evident to all: greater availability of manufactured goods imported at lower cost than by wagons on the Overland Trail; easier export of the territory's products and raw commodities to bigger markets; and fast, low cost, transportation of people—immigrating converts, miners, businessmen, and tourists.

Fifteen years and a Civil War later, when the transcontinental railroad was finally joined in May 1869, the tracks passed through Ogden to the golden spike site at Promontory Summit, bypassing Salt Lake City entirely and leaving a forty-mile gap between Utah's capital and the new national transportation link.[1]

Speaking at the general conference in April 1869, as the completion of the railroad neared, Daniel told his listeners that, they would benefit most in the changing economy by producing more goods locally and remaining independent of outside economic forces they could not control.

> Just think how many things could be raised and manufactured here, that, if we had them today, would fetch very remunerative prices. Butter, for instance, that at the present time is selling for a dollar and a quarter a pound, in a country like this

should not bring more than twenty-five cents. Cheese the same. These two articles are imported twelve or fifteen hundred miles, and then the Territory is not near supplied . . . There is not near enough grain raised in the Territory. Wheat is selling today at four dollars a bushel, when it should not be more than half that price, and even then would well remunerate the producer. It is so with every other article of our own consumption . . . If a person has a farm his produce will keep until he can obtain remunerative prices, and he is more free and independent than the merchant; for the earth being his banker, he is not called upon to meet his bills and obligations by any particular and specified time, as the merchant is . . .

By industry we thrive; industry, in the mechanical and agricultural pursuits, is the foundation of our independence, and they who obtain a livelihood by habits of industry are far more honorable members of society than they who live by their wits.[2]

Even while the transcontinental railroad was under construction, Daniel began using it to advantage for immigration and transport of goods. Beginning in 1860 and continuing through the Civil War years, the church trains that brought immigrants to Utah traveled east to the Wyoming-Nebraska depot the church set up near the Omaha rail terminus. As construction of the transcontinental railway progressed, the rail terminus moved west and new temporary depots for the church trains were established at locations the tracks were projected to reach by the start of each season. Daniel monitored the progress of the railroad, determined where the next depot would be, and arranged for sufficient wagons to arrive there on time. By June 1867 the Union Pacific rails had advanced 273 miles from Omaha, to North Platte, Nebraska. Immigrants that year traveled to North Platte by rail and met the church trains there for the final leg of their journey to Utah.

As the length of the difficult wagon trek decreased, the number of Saints riding the lengthening rails increased. In a March 1868 letter to LDS bishops, the First Presidency wrote:

In consideration of the great number who anticipate immigrating to this Territory from Europe and the United States during the ensuing season, it is deemed necessary to send 500 teams to the terminus of the U. P. R. R . . . It is well known that the Union Pacific Railroad is now prepared to convey passengers and freight upwards of 500 miles west of Omaha, on the Missouri River. With these great facilities for transportation there are some inconveniences which must be provided for, viz., a depot should be formed at a spot deemed most suitable, near the terminus of the railroad, where provisions may be stored and which will afford good camping facilities for our immigrants.

We do not anticipate purchasing provisions and other supplies for the people from the eastern market, but propose sending means of subsistence with the teams which will meet them at the terminus of the U. P. R. R.[3]

The 1868 depot was actually established at Benton, Wyoming Territory, some 800 miles west of Omaha and 530 miles beyond the 1867 depot at North Platte. Benton was only 165 miles from Ogden, Utah, but those miles were the most difficult of the western route. The church trains still needed an average of sixty days to transport immigrants to Great Salt Lake City that year. By May 1869 the transcontinental line was completed at Promentory, Utah, and immigrants could then ride in relative comfort and at increased speed all the way to Ogden. Within the next two years, Utah railroads were completed to carry passengers to Salt Lake City and many other settlements.

The completion of the railroad proved to be at least a temporary financial disaster for the Saints who had contracted with both the Union Pacific and Central Pacific companies to build and grade some five hundred miles of the road bed through Utah and Nevada. After the rails were joined, both companies defaulted on their construction contracts, leaving their Mormon contractors, subcontractors, and businessmen, including Daniel, to absorb over $1.5 million in losses—much of it unpaid wages to Mormon workers who labored on the two lines, and the balance in unpaid bills for ties, lumber, coal, food, and supplies for the track gangs who laid and spiked down the rails.

For the first time since he purchased land on credit in Nauvoo, Daniel found himself in debt and without the means to pay. He paid the wages of all his workers on time, but doing so left him without sufficient cash to continue the full scope of his businesses and he was obliged to close some enterprises while reducing the scale of others. He recovered within a year or two, but the experience was a foretaste of worse reverses to come.[4]

The bankrupt Union Pacific Company offered Brigham Young $600,000 worth of rails, ties, construction equipment, and rolling stock in part payment of its portion of debt. He accepted and immediately organized the Utah Central Railroad with himself, Daniel H. Wells, and three other Mormon businessmen as directors. Nine other men were brought into the venture as shareholders. Most of these men had lost money due to the railroad companies' default, but still supported the new venture as a means of possibly earning back some of their money in profits from the Utah Central.[5]

Within seven months the new company constructed a track from Ogden to Salt Lake City. When the line opened on January 10, 1870, Utah's capital was finally connected to the national transportation system.[6]

On the day the Utah Central track was completed, another company, the Utah Southern Railroad, was organized, with Daniel as one of the five incorporators, directors, and principal shareholders, to construct a railroad line south to Provo and eventually to Chicken Creek in Juab County. Daniel invested $5,000 in this line, his last railroad venture. Track was laid to Sandy (originally Sandy's Station) by September 1870 and to Draper by December. As soon as this line opened, it began carrying ore from the mines at Alta to smelters in the Salt Lake Valley and beyond.[7]

More importantly for Daniel, in his role as superintendent of public works, the railroad could haul granite blocks to the Salt Lake Temple site. At the same time tracks were being laid to Draper, a standard gauge spur line was built from that station to Granite, located at the stone quarry in the mouth of Little Cottonwood Canyon. Due to the extreme difficulty in transporting the multi-ton stones by wagon or floating them on canal rafts, construction of the temple had progressed slowly during the dozen years since building was restarted in 1860. The new rail line turned a four-day trip into one of mere hours and virtually eliminated the constant breakdowns of wagons that were often overloaded by the weight of a single stone.[8]

Another spur was constructed from the Southern Utah depot in Salt Lake City east on South Temple Street to the building site on Temple Square. These spurs, which were completed in April 1873, allowed granite stones to be carried by rail from the quarry direct to the building site with only a single transfer from narrow gauge cars to standard gauge.[9]

The Southern Utah Railroad was later extended to the Stockton mines, then on to Provo, and finally to Frisco to carry silver and lead ore from new mines there. A third company, the Northern Utah Railroad built north from the Utah Central Railroad terminus at Ogden, adding a track to Logan and then to Franklin, Idaho. The northern track eventually reached Dillon, Montana, and connected to the Northern Pacific Railroad there. None of the Mormon railroads were notably profitable in themselves, but they vastly improved transportation of people and goods throughout Mormon country and thereby promoted commerce and trade in all the settlements. They also helped tie the distant Mormon congregations more closely to central church leaders, who could visit them more easily and send them essential supplies more readily. Daniel and the other directors never became wealthy railroad magnates, but they earned modest profits and their railroads vastly improved and helped develop the territory over which they presided.[10]

In 1869, about three years after he was elected mayor, Daniel took on another church assignment as chancellor of the University of Deseret. He had been a member of the institution's Board of Regents since its creation by the territorial legislature in 1850, but due to the press of other duties, had not been able to take active part in the development of the institution.[11]

The university held its first classes in the home of John Pack, who accepted tuition of $8.00 per quarter (cash or kind) from forty male students. The school moved to the Council House in 1851 and soon thereafter to the newly-completed 13th Ward Schoolhouse.[12]

After struggling to secure financial support and hold classes in its early years, the university suspended operations in 1853 as the territory's people grappled with severe weather, crop failures, military operations against Indians and the Utah Expedition, the Move South, and simple survival.[13]

Classes were again held intermittently beginning in 1859, but at the time Daniel became chancellor in 1866, the institution still had no permanent home and no secure source of funding. He set about overcoming those difficulties. All classes were consolidated at the Council House and the original curriculum of commercial courses was gradually expanded to include history, natural philosophy, sciences, and the arts.[14]

Under Daniel's direction, new faculty was added, including Dr. John R. Park who was hired as principal in 1869. He spent two years touring universities in Europe, at his own expense, studying their organization and curriculum, and returned to Utah to organize a dozen new professors into a full university with himself as president.[15]

While Dr. Park was absent abroad, Daniel built up the enrollment and support of the university and even taught some courses himself. Although his own formal education was not as great as some other Utah residents, he had studied extensively since leaving school and by his own efforts had made himself qualified to teach others. In November 1869, the first academic paper produced by Deseret University students and edited by Daniel H. Wells, titled "the Prickly Pear," was read to the assembled faculty and students.[16]

Several of Daniel's sons were students at the university during the 1870s and the enrollment at Deseret University increased each year from 115 in the fall term of 1869 to 200 the next fall and 375 in 1873. In addition to enrolling his children at the institution, Daniel hired out some of them to assist faculty members in transcribing lectures and preparing curriculum materials, tasks that benefited their own education as well.[17]

In 1874, Daniel's annual report to the governor and territorial assembly noted that the university had spent its appropriated budget of $10,000 from the legislature and was still almost $5,000 in debt for expenses already accrued. The money was spent mainly for faculty salaries and the acquisition of books and teaching apparatus. The institution still had no campus and was still housed in the Council House where its six hundred–volume library and other equipment was also stored. Branches were established at Provo and St. George, and Daniel pleaded with the authorities to continue their financial support and help the institution obtain a permanent home.[18]

> The University has now become a necessity; there are now more advanced students pursuing the higher branches of education than at any previous date. It can no longer be urged that our young men are obliged to go to distant States in order to procure a thorough collegiate course of education; as good opportunities can be procured at our home institutions in many branches as elsewhere . . . In its present struggle for existence, the University therefore commends itself to our Legislators as an institution worthy of their nourishing care and regard, as also the patronage of the people.[19]

In 1876, the school moved out of the Council House and into the Union Academy, an adobe building located at 200 West 400 North in Salt Lake City. The University of Deseret in Provo was closed in 1877 and replaced by another church-sponsored school, Brigham Young Academy, forerunner of Brigham Young University. Property was purchased at the present site of West High School from Salt Lake City, and a University Hall was built there by 1884, but it was not until 1894 that Congress deeded sixty acres of Fort Douglas on the city's east bench to the university. Classes were held there when the first building was completed in 1900.[20]

Daniel continued his duties as chancellor until 1878 when, after submitting to the legislature the annual report of the university he also submitted his resignation to them: "Gentlemen—Having discharged at the instance of your honorable body, the duties of Chancellor of the University of Deseret for some ten years, I now feel to decline the further continuance in that important position."[21]

After more than twenty years of service as superintendent of public works, Daniel was finally released from that office at the October conference of 1870. The only major church construction projects that were unfinished when he vacated the position were the Salt Lake Temple and some of the forts being built in Mormon settlements as part of their defenses against Indian depredations. The walls of the temple were then only a few feet above ground level and another twenty-four years of labor was required to complete the edifice. Church Architect Truman O. Angell continued in charge of the temple construction, but Daniel did not live to see it dedicated. So complete had his work been as superintendent of public works that the office was left open upon his release and no other church member was ever called to fill it.[22]

Daniel's duties as a member of the First Presidency increased after his release from public works as Brigham Young, who was sixty-eight years old and in gradually weakening health, relied ever more extensively on his counselor. When the president visited settlements in the outlying areas of the territory, Daniel nearly always went with him. These journeys were major undertakings and often lasted a month or longer.

A typical conference trip began on April 14, 1869 when President Young and his party left Salt Lake City bound for the "Cotton Country." The next day President Wells, who had been detained from going earlier by the press of other business, left with another group who expected "to join Brother Brigham at Provo." They arrived on the 17th and Brigham, Daniel, and others spoke at an evening meeting there. The combined companies then left Provo for Springville where another conference was scheduled. This meeting opened on the 18th with a dedicatory prayer by President Wells, who also gave an address to the congregation. On the 20th, Daniel spoke again at a meeting in Scipio; on the 21st, he delivered an address at Fillmore; on the 23rd, another at Kanosh; on the 25th, another at Parowan; and on May 1, another at St. George. The company stayed several days in St. George and then visited other southern settlements around it. They then returned north, traveling through the valleys on the eastern side of the Wasatch Mountains. The First Presidency visited and spoke in conferences in Manti, Ephraim, and other communities along the way. They returned to Salt Lake City a month after their departure and Daniel was soon engaged in preparing for a similar trip to the northern settlements.[23]

The new railroads made some of the Presidency's travel easier after 1872, but by then Brigham's health had declined enough that he reduced his schedule of visits somewhat and began spending the winter months of each year at his new home in St. George. Thereafter, Daniel and other apostles often visited northern settlements and attended conferences without him.

The anti-Mormon faction in Utah received a new ally in the appointment of John Wilson Shaffer as governor of the territory on March 20, 1870. Governor Shaffer arrived in Utah with the express determination to make himself "the Governor of Utah in fact, and the commander in Chief of the militia." Most of the governor's actions during his short time in office were directed against Daniel as lieutenant general of the Nauvoo Legion.[24]

The governor's attempt to exert his control over the Legion began when General Wells issued orders for the annual muster of the Legion's forces for training, inspection, and drill.

> Adjutant General's Office, U. T.,
> Salt Lake City, Aug. 16th, 1870
>
> General Order No 1.
>
> No, 1.—Major-General Robert T. Burton, commanding 1st Division Nauvoo Legion, Salt Lake Military District will cause to be held a general muster, for three days, of all the forces within said district, for the purposes of drill, inspection, and camp duty.
>
> No. 2.—The commandants of Utah, Juab, Sanpete, Parowan, Richland, Tooele, Summit and Wasatch military districts, will cause to be held a similar muster, not to exceed three days, of the forces in their respective districts, to be held not later than the 1st day of November . . .
>
> No. 6.—District commandants will cause all vacancies to be filled in their respective districts; they will have a rigid inspection of arms and equipment, and make full and complete returns to this office, on or before the fifteenth day of November. They are also enjoined to enforce good order and sobriety and to take every precaution to avert the occurrence of accident from any cause whatever during the muster.
>
> By order of
> Lieut.-Gen. Daniel H. Wells
> Commanding Nauvoo Legion.[25]

Upon learning of this muster, which had been held annually since 1850, Governor Shaffer issued two proclamations: the first refused to recognize Daniel's position or that of any other Nauvoo Legion officers as territorial militia officers and appointed others in their places; the second banned all musters or other assemblies of militia in Utah except by his order and ordered all arms held by the militia to be turned over to his newly appointed officers.

> Executive Department, Salt Lake City, Utah Territory
> September 15th, 1870

Know ye, that I, J. Wilson Shaffer, Governor of the Territory of Utah, and commander-in-chief of the militia of said Territory; by virtue of the power and authority in me vested by the laws of the United States, have this day, appointed and commissioned P. E. Connor, major general of the militia of Utah Territory; and W. M. Johns; colonel and assistant adjutant-general of the militia of, the Territory. Now, it is ordered that they be obeyed and respected accordingly.

    Witness my hand and the great seal of said Territory, at Salt Lake City, this the 15th day of September, A. D. 1870
    J. W. Shaffer,
    Governor
    Attest: Vernon H. Vaughn[26]

    Executive Department, Salt Lake City, Utah Territory
    September 15th, 1870

 Know ye that I., J. Wilson Shaffer, Governor of the Territory of Utah, and commander-in-chief of the military of the Territory of Utah, do hereby forbid and prohibit all musters, drills or gatherings of militia of the Territory of Utah, and all gatherings of any nature, kind or description of armed persons within the Territory of Utah, except by my orders, or by the orders of the United States marshall, should he need a posse commitatus to execute any order of the court, and not otherwise. And It is hereby further ordered that all arms or munitions of war belonging to either the United States or the Territory of Utah, within said Territory, now in the possession of the Utah Militia be immediately delivered by the parties having the same in their possession to Col. Wm. M. Johns, assistant adjutant-general; and it is further ordered that, should the United States marshal need a posse commitatus to enforce any order of the courts, or to preserve order, he is hereby authorized to make a requisition upon Major-General P. E. Conner for such posse commitatus or armed force; and Major-General P. E. Connor is hereby authorized to order out the militia, or any part thereof for said purposes and no other.

    Witness my hand and the great seal of said Territory, at Salt Lake City, this the 15th day of September, A. D. 1870
    J. W. Shaffer,
    Governor
    Attest: Vernon H. Vaughn[27]

Responding to the Governor's proclamations, General Wells respectfully requested that its implementation be delayed until after the currently called muster.

> Adjutant General's Office, U.T.
> Salt Lake City, October 25, 1870
>
> His Excellency, J. W. Shaffer,
> Governor and Commander-in-Chief of the Militia of
> Utah Territory
>
> Sir:
>
> Whereas a Proclamation has been published emanating from your Excellency, in which the holding of the regular musters in this Territory is prohibited except by your order, and
>
> Whereas, to stop the musters now, neither the terms of the proclamation, the laws of the Territory, nor the laws of Congress requiring reports of the force and condition of the militia of the Territory could be complied with,
>
> We therefore, the undersigned, for and in behalf of the militia of said Territory, respectfully ask your Excellency to suspend the operations of said proclamation until the 20th day of November next, in order that we may be enabled to make full and complete returns of the militia as aforesaid.
>
> Daniel H. Wells
> Lt.-Gen., Com'd'g Militia
> H. B. Clawson
> Adjt-Gen., Militia, U.T.[28]

Governor Shaffer replied to "D. H. Wells, Esq.," again refusing to recognize the elected officers of the militia. He claimed that the entire organization of the Nauvoo Legion was illegal and was not acting under the authority of the governor, but by order of Brigham Young. He also asserted that President Young and his associates had "denounced the Federal officers of this Territory with bitter vehemence" and refused to recognize the authority of Congress or that of himself, the appointed governor. He concluded by declaring that "as long as I continue to hold that office, a force so important as that of the militia shall not be wielded or controlled in disregard of my authority, which by law and my obligation it is my plain duty not only to assert, but, if possible, to maintain."[29]

General Wells responded with a long letter in which he attempted to educate the new governor and the public (his letter and all the subsequent correspondence in the matter was published in the *Deseret News*) regarding the legal basis of the territorial militia in Utah and its recognition and use over the preceding two decades by Governor Young and several of his successors, including Frank Fuller and the strongly anti-Mormon Steven S. Harding. He pointed out that his order for the annual muster was given "in order that I might comply with the request of the Department made through the Adjutant-General's Office, for Washington City, asking for the Annual Return of the Militia of Utah Territory, in accordance with the provisions of the act of Congress (Sec. 1), approved March 2, 1803. How this can be construed into an attempt to 'nullify' the laws of Congress, escapes my penetration, but, on the contrary, it appears to me that the proclamation of Governor Shaffer is calculated to produce that result."[30]

Governor Shaffer refused to alter his proclamations and his note confirming that they were still in force was dictated on October 31, two days after General Wells's public letter asking him to reconsider. The governor, who had been ill for some time, died suddenly on the same day, still determined to subdue the rebellious Mormons and assert his authority over the militia. From his point of view, as described in his dying words, "they are traitors, and I only regret that I shall not live to help bring them to justice."[31]

With the governor's death, General Wells could not further question his actions and felt obligated to respect the proclamation he had issued. On November 12, he issued the following order:

Adjutant General's Office, U. T.,
Salt Lake City, Aug. 16th, 1870

General Order No 2.

No, 1.—So far as the general musters in various military districts have not already been held, as contemplated in General Orders, No. 1, of August 16th, 1870. They are hereby postponed until further orders.

By order of
Lieut.-Gen. Daniel H. Wells
Commanding Nauvoo Legion.[32]

All the musters had, in fact, taken place by the time the order to postpone was received except that in Salt Lake County. The anti-Mormon faction there hoped that General Wells would defy the governor and order the Salt Lake City muster held, thereby provoking a conflict with the US Army stationed at Fort Douglas, but the Saints sustained the governor even though they did not like his actions concerning the militia or believe them to be legal.[33]

Governor Shaffer's death left the Territorial Secretary, Vernon H. Vaughan, to fill the four remaining months of Shaffer's term. He was not reappointed to another full term, however, and George L. Woods, an even more virulent anti-Mormon politician than his predecessor, was appointed governor on March 10, 1871. Governor Woods continued the ban on meetings of the militia and claimed that it was he who initiated it on his arrival in Utah. Thus, a new collision between Mormons and the governor was soon in the making.

Mayor Wells and the city council proposed to celebrate the nation's birthday in 1871 with more than usual pomp and ceremony and a committee representing the citizens was appointed to plan and organize the festivities. The anti-Mormons in the city refused to participate with the Mormon majority and instead appointed another committee representing their own group to organize a separate celebration. City officials tried to join the two celebrations together for the observance but were not successful.[34]

Daniel H. Wells as lieutenant general, at the request of the municipal committee, ordered out a few companies of militia to march in the holiday parade.[35] Governor Woods, who had been chosen as the chairman of the Gentile committee, was in the east and Territorial Secretary George A. Black, as anti-Mormon as Woods, was acting governor. He immediately issued a proclamation forbidding "the said military parade under the said order of the said Daniel H. Wells." Black added further insult by noting "no such office or officer [was] recognized by the commander-in-chief of the militia of the Territory as that of lieutenant-general."[36]

Fearing, or perhaps hoping, that Daniel would rise up in anger and defy the ban, Acting Governor Black called upon Gen. Philippe Regis DeTrobriand, commanding officer at Camp Douglas, to enforce his decree by having all his troops present in the city and ready to move against the militia companies that were preparing to parade on the Fourth of July.

General DeTrobriand, who had a cordial relationship with LDS Church leaders and did not have any serious issues with them, informed the acting governor that his command would be present at the celebration and ready up to the point of presenting arms, but that he would not give any order to fire on the civilian population. Acting Governor Black would have to do that himself. The matter was finally resolved with a compromise that allowed the governor to save face and the Legion to march in the parade. The companies called out by Daniel marched unarmed, carrying only wooden sticks in place of their rifles. General DeTobriand gave all the soldiers from Fort Douglas leave to attend, but only as spectators observing the celebration and not under arms.[37]

In a brief note to Brigham Young, Daniel described the day's events:

> The Celebration has passed off without disturbance—programme fully carried out—Majors & Fitch made very good speeches—procession very long, & very good—New Tabernacle filled to overflowing; no accident occured and no one as yet hurt; although about one dozen arrests have been made, chiefly for drunkeness. Probably will be more arrests, as there is quite a number on the street drunk, but we think we have the nosiest ones in custody, and at present they are thinning out. Our streets have been very full of strangers to day. Quite a good many participated with us in the celebration. General De Trobriand [sic] came down with a company of troops stationed near Townsend House—He rode round viewing the procession, and I presume thinking all right. He returned to camp between 12 & 1 o'clock. From threats, and misrepresentations, he was very fearful of a collission.[38]

Governor Woods, speaking to the historian H. H. Bancroft, later described the entire affair as if he had been present and had personally issued orders preventing the militia's march, a complete fabrication on his part.

Governor Woods' administration lasted for about four years, but during that period he sought no opportunity of making the acquaintance of Brigham Young. When invited by the first councillor [George A. Smith] to call, as had been the custom with his predecessors, he replied that the lowest subordinate in the United States ranked higher than any ecclesiastic on earth, and that he should not call until the president first called on him. The reader may judge the chief magistrate by his own words. "My first conflict with the church occurred," he says, "July 4, 1871. The organic act of the territory made the governor commander-in-chief of the militia. The Mormon legislature, prior to that time, usurped that authority, and invested it in Daniel H. Wells, the third in the church. (They had a pantomime, in which B. Young played God the Father, Daniel H. Wells God the Son, and John H. Smith the Holy Ghost.) That law was in force on my arrival. On July 1, 1871, Wells issued an order as commander-in-chief to the militia of the territory to assemble at Salt Lake City July

4th to participate in the celebration. I resented this usurpation, and forbade them to assemble, but my prohibition was disregarded. Thereupon I ordered to the rendezvous three companies of infantry, one of cavalry, and a battery of artillery, and dispersed them [the militia] at the point of the bayonet. This practically ended the Nauvoo legion.[39]

Like the anti-Mormon sentiments of Gen. Patrick Connor and some of the other officers who commanded the Camp Douglas garrison, the more favorable attitude of Gen. DeTrobriand percolated down to the lower-ranking officers of his command. The general even permitted his officers to socialize with the Mormons of Salt Lake City, a practice that was actively discouraged by the anti-Mormon commanders that preceded him. The Saints responded to the hostility of the soldiers by shunning any unnecessary contact with them, and when the men in uniform were allowed to fraternize, church leaders found it difficult to overcome their long-held wariness of social contact with them. Daniel, as mayor of Salt Lake City, was obliged to be a cordial host to the army men who protected the city, but as a church leader and a conservative Mormon father, he was also concerned lest his children, especially his daughters, become too familiar with the soldiers. An incident described by Annie Wells Cannon illustrates how members of Daniel's family could be hospitable and charming while the patriarch mayor limited their enthusiasm to the length of a single visit.

> In these early days it was quite the custom for young ladies to keep "open house" on New Year's Day, and for the young men to go calling from house to house, partaking of light refreshments, give a greeting, and leave a card on departure. Father thought such formality very foolish, but one year some of the girls, Kate, Emmie, Dessie and Abbie, persuaded him to let them entertain. They chose one of the small parlors, decorated it prettily, closed the shutters and lighted the room only with the firelight and candles in brass and crystal holders. In the early afternoon father saw a smart trap stop in front and a group of young officers from Ft. Douglas step out, all in dress uniform with side arms. They approached the front hall door. Father was alone in the big parlor. These officers had come to pay their respects to the Mayor of the city.
> He met them at the door and was very glad to escort them along the porch where he knew his daughters had prepared something of entertainment. There they were, quite expectant,

for they had wondered what father would do with these young gallants, knowing his prejudice against the girls' meeting "Gentiles." Introductions were soon over. These young men seemed so delighted with everything, the dainty sandwiches, small cakes, shiny apples, and glasses of cider, that the call was quite prolonged. That father went back to his reading in the other parlor rather surprised the girls, who seemed to be having "the time of their lives." He told them afterward he was quite satisfied with their deportment, but "hoped there would be no repetition of the visit." Not long after the regiment was transferred.[40]

Word reached Salt Lake City in October of the Great Chicago Fire that occurred over a three-day period and consumed more than three square miles of the city. Hundreds of people were killed and more than a hundred thousand were made homeless. Daniel immediately initiated a relief effort for Chicago's destitute by issuing a proclamation seeking subscriptions:

Proclamation

The news having been confirmed of the terrible conflagration by which a great portion of the city of Chicago has been reduced to ashes, and one hundred thousand people have been stripped of their homes, clothing, and means of subsistence, therefore,

I, Daniel H. Wells, Mayor of Salt Lake City, by the wish of the city council of said city, call upon all classes of the people to assemble in mass meeting tomorrow, Wednesday, October 11th, at one o'clock p. m, in the old tabernacle in this city, for the purpose of making subscriptions and taking such measures as are demanded for the relief of our fellow citizens who are sufferers by this dreadful visitation.

Daniel H. Wells, Mayor
October 10, 1871[41]

More than $6,200 was raised at the meeting, nearly all of it from prominent Mormon leaders and businessmen including Daniel who gave $500. Another $1,500 was given by the city council at Daniel's suggestion and the Masonic Brotherhood also raised a substantial sum. As word spread of the need, hundreds of citizens gave cash or in-kind donations. While funds were still being collected, Mayor Wells was arrested on a charge of murder, but after his release, he was able to complete the subscription drive and ultimately send more than $20,000 raised in Salt Lake City to help feed and house those in need.[42]

Grace Greenwood Lippincott, a prominent visitor who attended the tabernacle meeting, later wrote to the *New York Herald* concerning the irony of the Saints giving money to the people who were trying to imprison many of them for polygamy.

> In the old tabernacle, yesterday, we attended a mass meeting, called by the Mayor, to raise money for the relief of the Chicago sufferers. Here we saw Brigham Young, and I must confess to a great surprise . . .
>
> I could see in his face or manner none of the profligate propensities, and the dark crimes charged against this mysterious, masterly, many-sided and many-wived man. The majority of the citizens of Salt Lake present on this occasion were Mormons, some of them the very polygamists arraigned for trial, and it was a strange thing to see these men standing 'at bay, with the people of the United States' against them, giving generously to their enemies. It either shows that they have underlying their fanatical faith and Mohammedan practices a better religion of humanity, or that they understand the wisdom of a return of good for evil just at this time. It is either rare Christian charity or masterly worldly policy.[43]

On Saturday, October 28, 1871, Mayor Daniel H. Wells was arrested on a charge of murder. The arrest warrant, issued by Chief Justice James B. McKean in compliance with an indictment issued by a grand jury impaneled in the district court, included the same charge against Brigham Young, Joseph A. Young, Hosea Stout, and William Adams Hickman. All four Mormons were accused of complicity in the murder of Richard Yates, who Hickman, an ex-Mormon, claimed he killed in 1857 for trying to transport munitions to the US Army during the Utah War.[44]

According to Acting US Attorney Robert N. Baskin, as recorded in his Reminiscences, written years later:

> . . . Hickman came to him asking for professional representation, out of fear of being killed by his former Danite associates, Hickman confessed to killing Yates, who sold supplies to the U.S. troops headed to Utah, since Mormons considered this activity to be treason during the Utah War. Hickman

insisted he killed Yates on orders from Mormon leaders. Baskin described writing the details of several interviews with Hickman and finding no contradictions among the versions, he was "satisfied that Hickman told me the truth." Hickman consented to testify before the grand jury, Baskin placed this confession "in the hands of Major Hampstead, who was the United States district attorney" but Hampstead did not act on the evidence. It was at this time that Hempstead resigned and Baskin was appointed, circumstances that support Bigler's claim that Hempstead feared Mormon reaction.[45]

Baskin encouraged the indictment and claimed that Hickman's confession was corroborated by statements of other persons, although he never produced any such documents in court. Justice McKean, a bitter opponent of what he termed the "Mormon theocracy," who was eventually removed from office due to his anti-Mormon bias by the same president who appointed him, regarded the charges as a convenient means of putting Brigham Young and Daniel H. Wells in prison and thus removing them from their positions of influence and control over the Mormon people.[46]

The case against the defendants rested entirely on the dubious statements of Hickman and as one Mormon writer noted:

> There is little doubt but that Yates was killed, but no sane man in Utah, today, at all acquainted with the facts or the men, believes for a moment that either Daniel H. Wells or Hosea Stout had anything to do with the killing of Yates. "But," to use the words of the *Salt Lake Herald*, "the infamous proceedings adopted to carry out effectively the crusade against the 'Mormons' has another exemplification in these arrests, the determination of the public prosecutor to have, if not convictions, at least public odium cast upon the leading men of the community being apparent at every step taken . . .
>
> President Wells and Elder Stout having been arrested, were taken to the Third District Court room, the court being then in session, and by their counsel made application to be liberated on bail. As it was then late, about four or half past four o'clock, the court said it would be impossible to entertain the question then. Counsel asked that a time be fixed for the hearing of the application, and ten o'clock on the Monday morning following was fixed for that purpose. The arrested parties were taken by the Marshal to Camp Douglas, and there held in confinement.[47]

On Monday, October 30, after having been forced by the timing of the arrest to spend the Sabbath in confinement, Daniel was brought before the court and his counsel argued for bail on his behalf. His attorney assured Daniel that Judge McKean would never allow him to be released on bail, an opinion shared by almost everyone in the courtroom and throughout the city, but the mayor insisted that the attempt be made.[48]

To the surprise of nearly everyone except the defendant, Judge McKean agreed that the mayor could not perform the duties of his office while incarcerated and allowed himself to be convinced that bail for Daniel was necessary.

> In the case of the people against Daniel H. Wells, his counsel properly say that the defendant is the Mayor of the city, and is at the head of the police force. Camp Douglas, the place where prisoners awaiting trial in this court are usually detained, is some miles distant from the City Hall, and from the residence of the Mayor. In that camp it would be practically impossible for the Mayor to attend to any of the duties of his office, and therefore he could not be held responsible for the quietude and good order of the city. I will therefore admit him to bail.[49]

George Maxwell, now serving as marshal in addition to his appointed position as Land Registrar, asked that bail be fixed at $500,000, but Judge McKean, over the objection of the prosecutor, Mr. Baskin, set a lower figure, but stated his decision could not be used as a precedent in any other case. Daniel was then admitted to bail in the sum of $50,000. William Jennings and Horace S. Eldredge, prominent Mormon businessmen, acted as his bondsmen putting up their personal assets to guarantee his appearance.[50]

Judge McKean's unpredictable handling of bail for the defendants was typical of his anti-Mormon sentiment. He allowed bail for the mayor only after hearing the statements of other city officials and businessmen that Daniel was then in the process of securing land titles for the entire city from the federal government. But he then denied bail for the seventy-one-year-old Brigham Young, even after US District Attorney Baskin requested that it be granted.[51]

Daniel was released upon posting the required bail and President Young was held under house arrest at his home in the Beehive House. Hickman, who had confessed to more than twenty murders and had been promised immunity from prosecution in return for his unsubstantiated accusations against the Mormon leaders, was held at Camp Douglas for his own protection. He was, in fact, never tried for any of his crimes, including the murder for which he was indicted with Daniel. Before the case could come to trial, the US Supreme Court handed down its decision in *Clinton v. Englebrecht*, which overturned all the criminal proceedings in Utah for the previous eighteen months (1870 and 1871) on grounds that the grand juries had been improperly impaneled. The indictments handed down during the period, including the murder charge against Mayor Wells, were declared void. The accusation was never brought again.[52]

Following his release, Daniel stated his view of Judge McKean in an interview published in the *Deseret News*:

> In the estimation of the Chief Justice of that [the Utah federal] court, there is but one crime in the world, and that is polygamy. There is but one set of criminals, and they are Mormons. He has mustered around him all the other vices, and adopted them as allies to move upon our one offense. Rum, prostitution, rapacity, incivility—these are the adherents of the supreme court of Utah in its holy war upon our marriage relation. The court entertains every complaint made against us. It gives Godbe an injunction forbidding us to sue him as a corporation, and a score of unlicenced liquor dealers seem emboldened to defy us. The liquor-sellers have now, I am told, by the advice of the satellites of the court, raised a fund to sue the city when we interfere with them. The prostitutes newly landed among us, rise up in that court to assail our every complaint, and those too preposterous for us to treat with seriousness, it puts in its pocket and staves off, while crime takes advantage of the interregnum. Our Alderman's courts have been delegalized and, we are told by [Chief Justice] McKean that a legislature has no right to bestow discretionary powers on a jury or a civic corporation. In short . . . there is an end in Utah to any equity before the law. The end of the law is to reach polygamy. All are hailed as friends of the government, however notorious, who will leave the great and decent body of the Gentiles and persecute us. Our probate courts are declared to have no power to grant divorces and yet Mr. Baskins, the United States Prosecuting Attorney, is married to a woman divorced by a probate court. But, then, we are Mormons! Finally, professional murderers like Bill Hickman are permitted to give themselves up by collusion with the

courts, and affect to turn State's evidence against us to prejudice us in the eyes of civilization."[53]

Although the *Engelbrecht* decision saved Daniel from trial on a trumped-up murder charge, anti-Mormon efforts in Congress to pass laws detrimental to the LDS Church were so pervasive, and the radical Republican majority so willing to consider them favorably, that the First Presidency felt compelled to delay or defeat some of their attempts by using outright bribery. George Q. Cannon, Utah's Congressional Delegate, was fearful, that if the Voorhees anti-polygamy bill or any like it were to pass, Mormon polygamists would be "launched again upon a sea of troubles."[54]

In a letter to Daniel H. Wells, Cannon left unequivocal evidence that Mormons did not rely solely on strength of argument to ward off damaging legislation:

> [It would] be well for us to fee some of the members of Congress, for them to stay proceedings on this infamous Bill . . . We think its defeat is important, and we think we can defeat said Bill by giving a few thousand dollars . . . If you (the brethren) wish us to do this, it would be well for you (bro Wells) to arrange . . . with Kountze Bro's. at New York, depositing the money with them in my name.[55]

With funds available to Cannon for bribery, and with it approval from those in Salt Lake City to put the money to such use, it was not surprising that the Voorhees proposal failed—as did many bills directed at the "Mormon problem."

With the governor's ban on any muster of the territorial militia still in effect, the Nauvoo Legion did not march in a parade on the Fourth of July 1872, nor on Pioneer Day, the twenty-fourth, but the latter holiday brought personal tragedy to the Wells family. On that date, George A. Wells, the twelve-year-old son of Daniel and Susan Alley Wells accidentally shot himself while celebrating with a group of his friends. George loaded a pistol that one of the boys had with powder and gravel, intending to shoot pigeons. He thought the weapon was only half-cocked as he looked for a suitable target amid loud encouragement from his fellows. But it was, in fact, fully cocked and when he turned it about, thinking to lower the hammer on the cap, he touched the trigger and the gun fired into his abdomen.[56]

George was carried home still alive by the others in the group, but there was little else they or anyone could do. Abby Wells Cannon, George's half-sister, described the family's grief:

The wound was fatal, notwithstanding the skill of the physician and the prayers of the Priesthood. In the afternoon President Brigham Young and his Counselor, George A. Smith, came in and blessed George, and dedicated him to the Lord. On this occasion the tender ministrations of the mothers, and their kind attentions to Aunt Susan, seemed to bring us all nearer and dearer to each other. I well remember, even after all these years, the hushed silence and sorrowful fears of the family as we waited in the parlor for word from the room above. Aunt Lydia Ann and Aunt Louisa were there with Aunt Susan, and I noted Aunt Hannah and mother going up the long stairs with fresh linen and water, and Aunt Martha carrying a tray of savory things for the anxious watchers. Finally, in the late afternoon, father came into the room, told us all was over, spoke kindly, comforting words, and we all knelt in prayer. Each one present felt this a great personal loss.[57]

Around the time of George's death, another of Daniel's sons, Junius Wells, was called to serve a mission to Great Britain, the same area in which his father had served as Mission President seven years earlier. Junius, who was one of Hannah Wells's children, was the first of the Wells boys to go into missionary service and was followed soon afterward by Rulon Wells, the son of Daniel and Louisa, who was called to the Swiss and German mission. Additional sons were called in succeeding years: Joseph S. Wells, Martha's son, to the England and Wales Mission; Louis R, Wells, Lydia's son, to the Southern States Mission; Gershom Wells, Hannah's son, to the Swiss and German Mission, and finally, Melvin D. Wells, Louisa's son, to the England and Wales Mission in company with his father when Daniel was called as European Mission President for the second time in 1884.[58]

As mayor, Daniel was continually interested in the development of Salt Lake City, both by improving city services, such as police and fire protection, and by adopting new technology as conditions made it practical to do so. The first city in the western United States to make gas lighting available to private users was San Francisco, which began manufacturing and using gas for illumination in 1854. A second California city, Los Angeles, began providing gas lighting in 1867. In 1872, Daniel made Salt Lake City the third western city to have gas lighting in businesses, in homes, and on city streets.[59]

With himself as principal stockholder, Daniel and some other businessmen incorporated the Salt Lake City Gas Company. The initial paid-up capital was $50,000 and Daniel supplied most of that sum, for which he received stock giving him a controlling ownership of the new company.

Daniel persuaded the city council to grant his company a franchise to manufacture and distribute illuminating gas to the residents of Salt Lake City. The firm used a recently patented process to make gas from Summit County coal mined principally by the Wells and Taylor Coal Company, another of Daniel's business enterprises. The ordinance for the company's franchise also granted it the right to construct a railroad siding to bring coal to its plant, gave it control of a water source to provide for its needs, and set the price of the manufactured gas at four dollars per one thousand cubic feet for private users. Cost for city streetlights was fixed at $60 per year per lamp including fixture, piping, gas, and maintenance. These prices could not be increased for twenty years, a restriction that kept gas an affordable alternative to coal oil for lighting, but made the company unprofitable in the beginning years when installation costs were high.[60]

A gas-manufacturing plant was assembled near the corner of North Temple and Fourth West as soon as the needed components were shipped by rail from St. Louis. These included a metal storage tank sixty-eight feet in diameter and twenty feet high that could contain over seventy thousand cubic feet of uncompressed gas. The gas-making process involved roasting coal to drive off a mixture of hydrogen, methane, and a non-flammable waste gas, carbon dioxide. The gas was stored in the holding tank and the remaining "coke" residue was sold as a high temperature fuel for melting metal.[61]

In July 1873, the company started pumping gas into mains under Salt Lake City streets. Among the first buildings connected was the Salt Lake Theatre, which had previously used some 385 coal-oil lamps to illuminate its stage and interior. The theater's new gaslights were brighter and less likely to flare out of control creating a fire hazard. The buckets of sand, water, and salt kept ready for an emergency were retained, however, as fluctuations in gas pressure could also cause flaring in the new lamps. About 120 public buildings, hotels, stores, and warehouses adopted gas lighting at the opening of the service and the number increased rapidly as more pipes were installed.[62]

The city streetlights, which began functioning in the fall, were hailed by newspaper reports as "brilliantly illuminating," although they did not provide as much light on city streets as the full moon and were consequently not used every night. Gas lighting also had other drawbacks, such as flaming out when pressure was too low, overheating and cracking fixtures when it was too high, and depositing dimming soot on protective glass, but it was still much better than coal oil or candles.[63]

The company had expended most of its capital on infrastructure by the end of 1873 and found itself short of cash with an insufficient revenue stream to provide for future expansion. When he started the company, Daniel was assured by Brigham Young and other leading church and civic officials that the community would stand behind the project and see it through to completion. Relying on that promise, he asked the city council to furnish the company an additional $50,000 in return for new stock issued to the city. Within days of the new stock being delivered, the Panic of 1873 shut down the New York Stock Exchange for the first time in its history and led to an economic downturn that lasted for several years.[64]

The gas company continued to grow and expand its customer base, but more slowly than had been anticipated due to the recession. The difficult economic times prevented any increase in gas rates and the company continued to operate unprofitably. The value of its stock declined and Daniel invested more of his own money in order to keep the company afloat. He also continued to supply it with coal from his mine at less than market value. Within a year, the company was deeply in debt and so was Daniel.

To save the company and himself from bankruptcy, Daniel transferred his 850 shares of stock to the church giving it the controlling interest that he had exercised from the firm's inception. The stock was valued at slightly less than $85,000 and it was accepted by the church as a tithing donation, free and clear of any of Daniel's obligations acquired in founding or operating the company.[65]

His debts, Daniel kept and resolved to pay himself. For several years he was chronically cash poor, although he was never foreclosed upon by any of his creditors, all of whom apparently felt that he would make good what he owed. He did so over a period of years reducing his burden to a manageable level by 1878 and finally paying off the last of his debts about 1888 when he sold two of his homes and some other properties.[66]

Daniel's efforts to pay his obligations and maintain his businesses were often hamstrung by the actions of anti-Mormon officials. One of the most diligent of these was US Land Office Registrar Oliver Patton who replaced George Maxwell in that position during the administration of President Ulysses S. Grant. Although The Big Cottonwood Lumber Company had been cutting timber in the canyon for more than fifteen years and that action had been approved by instructions from the Commissioner of the Land-Office in Washington, DC, in 1870 and again in 1874, Patton swore out a complaint against Daniel H. Wells, the company's owner, charging him with illegally cutting timber on the public lands because he did not have a federal patent proving ownership of the canyon property. A warrant was served on Daniel and he appeared before US Commissioner Sprague. He was released on a $1,000 bond, until he could answer the charge to the grand jury.[67]

Registrar Patton next attached all the lumber in the sawmill yards and advertised it for sale in the name of the US Government. Daniel then posted a bond of $9,000 to guarantee that he would relinquish the lumber or pay the full value of it, if he were found to have acquired it illegally. He also paid the court costs of the case in the amount of $312.[68]

The *Deseret News* reported the outcome of the matter:

> Registrar Patton was allowed five days by the court to file a counter-bond of $18,000. In the event of his not doing so within the specified time, as a matter of course the lumber would be released to its owner. The counter-bond was not filed, and President Wells commenced to haul away the property. The Registrar then resorted to the extraordinarily foolish proceeding of making application to the military for troops to prevent the taking away of the property, receiving the reply, however, from the commandant that he had better first exhaust the civil process before making application for military aid, and that there were no troops to spare from the garrison for the purpose for which they were desired by the Registrar.[69]

Registrar Patton, unable to prevent Daniel from taking possession of his property legally, then proceeded to sell the same timber and cut lumber shipment a second time to John Nickles, a non-Mormon buyer whom he seems to have recruited to obstruct Daniel's title and possession. Nickles then sued Daniel in the district court claiming that the timber belonged to him because the first sale to Daniel by Patton was illegal. The district court, still dominated by anti-Mormon judges, ruled that Nickles was the legal owner and the supreme court of the territory of Utah, to which Daniel appealed the ruling, affirmed the ruling of the lower court.[70]

Still maintaining that he was the rightful owner of timber that he had paid for and harvested himself, Daniel appealed to the US Supreme Court. Five years after Patton's original warrant was issued (and after Patton himself had been dismissed for malfeasance in his office), the decisions of the district court and the Utah Supreme Court were reversed and the matter was decided in Daniel's favor. The high court ruled that the right given him by the Territorial Legislature to harvest timber in the canyon was valid and had not been rescinded or impeded by any act of Congress. The "stumpage fee" and court costs he had paid to gain possession of his timber constituted a contract of sale by an authorized agent of the US Government and Patton had no right to deny Daniel the use of his property.[71]

In October 1878 the *Salt Lake Herald* finally noted that, "Yesterday Ex-Mayor Wells received from the Marshal an order for his lumber in Big Cottonwood Canyon. After all the fuss and trouble made in this matter, Mr. Wells still has the privilege of selling his own lumber."[72]

19

Daniel Opposes the GLU, Defends Brigham, Escapes Drowning, and Dedicates a Temple

1875–1878

In his dual capacity as a member of the First Presidency of the Church of Jesus Christ of Latter-day Saints, and mayor of Salt Lake City, Daniel H. Wells was host to many prominent visitors. Among the most notable of these were Horace Greeley, the founder and editor of the *New York Tribune*, who arrived in the summer of 1859; author and adventurer Richard Burton, who wrote *City of the Saints* after his three-week visit in 1860; Mark Twain, who came with his older brother in 1861 and wrote of his experiences in the 1872 book *Roughing It*; Prince Iwakura, chief ambassador of the Empire of Japan to the United States, who arrived in 1872, accompanied by US Minister DeLong; and his Majesty, King Kalakaua, who came in 1874 from the Sandwich Islands (Hawaii), where church missionaries first made Mormon converts in 1850.[1]

In the autumn of 1875, Ulysses S. Grant became the first president of the United States to set foot within Utah Territory. Grant's views toward Utah and its mostly Mormon population were negative at the beginning of his administration and did not improve significantly after his reelection in 1873.[2]

Soon after his election in 1869, he appointed John W. Schafer as governor to replace Charles Durkee, who was appointed by Andrew Johnson. Unlike Governor Durkee and his predecessor James D. Doty, both of who had maintained amicable relations with their Mormon and Gentile constituents in the territory, Schafer was determined to carry out Grant's policy of suppressing what he thought was rebellion among the Mormon population. As described previously, Governor Schafer was in constant conflict with the Saints until his sudden death in 1870. Vernon H. Vaughan, whom Grant appointed to fill the remainder of Schafer's term, pursued the same policy with equally negative results.[3]

Grant's next appointment as governor was George L. Woods who quarreled with Daniel H. Wells over the Nauvoo Legion, criticized the lack of public schools in the territory and spoke frequently against polygamy. None of these actions, which again reflected President's Grant's views about Utah, endeared Woods to the Mormon majority and his ineffective efforts to increase Gentile power in the territory left them unwilling to press for his reappointment. When Grant appointed the more moderate Governor Samuel B. Axtell in 1875, Utah's anti-Mormon faction was furious and pressed to have him removed. After a few months, Axtell was appointed governor of New Mexico Territory, where the Mormon conflict did not exist, and Grant replaced him in Utah with his fifth appointment to the territory, Governor George W. Emery. Governor Emery had taken office only a few months before President Grant arrived in Utah and he wanted to make a good impression on the commander in chief.[4]

Governor Emery and a committee of ten non-Mormons, riding on a Central Pacific train, met the president and his party at Peterson in Weber Canyon in an effort to preempt his welcome by Mormon leaders. Mayor Wells and the city council committee, with President Young and other church and civic officials, rode from Salt Lake City to Ogden on a Utah Central Railway train. They greeted the president there and the Central Pacific cars carrying the presidential party were attached to the Utah Central train. Mayor Wells and his committee extended the hospitality of the city, but Grant had already accepted an invitation to be the guest of the governor during his two-day stay. After introductions were completed both groups of Utahns proceeded with the president by train to Salt Lake City.[5]

October 3 was a Sabbath Day, and a multitude of children, just released from Sunday School services lined the streets and gave the president and his wife, who were riding in a carriage with Governor Emery, an ovation as they drove from the Utah Central depot to the Walker House on Main Street. Observing the happy and well-dressed throng, the president inquired of the governor, "Whose children are these?"

"Mormon children," he replied.

Grant gazed a few moments upon the unexpected throng of happy well-wishers, accompanied by many of their teachers and parents, as Governor Emery reported, and murmured, "I have been deceived."[6]

His experiences in Utah softened Grant's attitude toward Utah's citizens and for the remainder of his presidency he heard anti-Mormon complaints and diatribes with an enlightened understanding of what the Saints were really like. His policy of upholding federal laws, supporting his appointees to the courts and opposing polygamy did not change and he directed Governor Emery to pursue these objectives, but he no longer seemed to view Mormons as the wicked, anti-Christian rebels they were depicted as being by their detractors.[7]

This negative view of the Saints was propounded to Grant for years by his Methodist minister, Rev. John T. Newman, who visited Salt Lake City in 1870 and preached vehement anti-Mormon sermons in Independence Hall of the First Congregational Church, which was first organized in Utah by the equally anti-Mormon missionary, Rev. Norman McLeod, in 1865. Neither Newman nor McLeod had any success winning Mormons away from their religion, but both were influential in maintaining the harshly anti-Mormon attitude of American society and government in the eastern states and in Washington.[8]

Grant's comment to Governor Emery about "being deceived" appears to refer to his own similar view that, after seeing and interacting with large numbers of Saints and their children, he no longer held. The president's wife Julia Grant was equally affected by her Utah visit and herself offered a prayer for the Mormons in a Tabernacle meeting.[9]

After his weekend stay, President Grant rode back to Ogden on the Utah Central, accompanied by Mayor Wells, the city council committee, Governor Emery and the non-Mormon committee. Once Grant's special car had departed eastward up Echo Canyon, the Gentile group, who had arrived separately to greet the president the previous day, accepted the LDS leaders' invitation to ride home on the Utah Central train. The short trip marked one of the few occasions when the leaders of the two factions of Utah's populace sat side by side and spoke freely to one another without the presence of any outsiders they needed to impress.[10]

Five years later, in September 1880, President Rutherford B. Hayes also visited Utah. By this time, Daniel's term as mayor had ended and he had also been released from his calling in the First Presidency, but he was still included with President John Taylor and other officials in the Mormon group that greeted the chief executive in Ogden, hosted him during his two-day visit, and journeyed north again to see him off on the transcontinental rail line.[11]

The anti-Mormon faction in Utah grew stronger during the 1870s as non-Mormons flocked to the rich mines of the territory and its expanding railroad industry. In early 1872, the most extreme anti-Mormon federal officials and Gentiles in Salt Lake City, Ogden and several mining camps organized themselves in a secret society that they called the "Gentile League of Utah" or GLU. The group was known to Mormons, who saw it as a corrupt and sometimes criminal political machine, as the "Gentile Ring." Its stated mission was to end "Mormon Theocracy," the dominance and political control of Mormons in Utah and of President Brigham Young in particular. Mormons still outnumbered Gentiles in Utah Territory by at least a five to one margin, so the GLU and its supporters had little hope of wresting control from the Saints in a fair election.[12]

Recognizing that truth, the GLU adopted tactics designed to disenfranchise Mormons by preventing them from voting, thus allowing Gentile candidates to be elected by the non-Mormon minority. They sponsored legislation in Congress that would strip Mormons of their right to vote, contested the election of any Mormon who practiced or supported plural marriage, and promoted changes in federal laws governing territories that would have made all territorial office holders federal appointees rather than being elected by the local citizens. Until these legal maneuvers could succeed in breaking Mormon power, the GLU members sought to accomplish their objective by extra-legal methods: intimidation of voters at the polls and intimidation of elected Mormon officials. Daniel H. Wells was a principal target of the GLU in both of these endeavors.[13]

Joseph Salisbury, an associate editor of the anti-Mormon *Salt Lake Tribune*, described in an affidavit a typical effort to intimidate Mayor Wells and the city council in one of their weekly meetings.

I, Joseph Salisbury . . . make the following statement, to-wit:

> That on the evening of the 26th of July, 1872, I attended a meeting of the city council, held in the council chamber, in the city hall, Salt Lake City, and made a report of its proceedings;
>
> That on the 30th instant, I attended again, when that honorable body, taking exceptions to my previous report, demanded of me a public recantation on pain of expulsion. This I refused when the vote of the council was passed to that effect;
>
> That I was afterwards directed by Mr. Fred. T. Perris, manager of the paper, to attend at the next regular meeting of the council, and report as usual, I said, in answer, that I presumed the council would adopt parliamentary rules and close its doors; whereupon the manager informed me that General Geo. R. Maxwell had promised to be there with 100 men, from the "G. L. U's" and other secret orders to force an entrance and insist on my taking the minutes;
>
> That, on the day previous to the meeting, I was in the editor's office writing, when General Maxwell came in and asked me if I was ready to go to the council the following evening. I replied, "I shall go anyhow." He intimated that he was ready, and the "boys" would be there;
>
> That I understood the programme to be that, if any hostile demonstration were made by the mayor and council, each of them

would be immediately covered by a pair of pistols, in the hands of the 100 men present;

And furthermore, that, if Brigham Young was present, he would be a special mark;

That, for some reason, the project was abandoned;

That myself, accompanied by Mr. F. T. Perris and Mr. Abrahams, went to said meeting, when the motion of the preceding council was confirmed and the Tribune men again expelled.

(Signed) Joseph Salisbury[14]

Edward W. Tullidge, who replaced Salisbury as associate editor of the *Salt Lake Tribune*, says that the explanation why the one hundred men did not appear was not the "fault of the agitators, but simply because certain well-known conservative business men did not enthusiastically take the responsibility. Without these influential citizens, Maxwell knew that his 100 men would have been but an armed band of rioters."[15]

The GLU made strong attempts to intimidate voters during the 1872 election for Utah's Congressional Delegate, but they were not successful. George Q. Cannon, the People's Party (Mormon) candidate, an apostle in the LDS Church and a practicing polygamist, defeated the Liberal Party (Gentile) candidate, George R. Maxwell (the same person as named in the affidavit above), by 20,000 votes to 3,500, despite the GLU's attempts to provoke violence before the election, deter voters at the polls, and induce federal troops to intervene in the election. After his defeat, Maxwell challenged the seating of Cannon in Congress, but even the anti-Mormon Republican majority laughed at his complaint and promptly gave Cannon their approval. Maxwell also agitated to unseat Cannon during the congressional session, but again failed.[16]

On an election day in 1874, the riot that the GLU had attempted to provoke in 1872 actually happened and Mayor Daniel H. Wells found himself literally in the middle of it. The municipal election to select county officers and representatives to the territorial legislature was held in February without serious incident and the People's Party candidates all won office by a comfortable margin. But the August congressional delegate election, in which George Q. Cannon was running for re-election against the Liberal Party candidate Robert N. Baskin, the appointed US attorney for Utah, was a different matter. The Liberal Party and its GLU supporters were determined to win this contest by any means necessary and thought they had found a way to block the Mormon majority from the polls.

Under Section 4 of the so-called "bayonet law," a federal statute then in force that was enacted in 1870 to prevent voting fraud during the reconstruction period in the South, but later declared unconstitutional,

US marshals were authorized to appoint special deputies to keep the polls open and clear of obstruction on election day. Marshall Metcalf in Utah selected a large number of the most violent anti-Mormons and swore them into office as deputy US marshals under the pretense that they were needed to preserve the peace on election day. During the day it became evident that their real object was to frighten Mormon citizens away from the polls. Mayor Wells and the local Salt Lake City police, whose normal duties included keeping the peace and the polls open and clear on Election Day, were forcibly prevented by the deputy marshals from doing so. Every measure to preserve the peace was construed by Marshal Metcalf as resistance to the US deputy marshals, who were themselves fomenting riot and abusing voters. A large crowd of anti-Mormons soon gathered at the Council House where the polls were open and, with the encouragement of the marshals, threatened to take forcible possession of the ballot box and break up the election.[17]

Dan W. Jones, who was present that morning at the polls, afterward wrote a graphic account of the day's events, which accurately describes Daniel H. Wells's central role:

> The Liberals were on their "high heels" and believed that they had now the right and power to put down Mormon rule in Salt Lake City. During the day there was continued contention as to who should act as police or protectors of the polls. The marshals interfered continually, and when the police attempted to do their duty they were arrested by the deputies and taken before the U. S. Commissioner and put under bonds. Several times during the day the spirit of lawlessness ran so high that a collision seemed inevitable . . .
>
> Late in the afternoon the mob became so aggressive and the polls so obstructed that people wishing to vote could not get in. The marshals headed [led] this obstruction. The police seemingly had no power to keep order. Captain Burt sent word to Mayor Wells asking for instructions. Mayor Wells soon appeared on the ground and managed to work his way through the crowd and get into the door of the polling room. The regular police were mostly on the inside of the City Hall at that time. The Mayor commanded the crowd to disperse and leave the entrance clear. This he uttered by authority of his office. There were possibly two hundred persons in the crowd. The room was full and the doors completely blocked and the sidewalk crowded. Many were in the street and more coming, cursing and yelling. Some of the leaders, now more

or less intoxicated, when the order was given to disperse, instead of obeying, made an attack on the Mayor. They were led by Milton Orr, who seized hold of Mr. Wells and attempted to drag him from his position. Mayor Wells resisted this move. Several others now caught hold of him, tearing his clothes.

I was just at the outer side of the sidewalk in company with George Crismon. As we saw this violent move against the Mayor we started through the crowd, George taking the lead. And I always remembered his expertness in opening the way, for we soon were on hand. The noise was so terrific that I had to put my mouth close to Mr. Wells's ear. I asked him which way he wished to go. The jam was on both sides of him. I naturally supposed he wanted to get away, for the mob seemed to want to rend him in pieces and were doing their best to accomplish it.

Brother Wells answered, "I do not want to go either way. I shall stay here if I can; you help me to keep my place."

Brother Crismon did all he could to keep the mob off. I caught Brother Wells around the waist and held him against those pulling at him. His clothes were badly torn in the scuffle.

While this was going on, Brother Andrew Smith, of the police force, managed to get near us from the inside. He called to me to push Brother Wells to him. I said, "He don't want to come in."

Brother Smith said, "Never mind" at the same time reaching and getting hold of Brother Wells, telling me to shove him in. This we did. I always believed that Mayor Wells would have died before he would have given way to the mob of his own free will.

As the Mayor went in, the door was shut and I was crowded outside with the mob. I now felt quite small, jammed in the doorway, all alone with the mob. I could see no friend with me, so I kept very quiet. Soon Mayor Wells appeared on the balcony of the Court House. He looked rather dilapidated, but in a clear, steady voice he commanded the rioters to disperse. At this they only shouted louder, cursing and defying his authority. He then turned to Captain Burt and said in substance: "Captain Burt, disperse this mob and clear the sidewalk of obstruction." The mob had given way from just in front of the hall door, as the balcony was immediately over it and those under the balcony had crowded out so as to get a view of the Mayor.

In a moment after the order was given, Captain Burt stepped out onto the sidewalk in front of the hall door, followed by a few regular police. Addressing the crowd immediately in front of the polling room, he commanded them to disperse.

Instead of obeying the order, the mob with a howl of defiance rushed at the captain, who stood with his arms folded. I was looking from a slight elevation, being on the doorsteps, and powerless to do anything but watch, so that what I am writing is just as I saw it. As the mob rushed at Captain Burt he let drive with his police club; instantly others of the police pitched in. I have seen a good many knock-downs, but men fell as fast for a short time as I ever saw them. Most of them were U. S. Marshals. The police were making a clearing toward the door where I was jammed in. The mob almost instantly gave way. They were so taken by surprise at seeing their leaders falling that many, who were seemingly brave as lions a minute before, took to their heels and ran away . . .

All the police were arrested and brought to trial before the Commissioners, but were cleared. There were many sore heads, but no one was killed. The man's name who did the hardest hitting that day never came up, and, without his permission, I will not mention it.[18]

Once again Daniel was able to control a violent confrontation with a minimum of casualties and no lives lost, but this was not the response the anti-Mormons had hoped to provoke and they immediately sought revenge against the mayor. While the rioters were being subdued, others of their number prepared the legal papers for their next assault on the mayor who had foiled them.

As soon as the crowd was dispersed, Deputy US Marshal Bird served a warrant upon Mayor Daniel H. Wells, arrested him on the charge of resisting a deputy US marshal in the discharge of his duty, and took him before US Commissioner Toohey, who released him on $1,000 bond to appear in one week to answer to the charge.

On August 24, Mayor Wells appeared in court for a preliminary investigation of the charges against him. After hearing a number of witnesses, who testified both for and against the accused, the commissioner summarized their evidence and ruled: "I am also satisfied that the evidence does not present to me plausible cause for the detention of Mr. Wells. I think that the resistance, or the assault, or whatever other offense was committed, if any at all, does not amount to sufficient to warrant my holding him, and he is discharged."[19]

As Brigham Young grew older and his health became more fragile, Daniel increasingly felt the need to not only carry as many of the president's administrative responsibilities as he could, but also to keep in his company as much as possible, when he was engaged in church business, so as to be near at hand in the event his help was needed or desired. From 1860 onward, Daniel also came to feel that he was responsible for Brigham's personally safety and he assumed the role of chief of security for the prophet, a position that would not formally exist in the church for another century. Nevertheless, Daniel saw to it that suitable protection was provided whenever the anti-Mormon faction's actions raised the possibility of harm to Brigham. Whether he was surrounded by hostile Indians while negotiating peace during the Black Hawk War or confronted with equally hostile Gentiles seeking to overthrow him, Daniel kept close to him and provided a sufficient force of bodyguards to secure the president's person from harm. And at last, when Brigham's foes finally managed to arrest and incarcerate him, his counselor went with him.

Daniel's next visit to prison was not as an accused defendant, but as an assistant and bodyguard for President Young who was sent to the penitentiary for contempt of court in March 1875. One of Brigham's wives, Ann Eliza Webb Young, instituted divorce proceedings against him in the district court in July 1873. As a plural wife, she sued for divorce and to obtain alimony. A year and a half of legal proceedings followed to determine whether plural marriages in general and this marriage in particular were valid. In February 1875, Judge McKean ruled that the marriage (and by implication plural marriage as well) was valid and the divorce trial could proceed. At the same time, he also directed the defendant to pay Ann Eliza Young $3,000 attorney fees and $500 a month from the date the suit was filed for her support and the education of her children. Brigham was given ten days to pay the fee, and twenty to pay $9,500 accumulated alimony. He appealed the decision to the supreme court of the territory and filed a motion to stay execution of the order to pay issued by Judge McKean in district court.[20]

The allotted time expired before the appeal was heard and, as no payment had been made, Brigham was required to show cause why he should not be held in contempt. On March 11, 1875, he appeared in court, where his attorney, asked that further proceedings be stayed until the appeal had been determined.[21]

Judge McKean denied the stay, found President Young guilty of contempt, fined him $25, and sentenced him to twenty-four hours imprisonment in the penitentiary. The fine and the attorney fee imposed were promptly paid and the president left the courtroom in company with US Marshal A. K. Smith. Brigham, who was in poor health, was taken in his own carriage to his residence, where he had dinner and obtained the bedding and other articles he would need in his cell. He was then driven through a heavy snowstorm to the Territorial prison.[22]

President Young's first and only night in prison (he was held under house arrest in his own home when arrested in the Yates case) is described in the Journal History of the Church:

> At about 3 o'clock, President Brigham Young started out in his own carriage, in company with Marshal A. K. Smith and President Daniel H. Wells, for the penitentiary . . . "This being the first time that President Young was ever confined to prison by order of the court, I had a desire," writes Wilford Woodruff, "to spend the night with him, but my desire was not granted. President Daniel H. Wells, [Dr.] Seymour B. Young, and another man, William A. Rossiter (his son-in-law) were all that were allowed with him through the night. The rest of us rode home."[23]

A week after Brigham and Daniel's night in the Sugar House penitentiary, President Grant removed Judge McKean from office, reportedly for acts "which are considered ill advised and tyrannical, and in excess of his powers as a judge." George R. Maxwell, the registrar of the Territorial Land Office and the instigator of the suit by Ann Eliza Young, was also replaced, "for fanatical and extreme conduct."[24]

Over the next two years Brigham Young appeared before four successive judges who repeatedly reversed or altered one another's decisions. In April 1877, nearly four years after the divorce suit was filed, it finally came to trial. The marriage was declared void from the beginning, and all alimony was revoked. The anti-Mormon faction was so upset by Judge Schaeffer's decision that they successfully lobbied for his removal after the trial.[25]

In June 1875, soon after Junius F. Wells, Daniel and Hannah Wells oldest son, returned from his mission to England, he was called at age twenty-one to organize societies to teach missionary preparation and mutual improvement to young men in the Church. Junius's own missionary experience had demonstrated to him that he, like many young missionaries, lacked the needed skills and knowledge to preach effectively when they were called. Of his own mission introduction experience he wrote:

> I found myself upon a mission before I was eighteen years old, standing for the first time in my life before an audience to speak. I was in Liverpool, six thousand miles away from home. I was introduced by the President, and being a son of President Wells, there was much expected of me, but it took

me just one and one-quarter minutes to say all that I knew. I desired in my heart that my brothers should be better prepared than I was for such a position.[26]

According to Junius, his father, Daniel H. Wells, and Brigham Young instructed him about what they wanted him to accomplish in his calling:

> We want to have our young men enrolled and organized throughout the Church, so that we shall know who and where they are, so that we can put our hands upon them at any time for any service that may be required. We want them to hold meetings where they will stand up and speak—get into the habit of speaking—and of bearing testimony. These meetings are to be for our young men . . . for their mutual improvement. There is your name: The Young Men's Mutual Improvement Soci— Association.[27]

Beginning at the Thirteenth Ward meetinghouse, Junius called a public meeting to establish the organization. Henry A. Woolley, son of the Thirteenth Ward bishop, was chosen president with B. Morris Young, a son of Brigham Young, and Heber J. Grant, Rachel Grant's son and future president of the church, as counselors. From there he went on to organize other associations in each of the wards in Salt Lake City, and then in other wards north and south of the central city, visiting about a hundred congregations within a few months.

After many units were functioning, general officers were appointed to supervise all the ward and stake Mutual Improvement Associations. The name, which was soon shortened to MIA, became so popular that the young ladies adopted it and their improvement organization, The Young Ladies Retrenchment Association, became the Young Ladies' Mutual Improvement Association and later the Young Women's MIA.[28]

In the late summer of 1875, Daniel started on a trip to the southern settlements, accompanied by Apostles Lorenzo Snow and Franklin D. Richards. Elder Robert T. Burton went along as bodyguard and others joined the company as it traveled south. Brigham, perhaps out of concern for the illness of his First Counselor George A. Smith, or burdened by the press of other business, did not accompany them. On the evening of their first day's travel, a rider reached their camp with news that President Smith had died. Daniel and the others returned to Salt Lake City the following day and did not resume their journey until after President Smith's funeral. His death was unexpected, as he was only fifty-six years old, and it left a vacancy in the leadership of the church for the third time since Brigham Young became president.[29]

Brigham had called three assistant counselors to the First Presidency as church growth continued and the group's responsibilities correspondingly increased: George Q. Cannon and Brigham Young Jr. in 1873; and John Willard Young, another of his sons, in May 1874. Although Cannon was the oldest in both age and church experience, Brigham called his son John as first counselor and he was sustained in conference in October 1876. Daniel remained as second counselor while Brigham Young Jr. and George Q. Cannon continued as assistant counselors.[30]

When Daniel and other church leaders resumed their trip to southern Utah in late September, after the funeral of President Smith, Junius Wells went with them. Having organized a large number of Young Men's MIA groups in the wards of Salt Lake City, Junius continued his missionary labors by setting up similar organizations in each of the communities where the company stopped to preach and hold meetings. When they reached St. George, the southern limit of this trip, he also organized an MIA there. After their return to Salt Lake City, Junius accompanied his father on another tour of northern Utah settlements where Daniel spoke and his son organized improvement associations in Brigham City, Mantua, and other towns.[31]

At the next October conference, Junius was called on another mission to continue his work in wards and branches in the eastern states beginning with Iowa, Missouri, and Illinois, and continuing to New England.[32]

Daniel H. Wells, in company with the ailing Brigham Young, visited St. George again in May 1876 and there inspected the temple that was nearing completion. The building was constructed of red native sandstone and the entire exterior was plastered a brilliant white that looked beautiful in contrast with the surrounding landscape. After touring the building and planning for its dedication and opening the following year, the First Presidency presided at a conference of the Southern Utah Mission.

Daniel, who was one of the principal speakers, noted that progress of the church was apparent as the members showed their willingness to again organize according to principles given by the Lord years ago. Some of these, he said, had not been lived up to previously, but were now being more faithfully observed. He noted that the Lord requires nothing more of his people but that they be willing and obedient and added, "Our true progress in the work of the Lord is marked by the extent of our obedience to divine counsel. The Lord desires to establish the principles of righteousness upon the earth, and we have the privilege given to us of assisting to bring about the time when His will shall be done on earth as it is in heaven."[33]

Figure 19.1. Wagon and team crossing the Colorado River on Lee's Ferry at low water, ca. 1875. Daniel H. Wells narrowly escaped drowning on a similar crossing at high water.

While at St. George, Brigham placed Daniel in charge of a company that journeyed to visit and encourage the new settlements in Arizona that had been pioneered in 1874, partly by Mormons from settlements abandoned in Nevada. Another large company of new settlers was called by the First presidency in January 1876 to move to Arizona with their families. These missionary families founded four new settlements along the Little Colorado River and were already tending their first crop by the time Daniel and his associates reached them in July with additional supplies they would need for the coming winter months. At open-air services, Daniel and the others complemented the colonists on the work they had accomplished and assured them that they were well remembered in the thoughts and prayers of the First Presidency and other leaders. He promised additional settlers would be called the following year to reinforce the established settlements and provide manpower for opening new ones.[34]

On the return journey, while crossing the Colorado River at Lee's Ferry, the boat transporting Daniel and a number of the party, as well as their wagon and outfit, capsized in the high water of the turbulent river and they were thrown into the rushing water. In a letter sent just after the event Daniel described what followed:

> We found the large boat in pretty good repair and the large sweeps which we brought enabled us to load up & commence operations almost immediately. Sent over two loads of horses, 14 and 7 head. Third trip Bro Wells carriage the heavy baggage wagon and Bro. Roundy's wagon were put on the boat which was maned [manned] by Bro. Wells, Roundy, Hatch, Nutall, Johnson (who keeps the ferry), Hamblin, Carter and Wilkbanks, To make a safe trip and land just where we desire it is necessary to tow the boat half mile up the stream most of the way in an eddy, but there is a rocky point to pass where the current is very swift. Bro. Roundy and Carter were keeping the boat away with poles and oars. Bro. Emmet was assisting at the tow rope with his pony, pulling by the horn of the saddle. The current at this point was too much for the boat and the bow began to dip water, the raft was immediately tossed but caught between two rocks and held the boat fast and the boat went down almost instantly until released of the wagons which floated off. Bro Wells, Hamblin & Nutall swam ashore. Bro. Hatch and Carter were supported by clinging to Bro. Wells' carriage & Bro. Wilkbank jumped ashore before boat then swung out. Bro. Roundy ran along the rail towards the rear of the boat which was nearest shore and when about half way called out "come on boys all who can swim," and then plunged into the water and struck out for the shore. After swimming a short distance he was seen to throw up his hands and he sank out of sight. Our small boat reached the spit in a few moments but nothing could be found of Bro. Roundy. As far as possible, under the circumstances the bank and islands below have been searched in hopes of finding the body but no success. Bro. Hatch, Carter and Johnson were recued [rescued] from their perilous situation with the small boat which then followed the wagons and succeeded in grounding Bro Roundy & Hatch's wagon on a bar where they left it as it was now dark . . .

> The main part of our provisions, all the bedding, guns & cloths of the St. George boys, went down with the wagons. Bro. Wells harness and entire outfit with the exceptions of his mules, their halters and briddles, were lost.

> The St. George boys will return from this point. The following brethren will continue: D. H. Wells & son, E. Snow, L. H. Hatch,

D. D. McArthur, J. Hamblin, B. Y. Jr. & son, L. D. Young, Bro. Ensign. We can make out pretty well for provisions and have plenty of grain. We have ferried over our four wagons and luggage on the small boat which we brought with us and which has done excellent service . . .

We are now all accross the river and Bro. Perkins is waiting to take our letters. We shall go to Navajo Springs 8 miles when we expect to camp and let our animals have something to eat. They have had but little but grain since we came here.

> We are in good health and trust in God for ability to accomplish our mission, praying God to bless you we remain your brethren—
> Daniel Wells
> Erastus Snow
> Brigham Young, Jr.[35]

Daniel was not a good swimmer in any circumstances and on this occasion he was weighed down by his boots and clothing. He was also past sixty years of age, but still in good physical condition. He did not panic and calmly struck out for the shore, holding his breath and keeping his face in the water as was his usual practice. Within a minute he reached the shallows, climbed out onto the steep bank, and ever afterward regarded his escape as miraculous.[36]

Bishop Roundy, who drowned despite being an expert swimmer, told his family before leaving on the trip that he would not complete it. "My father said goodby to Susannah his 2nd wife, and to my mother Prisilla (his 3rd wife) and to each of us children for a total of three times each. My father said he would never see us alive again and he would 'die with his boots on.' His wives told him to tell the Authorities then how he felt but he said he would rather die with his boots on than to go against the Authority's wishes."[37]

Brigham Young left Salt Lake City again for St. George on November 1, 1876. Through the winter he devoted his time and energy to overseeing the completion of the temple there and the strengthening of the southern settlements in Utah and Arizona. The day-to-day administration of church affairs in Salt Lake City, he left to Daniel and a staff of clerks working with him. Daniel issued mission calls, sent instructions to church-owned farms, managed church work projects, settled marital disputes, and handled many other similar matters. He kept in touch with Brigham by letter and, concerning urgent matters, by telegraph. A typical note to the president says: "I have not forgotten your instructions with regard to raising means to pay for the flour sent to the Little Colorado [Arizona] settlements and we expect to deposit the same to your credit at Z.C.M.I. within a few days as you directed."[38]

Brigham also wrote Daniel his thoughts on future projects that he wanted to pursue including a history of the church:

> As soon as we can we must have someone of our brethren take hold of the matter of getting out a History of the Church in a condensed form. Though we have very much published history of the rise and progress of the Church in sundry books and publications, we are yet without a History to place in the hands of our own people or of the enquirer out in the world.[39]

In March 1877 Daniel journeyed south again with many of his family to attend the April general conference of the church that was held in the newly completed St. George Temple. The entire First Presidency and all of the apostles who were not abroad in missionary service also came to participate in this memorable occasion. Some parts of the temple had been dedicated on New Year's Day and were placed in use from that time on, but the formal dedication of the entire building took place on April 6, the forty-seventh anniversary of the founding of the Church of Jesus Christ of Latter-day Saints. President Young, now in seriously weakened condition, but gratified to see the first Utah temple completed in his lifetime, presided at the dedication.[40]

Brigham asked Daniel H. Wells to give the dedicatory prayer, in which he said:

> We thank Thee, O Lord, that Thy people whom Thou hast led to this distant land, and whom Thou hast preserved by Thine own right arm, have been permitted to establish themselves . . . and erect . . . a Temple, which we dedicate and now consecrate to Thee that it may be holy unto Thee the Lord our God, for sacred and holy purposes, and that the blessing, even life for evermore, may be commanded here from heaven, even from Thy presence, and may flow through the ordinances which appertain unto Thy holy place, unto us Thy children . . .
>
> We acknowledge Thee and the great deliverance Thou hast wrought out for us, and we pray Thee, O God, in the name of Jesus . . . let Thy grace and power be upon us that we may walk in the paths of purity and holiness, and be enabled to bring forth Thy purposes and establish Thy kingdom in all its fullness . . .

Figure 19.2. St. George Temple as it neared completion in 1876. Sandstone walls were faced with white lime plaster, and the building was dedicated by Daniel H. Wells in 1877.

Accept, O God, of this tribute of our hearts, and let Thy peace and blessing dwell and abide here in this Holy Temple, which we now, with uplifted hearts and hands, present and consecrate and dedicate entire as a sacred offering unto Thee for Thine acceptance. May it stand as a monument of purity and holiness as long as the earth shall remain, commemorative of Thy great goodness towards us, Thy people, and Thy name shall have the honor, the praise and glory, for we ask all in Jesus' name, and unto Thee and our blessed Lord and Savior, and to the Holy Spirit be all power, might and dominion worlds without end. Amen.[41]

As soon as the temple was dedicated, Daniel began visiting it frequently to perform work on behalf of deceased members of his family. During the years since he came west he had requested relatives to send him as much information as they could find concerning his ancestors and had accumulated enough to begin temple work for some of them at St.

George. He was also assisted in this effort by having a copy of a genealogy of the Welles family written by Albert Welles, president of the American College of Heraldry and Genealogical Registry in New York. This Albert was not Daniel's eldest son, but a cousin whose book contained accurate information about hundreds of family members. Albert Welles visited the Wells family in Salt Lake City in 1876 and Daniel purchased a copy of his book. Using this data, members of the Wells family spent several days at the temple before starting back with Brigham Young and some of the apostles to Salt Lake City.[42]

Daniel organized a guard of about twenty-five men to accompany the travelers on their journey. The extra security he deemed necessary because of alleged threats against Brigham Young by the sons of John D. Lee who had been recently tried and executed for his part in the Mountain Meadows Massacre. The escort followed the First Presidency's party all the way to Salt Lake City, but no significant danger emerged during the journey.[43]

The returning party stopped in Manti where Brigham dedicated another site for a temple, the third to be built in Utah. A few weeks later Daniel accompanied him to Logan where he dedicated the site for a fourth temple. Brigham also gave instructions that both temples were to be completed as quickly as possible, perhaps hoping that he might remain alive long enough to dedicate one or both of them.[44]

20

From Counselor to Assistant, Trapped in Court, Imprisoned, and Paraded Home

1877–1879

On August 29, 1877, President Brigham Young, who had led the Church of Jesus Christ of Latter-day Saints for more than thirty years, died at his home in Salt Lake City at the age of seventy-six. At his passing, the First Presidency of the church was dissolved and leadership was taken by the Quorum of the Twelve Apostles until a new Presidency could be organized and sustained.[1]

President Young, acting on inspiration he had privately received, reorganized the Quorum of Twelve Apostles in June 1875 by designating John Taylor, a close associate of Joseph Smith who was wounded in the same attack in which Joseph was murdered, as the president of the Twelve. Until Brigham's action, Orson Hyde was president of the Twelve with Orson Pratt next in line and Taylor third, but both Hyde and Pratt had apostatized from the church and left their callings for brief periods. When they returned, they were taken back into the Quorum in their former places of seniority, and Hyde became president of the Twelve Apostles in late 1847 after Brigham chose Heber C. Kimball, who was then president of the Twelve, as his counselor.[2]

More than twenty-four years later, Brigham Young explained to the Twelve that Hyde and Pratt should not have resumed their former places in the Quorum, but should have re-entered it as though they were newly called—as the least senior members. He then turned to John Taylor and said, "Here is the man whose right it is to preside over the council in my absence, he being the senior apostle." The Twelve unanimously accepted this restructuring and it was sustained by the church membership in the October 1875 conference.[3]

With Brigham's death, John Taylor thus became the acting head of the church as president of the Twelve. Daniel H. Wells, George Q. Cannon, Brigham Young Jr., and John W. Young were all released from their positions as counselors in the presidency. At a meeting of all the apostles (members of the Quorum of Twelve and Brigham Young's former counselors) a month after Brigham's death, Daniel stated that Brigham Young never intended that John Taylor succeed him in leading the church. Instead he proposed that Joseph F. Smith, the son of Hyrum Smith and one of the youngest apostles (ordained in 1866), be appointed president of the church.[4]

The Twelve voted against Daniel's suggestion and some, including John Taylor may have been offended by it. Daniel had worked closely with Joseph F. Smith in the First Presidency and knew him to be a strong, capable leader. He was less impressed with some of the older apostles who, though they had served many years in the Quorum, had also sometimes been at odds with Brigham Young's leadership style and, consequently, with his counselors. Daniel was not a church member at the time of Brigham Young's succession to the Presidency and evidently saw individual merit as preferable to seniority in choosing the Lord's prophet.[5]

At the following October conference, George Q. Cannon and Brigham Young Jr., two of Brigham's counselors, were sustained as members of the Quorum of the Twelve in the seniority positions they held at the time they were called to the First Presidency. Daniel H. Wells and John W. Young, Brigham's other counselors, were not sustained as members of the Twelve, even though Daniel had been ordained an apostle before either Cannon or Brigham Jr. and was senior to both as an apostle by several years. It is possible that his lack of regard for the seniority principle in the succession question may have caused the Twelve to exclude him from their number.[6]

The Twelve specified that Daniel and John W. Young "are to stand as Counselors to the Twelve as they did to Brigham Young." Both men were sustained as counselors to the Twelve Apostles in the October conference. Both were also sustained with John Taylor and George Q. Cannon as members of an administrative committee to supervise the building of temples, public works, and other church financial affairs. Neither was ever made a member of the Quorum of the Twelve although Daniel held the position of counselor to the Twelve for the rest of his life. John W. Young was released in 1891 and never held another high church office, although he lived until 1924.[7]

Because many, if not most, of the apostles were not comfortable reorganizing the First Presidency immediately, John Taylor continued as president of the Twelve to direct the affairs of the church for the next three years. When Taylor pressed to be appointed president during meetings of the apostles held before general conference in October 1880, some apostles were "unsettled" about doing so; several approved, and a few openly suggested a younger man. Daniel was still of this opinion, even when most other apostles had agreed on Taylor's ascension. When George Q. Cannon said that he "thought he had heard [Brigham Young] say that 'John Taylor would be his successor,'" Daniel replied that he "did not believe that any man ever heard President Young say that,—for he knew that he never thought so."[8]

John Taylor was finally sustained as president in October 1880. He chose George Q. Cannon as his first counselor and Joseph Fielding Smith as his second counselor. Moses Thatcher and Francis M. Lyman were sustained as new members of the Twelve Apostles, but Daniel H. Wells and John W. Young were again not sustained as members of the Twelve. They retained their callings as assistants to the Twelve.[9]

It seems apparent to any outside observer that Daniel was abruptly turned out of the top leadership of the church and relegated to a secondary role far less significant than his seniority and previous service in the hierarchy warranted. But if Daniel felt slighted by his brethren, none of his extant writings express any bitterness, either following Brigham's death or at any time thereafter. He had not sought his calling as an apostle or as a member of the First Presidency and, although he had served in both capacities for more than twenty years, he did not see himself entitled to any appointment that his brethren were not willing to give him. In the meeting where the Twelve reorganized the seniority order of the apostles and created Daniel's position as counselor to the Twelve, he voted to sustain these actions and reaffirmed his acceptance of his own calling by voting to sustain the new First Presidency in conference. At age sixty-three, he felt relieved to be released from some of the heavy burdens of church administration and to have more time available for his family and for the temple ordinances that he knew were needed on behalf of his ancestors.[10]

Some of Daniel's relatives, from whom he requested family information, were vehemently opposed to Mormon doctrines regarding salvation for the dead and refused to send him any data that would assist him in practicing them. They continued to insist that he abandon the LDS faith and return to his Protestant roots. Others, including his sister Catherine and a few cousins, became reconciled to Daniel's religion and, while they did not accept Mormonism themselves, they helped him compile a genealogy of deceased family members who might benefit in the afterlife from his efforts. Some may have felt that Joseph Smith revealed correct principles, but more probably reasoned that, at worst, anything done by the living on behalf of the dead could do no harm.[11]

Daniel was certain that temple ordinances were the means of bringing salvation to the members of his family who had died before the restoration of the gospel. He was equally sure that, as the only one who understood the doctrine of universal salvation, he was responsible for bringing that knowledge to the rest of the family, both living and dead. He tried mightily without success to convert some of his living relatives, but for those who had died without an opportunity to accept the restored Church of Jesus Christ, he could facilitate redemption.[12]

The Wells genealogy book that Daniel purchased from Albert Welles provided more knowledge of his family's beginnings and his ancestors than he had been able to accumulate in the previous ten years. When Albert Welles visited Salt Lake City, Daniel presented him with an album containing photographs of every member of his immediate family, some forty-five persons. Seventy years later that album, which had returned to New York with Welles and his wife when they left Utah, came again into possession of Daniel's grandchildren.[13]

Daniel and several members of his family returned to perform ordinances in the St. George Temple several times during the years following its dedication. They were able to complete temple work for Daniel's sisters and his parents, his grandparents and many of his earlier ancestors. They also did work for deceased members of the families of Daniel's wives: the Free family, the Alley family, the Harris family, and the Woodward family. They did not do work for the family of Eliza Robison Wells, Daniel's first wife, because that was being done by his brother-in-law, Lewis Robison. They continued to do temple work periodically in St. George and later also in the Manti Temple. Daniel did not live long enough to see the Salt Lake Temple dedicated and he was released as president of the Endowment House in 1877, although he continued to perform marriages there as he had since 1857. During his later years, Daniel and his family labored on behalf of their dead ancestors in the Endowment House and the two southern temples.[14]

Shortly after Daniel and his family returned to Salt Lake City, they were saddened by the unexpected demise of Emma W. Wells, the daughter of Daniel and Emmeline Wells. Emma, who was only twenty-four and unmarried at the time of her death from pneumonia, was a founding member of the Wasatch Literary Society, which frequently met in her mother's home. She also worked as a volunteer bookkeeper for several church organizations such as the *Juvenile Instructor* and ZCMI. In her obituary, the *Deseret News* wrote of her, "Miss Emma Wells was a most amiable and accomplished young lady, and we sincerely sympathize with the parents and the relatives generally." Emma was the first of Daniel's adult children to die and her passing, almost six years after the accidental death of young George Wells, stunned the family. Apostle Joseph F. Smith spoke at her funeral, which was also attended by a number of other apostles and general church authorities.[15]

Two plural marriages that Daniel solemnized in the Endowment House in the 1870s became the focus of court battles that confirmed the government's power to outlaw polygamy and brought Daniel into open confrontation with a federal judge.

The first case was *Reynolds v. United States* which came before the US Supreme Court on appeal in 1878 after being tried in Utah territorial courts beginning four years previously. Daniel was not involved in the Supreme Court trial or in the lower court proceedings that preceded it, but he was the man who married George Reynolds to his second wife, Amelia Jane Schofield, in the Endowment House on August 3, 1874. Reynolds had married his first wife, Mary Ann Tuddenham, in July 1865, shortly after his arrival in Utah from England. Brigham Young hired Reynolds as secretary to the First Presidency and also appointed him as manager of the Salt Lake Theatre. In 1875, Reynolds was also elected as a member of the Salt Lake City Council.[16]

The Morrill Anti-Bigamy Act, under which Reynolds was prosecuted, was passed by Congress and signed into law on July 8, 1862 by President Abraham Lincoln. It banned bigamy and limited churches and non-profit organizations in any territory of the United States to a maximum ownership of $50,000 in property. The act specifically targeted the Mormon practice of plural marriage, but Lincoln chose not to enforce the law and actually gave Brigham Young tacit permission to ignore the Morrill Act as a means of encouraging the Saints to remain loyal to the Union during the Civil War. Lincoln's successors, burdened with Reconstruction and other post-war problems, followed his example and let the Morrill Act remain dormant. By 1874, however, anti-Mormon sentiment in Congress and across the nation had become so strong that President Grant was pressured to prosecute offenders under the act, using military force to apprehend and try them, if necessary.[17]

In the hope of avoiding wholesale prosecutions, the First Presidency, who believed the law an unconstitutional denial of first amendment rights to practice religion freely, agreed to furnish a defendant for a test case. Brigham Young asked George Reynolds if he would be willing to serve as the test defendant. Reynolds agreed and was indicted for bigamy by a grand jury on October 23, 1874. He supplied the evidence that resulted in his conviction, but still had to be tried twice because of a faulty first indictment. His second conviction was appealed to and confirmed by the Utah Territorial Supreme Court so the case could be appealed on constitutional grounds to the US Supreme Court.[18]

The court heard arguments in November and on January 6, 1879 unanimously affirmed Reynold's conviction. Reynolds's argument that, as a Mormon, it was his religious duty as a male member of the church to practice polygamy if possible, was not accepted. The Court noted that the fact that a person could only be married to one person had existed in English law since at least the time of King James I of England and that the United States law was based on this common law. The Court quoted Thomas Jefferson's writings that there was a distinction between religious belief and actions that followed from religious belief. The former "lies solely between man and his God," and therefore, "the legislative powers of the government reach actions only, and not opinions." The court held that, if polygamy was allowed, someone might eventually argue that human sacrifice was a necessary part of their religion, and "to permit this would be to make the professed doctrines of religious belief superior to the law of the land, and in effect to permit every citizen to become a law unto himself." The Court concluded that the First Amendment forbade Congress from legislating against opinion, but allowed it to legislate against action.[19]

As soon as the Reynolds decision was announced, federal prosecutors in Utah began to arrest Mormons who had more than one wife and charge them with bigamy. They did not commence by accusing church leaders or those Saints who had many wives, but instead concentrated on a few Mormons who had two or three wives and limited resources to hire legal defense counsel. Against these, the prosecutors reasoned, a charge of bigamy could be brought and more easily proved, and precedents established that would make the later prosecutions of the First Presidency, apostles, and other Mormons with several wives more likely to succeed.[20]

One such Saint was John H. Miles, a resident of St. George, who came to Salt Lake City in October 1878 and while there married Miss Caroline Owen, a convert from London, England, in the Endowment House. On the same day, just prior to his wedding with Miss Owen, Miles also married Miss Emily Spencer, of St. George. Both ceremonies were performed by Daniel H. Wells. In her later divorce complaint, Miss Owen stated that she had not witnessed the first ceremony, but declared that she had consented to it, and had seen Emily Spencer in the Endowment House that day.[21]

Caroline Miles testified that just before her marriage ceremony was performed by Daniel H. Wells, he said to her husband-to-be, John Miles, "Your first wife ought to be present at this ceremony"; and that afterward, during a reception held that evening, Emily Spencer was referred to as "Mrs. Miles." The two women had a disagreement and Caroline went to the US marshal the next morning. She made statements to him that resulted in the arrest of her new husband for polygamy.[22]

Caroline quickly realized how serious her accusations were and recanted them in order to protect the man she had married. She wrote a letter, which was published in the *Salt Lake Herald*, denying all that she had previously asserted to the injury of her husband. They became reconciled, and she accompanied him to his home in southern Utah. Soon, however, she again left him, and at the time of his trial was as much opposed to him as before.[23]

The Miles bigamy trial took place before Associate Justice Emerson, at Salt Lake City, beginning late in April 1879. Miles admitted his marriage to Caroline Owen and her testimony was therefore not available at the trial since, as his wife, she could not legally testify against him. The prosecution sought to prove that the earlier marriage ceremony was performed between John Miles and Emily Spencer so that the defendant would be convicted of bigamy for also marrying his admitted wife Miss Owen. Miles denied that he was married to Miss Spencer. She also was not called to testify because, if she was his wife, as the prosecutors alleged, she could not testify against him and if she was not, as Miles claimed, then he was innocent of the charge.

The prosecution was thus required to prove the bigamy charge without the direct testimony of any of the three participants. Caroline Owen Miles gave a description of the clothing worn by those passing through the Endowment House and stated that Emily Spencer was dressed in exactly the same manner. The prosecution sought to show that such apparel was invariably worn in that place by persons there to be married, and to establish this point and corroborate the testimony of Mrs. Miles, Daniel H. Wells, the then president of the Endowment House, was called to the stand by US Attorney Van Zile.[24]

Daniel testified that it was customary for persons married in the Endowment House to wear certain robes. He was asked to describe the robe but declined to do so. Over a defense objection, the court decided that the questions were proper, but still Daniel would not answer. His refusal was based on his belief that he was under a sacred obligation not to reveal any of the proceedings of the Endowment House outside that edifice and that to be forced to do so was a violation of his right of religious freedom. Judge Emerson disagreed, however, and Daniel was judged to be in contempt of court. He was committed to the custody of the marshal for the rest of the day's court proceedings, and the next day was brought back into court with his attorney. Judge Emerson stopped the progress of the Miles case and gave Daniel an opportunity to purge himself of the contempt in which he had placed himself the day before. The prosecutor, angry that the conviction of Miles was in jeopardy and sensing correctly that Daniel still would not answer queries concerning temple ceremonies, phrased his questions so as to assure that result and quickly backed Daniel into a legal and moral conflict for which he could give only one response.[25]

He took the witness stand, stating that he would try to answer the questions if possible. At the prosecutor's request the court reporter read the question that Daniel had previously refused to answer, "Do candidates for marriage wear a green apron at that time?"

Answer: At what time? I have performed that ceremony without such attire, at the bedside of the dying.

Question by Attorney Van Zile: Do they wear a green apron at marriage in the Endowment House?

Mr. Hagan here objected to the introduction of testimony relating to the Miles case, as the prosecution had closed its evidence and wished to know whether the witness was being examined on the matter of contempt or in regard to the case for which he was one of the attorneys for the defense.

The Court [Judge Emerson] replied: Both.

The defense objected, and the court overruled the objection.

The question was again put, when the witness declined to answer, stating that he was under a sacred obligation to preserve secret the things he was now required to reveal.

Attorney Van Zile: Thus we are to understand that you have taken an oath not to reveal what takes place in the Endowment House?

Witness [Wells]: I did not say so. I said a sacred obligation. I consider it as sacred as any oath taken in a court of justice.

The court said the witness had not purged himself of contempt, but was again in contempt.

Witness: I consider any person who reveals the sacred ceremonies of the Endowment House a falsifier and a perjurer, and it has been, and is, a principle of my life never to betray a friend, my religion, my country, or my God. It seems to me that this is sufficient reason why I should not be held in contempt.

The court then explained that this was no legal reason why the question which had been declared relevant should not now be answered, and though not disposed to be vindictive or severe, the dignity of the court must be maintained, and was about to pronounce sentence when Judge Sutherland interposed and requested time to prepare an argument on the case, to which the court at length consented, and fixed the time for the hearing at 7 o'clock that evening.[26]

With the help of his attorney, Daniel composed an affidavit that would answer the prosecutor's demand without revealing specifics about the temple marriage ceremony. When he returned to court that evening, the affidavit of the defendant was filed:

In the Third Judicial District Court of Utah Territory
The People vs. Daniel H. Wells
Salt Lake County ss

Daniel H. Wells, being duly sworn, says: "In respect to the charge of contempt now pending against me for refusing to answer the two questions relating to the apron and slippers of persons going through the ceremony of the Endowment House of the Mormon Church, I meant no disrespect of this court. I declined wholly upon conscientious grounds. I was willing to testify to any material fact not covered by any previous obligation, and had I been interrogated while on the witness stand to elicit these facts, I should have stated, and the truth is, that persons going through such ceremonies wear special garments, and these are precisely the same whether the wearer in the course of those ceremonies is united in plural marriage or otherwise, or not, and those married are not distinguished by any difference of dress from those who do not enter into the marriage relation.

Daniel H. Wells[27]

After the affidavit was entered, Daniel's attorney, J. D. Sutherland, argued to the effect that the questions put to him were irrelevant, immaterial, and unimportant; and he contended that the same delicate consideration should be shown to what Daniel religiously cherished, as was due to all other private and sacred affairs not within the proper scope of judicial inquiry. Judge Emerson again rejected the argument for religious freedom from government inquiry and stated:

> The question was not a personal one between the defendant and himself, but between the defendant and the court as a representative. General Wells had defied the mandate of the court and it was necessary that the supremacy of the law should be maintained. The question of the materiality of the question, as he had previously stated, was closed, and did not enter into this matter, but he was even now more firmly convinced than before that the question was a material one. The law as to what should constitute a contempt could not be expressed with more force or propriety than it had been by counsel for the defendant. Though it was a very disagreeable duty, it was nevertheless incumbent upon the court to see that the orders of the court were respected as they should be. He therefore ordered the defendant pay a fine of $100 and be confined for a period of two days.[28]

Daniel was then placed in the custody of the marshal, who immediately took him out to the Sugar House penitentiary. The term of imprisonment was short, but the anti-Mormon authorities had finally succeeded in remanding the sixty-five-year-old Daniel to prison, as they had an aged Brigham Young before him, as a means of reducing his standing among members of the church and in the community and demonstrating that polygamy was not to be further tolerated.[29]

The actual result, as reported under the headline "In the Penitentiary" in the *Deseret News* the following day, was not what the judge and prosecutors had intended:

> The friends of President Daniel H. Wells visited him in prison yesterday, bringing presents of flowers and table delicacies, to cheer the hours of his confinement. They found him in comfortable circumstances with every convenience of the place at his service, and quite cheerful in disposition. Marshal Shaughnessy and his assistants, though strict in the performance of the duty imposed upon them, have acted with all possible courtesy toward their prisoner, and many prominent Gentiles have freely expressed their admiration of General Wells' conduct in preferring to go to prison rather than betray a sacred trust . . . The fine of $100 has been offered repeatedly by a number of the prominent citizens, but we believe it is the intention to raise the sum by subscription, 5 cents to be the highest sum accepted from one person, in order to give a greater number the chance to subscribe. The term of imprisonment (two days) expires at 8 o'clock tonight, when the brave man who dared to do right will emerge from his prison, covered with new honors and upheld by the plaudits of the people whose spirit he has so faithfully represented.[30]

On the day Daniel entered the penitentiary, a special meeting of the city council was called, in which the mayor asked that an expression of support be made in response to the imprisonment in the penitentiary of one of the city's prominent citizens, "a man long associated with the Council as its president, and honored by the suffrages of the citizens of Salt Lake as Mayor for five consecutive terms, covering a period of ten years."[31]

A committee drafted a resolution expressing the feelings of the council and inviting the citizens of the city to join with them in support of Daniel and his actions:

Whereas our much respected friend and fellow citizen, Honorable Daniel H. Wells, ex-Mayor of Salt Lake City, is at present suffering what we deem to be an unjust imprisonment in the Territorial penitentiary, under the order of the Acting Judge of the Third Judicial Court of this Territory for alleged contempt of court, in refusing to answer questions which would violate what he esteemed to be sacred obligations, as set forth in his affidavit filed with said court, May 3, 1879, and,

Whereas we further approve of his declaration, "I am under moral and sacred obligations to not answer, and it is interwoven in my character never to betray a friend, a brother, my country, my religion, or my God," and honoring his determination rather to suffer imprisonment than to do violence to sacred principles,

Therefore, be it resolved by the City Council of Salt Lake City that, to manifest our sympathy, respect and honor for the man who would rather suffer wrong than to do wrong, we proceed in a body to meet him upon his liberation from custody, and escort him back to his home and to the society of his family and friends.

And be it further resolved that we invite all citizens sympathizing in the movement to participate in this demonstration of respect.

Feramorz Little, Mayor[32]

The document was unanimously adopted and word of it spread rapidly throughout the city. The council committees worked with quickly formed citizens' committees to make arrangements for a large popular demonstration. The same day the resolution was adopted, a notice was published in the *Deseret News*:

To the Merchants and Other Businessmen

It is particularly requested by the general public that stores, workshops, and all places of business and public labor be closed tomorrow morning, that those who desire may be at liberty to take part in the reception to General D. H. Wells, the true man whom the people delight to honor.[33]

In less than two days' time, the event developed into an outpouring of support for Daniel larger than any that Salt Lake City had seen up to that time. Many Gentiles participated in the belief that he had been unnecessarily wronged and humiliated by the court, but it was mainly a Mormon statement of outrage that their religion was being attacked through one of their leaders who was among the most revered of the city's residents. Daniel was, by all accounts, universally believed to be a man of honor who would defend his principles at any cost.[34]

The order of procession set by the city council committee and published in the *Deseret News* shows the scale that the demonstration attained:

1. The party invited to escort General D. H. Wells to the city will be organized and leave President Taylor's office in carriages only, on Tuesday, May 6, at 9 a.m.
2. The Bishops are requested to organize their respective wards, march them to East Temple Street between 3rd and 6th South Streets, and there report to the Marshal of the day at 9:30 a.m., who will place them in position to receive General Wells on his arrival in the city.
3. The escort will return by the State Road to 6th South Street, then west to East Temple Street, thence up East Temple to General Wells' residence.[35]

This Order of Procession was issued: Captain Burt, marshal of the day; band; President Taylor and escort; territorial, county, and city officers; mayors and city councils from various places and invited guests; representatives of the press; Salt Lake City Fire Brigade; band; relief societies with banners; band; Sabbath schools with banners; band; Mutual Improvement and Retrenchment Societies with banners; band; Seventies; high priests; elders; bishops and the lesser priesthood with banners; Scandinavian band; German citizens with banners; general citizens on foot and on horseback.[36]

Recognizing that a demonstration of such size might become overly enthusiastic or be exploited by anti-Mormons in the city to foment a riot or damage Mormon property, the committee added a note of caution to participants and an implied warning to observers to respect the peaceful intent of the organizers:

> It is to be hoped that everyone will aid in preserving order. It is to be a peaceable assemblage of citizens. It is not designed as a defiance to any person, government, society, or establishment. It is simply an expression of the popular sentiment towards an old and tried friend, true patriot, and an honorable, faithful Counselor in Israel. Care should be taken to preserve children from accident, from teams and other sources. Caution should be observed in regard to our homes; let none

be left unguarded. It is desired that the stores, workshops, and places of public business and labor be closed. Let us have a quiet, peaceful, orderly and lawful, if enthusiastic and earnest, assembly, that nothing may be done which has even the appearance of evil or can be construed into anything hostile or offensive to the honor, dignity, welfare or authority of any lawfully constituted power under the heavens. Glory to the brave, and good will to all honorable of the earth.[37]

Daniel was released from the penitentiary on Monday afternoon, but at the request of the city council, stayed overnight at the farm of John R. Winder in Sugar House so as to be ready to meet the cortege assembling to honor him on Tuesday morning. At nine o'clock, a large group of carriages and riders started from the vicinity of the church office on South Temple Street. Included were the First Presidency, Mayor Little and the city council committee, six apostles, the presiding bishop, ten mayors and city councils, county and territory officials, and a number of other priesthood and auxiliary leaders. They were joined by a group of press representatives, five bands, a company of mounted horsemen (members of the Nauvoo Legion that Daniel commanded, but not designated as such because any muster of the Legion was still banned), and a large number of other vehicles filled with ladies and gentlemen who wanted to be part of the parade.[38]

The weather was sunny and dry and such a huge moving train inevitably raised an enormous cloud of dust as it moved along South Temple to Third East and then south to the Winder farm. A strong breeze bore away most of the dirt, saving those in the procession from choking or blindness, but still covering everyone with a layer of fine grit. When they reached their destination, Daniel stepped forth to meet them and was formally received by President John Taylor.

> President Wells: In behalf of the community who feel outraged by the treatment you have received, I propose to present to you the confidence, the respect, the honor and the esteem of the people whose hearts, feelings and affections are with you.
> ... we have come to exhibit to you our esteem and to show you that whilst you are true to your friends, your principles, your country, and your God, that your friends are equally true to you ...
> We have come, General Wells, to wipe away a stain sought to be heaped upon you by the bigoted, unreflecting and

thoughtless, and this demonstration is the spontaneous impulse and action of a generous, patriotic, kind-hearted and friendly people. For this purpose we have assembled here today, and in behalf of this whole community, I tender to you our sincere regards and our most heartfelt sympathy.[39]

Had he not been forewarned, Daniel would probably have been speechless at this huge manifestation of public affection. Having had a little time to think of his response, he replied with sincere feeling, if not great eloquence:

> I will simply say that I should feel exceedingly sorry for myself if I felt for a single moment that any of my friends supposed or could entertain the idea that I could do otherwise than I have done . . . I can well afford to suffer bonds, fines, and imprisonment, and even death if necessary—which, by the way, has no terms for me—but to forfeit my fellowship with you, my brethren, or a single particle of the confidence which is reposed in me by the people of God, through violating the sacred and holy covenants we have entered into, I could not afford . . .
> I feel happy and well, and am rejoiced to meet you, though I did not expect any such demonstration as this. I thank you heartily; but not, however, so much for myself as the expression of your feelings to sustain the principle. I know that you are my friends and that you are the friends of the Most High God, and I pray that I may ever be worthy of your confidence and esteem, and be the friend of the Lord.
> I will not detain you, but in the fullness of my heart I say, God bless you forever; and again thank you for this expression of your kindness and love.[40]

Daniel stepped into President Taylor's carriage and the procession moved out at a fast trot toward the city. When it reached Sixth South, it turned west to Main Street where most of the crowd was waiting to observe its passage and join in at its end. More than three hundred carriages "moved at a walk up East Temple Street to the Council House." Behind them came the bands and a long train of men, women and children in the various organizations on foot, followed by a huge number of wagons, three deep, too numerous to count. When this multitude had passed, nearly all the observers watching from the sides fell into line behind the

Figure 20.1. Frank Leslie's Illustrated Newspaper: *"Great Mormon demonstration in Salt Lake City in honor of Daniel H. Wells . . . for his refusal to reveal secrets of the Endowment House," New York, May 31, 1879.*

wagons and marched with the procession past the Council House to the Tabernacle on Temple Square. This last contingent far outnumbered the rest of the procession combined and gave spontaneous proof of the genuine affection that almost all people in Utah felt for Daniel.[41]

Even the stridently anti-Mormon *Salt Lake Tribune* was compelled to acknowledge the size of the gathering while still disparaging its purpose:

> The streets of this city yesterday from nine o'clock in the morning until late in the day, presented a sight seldom, if ever witnessed before. Never has such a crowd thronged the streets, nor such a cavalcade of human beings and brutes, in point of numbers, promiscuousness and motley confusion, been witnessed before, as that presented on our public streets on the occasion of the triumphal entry into town from the penitentiary of Daniel H. Wells, first counsellor [*sic*] in the Mormon Church. So far as concerns the magnitude in a numerical point of view of this demonstration, not even the event of the death and funeral of Brigham Young could at all rival

it. Hundreds of poor dupes were forwarded by all the trains centering in this city, to participate in a celebration, which in spirit and substance, was designed as a public defiance of the national judicial authorities. The flag of our country was ruthlessly profaned by association with banners, upon which were inscribed incendiary mottoes and devices. The immense procession as it moved up Main Street, presented a spectacle which should have roused the patriotic heart to indignation, had its supreme ridiculousness not been so apparent.[42]

The *Salt Lake Herald*, an independent though usually pro-Mormon newspaper, gave a more objective account of the event:

> The demonstration was one of the most remarkable that has ever taken place in this or any other country or age. It is estimated that not less than ten thousand persons were in the procession, while more than that number lined the streets on either side from the Tabernacle to the suburbs. And yet there was no disorder, no accident, no brawling, nothing that indicated any other than the happiest peace. The brief addresses contained no incendiary word, and implied no offensive sentiment. We question if the world has ever before seen an impromptu demonstration of this magnitude, and this character, where nothing was said or done that could be found fault with, or which gave no occasion for alarm . . .
>
> The demonstration of May 6th, 1879, in honor of one who was regarded by the people as having been made to suffer unlawfully, to gratify the malicious spite of officials, will long be remembered in this Territory.[43]

The largest public gathering in Salt Lake history would not be satisfied merely to march in a parade and the committee had, consequently, planned a suitable program as a conclusion to the occasion.

> Turning west from the Council House, the vast concourse filed into the large Tabernacle, which was quickly filled in every part, and many thousands could not find admittance. It was a magnificent sight. Seven bands were seated in the choir; the firemen sat together in the body of the building to the left; the banners, flags and mottos were arranged around the gallery, and when Counselor Wells appeared on the stand,

deafening cheers resounded through the great house; Ladies waved their handkerchiefs, the banners and streamers were set in motion, and the enthusiasm for several minutes was unrestrained.[44]

After music played in succession by no fewer than seven bands from as far north as Logan and as far south as Nephi, and a prayer offered by President Taylor, Daniel was again called upon to acknowledge the tribute paid him. As earlier in the day, his remarks were brief and to the point:

> My friends, my brethren and sisters, and fellow citizens: I sincerely thank you for this demonstration of your love, sympathy and respect; probably this is a demonstration of such a character as never was seen before . . . Acts speak louder and are more expressive than words; therefore, after again thanking you in the name of insulted freedom and in accordance with the dictates of wisdom. we will soon close these proceedings and retire in silence to our happy and disturbed homes. And now may the peace of Heaven and the blessings of Israel's God rest in rich abundance upon you all and upon every one whose soul responds to the sound, the echoes of truth and integrity in the name of Jesus. Amen.[45]

Daniel's statement that the program would "soon close" was more an expression of his wish than of those who had organized the affair. His speech was followed by a musical rendition of *Hail Columbia* and an address by President Taylor, admittedly a better and more practiced speaker, which extended to more than seven times the length of Daniel's remarks. But the audience was well-accustomed to lengthy conference talks and applauded both speakers with equal enthusiasm. After three more band presentations and a benediction by Joseph F. Smith, the crowd finally was dismissed from the Tabernacle, the dignitaries to a meal prepared under the direction of the committee, and the bulk of the audience to socialize with family and friends through the conclusion of the unexpected holiday celebration. Said the *Deseret News*,

> The whole proceedings were carried out with perfect order; there was no brawling, no ill humor nor hard sayings, but everybody was delighted with the celebration, which was the most imposing ever witnessed in this city. Considering that it was a spontaneous outburst from an indignant people, the

executive effort of bringing this popular uprising into perfect order and attractive shape, was masterly. About 10,000 people took part in the procession, and fully 15,000 more were spectators. The committee on arrangements was deserving of great praise . . .

Thus ended a day long to be remembered in Israel, when the Latter-day Saints united in a grand manifestation of sympathy, admiration and support of a brother and counselor who set them a noble example of fidelity to the right.[46]

Despite the absence of Daniel's testimony in his trial, John Miles was convicted of bigamy on the same day that the procession honoring Daniel marched to the Tabernacle. He was fined $100 and sentenced to five years imprisonment, a harbinger of similar penalties that would be meted out to other polygamists convicted in the future.[47]

Although Miles's conviction was reported in newspapers across the country, it was the procession honoring Daniel that garnered by far the most prominent coverage. For once, a leading Mormon was given favorable national press exposure even though Daniel was a practicing polygamist of thirty years' duration and had solemnized more polygamous marriages than any other person.[48]

21

Wells Family Marriages, the Anti-polygamy Crusade, and a Second Mission in Europe

1880–1885

Following the signal honor paid him on the occasion of his release from prison, Daniel returned to his church and business duties, but at a reduced pace as befitted a man who had reached retirement age. He continued in his calling as an apostle and counselor to the Twelve and as president of the Endowment House. The latter assignment occupied an increasing portion of his time as the Mormon population of Utah grew and the children of immigrant converts reached marriageable age. The St. George Temple was now available for couples seeking a sealed-for-eternity wedding, but many could not afford to travel to the southwestern corner of the territory for their nuptials and the Endowment House remained the preferred choice of less affluent families, especially those who lived north of Nephi. Daniel presided at hundreds of weddings in the years after his brief incarceration and was not released from this assignment until he departed on his second mission in 1884.[1]

He also began to divest some of his commercial interests so as to have more time for family matters, social activities, and the temple work that he had commenced in 1877. In March 1880, Daniel closed down the Wells and Taylor Coal Company and sold the coal lands that he owned in Summit County to Angus M. Cannon. Daniel's partner, Steven W. Taylor, had previously sold his interest in the coal property to Cannon in 1874. This land included not only the Wells and Taylor claim, but also the claim known as the Old Church Mine that Daniel and Taylor had operated for the church since 1856. The purchase price for all his coal holdings was $8,100.[2]

Cannon and his associates continued to work the mine for many years. In 1897 they constructed a railway track extension to connect the mine with the Echo and Park City branch of the Union Pacific main line, thus enabling the transport of coal by rail from the mine head to Salt Lake City and other markets. In 1923 the rail extension was purchased by the Union Pacific Railroad. The mine was still in operation in 1934 when it was sold with a group of adjacent claims to the Grass Creek Coal Company for $10,000.[3]

Daniel also scaled back the logging operations of the Big Cottonwood Lumber Company, which by 1880 had cut and processed most of the easily accessible timber in the canyon. That year the 107 lumber mills operating in Utah Territory produced over 25 million board feet of lumber, with Big Cottonwood accounting for more than two million of the total. Thereafter, however, timber production declined each year until by 1890 only thirty-two mills remained in operation and the value of their production had declined by a third. Some of the logging companies resorted to extremely destructive practices when harvesting timber in order to keep costs down. They burned areas of forest to destroy obstructing undergrowth and strip the trees of their branches, then cut only the largest trees that survived the fire relatively intact, leaving the rest as waste on the hillsides. Daniel would not use such methods and the Big Cottonwood Canyon consequently yielded less timber at higher cost as the lower slope trees were depleted.[4]

Ironically, as Daniel's involvement in the lumber business was beginning to decline, his lawsuit against Mr. Nickles, the man to whom the Federal Land Registrar, Oliver Patten, illegally sold his lumber in 1876, was finally decided by the US Supreme Court. As noted previously, Daniel had posted a large bond to guarantee payment for the lumber to Nickles if the sale to him by Patton was found to be legal. This bond had obligated some of Daniel's assets and contributed significantly to the financial distress he suffered in the 1870s as the Salt Lake Gas Company and some of his other business interests turned unprofitable.

The Third District Court had ruled in favor of Nickles and the Utah Territory Supreme Court had affirmed the lower court's decision, both holding that Registrar Patton's sale of the lumber to Nickles was legal despite the compromise sale to Daniel that Patton had previously made. After waiting three years for a final decision, Daniel must have been both relieved and gratified that the nation's highest court understood and followed the law. Its decision stated:

> The compromise [sale] appears to have been framed in conformity with the language of the letter of Nov. 4, 1870.

Wells agreed to pay, and did pay, the expenses of seizure and the costs of suit, and nothing remained but for the judge who decided the demurrer to fix the amount of the stumpage and give judgment therefor against Wells. He had given bond to pay what was so ascertained. The case was settled in precise accordance with the instructions of the commissioner, and we think the settlement bound the United States, whose agent made the compromise.

The authority to make this settlement is quite as clear as the authority of the same officer to sell to Nickles; so that his right to sue depends upon the same authority on which Wells had the property delivered to him, on paying all costs and expenses and giving a bond, with surety, for the damages.

The instruction of the District Court held this settlement to be of no validity. The [Utah] Supreme Court held the same view; and the registrar who made the sale to Nickles evidently disregarded his own compromise and sold the property to Nickles under the same idea. All this, we think was erroneous . . .

We are of opinion that the instruction to the jury, which we have given in full, and the whole theory on which the effect of the stipulation of compromise was decided, is erroneous, and that the judgment of each of the courts below must be reversed, with directions to set aside the verdict and grant a new trial; and it is

So ordered.[5]

With this decision, Daniel was released from his bond and the nearly $10,000 of his assets that secured it were freed so that he could dispose of them. His victory was complete, but costly, as his property had been held for several years and he was also forced to pay the expense of appeal to the Supreme Court.

By 1880, all but the youngest four of Daniel's surviving children were in their teens or twenties. Unlike many second-generation Mormon girls, who often married well before the age of twenty, Daniel's daughters usually took more time in choosing a mate. The average age of his twelve daughters who married was 22.7 years at the time of their weddings and only one of them took a husband while still in her teens. The ten Wells sons who married waited even longer to do so; they were an average of twenty-six years old at their weddings. Two daughters married in the late 1860s and three more in the 1870s, along with two of the older sons. But the 1880s were the marriage decade for the Wells family. During the

Figure 21.1. Daughters of Daniel H. Wells: (top row, left to right) Susan Annette, Frances Louisa, Emmeline, Eliza Free, Mary Minerva, Clara Ellen, and Emily Harris; (center row) Elizabeth Ann, Abbie Corilla, Martha Deseret, and Catherine Chapin; (lower row) Louisa Martha, Emeline Young, Edna Margaret. Photo taken ca. 1874.

period between 1880 and Daniel's death in March 1891, six of his daughters and five of his sons found mates. The remaining five sons and one daughter all married in the decade after his death.[6]

The only teenage bride was Melvina Whitney, the daughter of Emmeline Wells and her second husband Newell K. Whitney whom Daniel had raised as his own child. She married William Dunford in 1867, at the age of seventeen, and with him had four children in five years. But the marriage foundered and the couple divorced in 1873. The following year Melvina married William Wells Woods, the son of Daniel's sister Catherine and her husband James W. Woods. William had followed his father and become a lawyer. He arrived in Utah not long after his discharge with the rank of major from the Union Army. He lived for a time with the Wells family and courted Melvina after her divorce. She was the mother of four small children, but only twenty-four years old at the time of her second marriage to Major Woods. They had two children together in the following four years, but both of them died before reaching their teens, as did one of Melvina's children from her earlier marriage. Around 1887 the Woods moved to Idaho where William became chief justice of the Idaho Supreme Court following that state's admission to the Union.[7]

Melvina's sister, Isabel M. Whitney, married Septimus W. Sears in 1869 at age twenty. Daniel H. Wells Jr., Daniel and Louisa's oldest child, married Emma G. Price in 1874, a few months before Melvina's second marriage, and their second child, Francis L. Wells, married George Naylor in 1875. Martha Wells, daughter of Daniel and Martha, married Charles Read in 1877, and Susan Wells, daughter of Daniel and Susan, married Henry Culmer on the last day of 1878. Junius Wells, Daniel and Hannah's son, married Helena Fobes in June 1879, a month after his father's stay at the territorial prison and triumphal return to the city. Except for Will and Melvina Woods, who had a civil marriage ceremony because he was not a Mormon, all of these marriages were performed by Daniel in the Endowment House.[8]

The new decade began with the marriage in January 1880 of Heber M. Wells, the son of Daniel and Martha, to Mary Elizabeth Beatie. Heber was only twenty and his wife barely eighteen, one of the youngest of the Wells family marriages. It was also short-lived as Mary Elizabeth died eight years later, soon after the birth of her third child. Heber married Theresa Clawson in 1892, but his second wife also died in 1897 after having two children. Heber, who had by then been chosen, at age thirty-seven, as the first governor of the new state of Utah, was left with four minor children (his oldest son died at age five) and no wife. He was reelected to a second four-year term as governor in 1900 and in June 1901 married Emily Katz who was a dozen years his junior. His third wife bore him three additional children and outlived him by more than twenty years.[9]

Elizabeth Ann Wells, the daughter of Daniel and Emmeline Wells, was known to family and friends as Annie and was, like her deceased sister Emma, a young lady of accomplishment and refinement. In March 1880 Annie married John Quayle Cannon, the son of Apostle George Q. Cannon and his wife Elizabeth Hoagland. John Q. Cannon was a handsome, bright, and well-educated young man who worked as an editor for the *Deseret News*. His marriage to Annie Wells, officiated in the Endowment House by Daniel H. Wells, linked two of the most prominent families in Utah. They had a large wedding reception that was the high point of the winter season even though John Q.'s parents could not attend. George Q. Cannon was then in Washington, DC, serving as Utah's Congressional Delegate, but he and his wife sent their regrets and best wishes to the newlyweds.[10]

John Q. and Annie lived during their first year of marriage in the home of Emmeline Wells and their first child was born there in February

Figure 21.2. Sons of Daniel H. Wells: (inserts, left to right) Albert Emory and Briant Harris; (standing, left to right) Louis Robison, Charles Henry, Gershom Britain F., Joseph Smith, Daniel Hanmer Jr., and Melvin Dickensen; (seated, left to right) Stephen Franklin, Heber Manning, Rulon Seymour, Junius Free, and Victor Pennington. Photo taken ca. 1887.

1881. They then moved to John Q.'s farm in the southwest area of the city where a new home had been constructed for them. Their stay on the farm was short, however, as John Q. was called on a mission to Europe in August 1881. Annie and her son George moved back to Emmeline's house while John Q. was away. He served first in Great Britain and then in Switzerland where he became mission president in August 1883. Annie joined him in Europe in October and stayed until they returned to Salt Lake City in June 1884.[11]

By the time the Cannons returned to Utah, no less than four additional Wells weddings had occurred. Daniel officiated at each of them in the Endowment House. Daniel and Louisa's daughter, Clara Ellen Wells, married William Sanford Hedges in October 1882 and their son Rulon S. Wells married Josephine Beatie, the sister of Heber's wife Mary Elizabeth, in January the next year.[12]

The next two marriages were different than any of those that preceded them in the Wells family. None of Daniel's children, sons or daughters, up to this time had contracted a polygamous marriage. Neither Daniel nor any of his wives were opposed to plural marriage and would undoubtedly have given their consent to any of their sons who desired to take a plural wife or any of their daughters who wanted to become one, but they did not attempt to arrange any unions or to seek prospective mates, polygamous or otherwise, for their children. Although several of Daniel's wives had married him under the duress of severe circumstances, he had a genuine affection for all of them that had endured through many years. He believed, as they did, in marrying for love and, as a parent, left his children free to seek their own relationships according to their own hearts. The first dozen marriages in the Wells family were, consequently, all monogamous and all among young couples of roughly similar age.[13]

The enactment of the Edmunds Act in 1882 foreshadowed an intense period of prosecution for any Latter-day Saint who was involved in polygamy. The act stipulated that any person with a living spouse who married again was guilty of polygamy and provided for a prison sentence up to five years and a $500 fine. It also made cohabitation, living together as husband and wife when not legally married, unlawful and designated that children born of polygamous parents before January 1, 1883 were to be considered legitimate, but those born after that date were not. The Edmunds Act and the still more proscriptive Edmunds-Tucker Act which followed it into law in 1887, turned Utah Territory into a judicial hunting ground in which federal prosecutors sought to arrest anyone suspected of plural marriage. Their quarry was often forced into hiding in "the underground," a network of concealed hideouts in private homes, remote farms, and other refuges, some of which were located in different states, territories, or countries. The result was a huge disruption in Mormon society.[14]

> Otherwise law-abiding men suddenly found themselves escaping to the underground—that is going into hiding, and frequently moving from place to place to escape the marshals who were hunting them. Hideouts were prepared in homes, barns and fields to serve as way stations for the fleeing "cohabs," as they were nicknamed by their pursuers. Secret codes were invented to warn of approaching deputies, and . . . scores of federal officers brought into the territory to conduct this all-out raid disguised themselves as peddlers or census-takers in order to . . . question children, gossip with neighbors and even invade the privacy of homes.[15]

The Edmunds Act placed many Mormons, especially their leaders who were the most prominent polygamists, outside the law. It produced a strong feeling among most of the Saints that the law would not protect them, but was being used as a tool to destroy their religion. As prosecutors began to enforce the act, the Mormon—Gentile divide that had characterized Utah society for years widened and intensified. The movement was mostly on the side of the Saints who, though formerly among the most law-abiding peoples anywhere, now regarded some laws as instruments of their enemies and consequently felt less need to obey any law that appeared to work against their interests. A spirit of defiance grew among many Mormons and the practice of evading or covertly defying the law, not previously common among them, became more so. Many people ignored the Edmunds Act and many more supported those who did so, hiding them from arrest or refusing to give information about them.[16]

Some Mormons also participated in other lawless acts seeking revenge for wrongs against Mormons. One of the worst of these incidents was the only lynching in Salt Lake City's history; it occurred in 1883 and was graphically described by Bill Heywood who was a witness:

> When I was about twelve I ran a fruit stand on Elephant Corner for old man Reese. Around dinner time one day I heard some shooting down the street and saw a crowd gathering in front of Griggs' restaurant. I ran down to see what the trouble was. Two policemen were bringing a Negro out of the restaurant. From what the crowd said I understood that he had killed one policeman and the watermaster, and had wounded another policeman.
>
> The policemen, with the crowd following, started toward Second South Street. I wondered why they did not go the shortest way to the jail; the route they took was nearly a block longer. As they went along Second South Street, a grocer left his store and joined the crowd, folding up his apron and tucking it into his belt as he walked along. This man, whose name I did not know, shouted: "Get a rope!" I thought to myself, "What do they want with a rope? The police have got him fast."
>
> The crowd was increasing and getting more excited at every step. The added distance increased the number of the mob. As the jail was reached, I could see the prisoner and the policemen on the steps that led up to the door. It seemed to me that the policemen, instead of pushing the Negro into the prison, pushed him into the hands of the mob. I did not see him again until I had crowded in under the arms of the mob, which was then standing hushed as though stricken with awe. Then I saw the Negro hanging by the neck in the wagon shed. His face was ghastly, and although he was light colored, it was turning

blue, with the eyes and tongue sticking out horribly. I looked at the swinging figure and thought over and over, "What have they done—what have they done." It was as though a weight of cold lead settled in my stomach.

The leaders of the mob were not satisfied with the death of the man. Some one cried out: "Drag him out and quarter him! Hang him to a telegraph pole!" They dragged the limp body by the neck to the corner of the street, where Mayor Wells drove up and read the riot act, ordering them to return the body at once to the jail. This was my first realization of what the insane cruelty of a mob could mean.[17]

Although Daniel witnessed the aftermath of the lynching and tried to disperse the mob, Heywood was mistaken in identifying him as the mayor. He was long out of office at that time and it was Mayor William Jennings who eventually broke up the crowd and ordered the body of Sam Joe Harvey, the victim, taken to a mortuary. The men who Harvey shot were City Marshal Andrew Burt and City Watermaster Charles H. Wilcken, both prominent Mormons. Burt was killed and Wilcken seriously wounded. Most of the police and the mob were also Mormons and were probably influenced by their mistaken belief that Harvey, known to be a non-Mormon, might not be punished for his crime. No member of the mob was ever charged with any offense in connection with the lynching.[18]

The Edmunds Act did not have any effect on President John Taylor's determination that the Saints should continue to practice polygamy. Taylor had been grievously wounded in the attack on the Carthage jail in which Joseph and Hyrum Smith were martyred, and he was ever afterward absolutely convinced that both men had died in defense of the principle of eternal marriage. He saw no reason, including what he regarded as the unconstitutional acts of Congress, to alter any aspect of the church's practice of plural marriage and to the end of his life continued to live and preach the principle.[19]

In October 1882, in response to his inquiry regarding the filling of vacancies in the Quorum of the Twelve Apostles and other matters, President Taylor said that he received a revelation that stated in part:

> Thus saith the Lord to the Twelve, and to the Priesthood and people of my Church.
> Let my servants George Teasdale and Heber J. Grant be appointed to fill the vacancies in the Twelve, that you may be fully organized and prepared for the labors devolving upon you . . . You may appoint Seymour B. Young to fill up the

vacancy in the presiding quorum of Seventies, if he will conform to my law; for it is not meet that men who will not abide my law shall preside over my priesthood.[20]

Within a few days after the revelation was read to the apostles and approved by them, Heber J. Grant was ordained an apostle and sustained as one of the Twelve and Seymour B. Young was set apart as one of the Seven Presidents of the First Council of the Seventy. Both men were already married, Young for more than fifteen years and Grant for five, to their first wives. Neither had previously intended to contract a plural marriage, but both agreed to follow the direction of President Taylor and began seeking additional wives. Eighteen months later both found the women they were seeking among the daughters of Daniel H. Wells.[21]

Seymour B. Young, who was a son of Joseph Young, Brigham's older brother, married Abby C. Wells, the daughter of Daniel and Hannah, on April 28, 1884. Although he was undoubtedly worried about the possible prosecution of his son-in-law under the Edmunds Act, Daniel officiated at their marriage in the Endowment House. Young's first wife, Ann Elizabeth Riter, with whom he already had seven children and was expecting an eighth, gave her reluctant consent even though she was not enamored of the plural marriage principle.[22]

A month later, Heber J. Grant married Emily H. Wells, the daughter of Daniel and Martha, as his third wife. They were married by Daniel one day after Grant was sealed to his second wife, Hulda Augusta Winters. Both Augusta and Lucy Stringham, Grant's first wife, gave their consent and were present at the ceremony in which he wed Emily. As with Abby's plural marriage, Daniel was concerned about the prosecution of Grant and about the legal status of any children born to the couple who would be considered illegitimate under provisions of the Edmund Act.[23]

His concerns were well-founded. By the end of the year Abby Young was expecting her first child and, within a few months thereafter, so was Emily Grant. Although the good news of the pending births that would ordinarily have been publicly announced was kept secret from all but family members, word of the plural marriages of church authorities to members of the prominent Wells family could not be long suppressed. It soon became widely known in the community and the federal anti-polygamy prosecutors began building cases against Young and Grant. Both were obliged to maintain a low public profile to avoid arrest.[24]

Daniel and several members of his family attended the dedication of the Logan Temple in May 1884, traveling most of the distance by rail on the Utah Northern Railroad in company with the First Presidency and other general authorities. The anti-polygamy crusade that developed following the passage of the Edmunds Act was by then well underway and federal marshals were actively seeking to arrest church leaders who had long practiced polygamy. Although Daniel traveled openly with his wives and children, as did President John Taylor who dedicated the temple, they were not approached by any lawmen and the three dedicatory sessions were completed without incident.[25]

By February of the following year, however, warrants for the arrest of many LDS general authorities were issued and they went into hiding to avoid arrest. Daniel did not leave Salt Lake City, but he avoided most public appearances where he might be apprehended by federal marshals. He was one of the most well-known polygamists in the territory and his distinctive appearance made it impossible for him to travel anywhere without being recognized. Consequently, he kept mostly to his home and relied on family members and friends to give him warning of any threat. That threat was in the making, but before it became imminent another crisis arose that seriously disrupted the lives of all Daniel's family members and ultimately cost the life of one of them.[26]

A month after her return from Europe with her husband, John Q. Cannon, Annie Wells Cannon gave birth to her second child in July 1884. She named her new daughter Louise after her younger sister Louisa Wells, universally known as Louie, to whom she was very close.

At the October conference that year, Rob Sloan, a long-time suitor of Louie Wells, was called on a mission to Great Britain. John Q. Cannon reported in the conference on his mission in England and was sustained as second counselor in the church's Presiding Bishopric, making him, at age twenty-seven, one of the youngest general authorities.[27]

On November 2, 1884, the *Salt Lake Tribune* published an article by city editor Joseph Lippman in which he claimed that John Q. Cannon and his wife's sister, Louie Wells, had traveled separately to Logan in September or October and had secretly married one another in the temple there. Lippman cited as his source the "son of a Mormon high up in authority in the Mormon Church." He also claimed that John Q. had been pushed to secretly court and marry Louie by his father, Apostle George Q. Cannon, who was first counselor to President John Taylor. The senior Cannon was anxious to have his sons enter plural marriages in accordance with President Taylor's revelation that only men who did so were worthy to be called as general church authorities. According to Lippman, George Q. had even smoothed the way for his son John Q. to win Louie as his bride by sending her current suitor on a mission to get him out of the way, even though, as the article stated, "it was well known that the habits of this journalist were anything but in accord with those of a person one would expect to be sent on a mission for any faith."[28]

The day after the article appeared, Louie Wells's mother, Emmeline B. Wells, accompanied by her non-Mormon lawyer and son-in-law, Maj. William W. Woods, personally visited the *Tribune*'s editor-in-chief, accused him of printing lies that defamed Louie and John Q, and demanded a retraction of Lippman's article. Major Woods also published a statement in the next day's *Tribune* stating that he was in a position to know the facts of the matter and knew that the article was false. He also said that he had "the positive statement of Mrs. Wells—a lady whose word neither Mormon nor Gentile will question, that it is not true." Woods's "card" was accompanied in the *Tribune* by the paper's weak retraction to the effect that the major's information was entirely trustworthy while their reporter's informant was not.[29]

The main premise of Lippman's article was a lie; John Q. Cannon and Louie Wells were not married. Louie would never have deceived her parents, with whom she had a happy and close relationship, about her marriage and would certainly have wanted her father to perform her wedding ceremony. John Q., although he had some weaknesses, deeply loved his wife Annie and would not have disgraced her and her sister by a secret marriage that would also have subjected him to prosecution under the Edmunds Act.

The source of the article was revealed a few days later to be Angus Cannon Jr., a cousin of John Q. who was known to be fond of liquor and to have a loose tongue. Angus Jr.'s father, according to John Q.'s brother Abram Cannon, had long been "greatly troubled about his son Angus, who lies, steals, drinks and even commits adultery without scruple."[30]

The *Tribune*'s article and Will Woods's response produced a number of editorials from the *Deseret News* and the *Salt Lake Herald*, but the most direct reaction came from John Q. Cannon himself. He was out of town when the *Tribune*'s article appeared and was furious to learn of it on his return. He went to the *Tribune*'s offices several times looking for Lippman, who wisely absented himself. On November 9, however, John Q. encountered Lippman in front of City Hall on the corner of First South and First East. What followed was later written up in the *Deseret News* by John Q. himself, who had resumed his job as editor of the paper upon his return from Europe.

> Mr. Cannon accosted the Tribune Scribe with: "Your name's Lipman [sic], I believe."
>
> "It is," replied the one addressed.
>
> "Mine is Cannon and I want you to get right down on your knees and apologize for the lie you published about me last Sunday."
>
> "I never published any lie about you."

"You did and you knew it was such at the time. Now I want you to apologize."

"I will not."

The words were not out of his mouth when he found himself flying through the air as if a cannon-ball had struck him. He was knocked about ten feet and lit on the back of his neck and shoulders. Before he could scramble to his feet, Mr. Cannon stood over him and was reaching for a little rawhide in his pocket, with the intention of giving him a taste of its keenness, when the prostrate reporter began to cry piteously and beg for his life, making all sorts of promises about future good conduct, and at the same time wriggling his fingers in front of him as if he expected the grim visage of death to stare at him from the muzzle of a revolver.[31]

Police from City Hall broke up the fight and arrested John Q. for assault. He pled guilty the following week and paid a $15 fine. Strangely, John Q. seems to have seen only himself as the injured party and said nothing to defend the character and reputation of Louie Wells. He did not publish any card personally denying the *Tribune*'s accusations even though news reports of the fracas with Lippman restated them in more lurid form. His actions only served to intensify the defamation of Louie Wells in the press. John Q.'s subsequent behavior confirmed that his main concerns were his own and his family's reputations and church positions, not those of his wife Annie or her sister Louie.

The reason John Q. did not publish a complete denial of Lippman's article nor rise to defend the honor of Louie Wells was probably because, among the story's false claims about his alleged courtship and secret plural marriage were several grains of truth. John Q. and Louie were very close to one another and had lived in the same household off and on ever since his marriage to Annie. George Q. Cannon did want his sons to enter plural marriage and had pressured them to do so in order to be worthy, as defined by President Taylor, of being called as general authorities. John Q. had been called as a general authority and so was presumed to be seeking to comply with the plural marriage requirement. Rob Sloan, Louie's erstwhile boyfriend, had been called on a mission by George Q. Cannon and served honorably for the next two years under the leadership of Daniel H. Wells. Annie Wells loved her sister Louie and wanted her to marry John Q. And finally, Louie and John Q. cared deeply for one another and may well have been romantically involved by the time the *Tribune*'s incendiary article was published. The publicity surrounding them eventually died down, but all of these factors remained active and over time led to tragedy.[32]

In late November, Daniel H. Wells was called to again preside over the European Mission. His appointment, made by President Taylor and his counselor, George Q. Cannon, was both sudden and secretive. As Daniel described it in a letter to his wife sent from New York after his hasty departure from Utah, it was also a surprise to almost everyone.

> Whatever may have been the motive, or seeming impossibility of my leaving, I could do no other than to accept the appointment at once, which I did, and it was very secret. I was taken aside, even from the Council, to make it known to me, with no one present but Brothers Taylor and Cannon and I was desired to go at once. It was on Thanksgiving Day. You can judge what my feelings were, and what would have been the feelings of all the family on that occasion if they had known of it. I had to drop everything and arrange matters as speedily as possible.[33]

At least two possible reasons for Daniel's call, beyond the obvious need for a qualified person to fill the position, are evident. Taylor and Cannon may have had warning of his imminent arrest or they may have feared some reaction on his part regarding John Q. Cannon's relationship with his daughter. Both of these factors likely influenced the call, or at least the haste in which it was done, but Daniel chose to accept the assignment as coming from the Lord and acted as quickly as he could.

The respect in which he was held by the Mormon and non-Mormon portions of the community alike made federal authorities reluctant to charge him, perhaps fearing it would be difficult to impanel a jury, even of non-Mormons, who would convict him. They also hesitated to call him as a witness against other polygamists in view of his refusal to testify in the Miles case, even when he was sent to prison. The public outpouring of support that followed his incarceration proved that he was not a good defendant or witness to pursue in future prosecutions.

The fact that none of Daniel's children had, through the end of 1883, contracted a plural marriage may also have persuaded federal authorities that he and his family were trying to obey the anti-polygamy statute. But the 1884 plural marriages of Abby Wells to Seymour B. Young and Emily Wells to Heber J. Grant greatly increased the probability that Young, Grant, and Daniel H. Wells, who performed their plural marriages, would be arrested and charged with open defiance of the law.[34]

Daniel's calling gave him a valid reason to leave Utah and thereby avoid prosecution under the Edmunds Act or being summoned to testify in any trials, but he had to vanish from the city like a thief in the night. "It was necessary for him to go at once and in absolute secrecy. He would have been stopped if the least intimation of his departure became known. Hence, the haste and secrecy was imperative."[35]

Having left without telling anyone, Daniel wrote home to explain his actions and ask his wife Louisa to join him in England. "I have taken berth on the Steamer 'Arizona' and expect to sail on Tuesday the 23rd at 9 a.m. Only wish you were with me . . . I should have had you along, though it might have looked a little like kidnapping to take you off in that way . . . and so I thought I would get away myself as easy as I could, and have you, if you would conclude to come, to come afterwards."[36]

Louisa did agree to join him, was in fact pleased to be asked and immediately wrote her acceptance and set about making ready to go. Daniel was both relieved and pleased by her response. "Now I am delighted to learn that you take it all so kindly, and look forward to joining me in Liverpool so favorably . . . I believe it will do you good, and that you can do good by coming . . . May the God of Heaven bless and sustain us all is my constant prayer."[37]

Louisa's only request was that her youngest son, Melvin, accompany her on the trip. To this Daniel gladly acceded. "Your very welcome letter came today with Melvin's enclosed. Certainly I would be very glad to have Mell come with you on a mission, wouldn't I tho. He could do a great deal of good and be a comfort to us both. I did think that I would like him to go to school for another year as he is rather young to go on a mission, but I do not know but that it will be the best school that he can go to."[38]

Melvin D. Wells, age seventeen, was called on a mission to England and was also delegated to assist his mother on the journey across the Atlantic. Because, under the civil law, Louisa was Daniel's only legal wife (his first wife, Eliza, had divorced him in 1853), she could travel openly without fear of anti-polygamy difficulty in America or Europe. But she definitely felt more at ease traveling with a male escort rather than alone.

Although Daniel was still angered about the maligning of his daughter Louie and John Q. Cannon and was reluctant to leave her and the rest of his family while the scandal remained current, he obeyed the counsel of John Taylor and George Q. Cannon, to get out of town before the marshals could apprehend him. He departed alone in early December, traveled by train to New York City in a week, and embarked on the *Arizona* within a few days. After a pleasant voyage, he arrived in Liverpool about midnight on New Year's Eve.[39]

He immediately plunged into the work of the European Mission, presiding at conferences in various cities, supervising the work of the missionaries in Great Britain and on the European Continent, editing the *Millennial Star* newspaper, directing the leasing and provisioning of emigration ships, and organizing the companies of Saints who set sail each spring on their way west to the gathering in Zion. His statement to the

Saints published shortly after his arrival indicates how unexpected was his call and with what haste he was obliged to begin his new assignment. Also clear in his remarks are his continuing dedication to missionary work and his determination to fulfill the assignment given him:

> Quite unexpectedly to myself, I assure you, have I been called by the First Presidency of the Church of Jesus Christ of Latter-day Saints to a mission in a foreign land. I am required by my appointment and instructions to take charge of, and preside over the European Mission.
>
> It is with an unfeigned feeling of distrust in my own ability and powers, that I assume so great and onerous a responsibility, and I can therefore rely only upon the faith, prayers and patience of the Saints, and the blessings and power of Almighty God for aid to enable me, in any degree, to successfully perform the duties to which I am so suddenly called . . . I call upon all the Elders and Saints now in these lands to come up to the help of the Lord against the mighty, for He has given us the privilege to be coworkers with Him in this great work, and we should be submissive to His will, and work in accordance with His laws.[40]

The European Mission was considerably larger in 1885 than when Daniel began his labors there in 1864. That year only fifty-two missionaries were called in the entire church and seventy-one the following year. When Daniel became president of the European Mission for the second time, there were seventy-eight missionaries laboring in thirteen conferences in Great Britain and dozens more at work in Scandinavia, Germany, Switzerland, and other countries across the continent as far east as Turkey.[41]

Four days after his arrival in Liverpool, Daniel traveled to Glasgow and was the concluding speaker at a conference held in that city. He told those present that he was pleased to again meet with church members in Scotland after an absence of twenty-five years. Three weeks later he presided at the London Conference held at Whitechapel where he spoke of his personal knowledge of the Prophet Joseph Smith and his testimony that Joseph's mission of restoration of the gospel was divinely inspired. His remarks were particularly moving to many recent converts who had never before heard the witness of a man who was a close friend of Joseph and had himself been converted through the teachings he had received from the first Mormon prophet.[42]

Daniel had also planned to be present at the Welsh Conference held at Merthyr Tydfil, in the Railway Inn Assembly Rooms, on the first Sunday in March, but the preceding day he received word that the steamship

City of Berlin was arriving in port and that his wife Louisa and son Melvin were on board. He went to meet them, leaving the Welsh Conference President, W. D. Williams, to preside at the meeting in his stead.[43]

Louisa and Melvin had departed New York on February 12 aboard the *City of Chester* bound for Liverpool with several missionaries. The voyage started well, but three days out, a violent storm struck that smashed the cabin skylights and flooded the passenger compartments. One of the ship's lifeboats was carried away and the passengers dared not go on deck again until the storm had blown over. The following Saturday a worse tempest hit the *Chester*. The ship's rudder was torn off and the bowsprit was also carried away. The wheelhouse was heavily damaged and the ship remained without steering for three days until a tug boat sighted it and took it in tow into Queenstown. There the passengers disembarked and boarded the *City of Berlin*, which took them on to Liverpool, completing a harrowing voyage of sixteen days that left all the Saints and particularly Louisa, considerably worse for the experience.[44]

Daniel's daughter, Abby Wells Young, now the plural wife of Seymour B. Young and pregnant with her first child, also arrived in Liverpool in early 1885 to reside temporarily with her father. Abby traveled under the assumed name Abby Wells Chapin and left Utah to avoid involvement in any attempt to prosecute her husband for polygamy. Her daughter, Hannah Louisa Young, was born in Liverpool in September 1885. So serious was the ongoing threat of prosecution for Seymour B. Young that Abby and her daughter continued to use the surname Chapin while in England and for many years after their return to America. Even Abby's 1930 death certificate listed her as "aka Abbie Wells Chapin."[45]

The new arrivals quickly settled in at the mission headquarters and Melvin Wells took up his duties as a traveling elder in the Liverpool Conference. He also attended conference meetings with Daniel, beginning with the Manchester Conference a week after his arrival, at which he and Daniel both spoke.

Two weeks after her arrival, Louisa accompanied Daniel, Charles W. Penrose and a few other Mormons on a tour of the Mersey River Railway Tunnel then under construction beneath the river in Liverpool. The excursion required a seventy-foot descent by elevator followed by a walk of more than a mile through the tunnel and an equal ascent on the other side of the river. Louisa and Daniel were fatigued enough by their exertions to opt for a tram ride back to their quarters while the others in the group walked home.[46]

In April, Daniel presided at another Glasgow Conference meeting and spoke more extensively than he had just after his arrival. On the same day, the ship *Milo*, which had sailed from Copenhagen on April 2 with seventy-three Saints on board, completed its voyage across the North

Sea and arrived in Hull, England. The emigrants, joined by ten more who had come from Christiania, Norway, continued their journey to Liverpool the following day. There Daniel and his counselor Charles W. Penrose arranged a week's accommodations for them until they could board the S. S. *Wisconsin*, the first ship of the 1885 transatlantic emigration season. A total of 187 Mormons, including more than a hundred from Great Britain along with nineteen missionaries returning home, made the ten-day voyage on the *Wisconsin* and arrived in New York on April 22. Another six days of travel was required for the entire company to reach Salt Lake City by train before the end of the month.[47]

There were fewer converts made in the European Mission during Daniel's second term as president than were baptized during his first mission and, consequently, a smaller number of Saints who immigrated to Utah each season. But the testimonies of the new converts were as deep and sincere as those of any who had gone before them. Prior to leaving on a later ship, one recently confirmed member wrote Daniel to express his feelings upon receiving the gospel from the elders:

> I was baptized into the Church of Jesus Christ of Latter-day Saints and confirmed a member on the 17th April, 1884. Since then, have been the happiest and also the most painful times I have experienced in all my life. Happiest: in that I know I have passed from death unto life and have been made an heir to eternal glory, in as much as I am willing to endure unto the end. Most painful: in that some of the dearest ties of affection I ever formed have been severed, and I have been branded as a blackguard, a deceiver, a deluded fool and everything that is associated with evil. Yet, notwithstanding, I rejoice in the position wherein I stand, and think myself honored to be accused of all such things for the Gospel's sake. How truly can they who are born of the spirit say: "Old things are passed away; behold, all things are become new." Compared with the darkness we once walked in, the light in which we now walk is indeed a marvel and a wonder . . .
>
> In conclusion, my desire is to leave here and gather to Zion, that I may be the more able to assist in advancing the work of the Lord, and hoping soon to meet in Zion many of those I have formerly associated with in the land of my birth,
>
> > I remain your brother in the Gospel,
> > James Gillespie[48]

As Gillespie stated, opposition to the Mormons was strong in Britain, as well as in other European countries. Antagonism was often especially fierce among the relatives of those converted. Whole families and whole congregations were less frequently brought into the church and the missionaries usually found only one or two individuals in a family who would accept the gospel, only to be ostracized and disowned by their relatives when they did so. The rejection of their new faith by friends and family led many new converts to seek immigration to Zion as soon as possible. They were joined by others who had previously delayed going or been unable to pay their passage. The result was that more Saints actually immigrated to America from Great Britain than joined the church in that country during Daniel's tenure as president of the European Mission. The exodus left fewer members remaining in Britain when he left to come home than when he arrived, but enough congregations still functioned for the missionaries to have adequate pulpits from which to preach and to bring new investigators into the church.[49]

The second company of the 1885 season's emigrants also sailed from Liverpool on the S. S. *Wisconsin*, on May 16 after its return from New York following the April voyage. Having found the *Wisconsin* a seaworthy and well-handled ship, the mission presidency arranged passage on it whenever possible. The church no longer leased an entire ship, as had been done in the 1850s and 1860s, but members still traveled as an organized group under a chosen leader and counselors, in the same manner as in past years. This second company, organized by Daniel under the leadership of Nathaniel M. Hodges, included 197 British, 1 Swedish, and 61 Swiss and German emigrants, plus 15 returning missionaries. The ship arrived without incident before the end of May and most of the company reached Salt Lake City by the second week of June.[50]

The S. S. *Wisconsin* made a third voyage in June carrying a company of Saints assembled from Scandinavia, Germany, Switzerland, and Great Britain. The steamship *Cato* brought two Danish Mormons from Copenhagen to Hull and the steamship *Angelo* brought forty more from Christiana. These groups arrived in Liverpool by rail in mid-June and the Mission Presidency arranged accommodations for them until the rest of the transatlantic company was assembled. Two hundred sixty-three more Danish and Swedish members sailed from Copenhagen on the chartered steamer *Panther* and arrived in Hull on June 19 after a stormy four-day trip. They went directly to the *Wisconsin* in Liverpool and boarded the ship the same day. The next day the other Scandinavian passengers boarded along with 18 Swiss and German emigrants and 158 more from the various conferences in Great Britain. Some 30 returning missionaries also joined the company bringing the total number of Saints on board to 541.[51]

Daniel called all the traveling Saints of this voyage to a meeting on board at which he proposed Jorgen Hansen as president of the company with W. C. A. Smoot as his first, and J. G. M. Barnes as his second counselor. They were sustained by unanimous vote and, after songs were sung in several languages, Daniel blessed the company and the ship that would carry them. The *Wisconsin* departed Liverpool on June 20 and arrived in New York on the first day of July. The company reached Salt Lake City on July 7.[52]

While he was assembling emigrant companies and arranging for their accommodations and passage to America, Daniel also maintained a grueling travel schedule around the British Mission. Between April 11, when the *Wisconsin* sailed on the season's first emigrant voyage, and the end of August when the ship made its fourth crossing, he presided and spoke at no less than twelve conferences: he was at Liverpool on April 12, Nottingham on April 19, London on April 26, a district meeting in Liverpool on May 10, Leeds on May 17, Norwich on June 14, Glasgow on July 12, Birmingham on July 26, London on August 2, Sheffield on August 15, Liverpool on August 23, Merthyr Tydfil in Wales on August 30, and Manchester on September 13.[53]

Although opposition to Latter-day Saint beliefs was strong in many parts of Britain, most Mormon meetings were peaceful occasions at which members could hear sermons delivered by their leaders and outsiders could observe the faith in operation. The Sheffield conference, however, proved an exception. A previous meeting in that city had been broken up by the actions of an apostate former Mormon, as described in the *Millennial Star*:

> It will be remembered by our readers, that on the occasion of a Conference of the Latter-day Saints in Sheffield, last December, the passions of the rough element of society in that town were so inflamed by a miserable, lowlived apostate, whose name we will not honor by mentioning, that the meeting of the Saints was broken up almost as soon as commenced, and it required the utmost efforts of the Elders to preserve themselves from personal violence, a task for which, fortunately, they were physically well qualified.[54]

The August 1885 Sheffield conference was held in the Albert Hall, a meetinghouse with seating for five hundred persons and standing room for perhaps two hundred more. Having learned the necessity from previous experience, Daniel and his counselors arranged for a number of police to attend all three sessions. The precaution was well justified as the afternoon meeting was filled to capacity and not entirely with Saints.

> ... the same contemptible creature who created the disturbance last year put in an appearance on the outside of the hall, where he was destined to remain, as the police would not admit him, so he harangued an ever increasing multitude in the street. So vehement was he in his denunciation of the Elders that the curiosity of many of his hearers was aroused, and they were induced to leave him and enter the hall. An immense audience was the result, some appearing to be much interested in the meeting, while others were evidently there for the purpose of creating a disturbance ... Brute force and ruffianism were there like hounds in their leashes, ready to howl and rend and tear as soon as the apparently slight restraints should be removed or weaken in their moral force. Even the Saints moved uneasily in their seats and craned their necks with anxious expectancy at every little unusual sound, thinking that the storm was about to burst upon them, so that the speaker did not have even the benefit of their undivided attention ... Occasionally, when the rough element seemed about to break forth into tumult, a timely and energetic rebuke from Elder Penrose would restore comparative quiet, and thus the meeting went on until the close of the discourse, which was replete with instruction and accompanied by the power and demonstration of the Holy Spirit.
>
> But with the end of the discourse came the end of that moral control which had been so marvelously exhibited. The meeting was dismissed, and when the Elders left the hall, they were immediately assailed with shouts and cries of a most demoniac character.[55]

Daniel, who had been identified to all as the highest-ranking Mormon in Great Britain and who was easily recognized, was the principle target of the crowd. What happened next is described by Elder Reuben S. Collett, a missionary who stood about six feet, four inches tall and weighed over two hundred pounds:

> While the meeting was going on a mob gathered on the outside. The question was, how to get the Elders out and evade the mob. As we have said, the hall was a large one. It had two departments on the ground floor. The Salvation Army occupied the south side and the Latter-day Saints the north side. The manager of the building suggested that we dismiss our meeting at the same time they dismissed theirs and that the two congregations go out together.

We did this, but fearing for President Wells, slipped him out of the side door with some of the Elders, hoping he would escape unnoticed. Soon he was surrounded by a dozen or fifteen men. His white hair and beard were conspicuous above the heads of the mob. They were pushing and jostling him about trying to knock him off his feet and then if they trampled him to death no one person could be held responsible for it.

From the door, I had about ten feet clear space and, making a lunge for the mob surrounding President Wells, I hit them with all the force I had, broke through and reached his side. He had lost his hat. His hair and clothes were disheveled, but he was perfectly cool and calm and was using his heavy walking stick to parry the men off. I succeeded in getting him into a cab, gave the driver a silver crown and the address of the conference house, and told him to get away quickly, which he did.[56]

Daniel was not injured, but so threatening and violent was the opposition at the close of the afternoon meeting, that some suggested that the evening meeting be canceled. After being assured by the police of their continued protection, it was decided to go ahead with the concluding session. Out of concern for his age and physical health, however, "President Wells was induced, by the persuasions of the brethren, to retire to his lodging and not expose himself again to the violence of the mob, who seemed to direct their fury principally against him."[57]

The evening meeting, though not as well-attended as the afternoon session, was orderly and reverent. A crowd again formed outside the building and accosted the elders when they came out. Escorted by the police, they moved away, surrounded and pursued by a howling mass that soon numbered several thousand persons. The police felt it unwise for the elders to proceed directly to their lodgings and thereby expose their homes to an attack and they instead took refuge in a police station until the anti-Mormon crowd dispersed.[58]

On August 23, the steamship *Cato* brought another company of emigrant Saints, ninety-three in number, from Copenhagen. They arrived in Hull and continued by rail to Liverpool where they rested a few days in rooms arranged for them by the Mission Presidency. Another group, numbering thirty-eight, sailed from Christiania on the *Angelo* and joined the larger Copenhagen contingent in England. On August 28 the Scandinavians boarded the *Wisconsin*, together with a number of British Saints and several returning missionaries. The company was organized by Daniel with Elder J. W. Thornley as president and Niels C. Mortensen and

Thomas Biesinger as his counselors. The ship sailed on August 29 and the company arrived in Salt Lake City on September 14.[59]

In late September, Daniel left on tour to visit Mormon congregations in Scandinavia. He was accompanied by Charles W. Penrose and George Osmond, as well as Melvin, who served as his assistant in both church duties and temporal needs. Melvin sent a letter back to Liverpool soon after the party arrived in Denmark.

> We are having a most excellent time among our Scandinavian brethren and sisters. Of course we cannot understand them, nor they us; but the very same spirit (that of the Gospel) is prevalent among them. We held two good meetings in Christiania, and Brother Penrose delivered two excellent sermons. Brother Lund took notes and then interpreted to the people. They paid marked attention all the time, although they could not understand anything that was said. We have visited some very interesting places here as well as in Copenhagen, and have enjoyed ourselves exceedingly. The brethren have been and are as kind to us as they can be. We expected to leave here for Stockholm this morning [October 1], but we found on our arrival at the station that the time of starting was changed, so we have to wait until 4 p.m., and will thereby lose one day which we would otherwise have had in Stockholm. It has rained all the time since we came here, so you can imagine it is not so pleasant to get around as it might be.[60]

After spending about two weeks in Denmark, one in Sweden, and a few days in Oslo, Norway, Daniel and the other elders returned to Liverpool. Daniel did not visit the other countries encompassed within the European Mission, apparently feeling that his lack of language skills made him less effective as a church leader among foreign cultures than those converts who were native born or missionaries who had mastered a new tongue.

The fifth and final company of emigrating Saints in the 1885 season sailed from Liverpool on October 24 aboard the S. S. *Nevada*. It consisted of 162 British, 119 Scandinavian, 6 Swiss and German Saints, and 26 returning missionaries. The Scandinavian group had previously sailed from Copenhagen on the steamship *Bravo*, under the leadership of Fred T. Christensen.[61]

One of the returning missionaries was Melvin D. Wells, who had arrived in England with his mother Louisa only eight months previously. He had planned on two years of missionary service, but was asked by his

Figure 21.3. Portrait of Daniel H. Wells made in Copenhagen, Denmark, during his second mission as President of the European Mission, 1885.

father to accompany his seriously-ailing mother Louisa as she returned home.

Louisa had considered Daniel's request for her to accompany him to England as a missionary calling, but her health was fragile when she left Salt Lake City and the English climate did not agree with her. She took great interest in the labors of the missionaries, and she did everything in her power to help and encourage them, including on several occasions, supporting the elders when they held outdoor meetings in the parks and streets. She stood by her brethren and faced the ridicule and abuse that was sometimes heaped upon them. Her testimony of Mormonism, backed by more than forty years of enduring the trials of the faith strengthened the missionary work, but with each passing month she grew weaker and less able to continue. She did not accompany Daniel on his trip to the Continent and when he returned in late October, he was so concerned at the change in her appearance that had been wrought in a month's time that he insisted she return home as soon as possible.[62]

At an organizing meeting held on board the *Nevada*, instructions were given by Daniel and Elder Penrose. They then proposed Elder Anton H. Lund as president of the company, with Elders C. J. Arthur and Samuel Bennion as his counselors. After singing several songs, Daniel closed the meeting with prayer, asking divine protection for the travelers. He then bid Louisa an affectionate farewell and was visibly affected as he took a last look at her white and tear-stained face. Her sorrow at their parting was likely caused more by her feeling that she was leaving her husband in a weakened condition than for her own failing health. Although Daniel said nothing, he probably knew they would not meet again in life.[63]

In contrast with Louisa and Melvin's previous tempestuous voyage on the *City of Chester*, the *Nevada* had an easy crossing and reached New York on November 4. The company of Saints arrived in Salt Lake City six days later. Louisa was exhausted, but very glad to be home and again among her sister wives and children.[64]

22

Defending against Opposition in England while Tragedy Unfolds at Home

1886–1888

A week after Louisa and Melvin Wells's departure, another of Daniel's sons, Joseph S. Wells, arrived in company with twenty-four other missionaries on the *Wisconsin*. Like his brother Melvin, he was assigned to the Liverpool Conference in the British Mission and, also like Melvin, he sometimes accompanied Daniel to other conference meetings as an assistant. This was Joseph's second European mission; he had served in Germany and Switzerland in the 1870s.[1]

Daniel did not travel outside of Britain in the following year, but maintained his heavy schedule of presiding and speaking at conferences around that country. He attended two more conferences in 1885 after his return from Scandinavia and eighteen during 1886 and early 1887. He did not attend the Liverpool Conference in April due to illness and he must have been seriously sick and confined to miss this meeting, as it was the only one that did not require him to travel. No conference was held in Sheffield due to the continuing violent opposition to the church that persisted there, but the Saints in that area held their regular weekly meetings and missionaries assigned by Daniel continued to work quietly among the people. Daniel also assigned local leaders and missionaries to preside over the conferences held in Scandinavia and the Swiss-German Mission, but he did not personally attend any of them.[2]

He sent Elder Joseph M. Tanner and Elder Jacob Spori to Turkey to investigate the prospects there for teaching Eastern Orthodox Christians about the restored gospel. They were politely, even warmly received, and the elders made use of newspaper interviews and public meetings to introduce Mormonism to Constantinople residents. Editors seemed anxious to give the message of the elders a fair hearing and they soon had to rent a room where they could meet with those who came to inquire further. Even the Minister of Public Instruction, Munif Pasha, requested an interview with them in order to learn more of their religious beliefs and history. Most of their conversations, however, were with French and German natives living in Constantinople.[3]

The two missionaries wanted to teach Turkish nationals whom, as Elder Tanner later wrote to Apostle Franklin D. Richards, were usually more Christian in their attitudes and behavior than most Europeans.

> So far as I have the spirit of discernment the Turks are the only ones, as a nation, that live so as to receive the gospel. They are far above Europeans in real Christian ethics... I cannot say what the will of the Lord may be regarding the spread of the Gospel among the Turks; but I have a great desire that they should have it in their own language, for I feel that if an opening can be made among them, there will be a great work accomplished in these lands. They are very reticent, but very courteous.[4]

Sadly, the interest level of Turkish Christians and Muslims rarely went beyond a few courteous questions. It quickly waned to indifference or even hostility when investigators learned that the Mormon Church had no paid clergy and all members were commanded to tithe.

During a visit to the Holy Land in the company of Elder Francis M. Lyman Jr., Elder Tanner had been greatly impressed by the Christian members of German-speaking colonies there who, several years earlier, had gathered in Palestine to await the second coming of Christ. Having had little success in Turkey, Elder Tanner received Daniel's permission for Elder Spori to travel to Haifa and introduce the gospel there. He arrived at his destination in August 1886, but found that his reception by both the German and Swiss Christians in Palestine was much the same as in Turkey: a general feeling of disinterest. They saw no need for priesthood authority or proper baptism and having heard negative reports about polygamy, did not find the Mormon faith appealing. Elder Spori was not discouraged, however, and spent his time visiting Jerusalem and other sacred sites where he continued to discuss the gospel and bear testimony to numerous Jews, Arabs, and German-speaking pilgrims.[5]

Five companies of Saints sailed from Liverpool to America in 1886, but together they contained fewer travelers than made the trip the previous year. The reduced emigration was caused partly by the fact that fewer converts were baptized in Great Britain during the year and partly by the relentless prosecution of the Saints by federal authorities in Utah, which made some European members hesitant to go. The first company went aboard the steamship *Nevada*, which sailed from Liverpool for New York on April 17. The group included eighty-nine Scandinavian Saints who had arrived in England from Christiana and Copenhagen, and one member from Switzerland. The rest of the 179 emigrants were from Great Britain and 17 returning missionaries were also in the company. Daniel called three of them to lead it: Elder E. T. Wooley as president, and Elders C. J. Stromberg and J. L. McMurrin as his counselors. The *Nevada* made an uneventful ten-day crossing and the company arrived in Utah in early May after some delay caused by a strike of railroad workers in Wyoming.[6]

The *Nevada* returned immediately to Liverpool and the second company of emigrants left aboard it on May 22. Daniel was still recovering from his late April illness and did not see this company off, but he sent Elders George Osmond and Frederick Schoenfeld to organize it. The diverse company included 144 members from Great Britain, 106 from Switzerland and Germany, 14 from Scandinavia, 2 from Iceland, and 1 from Holland. Twelve returning missionaries completed the complement of 279 Saints. The *Nevada* made another rapid voyage and arrived in New York on June 2.[7]

Again the *Nevada* hastened back to England to pick up the third company of Saints who boarded on June 26. three hundred seventeen Saints from Scandinavia and 101 from Great Britain plus 18 returning missionaries made up the total of 426 members. At a meeting on board ship, Daniel made a few remarks, which were interpreted in Swedish by Elder C. F. Olsen, and then organized the company with Elder Olsen as president, and Elders L. John Nuttal Jr. and R. S. Collett as counselors. The reliable *Nevada* made the crossing in eleven days and, although there were four deaths on the way, the remainder of the company reached Utah in good spirits.[8]

A small company of Saints from Iceland arrived in England too late to join the third company of emigrants aboard the *Nevada* and Daniel was obliged to make separate arrangements for them on the steamship *Alaska*. Since none of the Icelanders spoke English well, he felt that some American Mormons were needed to lead them and called Elder John D. Burt and Robert Campbell for that purpose.

> After presiding in Scotland a year, President Wells sent a telegram directing me to come to Liverpool and take charge of a company of Iceland Saints, twenty-three in number, who were going to Utah. On receipt of this telegram I left Brother

Richie in charge of the office and hastened to Liverpool, where I found the emigrants were already on board the ship which was ready to sail. There was little time for exchanging compliments with our co-laborers in England, so after shaking hands with President Wells and the brethren and sisters in the office, Brother Robert Campbell and myself boarded a tug in the harbor and steamed out to the noble and majestic Guion [Company] liner, Alaska, which sailed out of the harbor in about an hour with we two and the Icelanders abound for America, this being the 10th of July, 1886.[9]

Finally, on October 13 Daniel placed the final company of the year aboard the steamship *British King*. It numbered 307 Saints, including some returning missionaries; 103 Scandinavians and others from Great Britain, Germany, and Switzerland. After a rough fourteen-day voyage, this company arrived at Philadelphia in late October. The same day they landed, the emigrants started westward by rail via Baltimore, Chicago, and Omaha and arrived in Salt Lake City on November 1.[10]

As Daniel pursued his labors through the year, the news he received from home was grim. A number of church leaders were being prosecuted for polygamy under the Edmunds Act. The still more oppressive Edmunds-Tucker Act, which disenfranchised church members and enabled the federal government to seize church property and assets, was pending before Congress. President Taylor and several other general authorities were in hiding to avoid arrest and Daniel's two polygamous sons-in-law had been obliged to maintain their plural wives outside of Utah for the same reason.

Mrs. Emily Wells Grant, third wife of Apostle Heber J. Grant, arrived in England early in 1886 to reside with Daniel until after the birth of her first child. Martha Deseret Grant was born in April and she and her mother remained in England through the rest of the year. Like Abby Wells Young, Emily Wells Grant was able to obtain a birth record for her daughter in the United Kingdom without fear of prosecution for polygamy.

Seymour B. Young's wife Abby Wells Young, who had come to England in 1885 for the birth of her first child, was expecting again and was relocated by her husband to Denver. She was still using the surname Chapin and her second child was due in mid-1887.[11]

On June 19, Daniel received a cablegram telling him that Louisa Free Wells had died the previous day. He had feared for her health since sending her home with Melvin the previous October. Her letters to him since then had remained cheerful, but other family members advised him privately that she was declining. Her death was not a surprise, but it was nevertheless a severe shock. They had been married more than thirty-seven years and Louisa, who was at least four years older than any of Daniel's other wives except Eliza, was the acknowledged anchor of the family structure. Daniel grieved her passing deeply and the family events which followed no doubt made the absence of her stabilizing influence still more keenly felt.[12]

The scandal caused by the *Salt Lake Tribune*'s assertion that John Q. Cannon and Louie Wells were secretly married, that had erupted just before Daniel left for England, had died down within a few weeks, but the grain of truth contained within the newspaper article continued to develop. John Q. and Louie were, in fact, romantically attracted to one another, possibly before the *Tribune*'s story broke, and definitely after it. John Q. was still in love with his wife Annie and their third child was born in 1886, but he also fell in love with Louie and, with Annie's encouragement, they pursued the relationship that all three young people hoped would culminate by John Q. marrying Louie and the sisters living together with their husband. All were devout in their belief in polygamy; all came from polygamous family backgrounds, and all felt certain that their parents would approve their plans to marry.[13]

But John Q.'s father, George Q. Cannon, first counselor in the Presidency of the Church, would not give him approval to marry Louie while the threat of prosecution under the Edmunds Act remained large. He wanted his eldest son, a recently called member of the Presiding Bishopric, to wait until a more auspicious time to wed Louie. George Q. was under constant threat of arrest; his brother Angus was already in prison on a conviction for polygamy and he did not want John Q. to suffer the same penalty. He felt that, in time, the Lord would provide the way for John Q. and Louie to marry.[14]

As often happens, however, passion overcame restraint. Deeply in love and sure they would eventually marry, John Q. and Louie became intimate and Louie became pregnant. Sometime during the summer of 1886, Louie miscarried. No record exists of exactly when this event happened or who may have known about her condition and treated her medically for it. Louie's mother, Emmeline, was almost certainly aware of her relationship with John Q., but her father was not available to counsel her. In the male-dominated Mormon society of that time, Daniel's absence left the welfare of his daughter to the judgment of other older men who did not have her protection or even her best interests as their first priority.[15]

If Daniel had been available and aware of John Q. and Louie's situation, he would undoubtedly have advised them to marry immediately; would have performed the ceremony for them and then let them commence their repentance for the sin of premarital sexual relations in private, counseling with their bishop or other church leaders. Daniel had himself married Louisa before she was divorced from her first husband

and Hannah when she was eight months pregnant with another man's child. He had also presided at marriages that had been consummated before the couple wed. He understood clearly that church doctrine did not require the public humiliation of the sinner before forgiveness could be obtained but rather the best restitution possible in the circumstances followed by sincere repentance.

The puritanical George Q. Cannon and other members of his family did not share that view, however, either for Louie or for John Q. When he confided to his younger brother Abram that he had committed adultery (he did not name Louie as his partner), the latter insisted he repeat his statement to their father, to Presiding Bishop William B. Preston, and to Stake President Angus Cannon, George Q.'s brother. Unable to face his father, John Q. made his confession to him in a letter and indicated that he planned to immediately leave Utah and go abroad with his family and Louie.[16]

George Q. forbade his son to leave and, instead, insisted that he publicly confess his transgressions at the Sunday meeting in the Tabernacle on September 5. John Q. did as his father asked, though he must surely have been in agony when he spoke.

> I have violated my covenants. I have sinned against the Lord. I have committed a grievous sin, next in our belief to the shedding of blood, and I, according to what I conceive to be right, feel to say that I have been thus guilty, and I desire to lay down my priesthood, the priesthood I have dishonored. As you, my brethren and sisters, will be called upon to pronounce judgment upon me, I ask that you will, after pronouncing judgment upon me, at least give me a chance to show that there is also some good to me.[17]

On the motion of Angus Cannon, John Q. was excommunicated from the church by a vote of the congregation. The same afternoon he "suffered a thousand deaths in telling Annie, Louie, and Sister Wells . . . of his fall from the Church." They had not been at the Tabernacle meeting and probably had no knowledge of the course of action that George Q. Cannon and his family had determined upon. All must have been both stunned and horrified to be indirectly condemned in such a public spectacle, but no record of their reaction remains.[18]

Worse was to come for the Wells women and John Q. Cannon over the next few days. According to Abram Cannon, George Q. "encouraged and advised [John] to remain right here and live down the sin he has committed as far as possible. John Q. promised to do as told." No consideration appears to have been given to the effect of this demand on John Q., his wife, Louie or anyone in the Wells family. George Q. appears to have been solely concerned about maintaining his own church position and restoring the reputation of the Cannon family. He regarded John's fall as a blot on the family name that must be expunged regardless of the cost to him or others. His next actions made that agenda even more clear.[19]

> . . . apparently at George Q. Cannon's direction, Annie Wells Cannon filed for divorce. The complaint and waiver of issuance of summons were filed on Wednesday, September 8. The findings and uncontested decree of divorce were issued on Thursday, by probate judge (and LDS bishop) Elias Smith. Federal prosecutors later claimed that this overnight divorce was improperly administered and therefore invalid. According to Louie's testimony at John Q.'s preliminary hearing a month later, John Q. then immediately asked Louie to marry him; she testified that she had told him she would "think of it." Within twenty-four hours, however, on Friday, September 10, Abram Cannon performed the marriage of John Q. and Louie Wells at the home of the now-divorced John Q. and Annie. The only witness in attendance was apparently Emmeline B. Wells. There is no record of the marriage in the Salt Lake County marriage records.[20]

The Wells and Cannon families were both wounded and grieved by the events that swirled around John Q. Cannon and Louie Wells. All of George Q.'s efforts to shield the Cannons from the fallout proved useless. The newspapers, particularly the *Tribune*, had a field day reporting on John Q.'s confession, excommunication, divorce, and marriage. He moved out of his house, again at his father's direction, and was soon arrested on a charge of violating the Edmunds Act. Annie, Louie, and Emmeline were served subpoenas to testify at his trial and placed under $1,500 bonds to assure their appearance.[21]

The preliminary hearing for John Q. was held on October 8 and featured less than truthful testimony from several witnesses, as well as weak arguments from the prosecutors who tried to establish that John Q. was a polygamist both because he had been married to Louie Wells in 1883 and because his divorce from Annie prior to marrying Louie in 1886 was invalid. Although the evidence was anything but conclusive, Judge McKay bound John Q. over, stating he was satisfied that the grand jury should determine whether to indict him. In December the grand jury issued two indictments for polygamy. John Q. was one of those charged.[22]

Daniel, still in England, was kept informed about the disaster that had befallen his family through letters that arrived after the events. He was extremely angry with John Q. and George Q.'s treatment of his daughters, but there was little he could do to help the situation from a distance. He decidedly felt that George Q. had handled the matter badly and ignored the feelings and welfare of Wells family members in the process. His opinion of John Q. as a son-in-law and George Q. as a church authority diminished as each new report of their ineptitude arrived.[23]

In November, another of Daniel's sons, Gershom B. Wells, arrived in England. He worked in the Liverpool mission office with Daniel for a few weeks and spoke at a few church meetings in the area. After that he was assigned by Daniel to work in the Swiss Mission and departed for Bern before the end of the year.[24]

Gershom brought the news that Louie was again pregnant with John Q.'s child, and probably had been since before John Q. made his confession in September. For Daniel, this development confirmed his belief that John Q. and Louie should have married immediately when her pregnancy became evident. It also convinced him that the Cannons would sacrifice Louie's interests to protect John Q. and his father in the former's coming trial. She would be pressured to lie for him and the false allegation of her earlier marriage to John Q. would be raised again. His lawyers might be able to preserve John Q.'s freedom (although not his reputation), but for Louie no good ending to the debacle was possible. The prosecution would present her condition as proof of his guilt and if, by a miracle, John Q. were found innocent of polygamy, Louie would be branded the adulteress who had broken up his marriage to her sister Annie.[25]

In November, Heber J. Grant wrote Daniel that he felt John Q. was getting poor legal advice from his lawyers and from his father George Q. Other members of the Wells family, particularly William W. Woods, felt that John Q. had behaved badly throughout the entire affair and that other members of the Cannon family had supported him with equally perverse statements and actions. Will Woods, being non-Mormon, had no interest in protecting the Cannons's reputation in the church. His testimony was a decisive factor in John Q.'s indictment for polygamy and he also threatened to prosecute his brother-in-law for his statements that damaged Louie's reputation.[26]

Daniel wrote Louie to flee and she immediately took his advice. Without the consent of John Q. or any of the Cannons, and probably without even telling them, she boarded a Central Pacific train for San Francisco and went to live with the family of her half-sister Belle W. Sears. Her mother, Emmeline, saw her off and wrote in her diary, "This is a sad beginning for the New Year. Louie gone and all so desolate. House and home left as it were forsaken."[27]

The day after Louie left Salt Lake City, Daniel's two year calling as European Mission President was completed, but he did not receive written confirmation of his release by the First Presidency until January 17. His release letter was delivered while he was attending the London conference with his replacement, Apostle George Teasdale, who had arrived in England in November from Mexico where he had been laboring as a missionary. Elder Teasdale had anticipated working for several months with his predecessor, but Daniel was extremely anxious to be gone and at once turned over his duties to the new president.[28]

When he returned to Liverpool on January 19, he immediately made arrangements to travel home, but was not able to start his journey until the latter part of February. He was exhausted and sick when he boarded the homeward bound vessel and did not improve on the voyage.[29]

Daniel's farewell statement, published in the *Millennial Star* after his departure, indicates that, despite the rigor of his labors during his presidency, he had not accomplished as much as he hoped and gave extensive credit to those who had helped him in his service. It also showed his uncertainty about his homecoming and his continued willingness to share whatever trials the Saints were enduring.

> More than two years have elapsed since our arrival in these lands, and from that time until the present we have labored to the best of our ability to promote the interests of the Cause of God and the salvation of the children of men. We do not know that the work accomplished during our presidency would be counted as a very brilliant success. Surely, so far as additions to the Church are concerned, the number falls considerably below what have been baptized in former years during a like period, and particularly is this the case in the British Isles. But if, as Jesus said, there is joy in heaven over one sinner that repenteth, and the souls of men are precious in the sight of God, then after all we may congratulate the Elders and ourselves upon the labor that has been accomplished . . .
>
> And now we go home, perhaps not to the immediate gathering place of the Saints, but to America . . . It is the desire of our heart to be at least in that land to watch the development of those circumstances which will lead to the accomplishment of Jehovah's purposes, and to assist so far as God shall give us ability and strength, in working out to a successful issue His righteous designs—and to share whatever of trial, or of

imprisonment, or distress may befall the Saints, that we may share, too, in the triumphs and blessings that will at last be awarded them.[30]

Having been warned by the First Presidency that he would be subject to arrest on his return to Salt Lake City, Daniel stayed for a time in the East after arriving in New York, first to recover his health as much as possible and then to visit relatives and congregations of the Saints along his route home. The family members he found still living were mostly distant cousins whom he had not seen in a quarter century or more. Abby Rockwell, the last of his six sisters, had died during his time in England, but he was able to visit with her children and those of Eliza Ross and Honor Raphel. He spent several months as a guest in their homes recuperating from his illness and at the same time watching reports of the government's enforcement of the newly-enacted Edmunds-Tucker Act. When it became evident that the provisions of the act would be prosecuted vigorously, Daniel determined to return home anyway, regardless of the threat of imprisonment. He finally reached Salt Lake City in July and was warmly welcomed by members of his family.[31]

Despite their happiness over his return, Daniel's family was in mourning over the death of Louie Wells, whose life ended in San Francisco in May 1887, far removed from most of her family and disgraced by the man she loved and his family. Louie had gone to California to escape the scandal of her marriage to John Q. Cannon and his subsequent indictment and trial for polygamy, but the change of locale did not help her emotional or physical health. Almost from her arrival, when she was about four months pregnant, Louie felt weakened by the separation from her family and by the maneuvering of John Q.'s lawyers, who used her absence from Utah as an excuse to delay his trial and asked her to sign an affidavit containing false statements about their relationship. By March she was physically sick as well and by April too debilitated to write to her mother. On April 5 she gave birth to a stillborn son and Belle wrote to Emmeline that her life was in danger following the delivery. Emmeline rushed to San Francisco and over the next six weeks tried desperately to nurse her daughter through the crisis. But Louie did not improve and her body began to retain fluids to an extent that soon became life-threatening. After Louie's doctors removed fourteen quarts of liquid from her failing body, she rallied briefly, but Emmeline telegraphed John Q. on May 15 to come quickly to be with his wife. He was too late. Louie died the next morning with only her mother and sister at her side.[32]

The funeral of Louie Wells proved to be another disaster for her reputation and for the Wells family, again caused by the actions of George

Q. Cannon. Daniel was still in the east when Louie's funeral was held on May 21, the same day that the casket containing her remains arrived in Salt Lake City by train from San Francisco. The service was held in John Q. Cannon's farmhouse and was attended by most of the leading Mormon families of the city. Louie's mother, Emmeline Wells, noted that the funeral was lovely, with beautiful music played and sung by Louie's friends, but she also long remembered the day in her diary as "one of the most dreadful heart-rending days of my life—the agony, the misery, the tearing asunder of the most delicate fibres of my nature was beyond all that I have ever known."[33]

The principal cause of Emmeline's distress was the address delivered to the mourners by Angus Cannon in which he publicly identified Louie Wells as an adulteress for her relationship with John Q. Cannon. This incredible statement by Cannon brought cries of "shame" from some in the audience and caused both Emmeline and Annie to faint, but Angus took no notice and went on to relate that he was revealing Louie's role at the behest of his brother George Q. Cannon. George Q. apparently felt that Louie's name should be blackened, even at her funeral, with the same sin that he had demanded his son John Q. admit publicly. This public denigration of the dead was too much even for the anti-Mormon press in Salt Lake. No newspaper in the city or in the whole territory reported Angus Cannon's disclosure, but word of it still spread widely through the comments of those who were in attendance at the funeral. To add insult to the injury, another rumor started soon after Louie's funeral that Annie Cannon had become pregnant after her divorce from John Q., creating the false impression that he had had sex outside of marriage with both Wells sisters.[34]

When Daniel arrived home in July, he was still furious at the manner in which George Q. Cannon had interfered in his son's marriages and tried to protect his own reputation and church standing at the expense of John Q. and both of his wives. Other Wells family members were also extremely angry, including Heber J. Grant and Will Woods. Grant was so incensed at the behavior of George Q. Cannon that he questioned whether he should be sustained as a counselor in the First Presidency of the church.[35]

Apostle Francis M. Lyman wrote to Joseph F. Smith that "these terrible things will, I fear, prove a death blow to Bro. D. H. Wells and bring his silver locks in sorrow to his grave. There is universal horror felt throughout Israel at the developments in that case." While he felt that "there is general sympathy for Prest. Cannon and all the innocent and injured parties," he was worried about the effect of recent statements on relations between the Wells and Cannon families.[36]

Lyman wrote again to Joseph F. Smith a month later that he was concerned that "mortal enmity" would arise between the Cannon and Wells clans. Lyman noted that, "John Q.'s doings" had shocked "all Israel" and appeared to be getting worse. "Nothing turns up to mitigate his offenses but . . . every new rumor seems to blacken the record."[37]

President John Taylor died on July 25, 1887 and his counselors in the First Presidency were released. George Q. Cannon returned to his position in the Quorum of the Twelve, but expected (and wanted) to be called again as first counselor when the First Presidency was reorganized under the leadership of Wilford Woodruff. The questions that arose about his judgment in handling the situation of John Q. Cannon and his wives did not enhance George Q.'s prospects and he attempted to soothe the feelings of the Wells family by maintaining silence concerning the matter after Louie's funeral. The Wells family also grieved privately and the fires of indignation on both sides gradually subsided until they were reignited by a chance meeting.[38]

Daniel H. Wells met with The Quorum of the Twelve and John Taylor's two counselors on August 3, 1887. The counselors, George Q. Cannon and Joseph F. Smith, were reinstated in their respective positions among the apostles, but Daniel learned in the meeting that no less than five other apostles (including Grant) were opposed to Cannon being again sustained as a member of the First Presidency. His handling of church affairs without consulting the apostles during the last days of President Taylor's administration had angered other church leaders as much as his callous handling of the Wells-Cannon tragedy had infuriated Daniel and the apostles made no effort to reorganize the First Presidency at this meeting or for months afterward.[39]

Heber J. Grant recorded that Daniel recounted to the Twelve and others in the meeting a dream he had while still in England. In the dream he saw a black rattlesnake and a young woman standing near its head while another young woman stood near its tail. Daniel held a strong hoe in his hands but did not believe he could kill the snake with one blow from the weapon. He wanted to get the two girls away from danger and then kill the snake. He had awakened at that point, before taking any action, and had soon forgotten about the dream, not believing it significant. While discussing John Q. Cannon with the apostles in the meeting, Daniel suddenly recalled the dream and realized that John Q. was the snake and the endangered girls were his daughters, Annie and Louie. Neither his grief over the treatment of his family nor his anger at John Q. and other members of the Cannon family was tempered by George Q.'s assertion that his son's "fall" had happened in "an unguarded moment" and that he was then worthy to be readmitted to church membership.[40]

The final injury in the growing feud was delivered in September by Angus Cannon, the man who had branded Louie Wells as an adulteress at her funeral. Louie's sister Mell Whitney Woods, wife of Will Woods, encountered Angus on the street in front of the Woman's Exponent office.

> Still angry about what President Cannon had said at Louie's funeral, she began scolding him, becoming so wrathful that she finally struck him on the side of the face. Almost unbelievably, President Cannon, known for his sometimes ill temper, "returned the blow" and told her that, if she did not desist, he would publish a "card," "giving all the facts in the case of John Q. . . . charging Louie with being the guilty party with him." Emmeline was "almost paralyzed" when Ort Whitney brought the news. As Emmeline described the conversation, Whitney advised Emmeline "to go up to see her [Mell] immediately and if possible to keep it out of the papers. I went and passed thru a most severely trying ordeal, one that no language can portray." When Emmeline visited Mell the next day, Mell was still sore from the blow, though "a little better—her neck is hurt & she holds her head much to one side."
>
> Abram Cannon heard the same story from Annie Wells Cannon. "At Annie's request, I went to see Father about it, and he told me to see and talk to Uncle Angus about it, and urge him for the love he bears Father to avoid resenting anything he deems an insult from the Wells family." Abram did not find Angus, but he did find John Q., who was "desperate. He says that if Uncle Angus publishes the card of which he speaks he (John) will kill him, while Annie says if such an announcement is made she will kill herself."[41]

Angus Cannon's violent and threatening response to Mell Woods's diatribe, left little doubt among any of the Wells family, including Daniel, that the Cannons meant to continue placing as much blame as possible on Louie for John Q.'s errant behavior. Daniel was deeply offended by John Q.'s callous treatment of both his daughters and still more wounded by George Q. Cannon's senseless handling of the entire matter. For the next eight months, Daniel did not speak to any member of the Cannon family except on occasions required for church business. The estrangement of the two families continued to fester as they grieved over Louie's death and John Q.'s public disgrace. It might have continued indefinitely had not the principle figures in the drama decided otherwise.

Despite the horrendous blows their relationship had endured—infidelity, divorce, excommunication, public shaming—Annie Wells and John Q. Cannon still loved one another and wanted to restore their family.

Annie's mother, Emmeline Wells, was also fond of John Q. and was very concerned for her daughter's happiness and the welfare of her grandchildren. In May 1888, at the urging of Annie and John Q., Emmeline made arrangements for reconciliation between John Q. Cannon and her husband, Daniel H. Wells. She was probably the only one who could have facilitated such a meeting as the one that occurred in the parlor of her home. No record exists of what was said but Emmeline reported afterward that things were "different than they were before," and that she could "feel much easier."[42]

The day after Daniel and John Q. resolved their differences, George Q. Cannon baptized his eldest son and confirmed him into the church again. His priesthood blessings were restored to him by Apostle Wilford Woodruff. Two days later, Daniel presided at the marriage of Annie and John Q. Cannon in the Endowment House. They were also married civilly in a ceremony presided over by Judge Elias Smith, the same person who had granted their divorce two years before. Their re-confirmed union endured for another forty-three years during which they had nine more children, a total of twelve when added to the three born before their divorce.[43]

Wilford Woodruff proposed that the First Presidency be reorganized at a meeting of the Twelve on March 20, 1888 with himself as president, George Q. Cannon as first counselor and Joseph F. Smith as second counselor. Five apostles opposed Cannon and the group spent four rancorous days arguing over his past actions and fitness for the position. Woodruff adjourned the meetings for a weekend cooling-off period and when the apostles met again on Monday, they finally came to an understanding, forgave one another for past animosities, and agreed to the reorganization proposed by Wilford Woodruff. Daniel H. Wells sustained the agreement.[44]

On April 7, 1889, after a two year delay occasioned in part by the apostles' questioning the fitness of George Q. Cannon, Wilford Woodruff was sustained as president of the LDS Church with George Q. Cannon as his first counselor and Joseph F. Smith as his second counselor. The First Presidency was sustained by Daniel H. Wells, Heber J. Grant, Seymour B. Young, and other members of the Wells family. Although Will W. Woods did not participate in the sustaining, he had by that time also become reconciled to John Q. Cannon as a member of the Wells family. In May 1892, a year after Daniel's death, John Q. Cannon was sealed to Louie Wells with Annie standing as proxy for her sister. The ceremony took place in the Manti Temple where Daniel had served as president until his death.[45]

23

Preparing for His Passing, President of the Temple, Death while still in Harness

1887–1891

Daniel was seventy-two years old when he returned to Salt Lake City in July 1887. His illness during his second term as president of the European Mission and the months he spent recuperating in New York made him keenly aware that his remaining time was limited. He began setting his affairs in order so that his family would be secure and adequately provided for in the future.

President Grover Cleveland did not sign the Edmunds-Tucker Act, believing it might be unconstitutional, but he allowed it to become law without his signature and federal prosecutors immediately began prosecuting cases based on its provisions. Daniel realized that, with this punitive law in place, his family could no longer live safely in the Big House on South Temple Street that had been their principle home for more than twenty years. He needed to provide separate residences for each of his wives and another for himself, preferably in a different town, so that he could not be charged with unlawful cohabitation.

The houses Daniel sought to acquire did not need to be large since they would each be occupied by only one wife and her children still at home. Most of the Wells children were already married and living with their families in their own homes. The youngest of those still single were in their late teens and within a few years most of them would marry and start families.

Daniel had often remarked to members of his own family and to friends that "I propose to give my children a good education, but that is all I expect to give. They must earn their own living." He had expended enormous resources in educating his two dozen sons and daughters who lived to adulthood and in giving them broad exposure to musical training and dramatic arts. Their education, as Daniel told them, was their inheritance. He did not intend to bequeath any large amount of wealth to any of them.[1]

He could not have done so even if he had wished. Daniel was still in debt in the summer of 1888. He had been able to repay some of the loans he had taken out to finance the Salt Lake Gas Company in the 1870s, but he still owed more than $100,000 when he departed on his second mission in 1884. That sum did not decrease substantially during the years he was gone, although his remaining business enterprises generated enough income to pay the interest and a small amount of the principal. To clear himself of his remaining obligations, Daniel began selling off his assets.

The first business he sold was the Wells Coal Company, which brought him a little over $8,000 and enabled him to pay for his travel and support himself and his family in England. He also sold his shares in the San Pete and Sevier Railroad Company, which he helped organize in 1872, with Brigham Young and others. The metal-working machinery and other assets of the nail factory were sold off and that business was shut down.[2]

Soon after his return from Great Britain, Daniel sold his farm in Pleasant Grove, which had been managed for him by Alexander Bullock since 1870. Bullock, who had worked for the Wells family for thirty-three years, then purchased his own thirty-acre farm in the same community.[3]

Daniel also sold his farm in the Sugar House area of Salt Lake City. By 1887 this property had become part of the city and farms around it were being subdivided into building lots for homes. The two-acre lot on which the Wells Mansion stood at No. 8 East South Temple was located in the center of the city and was suitable for a large commercial building. Daniel sold this home to the church for $7,150, considerably less than it was worth at the time. The difference between it's true value and what he received for it he may have considered a tithing donation for other income.[4]

Most of the Wells family moved into a new home at 349 East First South. Emmeline Wells took a small home at 25 East South Temple, and Hannah, who still had two children living at home, moved to a new home Daniel purchased at 140 A Street in the avenues section of the city.[5]

Daniel also bought a home at 335 West North Temple Street in which Lydia Wells and her sister Susan both resided for a short time. But they did not like living away from the city center. Daniel soon sold this home and purchased a house at 51 Second Avenue, a block from Hannah's home on A Street and Emmeline's on South Temple, where Lydia and Susan lived for many years.[6]

Figure 23.1. Salt Lake City Main Street, looking southeast from atop the temple construction site, 1887. The Wells Mansion is at the lower left. Engraving from a photo by F. J. Monson Company.

Shortly before his death Daniel sold his First South home and the two-acre lot on which it stood for $36,500 and, after dutifully paying tithing on the full amount, retired the last of his outstanding obligations. The rest of the money he used to purchase two additional homes in which Martha and Emmeline Wells lived for the remainder of their lives. Martha's home was at 90 First Avenue and Emmeline's was at 327 Second Avenue.[7]

The Manti Temple was dedicated by Wilford Woodruff, in a private ceremony on May 17, 1888. The semi-secret dedication was necessary because Woodruff and other members of the Quorum of the Twelve were in hiding and under threat of arrest by federal prosecutors. Several public sessions, in which the president's dedicatory prayer was read by Apostle Lorenzo Snow, were held the following week. Only a few church authorities, those who thought they were not being actively pursued, attended these sessions.[8]

Daniel spoke briefly at the last session on Wednesday, May 23, and noted that this was the fourth temple dedication he had attended. Since Manti was the third temple built since Daniel had joined the church, he was presumably referring to his attendance at the dedication of the Nauvoo temple, which occurred before his baptism. He added that he might live to attend many more, undoubtedly thinking of the Salt Lake

Figure 23.2. Manti Temple, 1888. Final home of Daniel H. Wells, who served as temple president from its opening until his death in 1891.

Temple, which had begun construction under his supervision in 1853, but was still unfinished.[9]

Daniel had also been present for the groundbreaking of all four Utah temples and had performed temple work for his own family in each of the functioning temples from the time of their openings. He had presided as president of the Endowment House for more than twenty years and had performed more marriages than any other church authority. Although he must have known that he would not live to see many more temples built and was not likely to see even the Salt Lake Temple dedicated, he was still determined to dedicate what remained of his life to the doctrine that most appealed to him at his conversion: the sealing of men and women into families that he believed would endure through eternity. When President Woodruff called him to become president of the new Manti temple, he accepted without hesitation.[10]

Daniel's calling required him to live in Manti so as to be present in the temple daily, but he did not buy a home or rent rooms in the town. He lived at the temple in a single furnished room on an upper floor. For the next three years he was almost always on duty directing baptisms and ordnance sessions or available to perform marriages. He seldom left the temple except to visit his family in Salt Lake. They more often came to see him, staying nights at a hotel or as guests of local church members and participating with him in temple work for family members and others during the days. Though his health continued to decline during his time in Manti, Daniel's calling as temple president was greatly to his liking.

The nature of the work and the congenial surroundings prolonged and sweetened his days.[11]

Owing to the prosecution church members continued to suffer at the hands of federal prosecutors and the personal tragedy of his daughters Louie and Annie Cannon, not to mention the continued trials of Emily Grant and Abby Young, who were still living in hiding, Daniel felt that no more of his children should enter into polygamous marriages until the laws forbidding it were repealed or altered. He still believed that the Lord would provide a way for the Saints to go on living the law of celestial marriage and counseled his family to be patient until the way forward was revealed.

Although he probably had some anxiety about it, Daniel gave his approval soon after beginning his service in Manti for Apostle Orson F. Whitney to marry Mary Minerva Wells as his second wife. Mary was the daughter of Daniel and Lydia Wells and was thirty-four years old at the time Ort Whitney asked for her hand. He had married his first wife, Zina Smoot, in 1879 and already had four children with her. He was a rising leader in the church, having been on two missions, served as a bishop, edited both the *Millennial Star* and *Deseret News* newspapers, and been elected to several terms as treasurer of Salt Lake City. Daniel was fond of Ort Whitney and felt that he would make an excellent husband for Mary who otherwise might not marry at all. But he still requested, and Ort agreed, that his marriage to Mary should not be performed in Utah in open defiance of the law.

In July 1888, Mary and Ort journeyed quietly to Colonia Juarez in Chihuahua, Mexico, and were married there in a church, but not a temple ceremony. Neither the bride's parents nor the groom's were present at the wedding, which was performed by a local bishop.[12]

Although polygamy was illegal in Mexico under the Spanish legal code adopted by the federal government and most states, it was rarely prosecuted and usually viewed tolerantly by legal authorities as was adultery and the keeping of mistresses. Colonia Juarez was one of a dozen Mormon settlements founded in 1886 by Saints seeking to live openly in plural marriage without fear of prosecution. These colonies were successful and prosperous until the Mexican revolution forced many foreigners to flee the country in 1911.[13]

Ort Whitney could have moved his family to Mexico, as a number of LDS families did in the 1890s, but he did not want to be so far removed from the center of the church. Neither he nor Mary remained in Colonia Juarez after their marriage. They returned to Utah and Ort established a separate home for her in Logan, where he lived with her for short periods during the next few years. Ort and Mary would eventually have two children together (Ort and Zina had a total of nine), but their first son,

Murray Wells Whitney, was not born until 1892, after Daniel's death and after the Manifesto issued by President Woodruff ended Mormon polygamy in the United States in 1890. Zina died in May 1900 and Ort and Mary were sealed to one another in the Salt Lake Temple in October the same year.[14]

Mary and Ort Whitney's was the last plural marriage among Daniel's children. Joseph Smith Wells, Martha's son, returned from his second mission in England while Daniel was still serving as president of the European Mission. A few months after Daniel was released, Joseph married Anna Elizabeth Sears. His was the final marriage among Daniel's children to occur while he was alive. Daniel returned from Manti to Salt Lake for the October general conference, then traveled north to Logan with his family and presided at the marriage of Joseph and Anna. Another six of his children married during the next decade, the last in 1901, but Daniel did not live to attend any of their weddings.[15]

Orson F. Whitney, now his son-in-law, said in reference to Daniel's appointment as Manti Temple President: "The choice of such a man for such a place was most happy. Familiar with Temple work for many years, he had taken great delight in it. The doctrines embracing salvation for the dead—one of the main purposes for which our Temples are erected—were the ones that originally attracted him to Mormonism; and the performance of sacred ordinances in behalf of his kindred dead and friends who had passed away, was to him a source of unalloyed happiness."[16]

Slowed by age and infirmity, Daniel nevertheless went on with his work in the temple with the same dedication that he had exhibited in his other callings. He became a much loved figure in Manti as he had been for years in Salt Lake City. His courtesy and concern was equal for those who worked at the temple and those who came to it for ordinances. His coachman, writing many years after his term of service, described his feelings for Daniel:

> When the Manti Temple was dedicated I was retained as a worker. I was happy beyond words, though I worked early and late every day in the week at $20.00 per month. But I loved the place and the dear people. However, President Wells tried to make it up to me in many ways.
>
> One cold morning a dear old brother rode up the hill with me. On getting out he threw a quarter over on my seat. "How dare you take money when the team is not yours? I shall report you to the President," some officious brother exclaimed. And he did. In a moment President Wells came out without hat though it was very cold. He was followed by the informer.

> President Wells said: "Brother Christian I want you never to forget when a kind-hearted person wants to bestow a gift on you to never refuse it, for if you do you will deprive that person of a blessing."
>
> The best loved person I ever knew was General Daniel H. Wells, who was always a champion of the poor and troubled ones of humanity . . .
>
> He treated me as one of the family. How I appreciated the good words and the kindly handclasp! If he kept me waiting or put me to any extra trouble, he invariably left a coin in my hand . . .
>
> I served General Wells for about three years. When he passed away strong lips quivered and eyes filled with tears, for many felt they had lost a father and a true friend. He was mourned by thousands for he was beloved by all.[17]

Despite the periods of separation caused by his residence in Manti, Daniel's personal relationship with his family improved during his time as temple president. With only a single calling to attend to, rather than the many that had consumed nearly all of his time during the previous forty years, he was able to devote more attention to his wives and children. He usually stayed on his return to Salt Lake City at the home of Emmeline Wells who now resided alone. She was both surprised and pleased at the renewed intensity of their love, a flowering of affection that she had longed for in previous years and, in her eyes, without adequate response. "Strange indeed" she wrote after one of his visits "that after all my younger years have been past in comparative seclusion that when I am past three score even he should seem so devoted."[18]

Although Daniel's renewed fervor may have been belated, it was none the less a welcome joy to him and his wives. They visited him frequently and stayed in his one-room temple apartment.

> O the joy of being once more in his dear presence—his room is so nice and we are so cosy by the large grate and such a comfortable fire in it. We are more like lovers than husband and wife for we are so far removed from each other there is always the embarrassment of lovers and yet we have been married more than 37 years—how odd it seems I do not feel old neither does he—we are young to each other and that is well.[19]

The end came slowly for Daniel and he accepted death's approach with the same grace that he had lived. Although he was aware for many months that his condition was deteriorating, he said nothing about it to any of his wives or other family members. He sought treatment for the pain that his illness caused him, but he did not expect a cure. He saw his passage out of the mortal world as a natural and necessary part of his eternal journey and he had no fear of taking the next step. A non-Mormon writer, Charles Ellis, who visited Daniel shortly before his death, described his declining health and his desire to carry on as long as he could:

> When I met him last it was at the scene of his latest labors, in Manti. So feeble had his physical powers grown that, if left to himself, he would fall into a half-conscious doze. But a word would wake his mind to its wonted action, and that quiet, unostentatious will that made him so long a tower of strength, rose superior to the weakness of the body. I said to myself that he would never again hear the birds sing their songs in the spring, and I was astonished at the light-heartedness of the aged man. He was full of joke and mental play. I rode with him up to the beautiful Temple, where his last work was being done. He was so weak that he staggered as he stepped to the ground, but there was no evidence of it in his merry eye and his cheerful conversation.
>
> I shook hands, and parted with him at the door of the Temple, and felt that we should meet no more in the flesh. But if ever I have seen or known a man who, from the threshold of the grave at seventy-seven years, looked backward and forward without regret or fear, certainly Daniel H. Wells was such a man.[20]

Daniel continued his labors in the temple until early March 1891. By then he was too weak to stand unaided and members of the temple staff brought him to Salt Lake City. His wives took over his care, at least one of them constantly at his bedside, but pneumonia soon developed and he lingered only long enough to bid farewell to each of his family who came to see him. He died peacefully at Emmeline's home on March 24, 1891. After his passing, although reconciled to his loss and well-schooled in the Mormon understanding of death's place in the eternal scheme of things, she reflected sadly that she was again left alone:

> only memories, only the coming and going and parting at the door, the joy when he came the sorrow when he went as though all the light died out of my life. Such intense love he

has manifested towards me of late years. Such a remarkable change from the long ago, when I needed him so much more, how peculiarly these things come about.[21]

All five of Daniel's surviving wives outlived him by at least a dozen years. Martha, the youngest lived until 1908; Lydia, who was four years older, until 1909; Susan lived to the age of ninety-four and died in 1930; Hannah died in 1913 and Emmeline in 1921 at the age of ninety-three. At the time of Daniel's death, twenty-four of his thirty-seven children were still living and he had twenty-five grandchildren.[22]

The funeral of Daniel H. Wells was held in the Tabernacle whose construction he had supervised and whose acoustics he had modified, on March 29, 1891. The building was filled to capacity and those who attended heard President Wilford Woodruff describe Daniel as a man who "has lived to a good old age, and has gone down into the grave like a shock of corn fully ripe, and with the harness upon him."[23]

The room that Daniel occupied in the Manti Temple, and the furniture that he used in it, remained for more than half a century much as they were when he departed for the last time. The small apartment stood as a symbol of the respect and veneration in which he was held by those who succeeded him as president of that temple.[24]

> Daniel H. Wells' life was not an easy one, he had his full measure of trouble; his cup was not free from the dregs of bitterness. He knew by personal experience the grim realities that go with pioneering and colonizing a hard and barren land; he knew what it was to fight the treacherous and ambushed savage, to face mob violence, to suffer slander and imprisonment for conscience sake, to meet in battle the armed foes of his people, to bare his cheek to the summer sun and the winter's blast. Droughts did not discourage him, the angry floods did not terrify him. He was inwardly fortified and constantly sustained by a settled and perfect faith in his Creator.[25]

Daniel H. Wells died as he lived, enduring to the end in the Mormon religion he had embraced and defended. Although none of his sisters, cousins, or earlier ancestors accepted the teachings of Joseph Smith and became members of the LDS Church, most of his descendants remained true to the faith he bequeathed them. Today, at least seven succeeding generations of Wells family members revere his name and a few, of which this writer is one, occasionally still pay homage at his grave in the Salt Lake City Cemetery that he founded.

Appendix A

THE WELLS FAMILY IN ENGLAND AND AMERICA

1484–1814

Thomas Wells, the first of his family to immigrate to America, descended from a family that had lived in Warwickshire for at least four generations. Thomas Wells's great grandfather, Robert Wells, was born about 1484 in Warwickshire. He and his wife Elizabeth had at least three children: Walter, born about 1510; Thomas, born about 1512; and William, born about 1514.

Robert Wells's son, Thomas, married Elizabeth Bryan in Warwickshire in 1535 and they had at least three children: Ann, born about 1537; Robert, born about 1538; and Walter, born about 1542. Robert Wells married Alice Harbourne in 1572. He and his wife had at least seven children: Mary, born about 1570; Jane, born 1573, Alice, born 1575; Robert, born about 1580; Hugh, born 1590; Thomas, born 1598; and Elizabeth, born 1611. Thomas Wells, the son of Robert and Alice Wells, immigrated to America with his family in 1635.[1]

The identities of these early generations of the Wells family are all known principally from the pleadings of a lawsuit regarding the ownership of property sold by Thomas Wells before he left England. In 1648, John Wells, a nephew of Thomas Wells, filed suit in the English courts claiming that the land Thomas Wells sold before he left England belonged by right to him, John Welles, through inheritance from his late father, Robert Wells, an older brother of Thomas Wells.[2]

The Wells family owned land in Warwickshire, some of which was deeded to Thomas by his father and his older brother at the time of his marriage to Alice Tomes. His family and the generations of Wells that preceded him in Stourton were likely sheep farmers and wool merchants, occupations that produced a generous income and enabled family members to acquire a quality education and live a comfortable lifestyle. Thomas's work activities in his later life demonstrate conclusively that he could read and write in Latin as well as English and his personal library, as noted in the inventory of his will, shows that the scope of his education was well above that of most of his contemporaries in America.

Thomas Wells and his wife probably converted to the Puritan faith about 1620, some five years after their marriage. Some of their neighbors, among them George Wyllys, the Griswolds, Rev. Ephraim Huit and Daniel Clark, also embraced Protestant doctrine and worshiped with Lord Saye and Sele (an English nobleman sympathetic to the Puritans), and with the group around Rev. Thomas Hooker.[3]

Thomas was a moderate Puritan. He decided to leave England after King Charles I appointed William Laud as Archbishop of Canterbury in 1633 and the latter's ecclesiastical reforms attempted to pull the Church of England back toward Catholic doctrine and away from nonconformist theology and protestant Calvinism. As the crown enforced religious uniformity by closing down Puritan organizations and replacing recalcitrant clergymen, a number of Puritans and other dissidents left England for the relative freedom from religious persecution in America. Among them were Rev. Thomas Hooker and Rev. John Cotton, who arrived in Massachusetts in 1633 with about two hundred others. The Wells family followed about two years later.

Ironically, Thomas may also have been influenced to leave the Old World for the New by the political and religious views of his wife's family. Alice Tomas's half-brother John was a fierce Cavalier (Royalist adherents to the Church of England led by Charles I and the nobility who supported him) who later provided shelter to the fugitive King Charles II during his escape to France. Loyalists were frequently treated as traitors by the Roundheads (Puritan adherents supported by Parliament and led by Oliver Cromwell) during the turbulent years of religious conflict between King Charles I's accession in 1625 and his execution in 1649. Thomas probably thought that whether Roundheads or Cavaliers emerged victorious, his family might be persecuted for being on the losing side. He thus was doubly encouraged to quit England for more tolerant shores.[4]

When he got there, Massachusetts did not meet his expectations and Thomas Wells stayed only a few months in Boston before moving to Saybrook, Connecticut, and then, in June 1636, to Hartford. There he prospered, acquiring a home on the east side of Governor's Street and becoming a member of the Court of Magistrates in 1637, an office he continued to hold until his death. He was also a member of the Court that in 1639 issued the Fundamental Orders or Constitution of Connecticut

Colony, the original manuscript copy of which is in his handwriting. On April 11, 1639, he was appointed treasurer of the colony and held that office for two years.[5]

In 1646, Thomas's wife Alice Wells died, leaving him with four minor children, and he soon married Elizabeth Deming, who was the widow of Nathaniel Foote, one of the first settlers of Wethersfield, Fairfield, Connecticut. Thomas Wells had no children with his second wife who survived him by more than twenty years.[6]

John Wells, the eldest son of Thomas Wells, was born in 1621 and was a teenage youth at the time his family immigrated to America. In 1647 he married Elizabeth Bourne, born about 1626, probably in Stratford, Fairfield, Connecticut. She was the daughter of Elisha Bourne and Elizabeth Collyer. The same year John moved from Wethersfield to Stratford to manage his father's properties there and to be nearer his wife's family who resided there. John and Elizabeth Wells had seven children, four sons and three daughters, born between 1648 and 1660.[7]

John Wells died about five months before his father and left most of his property to his wife and three of his sons: John, the eldest, Thomas, the third, and Samuel, the fourth. His daughters shared with their brothers bequests of household goods and cash. John's second son Robert must have been the favored grandson of Thomas Wells as the following paragraph concerning him appears in John's will: "I freely give to my dear and loving father my sonn Robert to be educated and brought up as he see good."[8]

At the time his will was made, John expected that his father would long outlive him, but events proved otherwise. About five months after John's death, Thomas Wells also succumbed suddenly one evening after being, as attested by Governor John Winthrop, "very well at supper and dead before midnight."[9]

Perhaps prodded by his son's unexpected demise, Thomas had written his own will on November 7, 1659, a few weeks after John's passing. His grandson Robert, then age eleven, was the principal beneficiary, being given Thomas's home and its contents with a provision that Robert eventually pay each of Thomas's children or their heirs the sum of twenty pounds. Thomas's sons also shared his farm lands among them.[10]

After reaching adulthood and gaining control of his inheritance, Robert Wells quarreled with his step-grandmother over the administration of the home and adjacent buildings in which they shared occupancy. On June 9, 1675, Robert Wells married Elizabeth Goodrich, the daughter of William Goodrich the Younger and his wife, Sarah Marvin. Robert was almost twenty-six years old at the time of his marriage, but his wife was only eighteen. The conflict between Robert and his step-grandmother intensified when he desired to place his new wife in charge of his household and Elizabeth Wells resisted that change in her standing as head of the household.[11]

Robert Wells prospered rapidly after his marriage. He and his wife had three sons by 1681, the year Robert was made a freeman[12] and two more sons and a daughter by 1691. Robert's wife Elizabeth died February 17, 1697, while all but one of their five children were still minors. On October 13, 1698, Robert married Mary Stoddard, who was born March 25, 1668 in Salem, Essex, Massachusetts. Mary was thirty years old and twenty years Robert's junior at the time of their marriage. Although she proved an able and loving stepmother to Robert's children, the couple had no additional children of their own.[13]

Robert Wells died June 22, 1714 while serving a final term as justice of the peace in Wethersfield. He was survived by Mary, his second wife, and four of his five children. Robert's will directed that the family harmony continue. Mary was given a small plot of land, livestock, a "sixth part of all my silver, bills, and plate," and an annuity of eight pounds to be paid in equal shares by Robert's four sons. He concludes: "My will is that my wife live with some of my children and they to take care of her," a directive that the children followed until Mary's death.[14]

Joseph Wells, the third son of Robert and Elizabeth Wells, was born in Wethersfield September 1680 and spent his entire life there living in the home and farming the land he inherited from his father. He was made a freeman and served a one-year term as lister (tax assessor) in 1712. He also served one year as a tax collector in 1715, but perhaps burdened by his duties in these necessary but reviled offices, he was never appointed to any others. His brothers, Thomas, Robert, and Gideon, all served as captains of Wethersfield militia companies and in other municipal offices, but Joseph was content with life of a prosperous farmer.

He married Hannah Robbins, the daughter of another militia captain, Joshua Robbins, and his wife, Elizabeth Butler, on January 6, 1709. They had eight children evenly divided between sons and daughters. The youngest child, Christopher, appears to have predeceased his father, but all the others are named as heirs in Joseph's will.[15]

Joshua Wells, born September 3, 1726, was Joseph's youngest son and was still a minor at the time of his father's death. He chose a close family friend, Joseph Hurlbut of Wethersfield, to be his guardian until he reached majority age.[16]

Joshua gained full control of his inheritance in 1747, but did not marry for another ten years. He worked the land he had received from his father and, in 1757, married Experience Dickenson, the daughter of Elihu Dickenson and his wife, Lucy (Eunice) Deming. Experience was born April 17, 1736 in Wethersfield and was the sixth of eight children in her family.

Joshua and Experience had nine children, all born in Wethersfield during the years 1759 to 1773. Their youngest child Daniel Wells, born June 15, 1773, was the father of Daniel Hanmer Wells. Less than two weeks after Daniel Wells's birth, his mother died on June 27, 1773, whether as a consequence of childbirth complications or from other causes is not known.

Although the oldest of Joshua and Experience Wells's nine children was only fourteen years of age at the time of her death, Joshua did not remarry. He relied instead on the homemaking and parenting skills of his two eldest daughters, Experience Welles, born September 14, 1758, and Hannah Wells, born October 26, 1759, to care for and help educate their younger siblings. They seem to have accepted this heavy burden willingly and to have performed it admirably.[17]

Joshua Wells was confident enough in the capacity of his family to manage without him (probably with the assistance of other family members and friends) that he volunteered to go to war. He was older than most of those who enlisted to fight in the Revolution, almost fifty when the Declaration of Independence was signed, but he still served throughout the conflict and survived another fifteen years beyond it.[18]

After the Revolution, Joshua Wells resumed his active leadership as patriarch of the family and continued to operate his farm as, one by one, his children married and began their own families. Daniel Wells, the father of Daniel Hanmer Wells, was the last sibling to marry. He married Honor Francis, born September 19, 1774 in Wethersfield, on March 26, 1799, six months after his father Joshua's death at age seventy-one.[19]

Eliza Wells, Daniel and Honor's first child, was born in Oneida County, New York, September 24, 1800. Four additional daughters were born in Trenton during the following years as Daniel developed his property and prospered as a farmer. Pamela Wells arrived on May 7, 1803, Abigail Wells on March 15, 1805, Lucy Ann Wells on August 17, 1809, and Honor Francis Wells on August 20, 1812.

On September 8, 1812, less than three weeks after the birth of her fifth child, Honor Wells died, probably as a result of complications from childbirth. She was eleven days short of being thirty-eight years old.[20]

On November 30, 1813, Daniel Wells and Catherine Chapin, born March 15, 1788, were married in Trenton. Catherine was the daughter of David Chapin, born in New Hartford, and his wife Ruth Seymour.[21]

Daniel and Catherine's first child, Daniel Hanmer Wells, was born on October 27, 1814.[22]

Appendix B

THE CHAPIN FAMILY IN ENGLAND AND AMERICA

1484–1814

David Chapin was a direct descendant of Deacon Samuel Chapin, born 1598 in Paignton, Devonshire, England, and his wife Cicily Penney, born 1601. Samuel and his family immigrated to Massachusetts in 1635, the same year that Thomas Wells arrived in the colony. Like the Wells family, the Chapins were Puritans seeking refuge from religious persecution in England. Unlike the Wells, who soon relocated to Connecticut, Samuel Chapin remained in Massachusetts. In 1642 he moved with his family from Roxbury to the new Agawam settlement, which by the time of their arrival had been renamed Springfield.

Samuel and Cicily Chapin had eleven children. Two of the six who were born in England died prior to 1635 and the remaining four immigrated with their parents. Four additional children were born in Roxbury and the youngest child joined the family in Springfield a year or so after their move.[1]

Samuel became a prominent citizen of Springfield where he lived for the remainder of his life. He was elected selectman for several years until 1652 when he was appointed a magistrate and as such could no longer serve on the board. In addition to his court responsibilities, he shared the duties of minister with two other citizens after the departure of the settlement's regular minister following a dispute about Calvinist doctrine in 1651. This religious calling gained him the title of Deacon which he retained throughout his life.

In 1660, when the towns of Springfield, Northampton and Hadley were constituted a county, Samuel was sworn in as one of the three judges of the new County Court. He served in this capacity until 1666 when, at age sixty-eight, he retired from active life, deeded most of his property to his youngest son Japhet, and also relinquished his civic responsibilities to Japhet and his sibling Henry. He lived quietly thereafter until October 5, 1675 when he survived a powerful attack on Springfield by the Agawam Indians who killed several settlers and burned more than fifty homes and barns. Samuel was not wounded in the action, but at age seventy-seven, he was traumatized by the event and it probably contributed to his death on November 11, 1675.[2]

Japhet Chapin resided all but the first year of his life in Springfield. Like his father he was primarily a farmer but also had civic and military duties. He was in the Battle of Turner Falls in May 1676 in which the colonists defeated the Indians who had attacked Springfield the previous year, but at a high cost in casualties to their own force. Japhet noted the battle thus in his own hand:

> "I went out Volenteare against injens the 17th of May, 1676 and we ingaged batel the 19th of May in the morning before sunrise and made great Spoil upon the enemy and came off the same day with the Los of 37 men and the Captin Turner, and came home the 20th of May."[3]

Japhet married Abilenah Cooley, born 1642 in Springfield, on July 24, 1664 and they had a total of ten children. Two of these died in infancy, but the surviving eight children all lived long lives.[4]

Ebenezer Chapin, the fifth child of Japhet and Abilenah Chapin, lived most of his life in Springfield and made his living as a farmer. He married Ruth Janes, born 1682, in 1702. Ruth was the daughter of Abel Janes, born about 1642, and his wife Mary Judd, born 1660. Ebenezer and Ruth Chapin had thirteen children born between 1703 and 1726.

About 1721 Ebenezer and Ruth Chapin moved to Enfield, a town about ten miles south of Springfield, that was first settled in 1679 and was then part of Massachusetts. Their three youngest children were born in Enfield.[5]

In 1749, some twenty-eight years after the Chapins settled in Enfield, a lawsuit was concluded concerning the border between Massachusetts and Connecticut colonies. In the decision, a surveyor's error was determined to have placed part of Hartford County, Connecticut, in Massachusetts and the boundary was ordered to be corrected. The town of Enfield, which was in the affected area, seceded from Massachusetts and became part of Connecticut Colony. The Chapins thus became Connecticut citizens without changing their place of residence and lived the remainder of their lives in Connecticut.

Ruth Chapin died in 1736, but Ebenezer lived to see all his eleven surviving children married and the birth of well over fifty grandchildren. He died in Enfield in 1772, a little more than two years before the shots fired at Concord and Lexington marked the start of the American Revolution.[6]

David Chapin, born 1722 in Enfield, was the youngest of Ebenezer and Ruth's children to survive into adulthood. David's life was also short in comparison with his other siblings: he died at age forty, more than ten years before his father's passing.

David married Martha Allen, born 1728 in Enfield, on October 5, 1749 when he was twenty-seven years old and she was twenty. Martha was the daughter of Azariah Allen, born 1701 and his wife Martha Burt, born 1707, both of whom were among the original settlers of Enfield.

After their marriage, David and Martha immediately relocated to New Hartford, Litchfield, Connecticut, about thirty-five miles west and a few miles south of Enfield. They had eight children over the next dozen years, all born in New Hartford. The last of these, David Chapin, was born on August 1, 1762, just six weeks before his father's death.[7]

On March 1, 1778, David Chapin enlisted as a private in the Revolutionary Army for a period of three years serving in Captain Joseph Walker's company. His enlistment at age fifteen was exactly three days after that of fifty-one-year-old Joshua Wells in the same company.

David was honorably discharged from service at Newburg, New York, on February 19, 1781. He married Ruth Seymour, born January 2, 1767 in New Hartford, in 1784. Their first five children were born in New Hartford between 1786 and 1793. They had three additional children after their move to Sangerfield, bringing their total family to eight.

On November 30, 1813, Daniel Wells and Catherine Chapin, the eldest child of David Wells, were married in Trenton. Their first child, Daniel Hanmer Wells, was born the following year on October 27, 1814.[8]

Notes

Chapter 1

1. For a more detailed description of the Wells family background in England and America, see appendix A.
2. Charles William Manwaring, *Digest of Early Connecticut Probate Records*, vol. 3, *Hartford District, 1729–1750* (Hartford: M.S. Pack & Co., 1906), 473.
3. Junius F. Wells, "The Wells Family Genealogy," in *The Utah Genealogical and Historical Magazine* (Salt Lake City: The Church of Jesus Christ of Latter-day Saints Genealogy Department, 1915), 6:9–10.
4. Ibid.
5. *Connecticut Military Record, 1775–1848, Record of Service of Connecticut Men in the War of the Revolution, War of 1812, Mexican War* (Hartford: The Case, Lockwood & Brainard Company, 1889), 424.
6. Ibid., 383.
7. Ibid., 497–98.
8. Ibid., 245, 251, 539.
9. Ibid., 302–7, 335.
10. Ibid., 307.
11. *Lists and Returns of Connecticut Men in the Revolution, 1775–1783* (Hartford: Connecticut Historical Society, 1909), 44, 176, 271.
12. Wells, "The Wells Family Genealogy," 9–10.
13. Ibid.
14. Joshua Wells, Will, Barbour Collection: Connecticut Vital Records Prior to 1850, Vital Records Waterbury-Wethersfield, Microfilm of original records at the State Library Hartford, Connecticut (Salt Lake City: Family History Library, The Church of Jesus Christ of Latter-day Saints), US/CAN Film #2982, 230–31.

15. Daniel F. Littlefield Jr. and James W. Parins, *Encyclopedia of American Indian Removal* (Santa Barbara, CA: ABC-CLIO, 2011), 152.
16. Daniel Wells, Letter to Honor Francis, December 12, 1797, "Trenton," in *The Contributor* (Salt Lake City: The Contributor Company, 1892), 13:45–46.
17. Ibid.
18. Rev. Frederick W. Bailey, *Wethersfield, Hartford Co., CT, Marriages 1739–1799, Early Connecticut Marriages as Found on Ancient Church Records Prior to 1800*, vol. 3, 1898, accessed June 11, 2015, https://archive.org/stream/earlycon necticut03bail/earlyconnecticut03bail_djvu.txt.
19. Junius F. Wells, "Trenton," in *The Contributor* (Salt Lake City: The Contributor Company, 1892), 13:46.
20. Samuel W. Durant, *History of Oneida County, New York: With Illustrations and Biographical Sketches of Some of Its Prominent Men and Pioneers* (Oneida, NY: Higginson Book Co., 1878), 534–35. Utica was first settled in 1773. Rome, to the east, was fortified by the British in 1758, but had been occupied long before that. Oneida County was created by the New York state government in 1798 from a part of Herkemer County, which was itself split off from Montgomery County, the renamed Tryon County of pre-Revolutionary days. Most of the pre-war Loyalist residents of Tryon County had fled to Canada during and after the Revolution, leaving the area largely depopulated.
21. Ibid.
22. Joshua Wells, Will; and Daniel Wells, Deed in Deeds, 1791–1901, Oneida County, NY, Microfilm of original records in the Oneida County Courthouse, Utica, New York (Salt Lake City: Family History Library, The Church of Jesus Christ of Latter-day Saints), US/CAN Film #364859.
23. Daniel Wells, Deed.
24. Wells, "The Wells Family Genealogy," 10.
25. "Oneida County Cemeteries, Trenton, Holland Patent Cemetery, Transcription S thru Z" (Provo: Rootsweb, Ancestry.com Operations, Inc.), accessed June 11, 2015, http://freepages.genealogy.rootsweb.ancestry.com/~townoflee/cemeteries/Trenton/hollandpatents-z.html.
26. C. Edward Skeen, *Citizen Soldiers in the War of 1812* (Lexington: University Press of Kentucky, 2015), 78–101.
27. Wells, "The Wells Family Genealogy," 4.
28. Skeen, *Citizen Soldiers in the War of 1812*, 78–101.
29. Wells, "The Wells Family Genealogy," 10. For a more detailed description of the Chapin family background in England and America, see appendix B.
30. *Connecticut Military Record, 1775–1848*, 245–48.
31. Ibid., 333, 641.
32. Ibid.; and Revolutionary War Record of David Chapin, Revolutionary War Pension and Bounty-Land Warrant Application Files, 1800–1900, National Archives and Records Administration, NARA microfilm publication M804, Records of the Department of Veterans Affairs, Record Group 15 (Washington, DC: National Archives), 1–16.
33. Revolutionary War Record of David Chapin, 1–16.
34. *Lineage Book–National Society of the Daughters of the American Revolution* (Washington, DC: National Society of the Daughters of the American Revolution, 1908), 25:148.

35. Durant, *History of Oneida County, New York*, 515. Sangerfield was named for Col. Jedediah Sanger, a Revolutionary War veteran from New Hartford, who founded it with Michael Myers and John J. Morgan. They purchased the land from the State of New York on speculation in 1789 for a cost of about three shillings three pence per acre with payment spread over five years. The three proprietors then invited residents of New Hartford and other towns to purchase parcels in Sangerfield on similarly easy terms. The town was annexed into Oneida County in 1804.
36. Gilbert Warren Chapin, *The Chapin Book of Genealogical Data* (Hartford: Chapin Family Association, 1924), 1:175; and Abigail Wells, "Genealogy of the Wells and Chapin Family" (Salt Lake City: unpublished document in author's possession, 1970).
37. Wells, "The Wells Family Genealogy," 10.

Chapter 2

1. W. W. Canfield and J. E. Clark, *Things Worth Knowing about Oneida County* (Utica, NY: Thomas J. Griffiths, 1909), 126.
2. Wells, "Trenton," 47.
3. Ibid., 48.
4. Hamilton Child, "History of Trenton, New York," in *Gazetteer and Business Directory of Oneida County, N. Y.* (Syracuse, NY: 1862).
5. Wells, "Trenton," 47.
6. Ibid., 48.
7. Ibid.
8. New York, Land Records, 1630–1975, Oneida, Owners of Land (Trenton) 1814; "Salt Lake City: Family History Library, The Church of Jesus Christ of Latter-day Saints," accessed February 12, 2015, https://familysearch.org/pal:/MM9.3.1/TH-1961-25923-10273-80?cc=2078654&wc=M7HP-QZS:358132601,358165501; and Catherine Wells, et al., Grantors, to Oliver Coombs, Grantee, Indenture and Deed, June 4, 1832. (Salt Lake City: unpublished document, copy in author's possession).
9. Catherine Wells, et al., Grantors, to Oliver Coombs, Grantee.
10. Wells, "Trenton," 47.
11. "The Erie Canal, Images, Other Images of the Erie Canal, Tolls, Fares, Distances, etc.," accessed June 17, 2015, http://www.eriecanal.org/misc-1.html#toll.
12. Ibid.
13. Wells, "The Wells Family Genealogy," 5–6.
14. Ibid.
15. Bryant S. Hinckley, *Daniel Hanmer Wells and Events of His Time* (Salt Lake City: The Deseret News Press, 1942), 391–92.
16. Daniel H. Wells, "The Narrative of General Daniel H. Wells" (Berkeley, CA, Bancroft Library, unpublished manuscript, copy in author's possession), 1.
17. Patent Certificate #6726, United States General Land Office, Springfield, Pre Emp. Act of May 29, 1830, Re-recorded June 18, 1846 (Springfield, IL).

18. Catherine Wells and Daniel H. Wells, Letter to Pamela Wells, July 7, 1835, in the Daniel H. Wells File (Salt Lake City: Church History Department, The Church of Jesus Christ of Latter-day Saints).
19. Daniel H. Wells and Catherine Wells, Letter to Pamela Wells, March 12, 1836, in the Daniel H. Wells File (Salt Lake City: Church History Department, The Church of Jesus Christ of Latter-day Saints).
20. Ibid.
21. Ibid.
22. Daniel H. Wells and Catherine Wells, Letter to Pamela Wells, August 28, 1836, in the Daniel H. Wells File (Salt Lake City: Church History Department, The Church of Jesus Christ of Latter-day Saints).
23. Ibid.
24. Edward W. Tullidge, *Life of Brigham Young: Or, Utah and Her Founders* (New York: 1876), 421.
25. *Biographical Record of Salt Lake City and Vicinity* (Chicago: National Historical Record Company, Chicago, 1902), 52.
26. Daniel H. Wells, Letter to Horace S. Eldredge, January 24, 1871 (Salt Lake City: unpublished document, copy in author's possession).
27. Martha L. Banner and Cullom Davis, et al., eds., *The Law Practice of Abraham Lincoln: Complete Documentary Edition* (Urbana: University of Illinois Press, 2000); File ID L01846, People v. Fraim.
28. Albert Emory Wells, Letter to the Chicago Historical Society (Salt Lake City: 1903, unpublished document, copy in author's possession).
29. Wells, "The Wells Family Genealogy," 5–6.
30. Ibid.
31. Joseph D'Ortique Raphel, "Record L7GV-QR3, Salt Lake City, Church History Library, The Church of Jesus Christ of Latter-day Saints," accessed February 13, 2015, https://familysearch.org/tree/#view=ancestor&person=L7GV-QR3&spouse=24W4-YZT.
32. William MacDonald, *Documentary Source Book of American History, 1606–1913* (New York: The Macmillan Company, 1916), 359.
33. Joseph Thorpe, *Early Days in the West Along the Missouri One Hundred Years Ago* (Liberty, MO: Irving Gilmer [reprint], 1924), 85–86.
34. Wells, "The Wells Family Genealogy," 2, 11.
35. Wells, "Genealogy of the Wells and Chapin Family."
36. Daniel H. Wells, Letter to Brother and Sisters, April 30, 1838, in the Daniel H. Wells File (Salt Lake City: Church History Department, The Church of Jesus Christ of Latter-day Saints).
37. Joseph Smith, *History of the Church of Jesus Christ of Latter-day Saints, Period 1 History of Joseph Smith, the Prophet* (Salt Lake City: The Deseret Book Company, 1965), 3:175.
38. Rollin J. Britton, *Early Days on the Grand River and the Mormon War* (Columbia: The Missouri State Historical Society, 1920), 39.
39. Donna Hill, *Joseph Smith the First Mormon* (Garden City, NY: Doubleday and Company, Inc., 1977), 235.
40. The Joseph Smith Papers, History, 1838–1856, vol. C-1 [2 November 1838–31 July 1842], entry of 4 April 1839, accessed February 15, 2015, http://josephsmithpapers.org/paperSummary/history-1838-1856-volume

-c-1-2-november-1838-31-july-1842?p=38&highlight=hauns#!/paper
Summary/history-1838-1856-volume-c-1-2-november-1838-31-july-1842&
p=38.
41. The Joseph Smith Papers, Petition to United States Congress, 29 November 1839, 31–32, accessed February 15, 2015, http://joseph smithpapers.org/paperSummary/petition-to-united-states-congress-29 -november-1839?p=32&highlight=hauns#!/paperSummary/petition-to -united-states-congress-29-november-1839&p=33.
42. Britton, *Early Days on the Grand River and the Mormon War*, 51.

Chapter 3

1. Lyndon W. Cook, "Isaac Galland, Mormon Benefactor," *BYU Studies* 19, no. 3 (1979): 261–84; The Joseph Smith Papers, History, 1838–1856, vol. C-1 [2 November 1838–31 July 1842], entry of 28 November 1838, accessed February 15, 2015, http://josephsmithpapers.org/paperSummary/history -1838-1856-volume-c-1-2-november-1838-31-july-1842?p=89&highlight =galland.
2. Hill, *Joseph Smith the First Mormon*, 264–67.
3. The Joseph Smith Papers, Bond from Horace Hotchkiss, 12 August 1839-B, accessed February 15, 2015, http://josephsmithpapers.org/paperSummary /bond-from-horace-hotchkiss-12-august-1839-b.
4. The Joseph Smith Papers, Nauvoo Post Office, Nauvoo, Illinois, Summary, accessed February 15, 2015, http://josephsmithpapers.org/place?name= Nauvoo+post+office,+Nauvoo,+Illinois.
5. Gustavus Hill Esq., *City of Nauvoo Map, Lithographed Reproduction from the Original Entered in the Hancock County Clerk's Office, Carthage, Illinois, 1841* (Nauvoo: Nauvoo Restoration, Inc., 1971).
6. Ibid.
7. Junius F. Wells, "Daniel H. Wells," in *The Contributor* (Salt Lake City, Deseret News Co., 1891), 12:242; and *Biographical Record of Salt Lake City and Vicinity*, 52.
8. Robert Bruce Flanders, *Nauvoo, Kingdom on the Mississippi* (Urbana: University of Illinois Press, 1965), 125. Wells's land dealings are recorded in Deed Book 12G, 137, 367; Deed Book M, 397; Deed Book K, 189, 361; Deed Book L, 222, 311; Bond and Mortgage Book 1, 403, 521. Wells, like most Nauvoo land dealers, also bought and sold farm lands outside the city.
9. The Joseph Smith Papers, Journal, December 1842–June 1844; Book 1, 21 December 1842–10 March 1843, 183–85, accessed February 15, 2015, http://josephsmithpapers.org/paperSummary/journal-december-1842 -june-1844-book-1-21-december-1842-10-march-1843?p=193&highlight =upper%20part%20of%20the%20town#!/paperSummary/journal-dec ember-1842-june-1844-book-1-21-december-1842-10-march-1843&p=192.
10. Ibid., 205–6.
11. Mary Ann Sterns Winter, Journal, 11 (Salt Lake City: Nauvoo Restoration Inc. Collection, Church History Department, The Church of Jesus Christ of Latter-day Saints).

12. Parley P. Pratt, *Autobiography of Parley P. Pratt* (Salt Lake City: Deseret Book Company, 2000), 426.
13. Samuel Bennion, *Samuel's Day Book, Bennion Family Papers* (Salt Lake City: Utah State Historical Society).
14. The Joseph Smith Papers, Oaths, Oath of Office as an Alderman of the City of Nauvoo, 3 February 1841, accessed February 15, 2015, http://josephsmithpapers.org/paperSummary/oaths-3-february-1841?p=1&highlight=Daniel%20h%20wells.
15. Alex Beam, *American Crucifixion: The Murder of Joseph Smith and the Fate of the Mormon Church* (New York, Public Affairs, 2014), 67.
16. John Hajicek, "Daniel H. Wells Justice Court Record Book, Synopsis of Content, Mormonism.com," accessed June 17, 2015, http://www.mormonism.com/Court.htm,
17. Wells, "The Wells Family Genealogy," 10.
18. Charles Mansfield Thompson, "The Illinois Whigs Before 1846," in *University of Illinois Studies in the Social Sciences* (Urbana, University of Illinois Press, 1915), 4:78.
19. Hill, *Joseph Smith the First Mormon*, 281–82.
20. The Joseph Smith Papers, History, 1838–1856, vol. C-1 [2 November 1838–31 July 1842] 1159, accessed February 19, 2015, http://josephsmithpapers.org/paperSummary/history-1838-1856-volume-c-1-2-november-1838-31-july-1842?p=331&highlight=Daniel%20h%20wells.
21. The Joseph Smith Papers, Nauvoo City Officers Chart, accessed June 17, 2015, http://josephsmithpapers.org/bc-jsp/content/jsp/images/content/library/pdf/chart11.pdf.
22. The Joseph Smith Papers, The Nauvoo City Charter, Section 16, History, 1838–1856, vol. C-1 [2 November 1838–31 July 1842], 1126, accessed February 16, 2015, http://josephsmithpapers.org/paperSummary/history-1838-1856-volume-c-1-2-november-1838-31-july-1842?p=302&highlight=charter#!/paperSummary/history-1838-1856-volume-c-1-2-november-1838-31-july-1842&p=298.
23. Ibid., Section 24, 1127; and The Joseph Smith Papers, History, 1838–1856, vol. C-1 [2 November 1838–31 July 1842], 1160, accessed February 19, 2015, http://josephsmithpapers.org/paperSummary/history-1838-1856-volume-c-1-2-november-1838-31-july-1842?p=332&highlight=Daniel%20h%20wells.
24. The Joseph Smith Papers, History, 1838–1856, vol. C-1, 1199; and "Old Nauvoo Cemetery," *FindAGrave.com*, accessed February 19, 2015, http://www.findagrave.com/cgi-bin/fg.cgi?page=cr&GSln=wells&GSbyrel=all&GSdyrel=all&GSst=16&GScnty=723&GScntry=4&GSob=n&CRid=107486&df=all&pt=Old%20Nauvoo%20Burial%20Grounds&. The cemetery has also been known as the Nauvoo Cemetery, Old Mormon Cemetery, Pioneer Saints Cemetery, among other names.
25. The Joseph Smith Papers, The Nauvoo City Charter, Section 25, History, 1838–1856, vol. C-1 [2 November 1838–31 July 1842], 1127, accessed February 16, 2015, http://josephsmithpapers.org/paperSummary/history-1838-1856-volume-c-1-2-november-1838-31-july-1842?p=302&highlight=

charter#!/paperSummary/istory-1838-1856-volume-c-1-2-november-1838-31-july-1842&p=298.
26. Hamilton Gardner, "The Nauvoo Legion, 1840–1845: A Unique Military Organization," in *Journal of the Illinois State Historical Society*, no. 54 (Summer 1961), 181–197.
27. The Joseph Smith Papers, Minutes of a Court Martial, 4 February 1841, accessed February 16, 2015, http://josephsmithpapers.org/paperSummary/minutes-of-a-court-martial-4-february-1841?p=2&highlight=daniel%20h%20wells#!/paperSummary/minutes-of-a-court-martial-4-february-1841&p=1.
28. "The Nauvoo Legion on Parade," *The Joseph Smith and Emma Hale Smith Historical Society*, accessed February 16, 2015, https://www.josephsmithjr.org/.
29. Hill, *Joseph Smith the First Mormon*, 286.
30. John Nevius, Letter, May 2, 1841, Stanley Kimball Collection, Southern Illinois University.
31. Wells, Letter to the Chicago Historical Society.
32. Ibid.
33. Ibid.
34. Smith, *History of the Church*, 4:186, 205.
35. County Deeds, Book M, 397–98, recorded in Nauvoo on Feb 8, 1844, and in the Hancock County Courthouse on 8 Jul 1844. The last date is after the murder of Joseph Smith.
36. *Times and Seasons* 2, no. 12 (April 15, 1841): 375–77, 380–83, accessed September 8, 2015, http://www.centerplace.org/history/ts/v2n12.htm.

Chapter 4

1. The Joseph Smith Papers, History, 1838–1856, vol. C-1 [2 November 1838–31 July 1842], 1167, 1168, accessed February 19, 2015, http://josephsmithpapers.org/paperSummary/history-1838-1856-volume-c-1-2-november-1838-31-july-1842?p=339&highlight=Daniel%20h%20wells#!/paperSummary/history-1838-1856-volume-c-1-2-november-1838-31-july-1842&p=339.
2. Davison Hibbard Lease, "Old Nauvoo Collection, Rick Grunder Books," accessed June 17, 2015, http://www.rickgrunder.com/OldNauvoo/oldnauvoo.htm#hibbardfieldpoint.
3. Daniel H. Wells, Letter to Pamela Wells, 1841, Daniel H. Wells Papers (Logan: Utah State University).
4. Wells, "Daniel H. Wells," 247.
5. Hill, *Joseph Smith the First Mormon*, 298.
6. The Joseph Smith Papers, History, 1838–1856, vol. C-1 [2 November 1838–31 July 1842], 1344, accessed February 19, 2015, http://josephsmithpapers.org/paperSummary/history-1838-1856-volume-c-1-2-november-1838-31-july-1842?p=508&highlight=Daniel%20h%20wells#!/paperSummary/history-1838-1856-volume-c-1-2-november-1838-31-july-1842&p=508.
7. John C. Bennett, *The History of the Saints: Or, an Exposé of Joe Smith and Mormonism* (Boston: Leland & Whiting, 1842), 287–89

8. The Joseph Smith Papers, History, 1838–1856, vol. C-1 [2 November 1838–31 July 1842], 1357, accessed February 19, 2015, http://josephsmithpapers.org/paperSummary/history-1838-1856-volume-c-1-2-november-1838-31-july-1842?p=531&highlight=Daniel%20h%20wells.
9. *Times and Seasons* 3, no. 19 (August 1, 1842): 870–74, accessed September 8, 2015, http://www.centerplace.org/history/ts/v3n19.htm.
10. The Joseph Smith Papers, History, 1838–1856, vol. C-1 [2 November 1838–31 July 1842], 1359, 1360, accessed February 19, 2015, http://josephsmithpapers.org/paperSummary/history-1838-1856-volume-c-1-2-november-1838-31-july-1842?p=534&highlight=Daniel%20h%20wells.
11. Hill, *Joseph Smith the First Mormon*, 310–311.
12. The Joseph Smith Papers, Appendix: Missouri Extradition Attempt, 1842–1843, Selected Documents, accessed February 19, 2015, http://josephsmithpapers.org/paperSummary/appendix-missouri-extradition-attempt-1842-1843-selected-documents?p=5&highlight=rockwell#!/paperSummary/appendix-missouri-extradition-attempt-1842-1843-selected-documents&p=5.
13. Daniel H. Wells, Letter to Joseph Coombs, March 31, 1844, in the Daniel H. Wells Papers (Logan: Utah State University).
14. The Joseph Smith Papers, Journal, December 1841–December 1842, 129–35, accessed February 19, 2015, http://josephsmithpapers.org/paperSummary/journal-december-1841-december-1842?p=34&highlight=rockwell#!/paperSummary/journal-december-1841-december-1842&p=34.
15. Hill, *Joseph Smith the First Mormon*, 320–23.
16. Flanders, *Nauvoo, Kingdom on the Mississippi*, 225–32.
17. Ibid.
18. *2013 Church Almanac* (Salt Lake City: The Deseret News, 2013), 211.
19. William Clayton, *Nauvoo Temple History Journal* (Salt Lake City: Church History Department, The Church of Jesus Christ of Latter-day Saints), 20.
20. Hill, *Joseph Smith the First Mormon*, 324.
21. Ibid., 325–29.
22. Ibid., 330.
23. Smith, *History of the Church*, 6:221.
24. The Joseph Smith Papers, Journal, December 1842–June 1844; Book 1, 21 December 1842–10 March 1843, 219–22, accessed February 20, 2015. http://josephsmithpapers.org/paperSummary/journal-december-1842-june-1844-book-1-21-december-1842-10-march-1843?p=230&highlight=daniel%20h%20wells#!/paperSummary/journal-december-1842-june-1844-book-1-21-december-1842-10-march-1843&p=230.
25. Hajicek, "Daniel H. Wells Justice Court Record Book."
26. Ibid.
27. Ibid.
28. James B. Allen, "One Man's Nauvoo: William Clayton's Experience in Mormon Illinois," in *The Journal of Mormon History* (Salt Lake City: Mormon History Association, 1979), 6:42–43.
29. Smith, *History of the Church*, 6:6–7.
30. Ibid.
31. Hill, *Joseph Smith the First Mormon*, 364.

32. Daniel H., Letter to Joseph Coombs, March 31, 1844.
33. Quentin Thomas Wells, "Genealogy of the Wells, Thomas, Young, Coon and related Families" (Salt Lake City: unpublished manuscript in author's possession).

Chapter 5

1. *Doctrine and Covenants*, Section 132 (Salt Lake City: The Church of Jesus Christ of Latter-Day Saints, 1985).
2. *Journal of Discourses*, 3:266, accessed September 10, 2015, http://jod.mrm.org/3/264.
3. Hill, *Joseph Smith the First Mormon*, 338.
4. Brian C. Hales, "Joseph Smith's Polygamy, Nauvoo Polygamy—1843, Emma Learns that Plural Marriage Has Been Restored," accessed February 23, 2015, http://josephsmithspolygamy.org/history-2/changes-in-june-1842/.
5. Ibid.
6. Hinckley, *Daniel Hanmer Wells and Events of His Time*, 343.
7. Brian C. Hales, "Joseph Smith's Polygamy, Nauvoo Polygamy—1843, Knowledge of the Revelation Spreads," accessed February 23, 2015, http://josephsmithspolygamy.org/history-2/changes-in-june-1842/.
8. The Joseph Smith Papers, History, 1838–1856, vol. C-1 [2 November 1838–31 July 1842], 1344, accessed February 19, 2015, http://josephsmithpapers.org/paperSummary/history-1838-1856-volume-c-1-2-november-1838-31-july-1842?p=508&highlight=Daniel%20h%20wells#!/paperSummary/history-1838-1856-volume-c-1-2-november-1838-31-july-1842&p=508.
9. The Joseph Smith Papers, History, 1838–1856, vol. C-1 [2 November 1838–31 July 1842], 1359, 1360, accessed February 19, 2015, http://josephsmithpapers.org/paperSummary/history-1838-1856-volume-c-1-2-november-1838-31-july-1842?p=534&highlight=Daniel%20h%20wells.
10. Hinckley, *Daniel Hanmer Wells and Events of His Time*, 234–35.
11. Ibid., 239–40.
12. Ibid., 343–44; *Pearl of Great Price, The Articles of Faith*, no. 3 (Salt Lake City: The Church of Jesus Christ of Latter-Day Saints, 1985).
13. Hinckley, *Daniel Hanmer Wells and Events of His Time*, 343.
14. Wells, Letter to the Chicago Historical Society.
15. Eliza R. Wells, Petition for Divorce, Des Moines County Circuit Court, IA, March 1851 (Salt Lake City: Church History Department, The Church of Jesus Christ of Latter-day Saints).
16. Hill, *Joseph Smith the First Mormon*, 372–73.
17. Smith, *History of the Church*, 6:64.
18. Ibid., 187–88.
19. Daniel H. Wells, Letter to Joseph Coombs, March 31, 1844.
20. Hill, *Joseph Smith the First Mormon*, 387–90.
21. John S. Dinger, ed., *The Nauvoo City and High Council Minutes* (Salt Lake City: Signature Books, 1995), Special Session, December 29, 1843.
22. Smith, *History of the Church*, 6:149–53.
23. Ibid, 334.

24. Dinger, *The Nauvoo City and High Council Minutes*, Regular City Council meeting, Monday, June 10, 1844; see also Smith, *History of the Church*, 6:443.
25. Dinger, *Nauvoo City*; Prospectus of the Nauvoo Expositor read before the Nauvoo City Council meeting of June 10, 1844; see also Smith, *History of the Church*, 6:443–45.
26. Dinger, *Nauvoo City*; Resolution of the Nauvoo City Council passed June 10, 1844; see also Smith, *History of the Church*, 6:448.
27. Smith, *History of the Church*, 6:532.
28. Ibid.
29. The Joseph Smith Papers, Nauvoo City Officers Chart, accessed June 17, 2015, http://josephsmithpapers.org/bc-jsp/content/jsp/images/content/library/pdf/chart11.pdf.
30. "The Warsaw Signal," June 12, 1844, *Uncle Dale's Readings in Early Mormon History Newspapers of Illinois*, accessed February 26, 2015, http://www.sidneyrigdon.com/dbroadhu/IL/sign1844.htm#0612.
31. "The Warsaw Signal," Extra, 14 June 1844, *Uncle Dale's Readings in Early Mormon History, Newspapers of Illinois*, accessed February 26, 2015, http://www.sidneyrigdon.com/dbroadhu/IL/sign1844.htm#0612.
32. Hill, *Joseph Smith the First Mormon*, 396; see also Smith, *History of the Church*, 6:488–91.
33. Smith, *History of the Church*, 6:488.
34. Wells, *The Narrative of General Daniel H. Wells*, 2.
35. Smith, *History of the Church*, 6:534.
36. Ibid., 536–37.
37. Hill, *Joseph Smith the First Mormon*, 402–3.
38. *The Latter-Day Saints Millennial Star* 24 (London: Islington, The Church of Jesus Christ of Latter-day Saints, May 31, 1862): 342.
39. Hinckley, *Daniel Hanmer Wells and Events of His Time*, 343.
40. Hill, *Joseph Smith the First Mormon*, 410–21.

Chapter 6

1. Eudocia Baldwin Marsh, "When the Mormons Dwelt Among Us," in *The Bellman* 20, nos. 507–8 (Berkeley: Bancroft Library, University of California, April 1, 1916), 403.
2. Hill, *Joseph Smith the First Mormon*, 427–31.
3. Ibid.
4. Smith, *History of the Church*, 6:628.
5. Hill, *Joseph Smith the First Mormon*, 421–23.
6. Thomas Ford, *A History of Illinois from Its Commencement as a State in 1814 to 1847* (Chicago: S. C. Griggs & Co., 1854), 361.
7. Thomas Gregg, *History of Hancock County, Illinois* (Chicago, Chas. C. Chapman & Co., 1880), 450.
8. *2013 Church Almanac*, 211.
9. *Church Historian's Office Register of General Church Minutes, 1839–1877* (Salt Lake City: Church History Library, The Church of Jesus Christ of Latter-day Saints).
10. Hill, *Joseph Smith the First Mormon*, 427.

11. Edward W. Tullidge, "Daniel H. Wells," in *Tullidge's Quarterly Magazine* 3, no. 2 (Salt Lake City: Edward W. Tullidge, April 1884): 114.
12. Ford, *A History of Illinois from Its Commencement as a State in 1814 to 1847*, 341–44.
13. William Clayton, *Nauvoo Temple History Journal*, 30.
14. Hill, *Joseph Smith the First Mormon*, 429, 431.
15. Mrs. Minor Deming, Letter, September 29, 1845 (Urbana: Minor Deming Papers, Illinois Historical Survey, University of Illinois Library).
16. Wells, *The Narrative of General Daniel H. Wells*, 1.
17. Hill, *Joseph Smith the First Mormon*, 434.
18. Wells, *Genealogy of the Wells, Thomas, Young, Coon and Related Families*.
19. Wells, *The Narrative of General Daniel H. Wells*, 2.
20. *The Latter-Day Saints Millennial Star* 6 (Liverpool: The Church of Jesus Christ of Latter-day Saints, December 1, 1845): 188.
21. Hill, *Joseph Smith the First Mormon*, 435.
22. "Nauvoo Temple Endowment Name Index," accessed June 12, 2015, http://user.xmission.com/~research/family/familypage.htm.
23. Wells, *The Narrative of General Daniel H. Wells*, 1.
24. Brigham H. Roberts, *The Rise and Fall of Nauvoo* (Salt Lake City: Deseret News Publishers, 1900); and Ford, *A History of Illinois from Its Commencement as a State in 1814 to 1847*, 411–12.
25. Wells, "The Wells Family Genealogy," 2. Almon W. Babbitt was later presumed killed by Indians while he was returning from Great Salt Lake City to St. Louis. His body was never found.
26. William Clayton, *Journal of William Clayton* (Salt Lake City: Church History Department, The Church of Jesus Christ of Latter-day Saints), entry for August 25, 1846.
27. Richard Van Wagoner and Steven C. Walker, *A Book of Mormons* (Salt Lake City: Signature Books Library, Salt Lake City, 1982), page W, online edition, accessed March 3, 2015, http://signaturebookslibrary.org/?p=17795.
28. Roberts, *The Rise and Fall of Nauvoo*, 360–61.
29. Ibid.
30. Ibid.
31. Wells, *The Narrative of General Daniel H. Wells*, 2.
32. John S. Fullmer, *A Condensed History of the Expulsion of the Saints from Nauvoo* (pamphlet) (Liverpool: Printed by B. James, 1855).
33. Clayton, *Journal of William Clayton*, entry for August 25, 1846.
34. Fullmer, *A Condensed History of the Expulsion of the Saints from Nauvoo*.
35. Clayton, *Journal of William Clayton*, entry for August 25, 1846.
36. Roberts, *The Rise and Fall of Nauvoo*, 364.
37. Fullmer, *A Condensed History of the Expulsion of the Saints from Nauvoo*.
38. Philo Johnson, *Autobiographical Sketch of the Life of Philo Johnson* (Payson, UT: 1894), accessed June 15, 2015, http://www.rootcellar.us/johnsnph.htm.
39. Roberts, *The Rise and Fall of Nauvoo*, 364.
40. Clayton, *Journal of William Clayton*, entry for August 25, 1846.
41. Fullmer, *A Condensed History of the Expulsion of the Saints from Nauvoo*.
42. Roberts, *The Rise and Fall of Nauvoo*, 365.

43. Hinckley, *Daniel Hanmer Wells and Events of His Time*, 42–43.
44. Wells, *The Narrative of General Daniel H. Wells*, 2.
45. Johnson, *Autobiographical Sketch of the Life of Philo Johnson*.
46. Hinckley, *Daniel Hanmer Wells and Events of His Time*, 42–43.

Chapter 7

1. Josiah B. Conyers, *A Brief History of the Leading Causes of the Hancock Mob in the Year 1846* (St. Louis: Cathcart & Prescott, 1846), 73–74.
2. Wells, *The Narrative of General Daniel H. Wells*, 2.
3. Hinckley, *Daniel Hanmer Wells and Events of His Time*, 45–47.
4. Ibid, 26.
5. Wells, *The Narrative of General Daniel H. Wells*, 3.
6. Coombs, Lucy Ann, Letter to Daniel H. Wells, 1846 (Logan: Daniel H. Wells Papers, Utah State University).
7. Ibid.
8. Acknowledgements of deeds and property sales made or witnessed by Daniel H. Wells during 1846 and 1847 appear in Hancock County Deed Books H, L, M, O, Q, R, and T.
9. Fred C. Collier, ed., *Manuscript History of Brigham Young 1847–1850* (Salt Lake City: Colliers Publishing Co., 1997), 18.
10. Edward W. Tullidge, *Tullidge's Histories* (Salt Lake City: Juvenile Instructor Press, 1889), 2:116; and "Heritage Gateways, Pioneer Date Summary, 14 July 1847," Utah State Office of Education, Salt Lake City, accessed March 9, 2015, http://heritage.uen.org/resources/Wc9f599d2aae0e.htm.
11. "Heritage Gateways, Pioneer Date Summary, 25 July 1847," Utah State Office of Education, Salt Lake City, accessed March 9, 2015, http://heritage.uen.org/resources/Wca6be5da9544.htm.
12. Abigail Rockwell and Lucy Ann Coombs, Letter to Daniel H. Wells, 1848 (Logan: Daniel H. Wells Papers, Utah State University).
13. "What man is this?" in *The Improvement Era* (Salt Lake City: The Church of Jesus Christ of Latter-day Saints, March 1964), 223; and Hinckley, *Daniel Hanmer Wells and Events of His Time*, 47.
14. Hinckley, *Daniel Hanmer Wells and Events of His Time*, 88.
15. Ibid, 49.
16. Collier, 18.
17. Ibid., 89.
18. Wells, Letter to the Chicago Historical Society.
19. Mark 10:22
20. "Nauvoo Neighbor, 29 October 1845," cited in B. H. Roberts, *A Comprehensive History of the Church of Jesus Christ of Latter-day Saints* (Provo: Brigham Young University Press, 1965), 1:539–40.
21. Collier, *Manuscript History of Brigham Young 1847–1850*, 106.
22. Ibid., 107.
23. Roberts, *A Comprehensive History of the Church of Jesus Christ of Latter-day Saints*, 319.
24. Collier, *Manuscript History of Brigham Young 1847–1850*, 106.

25. Thomas Bullock, "Journals 1843–1849" (Salt Lake City: Church History Department, The Church of Jesus Christ of Latter-day Saints), June 15, 1848, accessed March 10, 2015, http://history.lds.org/overlandtravels/trail ExcerptMulti?lang=eng&sourceId=4546.
26. John D. Lee, *A Mormon Chronicle: The Diaries of John D. Lee, 1848–1876*, ed. Robert Glass Cleland and Juanita Brooks (Los Angeles: Huntington Library Press, 2004), 30–79.
27. Bullock, "Journals 1843–1849," 29 June 1848 (Salt Lake City: The Church of Jesus Christ of Latter-day Saints, Church History Archives), accessed March 10, 2015, http://history.lds.org/overlandtravels/trailExcerptMulti?lang=eng&sourceId=4546.
28. Lee, *A Mormon Chronicle: The Diaries of John D. Lee, 1848–1876*, 30–79.
29. Ibid.
30. Lorraine Richardson Manderscheid, "Divorce of Louisa Free, Some Descendants of John Doyle Lee," accessed March 10, 2015, http://www.wadhome.org/lee/chapter_04.html. At the time of Lee's execution in October 1877 for his part in the Mountain Meadows Massacre, only three of his nineteen wives were reportedly still with him.
31. Emeline Y. Wells, "Sketch of the Life of Louisa Free Wells" (Salt Lake City: unpublished manuscript, 1928).
32. Edward W. Tullidge, *Women of Mormondom* (New York: Tullidge & Crandall, 1877), 336–38.
33. Martha Givens Harris and Josephine Wells Lyman, "Martha Givens Harris Autobiographical Life Sketch," in *Our Pioneer Heritage*, vol. 8, *That They May Live Again* (Provo: Brigham Young University Press, 1965), 188–91.
34. Ibid.
35. Collier, *Manuscript History of Brigham Young 1847–1850*, 110–11.
36. Bullock, "Journals 1843–1849," 26, 27, 28, and 30 August 1847.
37. Ibid.
38. Wells, *The Narrative of General Daniel H. Wells*, 3.

Chapter 8

1. Collier, *Manuscript History of Brigham Young 1847–1850*, 124.
2. Wells, *The Narrative of General Daniel H. Wells*, 3.
3. Orson F. Whitney, *History of Utah* (Salt Lake City, George Cannon & Sons Co., 1904), 4:177.
4. Hinckley, *Daniel Hanmer Wells and Events of His Time*, 64.
5. Ibid., 65.
6. "The Day the Sky Fell in Salt Lake City: April 5, 1876, The Mystery of Utah History," accessed March 10, 2015, http://mysteryofutahhistory.blogspot.com/2013/10/the-day-sky-fell-in-salt-lake-city.html.
7. "Salt Lake City Cemetery," FindAGrave.com, accessed March 10, 2015, http://www.findagrave.com/cgi-bin/fg.cgi?page=cr&CRid=77424&CScn=salt+lake+city+cemetery&CScntry=4&CSst=47&.
8. "Ancestors of Henry Grow," HenryGrowFamily.com, 9, accessed March 10, 2015, http://www.henrygrowfamily.com/documents/Henry%20Grow.pdf.

9. "Lewis Robison 1816–1883," *FamilySearch.org*, Memories, accessed March 10, 2015, https://familysearch.org/photos/stories/1324458.
10. Hinckley, *Daniel Hanmer Wells and Events of His Time*, 55; and Collier, *Manuscript History of Brigham Young 1847–1850*, 164. The animals harvested included 783 wolves, 409 foxes, 31 minx, 2 bears, 2 wolverines, and 2 wildcats, as well as 1565 scavenging birds.
11. Collier, *Manuscript History of Brigham Young 1847–1850*, 165–73.
12. Ibid., 173.
13. Wells, *The Narrative of General Daniel H. Wells*, 4.
14. Collier, *Manuscript History of Brigham Young 1847–1850*, 203–4.
15. Wells, *The Narrative of General Daniel H. Wells*, 3–4.
16. Hinckley, *Daniel Hanmer Wells and Events of His Time*, 136–39.
17. John A. Sutter, "The Discovery of Gold in California," The Virtual Museum of the City of San Francisco, accessed March 10, 2015, http://www.sfmuseum.org/hist2/gold.html.
18. "Heritage Auctions, All Auction Archive, Territorial Gold, 1849 $10 Mormon Ten Dollar AU58 NGC," accessed March 10, 2015, http://coins.ha.com/itm/territorial-gold/1849-10-mormon-ten-dollar-au58-ngc-k-3-r7/a/1204-5455.s.
19. Ibid.; and "Coin Community Family, Main Coin Forum, Heritage Seldom Seen Selections: Rare 1849 Mormon $20 Gold," accessed March 10, 2015, http://www.coincommunity.com/forum/topic.asp?TOPIC_ID=160791.
20. Wells, *The Narrative of General Daniel H. Wells*, 3.
21. "Gold Mormon Coins," accessed March 10, 2015, http://goldmormoncoins.com/Gold_Mormon_Coins.html. Mormon gold coins are rare collectors' treasures today. In 2014, an 1848 $10 eagle sold at auction for over $700,000.
22. Wells, *The Narrative of General Daniel H. Wells*, 4.
23. Hosea Stout, "The Diary of Hosea Stout, 5 March 1849," Rob and Susan Johnson Family Pages, accessed March 11, 2015, http://robandsusanpages.com/History/Stout/Hosea_1849_03.html.
24. Peterson, *Utah's Black Hawk War*, 49–50.
25. Ibid., 51–52.
26. "Journal History of the Church: 1850–1859; 1850, 9 January 1850" (Salt Lake City: Church History Library, The Church of Jesus Christ of Latter-day Saints), accessed March 11, 2015, https://dcms.lds.org/delivery/DeliveryManagerServlet?dps_pid=IE293668.
27. Hinckley, *Daniel Hanmer Wells and Events of His Time*, 77–78.
28. Peterson, *Utah's Black Hawk War*, 53.
29. Daniel H. Wells, Major General, Special Order No. 2, Headquarters, Nauvoo Legion, Major General's Office, GSL City, January 31, 1850 (Utah Territorial Militia Records, Utah State Archives Record Series 2210), *FamilySearch.org*, The Church of Jesus Christ of Latter-day Saints, accessed March 12, 2015, https://familysearch.org/search/image/index#uri=https://familysearch.org/recapi/sord/collection/1462415/waypoints.
30. Hinckley, *Daniel Hanmer Wells and Events of His Time*, 78.
31. Peterson, *Utah's Black Hawk War*, 54.
32. Wells, *The Narrative of General Daniel H. Wells*, 4–5.

33. Collier, *Manuscript History of Brigham Young 1847–1850*, 286–87.
34. Peterson, *Utah's Black Hawk War*, 55–56.
35. Hinckley, *Daniel Hanmer Wells and Events of His Time*, 79.
36. Peterson, *Utah's Black Hawk War*, 56–57.
37. Daniel H. Wells, Letter to Bishop Higbee and Peter Conover, March 21, 1850 (Utah Territorial Militia Records, Utah State Archives Record Series 2210, No. 57), *FamilySearch.org*, The Church of Jesus Christ of Latter-day Saints, accessed March 12, 2015, https://familysearch.org/pal:/MM9.3.1/TH-1951-22024-4969-52?cc=1462415&wc=MXM3-R38:42653001.
38. Daniel H. Wells, Letter to Petetenete, Walker, Sowiette, and Black Hawk (Utah Territorial Militia Records, Utah State Archives Record Series 2210, No. 61), May 13, 1850, *FamilySearch.org*, The Church of Jesus Christ of Latter-day Saints, accessed March 12, 2015, https://familysearch.org/pal:/MM9.3.1/TH-1951-22024-4969-52?cc=1462415&wc=MXM3-R38:42653001.
39. Hinckley, *Daniel Hanmer Wells and Events of His Time*, 79.
40. Peterson, *Utah's Black Hawk War*, 58–59.
41. Hinckley, *Daniel Hanmer Wells and Events of His Time*, 80.
42. Collier, *Manuscript History of Brigham Young 1847–1850*, 326–27.
43. William W. Terry, William W. Terry Collection, MS 116 (Ogden: Weber State University, Special Collections); and Ambrose A. Shaw, *FamilySearch.org*, Memories, The Church of Jesus Christ of Latter-day Saints, accessed March 28, 2015, https://familysearch.org/photos/people/2106136.
44. Hinckley, *Daniel Hanmer Wells and Events of His Time*, 80.
45. Collier, *Manuscript History of Brigham Young 1847–1850*, 330.
46. Leonard J. Arrington, *Brigham Young, American Moses* (Urbana: University of Illinois Press, 1985), 226–27.
47. Hinckley, *Daniel Hanmer Wells and Events of His Time*, 143–44.
48. "Journal History of the Church, 1896–2001: 1850–1859" (Salt Lake City: Church History Library, The Church of Jesus Christ of Latter-day Saints), March 28, 1851, accessed March 11, 2015, https://dcms.lds.org/delivery/DeliveryManagerServlet?dps_pid=IE2112771.
49. "Journal History of the Church, 1896–2001: 1850–1859" (Salt Lake City: Church History Library, The Church of Jesus Christ of Latter-day Saints), October 21–23, 1851, accessed March 11, 2015, https://dcms.lds.org/delivery/DeliveryManagerServlet?dps_pid=IE2112771.
50. Norman F. Furniss, *The Mormon Conflict 1850–1859* (New Haven: Yale University Press, 1966), 24.
51. "Journal History of the Church, 1896–2001: 1850–1859" (Salt Lake City: Church History Library, The Church of Jesus Christ of Latter-day Saints), October 21–23, 1851, accessed March 26, 2015, https://dcms.lds.org/delivery/DeliveryManagerServlet?dps_pid=IE2112771.
52. Arrington, *Brigham Young, American Moses*, 128–29.
53. Furniss, *The Mormon Conflict 1850–1859*, 25–26.
54. Ibid.
55. Hinckley, *Daniel Hanmer Wells and Events of His Time*, 150.
56. Ibid., 147–50.

Chapter 9

1. Wells, "The Wells Family Genealogy," 10.
2. Arrington, *Brigham Young, American Moses*, 233.
3. Hinckley, *Daniel Hanmer Wells and Events of His Time*, 344.
4. Lorraine Richardson Manderscheid, "Divorce of Louisa Free, Some Descendants of John Doyle Lee," accessed March 28, 2015, http://www.wadhome.org/lee/chapter_04.html.
5. Wells, "The Wells Family Genealogy," 11.
6. Ibid.
7. Hinckley, *Daniel Hanmer Wells and Events of His Time*, 344.
8. Lydia Ann Alley Wells, "Lydia Ann Alley Autobiographical Sketch," in *Our Pioneer Heritage*, vol. 8, *That They May Live Again* (Provo: Brigham Young University Press, 1965), 191–93.
9. Ibid.
10. Hinckley, *Daniel Hanmer Wells and Events of His Time*, 344–55.
11. Whitney, *History of Utah*, 4:67.
12. Hannah Free Wells, "Sketch of the Life of Hannah Corilla Free Wells," in *Our Pioneer Heritage*, vol. 8, *That They May Live Again* (Provo: Brigham Young University Press, 1965), 194–96.
13. LaRae Free Kerr, "Life of Lawrence Sterne Hotchkiss" (Salt Lake City: unpublished research in author's possession, 2013).
14. *The Latter-day Saints Millennial Star* 15:115–16.
15. Wells, "The Wells Family Genealogy," 11.
16. 1850 US Federal Census, Utah Territory, Great Salt Lake City, Provo, 86, Ancestry.com, accessed September 10, 2015, http://interactive.ancestry.com/8054/4181033-00179/1097974?backurl=http%3a%2f%2fsearch.ancestry.com%2f%2fcgi-bin%2fsse.dll%3findiv%3d1%26db%3d1850usfedcenancestry%26gss%3dangs-d%26new%3d1%26rank%3d1%26gsfn_x%3d1%26gsln%3dwells%26gsln_x%3d1%26msbpn__ftp%3dutah%26MSAV%3d1%26uidh%3djb1%26pcat%3d35%26fh%3d4%26h%3d1097974%26recoff%3d%26ml_rpos%3d5&ssrc=&backlabel=ReturnRecord.
17. Carol Cornwall Madsen, "Emmeline B. Wells: Romantic Rebel," monograph 12 in *Supporting Saints: Life Stories of Nineteenth-Century Mormons*, vol. 1 (Provo: Brigham Young University, Religious Studies Center, 1985).
18. Kate Carter, "Sketch of the Life of Emmeline Blanche Woodward," *Our Pioneer Heritage*, vol. 8, *That They May Live Again* (Provo: Brigham Young University Press, 1965), 196–201. James Harris later left the United States and accidentally drowned while fishing off the coast of Calcutta, India, in 1859.
19. Ibid.
20. Madsen, "Emmeline B. Wells: Romantic Rebel."
21. Carter, "Sketch of the Life of Emmeline Blanche Woodward," 196–201.
22. Madsen, "Emmeline B. Wells: Romantic Rebel."
23. Ibid.
24. Carter, "Sketch of the Life of Emmeline Blanche Woodward," 196–201. Melvina Whitney later married William Wells Woods, second son of Daniel's sister Catherine Woods.

25. Wells, "The Wells Family Genealogy," 11.
26. Eliza R. Wells, Petition for Divorce, Des Moines Circuit Court Record, 1851.
27. 1860 US Federal Census, Utah Territory, Great Salt Lake City, 18th Ward, 217; and 1860 US Federal Census, Wisconsin, Waukesha, Summit, Nashotah Theological Seminary, 28.
28. James W. Woods, Letter to Daniel H. Wells, March 31, 1849 (Logan: Daniel H. Wells Papers, Utah State University).
29. Pamela Wells and Abigail Rockwell, Letter to Daniel H. Wells, September 10, 1850 (Logan: Daniel H. Wells Papers, Utah State University).
30. James W. Woods, Letter to Daniel H. Wells, September 15, 1850 (Logan: Daniel H. Wells Papers, Utah State University).
31. "Nauvoo Today," *The Improvement Era* (Salt Lake City: General Board M.I.A., 1909), 12:604–5.
32. 1850 US Federal Census, Utah Territory, Great Salt Lake City, 86; and Hinckley, *Daniel Hanmer Wells and Events of His Time*, 367–71.
33. "Historical Note: The Canyon's First Resident?" *Emigration Canyon Community Council Newsletter*, August, 2000, accessed March 13, 2015, http://www.emigrationcanyon.org/newsletters.asp?newsid=4&org=ECC&ind=y.
34. Ibid.
35. Alonzo Delano, *Life on the Plains and Among the Diggings* (Buffalo: Miller, Orton, & Mulligan, 1854), 123.
36. *Acts and Resolutions of the Second Annual Session of the Legislative Assembly of the Territory of Utah* (Great Salt Lake City: George Hales, Printer, 1853), 17.
37. Furniss, *The Mormon Conflict 1850–1859*, 37.
38. *New York Weekly Tribune* 18, no. 896 (October 1, 1858).
39. Thomas G. Alexander, *The Rise of Multiple-use Management in the Intermountain West: A History of Region 4* (Washington, DC: Forest Service, US Department of Agriculture, 1987), 9.
40. Hinckley, *Daniel Hanmer Wells and Events of His Time*, 371.
41. Rod Morris, "Balsam Hill Cabin, Brighton, Utah, 2009," accessed March 13, 2015, http://balsam-hill-cabin.com/php/book/ch1.php.
42. Andrew Jenson, *Encyclopedic History of the Church of Jesus Christ of Latter-day Saints* (Salt Lake City: Deseret News Press, 1941), 250.
43. Hinckley, *Daniel Hanmer Wells and Events of His Time*, 65–66.
44. Roberts, *Comprehensive History of the Church*, 4:17–19.
45. Hinckley, *Daniel Hanmer Wells and Events of His Time*, 67–68.
46. Utah Division of State History, "Markers and Monuments Database, Early Magna Settlements," 1992, accessed June 18, 2014, http://heritage.utah.gov/apps/history/markers/detailed_results.php?markerid=2662.
47. "Journal History of the Church" (Salt Lake City: Church History Department, The Church of Jesus Christ of Latter-day Saints), entry of April 22, 1852, accessed March 13, 2015, https://dcms.lds.org/delivery/DeliveryManagerServlet?dps_pid=IE408166.
48. Hinckley, *Daniel Hanmer Wells and Events of His Time*, 301–2.
49. *Deseret News*, Salt Lake City, October 20, 1855.

Chapter 10

1. Wells, *The Narrative of General Daniel H. Wells*, 5.
2. Ibid., 6.
3. Peterson, *Utah's Black Hawk War*, 64–65.
4. Wells, *The Narrative of General Daniel H. Wells*, 8.
5. Peterson, *Utah's Black Hawk War*, 65–66.
6. Hinckley, *Daniel Hanmer Wells and Events of His Time*, 81.
7. *Deseret News*, July 30, 1853, 2.
8. Ibid.
9. *Deseret News*, October 15, 1853, 2.
10. Lieut. J. W. Gunnison, *The Mormons or Latter-Day Saints, in the Valley of the Great Salt Lake: A History of Their Rise and Progress, Peculiar Doctrines, Present Condition* (Philadelphia: Lippencott, Grambo & Co., 1852).
11. "John W. Gunnison Expedition, National Park Service, Curecanti NRA," accessed March 16, 2015, http://www.nps.gov/cure/learn/historyculture/explorer_gunnison.htm.
12. Ibid.
13. Wells, *The Narrative of General Daniel H. Wells*, 5–6.
14. E. G. Beckwith and J. W. Gunnison, *Report of Explorations for a Route for the Pacific Railroad: Near the 38th and 39th Parallels of North Latitude: From the Mouth of the Kansas River, Mo., to the Sevier Lake, in the Great Basin*, OCLC 8497072 (Washington, DC: War Dept., 1856), 74.
15. Gunnison, *The Mormons or Latter-Day Saints, in the Valley of the Great Salt Lake*, v–xiv.
16. Hinckley, *Daniel Hanmer Wells and Events of His Time*, 89–90.
17. Arrington, *Brigham Young, American Moses*, 215–17.
18. Hinckley, *Daniel Hanmer Wells and Events of His Time*, 89–90.
19. Wells, *The Narrative of General Daniel H. Wells*, 7.
20. Hinckley, *Daniel Hanmer Wells and Events of His Time*, 91.
21. Peter W. Conover, Letter to Daniel H. Wells, June 18, 1854 (Salt Lake City: Utah Territorial Militia Correspondence, Utah State Archives, 1849–1863).
22. Peterson, *Utah's Black Hawk War*, 69–70.
23. Arrington, *Brigham Young, American Moses*, 219–20.
24. Ronald W. Walker, Richard E. Turley Jr., and Glen M. Leonard, *Massacre at Mountain Meadows* (New York: Oxford University Press, 2008), 21.
25. Hinckley, *Daniel Hanmer Wells and Events of His Time*, 96.
26. Arrington, *Brigham Young, American Moses*, 246.
27. Ibid. 247–49.
28. Walker, *Massacre at Mountain Meadows*, 21.
29. Daniel H. Wells, Letter to Brigham Young, November 21, 1857 (Salt Lake City: Brigham Young Collection, Church History Library, The Church of Jesus Christ of Latter-day Saints).
30. Davis Bitton and Linda P. Wilcox, "Pestiferous Ironclads: The Grasshopper Problem in Pioneer Utah," *Utah Historical Quarterly* 46, no. 4 (Fall 1978): 336–55, accessed March 17, 2015, http://historytogo.utah.gov/utah_chapters/pioneers_and_cowboys/pestiferousironclads.html.
31. "Written for Louisa F. Wells," *Deseret News*, August 13, 1856, 182.

32. Wells, "The Wells Family Genealogy," 10.
33. Ibid., 11.
34. *2013 Church Almanac*, 121.
35. Gene Allred Sessions, *Mormon Thunder: A Documentary History of Jedediah Morgan Grant* (Urbana: University of Illinois Press, 1993).
36. *2013 Church Almanac*, 121.
37. Hinckley, *Daniel Hanmer Wells and Events of His Time*, 23–24.
38. "Journal History of the Church," April 6, 1857, 229–30, accessed June 1, 2016, https://dcms.lds.org/delivery/DeliveryManagerServlet?dps_pid =IE266732.
39. Ibid.
40. *Journal of Discourses* 5:93–101.
41. *2013 Church Almanac*, 113–18.
42. Hiram P. Kimball, ed., *On the Potter's Wheel: Diaries of Heber C. Kimball, Appendix A* (Salt Lake City: Signature Books, Inc., 1987), 176.
43. Ibid.
44. *Journal of Discourses* 8:183–87.
45. Ibid.
46. Wells, "The Wells Family Genealogy," 10.
47. Ibid., 11.
48. William G. Hartley, "Dangerous Outpost: Thomas Corless and the Fort Limhi/Salmon River Mission," in *Mormon Historical Studies* 2, no. 2 (Sandy, UT: Mormon Historic Sites Foundation, 2002), 147; and Thomas J. Williams, *Miracle of the Desert* (The Williams Family History, 1957), 11.
49. Richard Darrell Kitchen, *Mormon-Indian Relations in Deseret: Intermarriage and Indenture, 1847 to 1877* (Phoenix: Arizona State University, 2002), 165.
50. Hartley, "Dangerous Outpost: Thomas Corless and the Fort Limhi/Salmon River Mission."
51. David L. Bigler, "A Lion in the Path: Genesis of the Utah War, 1857–1858," *Utah Historical Quarterly* 76, no. 1 (Winter 2008):17–18.
52. Arrington, *Brigham Young, American Moses*, 252.
53. *Deseret News*, June 17, 1857.
54. *Journal of Discourses* 5:52–58.

Chapter 11

1. Hinckley, *Daniel Hanmer Wells and Events of His Time*, 93.
2. Leonard J. Arrington and Ronald W. Walker, *Great Basin Kingdom: An Economic History of the Latter-day Saints, 1830–1900* (Urbana: University of Illinois Press, 2004), 162–69. Most of the BYX stations were later used by the Pony Express Co.
3. Whitney, *History of Utah*, 1:597–99.
4. Ibid.; and "Journal History of the Church, 1896–2001: 1850–1859" (Salt Lake City: Church History Library, The Church of Jesus Christ of Latter-day Saints), 1857 May–July; July 24, 1857, accessed March 20, 2015, https://eadview.lds.org/findingaid/CR%20100%20137.
5. Whitney, *History of Utah*, 1:604.

6. Ira Ames, "Ira Ames' Journal," accessed March 20, 2015, http://www.huntsman-gifford.com/history/iraames/iraames.htm.
7. *Deseret News*, July 22, 1857, column 3; and Hinckley, *Daniel Hanmer Wells and Events of His Time*, 93.
8. "Journal History of the Church, 1896–2001: 1850–1859," (Salt Lake City: Church History Library, The Church of Jesus Christ of Latter-day Saints), 1857 May–July; July 24, 1857, accessed March 20, 2015, https://eadview.lds.org/findingaid/CR%20100%20137.
9. Richard D. Poll and Ralph W. Hansen, "'Buchanan's Blunder' The Utah War, 1857–1858," *Military Affairs* 25, no. 3 (1961): 121–31.
10. Arrington, *Brigham Young, American Moses*, 230.
11. Thomas W. Burns, "Initial Ithacans," *Ithaca: Press of the Ithaca Journal* 51, accessed April 1, 2015, http://www.archive.org/stream/cu31924030991487#page/n65/mode/2up.
12. Arrington, *Brigham Young, American Moses*, 234–35.
13. Ibid., 233; and Hubert Howe Bancroft, *History of Utah 1540–1886* (San Francisco: The History Company, 1889), 461–62.
14. Bancroft, *History of Utah*, 461–62.
15. Whitney, *History of Utah*, 1:578–79; and Arrington, *Brigham Young, American Moses*, 233.
16. Whitney, *History of Utah*, 1:578–79.
17. Furniss, *The Mormon Conflict 1850–1859*, 25–26.
18. *New York Tribune*, February 13, 1857; *New York Times*, April 22, 1857; *New York Times*, July 18, 1857; and *New York Herald*, May 24, 1857.
19. John Bassett Moore, ed., *The Works of James Buchanan* (Philadelphia & London: J. B. Lippincott Co., 1908–1911), 10:152 and 12:212–18.
20. Arrington, *Brigham Young, American Moses*, 251.
21. Furniss, *The Mormon Conflict 1850–1859*, 99.
22. Ibid., 96 and 97.
23. Ibid, 95.
24. Ibid., 99–100; and Raymond W. Settle and Mary Lund Settle, *War Drums and Wagon Wheels: The Story of Russell, Majors, and Waddell* (Lincoln: University of Nebraska Press, 1966).
25. Furniss, *The Mormon Conflict 1850–1859*, 100–101; and Harold Schindler, "Utah War Broke Hold Mormons Had on Utah," *The Salt Lake Tribune*, July 23, 1995, accessed April 7, 2015, http://historytogo.utah.gov/salt_lake_tribune/centennial_celebration/072395.html.
26. Moore, *The Works of James Buchanan*, 10:152 and 12:212–18.
27. Furniss, *The Mormon Conflict 1850–1859*, 101.
28. *Journal of Discourses* 5:95; and *Deseret News*, September 23, 1857, 228, column 1.
29. Citizens of Utah, broadside proclamation, August 5, 1857 (Salt Lake City: Church History Department, The Church of Jesus Christ of Latter-day Saints).
30. LeRoy Reuben Hafen and Ann Woodbury Hafen, eds., *Mormon Resistance: A Documentary Account of the Utah Expedition, 1857–1858* (Glendale: Arthur H. Clark Company, 1958), 195–96.

31. Will Bagley, *Blood of the Prophets: Brigham Young and the Massacre at Mountain Meadows* (Norman: University of Oklahoma Press, 2012), 84.
32. "Journal History of the Church, entries for 4 August 1857, 5 August 1857, and 6 August 1857" (Salt Lake City: Church History Department, The Church of Jesus Christ of Latter-day Saints), accessed April 8, 2015, https://dcms.lds.org/delivery/DeliveryManagerServlet?dps_pid=IE492947.
33. Bagley, *Blood of the Prophets: Brigham Young and the Massacre at Mountain Meadows*, 85–86.
34. Samuel W. Richards, Letter to Orson Pratt, October 4, 1857, in *The Latter-day Saints Millennial Star* 19, no. 42, 668–71.
35. Furniss, *The Mormon Conflict 1850–1859*, 105–6.
36. "Journal History of the Church, 9 September 1857," (Salt Lake City: Church Historians Department, The Church of Jesus Christ of Latter-day Saints), accessed March 13, 2015, https://dcms.lds.org/delivery/DeliveryManagerServlet?dps_pid=IE492947; and Pleasonton, Letter to Capt. Stewart Van Vliet, July 28, 1857, in "Secretary of War Report, 1857," *Message from the President of the United States to the Two Houses of Congress, 1st Session, Thirty-Fifth Congress, 1857–1858* (Washington, DC: Cornelius Wendell, Printer), 2:27–28.
37. "Journal History of the Church, 14 September 1857," (Salt Lake City: Church Historians Department, The Church of Jesus Christ of Latter-day Saints), accessed March 13, 2015, https://dcms.lds.org/delivery/DeliveryManagerServlet?dps_pid=IE492947; and *Deseret News* 7:221.
38. Walker, *Massacre at Mountain Meadows*, 162–63; and "Journal History of the Church, September 11, 1857," (Salt Lake City: Church History Department, The Church of Jesus Christ of Latter-day Saints), accessed March 13, 2015, https://dcms.lds.org/delivery/DeliveryManagerServlet?dps_pid=IE492947.
39. Walker, *Massacre at Mountain Meadows*, 183–86.
40. Ibid, 186, 225–26.
41. Ibid, 144–45.
42. Ibid.
43. Arrington, *Brigham Young, American Moses*, 257.
44. Walker, *Massacre at Mountain Meadows*, 193–209.
45. Ibid.; and Bigler, *A Lion in the Path: Genesis of the Utah War, 1857–1858*, 19–20.
46. Arrington, *Brigham Young, American Moses*, 259–61.
47. Furniss, *The Mormon Conflict 1850–1859*, 104.
48. Maj. Irwin McDowell, order to Col. Albert S. Johnston, August 28, 1857, in "Secretary of War Report, 1857," *Message from the President of the United States to the Two Houses of Congress, 1st Session, Thirty-Fifth Congress, 1857–1858* (Washington, DC: Cornelius Wendell, Printer), 2:23–24.
49. Col. Albert S. Johnston, Letter to Maj. Irwin McDowell, September 29, 1857, in "Secretary of War Report, 1857," *Message from the President of the United States to the Two Houses of Congress, 1st Session, Thirty-Fifth Congress, 1857–1858* (Washington, DC: Cornelius Wendell, Printer), 2:24.
50. Charts of the Actual Strength of the Army of the United States on the 1st of July, 1857, in "Secretary of War Report, 1857," *Message from the President of*

the United States to the Two Houses of Congress, 1st Session, Thirty-Fifth Congress, 1857–1858 (Washington, DC: Cornelius Wendell, Printer), 2:64–67.
51. Furniss, *The Mormon Conflict 1850–1859*, 136, 137.
52. Ibid., 134 and 135.
53. Ibid., 133.
54. Capt. Stewart Van Vliet, Letter to the Commanding General, September 16, 1857, in "Secretary of War Report, 1857," *Message from the President of the United States to the Two Houses of Congress, 1st Session, Thirty-Fifth Congress, 1857–1858* (Washington, DC: Cornelius Wendell, Printer), 2:24–27.
55. Col. E. B. Alexander, Letter to Col. S. Cooper, October 9, 1857, in "Secretary of War Report, 1857," *Message from the President of the United States to the Two Houses of Congress, 1st Session, Thirty-Fifth Congress, 1857–1858* (Washington, DC: Cornelius Wendell, Printer), 2:29–31.
56. Hinckley, *Daniel Hanmer Wells and Events of His Time*, 100–1.
57. Whitney, *Popular History of Utah* (Salt Lake City: The Deseret News, 1916), 143; and Furniss, *The Mormon Conflict 1850–1859*, 139–40.
58. "Wyoming State Historic Preservation Office, Emigrant Trails, Bridger Trail, Fort Bridger," accessed April 10, 2015, http://wyoshpo.state.wy.us/trailsdemo/fort_bridger.htm#.
59. Furniss, *The Mormon Conflict 1850–1859*, 141.
60. Gen. Daniel H. Wells, Letter to Col. E. B. Alexander, September 30, 1857, in "Secretary of War Report, 1857," *Message from the President of the United States to the Two Houses of Congress, 1st Session, Thirty-Fifth Congress, 1857–1858* (Washington, DC: Cornelius Wendell, Printer), 2:31.
61. Brigham Young, Letter and Proclamation to Col. E. B. Alexander, September 29, 1857, in "Secretary of War Report, 1857," *Message from the President of the United States to the Two Houses of Congress, 1st Session, Thirty-Fifth Congress, 1857–1858* (Washington, DC: Cornelius Wendell, Printer), 2:32–33.
62. Col. E. B. Alexander, Letter to Brigham Young, October 2, 1857, in "Secretary of War Report, 1857," *Message from the President of the United States to the Two Houses of Congress, 1st Session, Thirty-Fifth Congress, 1857–1858* (Washington, DC: Cornelius Wendell, Printer), 2:34; and Hinckley, *Daniel Hanmer Wells and Events of His Time*, 32–33.
63. Furniss, *The Mormon Conflict 1850–1859*, 141.
64. Ibid.
65. "The Nauvoo Legion," *The Contributor* 9, no. 10 (Salt Lake City: The Contributor Company, August 1888): 370.
66. Col. Randolph B. Marcy, *Thirty Years of Army Life on the Border* (New York: Harper Brothers Publishers, 1866), 271–72; and Col. E. B. Alexander, Letter to Col. S. Cooper, October 9, 1857, in "Secretary of War Report, 1857," *Message from the President of the United States to the Two Houses of Congress, 1st Session, Thirty-Fifth Congress, 1857–1858* (Washington, DC: Cornelius Wendell, Printer), 2:29–31.
67. Hafen, *Mormon Resistance: A Documentary Account of the Utah Expedition, 1857–1858*, 226–31; and "The Nauvoo Legion," *The Contributor* 9, no. 10 (August 1888): 370–71.
68. "The Nauvoo Legion," 370–71.
69. Whitney, *Popular History of Utah*, 146.

70. Arrington, *Brigham Young, American Moses*, 255.
71. "The Nauvoo Legion," *The Contributor* 9, no. 10 (August 1888): 368.
72. Furniss, *The Mormon Conflict 1850–1859*, 112–14.
73. Hamilton Gardner, ed., "A Territorial Militiaman in the Utah War," *Journal of Newton Tuttle*, entries for October 19 and 20, 1857, Hickman Family Museum, accessed April 15, 2015, http://hickmanmuseum.homestead.com/Tuttle.html. Microfilm and typescript copies of the journal are in the library of the Utah State Historical Society.
74. Furniss, *The Mormon Conflict 1850–1859*, 114–15.
75. Ibid., 116–17.
76. Whitney, *Popular History of Utah*, 148.
77. Ibid., 148–50.
78. Roberts, *Comprehensive History of Church*, vol. 4, chap. 107.
79. Whitney, *Popular History of Utah*, 149–50.
80. Hinckley, *Daniel Hanmer Wells and Events of His Time*, 108.
81. Ibid, 109.
82. Daniel H. Wells, Letter to Lot Smith, October 17, 1857 (Tucson: Lot Smith Collection, University of Arizona Library).
83. "The Nauvoo Legion," *The Contributor* 9, no. 10 (August 1888): 365–67.
84. FortWiki.com, "Camp Scott (2)," accessed April 10, 2015, http://fortwiki.com/Camp_Scott_%282%29.
85. "The Nauvoo Legion," *The Contributor* 9, no. 10 (August 1888): 370–74; and Whitney, *Popular History of Utah*, 149.
86. Daniel H. Wells, Letter to Brigham Young, November 21, 1857 (Salt Lake City: Brigham Young Collection, Church History Library, The Church of Jesus Christ of Latter-day Saints).
87. Edward W. Tullidge, *The History of Salt Lake City* (Salt Lake City: Star Printing Company, 1886), 367.
88. Gardner, "A Territorial Militiaman in the Utah War," *Journal of Newton Tuttle*, entries for November 26 and 30, 1857.
89. Roberts, *Comprehensive History of the Church*, vol. 4, chap. 107.
90. Ibid.
91. "The Nauvoo Legion," *The Contributor* 9, no. 10 (August 1888): 374.
92. Gardner, "A Territorial Militiaman in the Utah War," *Journal of Newton Tuttle*, entry of December 5, 1857.
93. Hinckley, *Daniel Hanmer Wells and Events of His Time*, 108.

Chapter 12

1. Furniss, *The Mormon Conflict 1850–1859*, 169–72.
2. Ibid., 158.
3. Ibid., 151–52.
4. Arrington, *Brigham Young, American Moses*, 261–62.
5. Ibid.
6. Albert L. Zobell Jr., *Sentinel in the East: A Biography of Thomas L. Kane* (Salt Lake City: Nicholas G. Morgan, 1965), 119.
7. Furniss, *The Mormon Conflict 1850–1859*, 178–79.
8. Arrington, *Brigham Young, American Moses*, 262–63.

9. Ibid.
10. Furniss, *The Mormon Conflict 1850–1859*, 179–81.
11. Ibid., 175–76.
12. Ibid., 173.
13. Ibid., 172–73.
14. "Journal History of the Church, 9 September 1857," (Salt Lake City: Church Historians Department, The Church of Jesus Christ of Latter-day Saints), accessed April 13, 2015, https://dcms.lds.org/delivery/DeliveryManagerServlet?dps_pid=IE285027.
15. Brigham Young, Letter to Thomas Kane, March 22, 1858 (Salt Lake City: Kane Collection, Church History Department, The Church of Jesus Christ of Latter-day Saints).
16. Arrington, *Brigham Young, American Moses*, 175–76; and Bigler, *Fort Limhi: The Mormon Adventure in Oregon Territory, 1855–1858*, 266.
17. Arrington, *Bringham Young*, 264–67.
18. Arrington, *Great Basin Kingdom: An Economic History of the Latter-day Saints, 1830–1900*, 186–87.
19. Ibid.
20. Furniss, *The Mormon Conflict 1850–1859*, 182.
21. Ibid., 184–85.
22. William Alexander Linn, "The Story of the Mormons from the Date of Their Origin to 1901" (Digi-Media-Apps, 2012), accessed April 14, 2015, https://books.google.com/books?id=vWMXBQAAQBAJ&pg=PT680&lpg=PT680&dq=%22Cumming%22+%22echo+canyon%22+deception&source=bl&ots=mmexbRuSKz&sig=knkIw4OZ9sKnJur63oVMejccXXI&hl=en&sa=X&ei=VJYtVeG8MMmYgwS89ICwCw&ved=0CCQQ6AEwAg#v=onepage&q=%22Cumming%22%20%22echo%20canyon%22%20deception&f=false; and Tullidge, *History of Salt Lake City*, 209.
23. Tullidge, *History of Salt Lake City*, 209–10.
24. Arrington, *Brigham Young, American Moses*, 263.
25. Governor A. Cumming, Letter to A. S. Johnston, commanding Army of Utah, April 15, 1858; Tullidge, *History of Salt Lake City*, 208–9; and Arrington, *Brigham Young, American Moses*, 267.
26. Michael Scott Van Wagenen, "Sam Houston and the Utah War," *Utah Historical Quarterly* 76, no. 1 (Winter 2008):67–70.
27. Governor A. Cumming, Letter to Hon. Lewis Cass, Secretary of State, May 2, 1858; and Tullidge, *History of Salt Lake City*, 208–12.
28. Sam Houston, *The Writings of Sam Houston, 1813–1863* (Austin: The University of Texas Press, 1941), 522–25. Houston's Mormon informant was Seth Blair, a former US Attorney for Utah Territory, 1850–1854. Houston also wrote to his wife, Margaret, in a private letter: "I am no Mormon, & the evil of the difficulty has grown out of the policy pursued by Pierce, and kept up by Mr. Buchanan. Men were sent there of worse morals, than the Mormons. For instance, a man by the name of Drummond, who left a wife, & family in Ill. starving, & from this place took a hussy (I will not call her a woman) and introduced her at various places, Independence, Mo, & Santa Fe, and San Francisco, as his wife, and at Salt Lake lived with her as such. Others were men [of] dissolute habits, and these facts were known

to the Mormons. Now my Dear, this Mormon war had been predicated, on the reports of such men, and the Mormons have never refused to receive Federal officers, and respect them. So upon these premises, the President has sent Troops to subdue them, and Genl A.S. Johns[t]on is sent to the work, and of all men living the least qualified for such business. If the Mormons chuse [*sic*] to do it, they can destroy the whole command. If blood is drawn, the Troops will be annihilated." Sam Houston, Letter to Margaret Houston, February 16, 1857, *The Personal Papers of Sam Houston*, vol. 4, 1852–1863 (Denton: The University of North Texas Press, Denton, 1996).

29. Houston, *The Writings of Sam Houston, 1813–1863*, 522–25.
30. Ibid.
31. Gerhard Peters and John T. Woolley, "The American Presidency Project, James Buchanan, Proclamation—Rebellion in the Territory of Utah," accessed April 6, 1858, http://www.presidency.ucsb.edu/ws/?pid=68308.
32. Furniss, *The Mormon Conflict 1850–1859*, 193–95.
33. Hinckley, *Daniel Hanmer Wells and Events of His Time*, 112.
34. Tullidge, *History of Salt Lake City*, 214, 215.
35. Arrington, *Brigham Young, American Moses*, 273.
36. Hinckley, *Daniel Hanmer Wells and Events of His Time*, 113.
37. Furniss, *The Mormon Conflict 1850–1859*, 196.
38. Tullidge, *History of Salt Lake City*, 216.
39. Arrington, *Brigham Young, American Moses*, 273–74.
40. Ibid.; and Hinckley, *Daniel Hanmer Wells and Events of His Time*, 114–15.
41. Arrington, *Brigham Young, American Moses*, 274; and Furniss, *The Mormon Conflict 1850–1859*, 197–98.
42. Joseph Fielding Smith, *Essentials in Church History* (Salt Lake City: Deseret News Press, 1922), chapter 45; and Furniss, *The Mormon Conflict 1850–1859*, 201–2.
43. Arrington, *Brigham Young, American Moses*, 275.
44. Furniss, *The Mormon Conflict 1850–1859*, 200–201.
45. Ibid., 208–9.
46. *The Executive Documents of the Senate of The United States, 36th Congress, 1st Session, Volume 2, Executive Document No. 32, 1859–1860* (Washington, DC: George W. Rowman, Printer, 1860), 58, 59; and Hinckley, *Daniel Hanmer Wells and Events of His Time*, 171–72.
47. Tullidge, *History of Salt Lake City*, 226.
48. Hinckley, *Daniel Hanmer Wells and Events of His Time*, 172.
49. Furniss, *The Mormon Conflict 1850–1859*, 214–17.
50. "Journal History of the Church, 24 March 1859," (Salt Lake City: Church History Department, The Church of Jesus Christ of Latter-day Saints), accessed April 15, 2015, https://dcms.lds.org/delivery/DeliveryManagerServlet?dps_pid=IE281195.
51. Arrington, *Brigham Young, American Moses*, 276.
52. Furniss, *The Mormon Conflict 1850–1859*, 97–98.
53. Hinckley, *Daniel Hanmer Wells and Events of His Time*, 172.
54. Furniss, *The Mormon Conflict 1850–1859*, 220.
55. Hinckley, *Daniel Hanmer Wells and Events of His Time*, 173.
56. Whitney, *Popular History of Utah*, 167.

57. *The Executive Documents of the Senate of The United States, 36th Congress, 1st Session, Volume 2, Executive Document No. 32, 1859–1860,* 58–59; and Hinckley, *Daniel Hanmer Wells and Events of His Time,* 3–4.
58. Smith, *Essentials in Church History,* chapter 45.
59. Whitney, *Popular History of Utah,* 167.
60. "Journal History of the Church, 7 March 1859," (Salt Lake City: Church History Department, The Church of Jesus Christ of Latter-day Saints), accessed April 15, 2015, https://dcms.lds.org/delivery/DeliveryManager Servlet?dps_pid=IE281195; and Hinckley, *Daniel Hanmer Wells and Events of His Time,* 175.
61. Roberts, *Comprehensive History of the Church,* vol. 4, chapter 118; and Hinckley, *Daniel Hanmer Wells and Events of His Time,* 175–76.
62. *The Executive Documents of the Senate of The United States, 36th Congress, 1st Session, Volume 2, Executive Document No. 32, 1859–1860,* 58–59.

Chapter 13

1. Wells, "The Wells Family Genealogy," 11.
2. "Early Utah Coal Discoveries," *UtahRails.net,* accessed April 16, 2015, http://utahrails.net/utahcoal/utahcoal-early.php.
3. *Summit County Old Records,* Book D, 187; and *Summit County Abstracts,* Book 1, 289.
4. "Utah History to Go, Coalville" (State of Utah, 2013), accessed June 15, 2015, http://www.onlineutah.com/coalvillehistory.shtml.
5. W. Dee Halverson, *Grass Creek Canyon Coal* (Coalville, UT: Summit County Historical Society, 2010), 19–24.
6. Tullidge, *Tullidge's Quarterly Magazine* 3, no. 1:441.
7. Hinckley, *Daniel Hanmer Wells and Events of His Time,* 320.
8. Mabel Jarvis, "Sketches from The Life of Brigham Jarvis, Sr., 1850–1933," *The George and Ann Prior Jarvis Family Web Site,* accessed April 16, 2015, http://www.george-and-ann-prior-jarvis.org/html_docs/brigham_young_jarvis.html.
9. Ibid.; and "History of William Tonks," *FamilySearch.org,* Memories, Church History Library, The Church of Jesus Christ of Latter-day Saints, accessed April 17, 2015, https://familysearch.org/photos/stories/5239812; and "Memories of Adolphus R. Whitehead by His Son George F. Whitehead," *FamilySearch.org,* Memories, Church History Library, The Church of Jesus Christ of Latter-day Saints, accessed April 16, 2015, https://familysearch.org/photos/stories/1208552.
10. *Journal of Discourses* 9:28.
11. "Slavery in Utah," *Utah History to Go,* accessed April 17, 2015, http://history togo.utah.gov/utah_chapters/pioneers_and_cowboys/slaveryinutah.html.
12. John P. Enyeart, *The Quest for "Just and Pure Law" Rocky Mountain Workers and American Social Democracy, 1870–1924* (Stanford: Stanford University Press, 2009), 33–34.
13. Arrington, *Brigham Young, American Moses,* 281–84.
14. *2013 Church Almanac,* 211; and Arrington, *Brigham Young, American Moses,* 286. In March 1860, Congress authorized the creation of Nevada Territory

by partitioning it from the western portion of Utah Territory at the thirty-ninth meridian west of Washington, DC. The border between Utah and Nevada was moved eastward to the thirty-eighth meridian in 1861 and again to the thirty-seventh meridian in 1862. In the same year Colorado Territory was created and the eastern border between Utah and Colorado Territories was fixed at the thirty-second meridian.

15. William Hooper, Letter to George Q. Cannon, December 10, 1860, *The Latter-day Saints Millennial Star* 23 (Liverpool, 1861): 28–30.
16. Arrington, *Brigham Young, American Moses*, 287.
17. Ibid.
18. "American Civil War: General Albert Sidney Johnston," *About.com*, About Education, Military History Biographies, Confederate Leaders of the Civil War, accessed April 17, 2015, http://militaryhistory.about.com/od/americancivilwar/p/asjohnston.htm.
19. Miriam B. Murphy, "Territorial Governors," *Utah History Encyclopedia* (Salt Lake City: University of Utah Press, 1994), cited in Utah Department of Administrative Services, Division of Archives & Records Service, Utah State Government, accessed April 17, 2015, http://archives.utah.gov/research/guides/governor.htm.
20. Ronald M. Walker, "Salt Lake Theatre," *Utah History Encyclopedia* (Utah: Utah History to Go, 2013), accessed April 17, 2015, http://historytogo.utah.gov/utah_chapters/utah_today/saltlaketheatre.html.
21. Arrington, *Brigham Young, American Moses*, 288.
22. Fitz Hugh Ludlow, *The Heart of a Continent* (New York: Cambridge Riverside Press, 1870), 370–71.
23. Tullidge, *History of Salt Lake City*, 743–44.
24. Hinckley, *Daniel Hanmer Wells and Events of His Time*, 323–24.
25. Ibid., 347.
26. Ibid., 393.
27. "The Salt Lake Temple," *Encyclopedia of Mormonism* (New York: Macmillan, 1992), 1252–53.
28. Ibid.; and Richard O. Cowan, "The Design, Construction, and Role of the Salt Lake Temple," *Religious Studies Center* (Provo, UT: Brigham Young University, 2011), accessed April 17, 2015, http://rsc.byu.edu/archived/salt-lake-city/4-design-construction-and-role-salt-lake-temple.
29. E. B. Long, *The Saints and the Union: Utah Territory During the Civil War* (Urbana: University of Illinois Press, 2001), 61–62; and Whitney, *History of Utah*, 2:40–42.
30. Whitney, *History of Utah*, 2:40–42.
31. "Struggle for Statehood Chronology," *Utah History to Go* (Utah: Utah History to Go, 2013), accessed April 20, 2015, http://historytogo.utah.gov/utah_chapters/statehood_and_the_progressive_era/struggleforstatehoodchronology.html.
32. Long, *The Saints and the Union: Utah Territory During the Civil War*, 82–83; and Margaret M. Fischer, ed., *Utah and the Civil War: Being the Story of the Part Played by the People of Utah in That Great Conflict* (Salt Lake City: Deseret Book Company, 1929), 112.
33. Fischer, *Utah and the Civil War*, 112–13.

34. Dispatch of L. Thomas, Adjutant General (Washington, DC: War Department, April 28, 1862), cited in Roberts, *Comprehensive History of the Church*, 4:551; and Long, *The Saints and the Union: Utah Territory During the Civil War*, 84.
35. Long, *The Saints and the Union: Utah Territory During the Civil War*, 82–86.
36. Fisher, *Utah and the Civil War: Being the Story of the Part Played by the People of Utah in That Great Conflict*, 25–26.
37. Long, *The Saints and the Union: Utah Territory During the Civil War*, 85–86.
38. Whitney, *History of Utah*, 2:46–47.
39. Long, *The Saints and the Union: Utah Territory During the Civil War*, 87–88.
40. Ibid.
41. Gustive O. Larson, *Outline History of Utah and the Mormons* (Salt Lake City: Deseret Book, 1958), 195.
42. Long, *The Saints and the Union: Utah Territory During the Civil War*, 90–91.
43. Whitney, *History of Utah*, 2:54–55.
44. Hinckley, *Daniel Hanmer Wells and Events of His Time*, 130–31.
45. Whitney, *History of Utah*, 2:56–57.
46. Ibid.; and Hinckley, *Daniel Hanmer Wells and Events of His Time*, 179–80.
47. Whitney, *History of Utah*, 2:56–57.
48. Ibid., 89–90.
49. Ibid., 95–96.
50. Furniss, *The Mormon Conflict 1850–1859*, 232.
51. Orson F. Whitney, *History of Utah*, 2:97.
52. The Morrill Anti-Bigamy Act was a federal enactment of the US Congress that was signed into law on July 8, 1862 by President Abraham Lincoln. The act banned bigamy and limited church and non-profit organization ownership of property in any territory of the United States to $50,000 (37th United States Congress, Sess. 2., ch. 126, 12 Stat. 501). No funds were allocated for enforcement of the Morrill Act and Lincoln chose not to enforce it, but instead gave Brigham Young tacit permission to ignore it saying "if he will let me alone, I will let him alone." Gen. Patrick Edward Connor, commanding officer at Camp Douglas beginning in 1862, was explicitly instructed not to confront the Mormons over this or any other issue.
53. Whitney, *History of Utah*, 2:97.
54. Hinckley, *Daniel Hanmer Wells and Events of His Time*, 179–80.
55. *Sacramento Daily Union*, March 12, 1863.
56. Hinckley, *Daniel Hanmer Wells and Events of His Time*, 181–83.
57. Whitney, *History of Utah*, 2:99–101.
58. Ibid.

Chapter 14

1. Wells, "The Wells Family Genealogy," 11.
2. Wells, Letter to the Chicago Historical Society.
3. Hinckley, *Daniel Hanmer Wells and Events of His Time*, 341.
4. 1860 US Census for Albert E. Wells, Summit, Waukesha, Wisconsin, 28; and 1860 US Census for Daniel H. Wells family, Utah Territory, Great Salt

Lake County, Great Salt Lake City, Eighteenth Ward, 217–18. For unknown reasons, Daniel H. Wells also listed his deceased daughter, Luna Pamela Wells (August 24, 1856–November 4, 1857) in the 1860 Census as a four-year-old child living with the family.

5. 1860 US Census for Daniel H. Wells family, Utah Territory, Great Salt Lake County, Great Salt Lake City, Eighteenth Ward, 217–18.
6. Hinckley, *Daniel Hanmer Wells and Events of His Time*, 346–56.
7. From an address given by Ezra Taft Benson of the Quorum of the Twelve at the Logan Temple Centennial, May 17, 1984, published in *The Ensign* (August 1985), 6. Heber J. Grant was the son of Jedidiah M. Grant, who was second counselor to Brigham Young before Daniel H. Wells. He was a teenager in 1862, and both he and his mother were close friends of Daniel H. Wells and Brigham Young who both assisted them often in the years following Jedediah Grant's death.
8. "History of Ezra T. Benson," *The Benson Family: The Ancestry and Descendants of Ezra T. Benson* (Logan: The Ezra T. Benson Genealogical Society, Inc., 1979), accessed April 22, 2015, http://etb.bensonfamily.org/histories/etb-alder.htm.
9. Hinckley, *Daniel Hanmer Wells and Events of His Time*, 345–46.
10. Ibid., 343, 344.
11. Ibid., 355, 356.
12. Emmeline B. Wells, *Diary, 13 September 1874* (Provo: Special Collections, Harold B. Lee Library, Brigham Young University).
13. Ibid., October 11, 1874.
14. Hinckley, *Daniel Hanmer Wells and Events of His Time*, 353–54
15. Ibid., 347.
16. Ibid., 368–69.
17. Arrington, *Brigham Young, American Moses*, 336–37.
18. Hinckley, *Daniel Hanmer Wells and Events of His Time*, 373–76.
19. Wells, "The Wells Family Genealogy," 11.
20. Catherine Chapin Woods, Letter to Daniel H. Wells, September 8, 1862 (Logan: Daniel H. Wells Papers, Utah State University).
21. N. Park Woods, Letter to Daniel H. Wells, September 20, 1863 (Logan: Daniel H. Wells Papers, Utah State University).
22. D. O. Calder, Letter to George Q. Cannon, March 11, 1863, *The Latter-day Saints Millennial Star* 25 (Liverpool, 1863): 301–2.
23. Ibid.
24. "Territorial Governors," *Utah History Encyclopedia*, accessed April 27, 2015, http://www.uen.org/utah_history_encyclopedia/t/TERRITORIAL_GOVERNORS.html; and Whitney, *History of Utah*, 2:104.
25. Young, Brigham Jr., Letter to George Q. Cannon, December 5, 1863, *The Latter-day Saints Millennial Star* 26 (Liverpool, 1864): 109–10.
26. Memorial for the Location of Indian Reservations to His Excellency Abraham Lincoln President of the United States, January 11, 1865; and Bancroft, *History of Utah 1540–1886* (San Francisco: The History Company, 1889), 635–36.

Chapter 15

1. "Journal History of the Church, 6 April 1864," (Salt Lake City: Church Historians Department, The Church of Jesus Christ of Latter-day Saints), accessed April 27, 2015, https://dcms.lds.org/delivery/DeliveryManager Servlet?dps_pid=IE271959.
2. Hinckley, *Daniel Hanmer Wells and Events of His Time*, 347–48.
3. "Alexander Hill Bullock Life History," *FamilySearch.org*, Memories, accessed April 28, 2015, https://familysearch.org/photos/stories/1664980. Alexander Hill Bullock met his wife, Emily Caroline Harris, at the home of Daniel H. Wells. She came to the Wells home in 1854 at age ten to live with her sister, Martha Harris, one of the wives of Daniel H. Wells. Alexander was then also living in the Wells home. Sandy and Emily were married by Daniel in the Endowment House on November 9, 1861. Sandy Bullock continued in the employ of Daniel H. Wells for about thirty-three years until 1887.
4. Craig S. Smith, "Joseph W. Young and the Mormon Emigration of 1864," *BYU Studies*, accessed April 28, 2015, https://ojs.lib.byu.edu/spc/index.php/BYUStudies/article/viewFile/6627/6276.
5. "Autobiography of Abram Hatch," *FamilySearch.org*, Memories, accessed April 28, 2015, https://familysearch.org/photos/stories/1504859.
6. Daniel H. Wells and Brigham Young Jr., "Salutory Message," *Latter-day Saints Millennial Star* 26 (Liverpool, September 1, 1864): 571.
7. *Mission President's Handbook* (Salt Lake City: The Church of Jesus Christ of Latter-day Saints, 2006); and Bruce A. Van Orden, "The Decline in Convert Baptisms and Member Immigration from the British Mission after 1870," *BYU Studies* 27, no. 2 (Provo, 1987): 97–98, accessed August 1, 2015, https://ojs.lib.byu.edu/spc/index.php/BYUStudies/article/view/5667.
8. Cheltenham Conference Report, August 21, 1864, *Latter-day Saints Millennial Star* 26 (Liverpool, 1864): 652–53.
9. *2013 Church Almanac*, 529.
10. Hinckley, *Daniel Hanmer Wells and Events of His Time*, 348–49.
11. Brigham H. Roberts, "History of the Mormon Church," *Americana* 9 (New York: The National Americana Society, 1914): 239; and *Latter-day Saints Millennial Star* 26 (May 21, 1864): 332; and 27 (January 21, 1865): 47.
12. Roberts, "History of the Mormon Church," 239; and *Latter-day Saints Millennial Star* 27 (September 9, 1865): 572.
13. "South Africa's Contribution to Utah," *Treasures of Pioneer History* 6 (Salt Lake City: Daughters of Utah Pioneers), 288–89.
14. "B. S. Kimball," *Mormon Migration*, accessed April 29, 2015, http://mormonmigration.lib.byu.edu/Search/searchAll/keywords:b.+s.+kimball.
15. "1865 Voyages," *Mormon Migration*, accessed April 29, 2015, http://mormonmigration.lib.byu.edu/Search/searchAll/keywords:1865; and Conway B. Sonne, *Ships, Saints, and Mariners: A Maritime Encyclopedia of Mormon Migration, 1830–1890* (Salt Lake City: University of Utah Press, 1993), 34.
16. Sonne, *Ships, Saints, and Mariners*, 26–27; and "Description of the Ship Belle Wood and its Voyage of April 29, 1865," *Jensen Family Genealogy*, Freepages, Rootsweb, *Ancestry.com*, accessed April 29, 2015, http://free

pages.genealogy.rootsweb.ancestry.com/~sjensen/jensen/references/ref 228.htm.
17. Sonne, *Ships, Saints, and Mariners*, 59; and *Latter-day Saints Millennial Star* 27, no. 21 (1865): 331.
18. "Bridgewater," *Mormon Migration*, accessed April 29, 2015, http://mormon migration.lib.byu.edu/Search/searchAll/keywords:bridgewater.
19. *2013 Church Almanac*, 211; Van Orden, *The Decline in Convert Baptisms and Member Immigration from the British Mission after 1870*, 97–98; and Arrington, *Brigham Young, American Moses*, 210. Missionaries called in 1861: 19, 1862: 27, 1863: 50, 1864, 52, 1865, 71, 1866: 32, 1867: 133, 1868: 32, 1869, 250.
20. Arrington, *Brigham Young, American Moses*, 342–33.
21. Young, Brigham, Letter to Daniel H. Wells and Brigham Young Jr., May 15, 1865, *Brigham Young Letterbook* (Salt Lake City: Church History Department, The Church of Jesus Christ of Latter-day Saints), 7:619–25.
22. Peterson, *Utah's Black Hawk War*, 148.
23. O. H. Irish, Letter to William P. Dole, June 29, 1865, *Report of the Secretary of the Interior 1865, House Executive Document 1* (Washington, DC: Government Printing Office, 1866), 2:317–320.
24. Peterson, *Utah's Black Hawk War*, 149–50.
25. "Treaty with The Utah, Yampah Ute, Pah-Vant, Sanpete Ute, Tim-P-Nogs and Cum-Nm-Bah Bands of the Utah Indians, 8 June 1865," *Indian Affairs: Laws and Treaties, Vol. 5: Laws* (Washington, DC: Government Printing Office, 1941). The chiefs who signed the treaty were Sowiette (Nearly Starved), Toquana (Black Mountain Lion), and Tabby (the Sun) representing the Yampa and Uinta Utes; Kanosh (Man of White Hair), Ankawakits (Red Rifle), Pean-up (Big Foot), Eah-land (Shot to Pieces), and Nar-i-ent (Powerful) representing the Pahvants; Pan-sook (Otter), and Que-o-gand (Bear) representing the "Utahs"; Joe, or Sow-ok-soo-bet (Arrow Feather), representing the Sanpitch Utes; An-kar-tew-ets (Red Boy) and Nanp-peads (Foot Mother) representing the Timpanogos Utes; Quibets (Mountain), who was Black Hawk's brother, representing the Spanish Fork Utes; and An-oosh representing the Weber Utes.
26. Peterson, *Utah's Black Hawk War*, 163–64.
27. Ibid., 139–40.
28. Ibid.
29. Schuyler Colfax, "Hon. Schuyler Colfax's Journey From the Missouri River to California in 1865," *Western Galaxy* (Salt Lake City, The Juvenile Instructor's Office, 1888), 1:32–41; and Arrington, *Brigham Young, American Moses*, 343–44.
30. Daniel H. Wells, "Valedictory, 2 September 1865," *Latter-day Saints Millennial Star* 27 (Liverpool, 1865): 553, 554.
31. Hinckley, *Daniel Hanmer Wells and Events of His Time*, 248.
32. "Journal History of the Church, 1896–2001: 1860–1869; 1865 July–December" (Salt Lake City: Church History Library, The Church of Jesus Christ of Latter-day Saints) September 25, 1865, accessed April 30, 2015, https://dcms.lds.org/delivery/DeliveryManagerServlet?dps_pid=IE282780.
33. Hinckley, *Daniel Hanmer Wells and Events of His Time*, 250.

34. "Passenger Manifest, City of New York, 11 September 1865," *Ancestry.com*; and "New York Passenger Lists 1820–1957," *Ancestry.com*, 2012, accessed April 30, 2015, http://interactive.ancestry.com/7488/NYM237_256-0097/5673934?backurl=http%3a%2f%2fsearch.ancestry.com%2fcgi-bin%2fsse.dll%3fgss%3dangs-c%26new%3d1%26rank%3d1%26gsfn%3dd%26gsfn_x%3d1%26gsln%3dwells%26gsln_x%3dNP%26msady%3d1865%26msady_x%3d1%26msapn_ftp%3dNew%2bYork%2bCity%2b%28All%2bBoroughs%29%252c%2bNew%2bYork%252c%2bUSA%26msapn%3d1652382%26msapn_PInfo%3d6-%257c0%257c1652393%257c0%257c2%257c3244%257c35%257c1652382%257c0%257c0%257c0%257c%26msapn_x%3dPS%26msapn_ftp_x%3d1%26cp%3d0%26MSAV%3d1%26uidh%3djb1%26pcat%3d40%26h%3d5673934%26recoff%3d8%2b10%26db%3dnypl%26indiv%3d1%26ml_rpos%3d4&ssrc=&backlabel=ReturnRecord#?imageId=NYM237_256-0096.
35. Hinckley, *Daniel Hanmer Wells and Events of His Time*, 348–49.
36. Ibid., 250.
37. Kimball, *On the Potters Wheel: Diaries of Heber C. Kimball*, appendix A, 176, entry of December 27, 1864.
38. *Deseret News*, October 12, 1865, 1.

Chapter 16

1. Peterson, *Utah's Black Hawk War*, 92–100.
2. Daniel H. Wells, General Orders No. 1, Head Quarters Nauvoo Legion, Adjutant General's Office, GSL City, April 25, 1865, Territorial Militia Records, #761.
3. Hinckley, *Daniel Hanmer Wells and Events of His Time*, 250.
4. Peterson, *Utah's Black Hawk War*, 218.
5. Ibid., 218–19.
6. Ibid., 219–222.
7. Ibid.; and George A. Smith and Erastus Snow, Letter to Daniel H. Wells, February 7, 1866, Utah Territorial Militia Papers #804.
8. Peterson, *Utah's Black Hawk War*, 224.
9. Daniel H. Wells, Letter to George A. Smith, February 3, 1866, "Journal History of the Church, 1896–2001: 1860–1869" (Salt Lake City: Church History Library, The Church of Jesus Christ of Latter-day Saints), 1866 January–June, accessed May 5, 2015, https://dcms.lds.org/delivery/DeliveryManagerServlet?dps_pid=IE286822; George A. Smith and Erastus Snow, Letter to Daniel H. Wells, February 7, 1866; and George A. Smith, Letter to Daniel H. Wells, February 19, 1866, Utah Territorial Militia Records, #808.
10. Daniel H. Wells, Letter to Warren Snow, March 19, 1866, Utah Territorial Militia Records, #1521.
11. Peterson, *Utah's Black Hawk War*, 231–32.
12. Ibid., 235–37.
13. Warren S. Snow, Letter to Daniel H. Wells, April 13, 1866, Territorial Militia Records, #832.
14. Warren S. Snow, Letter to Daniel H. Wells, April 14, 1866, Territorial Militia Records, #835.

15. Warren S. Snow, Letter to Brigham Young and Daniel H. Wells, April 21, 1866 (Salt Lake City: Brigham Young Collection, Church History Department, The Church of Jesus Christ of Latter-day Saints); and Warren S. Snow, Letter to Daniel H. Wells, April 21, 1866, Territorial Militia Records, #839.
16. Peterson, *Utah's Black Hawk War*, 241–42.
17. Ibid., 244–45.
18. Ibid., 245–46.
19. Daniel H. Wells, Letter to George A. Smith, May 3, 1866, "Journal History of the Church, 1896–2001: 1860–1869; 1866 January–June" (Salt Lake City: Church History Library, The Church of Jesus Christ of Latter-day Saints), accessed May 5, 2015, https://dcms.lds.org/delivery/DeliveryManagerServlet?dps_pid=IE286822; and Peterson, *Utah's Black Hawk War*, 247–53.
20. Peterson, *Utah's Black Hawk War*, 247–48.
21. Ibid.
22. Ibid.; and Daniel H. Wells, Letter to Erastus Snow, June 11, 1866, "Journal History of the Church, 1896–2001: 1860–1869; 1866 January–June," (Salt Lake City: Church History Library, The Church of Jesus Christ of Latter-day Saints), accessed May 5, 2015, https://dcms.lds.org/delivery/DeliveryManagerServlet?dps_pid=IE286822.
23. Peterson, *Utah's Black Hawk War*, 260–67.
24. Ibid.
25. Ibid.
26. George A. Smith, Letter to Daniel H. Wells, April 3, 1866; unnamed informant, April 22, 1866; William McFadden, Letter to *Deseret News*, April 24, 1866; Andrew Peterson, Letter to *Deseret News*, April 29, 1866; and "Journal History of the Church, 1896–2001: 1860–1869" (Salt Lake City: Church History Library, The Church of Jesus Christ of Latter-day Saints), 1866 January–June, accessed May 5, 2015, https://dcms.lds.org/delivery/DeliveryManagerServlet?dps_pid=IE286822.
27. Daniel H. Wells, Letter to Erastus Snow, May 2, 1866, cited in Hinckley, *Daniel Hanmer Wells and Events of His Time*, 124–26; and "Journal History of the Church, 1896–2001: 1860–1869" (Salt Lake City: Church History Library, The Church of Jesus Christ of Latter-day Saints), 1866 January–June, June 11, 1866, accessed May 5, 2015, https://dcms.lds.org/delivery/DeliveryManagerServlet?dps_pid=IE286822.
28. Peterson, *Utah's Black Hawk War*, 268–69.
29. Ibid., 270–73.
30. Ibid.
31. Ibid.
32. Ibid., 273–76.
33. Daniel H. Wells, Letter to Brigham Young, July 15, 1866 (Salt Lake City: Brigham Young Collection, Church History Department, The Church of Jesus Christ of Latter-day Saints).
34. Heber P. Kimball, Letter to General Robert T. Burton, June 20, 1866 (Salt Lake City: Theodore Albert Schroeder Papers, Church history Department, The Church of Jesus Christ of Latter-day Saints).
35. Peterson, *Utah's Black Hawk War*, 294–96.

36. Ibid., 296–301.
37. "Record of Provo Military District Command 1857–1858 and Campaign Record of Expedition to Sanpete and Piute Military District 1866–1867, under Command of William B. Pace," Special Collections, Harold B. Lee Library, Bringham Young University, Provo, UT.
38. Kate B. Carter, *Heart Throbs of the West* (Salt Lake City: Daughters of Utah Pioneers, 2001), 6:493.
39. Peterson, *Utah's Black Hawk War*, 299–301.
40. Ibid., 301–5.
41. Daniel H. Wells, Letter to Aaron Johnson, July 1, 1866, Territorial Militia Records, #895.
42. Peterson, *Utah's Black Hawk War*, 304.
43. Ibid., 305–7.
44. Aaron Johnson, Letter to Daniel H. Wells, July 8, 1866, Territorial Militia Records, #1536.
45. "Journal History of the Church, 1896–2001: 1860–1869" (Salt Lake City: Church History Library, The Church of Jesus Christ of Latter-day Saints), 1868 July–August, August 19 and 22, 1868, accessed May 5, 2015, https://dcms.lds.org/delivery/DeliveryManagerServlet?dps_pid=IE499609.

Chapter 17

1. Daniel H. Wells, Letter to Brigham Young Jr., October 21, 1866, *Latter-day Saints Millennial Star* 27:798.
2. Ibid.
3. Hinckley, *Daniel Hanmer Wells and Events of His Time*, 387.
4. Allen Dale Roberts, *Salt Lake City's Historic Architecture* (Charleston, SC: Arcadia Publishing, 2012), 16–17.
5. Arrington, *Great Basin Kingdom: An Economic History of the Latter-day Saints, 1830–1900*, 186–87.
6. Hinckley, *Daniel Hanmer Wells and Events of His Time*, 70.
7. "History of the Tabernacle," *Newsroom*, The Church of Jesus Christ of Latter-day Saints, accessed May 6, 2015, http://www.mormonnewsroom.org/additional-resource/history-of-the-tabernacle.
8. L. J. Arrington, "Brigham Young and the Transcontinental Telegraph," *The Improvement Era* (Salt Lake City: The Church of Jesus Christ of Latter-day Saints), 54:510–11, 529.
9. Arrington, *Brigham Young, American Moses*, 347–48.
10. Ibid.
11. L. J. Arrington, "The Deseret Telegraph—A Church-Owned Public Utility," *Journal of Economic History* (Philadelphia: Economic History Association, University of Pennsylvania), 11:117–39.
12. Roberts, "History of the Mormon Church," 454; and Hinckley, *Daniel Hanmer Wells and Events of His Time*, 155.
13. Hinckley, *Daniel Hanmer Wells and Events of His Time*, 160. After he was elected mayor of Great Salt Lake City, Daniel H. Wells developed the habit of "hanging out" frequently at the telegraph office to monitor incoming

news, a practice similar to that of Abraham Lincoln at the Washington office during his presidency.
14. Ibid., 155.
15. "Squire Newton Brassfield, Histories, Brasfield—Brassfield Genealogies," accessed May 6, 2015, http://www.brasfield.net/histories/Squire%20Newton%20Brassfield.htm.
16. Ibid.
17. "Synoptical History of the Congregational Church and The First Congregational Church," *The Church Review* 4 (Salt Lake City, 1895): 2–6; "The Murder of Dr. Robinson," *New York Times*, November 13, 1866.
18. Louwane VanSoolen, "Dr. J. King Robinson" (Salt Lake City: Museum Archives, Vedette, Fort Douglas Military Museum Association, 2011), vol. 36, no. 3, 2011, accessed May 6, 2015, http://www.fortdouglas.org/sites/fortdouglas.org/files/Vedette_Fall_2011%5B1%5D.pdf.
19. Ron Andersen, "Land Ownership in Salt Lake Valley (1847–1869)," *Historical Salt Lake City Walking Tour*, accessed May 6, 2015, http://www.mormontrails.org/Tours/Walking/slcity.htm.
20. T. B. H. Stenhouse, *The Rocky Mountain Saints: A Full and Complete History of the Mormons* (New York: D. Appleton and Company, 1878), 617–620; and Hinckley, *Daniel Hanmer Wells and Events of His Time*, 155–56.
21. *Deseret News*, May 10, 1866, 183.
22. Arrington, *Brigham Young, American Moses*, 344.
23. Ibid.; and "Journal History of the Church, 1896–2001: 1860–1869" (Salt Lake City: Church History Library, The Church of Jesus Christ of Latter-day Saints), 1866 January–June, May 8, 1866, accessed May 6, 2015, https://dcms.lds.org/delivery/DeliveryManagerServlet?dps_pid=IE286822.
24. Transcript of the Potter Young Meeting, Minutes, 1855–77 (Salt Lake City: Church History Department, The Church of Jesus Christ of Latter-day Saints, undated), 149–61, summarized in *Brigham Young Manuscript History, 1866*, 404.
25. Arrington, *Brigham Young, American Moses*, 345–46.
26. *Journal of Discourses* 12:270.
27. Arrington, *Brigham Young, American Moses*, 346.
28. "Story of Cooperation in the United States," *Johns Hopkins University Studies in Historical and Political Science* (Baltimore: Guggenheim Weil & Co., 1888), 6:427–30.
29. John Hanson Beadle, *Life in Utah, Or The Mysteries and Crimes of Mormonism* (Philadelphia: National Publishing Company, 1874), 215.
30. Memorial of the Legislative Assembly of the Territory of Utah, Document No. 45, *Miscellaneous Documents of the House of Representatives for the First Session of the Forty-Eighth Congress* (Washington, DC: Government Printing Office, 1884), 19:3.
31. Hinckley, *Daniel Hanmer Wells and Events of His Time*, 185.
32. Ibid.; and *New York Times*, April 29, 1872, 2.
33. Whitney, *Whitney's Popular History of Utah*, 263–69; and Hinckley, *Daniel Hanmer Wells and Events of His Time*, 185–86. See also US Supreme Court, Clinton v. Engelbrecht, 80 US 13 Wall. 434, 1871.
34. Hinckley, *Daniel Hanmer Wells and Events of His Time*, 186.

35. Daniel H. Wells, Letter to Horace S. Eldredge, January 24, 1871, *Latter-day Saints Millennial Star* 33:122–23.
36. Ibid.
37. Ibid.
38. *Deseret News* 19, no. 32, September 14, 1870, and no. 35, October 5, 1870, 1.
39. *Journal of the Executive Proceedings of the Senate of the United States of America* (Washington, DC: Government Printing Office, 1901), 17:267.
40. Ron Anderson, "Land Ownership in Salt Lake Valley (1847–1869)," *Mormon Trails.org*, Tours, Walking Tours, Salt Lake City, accessed May 7, 2015, http://www.mormontrails.org/Tours/Walking/slcity.htm; and *New York Times*, October 31, 1866, 1.
41. Original Land Titles in Utah Territory, Utah Department of Administrative Services, Division of Archives & Records Services, 2013, accessed May 7, 2015, http://archives.utah.gov/research/guides/land-original-title.htm.
42. Hinckley, *Daniel Hanmer Wells and Events of His Time*, 157–58.
43. "An Act for the Relief of the Inhabitants of Cities and Towns upon the Public Lands (March 2, 1867)," *The Statutes at Large, Treaties, and Proclamations, of the United States of America* (Boston: Little, Brown, and Company, 1868), vol. 14.
44. Original Land Titles in Utah Territory.
45. *Deseret News*, November 15, 1871, 6.
46. Original Land Titles in Utah Territory; and Anderson, "Land Ownership in Salt Lake Valley (1847–1869)."
47. Hinckley, *Daniel Hanmer Wells and Events of His Time*, 160.
48. Wells, "The Wells Family Genealogy," 11.
49. Ibid.
50. Hinckley, *Daniel Hanmer Wells and Events of His Time*, 350.
51. "Journal History of the Church, 1896–2001: 1860–1869" (Salt Lake City: Church History Library, The Church of Jesus Christ of Latter-day Saints), 1868 April–June, June 22, 1868, accessed May 19, 2015, https://dcms.lds.org/delivery/DeliveryManagerServlet?dps_pid=IE510070; and *Deseret News* 17:156.
52. Ibid.
53. Ibid., 25.
54. *2013 Church Almanac*, 118.
55. Wells, *Genealogy of the Wells, Thomas, Young, Coon and Related Families*.
56. Hinckley, *Daniel Hanmer Wells and Events of His Time*, 7–8; and *2013 Church Almanac*, 114.
57. Hickley, *Daniel Hanmer Wells and Events*, 8.

Chapter 18

1. Arrington, *Brigham Young, American Moses*, 348–49; and Hinckley, *Daniel Hanmer Wells and Events of His Time*, 316–17.
2. *Journal of Discourses* 13 (April 7, 1869): 22–29.
3. Hinckley, *Daniel Hanmer Wells and Events of His Time*, 243–44.
4. Arrington, *Brigham Young, American Moses*, 349–50.
5. Hinckley, *Daniel Hanmer Wells and Events of His Time*, 316–17; and "Utah

Railroads, Utah Central Railroad (1869–1881)," *UtahRails.net*, accessed May 8, 2015, http://utahrails.net/utahrails/uc-rr-1869-1881.php.
6. UtahRails.net, accessed May 8, 2015, http://utahrails.net/utahrails/uc-rr-1869-1881.php.
7. "Utah Railroads, Utah Southern Railroad (1870–1881)," *UtahRails.net*, accessed May 8, 2015, http://utahrails.net/utahrails/us-rr-1870-1881.php.
8. Ibid.
9. Ibid.
10. Ibid., and Hinckley, *Daniel Hanmer Wells and Events of His Time*, 24.
11. Hinckley, *Daniel Hanmer Wells and Events of His Time*, 24.
12. "Utah Chapters, Pioneers and Cowboys, the Beginnings of the University of Utah," *Utah History to Go*, accessed November 15, 2015, http://historytogo.utah.gov/utah_chapters/pioneers_and_cowboys/thebeginningsoftheuniversityofutah.html.
13. University of Utah J. Willard Marriot Library, "University of Utah Sesquicentennial, 1850–2000, Deseret University, 1850–1892," accessed November 15, 2015, http://www.lib.utah.edu/collections/photo-exhibits/deseret-university.php.
14. Ibid.; and Hinckley, *Daniel Hanmer Wells and Events of His Time*, 378.
15. "Utah Chapters, Pioneers and Cowboys, the Beginnings of the University of Utah," *Utah History to Go*, accessed November 15, 2015, http://historytogo.utah.gov/utah_chapters/pioneers_and_cowboys/thebeginningsoftheuniversityofutah.html.
16. MS 4291: University of Deseret (Salt Lake City) records 1869–1887, "Record book, 1869 March 1–1871 July 4, 8," Church History Library, The Church of Jesus Christ of Latter-day Saints, accessed November 15, 2015, https://dcms.lds.org/delivery/DeliveryManagerServlet?dps_pid=IE3226485.
17. Ibid., "Programmes, 1873–1874," 7, accessed November 15, 2015, https://dcms.lds.org/delivery/DeliveryManagerServlet?dps_pid=IE3226491; and Hinckley, *Daniel Hanmer Wells and Events of His Time*, 379.
18. "Programmes, 1873–1874"; and Hinckley, *Daniel Hanmer Wells and Events of His Time*, 228
19. Hinckley, *Daniel Hanmer Wells and Events of His Time*, 229.
20. University of Utah J. Willard Marriot Library, "University of Utah Sesquicentennial, 1850–2000, Deseret University, 1850–1892," accessed November 15, 2015, http://www.lib.utah.edu/collections/photo-exhibits/deseret-university.php.
21. *Journals of the Legislative Assembly of the Territory of Utah, Twenty-Third Session for the Year 1878* (Salt Lake City: Salt Lake Herald, 1878), 184, 381–91.
22. Hinckley, *Daniel Hanmer Wells and Events of His Time*, 72.
23. Tullidge, *Life of Brigham Young: Or, Utah and Her Founders*, 367–68.
24. Tullidge, *History of Salt Lake City*, 481.
25. Ibid., 482–83.
26. Ibid.
27. Ibid.
28. Hinckley, *Daniel Hanmer Wells and Events of His Time*, 203–4.
29. Ibid., 204–8.
30. *Deseret News*, October 29, 1870, 1.

31. Stenhouse, *The Rocky Mountain Saints: A Full and Complete History of the Mormons*, 682.
32. Tullidge, *History of Salt Lake City*, 489.
33. Stenhouse, *The Rocky Mountain Saints: A Full and Complete History of the Mormons*, 682.
34. Tullidge, *History of Salt Lake City*, 499–501.
35. Ibid., 502.
36. Ibid.
37. Hinckley, *Daniel Hanmer Wells and Events of His Time*, 192–93; and Stenhouse, *The Rocky Mountain Saints: A Full and Complete History of the Mormons*, 682.
38. Ardis E. Parshall, "Somali Pirates, Mormon Militiamen, and the US Military," *Keepapitvhinin*, accessed November 6, 2015, http://www.keepapitchinin.org/2009/04/21/somali-pirates-mormon-militiamen-and-the-us-military/.
39. Bancroft, *History of Utah 1540–1886*, 663.
40. Hinckley, *Daniel Hanmer Wells and Events of His Time*, 353–54.
41. Tullidge, *History of Salt Lake City*, 536–38; and Hinckley, *Daniel Hanmer Wells and Events of His Time*, 160.
42. Tullidge, *History of Salt Lake City*, 538.
43. Ibid.
44. Edwin Brown Firmage and Richard Collin Mangrum, *Zion in the Courts: A Legal History of the Church of Jesus Christ of Latter-Day Saints* (Urbana: University of Illinois Press, 2001), 247.
45. John Gary Maxwell, *Robert Newton Baskin and the Making of Modern Utah* (Norman: University of Oklahoma Press, 2013), 114.
46. Roberts, "History of the Mormon Church," 862.
47. *Latter-day Saints Millennial Star* 33:744.
48. Tullidge, *History of Salt Lake City*, 544–46.
49. *Latter-day Saints Millennial Star* 33:744.
50. *Deseret News* 20, no. 49 (January 10, 1872): 559.
51. Firmage, *Zion in the Courts: A Legal History of the Church of Jesus Christ of Latter-Day Saints*, 247.
52. Ibid.
53. *Deseret News*, November 15, 1871, 6.
54. Maxwell, *Robert Newton Baskin and the Making of Modern Utah*, 114.
55. Ibid., 119; and George Q. Cannon, Letter to Daniel H. Wells, April 26, 1872, cited in Bigler and Bagley, *Innocent Blood*, 309–10.
56. George Q. Cannon, "Editorial Thoughts," *The Juvenile Instructor*, August 17, 1872, 4, accessed May 13, 2015, http://www.findmypast.com/mocavo-info.
57. Hinckley, *Daniel Hanmer Wells and Events of His Time*, 349–50. Five years after George's death and a few days after Daniel dedicated the St. George Temple on April 6, 1877, he completed temple ordinances there for his deceased son. He also posthumously sealed in marriage George Alley Wells and Laura E. Coombs, the daughter of his brother-in-law Joseph Coombs and his second wife Arrietta Wetmore, who died a few months before George, also at age twelve, on March 29, 1872. In 1890, while Daniel was serving as president of the Manti Temple, he posthumously sealed in

marriage George Alley Wells and Ellen R. Reynolds. The LDS Church no longer permits persons to be posthumously sealed to one another who were not married while alive, but these two sealings are still listed as valid on church records.
58. Hinckley, *Daniel Hanmer Wells and Events of His Time*, 354–55.
59. Craig E. Taylor, Elliott Mittler, and Le Val Lund, *Overcoming Barriers: Lifeline Seismic Improvement Programs* (ASCE Publications, 2002), 198–99.
60. *Revised Ordinances and Resolutions of the City Council of Salt Lake City in the Territory of Utah, with Congressional and Territorial Laws of Townsites and Great Salt Lake City Charter, and Amendments* (Salt Lake City: Deseret News Printing, 1875), 96–106.
61. David Hampshire, "No Western Parallel: The Story of Questar Corporation" (Salt Lake City: Questar Corporation, 1998), 14.
62. *Deseret News*, August 23, 1873.
63. Hampshire, "No Western Parallel: The Story of Questar Corporation." 14.
64. Arrington, *Great Basin Kingdom: An Economic History of the Latter-day Saints, 1830–1900*, 291.
65. Ibid.
66. Hinckley, *Daniel Hanmer Wells and Events of His Time*, 322.
67. Charles L. Keller, *The Lady in the Ore Bucket: A History of Settlement and Industry in the Tri-Canyon Area of the Wasatch Mountains* (Salt Lake City: University of Utah Press, 2001), 93.
68. "John Nickles, Respondent v. Daniel H. Wells, et al, Appellants," *Reports of Cases Decided in the Supreme Court of the Territory of Utah* (Chicago: Callaghan and Company, 1882), 2:167–73.
69. *Deseret News*, September 27, 1876, 1.
70. "John Nickles, Respondent v. Daniel H. Wells, et al, Appellants," *Reports of Cases Decided in the Supreme Court of the Territory of Utah* (Callaghan and Company, Chicago, 1882), 2:167–73.
71. *Cases Argued and Decided in the Supreme Court of the United States* (Rochester: The Lawyers Co-operative Publishing Company, 1881), 26:825–27.
72. *Salt Lake Herald*, October 20, 1878.

Chapter 19

1. Hinckley, *Daniel Hanmer Wells and Events of His Time*, 330; and Tullidge, *History of Salt Lake City*, 559–60.
2. Thomas G. Alexander, "A Conflict of Perceptions: Ulysses S. Grant and the Mormons," *The Ulysses S. Grant Association Newsletter* 8, no. 4 (Ulysses S. Grant Presidential Library, Mississippi State University): 38–41, accessed May 14, 2015, http://www.usgrantlibrary.org/usga/newsletters/volume8.asp.
3. Thomas A. McMullin and David Walker, "Biographical Directory of American Territorial Governors. Territorial Governors, Utah History Encyclopedia," accessed May 14, 2015, http://www.uen.org/utah_history_encyclopedia/t/TERRITORIAL_GOVERNORS.html.
4. Ibid.; and Whitney, *History of Utah* 2:774, 775.

5. Alexander, "A Conflict of Perceptions: Ulysses S. Grant and the Mormons," 39.
6. Tullidge, *History of Salt Lake City*, 623–24; and Hinckley, *Daniel Hanmer Wells and Events of His Time*, 332–34.
7. Alexander, "A Conflict of Perceptions: Ulysses S. Grant and the Mormons," 39–40.
8. Ibid., 33–35; and Gordon Harrington and Mary Paulson, "Congregationalism in Utah," *Utah History Encyclopedia*, accessed May 15, 2015, http://www.uen.org/utah_history_encyclopedia/c/CONGREGATIONALISM_IN_UTAH.html.
9. Julia Dent Grant, unpublished memoirs (ca. 1891), US Grant 3rd Collection, US Grant Association (Starkville: Ulysses S. Grant Presidential Library, Mississippi State University), 336–39; and Tullidge, *History of Salt Lake City*, 624.
10. Tullidge, *History of Salt Lake City*, 621–23.
11. Arrington, *Brigham Young, American Moses*, 372–73; and Tullidge, *History of Salt Lake City*, 590–91.
12. Tullidge, *History of Salt Lake City*, 590–91; *2013 Church Almanac*, 211; and US Census Bureau, "Resident Population and Apportionment of the US House of Representatives," accessed May 15, 2013, https://www.census.gov/dmd/www/resapport/states/utah.pdf.
13. Tullidge, *History of Salt Lake City*, 591–92.
14. Roberts, "History of the Mormon Church," 732–33.
15. Tullidge, *History of Salt Lake City*, 592.
16. *George R. Maxwell v George Q. Cannon*, Papers in the Case of Maxwell V. Cannon for a Seat as Delegate from Utah Territory in the Forty-Third Congress, Document No. 49, *Miscellaneous Documents of the House of Representatives for the First Session of the Forty-Third Congress* (Washington, DC: Government Printing Office, 1874), 1:1–151.
17. Tullidge, *History of Salt Lake City*, 611–14.
18. Daniel W. Jones, *Forty Years Among the Indians* (Salt Lake City: The Juvenile Instructor Office, 1890), 214–17.
19. Hinckley, *Daniel Hanmer Wells and Events of His Time*, 167–68.
20. Ibid., 195–96.
21. Firmage, *Zion in the Courts: A Legal History of the Church of Jesus Christ of Latter-day Saints*, 250.
22. Arrington, *Brigham Young, American Moses*, 373.
23. "Journal History of the Church, 1896–2001: 1870–1879" (Salt Lake City: Church History Library, The Church of Jesus Christ of Latter-day Saints), 1875 January–March, March 11, 1875, accessed May 19, 2015, https://dcms.lds.org/delivery/DeliveryManagerServlet?dps_pid=IE498917.
24. Roberts, "History of the Mormon Church," 950–52.
25. Firmage, *Zion in the Courts: A Legal History of the Church of Jesus Christ of Latter-day Saints*, 251.
26. Susa Young Gates, *History of the Young Ladies' Mutual Improvement Association of The Church of Jesus Christ of Latter-day Saints from November, 1869 to June, 1910* (Salt Lake City: Deseret News Press, 1911), 80–83.
27. Junius F. Wells, "Historical Sketch of the Y. M. M. I. A.," *Improvement Era No. 28* (June 1925): 718–723.

28. Arrington, *Brigham Young, American Moses*, 370, 371; and A. Glen Humphreys, "Missionaries to the Saints," *BYU Studies* 17, no. 1, accessed May 19, 2015, http://byustudies.byu.edu/PDFLibrary/17.1HumpherysMissionaries-74641240-5247-43f2-94a6-9f26f2c9cb73.pdf.
29. Hinckley, *Daniel Hanmer Wells and Events of His Time*, 304; and Arrington, *Brigham Young, American Moses*, 384.
30. *2013 Church Almanac*, 118–22.
31. Humphreys, "Missionaries to the Saints."
32. Ibid.
33. Hinckley, *Daniel Hanmer Wells and Events of His Time*, 304–5; and Arrington, *Brigham Young, American Moses*, 384.
34. Arrington, *Brigham Young, American Moses*, 382–83; and *2013 Church Almanac*, 330.
35. Daniel Wells with Erastus Snow and Brigham Young Jr., Letter to Brigham Young, May 26, 1876, Brigham Young Letters, box 43, folder 20 (Salt Lake City: Church History Department, The Church of Jesus Christ of Latter-day Saints).
36. Hinckley, *Daniel Hanmer Wells and Events of His Time*, 305.
37. "The History of Lorenzo Wesley Roundy, Chapter 10," Archie Earl Buchanan / Florene Davis Family Organization Web Pages, Histories, accessed May 19, 2015, http://aeb.buchananspot.com/histories/LWR/LWR_Ch10.html.
38. Arrington, *Brigham Young, American Moses*, 391.
39. Brigham Young, Letter to Presidents Daniel H. Wells and John W. Young, February 13, 1877, *Brigham Young Letterbook* (Salt Lake City: Church History Department, The Church of Jesus Christ of Latter-day Saints), 16:26–29.
40. Hinckley, *Daniel Hanmer Wells and Events of His Time*, 305–6; and Arrington, *Brigham Young, American Moses*, 392.
41. "Journal History of the Church, 1896–2001: 1870–1879" (Salt Lake City: Church History Library, The Church of Jesus Christ of Latter-day Saints), 1877 April–June, April 6, 1877, accessed May 19, 2015, https://dcms.lds.org/delivery/DeliveryManagerServlet?dps_pid=IE439737.
42. Hinckley, *Daniel Hanmer Wells and Events of His Time*, 351–52; and Albert Welles, *History of the Welles Family in England and Normandy, with the Derivation from Their Progenitors of Some of the Descendants in the United States* (New York: 1876).
43. Arrington, *Brigham Young, American Moses*, 392, 393.
44. Whitney, *History of Utah*, 843.

Chapter 20

1. *2013 Church Almanac*, 118, 124–25.
2. Arrington, *Brigham Young, American Moses*, 376.
3. Ibid.
4. Gary James Bergera, "Seniority in the Twelve: the 1875 Realignment of Orson Pratt," *Journal of Mormon History* 18, no. 1 (1992): 52.
5. Ibid.

6. Steven H. Heath, "Notes on Apostolic Succession," *Dialogue: A Journal of Mormon Thought* 20, no. 2:45, accessed May 19, 2015, https://www.dialoguejournal.com/wp-content/uploads/sbi/articles/Dialogue_V20N02_46.pdf.
7. Roberts, "History of the Mormon Church," 118–19; and *2013 Church Almanac*, 118–21.
8. Bergera, "Seniority in the Twelve: the 1875 Realignment of Orson Pratt," 55.
9. *2013 Church Almanac*, 113, 114, 118.
10. Roberts, "History of the Mormon Church," 118–19.
11. Rulon Chapin, Letter to Daniel H. Wells, June 15, 1854; C. C. Woods, Letter to Daniel H. Wells, April 5, 1857; and C. C. Woods, Letter to Daniel H. Wells, April 21, 1860, Daniel H. Wells Papers (Logan: Utah State University).
12. Hinckley, *Daniel Hanmer Wells and Events of His Time*, 260, 344, 419.
13. Ibid., 352.
14. Wells, "The Wells Family Genealogy," 8–10.
15. *The Latter-day Saints Millennial Star*, May 13, 1878, 303.
16. Leonard J. Arrinton and Davis Bitton, *The Mormon Experience: A History of the Latter-Day Saints*, 2nd edition (New York: Knopf, 1992), 180.
17. "The Morrill Anti-Bigamy Act," *Statutes at Large, Treaties and Proclamations, 37th Congress, 2nd Session* (Boston: Little, Brown and Company, 1863), vol. 12, chapter 126:501–2; and Firmage, *Zion in the Courts: A Legal History of the Church of Jesus Christ of Latter-Day Saints*, 139.
18. Firmage, *Zion in the Courts: A Legal History of the Church of Jesus Christ of Latter-Day Saints*, 151–152.
19. US Supreme Court, Reynolds v. United States, 98 US 145 (1879).
20. Daniel H. Ludlow, *Encyclopedia of Mormonism* (New York: Macmillan, 1992), 1229.
21. Whitney, *Popular History of Utah*, 321.
22. Ibid., 322–23; and *Deseret News*, October 28, 1878, 3.
23. *Salt Lake Herald*, November 4, 1878, 3; and *Deseret News*, November 4, 1878, 2.
24. Whitney, *Popular History of Utah*, 321–22.
25. Ibid., 322–23; and "Journal History of the Church, 1896–2001: 1870–1879" (Salt Lake City: Church History Library, The Church of Jesus Christ of Latter-day Saints), 1879 May–June, May 3, 1879, accessed May 21, 2015, https://eadview.lds.org/findingaid/CR%20100%20137.
26. Hinckley, *Daniel Hanmer Wells and Events of His Time*, 267–68.
27. Tullidge, *History of Salt Lake City*, 820–21.
28. Hinckley, *Daniel Hanmer Wells and Events of His Time*, 270; and Whitney, *Popular History of Utah*, 323.
29. Whitney, *Popular History of Utah*, 323.
30. *Deseret News*, May 5, 1879.
31. Hinckley, *Daniel Hanmer Wells and Events of His Time*, 271.
32. Ibid., 272; and Tullidge, *History of Salt Lake City*, 821.
33. *Deseret News*, May 5, 1879; and Hinckley, *Daniel Hanmer Wells and Events of His Time*, 273.

34. Tullidge, *History of Salt Lake City*, 821–23.
35. Hinckley, *Daniel Hanmer Wells and Events of His Time*, 276–77.
36. Tullidge, *History of Salt Lake City*, 823.
37. Hinckley, *Daniel Hanmer Wells and Events of His Time*, 278; and *Deseret News*, May 5, 1879.
38. Hinckley, *Daniel Hanmer Wells and Events of His Time*, 279–80; and *Deseret News*, May 6, 1879.
39. Hinckley, *Daniel Hanmer Wells and Events of His Time*, 280–81.
40. Ibid.
41. Tullidge, *History of Salt Lake City*, 822.
42. *Salt Lake Tribune*, May 7, 1879.
43. Ibid.; and Tullidge, *History of Salt Lake City*, 822–23.
44. *Deseret News*, May 6, 1879.
45. Hinckley, *Daniel Hanmer Wells and Events of His Time*, 284.
46. *Deseret News*, May 6, 1879.
47. Whitney, *Popular History of Utah*, 324.
48. *Frank Leslie's Illustrated Newspaper*, May 31, 1879, 213–15.

Chapter 21

1. Hinckley, *Daniel Hanmer Wells and Events of His Time*, 25.
2. *Summit County Abstracts*, Book 1, 205; *Summit County Old Records*, Book K, 292; *Summit County Abstracts*, Book 1, 289; and *Summit County Old Records*, Book D, 302.
3. *Summit County Warranty Deeds*, Book N, 81; and *UtahRails.net*, accessed May 8, 2015, http://utahrails.net/utahrails/us-rr-18701881.php.
4. Alexander, *The Rise of Multiple-use Management in the Intermountain West: A History of Region 4 of the Forest Service*, 10–12.
5. US Supreme Court, Wells v. Nickles, 104 US 444 (1881).
6. Wells, "The Wells Family Genealogy," 12–16.
7. "Biography of William Wells Woods, Illustrated History of the State of Idaho," *AccessGenealogy.com*, accessed May 21, 2015, http://www.accessgenealogy.com/idaho/biography-of-william-w-woods.htm.
8. Wells, "The Wells Family Genealogy," 12–16.
9. Ken Cannon, "The Tragic Matter of Louie Wells and John Q. Cannon," *The Journal of Mormon History* (Spring 2009): 148–49.
10. Constance L. Lieber and John Sillito, *Letters from Exile, The Correspondence of Martha Hughes Cannon and Angus M. Cannon, 1886–1888* (Salt Lake City: Signature Books, 1989), xi–xii.
11. Ibid.
12. Wells, "The Wells Family Genealogy," 12–16.
13. Ibid.
14. James B. Allen and Glen M. Leonard, *The Story of the Latter-day Saints* (Salt Lake City: Deseret Book Company, 1976), 396.
15. Ibid.
16. Ibid.; and Whitney, *Popular History of Utah*, 364–78.
17. William D. Haywood, *Bill Haywood's Book—The Autobiography of William D. Haywood* (New York: International Publishers, 1929), 16–17.

18. *Deseret News*, August 25, 1883; and Hal Schindler, "Frenzied Mob Kills 'Murderer,'" Utah History to Go, *Salt Lake Tribune, In Another Time*, accessed May 22, 2015, http://historytogo.utah.gov/salt_lake_tribune/in_another_time/100895.html.
19. James G. Williams, "Defending Plural Marriage to Vice President Colfax, Champion of Liberty: John Taylor" (Provo: Religious Studies Center, Brigham Young University), accessed May 22, 2015, http://rsc.byu.edu/archived/champion-liberty-john-taylor/defending-plural-marriage-vice-president-colfax.
20. Richard Neitzel Holzapfel and Christopher C. Jones, "'John the Revelator': The Written Revelations of John Taylor," Champion of Liberty: John Taylor (Provo: Religious Studies Center, Brigham Young University), accessed May 21, 2015, http://rsc.byu.edu/archived/champion-liberty-john-taylor/john-revelator-written-revelations-john-taylor; and Fred C. Collier, ed., *Unpublished Revelations of Prophets and Presidents of the Church of Jesus Christ of Latter-Day Saints* (Salt Lake City: Collier Publishing, 1979), 1:138.
21. Collier, *Unpublished Revelations*, 138; and *2013 Church Almanac*, 114, 121.
22. Wells, "The Wells Family Genealogy," 12–16.
23. Ibid.
24. Whitney, *Popular History of Utah*, 430–49.
25. Frank Esshom, *Pioneers and Prominent Men of Utah* (Salt Lake City: Utah Pioneers Book Publishing Company, 1913), 1238; and *2013 Church Almanac*, 257.
26. Edward Perkins and Mary Jane Woodger, "Administration from the Underground, Champion of Liberty: John Taylor" (Provo: Religious Studies Center, Brigham Young University), accessed May 22, 2015, http://rsc.byu.edu/archived/champion-liberty-john-taylor/administration-underground.
27. Cannon, "The Tragic Matter of Louie Wells and John Q. Cannon," 149–51.
28. "On the Quiet," *Salt Lake Tribune*, November 2, 1884, 4.
29. Cannon, "The Tragic Matter of Louie Wells and John Q. Cannon," 151–52; and "Card from Major Woods," *Salt Lake Tribune*, November 4, 1884, 4.
30. "The Facts Concerning Cannon's Polygamous Marriage, Cannon's Trial for Assaulting a 'Tribune' Reporter," *Salt Lake Tribune*, November 11, 1884; and Abram Cannon, *Diary of Abram Cannon, 14 November 1883* (Provo: Harold B. Lee Library, Brigham Young University).
31. "A Reporter Rawhided," *The Deseret News*, November 10, 1884, 3. Reports in the *Tribune* and *Salt Lake Herald* added the further details that Lippman said he would go to hell before retracting the article and John Q. cried "Don't shoot" when he thought Lippman might pull a gun on him.
32. Cannon, "The Tragic Matter of Louie Wells and John Q. Cannon," 155–59.
33. Daniel H. Wells, Letter to Louisa Wells, December 21, 1884, quoted in a letter from Melvin D. Wells to Heber J. Grant, 1941.
34. Wells, "The Wells Family Genealogy," 12–16.
35. Melvin D. Wells, Letter to Heber J. Grant, 1941.
36. Daniel H. Wells, Letter to Louisa Wells, December 21, 1884, quoted in a letter from Melvin D. Wells to Heber J. Grant, 1941.
37. Ibid.

38. Daniel H. Wells, Letter to Louisa Wells, January 14, 1885, quoted in a letter from Melvin D. Wells to Heber J. Grant, 1941.
39. Hinckley, *Daniel Hanmer Wells and Events of His Time*, 252; and *The Latter-day Saints Millennial Star* 47:8.
40. *The Latter-day Saints Millennial Star* 47:72.
41. *2013 Church Almanac*, 579; *The Deseret News* (Salt Lake City, 2013), 210; and British Mission October 1885 Portrait Roster of Serving Missionaries, composite published photograph, 1885.
42. *The Latter-day Saints Millennial Star* 47:25, 60, 78.
43. Ibid., 165.
44. Ibid., 148.
45. 1910 US Federal Census, Utah Salt Lake City, Ward 4, 11B, record for Abbie W. Young in household of Hannah C. Wells; 1900 US Federal Census, Utah, Salt Lake City, Record for Abbie Wells Young or Chapin; and death certificate for Annie Wells Young aka Abbie Wells Chapin, Utah Administrative Services, Division of Archives and Records Service, accessed May 23, 2015, http://archives.utah.gov/indexes/data/81448/2259767/2259767_0000352.jpg.
46. *The Latter-day Saints Millennial Star* 47:191, 198.
47. Ibid., 245; Andrew Jensen, *Church Chronology*, 2nd ed. (Salt Lake City: Deseret News Company, 1899), 119; and Andrew Jensen, *History of the Scandinavian Mission* (Salt Lake City: Deseret News Press, 1927), 289–90.
48. James Gillespie, Letter to Daniel H. Wells, April 9, 1835; *The Latter-day Saints Millennial Star* 47:259–60.
49. *2013 Church Almanac*, 211.
50. *The Latter-day Saints Millennial Star* 47:314.
51. Jenson, *History of the Scandinavian Mission*, 290–91.
52. *The Latter-day Saints Millennial Star* 47:391; and Jensen, *Church Chronology*, 2nd ed., 121–22.
53. *The Latter-day Saints Millennial Star* 47:260, 300, 314, 334, 362, 394, 499, 517, 532, 536, 563, 579, 595.
54. Ibid., 536.
55. Ibid.
56. Hinckley, *Daniel Hanmer Wells and Events of His Time*, 252–53.
57. *The Latter-day Saints Millennial Star* 47:536.
58. Ibid., 537–538.
59. Jenson, *History of the Scandinavian Mission*, 291.
60. Melvin D. Wells, Letter to C. J. Arthur, October 1, 1885; and *The Latter-day Saints Millennial Star* 47:653.
61. "Mormon Migrations, Liverpool to New York, 24 Oct 1885–5 Nov 1885," accessed May 23, 2015, http://mormonmigration.lib.byu.edu/Search/showDetails/db:MM_MII/t:account/id:1041/keywords:John%20J%20Boyd; and *The Latter-day Saints Millennial Star* 47:587.
62. *The Latter-day Saints Millennial Star* 48:411.
63. Ibid.
64. Jenson, *History of the Scandinavian Mission*, 291–92.

Chapter 22

1. *The Latter-day Saints Millennial Star* 47:697.
2. Ibid., 748, 780, 842; vol. 48: 94, 157, 180, 155, 298, 256, 266, 299, 395, 412, 445, 558, 605, 629, 668, 676; and vol. 49: 49, 61. The 1885 conferences were held on November 1 in Nottingham and November 29 in Leeds. The 1886 conferences were held on January 3 in Glasgow, January 24 in Birmingham, February 21 in London, March 7 in Merthyr Tydfil, March 21 in Newcastle, April 4 in Nottingham, April 11 in Manchester, April 25 in Liverpool, June 6 in London, July 4 in Leeds, August 15 in Bristol, September 5 in Merthy Tydfil, September 19 in London, October 3 in Nottingham, and October 17 in Manchester. The 1887 conferences were held on January 2 in Birmingham and January 16 in London.
3. *The Latter-day Saints Millennial Star* 48:29–30, 75–76, 108–109, 443–444, 479.
4. Joseph M. Tanner, Letter to Franklin D. Richards, August 31, 1886; *Deseret News*, October 6, 1886, 606.
5. Joseph M. Tanner, Letter to Daniel H. Wells, June 22, 1886, *The Latter-day Saints Millennial Star* 48:443.
6. *The Latter-day Saints Millennial Star* 48:256.
7. Ibid., 336.
8. Ibid., 412; and Jensen, *History of the Scandinavian Mission*, 296–98.
9. *The Latter-day Saints Millennial Star* 48:447; and John Davidson Burt, [*Autobiography*], *An Enduring Legacy* (Salt Lake City: Daughters of Utah Pioneers, 1980), 3:289.
10. Jensen, *Church Chronology*, 2nd ed., 138; and Jensen, *History of the Scandinavian Mission*, 298–99.
11. Wells, "The Wells Family Genealogy," 12–16.
12. *The Latter-day Saints Millennial Star* 48:411.
13. Cannon, "The Tragic Matter of Louie Wells and John Q. Cannon," 158–59.
14. Ibid., 157–63.
15. Ibid.
16. Ibid.
17. "Sunday Services," *The Deseret News*, September 8, 1886, 533.
18. Cannon, "The Tragic Matter of Louie Wells and John Q. Cannon," 164–65.
19. Cannon, Diary of Abram Cannon, September 6, 1886.
20. Cannon, "The Tragic Matter of Louie Wells and John Q. Cannon," 167.
21. Ibid., 168–69.
22. Ibid., 170–79.
23. Heber J. Grant, Letter to Daniel H. Wells, November 21, 1886, cited in Ronald W. Walker, "Grant's Watershed: Succession in the Presidency," *Qualities That Count, BYU Studies* 43, no. 1 (2004): 226. Daniel H. Wells also showed his son-in-law, Heber J. Grant, correspondence that had passed between himself and George Q. Cannon. From this, Grant recorded in his diary, "Unless I am greatly mistaken . . . [President Cannon's] action has been wrong and someday there will be a squaring of accounting that will be anything but pleasant." Heber J. Grant, June 26–27, 1887, *Letterpress Diary, Heber J. Grant Papers* (Salt Lake City: Church History Library, The Church of Jesus Christ of Latter-day Saints).

24. *The Latter-day Saints Millennial Star* 49:76.
25. Cannon, "The Tragic Matter of Louie Wells and John Q. Cannon," 179.
26. Ibid., 173–78; and Grant, Letter to Daniel H. Wells, November 21, 1886.
27. Emmeline Wells, *Diary,* January 1, 1887.
28. *The Latter-Day Saints Millennial Star* 49:107 and vol. 48:778, 795.
29. *The Latter-Day Saints Millennial Star* 49:121.
30. Hinckley, *Daniel Hanmer Wells and Events of His Time,* 254–55.
31. Wells, "Daniel H. Wells," 245–46.
32. Cannon, "The Tragic Matter of Louie Wells and John Q. Cannon," 179–82.
33. Emmeline Wells, *Diary,* May 21, 1890, May 21, 1889, May 21, 1891, May 24, 1898, May 21, 1900, and May 21, 1901.
34. Cannon, "The Tragic Matter of Louie Wells and John Q. Cannon," 183–85. John Q. and Annie's fourth child was not born until 1889, a year after their remarriage.
35. Heber J. Grant, June 26–27, 1887, *Letterpress Diary, Heber J. Grant Papers* (Salt Lake City: Church History Library, The Church of Jesus Christ of Latter-day Saints).
36. Francis M. Lyman, Letter to Joseph F. Smith, May 25, 1887, cited in Cannon, "The Tragic Matter of Louie Wells and John Q. Cannon," 177.
37. Francis M. Lyman, Letter to Joseph F. Smith, June 27, 1887, cited in Cannon, "The Tragic Matter of Louie Wells and John Q. Cannon," 184.
38. *2013 Church Almanac,* 118; and Heath, "Notes on Apostolic Succession," 47.
39. Cannon, "The Tragic Matter of Louie Wells and John Q. Cannon," 186–87.
40. Kenneth L. Cannon II, "Wives and Other Women: Love, Sex, and Marriage in the Lives of John Q. Cannon, Frank J. Cannon, and Abraham H. Cannon," *Dialogue: A Journal of Mormon Thought* 43, no. 4 (Winter 2010): 80–81.
41. Emmeline Wells, *Diary, 25 and 26 April 1892.*
42. Cannon, "The Tragic Matter of Louie Wells and John Q. Cannon," 187–88.
43. Ibid.; and Wells, "The Wells Family Genealogy," 12–16.
44. Heath, "Notes on Apostolic Succession," 49.
45. *2013 Church Almanac,* 113, 114, 118; and Cannon, "The Tragic Matter of Louie Wells and John Q. Cannon," 188–89.

Chapter 23

1. Hinckley, *Daniel Hanmer Wells and Events of His Time,* 379–80.
2. "San Pete Valley Railway," *UtahRails.net,* accessed May 26, 2015, http://utahrails.net/utahrails/san-pete.php.
3. Kenneth C. Bullock, *A Genealogy of James Bullock and Mary Hill, Latter Day Saint Pioneers* (Provo: 1964), 98–99.
4. "Daniel H. Wells Residence, Utah Division of State History, Digital Collection, Wells, Daniel H.– Residence Page 1, Photo No. 8956, Caption Text," accessed June 15, 2015, http://content.lib.utah.edu/cdm/singleitem/collection/USHS_Class/id/19311/rec/1.
5. Salt Lake City Directory for 1890 (Salt Lake City: R. L. Polk & Co., 1890), 629–30.

6. Hinckley, *Daniel Hanmer Wells and Events of His Time*, 395; and *Utah Gazetteer 1892–93* (Salt Lake City: Stenhouse & Company, Salt Lake City, 1894), 740–41; and *Utah Gazetteer and Directory* (Salt Lake City: R. L. Polk & Co., 1884), 600–601.
7. Hinckley, *Daniel Hanmer Wells and Events of His Time*, 387; and 1880 US Federal Census, Salt Lake City, District 65, 18A, and District 39, 6B.
8. "Manti Temple Information, Sanpete County Government, Visitors' Pages," accessed May 26, 2015, http://sanpete.com/pages/temple.
9. Roberts, "History of the Mormon Church," 522; and *The Latter-day Saints Millennial Star* 50:383.
10. "Journal History of the Church, May 23, 1888" (Salt Lake City: Church History Library, The Church of Jesus Christ of Latter-day Saints), accessed May 26, 2015, https://eadview.lds.org/findingaid/CR%20100%20137.
11. Hinckley, *Daniel Hanmer Wells and Events of His Time*, 260.
12. Orson F. Whitney, "Orson F. Whitney Letters, 1868–1957," *Archive Grid* (Logan: Utah State University), accessed June 20, 2015, http://beta.worldcat.org/archivegrid/data/70969393.
13. B. Carmon Hardy, *Solemn Covenant: The Mormon Polygamous Passage* (Urbana: University of Illinois Press, 1992), 174–75.
14. Orson F. Whitney, "Orson F. Whitney Letters, 1868–1957," *Archive Grid* (Logan: Utah State University), accessed June 20, 2015, http://beta.worldcat.org/archivegrid/data/70969393.
15. Wells, "The Wells Family Genealogy," 12–16. The six marriages of his children that occurred after Daniel's death were: September 23, 1891, Gershom B. Wells married Ellen L. Sheets; June 22, 1892, Melvin D. Wells married Ann Elizabeth R. Young; November 3, 1892, Edna Margaret Wells married Thomas W. Sloan; May 15, 1895, Charles H. Wells married Susan D. Riter; December 30, 1896, Briant H. Wells married Mary Jane Jennings; January 1901, Louis R. Wells married Inga J. Hansen. Seven of Daniel's adult children did not marry: Albert Emory Wells, Emeline Young Wells, Eliza Free Wells, Catherine Wells, Stephen Franklin Wells, Victor Pennington Wells, and Emma Whitney Wells.
16. Hinckley, *Daniel Hanmer Wells and Events of His Time*, 260.
17. Christian N. Anderson, Letter to Heber J. Grant, January 21, 1927, cited in Hinckley, *Daniel Hanmer Wells and Events of His Time*, 406, 407.
18. Emmeline B. Wells, *Diary*, April 9, 1890.
19. Emmeline B. Wells, *Diary*, March 13, 1890.
20. Hinckley, *Daniel Hanmer Wells and Events of His Time*, 410.
21. Emmeline B. Wells, *Diary*, March 26, 1891.
22. Wells, "The Wells Family Genealogy," 12–16; and Hinckley, *Daniel Hanmer Wells and Events of His Time*, 424. Eliza Wells also outlived her husband, Daniel; she died in 1905 at age eighty-five in Alma, Michigan.
23. Hinckley, *Daniel Hanmer Wells and Events of His Time*, 415.
24. Ibid., 260–61.
25. Ibid.

Appendix A

1. Thomas Wells's children from oldest to youngest are Mary, born 1618; Anne, born 1619; John, born 1621; Robert, born 1624; Thomas, born 1625; Samuel, born 1629; Sarah, born 1631; and Joseph, born 1637.
2. Lemuel Welles, The English Ancestry of Gov. Thomas Welles of Connecticut, New England Historical and Genealogical Register 80, 1926, 279–447.
3. Tor Hylbom, Hylbom Family Ancestry Project, Welles #16118, Maternal Lines / Maternal We to Z / Welles #16118, Thomas Welles (1590–1660), accessed May 30, 2015, http://hylbom.com/family/maternal-lines/maternal-we-to-z/welles-16118/.
4. Ibid.
5. Ibid. Following his term as treasurer, Thomas was appointed secretary of the colony from 1640 to 1649. He was again appointed as treasurer on May 17, 1649 and held the office for three more years. He was elected deputy governor of Connecticut in 1654 and governor of the Colony in 1655. In 1656 and 1657 he served as deputy governor to John Winthrop the Younger, who was the son of the governor of Massachusetts Colony. In 1658 Thomas was again chosen governor of Connecticut Colony, and in 1659 deputy governor, the position he held at his death on January 14, 1660. Thomas Wells became involved in the settlement of Stratford, in Fairfield County, Connecticut, and sent his son John there to manage his affairs. John became a leading citizen in Stratford and remained there the rest of his life. Thomas was also listed as one of the first proprietors of Farmington, Connecticut, although he never lived there. It is likely that his investment in land in Farmington was made as a potentially profitable financial opportunity. In 1646 he gave his house there, along with the property on which it stood, to his daughter Ann, on the occasion of her marriage to Thomas Thompson.
6. William Richard Cutter and William Frederick Adams, *Genealogical and Personal Memoirs Relating to the Families of the State of Massachusetts*, vol. 1 (New York: Lewis Historical Publishing Company, 1910), 68–70. After his second marriage, Thomas Wells moved his residence from Hartford to Wethersfield where he lived the remainder of his life. His move was prompted by his new wife's reluctance to leave Wethersfield because she was still managing there the large estate of her first husband and presiding over the family of seven children that she had with him. Five of these children were minors at the time of Nathaniel Foote's death in 1644.
7. The youngest two children, daughters Sarah and Mary, are not mentioned by name in their father's will as are the other five, although they are heirs under his provisions in it for "all my children." Sarah and Mary were probably twins born after John's untimely death at age thirty-eight on August 7, 1659.
8. Barbara J. Mathews, "The Wills of John Welles and his Father, Governor Thomas Welles," *Wellesprings*, the newsletter of the Welles Family Association, April 2000.
9. Governor John Winthrop, Letter, April 3, 1660, *Massachusetts Historical Society Collection*, vol. 8, 5 Series:58; quoted in Genealogies and Biographies of Ancient Wethersfield, 2:761.

10. Mathews, "The Wills of John Welles and his Father, Governor Thomas Welles"; and Charles William Manwaring, *Digest of Early Connecticut Probate Records*, vol. 2, *Hartford District, 1700–1729* (Hartford: M. S. Pack & Co., 1906), 323–324. Robert Wells continued to live with his step-grandmother and was educated according to the directive in his grandfather's will. Thomas Wells's second wife Elizabeth was also given a life estate and an annuity of twelve pounds per year as long as she remained a widow. Thomas appointed two friends, John Talcott and Mr. Cotton, a teacher at Wethersfield, as overseers to carry out the provisions of his will for which they were each paid the sum of five pounds. They earned the stipend as Thomas's will ended with a provision that, in lieu of Elizabeth's annuity, she could if the overseers find it meet enjoy the use of his whole estate during her widowhood. Implementing that stipulation while at the same time preserving and improving the estate for its ultimate heirs, Robert Wells and the children of Thomas by his first wife Alice, must have proved challenging. Being amply provided for with a good home and income, Elizabeth Wells did not remarry after Thomas Wells's death. She lived comfortably on the estate he left her and died at Wethersfield on July 28, 1683 at the age of eighty-three.
11. Manwaring, *Digest of Early Connecticut Probate Records*, vol. 2, *Hartford District, 1700–1729*, 325. In 1676 Robert was ordered by the Wethersfield General Court to repair a damaged barn that Elizabeth was using and to "Make up ye annuity of £12 per annum," that by his grandfather's will he was to pay her. This order probably terminated the provision in Thomas's will that gave his wife full use of his entire estate and reinstated the alternate provisions that gave her a life estate in Thomas's home and her annuity of twelve pounds annually. The estrangement between Elizabeth Wells and her step-grandson Robert seems to have continued after the court settlement until Elizabeth's death in 1683. Her will, approved in August of that year, made no mention of any member of the Wells family and left all of her estate, consisting principally of the land she had inherited from her first husband, to her children and grandchildren by Nathaniel Foote.
12. A freeman took the citizen's oath and thereafter was given freedom of the City of Wethersfield, granted the right to vote and made eligible to hold public office.
13. William Richard Cutter, *New England Families, Genealogical and Memorial* (New York: Lewis Historical Publishing Company, 1914), 2:69–70. Robert was one of the patentees to whom the patent of Wethersfield was granted on February 17, 1686. In September 1689, he was chosen captain of the Wethersfield company of citizen-soldier militia, a designation that he retained despite holding other higher offices thereafter. When Indian hostilities threatened the town in June 1704, his home was one of six that were fortified on orders of the Wethersfield council. From 1690 until 1705 and again from 1708 to 1714 Robert was deputy for Wethersfield to the Connecticut general court. He was appointed commissioner for Wethersfield from 1692 through 1694, served as a member of the council in 1697 and 1698, and was appointed justice of the peace for the years 1702 through 1711.

14. Mathews, "The Wills of John Welles and his Father, Governor Thomas Welles." Robert's will includes an inventory of his estate valued at 3,667 pounds, a sum more than three times the 1,069 pounds inventoried in his grandfather Thomas Wells's estate, and one which put his heirs among the well-to-do families of early Wethersfield. Each of his surviving sons, Joseph, Robert, and Gideon, and his grandson Robert (son of his fourth son Robert) was given a house as well as land. His only daughter, Prudence, who probably received her share of the estate at the time of her marriage to the Rev. Anthony Stoddard in 1700, was not mentioned in his will except indirectly as one of the children.
15. Manwaring, *Digest of Early Connecticut Probate Records*, vol. 3, *Hartford District, 1729–1750*, 473. During his lifetime, Joseph Wells acquired considerable land in addition to the plots he received from his father and was able to comfortably meet his family's needs as well as accumulate an estate valued at 2,121 pounds in the inventory of his will. Joseph gave a third of his estate, real and moveable property, to Hannah for her lifetime, but she was able to enjoy the bequest only briefly if at all. Joseph died in January 1744 and his will was proven in February of the same year. His wife also died in 1744, after Joseph's will was proven, but before the inventory of his estate was taken. Joseph's sons were named as his executors and managed his property together for four years until formally dividing the estate after the inventory in 1749. All seven surviving children received equal shares of their father's property, but Joseph had previously given each of his three elder daughters their portions at the time of their individual marriages. His three sons were each given large tracts of land and considerable moveable property and were each directed to transfer a portion of their inheritance to their unmarried sister Eunice so as to make her an equal heir with the other daughters.
16. Ibid.
17. Wells, "The Wells Family Genealogy," 9–10. Experience did not marry until October 1786, when she was twenty-eight and her youngest sibling, Daniel, was thirteen. She lived less than five years after her marriage to Noah Stanley, born April 25, 1769, and had only two children of her own with him. Hannah married even later in January of 1788, also at age twenty-eight, when Daniel was fifteen, but lived to the age of eighty-three, dying May 4, 1844. She married Simeon Goodrich, born December 7, 1762. Simeon and Hannah Goodrich had five children.
18. As early as 1776, three years after his wife's death, Joshua Wells, along with many of his Wells, Deming, Dickenson, Goodrich, and Robbins relatives, is listed as a member of the Wethersfield company of Connecticut State troops headed by Captain H. Wells.
19. Wells, "The Wells Family Genealogy," 9–10. Experience Wells married in 1786 and Hannah in 1789. Between the two sisters' weddings, Joshua Wells Jr. in 1788 married his second cousin Judith Wells, the daughter of Hezekiah Wells and Mary Boardman. Hezekiah Wells, like Joshua Wells Sr. was a grandson of Capt. Robert Wells and Elizabeth Goodrich. In 1790 Levi Wells also married a second cousin, Sarah Deming, born May 26, 1765. She was the daughter of Moses Deming and Martha Wells, a granddaughter

of Captain Robert Wells and Elizabeth Goodrich. Gideon Wells married Emily Hart, born February 3, 1771, the daughter of Josiah Hart and Abigail Sluman in 1790, followed by Prudence Wells who married Justus Griswold, born April 26, 1768, in 1791. Joshua's three youngest children, Pamela Wells, born August 30, 1768; Abigail Wells, born January 20, 1771; and Daniel Wells, born June 15, 1773, were all very young at the time of their mother's death and appear to have formed an even closer bond with one another than they perhaps did with the older children in the family. All three married into the Francis and Hanmer families and named some of their children after one another. In 1793, Pamela Wells married James Francis, born May 25, 1767, the son of James Francis and Elizabeth Hanmer. Two years later in 1795 Abigail Wells married James Hanmer, born August 18, 1767, a first cousin of Pamela's husband James Francis. Daniel's wife, Honor Francis, was the younger sister of Pamela's husband James Francis and thus also a first cousin of Abigail's husband James Francis. Pamela and Daniel Wells both had large families, but Abigail and her husband, although they both lived into their eighties, had no children.

20. Unknown author, Wells Family Members in Holland Patent Cemetery, and Wells, "The Wells Family Genealogy," 10.
21. Wells, "The Wells Family Genealogy," 10.
22. Ibid.

Appendix B

1. Howard Millar Chapin, *Life of Deacon Samuel Chapin of Springfield* (Salt Lake City: compact disc online, Family History Library, L. C. Photoduplication Service, 1981), 4–6. The Chapin children who immigrated to or were born in Massachusetts in order from the eldest are David, born January 4, 1624; Catherine, born 1626; Sarah, born October 1628; Henry, born January 1630; Honor, born 1636; Josiah, born 1637; Samuel, born about 1638; Japhet, born October 15, 1642; and Hannah, born December 2, 1644.
2. Orange Chapin, *The Chapin Genealogy: Descendants of Deacon Samuel Chapin* (Northampton: Metcalf and Company, 1862), 4.
3. Unknown Author, *Ancestors of Henry Judson Chapin* (Washington, DC: The Media Research Bureau), 34–37.
4. Unknown Author, *Deacon Samuel Chapin, The Story of his Life* (Salt Lake City: typed manuscript in The Family History Library), 1–12. Hannah and Jonathan, died in infancy and their parents named a following child after each of them. Among the surviving eight children, Samuel, born 1665, and Sarah, born 1668, lived into their late sixties; Thomas, born 1671, and Jonathan, born 1688, into their late seventies; John, born 1674, Hannah, born 1680, and David, born 1682, into their late eighties; and Ebenezer, born June 26, 1677, to age ninety-five. This longevity, even in the absence of effective medical treatments for the conditions that usually precluded advanced age, persisted in succeeding generations of the Chapin family. Three of Ebenezer Chapin's sons lived past ninety, and two others past eighty. His grandson David Chapin, the grandfather of Daniel Hanmer Wells, lived to the age of ninety-five.

5. This move preceded by a few years the beginning of the Great Awakening, during which Protestant preachers such as Jonathan Edwards delivered fiery sermons that made Enfield and the surrounding area a focal point of Revivalist Christian teaching. It was probably made for economic reasons so that Ebenezer could more adequately support his large and still growing family.
6. Gilbert Warren Chapin, *The Chapin Book of Genealogical Data* (Hartford: Chapin Family Association, 1924), 1:11.
7. Ibid, 175. Martha Chapin married Joseph Merrill, born March 28, 1707 in West Hartford, Connecticut in February 1769, some seven years after her first husband's death. She had no children with Joseph, who was twenty years her senior and had been twice married previously. All of his children were adults by the time of his marriage to Martha, but he provided support and a father figure for her still-growing family. By the time Joseph and Martha both died in 1788, all of the Chapin children were married and on their own.
8. Abigail Wells, "Genealogy of the Wells Family" (Salt Lake City: unpublished manuscript in possession of the author, 1970).

Bibliography

1850 US Federal Census, Utah Territory, Great Salt Lake City.
1860 US Federal Census, Utah Territory, Great Salt Lake City.
1880 US Federal Census, Utah, Salt Lake City, District 65 and District 39.
1900 US Federal Census, Utah, Salt Lake City, Ward 4.
1910 US Federal Census, Utah, Salt Lake City, Ward 4.
2013 Church Almanac. Salt Lake City. The Deseret News, 2013.
Acts and Resolutions of the Second Annual Session of the Legislative Assembly of the Territory of Utah. Great Salt Lake City: George Hales, Printer, 1853.
Alexander, Thomas G. *The Rise of Multiple-use Management in the Intermountain West: A History of Region 4*. Washington, DC: Forest Service, US Department of Agriculture, 1987.
Allen, James B. "One Man's Nauvoo: William Clayton's Experience in Mormon Illinois." *The Journal of Mormon History*, vol. 6. Salt Lake City: Mormon History Association, 1979.
Allen, James B., and Glen M. Leonard. *The Story of the Latter-day Saints*. Salt Lake City: Deseret Book Company, 1976.
Alexander, Thomas G. "A Conflict of Perceptions: Ulysses S. Grant and the Mormons," *The Ulysses S. Grant Association Newsletter* 8, no. 4: 38–41. Starkville: Ulysses S. Grant Presidential Library, Mississippi State University. Accessed May 14, 2015. http://www.usgrantlibrary.org/usga/newsletters/volume8.asp.
"American Civil War: General Albert Sidney Johnston." *About.com*. About Education, Military History Biographies, Confederate Leaders of the Civil War. Accessed April 17, 2015. http://militaryhistory.about.com/od/americancivilwar/p/asjohnston.htm.
Ames, Ira. *Ira Ames' Journal*. Accessed March 20, 2015. http://www.huntsman-gifford.com/history/iraames/iraames.htm.

"An Act for the Relief of the Inhabitants of Cities and Towns upon the Public Lands (March 2, 1867)." *The Statutes at Large, Treaties, and Proclamations, of the United States of America*, vol. 14. Boston: Little, Brown, and Company, 1868.

"Ancestors of Henry Grow." *HenryGrowFamily.com.* Accessed March 10, 2015. http://www.henrygrowfamily.com/documents/Henry%20Grow.pdf.

Anderson, Ron. "Land Ownership in Salt Lake Valley (1847–1869)." *Mormon Trails.org.* Tours, Walking Tours, Salt Lake City. Accessed May 7, 2015. http://www.mormontrails.org/Tours/Walking/slcity.htm.

Arrington, Leonard J., and Davis Bitton. *The Mormon Experience: A History of the Latter-Day Saints.* 2nd ed. New York: Knopf, 1992.

Arrington, Leonard J., and Ronald W. Walker. *Great Basin Kingdom: An Economic History of the Latter-day Saints, 1830–1900.* Urbana: University of Illinois Press, 2004.

Arrington, Leonard J. *Brigham Young, American Moses.* Urbana: University of Illinois Press, 1985.

Arrington, L. J. "Brigham Young and the Transcontinental Telegraph." *The Improvement Era*, vol. 54. Salt Lake City: The Church of Jesus Christ of Latter-day Saints.

Arrington, L.J. "The Deseret Telegraph—A Church-Owned Public Utility." *Journal of Economic History*, vol. 11. Philadelphia: Economic History Association, University of Pennsylvania.

Bagley, Will. *Blood of the Prophets: Brigham Young and the Massacre at Mountain Meadows.* Norman: University of Oklahoma Press, 2012.

Bailey, Rev. Frederick W. *Wethersfield, Hartford Co., CT, Marriages 1739–1799, Early Connecticut Marriages as found on Ancient Church Records Prior to 1800*, vol. 3, 1898. Accessed June 11, 2015. https://archive.org/stream/earlyconnecticut03bail/earlyconnecticut03bail_djvu.txt.

Bancroft, Hubert Howe. *History of Utah 1540–1886.* San Francisco: The History Company, 1889.

Banner, Martha L., and Cullom Davis, et al., eds. *The Law Practice of Abraham Lincoln: Complete Documentary Edition*. File ID L01846, People v. Fraim. Urbana: University of Illinois Press, 2000.

Beadle, John Hanson. *Life in Utah, Or The Mysteries and Crimes of Mormonism.* Philadelphia: National Publishing Company, 1874.

Beckwith, E.G., and J.W. Gunnison. *Report of Explorations for a Route for the Pacific Railroad: Near the 38th and 39th Parallels of North Latitude: From the Mouth of the Kansas River, Mo., to the Sevier Lake, in the Great Basin.* OCLC 8497072. Washington, DC: War Dept., 1856.

Bennett, John C. *The History of the Saints: Or, An Exposé of Joe Smith and Mormonism.* Boston: Leland & Whiting, 1842.

Bennion, Samuel. *Samuel's Day Book, Bennion Family Papers.* Salt Lake City: Utah State Historical Society.

Bergera, Gary James. "Seniority in the Twelve: the 1875 Realignment of Orson Pratt." *Journal of Mormon History* 18, no. 1 (1992): 10–58.

Bigler, David L. "A Lion in the Path: Genesis of the Utah War, 1857–1858." *Utah Historical Quarterly* 76, no. 1 (Winter 2008): 4–21.

Biographical Record of Salt Lake City and Vicinity. Chicago: National Historical Record Company, 1902.

"Biography of William Wells Woods, Illustrated History of the State of Idaho." *AccessGenealogy.com.* Accessed May 21, 2015. http://www.accessgenealogy.com/idaho/biography-of-william-w-woods.htm.

Bitton, Davis, and Linda P. Wilcox. "Pestiferous Ironclads: The Grasshopper Problem in Pioneer Utah." *Utah Historical Quarterly* 46, no. 4 (Fall 1978): 336–55. Accessed March 17, 2015. http://historytogo.utah.gov/utah_chapters/pioneers_and_cowboys/pestiferousironclads.html.

Brassfield, Squire Newton. "Histories, Brassfield—Brassfield Genealogies." Accessed May 6, 2015. http://www.brasfield.net/histories/Squire%20Newton%20Brassfield.htm.

Britton, Rollin J. *Early Days on the Grand River and the Mormon War*. Columbia: The Missouri State Historical Society, 1920.

Bullock, Kenneth C. *A Genealogy of James Bullock and Mary Hill*. Provo: Latter Day Saint Pioneers, 1964.

Bullock, Thomas. "Journals 1843–1849." Salt Lake City: Church History Department, The Church of Jesus Christ of Latter-Day Saints. Accessed March 10, 2015. http://history.lds.org/overlandtravels/trailExcerptMulti?lang=eng&sourceId=4546.

Burns, Thomas W. *Initial Ithacans*. Ithaca: Press of the Ithaca Journal. Accessed April 1, 2015. http://www.archive.org/stream/cu31924030991487#page/n65/mode/2up.

Burt, John Davidson. *[Autobiography]*, An Enduring Legacy, vol. 3. Salt Lake City: Daughters of Utah Pioneers, 1980.

Canfield, W.W., and J.E. Clark. *Things Worth Knowing about Oneida County*. Utica, NY: Thomas J. Griffiths, 1909.

Cannon, Abram. *Diary of Abram Cannon*. Provo: Harold B. Lee Library, Brigham Young University.

Cannon, George Q. "Editorial Thoughts," *The Juvenile Instructor*, August 17, 1872. Accessed May 13, 2015. http://www.findmypast.com/mocavo-info.

Cannon, Ken. "The Tragic Matter of Louie Wells and John Q. Cannon." *Journal of Mormon History* (Spring 2009): 126–90.

Cannon, Kenneth L., II. "Wives and Other Women: Love, Sex, and Marriage in the Lives of John Q. Cannon, Frank J. Cannon, and Abraham H. Cannon." *Dialogue: A Journal of Mormon Thought* 43, no. 4 (Winter 2010).

Carter, Kate B. *Heart Throbs of the West*, vol. 6. Salt Lake City: Daughters of Utah Pioneers, 2001.

Carter, Kate. "Sketch of the Life of Emmeline Blanche Woodward." In *Our Pioneer Heritage*, vol. 8: *That They May Live Again*. Provo: Brigham Young University Press, 1965.

Cases Argued and Decided in the Supreme Court of the United States. vol. 26. Rochester: The Lawyers Co-operative Publishing Company, 1881.

Chapin, Gilbert Warren. *The Chapin Book of Genealogical Data*. vol. 1. Hartford: Chapin Family Association, 1924.

Child, Hamilton. "History of Trenton, New York." *Gazetteer and Business Directory of Oneida County*. Syracuse, NY, 1862.

Church Historian's Office Register of General Church Minutes, 1839–1877. Salt Lake City: Church History Library, The Church of Jesus Christ of Latter-day Saints.

Clayton, William. *Journal of William Clayton*. Salt Lake City: Church History Department, The Church of Jesus Christ of Latter-day Saints.

Clayton, William. *Nauvoo Temple History Journal*. Salt Lake City: Church History Department, The Church of Jesus Christ of Latter-day Saints.

"Coalville." *Utah History to Go*, 2013. Accessed June 15, 2015. http://www.onlineutah.com/coalvillehistory.shtml.

Coin Community Family. "Main Coin Forum, Heritage Seldom Seen Selections: Rare 1849 Mormon $20 Gold." Accessed March 10, 2015. http://www.coincommunity.com/forum/topic.asp?TOPIC_ID=160791.

Colfax, Schuyler. "Hon. Schuyler Colfax's Journey from the Missouri River to California in 1865." *Western Galaxy*, vol. 1. Salt Lake City: The Juvenile Instructor's Office, 1888.

Collier, Fred C., ed. *Manuscript History of Brigham Young 1847–1850*. Salt Lake City: Collier Publishing Co, 1997.

Collier, Fred C., ed. *Unpublished Revelations of Prophets and Presidents of the Church of Jesus Christ of Latter-Day Saints*. vol. 1. Salt Lake City: Collier Publishing, 1979.

Connecticut Military Record, 1775–1848. Record of Service of Connecticut Men in the War of the Revolution, War of 1812, Mexican War. Hartford: The Case, Lockwood & Brainard Company, 1889.

Conover, Peter W. Letter to Daniel H. Wells, June 18, 1854. Salt Lake City: Utah Territorial Militia Correspondence, 1849–1863, Utah State Archives.

Conyers, Josiah B. *A Brief History of the Leading Causes of the Hancock Mob in the Year 1846*. St. Louis: Cathcart & Prescott, 1846.

Cook, Lyndon W. "Isaac Galland, Mormon Benefactor." *BYU Studies* 19, no. 3 (1979).

Coombs, Lucy Ann. *Letter to Daniel H. Wells*. Logan: Daniel H. Wells Papers, Utah State University, 1846.

Cowan, Richard O. *The Design, Construction, and Role of the Salt Lake Temple*. Provo: Religious Studies Center, Brigham Young University, 2011., http://rsc.byu.edu/archived/salt-lake-city/4-design-construction-and-role-salt-lake-temple, Accessed April 17, 2015.

Delano, Alonzo. *Life on the Plains and Among the Diggings*. Buffalo: Miller, Orton, & Mulligan, 1854.

Deming, Mrs. Minor. Letter, September 29, 1845. Urbana: Minor Deming Papers, Illinois Historical Survey, University of Illinois Library.

"Description of the Ship Belle Wood and its Voyage of April 29, 1865." *Jensen Family Genealogy*. Freepages, Rootsweb, Ancestry.com. Accessed April 29, 2015. http://freepages.genealogy.rootsweb.ancestry.com/~sjensen/jensen/references/ref228.htm.

Dinger, John S., ed. *The Nauvoo City and High Council Minutes*. Salt Lake City: Signature Books, 1995.

Durant, Samuel W. *History of Oneida County, New York: With Illustrations and Biographical Sketches of Some of Its Prominent Men and Pioneers*. Oneida, New York: Higginson Book Co, 1878.

Doctrine and Covenants. Salt Lake City: The Church of Jesus Christ of Latter-day Saints, 1985.

"Early Utah Coal Discoveries." *Utah Rails.net*. Accessed April 16, 2015. http://utahrails.net/utahcoal/utahcoal-early.php.

Encyclopedia of Mormonism. New York: Macmillan, 1992.

Enyeart, John P. *The Quest for "Just and Pure Law": Rocky Mountain Workers and American Social Democracy, 1870–1924*. Stanford: Stanford University Press, 2009.

Esshom, Frank. *Pioneers and Prominent Men of Utah*. Salt Lake City: Utah Pioneers Book Publishing Company, 1913.

FamilySearch.org. "Memories, The Church of Jesus Christ of Latter-day Saints." Accessed March 10, 2015. https://familysearch.org/photos/stories.

Firmage, Edwin Brown, and Richard Collin Mangrum. *Zion in the Courts: A Legal History of the Church of Jesus Christ of Latter-Day Saints.* Urbana: University of Illinois Press, 2001.

Fisher, Margaret M., ed. *Utah and the Civil War: Being the Story of the Part Played by the People of Utah in That Great Conflict.* Salt Lake City: Deseret Book Company, 1929.

Flanders, Robert Bruce. *Nauvoo, Kingdom on the Mississippi.* Urbana: University of Illinois Press, 1965.

Ford, Thomas. *A History of Illinois from Its Commencement as a State in 1814 to 1847.* Chicago: S. C. Griggs & Co, 1854.

Fullmer, John S. *A Condensed History of the Expulsion of the Saints from Nauvoo (pamphlet).* Liverpool: Printed by B. James, 1855.

Furniss, Norman F. *The Mormon Conflict 1850–1859.* New Haven: Yale University Press, 1966.

Gardner, Hamilton. "The Nauvoo Legion, 1840–1845: A Unique Military Organization." *Journal of the Illinois State Historical Society* 54 no. 2 (Summer 1961): 181–97.

Gardner, Hamilton, ed. "A Territorial Militiaman in the Utah War." *Journal of Newton Tuttle,* entries for October 19 and 20, 1857, Hickman Family Museum. Accessed April 15, 2015. http://hickmanmuseum.homestead.com/Tuttle.html.

Gates, Susa Young. *History of the Young Ladies' Mutual Improvement Association of the Church of Jesus Christ of Latter-day Saints from November, 1869 to June, 1910.* Salt Lake City: Deseret News Press, 1911.

"George R. Maxwell v George Q. Cannon, Papers in the Case of Maxwell V Cannon for a Seat as Delegate from Utah Territory in the Forty-Third Congress, Document No. 49." In *Miscellaneous Documents of the House of Representatives for the First Session of the Forty-Third Congress,* vol. 1. Washington, DC: Government Printing Office, 1874.

Gold Mormon Coins. Accessed March 10, 2015. http://goldmormoncoins.com/Gold_Mormon_Coins.html.

Grandstaff, Mark R. "General Regis de Trobriand, the Mormons, and the US Army at Camp Douglas, 1870–71." *Utah Historical Quarterly* 64 (Summer 1996): 204–23.

Grant, Heber J. *Letterpress Diary, Heber J. Grant Papers.* Salt Lake City: Church History Library, The Church of Jesus Christ of Latter-day Saints.

Grant, Julia Dent. *Unpublished memoirs (ca. 1891).* US Grant 3rd Collection, US Grant Association, Ulysses S. Grant Presidential Library, Mississippi State University.

Gregg, Thomas. *History of Hancock County, Illinois.* Chicago: Chas. C. Chapman & Co, 1880.

Gunnison, Lieut. J. W. *The Mormons, or, Latter-Day Saints, in the Valley of the Great Salt Lake: A History of Their Rise and Progress, Peculiar Doctrines, Present Condition, and Prospects.* Philadelphia: Lippencott, Grambo & Co, 1852.

Hafen, LeRoy Reuben, and Ann Woodbury Hafen, eds. *Mormon Resistance: A Documentary Account of the Utah Expedition, 1857–1858.* Glendale: Arthur H. Clark Company, 1958.

Hajicek, John. "Daniel H. Wells Justice Court Record Book, Synopsis of Content." *Mormonism.com.* Accessed June 17, 2015. http://www.mormonism.com/Court.htm.

Hales, Brian C. "Joseph Smith's Polygamy, Nauvoo Polygamy—1843, Emma Learns that Plural Marriage Has Been Restored." Accessed February 23, 2015. http://josephsmithspolygamy.org/.

Halverson, W. *Dee. Grass Creek Canyon Coal.* Coalville, UT: Summit County Historical Society, 2010.

Hampshire, David. *No Western Parallel: The Story of Questar Corporation.* Salt Lake City: Questar Corporation, 1998.

Hancock County Deeds. Carthage: Hancock County Recorder's Office.

Hardy, B. *Carmon. Solemn Covenant: The Mormon Polygamous Passage.* Urbana: University of Illinois Press, 1992.

Harrington, Gordon, and Mary Paulson. "Congregationalism in Utah." *Utah History Encyclopedia.* Accessed May 15, 2015. http://www.uen.org/utah_history_encyclopedia/c/CONGREGATIONALISM_IN_UTAH.html.

Harris, Martha Givens, and Josephine Wells Lyman. "Martha Givens Harris Autobiographical Life Sketch." In *Our Pioneer Heritage,* vol. 8: *That They May Live Again.* Provo: Brigham Young University Press, 1965.

Hartley, William G. "Dangerous Outpost: Thomas Corless and the Fort Limhi/Salmon River Mission." *Mormon Historical Studies* 2, no. 2. Sandy, UT: Mormon Historic Sites Foundation, 2002.

Haywood, William D. *Bill Haywood's Book—The Autobiography of William D. Haywood.* New York: International Publishers, 1929.

Heath, Steven H. "Notes on Apostolic Succession." *Dialogue: A Journal of Mormon Thought* 20, no. 2. Accessed May 19, 2015. https://www.dialoguejournal.com/wp-content/uploads/sbi/articles/Dialogue_V20N02_46.pdf.

Heritage Auctions. "All Auction Archive, Territorial Gold, 1849 $10 Mormon Ten Dollar AU58 NGC." Accessed March 10, 2015. http://coins.ha.com/itm/territorial-gold/1849–10-mormon-ten-dollar-au58-ngc-k-3-r7/a/1204-5455.s.

Heritage Gateways. "Pioneer Date Summary, Utah State Office of Education, Salt Lake City." Accessed March 9, 2015. http://heritage.uen.org/resources/Wc9f599d2aae0e.htm.

Hill, Donna. *Joseph Smith the First Mormon.* Garden City, NY: Doubleday and Company, Inc, 1977.

Hill, Gustavus, Esq. *City of Nauvoo Map, Lithographed Reproduction from the Original Entered in the Hancock County Clerk's Office, Carthage, Illinois, 1841.* Nauvoo: Nauvoo Restoration, Inc., 1971.

Hinckley, Bryant S. *Daniel Hanmer Wells and Events of His Time.* Salt Lake City: The Deseret News Press, 1942.

"History of Ezra T. Benson." *The Benson Family: The Ancestry and Descendants of Ezra T. Benson.* Logan, UT: The Ezra T. Benson Genealogical Society, Inc., 1979. Accessed April 22, 2015. http://etb.bensonfamily.org/histories/etb-alder.htm.

Holzapfel, Richard Neitzel, and Christopher C. Jones. "'John the Revelator': The Written Revelations of John Taylor, Champion of Liberty: John Taylor." Provo: Religious Studies Center, Brigham Young University. Accessed May 21, 2015. http://rsc.byu.edu/archived/champion-liberty-john-taylor/john-revelator-written-revelations-john-taylor.

Houston, Sam. *The Writings of Sam Houston, 1813–1863.* Austin: The University of Texas Press, 1941.

Humphreys, A. Glen. "Missionaries to the Saints." *BYU Studies* 17, no. 1. Accessed May 19, 2015. http://byustudies.byu.edu/PDFLibrary/17.1HumpherysMissionaries-74641240-5247-43f2-94a6-9f26f2c9cb73.pdf.

Irish, O.H. *Letter to William P. Dole, June 29, 1865. Report of the Secretary of the Interior 1865, House Executive Document 1.* vol. 2. Washington, DC: Government Printing Office, 1866.

Jarvis, Mabel. "Sketches from The Life of Brigham Jarvis, Sr., 1850–1933." *The George and Ann Prior Jarvis Family Web Site.* Accessed April 16, 2015. http://www.george-and-ann-prior-jarvis.org/html_docs/brigham_young_jarvis.html.

Jensen, Andrew. *Church Chronology.* 2nd. Salt Lake City: Deseret News Company, 1899.

Jensen, Andrew. *History of the Scandinavian Mission.* Salt Lake City: Deseret News Press, 1927.

Jenson, Andrew. *Encyclopedic History of the Church of Jesus Christ of Latter-day Saints.* Salt Lake City: Deseret News Press, 1941.

"John Nickles, Respondent v. Daniel H. Wells, et al., Appellants." *Reports of Cases Decided in the Supreme Court of the Territory of Utah,* vol. 2. Chicago: Callaghan and Company, 1882.

Johnson, Philo. *Autobiographical Sketch of the Life of Philo Johnson.* UT: Payson, 1894., http://www.rootcellar.us/johnsnph.htm, Accessed June 15, 2015.

Jones, Daniel W. *Forty Years Among the Indians.* Salt Lake City: The Juvenile Instructor Office, 1890.

"Journal History of the Church." Salt Lake City: Church History Library, The Church of Jesus Christ of Latter-day Saints. Accessed March 11, 2015. https://eadview.lds.org/findingaid/CR%20100%20137.

"Journal of Discourses." Salt Lake City: The Church of Jesus Christ of Latter-day Saints. Accessed June 12, 2015. http://jod.mrm.org/1.

Journal of the Executive Proceedings of the Senate of the United States of America. vol. 17. Washington, DC: Government Printing Office, 1901.

Keller, Charles L. *The Lady in the Ore Bucket: A History of Settlement and Industry in the Tri-Canyon Area of the Wasatch Mountains.* Salt Lake City: University of Utah Press, 2001.

Kerr, LaRae Free. "Life of Lawrence Sterne Hotchkiss." Salt Lake City: unpublished research, copy in the author's possession, 2013.

Kimball, Hiram P., ed. *On the Potters Wheel: Diaries of Heber C. Kimball.* Salt Lake City: Signature Books, Inc, 1987.

Kitchen, Richard Darrell. *Mormon-Indian Relations in Deseret: Intermarriage and Indenture, 1847 to 1877.* Phoenix: Arizona State University, 2002.

Larson, Gustive O. *Outline History of Utah and the Mormons.* Salt Lake City: Deseret Book, 1958.

Lee, John D. *A Mormon Chronicle: The Diaries of John D. Lee, 1848–1876.* Ed. Robert Glass Cleland and Juanita Brooks. Los Angeles: Huntington Library Press, 2004.

Lieber, Constance L., and John Sillito. *Letters from Exile, The Correspondence of Martha Hughes Cannon and Angus M. Cannon, 1886–1888.* Salt Lake City: Signature Books, 1989.

Lineage Book–National Society of the Daughters of the American Revolution. vol. 25. Washington, DC: National Society of the Daughters of the American Revolution, 1908.

Linn, William Alexander. *The Story of the Mormons from the Date of Their Origin to 1901,* Digi-Media-Apps, 2012. Accessed April 14, 2015. https://books.google.com/books?id=vWMXBQAAQBAJ&pg=PT680&lpg=PT680&dq=%22Cumming%22+%22echo+canyon%22+deception&source=bl&ots=mme

xbRuSKz&sig=knkIw4OZ9sKnJur63oVMejccXXI&hl=en&sa=X&ei=VJYtVe G8MMmYgwS89ICwCw&ved=0CCQQ6AEwAg#v=onepage&q=%22Cumm ing%22%20%22echo%20canyon%22%20deception&f=false.
Lists and Returns of Connecticut Men in the Revolution, 1775–1783. Hartford: Connecticut Historical Society, 1909.
Littlefield, Daniel F., Jr., and James W. Parins. *Encyclopedia of American Indian Removal.* Santa Barbara, CA: ABC-CLIO, 2011.
Long, E.B. *The Saints and the Union: Utah Territory During the Civil War.* Urbana: University of Illinois Press, 2001.
Ludlow, Daniel H. *Encyclopedia of Mormonism.* New York: Macmillan, 1992.
Ludlow, Fitz Hugh. *The Heart of a Continent.* New York: Cambridge Riverside Press, 1870.
MacDonald, William. *Documentary Source Book of American History, 1606–1913.* New York: The Macmillan Company, 1916.
Madsen, Carol Cornwall. "Emmeline B. Wells: Romantic Rebel." Monograph 12 in *Supporting Saints: Life Stories of Nineteenth-Century Mormons,* vol. 1. Provo: Brigham Young University, Religious Studies Center, 1985.
Manderscheid, Lorraine Richardson. *Divorce of Louisa Free, Some Descendants of John Doyle Lee.* Accessed March 10, 2015. http://www.wadhome.org/lee /chapter_04.html.
Manwaring, Charles William. *Digest of Early Connecticut Probate Records,* 3 vols., *Hartford District, 1729–1750.* Hartford: M. S. Pack & Co., 1906.
Marcy, Col. *Randolph B. Thirty Years of Army Life on the Border.* New York: Harper Brothers Publishers, 1866.
Marsh, Eudocia Baldwin. "When the Mormons Dwelt Among Us." *The Bellman,* vol. 20, nos. 507 and 508. Berkeley: Bancroft Library, University of California, 1916.
"Manti Temple Information, Sanpete County Government." Visitors' page. Accessed May 26, 2015. http://sanpete.com/pages/temple.
Maxwell, John Gary. *Robert Newton Baskin and the Making of Modern Utah.* Norman: University of Oklahoma Press, 2013.
McMullin, Thomas A., and David Walker. "Biographical Directory of American Territorial Governors. Territorial Governors." *Utah History Encyclopedia.* Accessed May 14, 2015. http://www.uen.org/utah_history_encyclopedia /t/TERRITORIAL_GOVERNORS.html.
"Memorial of the Legislative Assembly of the Territory of Utah, Document No. 45." *Miscellaneous Documents of the House of Representatives for the First Session of the Forty-Eighth Congress,* vol. 19. Washington, DC: Government Printing Office, 1884.
Mission President's Handbook. Salt Lake City: The Church of Jesus Christ of Latter-day Saints, 2006.
Moore, John Bassett, ed. *The Works of James Buchanan.* 12 vols., 1908–11. Philadelphia: J. B. Lippincott Co.
"Mormon Migration." Accessed May 23, 2015. http://mormonmigration.lib.byu .edu/.
Morris, Rod. "Balsam Hill Cabin." Brighton, UT, 2009. Accessed March 13, 2015. http://balsam-hill-cabin.com/php/book/ch1.php.
Murphy, Miriam B. "Territorial Governors." *Utah History Encyclopedia.* Salt Lake City: University of Utah Press, 1994. Cited in "Utah Department of Administrative Services, Division of Archives & Records Service." *Utah State Government.* Accessed April 17, 2015. http://archives.utah.gov/research /guides/governor.htm.

"Nauvoo Temple Endowment Name Index." Accessed June 12, 2015. http://user.xmission.com/~research/family/familypage.htm.

"Nauvoo Today." *The Improvement Era*, vol. 12. Salt Lake City: General Board M.I.A, 1909.

New York, Land Records, 1630–1975, Oneida, Owners of land (Trenton) 1814. Salt Lake City: Family History Library, The Church of Jesus Christ of Latter-day Saints. Accessed February 12, 2015. https://familysearch.org/pal:/MM9.3.1/TH-1961-25923-10273-80?cc=2078654&wc=M7HP-QZS:358132601,358165501.

Nevius, John. Letter, May 2, 1841. Carbondale: Stanley Kimball Collection, Southern Illinois University.

"Old Nauvoo Cemetery." *FindAGrave.com*. Accessed February 19, 2015. http://www.findagrave.com/cgi-bin/fg.cgi?page=cr&GSln=wells&GSbyrel=all&GSdyrel=all&GSst=16&GScnty=723&GScntry=4&GSob=n&CRid=107486&df=all&pt=Old%20Nauvoo%20Burial%20Grounds&.

"Oneida County Cemeteries, Trenton, Holland Patent Cemetery, transcription S thru Z." Provo: Rootsweb, Ancestry.com Operations, Inc. Accessed June 11, 2015. http://freepages.genealogy.rootsweb.ancestry.com/~townoflee/cemeteries/Trenton/hollandpatents-z.html.

"Original Land Titles in Utah Territory." Utah Department of Administrative Services, Division of Archives & Records Services, 2013. Accessed May 7, 2015. http://archives.utah.gov/research/guides/land-original-title.htm.

Patent Certificate #6726. United States General Land Office, Springfield, Pre Emp. Act of May 29, 1830, Re-recorded June 18, 1846, Springfield, IL.

Pearl of Great Price. Salt Lake City: The Church of Jesus Christ of Latter-day Saints, 1985.

Perkins, Edward, and Mary Jane Woodger. "Administration from the Underground, Champion of Liberty: John Taylor." Provo: Religious Studies Center, Brigham Young University. Accessed May 22, 2015. http://rsc.byu.edu/archived/champion-liberty-john-taylor/administration-underground.

Peters, Gerhard, and John T. Wooley. *The American Presidency Project, James Buchanan, Proclamation—Rebellion in the Territory of Utah, 6 April 1858.* http://www.presidency.ucsb.edu/ws/?pid=68308

Peterson, John Alton. *Utah's Black Hawk War*. Salt Lake City: University of Utah Press, 1998.

Poll, Richard D., and Ralph W. Hansen. "'Buchanan's Blunder': The Utah War, 1857–1858." *Military Affairs* 25, no. 3 (1961): 121–31.

Pratt, Parley P. *Autobiography of Parley P. Pratt*. Salt Lake City: Deseret Book Company, 2000.

Revised Ordinances and Resolutions of the City Council of Salt Lake City in the Territory of Utah, with Congressional and Territorial Laws of Townsites and Great Salt Lake City Charter, and Amendments. Salt Lake City: Deseret News Printing, 1875.

Revolutionary War Record of David Chapin. Revolutionary War Pension and Bounty-Land Warrant Application Files, 1800–1900, National Archives and Records Administration. NARA microfilm publication M804. Records of the Department of Veterans Affairs, Record Group 15. Washington, DC: National Archives.

Roberts, B.H. *A Comprehensive History of the Church of Jesus Christ of Latter-day Saints*. Provo: Brigham Young University Press, 1965.

Roberts, Brigham H. "History of the Mormon Church." *Americana*, vol. 9. New York: The National Americana Society, 1914.

Roberts, Brigham H. *The Rise and Fall of Nauvoo.* Salt Lake City: Deseret News Publishers, 1900.
Roberts, Allen Dale. *Salt Lake City's Historic Architecture.* Charleston, SC: Arcadia Publishing, 2012.
Rockwell, Abigail, and Lucy Ann Coombs. *Letter to Daniel H. Wells.* Logan: Daniel H. Wells Papers, Utah State University, 1848.
"Salt Lake City Cemetery." *Findagrave.com.* Accessed March 10, 2015. http://www.findagrave.com/cgi-bin/fg.cgi?page=cr&CRid=77424&CScn=salt+lake+city+cemetery&CScntry=4&CSst=47&.
"Secretary of War Report, 1857." *Message from the President of the United States to the Two Houses of Congress, 1st Session, Thirty-Fifth Congress, 1857–1858,* vol. 2. Washington, DC: Cornelius Wendell, Printer.
Sessions, Gene Allred. *Mormon Thunder: A Documentary History of Jedediah Morgan Grant.* Urbana: University of Illinois Press, 1993.
Settle, Raymond W., and Mary Lund Settle. *War Drums and Wagon Wheels: The Story of Russell, Majors, and Waddell.* Lincoln: University of Nebraska Press, 1966.
Salt Lake City Directory for 1890. Salt Lake City: R. L. Polk & Co, 1890.
Shaw, Ambrose A. "FamilySearch, Memories, The Church of Jesus Christ of Latter-day Saints." Accessed March 28, 2015. https://familysearch.org/photos/people/2106136.
"Slavery in Utah." *Utah History to Go.* Accessed April 17, 2015. http://historytogo.utah.gov/utah_chapters/pioneers_and_cowboys/slaveryinutah.html
Skeen, C. Edward. *Citizen Soldiers in the War of 1812.* Lexington: University Press of Kentucky, 2015.
Smith, Craig S. "Joseph W Young and the Mormon Emigration of 1864." *BYU Studies.* Accessed April 28, 2015. https://ojs.lib.byu.edu/spc/index.php/BYUStudies/article/viewFile/6627/6276.
Smith, Joseph. *History of the Church of Jesus Christ of Latter-day Saints.* 6 vols. Salt Lake City: The Deseret Book Company, 1965.
The Joseph Smith Papers. Documents. http://josephsmithpapers.org/the-papers#/D2L.
The Joseph Smith Papers. Journals. http://josephsmithpapers.org/the-papers#/J2L.
The Joseph Smith Papers. Administrative Records. http://josephsmithpapers.org/the-papers#/A2L.
The Joseph Smith Papers. Revelations and Translations. http://josephsmithpapers.org/the-papers#/R2L.
The Joseph Smith Papers. Histories. http://josephsmithpapers.org/the-papers#/H2L.
The Joseph Smith Papers. Legal, Business, and Financial Records. http://josephsmithpapers.org/the-papers#/L2L.
Smith, Joseph Fielding. *Essentials in Church History.* Salt Lake City: Deseret News Press, 1922.
Sonne, Conway B. *Ships, Saints, and Mariners: A Maritime Encyclopedia of Mormon Migration, 1830–1890.* Salt Lake City: University of Utah Press, 1993.
"South Africa's Contribution to Utah." *Treasures of Pioneer History,* vol. 6, 288–89. Salt Lake City: Daughters of Utah Pioneers.
Stenhouse, T.B.H. *The Rocky Mountain Saints: A Full and Complete History of the Mormons.* New York: D. Appleton and Company, 1878.
"Story of Cooperation in the United States." *Johns Hopkins University Studies in Historical and Political Science,* vol. 6. Baltimore: Guggenheim Weil & Co, 1888.

Stout, Hosea. "The Diary of Hosea Stout, 5 March 1849." Rob & Susan Johnson Family Pages. Accessed March 11, 2015. http://robandsusanpages.com/History/Stout/Hosea_1849_03.html.

"Struggle for Statehood Chronology." *Utah History to Go*. State of Utah, 2013. Accessed April 20, 2015. http://historytogo.utah.gov/utah_chapters/statehood_and_the_progressive_era/struggleforstatehoodchronology.html.

Summit County Abstracts. Book 1.

Summit County Old Records. Book D.

Sutter, John A. "The Discovery of Gold in California." *The Virtual Museum of the City of San Francisco*. Accessed March 10, 2015. http://www.sfmuseum.org/hist2/gold.html.

"Synoptical History of the Congregational Church and The First Congregational Church." *The Church Review* 4 (Salt Lake City, 1895).

Taylor, Craig E., Elliott Mittler, and Le Val Lund. *Overcoming Barriers: Lifeline Seismic Improvement Programs*. ASCE Publications, 2002.

"The Nauvoo Legion on Parade." *The Joseph Smith and Emma Hale Smith Historical Society*. Accessed February 16, 2015. https://www.josephsmithjr.org/.

"Territorial Governors." *Utah History Encyclopedia*. Accessed April 27, 2015. http://www.uen.org/utah_history_encyclopedia/t/TERRITORIAL_GOVERNORS.html.

Terry, William W. William W. Terry Collection. MS 116. Ogden: Weber State University, Special Collections.

"The Day the Sky Fell in Salt Lake City: April 5, 1876." *The Mystery of Utah History*. Accessed March 10, 2015. http://mysteryofutahhistory.blogspot.com/2013/10/the-day-sky-fell-in-salt-lake-city.html.

"The Erie Canal, Images, Other Images of the Erie Canal, Tolls, Fares, Distances, etc." Accessed June 17, 2015. http://www.eriecanal.org/misc-1.html#toll.

The Executive Documents of the Senate of the United States, 36th Congress, 1st Session. Vol. 2, *Executive Document No. 32, 1859–1860*. Washington, DC: George W Rowman, Printer, 1860.

"The History of Lorenzo Wesley Roundy." Chapter 10 in *Archie Earl Buchanan / Florene Davis Family Organization Web Pages, Histories*. Accessed May 19, 2015. http://aeb.buchananspot.com/histories/LWR/LWR_Ch10.html.

The Latter-day Saints Millennial Star. Liverpool: The Church of Jesus Christ of Latter-day Saints, 1840–1970.

"The Morrill Anti-Bigamy Act." *Statutes at Large, Treaties and Proclamations, 37th Congress, 2nd Session*, vol. 12. Boston: Little, Brown and Company, 1863.

"The Nauvoo Legion." *The Contributor* 9, no. 10. Salt Lake City: The Contributor Company, August 1888.

"The Warsaw Signal." *Uncle Dale's Readings in Early Mormon History Newspapers of Illinois*. Accessed February 26, 2015. http://www.sidneyrigdon.com/dbroadhu/IL/sign1844.htm#0612.

Times and Seasons. Vols. 1–6. Nauvoo: 1839–1846. Accessed June 17, 2015. http://www.centerplace.org/history/ts/.

Thompson, Charles Mansfield. "The Illinois Whigs Before 1846." *University of Illinois Studies in the Social Sciences*, vol. 4. Urbana: University of Illinois Press, 1915.

Thorpe, Joseph. *Early Days in the West Along the Missouri One Hundred Years Ago*. Liberty, MO: Irving Gilmer, 1924 (reprint).

Transcript of the Potter Young Meeting, (undated). Minutes, 1855–77. Salt Lake City: Church History Department, The Church of Jesus Christ of Latter-day Saints.

"Treaty with the Utah, Yampah Ute, Pah-Vant, Sanpete Ute, Tim-P-Nogs and Cum-Nm-Bah Bands of the Utah Indians, 8 June 1865." *Indian Affairs: Laws and Treaties*, vol. 5, *Laws*. Washington, DC: Government Printing Office, 1941.

Tullidge, Edward W. *Tullidge's Histories*. Salt Lake City: Juvenile Instructor Press, 1889.

Tullidge, Edward W. *Life of Brigham Young: Or, Utah and Her Founders*. New York, 1876.

Tullidge, Edward W. "Daniel H. Wells." *Tullidge's Quarterly Magazine* 3, no. 2. Salt Lake City: Edward W. Tullidge, April 1884.

Tullidge, Edward W. *The History of Salt Lake City*. Salt Lake City: Star Printing Company, 1886.

Tullidge, Edward W. *Women of Mormondom*. New York: Tullidge & Crandall, 1877.

US Census Bureau. "Resident Population and Apportionment of the US House of Representatives." Accessed May 15, 2013. https://www.census.gov/dmd/www/resapport/states/utah.pdf.

US Supreme Court, Reynolds v. United States, 98 US 145 (1879).

US Supreme Court, Wells v. Nickles, 104 US 444 (1881).

Utah Division of State History. "Markers and Monuments Database, Early Magna Settlements, 1992." Accessed June 18, 2014. http://heritage.utah.gov/apps/history/markers/detailed_results.php?markerid=2662.

Utah Gazetteer and Directory. Salt Lake City: R. L. Polk & Co, 1884.

Utah Gazetteer 1892–93. Salt Lake City: Stenhouse & Company, 1894.

"Utah Railroads, Utah Central Railroad (1869–1881)." *UtahRails.net*. Accessed May 8, 2015. http://utahrails.net/utahrails/uc-rr-1869-1881.php.

"Utah Railroads, Utah Southern Railroad (1870–1881)." *UtahRails.net*. Accessed May 8, 2015. http://utahrails.net/utahrails/us-rr-1870-1881.php.

"Utah Territorial Militia Records, Utah State Archives Record Series 2210." *FamilySearch.org*. The Church of Jesus Christ of Latter-day Saints. Accessed March 12, 2015. https://familysearch.org/search/image/index#uri=https://familysearch.org/recapi/sord/collection/1462415/waypoints.

Van Orden, Bruce A. "The Decline in Convert Baptisms and Member Immigration from the British Mission after 1870." *BYU Studies* 27, no. 2 (1987): 97–98. Accessed August 1, 2015. https://ojs.lib.byu.edu/spc/index.php/BYUStudies/article/view/5667.

VanSoolen, Louwane. "Dr. J. King Robinson." *Vedette* 36, no. 3 (2011). Salt Lake City: Museum Archives, Fort Douglas Military Museum Association. Accessed May 6, 2015. http://www.fortdouglas.org/sites/fortdouglas.org/files/Vedette_Fall_2011%5B1%5D.pdf.

Van Wagenen, Michael Scott. "Sam Houston and the Utah War." *Utah Historical Quarterly* 76, no. 1 (Winter 2008): 66–78.

Van Wagoner, Richard S., and Steven C. Walker. *A Book of Mormons*. Salt Lake City: Signature Books Library, 1982., http://signaturebookslibrary.org/?p=17795, Accessed March 3, 2015.

Walker, Ronald M. "Salt Lake Theatre." *Utah History Encyclopedia*. Utah History to Go, State of Utah, 2013. Accessed April 17, 2015. http://historytogo.utah.gov/utah_chapters/utah_today/saltlaketheatre.html.

Walker, Ronald W., Richard E. Turley Jr., and Glen M. Leonard. *Massacre at Mountain Meadows*. New York: Oxford University Press, 2008.

Wells, Abigail. "Genealogy of the Wells and Chapin Family." Salt Lake City: unpublished document in author's possession, 1970.

Welles, Albert. *History of the Welles Family in England and Normandy, with the Derivation from Their Progenitors of Some of the Descendants in the United States.* New York, 1876.

Wells, Albert Emory. Letter to the Chicago Historical Society, 1903. Salt Lake City: unpublished document, copy in author's possession.

Wells, Catherine, and Daniel H. Wells. Letter to Pamela Wells, July 7, 1835. Salt Lake City: Daniel H. Wells File, Church History Department, The Church of Jesus Christ of Latter-Day Saints.

Wells, Catherine Wells, et al. Grantors to Oliver Coombs, grantee, Indenture and Deed, June 4, 1832. Salt Lake City: unpublished document, copy in author's possession.

Wells, Daniel. "Deed." In *Deeds, 1791–1901, Oneida County, New York, Microfilm of original records in the Oneida County Courthouse, Utica, New York.* US/CAN Film #364859. Salt Lake City: Family History Library, The Church of Jesus Christ of Latter-day Saints.

Wells, Daniel H., and Catherine Wells. Letter to Pamela Wells, March 12, 1836. Salt Lake City: Daniel H. Wells File, Church History Department, The Church of Jesus Christ of Latter-day Saints.

Wells, Daniel H., and Catherine Wells. Letter to Pamela Wells, August 28, 1836. Salt Lake City: Daniel H. Wells File, Church History Department, The Church of Jesus Christ of Latter-day Saints.

Wells, Daniel H. Letter to Brother and Sisters, April 30, 1838. Salt Lake City: Daniel H. Wells File, Church History Department, The Church of Jesus Christ of Latter-Day Saints.

Wells, Daniel H. Letter to Horace S. Eldredge, January 24, 1871. Salt Lake City: unpublished document, copy in author's possession.

Wells, Daniel H. Letter to Pamela Wells, 1841. Logan: Daniel H. Wells Papers, Utah State University.

Wells, Daniel H. Letter to Joseph Coombs, March 31, 1844. Logan: Daniel H. Wells Papers, Utah State University.

Wells, Daniel H. Letter to Brigham Young, November 21, 1857. Salt Lake City: Brigham Young Collection, Church History Library, The Church of Jesus Christ of Latter-day Saints.

Wells, Daniel H. Letter to Lot Smith, October 17, 1857. Tucson: Lot Smith Collection, University of Arizona Library.

Wells, Daniel H. Letter to Brigham Young, November 21, 1857. Salt Lake City: Brigham Young Collection, Church History Library, The Church of Jesus Christ of Latter-day Saints.

Wells, Daniel H. Letter to Louisa Wells, December 21, 1884. Quoted in a letter from Melvin D. Wells to Heber J. Grant, 1941.

Wells, Daniel H. Letter to Louisa Wells, January 14, 1885. Quoted in a letter from Melvin D. Wells to Heber J. Grant, 1941.

Wells, Daniel H. "The Narrative of General Daniel H. Wells." Berkeley, CA: Bancroft Library, unpublished manuscript, copy in author's possession.

Wells, Daniel, with Erastus Snow, and Brigham Young Jr. Letter to Brigham Young, May 26, 1876. Brigham Young Letters, box 43, folder 20. Church History Department, The Church of Jesus Christ of Latter-day Saints.

Wells, Eliza R. *Petition for Divorce, Des Moines County Circuit Court, Iowa, March 1851.* Salt Lake City: Church History Department, The Church of Jesus Christ of Latter-day Saints.

Wells, Emeline Y. "Sketch of the Life of Louisa Free Wells." Salt Lake City: unpublished manuscript, 1928.

Wells, Emmeline B. *Diary*. Provo: Special Collections, Harold B. Lee Library, Brigham Young University.

Wells, Hannah Free. "Sketch of the Life of Hannah Corilla Free Wells." In *Our Pioneer Heritage*, vol. 8: *That They May Live Again*. Provo: Brigham Young University Press, 1965.

Wells, Joshua. Will. Barbour Collection: Connecticut Vital Records Prior to 1850, Vital Records Waterbury-Wethersfield. Microfilm of original records at the State Library Hartford, CT. US/CAN Film #2982. Salt Lake City: Family History Library, The Church of Jesus Christ of Latter-day Saints.

Wells, Junius F. "Daniel H. Wells." *The Contributor* 12 (1891). Salt Lake City: Deseret News Co.

Wells, Junius F. "Historical Sketch of the Y. M. M. I. A." *Improvement Era*, no. 28 (June 1925).

Wells, Junius F. "The Wells Family Genealogy." *The Utah Genealogical and Historical Magazine* 6 (1915). Salt Lake City: The Church of Jesus Christ of Latter-day Saints Genealogy Department.

Wells, Junius F. "Trenton." *The Contributor* 13 (1892). Salt Lake City: The Contributor Company.

Wells, Lydia Ann Alley. "Lydia Ann Alley Autobiographical Sketch." In *Our Pioneer Heritage*, vol. 8: *That They May Live Again*. Provo: Brigham Young University Press, 1965.

Wells, Pamela, and Abigail Rockwell. Letter to Daniel H. Wells, September 10, 1850. Logan: Daniel H. Wells Papers, Utah State University.

Wells, Melvin D. Letter to Heber J. Grant, 1941. Copy is in author's possession.

Wells, Pamela. Letter to Daniel H. Wells, August 1850. Logan: Daniel H. Wells Papers, Utah State University.

Wells, Quentin Thomas. "Genealogy of the Wells, Thomas, Young, Coon and Related Families." Salt Lake City: unpublished manuscript in author's possession.

"What Man is This?" *The Improvement Era* (March 1964). Salt Lake City: The Church of Jesus Christ of Latter-day Saints.

Whitney, Orson F. *History of Utah*. Salt Lake City: George Cannon & Sons Co, 1904.

Whitney, Orson F. "Orson F. Whitney Letters, 1868–1957." *Archive Grid*. Logan: Utah State University. Accessed June 20, 2015. http://beta.worldcat.org/archivegrid/data/70969393.

Whitney, Orson F. *Popular History of Utah*. Salt Lake City: The Deseret News, 1916.

Williams, James G. "Defending Plural Marriage to Vice President Colfax." *Champion of Liberty: John Taylor*. Provo: Religious Studies Center, Brigham Young University. Accessed May 22, 2015, http://rsc.byu.edu/archived/champion-liberty-john-taylor/defending-plural-marriage-vice-president-colfax.

Williams, Thomas J. *Miracle of the Desert*. The Williams Family History, 1957.

Winter, Mary Ann Sterns. Journal. Salt Lake City: Nauvoo Restoration Inc. Collection, Church History Department, The Church of Jesus Christ of Latter-day Saints.

Woods, Catherine Chapin. Letter to Daniel H. Wells, September 8, 1862. Logan: Daniel H. Wells Papers, Utah State University.

Woods, James W. Letter to Daniel H. Wells, March 31, 1849. Logan: Daniel H. Wells Papers, Utah State University.

Woods, James W. Letter to Daniel H. Wells, September 15, 1850. Logan: Daniel H. Wells Papers, Utah State University.

Woods, N. Park. Letter to Daniel H. Wells, September 20, 1863. Logan: Daniel H. Wells Papers, Utah State University.

Wyoming State Historic Preservation Office. "Emigrant Trails, Bridger Trail, Fort Bridger." Accessed April 10, 2015. http://wyoshpo.state.wy.us/trailsdemo/fort_bridger.htm#.

Young, Brigham. Letter to Thomas Kane, March 22, 1858. Salt Lake City: Kane Collection, Church History Department, The Church of Jesus Christ of Latter-day Saints.

Young, Brigham. Letter to Presidents Daniel H. Wells and John W. Young, February 13, 1877. *Brigham Young Letterbook*, vol. 16. Salt Lake City: Church History Department, The Church of Jesus Christ of Latter-day Saints.

Young, Brigham. *Brigham Young Letterbook*. Salt Lake City: Church History Department, The Church of Jesus Christ of Latter-day Saints.

Zobell, Albert L., Jr. *Sentinel in the East: A Biography of Thomas L. Kane*. Salt Lake City: Nicholas G. Morgan, 1965.

About the Author

A descendant of Daniel H. Wells, **QUENTIN THOMAS WELLS** is a former CIA officer, film and video writer and producer, entrepreneur, and retired Director of Program Innovation and director of the Student Media Center at Salt Lake Community College. This is his sixth book.

Index

To avoid confusion, married women are listed only under their maiden names. Italics indicates a reference to a figure.

Abbott, Thomas, 195
Agreement to leave Illinois, Mormon, 81
Alaska, 400, 401
Alexander, Col. Edmund B., 189, 191–92, 193, 196, 197
Alley, George, 134, 135, 226, 446n7, 467n57
Alley, Lydia Ann, 134–35, *136*, 136–37, 138, 140, 141, 226, 246, 251, 308, 333, 413, 416, 420
Alley, Margaret Maria, 135
Alley, Susan Hannah, 135, *136*, 137, 138, 140, 141, 172, 246, 332
An-kar-tewets, 123–25
Ankawakits, Chief, 278–79, 459n25
Anderson, August L., 89, 90, 96
Anderson, William, 88–89, 90, 96
Arapeen, Chief, 154, 155, 172, 173
Arizona, 387
Arnold, Orson P., 195
Arthur, C. J., 397
atrocity, 30, 124, 179, 189, 220, 280; in Black Hawk War, 277, 279–80; in Indian War of 1850, 124; in Indian War of 1853, 158; at Mountain Meadows, 188–89, 354, 441n30; in slave trading, 155; in Salt Lake City, 380–81
Atwood, Miner Grant, 266
Axtell, Gov. Samuel B., 338

Babbitt, Almon W., 84, 91, 117, 177–78, 439n25
Backenstos, Jacob, 77, 80–81
Bagby, Walter, 57–58
Barlow, Israel, 31–32
Barnes, J. G. M., 392
Barnes, Mark, 254
Baskin, Robert N., 328, 329, 330, 331, 341
Battle Creek, 119
Battle of Crooked River, 28
Battle of Nauvoo, *89*, 100
Beadle, John H., 305–7
Bear River, 130, 131, 192, 194, 196, 197, 202, 269
Bear River, Battle of, 269
Beatie, H. S., 203
Beatie, Josephine, 378
Beatie, Mary Elizabeth, 377
Beckwith, Lieut. E. G., 159, 161
Belle Wood, 267
Bennett, Dr. John C., 40, 41, 45, 48, 49–50, 51, 52, 53, 57, 62, 67
Bennion, Samuel, 37, 397
Benson, Ezra T., 248, 457n7
Benson, Ezra Taft, 247
Bernhisel, Dr. John, 130, 180, 192, 231, 236
Bickford, Ezra, 37
Biesinger, Thomas, 395
Big Cottonwood Canal, 169

Index   499

Big Cottonwood Lumber Co., 147, *148*, 226, 232, 234, 290, 335, 374
Bishop, Indian named, 120, 121, 155
Black, Sec. George A., 324
Black, Att. Gen. J. S., 222–23, 225
Black Hawk, Chief, 119, 124–25, 154, 162, 269–70, 275, 277, 278–88, 459n25
Black Hawk War, Illinois (1832), 17, 119
Black Hawk War, Utah (1865–72), 270, 275, 278, 289–90, 345
Blake, Dr. James, 124
Boggs, Gov. Lilburn, 28, 39, 52, 77
Bowery, 112, *113*, 168, 171, 186, 199, 209, 210, 274, 292
Bowles, Samuel, 270
Brandebury, Judge Lemuel, 128, 129, 180
Brassfield, S. Newton, 295
Bridger, Jim, 147, 192
Bridgewater, 267
Brigham Young Express and Carrying Co. (BYX), 175
Brigham Young University, 318
Brighton (UT), 147, 149, 175
Brighton, William Stuart, 148
British King, 401
Brocchus, Judge Perry E., 129, 180
Brockman, Col. Thomas S., 87, 90, 91, 95
Brooks, George F., 254
Brown, Walter Henry, 254
B. S. *Kimball*, 266–67
Buchanan, Pres. James, 175, 176, 179–82, 190, 201, 204, 206, 207, 208, 212, 214, 216, 220, 221, 452n28
Buchanan's blunder, 177, 214
Bullock, Alexander (Sandy), 255, 263, 413, 458n3
Bullock, James (Jim), 254
Bullock, Thomas, 105, 106, 108, 109
Burt, Andrew (police captain), 342, 343, 344, 366, 381
Burt, John D., 400
Burton, Capt. Richard P., 337
Burton, Col. Robert T., 190, 192, 193, 194, 198, 199, 203, 227, 237, 238, 240, 241, 242, 320, 347

Cache Cave, 194, 199
Calder, D. O., 237, 259
Calhoun, John C., 65
Call, Anson, 159
Campbell, Robert, 118, 125, 400, 401
Camp Crittenden, 233
Camp Douglas, *240*, 240, 245, 276, 295, 297, 306, 324, 326, 329, 330, 331, 456n52

Camp Floyd, 196, 218, 219, 221, 223, 224, 230, 232, 233
Camp Scott, *200*, 200, 201, 202, 203, 205
Camp Winfield, 186, 192, 193, 196, 197
Cannon, Abram, 403, 404, 410
Cannon, Angus, 373, 403, 408, 409, 410
Cannon, Angus, Jr., 384
Cannon, Annie Wells, 235, 246, 248, 254, 263, 310, 326, 383, 404, 408, 410, 416
Cannon, George Q., 237, 259, 264, 266–67, 332, 341, 348, 355–56, 377, 383, 385–87, 402–5, 408–11, 474n23
Cannon, John Q., 377, 378, 383, 384, 385, 386, 387, 402–5, 407–11
Carlin, John, 86, 91
Carlin, Gov. Thomas, 40, 52
Carrington, Albert, 274
Carroll, Ada, 178
Carthage (IL), 19, 22, 31, 37, 40, 56, 58, 59, 66, 70, 71, 72, 73, 74, 75, 77, 79, 80, 381
Carthage Greys, 74
Cathedral of the Madeline, 308
Catholic Church, 308, 342
Cemetery, Salt Lake City, 114, 166, 308, 420
Chapin, Catherine, 9, 11, 12, 311, *376*, 425, 428, 480n1
Chapin, David, 10, 11, 60, 425, 426, 428, 480n4
Chapin, Deacon Samuel, 3, 10, 426
church trains, 231, 263, 268, 289, 293, 314, 315
City of Berlin, 389
City of Chester, 389, 397
City of New York, 265, 272, 272, 273
Civil War in Utah, 112, 232, 233, 238, 255, 257, 267, 268, 281, 292, 296, 314, 359
claim-jumping, 296, 303
Clawson, H. B., 322
Clawson, Theresa, 377
Clay, Henry, 65, 66
Clayton, William, 57, 85, 109, 237
Clements, Gilbert, 217
Cleveland, Pres. Grover, 412
Clifford, Captain William E., 99
coal mining, viii, 227, 228, 334
Colfax, Speaker Schuyler, 270
Collett, Reuben S., 393, 400
Collins, Lieut. Col. William O., 239
Colonia Juarez, 416
Commerce, town of (IL), ix, 17, 18, 19, 20, 21, 22, 23, 24, 32, 33, 39
Compromise of 1850, 229
Comstock Lode, 231, 302

500   Index

Conner, Col. Patrick E., 239–40, 242, 243, 259, 260, 270, 278, 321
Conover, Peter, 155, 164
Cooke, Col. Phillip St. George, 200, 218
Coombs, Joseph, 15, 39, 59, 66, 258, 466n57
Coombs, Oliver, 15, 39
Coon, Abraham, 150
Council Bluffs (IA), 83, 84, 107
Council House, 111, 112, *113*, 216, 236, 317, 318, 342, 368, 369, 370
Cradlebaugh, Judge John, 181, 219–20, 221, 222
Craig, Brig. Gen. James, 338, 339
Crismon, George, 343
Culmer, Henry, 377
Cumming, Gov. George Alfred, 176, 181, 200, 201, 206–8, 211–12, 214–25, 233
Cutler, William L., 93, 96, 97
Cutler's Park, 96

Dame, William, 184
David Hoadley, 267
Dawson, Gov. John W., 195, 233, 236
dedication: of Logan Temple, 382; of Manti Temple, 414, *415*; of St. George Temple, 149, 466n57; of Salt Lake Tabernacle, *358*; of Salt Lake Theater, 234
Deming, Minor, 4, 77, 79, 80, 479n18
Deseret, Provisional State of, 115, 126
Deseret News, 129, 144, 155, 156, 173, 202, 210, 272, 274, 323, 331, 336, 358, 364, 365, 366, 371, 377, 384, 416
Deseret, University of, 40, 112, 131, 317, 318
Deseret Telegraph Co., viii, 292, 293
DeTrobriand, Gen. Philippe Regis, 324, 326
Dewey, Albert, 286
Dittmore, Henry, 254
Dodge, Gen. Grenville M., 297
Doniphan, Gen. Alexander, 30
Doty, Gov. James D., 233, 259–60, 269, 337
Douglas, Stephen A., 40, 53, 81, 302
Drake, Judge Thomas J., 242–43, 2599
dresser-drawer deeds, 37
Drummond, Judge William W., 161, 163, 178–79, 180
Duncan, Huldah, 247
Dunford, William, 376
Dunham, Jonathan, 69
Durkee, Gov. Charles, 281, 337

Earl, Jesse J., 202
Echo Camp, 199, 202
Eckels, Judge Delana, 181, 201, 207, 219

Eckelsville, 205, 207, 215, 220
Edmunds Act, 379, 380, 381, 382, 383, 384, 386, 401, 402, 404
Edmunds-Tucker Act, 379, 401, 407, 412
Eldredge, Horace S., 115, 116, 301, 302, 330
Ellis, Charles, 419
Emerson, Judge Phillip H., 361, 362, 363
Emery, Gov. George W., 338, 339
Emigration Canyon, 110, 145, 203, 218
Emmons, Sylvester, 40, 68
Endowment House, *113*, 149, 210, 310, 358, 359, 360, 361, 362, 362, *369*, 373, 377, 378, 382, 411, 415, 458n3
Engelbrecht, Paul, 300
Episcopal Church, 308
Erie Canal, 15, 27, 47
executive order, specie, 26

Farr, Lorin, 125–26
Ferguson, James, 191, 193
Ferris, Sec. Benjamin G., 177
Fifth Infantry Regiment, 181, 182
Fillmore (UT), 128, 158, 159, 161, 184, 210, 220, 284, 286, 319
Fillmore, Pres. Millard, 126, 165, 177, 179
Finlayson, James, 228
fire, Chicago, 327
fire, at Wells mansion, 255–57
First Congregational Church, 295, 339
Floyd, Sec. John B., 217, 219
Fobes, Helena, 377
Ford, Gov. Thomas, 53, 54, 55, 72, 73, 74, 75, 77–79, 81, 86, 95–96
Forney, Jacob, 216
Fort Bridger, 147, 186, 190, 191, 192, *193*, 193–95, *197*, 197–200, *200*, 209, 239, 297
fort-building, 286
Fort Douglas, 256, 269, 270, 318, 323, 324
Fort, Farr's, 125
Fort Kearny, 185
Fort Laramie, 147, 176, 189, 203, 205, 239, 241
Fort Leavenworth, 181, 182, 185, 189, 205, 208
Fort Lemhi, 172, 173, 209
Fort Supply, 147, 194, 199, 200, 209
Fort Utah, *120*, 124, 125, 154, 155
Foster, Dr. Robert D., 57, 67, 68, 70, 72
Fourth Artillery Regiment, 181
Fraim, William, 23–24, 31
Francis, Honor, 7, 8, 25, 425
Free, Absalom P., 106
Free, Emeline, 107, 135, 137

Index 501

Free, Hannah Corilla, 107, *136*-38, 141, 167, 172, 226, 229, 246, 252, 257, 262, 264, 265, 271, 272-*73*, 308, 333, 346, 377, 382, 403, 413, 420, 425, 479n15, 479n17, 479-80n19
Free, Louisa, 106, 107, 108, 133, 134, 135-37, 141, 166, 172, 226, 229, 246, 253, 257, 308, 333, 377, 401
Fuller, Sec. Frank, 233, 236, 237, 241, 243, 323

Galland, Isaac, 31-32, 33, 39
gas works, Salt Lake, viii, 333-34, 335, 374, 413
general military orders, 186
Gibson, John, 247
Gilbert & Gerrish, 196
Gillespie, James, 390-91
gold coins, Utah, 118, 442n21
gold rush, California, 118, 231
Gooch, Samuel, 17, 21
Grant, George D., 122, 198
Grant, Heber J., 167, 247, 248, 310, 347, 381, 382, 386, 401, 405, 408, 409, 411, 457n7
Grant, Jedediah M., 116, 128, 151, 167, 168, 170, 294, 457n7, 474n23
Grant, Martha Deseret, 401
Grant, Rachel, 310, 311, 347
Grant, Pres. Ulysses S., 300, 302, 303, 335, 337, 338, 339, 346, 359
Great Basin, 115, 116, 117, 149, 173, 180, 302
Great Salt Lake City, 108, 110, 114-16, 118, 119, 124-29, 133, 135, 137, 138, 141, 142, 144, 147, 149, *150*, 173, 175, 176, 178, 179, 181-83, 185, 186, 187, 189, 191, 192, 196-98, 201-7, 209, 211-12, 214-18, *219*, 221, 224, 227-28, 230, 231, 238-40, 255, 258-59, 263, 264, 270, 273-74, 288, 289, 292-95, 299, 304, 315, 439n25, 462n13
Greeley, Horace, 337
Greene, John P., 50, 57, 70
Green River, 1131, 145, 195, 228
Green River Ferry, *146*, 289
Griffen, Thomas, 228
Grow, Henry, 290
Gunnison, Lt. John W., 121, 158-61, 165

Haight, H. D., 195
Haight, Isaac C., 184, 186, 187, 188
Half Breed Reservation, 32
Hancock County, viii, x, 7, 20, 22, 23, 24, 25, 26, 28, 31, 32, 35, 37, 38, 39, 40, 41, 43, 46, 47, 50, 56, 67, 68, 72, 77, 78, 80, 99
Hansen, Jorgen, 392
Hanson, Clara, 247
Harding, Gov. Stephen S., 233, 242, 245, 259, 323
Harness, Emily, 247
Harney, Gen. William S., 181, 182, 185, 189, 191
Harris, Secretary Broughton D., 188, 180
Harris, Eugene Henri, 138
Harris, James Harvey, 138, 444n18
Harris, Martha Givens, 107, 134, *136*, 141, 246, 263, 458n3
Harris, McGee, 107
Harrison, Pres. William H., 39
Harvey, Sam Joe, 381
Haslam, Captain James, 186, 188
Hatch, Abram, 264, 350
Hawes, Col. Alexander. G., 311-12
Hawks, Walter, 254
Hawn's Mill Massacre, 29-30
Hayes, Pres. Rutherford B., 339
Head, Franklin H., 281-82
Hedges, William Sanford, 378
Heywood, William "Big Bill," 380-81
Hibbard, Davison, 34, 46
Hickman, William Adams (Bill), 328-29, 330, 331
Higbee, Chauncey, 67, 68
Higbee, Francis, 51, 67, 68, 72
Hill, Archibald N., 295
Hill, Donna, 64
Hill, Mary Emma, 295
Hills, Gustavus, *34*, 51
Hinckley, Arza A., 254, 260
Hinckley, Bryant S., 199, 294
History of the Welles Family, 354, 358, 469n42
Hodges, Nathaniel M., 391
Hogsted, Hans C., 267
Holland Land Co., 8
Holland Patent, 7-8
Holman, John G., 264
Hooper, William H., 232, 237
Hotchkiss, Horace, 32
Hotchkiss, Dr. Lawrence Sterne, 137, 229
Houston, Sen. Sam, 212-14, 452n28
Huntington, Dimick, 119, 269
Hyde, Orson, 280, 283, 355
Hyner, Elizabeth, 247

Illinois Militia Code, 41
Indian children, 116
Indian customs, 153, 155, 159

Indian slaves, 154, 280
Indian tribes: Goshute, 116, 154; Pahvant, 154, 159, 459n25; Paiute, 154, 186, 188; San Pitch, 116; Shoshone, 116, 125, 126, 154, 172, 209; Uintah, 116, 280, 281, 286; Ute, 116, 119, 120, 123–25, 154, 155, 158, 163, 172, 269, 270, 278, 279, 281, 282, 288, 459n25
Indian War of 1850, 119–24
Indian War of 1853, 154
Indian War of 1864. *See* Black Hawk War, Utah
Irish, Orsemus H., 269–70
Ivie, James, 155
Ivie, James A., 285
Ivie, James R., 283
Ivie, Richard, 120
Iwakura, Prince, of Japan, 337

Jackson, Pres. Andrew, 26, 119
Jarvis, Brigham, Sr., 228
Jennings, William, 330, 381
Johns, Col. William M., 8, 270, 321
Johnson, Aaron, 184
Johnson, Philo, 92
Johnston, Gen. Albert Sidney, 189–90, 193, 197, 198, 199, 200, 201, 202, 203, 205, 206–8, 211–13, 215, 217, 218, 220, 221, 222, 225, 230, 232–33, 268
Johnston's Army, 201. *See also* Utah Expedition
Jones, Dan W., 342
Jones, Nathaniel V., 192
Jordan River bridge, 218

Kalakaua, King, of Hawaii, 337
Kane, Col. Thomas L., 180, 185, 192, 206–8, 211–12, 215
Kanosh, Chief, 116, 278, 279, 319, 459n25
Kansas-Nebraska Act, 180
Katz, Emily, 377
Kilyon, John, 145
Kimball, Heber C., 50, 62, 104, 105, 109–10, 115, 125, 127, 149, 151, 168, 170, 171, 172, 175, 176, 183, 201, 215, 216, 217, 236, 243, 259, 274, 309–11, 355
Kimball, Hiram, 39
Kington Fort, 241, 242
Kinney, Judge John F., 178, 180, 240, 243, 244, 245

Law, William, 56, 67, 68
Law, Wilson, 50, 57, 67, 68
Leaker, David William, 228
Lee, John Brigham, 106, 134

Lee, John D., 105, 106, 107, 115, 134, 186, 188, 354
Lincoln, Abraham, 23, 31, 39, 40, 53, 232, 233, 242, 243, 259, 260, 261, 268, 269, 359, 456n52, 462–63n13
Lippincott, Grace Greenwood, 328
Lippman, Joseph, 383, 384, 385, 472n31
liquor laws, 296–97
Little, Mayor Faramorz, 365, 367
Livingston & Kinkead, 196
Livingstone, Archie, 147
logging, 147, *148*, 175, 374
Lucas, Gen. Samuel, 30
Luce, Matthew, 254
lumber business, viii, 67, 130, 145, 147–49, 155, 226–27, 232, 234, 254, 290, 335–36, 374
Lund, Anton H., 395, 397
Lyman, Amasa M., 57, 115
Lyman, Francis M., 357, 399, 408–9
lynching, 75, 380–81

mail service, 175
manifesto, of 1890, 417
Manti (UT), 123, 151, 155, 158, 278–79, 283, 286, 319, 354, 415, 416, 417
Manti Temple, 358, 411, 414, *415*, 415, 417, 418, 466n57
Marks, William, 50, 57, 61, 67
martial law, 122, 183, 193
Maxwell, George R., 303, 305–7, 308, 335, 340–41, 346
Maxwell, William, 200
McAllister, John, 193, 194
McCulloch, Major Ben, 214, 216, 217, 219
McCurdy, Judge Solomon P., 295
McIntyre, Robert, 277
McKean, Judge James B., 300–301, 328, 329, 330, 331, 345, 346
McLeod, Rev. Norman, 295, 339
McMurrin, J. L., 400
Mexicana, 266
Mexican War, 100, 115, 128, 218
Miles, John H., 360, 361, 372
Miles case, 361, 362, 386
Millennial Star, The LDS, 264, 387, 392, 406, 416
Montrose, 93, 97
Moore, Dr. David, 125, 126
Morley attack, 80
Mormon Battalion, 100, 118, 128–29, 201, 218
Mormon Raiders, 194, 195, 196, 197, 200, 202, 204, 228

Morrill Anti-Bigamy Act, 359, 456n52
Morris, David, 90, 96
Morris, Joseph, 240, 241, 245
Morrisite War, 241–42, 244
Mortensen, Niels C., 394
Mountain, Chief, 287
Mountain Meadows Massacre, 189, 354, 441n30
Move South, 210, 211, 212, 215, 218, 226, 229, 317
Murdock, John R., 263

nail factory, 228, 247, 413
Nauvoo, Battle of, *89*, 100
Nauvoo Cemetery, 76, 81, 144, 434n24
Nauvoo Charter, 40, 41, 53, 55, 59, 77
Nauvoo City Council, 52, 55, 57, 71, 296
Nauvoo Expositor, 57, 68, 69, 72
Nauvoo Justice Court, Hancock County, 39, 40, 53, 56, 57, 71
Nauvoo Legion in Illinois, 41, 42, 45, 48, 55, 59, 65, 67, 69, 72, 78, 79
Nauvoo Legion in Utah, 111, 115, 116, 121, 154, 155, 156, 157, 161, 162, 164, 167, 183, 186, 189, *190*, 190, 192, 196, 198, 199, 204, 209, 211, 217, 218, 238, 269, 270, 271, 275, 277, 278, 279, 281, 283, 284, 285, 286, 287, 288, 320, 322, 323, 326, 332, 338, 367
Nauvoo Municipal Court, 52, 55
Nauvoo Temple, 414
Naylor, George, 254, 377
Neibauer, Ike, 254
Nevada, 395, 397, 400, 454–55n14
Nevada Territory, 302–3
Newman, Rev. John T., 339
Nickles, John, 336, 374–75
nuisance abatement: in Nauvoo, 72; in Utah, 296
Nuttal, John L., Jr., 400

Ogden (UT), 125, 129, 241, 274, 293, 313, 315, 316, 338, 339
Old Church Mine, 227, 373
Old Elk, Chief, 123, 125
Olsen, C. F., 400
Oneida County, New York, viii, 7, 9, 12, 39, 425, 430n20, 431n35
Oquirrh Mountains, 150
Orr, Milton, 306, 343
Osmond, George, 395, 400
Overland Stage, 311
Overland Telegraph Co., 232
Owen, Caroline, 360–61

Pace, James, 184
Pace, William B., 283–84
Pacific Telegraph Co., 232
Pack, John, 317
panic of 1837, 25–26, 32
Panikrey, 285
pardon, presidential, 214, 216, 217, 220
Park, John R., 317
Parker, Major J. R., 86, 92
Parsons, Steve, 254
Partridge, Edward, 41
patent for Salt Lake City, 304, *305*, 308
Patton, Oliver, 335–36, 374
Peace Commission, 215
Penrose, Charles W., 389, 390, 393, 395, 397
Perkins, William G., 105, 351
Perpetual Emigration Fund, 146, 169, 289
Perris, Fred T., 340, 341
Phelps, William W., 78
Pierce, Pres. Franklin, 165, 179, 452–53n28
Pleasant Grove, 119, 145, 254, 413
plural marriage doctrine, 61–62, 133, 139, 168, 299, 311
plural marriages, 49, 61, 62, 64–68, 129, 132, 133, 134, 135, 144, 165, 178, 180, 186, 242, 243, 245, 250, 251, 252, 268, 270, 277, 310, 311, 328, 331, 332, 338–39, 340, 341, 345, 359, 360, 363, 364, 372, 378, 379, 381–83, 385–87, 389, 399, 401, 402, 404, 405, 407, 416, 417. *See also* plural marriage doctrine
plural marriages: of John Q. Cannon, 383, 402–4, 411; of Heber J. Grant, 381–82; of John D. Lee, 106–7; of D. H. Wells, 133–38, 140–41; of Newel K. Whitney, 139–40; of Orson H. Whitney, 416; of Brigham Young, 107, 135, 345; of Dr. Seymour B. Young, 381–82
polygamy. *See* plural marriages
Pony Express, 447n2
popular sovereignty, 180, 229
posse comitatus, 180, 182, 221, 222
Potter, Col. Carroll E., 297
Powell, Sen. Lazarus W., 214, 216, 217, 219
Pratt, Orson, 37, 57, 264, 266, 355
Pratt, Parley P., 37, 57, 109, 115, 117
Preston, William B., 403
Price, Emma G., 377
Provo, *120*, 122, 124, 125, 155, 158, 184, 210, 215, 216, 218, 220, 221, 223, 269, 276, 293, 309, 316, 318, 319
public proclamation, 183
Pugmire, John, 243
Pulzipher, Zera, 105

Quincy (IL), 31, 54, 55, 87, 93
Quincy Committee, 87, 90, 91, 92, 95

railroad: Central Pacific, 315, 338, 405; Northern Pacific, 316; San Pete and Sevier, 413; transcontinental, 165, 313–15, 339; Union Pacific, 314, 315, 374; Utah Central, 315, 316, 338, 339; Utah Northern, 382; Utah Southern, 316
Ralston, James H., 39
Raphel, Joseph D'Ortigue, 25
Raymond, W. W., 264
Read, Charles, 377
reformation, Mormon, 167, 231
Reid, Judge Lazarus, 178
resolutions, anti-Mormon, 58, 59, 70–71, 84
Revolutionary War, viii, 6, 10, 25, 431n35
Reynolds, George, 359
Reynolds case, 359–60
Rich, Charles C., 50, 196
Richards, Franklin D., 243, 347, 399
Richards, Samuel W., 185
Richards, Willard, 69, 82, 97, 115, 125, 149, 167, 168, 170, 177
Richardson, Albert, 270
Rigdon, Sidney, 32, 57, 76
Riter, Ann Elizabeth, 382
Riter, William W., 266
Robison, Eliza Rebecca, 24, *25*, 26, *27*, 43, 44, 102, 108, *136*, 141, 246, 258
Robinson, George W., 34
Robinson, Dr. J. King, 295–96, 303, 306
Robison, Rev. Charles, 24, 43, 44, 81
Robison, Lewis, 24, 39, 43, 44, 102, 108, 114, 144, 147, 192, 193, 202, 258
Rockwell, Orrin Porter, 52, 57, 108, 176, 190, 194
Rockwell, Stephen, 21, 172
Rogers, David, 32
Romney, Miles P., 264
Rose, Steven B., 128
Ross, Henry Wells, 47, 60, 172
Ross, Dr. James S., 26, 47
Rossiter, William A., 346
Roundy, Bishop, 350, 351
Runaways, 177–78
Russell, Majors, and Waddell Freight Co., 181

St. George Temple, 149, 352, *353*, 358, 373, 466
Salisbury, Joseph, 340–41
Salt Lake City Cemetery, 114, 166, 308, 420
Salt Lake City Gas Co., 333–34
Salt Lake Herald, 329, 336, 360, 370, 384, 472n31
Salt Lake Tabernacle, 112, *113*, 170, 186, 210, 243, 290, *291*, 292, 300, 310, 325, 327, 328, 339, 369–71, 403, 420
Salt Lake Temple, 111, 149, 210, 235, *291*, 316, 318, 358, 415, 417
Salt Lake Theater, 233, 234, 235, *291*, 334
Salt Lake Tribune, 340–41, 369, 383–84, 385, 402, 404, 472n31
San Diego, 100, 118
Sangerfield, 9, 11, 428, 431n35
Sanpete Valley, 283, 286
Sanpitch, Chief, 278–80, 282, 283, 459nn25
Schoenfeld, Frederick, 400
Schofield, Amelia Jane, 359
Scott, John, 122
Scott, Gen. Winfield, 181
Sears, Anna Elizabeth, 417
Sears, Septimus W., 377
Sebastopol Plan, 209, 210
Second Dragoon Regiment, 181, 218
Seymour, Ruth, 10, 425, 428
Shaffer, Gov. John Wilson, 319, 320, 321, 322, 323, 324
Sharp, Thomas, 70, 79
Shaver, Judge Leonidas, 178
Shearman, William H., 267
Sherman, Gen. William T., 281, 297
Shirts, Peter, 276
Shurtliff, Harrison, 264
Sinclair, Judge Charles E., 181, 219–20, 222
slavery, in United States, 154, 180, 229. *See also* Indian slaves; slave trade in Utah
slave trade in Utah, 154–55, 229
Sloan, Rob, 383, 385
Smith, Andrew K., 343
Smith, Catherine, 247
Smith, Daniel, 254
Smith, Don Carlos, 41, 57, 76
Smith, Elias, 237, 404, 411
Smith, Emma, 55, 61, 76
Smith, George A., 78, 127, 161, 183, 188, 193, 228, 231, 269, 277, 280, 311, 325, 333, 347
Smith, Hyrum, ix, 33, 48, 49, 51, 57, 61, 71, 72, 74, 75, 77, 79, 92, 224, 297, 356, 381
Smith, John (patriarch), 85, 97, 115
Smith, Joseph, ix–x, 30, 31–33, 35–36, 38–45, 48–59, 61–63, 65–74, 75–76, 78, 97, 102, 120, 133, 138, 213, 224, 246, 296–97, 355, 357, *378*, 388, 420, 435n35
Smith, Joseph F., 356, 357, 358, 371, 408–9, 411

Smith, Major Lot, 190, 193, 194, 199, 238–39
Smith, Samuel H., 57
Smith, William, 57, 64, 76
Smoot, Abraham O., 175, 176, 181, 293, 294, 297
Smoot, W. C. A., 392
Smoot, Zina, 416
Snarr, James T., 254
Snow, Erastus, 277, 283, 350, 351
Snow, Lorenzo, 105, 123, 347, 414
Snow, Warren, 278, 279, 282, 283, 284–85
Snow, Judge Zerubbabel, 177, 237
Social Hall, 112, *113*
Sowiette, Chief, 281, 288, 459n25
Spanish Fork, Treaty of, 269, 270, 278, 280
specie, use of: in Nauvoo, 26, 35, 55; in Utah, 117–18
Spencer, Daniel, 117
Spencer, Emily, 360–61
Spencer, George Boardman, 264
Spori, Jacob, 398, 399
Staine, William C., 216
Stansbury, Capt. Howard C., 121, 122, 124, 131
State House, *113*, 130
State of Deseret organized, 115, 116, 126, 236
Steptoe, Col. Edward J., 165–66, 177, 180
Stewart, Levi, 303
Stewart, Urban, 125
Stiles, Judge George P., 72, 178–79, 180
Stoddard, John, 240
Stoddard, Judson L., 176, 181
Storrs, William, 8, 14–15, 21
Stout, Hosea, 328, 329
Strang, James J., 76
Stringham, Briant, 227
Stringham, Lucy, 382
Stromberg, C. J., 400
Sutherland, Judge J. D., 362, 363
Swensen, John, 267

Tabby, Chief, 281–82, 287–88, 459n25
Tabernacle, "New," 290, *291*, 292, 300, 310, 325, 327, 328, 339, 369–71, 403, 420
Tabernacle, "Old," 112, *113*, 170, 186, 210, 243
Tamaritz (Shenavegan), Chief, 284, 288
Tanner, Joseph M., 398, 399
Taylor, Allen, 105, 110
Taylor, Charles, 267
Taylor, John, 115, 193, 231, 260, 269, 339, 355–57, 366, 367, 368, 371, 381–83, 385, 386, 387, 401, 409

Taylor, Joseph, 14, 50, 194, 195, 196
Taylor, Maria, 247
Taylor, Stephen W., 145, 227, 254–55, 373
Teasdale, George, 381, 406
Temple Square, 88, 112, 149, 169, 210, 303, 308, 316, 369
Tenth Infantry Regiment, 181, 182, 195
Terikee, Chief, 125
Territory of Utah created, 126
Thatcher, Moses, 357
Third California Volunteers, 276
Thomas, Adj. Gen. Lorenzo, 237
Thornley, J. W., 394
Titus, Judge John, 296
Tonks, William, 228
Tooele, 150, 153, 248, 320
Toquana, Chief, 281, 459n25
Treaty of Guadalupe Hidalgo, 115, 304
Trenton, New York, viii, 8, 9, 11, 12, *13*, 14, 15, 16, 20, 21, 26, 27, 39, 47, 98, 101, 142, 172, 264, 425, 428
Tuddenham, Mary Ann, 359
Tullidge, Edward W., 341
Twain, Mark, 337
twin relics of barbarism, 180

Underwood, William, 267
United States Land Office, 303, 304, 306, 307, 335
University of Deseret, 40, 112, 131, 317, 318
Utah Expedition, *182*, 182, *197*, 208, 211–15, *219*, 219, 233, 235, 317
Utah Territory, viii, 40, 85, 117, 127, 128, 129, 130, 137, 149, 154, 158, 166, 167, 173, 174, 175, 176, 177, 179, 182, 190, 192, 193, 201, 205, 206, 207, 211, 212, 215, 216, 217, 219, 221, 228, 229, 231, 232, 233, 236, 243, 259, 269, 270, 275, 277, 293, 295, 299, 300, 301, 303, 313, 320, 321, 322, 323, 337, 340, 363, 374, 379, 452–53n28, 454–55n14
Utah Valley, 118, 119, 121, 122, 123, 124, 125, 145, 155, 162, 210
Utah War, 112, 141, 147, *190*, 190, 206, 214, 215, 218, 219, 220, 226, 227, 228, 229, 231, 238, 328. *See also* Utah Expedition

Van Buren, Pres. Martin, 26, 38, 39, 53, 65–66
Vance, John, 195
Van Vliet, Capt. Stewart, 185–86, 187, 191–92, 196
Van Zile, Attorney Philip T., 361, 362
Vasquez, Louis, 147, 192

506   Index

Vaughn, Sec. Vernon H., 321
Venus (IL), 17. *See also* Commerce (IL)
Voorhees anti-polygamy bill, 332

Waite, Judge Charles B., 242, 259
Wakara (Walker), Chief, 154–55, 163
War of 1812, 8–9, 17
Warrington, Benjamin, 34, 40, 68–69
Warsaw (IL), 17, 43, 66, 70, 74, 75, 77, 79, 80
Wasatch Hot Springs, 295–96, 303
Wasatch Literary Association, 252
Washington Square, 114, 308
Weber County, 125–26, 194
Weber River, 131
Webster, Daniel, 177
Welles, Albert, 354, 358
Wells, Abigail (sister), 8, 21, 47, 60, 101, 144, 172, 264, 425, 479–80n19
Wells, Annie, 235, 246, 248, 254, 263, 310, 326, 377–78, 383–85, 402–5, 408–11, 416, 473n45, 475n34
Wells, Abby Corilla (aka Abby Wells Chapin) (child), 138, 257, 382, 386
Wells, Albert Emory (child), 26, 27, 43, 60, 64, 84, 85, 99, 101, 103, 132, 141, 144, 246–47, 258, 378, 476n15
Wells, Arthur Deming (child), 308
Wells, Briant Harris (child), 308–9, 378, 476n15
Wells, Brigham, 226, 257
Wells, Catherine Chapin (mother), 9, 11, 15, 24, 47, 81
Wells, Charles Henry (child), 308
Wells, Clara Ellen (child), 246, 376, 378
Wells, Daniel, 3, 6–9, 11, 15, 85, 171, 351, 425, 428, 479–80n19
Wells, Daniel H., viii, 3, 6, 11, 435, 428, 480n4; admitted to Bar, 129; affidavit regarding John C. Bennett, 50–51; aide-de-camp to Brigham Young, 104; alderman, viii, 40, 49–52, 55, 63, 77; apostle, ordained as, 168, 356; arrested, 326–28, 361–64; assaulted, 342–44, 392–94; Attorney-General, 115–16, 128, 129; baptism of, 84; Battle of Nauvoo and, 87–94; Bernhisel, letter to, 130–31; birth of, 3, 11–12; captain of the camp, 151, 176; Chancellor University of Deseret, 317–18; children of (see *individual names*); constable, viii, 22–23; Constitutional Convention of 1856, President of, 231; Constitutional Convention of 1862, President of, 236; Constitutional Convention of 1872, President of, 238; contempt, found guilty of, 361–64; Counselor to Brigham Young, 168, 170, 248, 309, 319, 345, 355; Counselor to Twelve, 356–57, 373; death of, 418; defends Brigham Young, 243–45, 259–60, 330–31, 344–46, 354; demonstration in behalf of, 361–71; description of, 13–15; Deseret Telegraph Co., director of, 293; discourses of, 91–92, 169–71, 368, 371, 387–88, 406; divorce of, 64, 141; education of, 12–14, 23, 116; Horace Eldredge, letter to, 301–3; family left in Illinois, 100–103; farm in Pleasant Grove, 145, 254, 413; farm in Sugar House, 144–45, 228, 413; ferry business of, 145–47; First Presidency, member of, 168; funeral of, 420; Grant, US President, hosted by, 338–39; harem of, 179; Hayes, President R. B., met by, 339; hired laborer, 14; lawyer, 23, 115; Legislature, member of, 115, 201, 231, 236–37; Lieutenant-General Nauvoo Legion, 115, 151–52, 156–57, 183–84, 190, 192–95, 198, 200–203, 275, 320, 322–24; Lincoln, friendship with, 23; Logan Temple, attended, 382; lumber business of, 149, 226–27, 232–34, 290, 335–36, 374–75; manufacturing by, 228, 413; marriage to Eliza R. Robison, 24; marriage to Emmeline B. Woodward, 140; marriage to Hannah C. Free, 137; marriage to Louisa Free, 133; marriage to Lydia A. Alley, 136; marriage to Martha G. Harris, 134; marriage to Susan Alley, 136; memorial to President Lincoln, 260; military actions in Black Hawk War, 275–77, 280–88; military actions in Indian War of 1850, 121–25; military actions in Indian War of 1853, 153–64; military actions in Nauvoo, vii–viii, 86–94; military actions in Utah Expedition, 176, 183–84, 189–90, 192–203, 211–12, 216–17; mining by, 227, 333, 373–74; missionary labors of (1864–65), 262–66, 271–72; missionary labors of (1885–87), 386–402, 405–7; Nauvoo Legion organized by, 41, 115–16, 156–57, 161–62, 183–84, 190–91, 238–39, 276, 284–86, 320, 321–23; near drowning of, 349–51; Ohio, arrival in, 16; patriarchal blessing of, 97; penitentiary, confined in, 345–46, 364, 367; Perpetual Emigration Fund,

support of, 146, 169, 289; priesthood, ordained to, 97; railroad investments by, 315–17; real estate business, 17–18, 33–38, 53–56, 85–86, 98, 103; Salt Lake City, arrival in, 110; Shaffer, Gov. John W., conflict with, 319–23; sisters of (see *individual names*); Squire, given title of, 23, 56; St. George Temple dedicated by, 352–53; Superintendent of Public Works for LDS church, 111–12, 118, 149–50, 210, 232–33, 261, 290–92, 318–19; Superintendent of Public Works for Utah Territory, 127–28, 149; surrender of Nauvoo, arranged by, 91–92; Tooele Valley, explored by, 150; University of Nauvoo, trustee of, 40; Utah Territorial Council, President of, 260; Winter Quarters, arrival in, 96–97, 104
Wells, Daniel Hanmer, Jr. (child), 134, *378*
Wells, Edna Margaret (child), 308, *376*, 476n15
Wells, Eliza (sister), 26, 27, 43, 47, 100, 172, 257
Wells, Elizabeth Ann (child), 226, *376*, 377
Wells, Eliza Free (child), 226, *376*, 425, 476n15
Wells, Emily Harris (child), 172, 376
Wells, Emeline Whitney (child), 141
Wells, Emeline Young (child), 107, 135, 137–38, 172, *376*, 476n15
Wells, Ephraim Willard (child), 246, 257, 265
Wells, Francis Louisa (child), 136, 377
Wells, George Alley (child), 226
Wells, Gershom Britain Finley (child), 265–66, 271, *273*, 273, 308, 333, *378*, 405, 476n15
Wells, Gideon, 6, 10, 424, 479n14, 479–80n19
Wells, Heber Manning (child), 226, *378*
Wells, Herman Chapin (child), 308
Wells, Honor Francis (Frank) (sister), 7–8, 9, 15, 25, 47, 60, 74, 100, 425, 479–80n19, 480n1
Wells, John Brigham (aka John Brigham Lee) (child), 134, 166
Wells, Joseph Smith (child), 246, 417
Wells, Joshua, 3–7, 10–11, 424–25, 428, 479n18, 479–80n19
Wells, Junius Free (child), 14–15, 141, 257, 333, 346–47, 348, 377, *378*
Wells, Louisa Martha (child), 257, *376*, 378
Wells, Louise (Louie) (child), 383
Wells, Louis Robison (child), 246, *378*

Wells, Lucy Ann (sister), 8, 15, 25, 28, 39, 47, 60, 98, 101, 166–67, 226, 425
Wells, Luna Pamela (child), 167, 172, 456–57n4
Wells, Martha Deseret (child), 141, *376*, 377
Wells, Mary Minerva (child), 141, *376*, 416–17
Wells, Melvin Dickenson (child), 308, 333, *378*, 387, 389, 395, 397, 398, 401, 476n15
Wells, Pamela (sister), 8, 18, 20, 21, 47, 60, 98, 101, 142, 144, 172, 425
Wells, Preston Strait (child), 246, 265
Wells, Rulon Seymour (child), 141, 147, 235, 253, 254, 255, 257, 333, *378*, 378
Wells, Stephen Franklin (child), 308, *378*, 476n15
Wells, Susan Annette (child), 141, 172, *376*, 377
Wells, Governor Thomas, 3, 10, 421–23, 424, 426, 477n1, 477n5–n6, 478n10–n11, 479n14, 480n4
Wells, Victor Pennington (child), 308, *378*, 476n15
Wells, Wilford Woodruff (child), 308
Wells and Taylor Mine, 227–28, 373
Wells Mansion, 249, 413, *414*
Wells Survey, 33, 35, 37, 44, 46, 53
West, Chauncey, 237
Wethersfield, 3, 5–9, 14, 15, 423–25, 477n6, 478–79n10–n14
White, Hugh, 32, 33
White, Captain James, 17
Whitehead, Adolphus R., 228
Whitney, Isabel M. (Belle) (child), 139, 377
Whitney, Mary Hyner, 247
Whitney, Melvina C. B. (child), 139, 311, 376, 410, 444n24
Whitney, Murray Wells, 417
Whitney, Newell K., 39, 50, 115, 120, 138, 139–40, 311, 376
Whitney, Orson F., 416, 417
Whitmore, James, 277
Wilcken, Charles H., 381
Willes, William S. S., 267
Williams, Frederick G., 57
Williams, Ruth, 267
Wilson, Alexander, 220
Wilson, James T., 254
Winberg, Anders, 267
Winder, John R., 203, 367
Winter Quarters, 10, 96, 97, 99–104, *104*, 107, 108, 110, 139, 193, 200, 208
Winters, Hulda Augusta, 382
Wisconsin, 390–92, 394, 398

Woman's Exponent, 410
Wood, Daniel, 105
Woodruff, Wilford, 50, 308, 346, 409, 411, 414, 415, 417, 420
Woods, Catherine Wells, 12, 14, 18–24, 26, 64, 85, 141–42, 143, 144, 247, 257, 444n24
Woods, Eliza Jane, 64, 257, 258
Woods, Gov. George L., 324–25, 338
Woods, James Dan, 258, 311
Woods, James Weston, 21–22, 23, 24, 44, 85, 103, 142–43, 144, 376
Woods, Nehemiah Park, 64, 257, 258, 311
Woods, William Wells, 64, 257, 311, 376, 384, 405, 408, 410, 411, 444n24
Woodward, David, 138
Woodward, Emmeline Belos, *136*, 138–41, 226, 247, 249, 252, 257, 311, 358, *376*, 376–78, 384, 402, 404, 405, 407–8, 410–11, 413–14, 418–20
Woodward, Henry, 202–3
Wooley, E. T., 277, 400
Woolley, Henry A., 347
Wooton, Sec. Francis, 233

Yates, Richard, 328–29, 346
Yenson, Anna, 247
Young, Ann Eliza Webb (case), 345–46, 476n15
Young, B. Morris, 347
Young, Brigham, ix, 50, 61, 76–78, 81–82, 84, 96–97, 100, 102–4, 106–8, 110, 111, 115–16, 119, 125–27, 129, 133–38, 140, 147, 149–52, 153–55, 157, 162, 165, 167–68, 170–71, 173, 175–79, 181, 185–88, 191–92, 199, 201, 203–5, 207, 212–13, 215–16, 218, 220, 223–24, 228–30, 234, 236–39, 243, 245, 248, 255, 259, 262, 269, 270, 278, 280, 281, 288, 292, 293, 296–97, 303, 308–10, *309*, 315, 318–19, 322, 325, 328–30, 333, 334, 340–41, 344, 346–48, 351, 354, 355–57, 359, 364, 369, 413, 456n52, 457n7
Young, Brigham, Jr., 260, 262, 264, 271–72, 276, 289, 348, 351, 356
Young, Evelyn Louisa, 135
Young, Hannah Louisa, 389, 403, 413, 420
Young, John Willard, 348
Young, Joseph A., 274, 328, 382
Young, Mahonri M., 136
Young, Dr. Seymour B., 346, 381–82, 386, 389, 401, 411
Young Men's Mutual Improvement Association (YMMIA), 347–48
Young Women's Mutual Improvement Association (YWMIA), 347

Zion's Cooperative Mercantile Institution (ZCMI), 248, *249*, 299, 358

www.ingramcontent.com/pod-product-compliance
Lightning Source LLC
Chambersburg PA
CBHW071226070526
44583CB00017B/2067